WARFARE IN HISTORY

The Dutch Army and the Military Revolutions, 1588–1688

The Dutch army is central to all discussions about the tactical, strategic and organisational military revolution of the early modern period, but this is the first substantial work on the subject in English. This book addresses the changes that were effected in the tactics and organisation of the Dutch armed forces between 1588 and 1688. It shows how in the first decades of this period the Dutch army was transformed from an unreliable band of mercenaries into a disciplined force that could hold its own against the might of Spain. Under the leadership of Maurits of Nassau and his cousin Willem Lodewijk a tactical revolution was achieved that had a profound impact on battle. However, the Dutch army's organisational structure remained unchanged and the Dutch Republic continued to rely on mercenaries and military entrepreneurs. It was not until the latter half of the seventeenth century that the Dutch, under William III of Orange, Captain-General of the Union, introduced revolutionary changes in military organisation and established an efficient standing army. This army withstood attacks by Louis XIV and the Dutch reforms were copied by the English.

OLAF VAN NIMWEGEN has held a number of research posts in the Netherlands. He has an extensive publication record in Dutch and has published several articles on the Dutch army in English. In 2004 he was awarded the Schouwenburg Prize for an outstanding publication on Dutch military history for *De Republiek der Verenigde Nederlanden als grote mogendheid* (The Republic of the United Netherlands as a great power), about the role and position of the Dutch Republic in the European system of states in the period 1713 to 1756.

WARFARE IN HISTORY
ISSN 1358–779X

Series editor
Matthew Bennett, Royal Military Academy, Sandhurst

This series aims to provide a wide-ranging and scholarly approach to military history, offering both individual studies of topics or wars, and volumes giving a selection of contemporary and later accounts of particular battles; its scope ranges from the early medieval to the early modern period.

New proposals for the series are welcomed; they should be sent to the publisher at the address below.

Boydell and Brewer Limited, PO Box 9, Woodbridge, Suffolk, IP12 3DF

Previously published volumes in this series are listed at the back of this volume

The Dutch Army and the Military Revolutions, 1588–1688

Olaf van Nimwegen

Translated by Andrew May

THE BOYDELL PRESS

Originally published in Dutch as *'Deser landen crijchsvolck' Het Staatse leger en de militaire revoluties 1588–1688*

© Olaf van Nimwegen 2006
English edition © The Boydell Press 2010

The translation of this book was made possible by a generous grant from the Netherlands Organisation for Scientific Research (NWO)

All Rights Reserved. Except as permitted under current legislation no part of this work may be photocopied, stored in a retrieval system, published, performed in public, adapted, broadcast, transmitted, recorded or reproduced in any form or by any means, without the prior permission of the copyright owner

The right of Olaf van Nimwegen to be identified as the author of this work has been asserted in accordance with sections 77 and 78 of the Copyright, Designs and Patents Act 1988

First published 2010
The Boydell Press, Woodbridge

ISBN 978–1–84383–575–2

The Boydell Press is an imprint of Boydell & Brewer Ltd
PO Box 9, Woodbridge, Suffolk IP12 3DF, UK
and of Boydell & Brewer Inc.
668 Mt Hope Avenue, Rochester, NY 14620, USA
website: www.boydellandbrewer.com

A CIP catalogue record for this book is available from the British Library

The publisher has no responsibility for the continued existence or accuracy of URLs for external or third-party internet websites referred to in this book, and does not guarantee that any content on such websites is, or will remain, accurate or appropriate.

This publication is printed on acid-free paper

Printed in Great Britain by
CPI Antony Rowe, Chippenham and Eastbourne

Contents

List of illustrations	ix
Foreword	xiii
Preface to the English edition	xv
Acknowledgements	xvii
List of abbreviations	xix
Notes: Dates, Currency, Holland and the Netherlands, Personal names and place names, Weights and measures	xxi
Introduction: The Notion of a Military Revolution in the Early Modern Era	1

Part I 1588–1648

1 The Organisation and Remuneration of the Dutch Army (1588–1648) — 21

The officers of the Dutch army	22
The raising of companies and regiments	30
A melting-pot of nationalities	33
Special forms of recruitment: *waardgelders*, Spanish mutineers and military enterprisers	37
The size of the Dutch army: the difference between paper and effective strengths	45
Muster and direct payment: prerequisites for efficient military management	47
Company management	51
Prisoners of war	61
The *solliciteurs-militair*	64
'This great and cankerous malady of negotiation': financing the Republic's war effort and the question of army reduction	69

2 The Dutch Army and the Revolution in Infantry Tactics (1592–1618) — 85

The types of soldier and their weaponry	85
The tactical revolution: Dutch infantry tactics and drill	100
Cavalry and artillery	113

3 Field Operations (1590–1648) — 117

The conduct of warfare	117
The campaign and the logistical organisation of the Dutch army	123

Fortifications and siege warfare	132
The war's impact on the countryside: fire-tax, contribution and plundering	146

4 The Dutch Offensive and the Spanish Counter-Offensive (1590–1609) 151

Ten successful years (1590–1600)	154
The struggle of attrition for Ostend (1601–1604)	171
Spinola on the offensive (1605–1606)	189
Hostilities are suspended for twelve years (1607–1609)	196
Conclusion	198

5 The Republic Escalates Her War Effort (1610–1634) 201

The Republic intervenes in the Jülich War of Succession – internal strife in the Republic (1610–1621)	201
War is resumed: Spinola goes on the offensive again (1621–1625)	207
The Dutch counterattack tentatively gathers momentum (1626–1628)	212
The great Dutch offensive: 's-Hertogenbosch and the Spanish-Imperial incursion into the Veluwe – the siege of Maastricht (1629–1632)	217
The Dutch offensive stalls (1633–1634)	234
Conclusion	240

6 Warfare Hits a Strategic Ceiling (1635–1648) 243

The Dutch-French invasion of the Spanish Netherlands founders (1635)	243
Besieging Dunkirk proves impossible – the siege of Breda (1636–1637)	251
Frederik Hendrik has limited success in the east – Antwerp and the major Flemish towns remain beyond his reach (1638–1641)	255
Francisco de Melo goes on the offensive (1642–1643)	266
Antwerp for the last time – the Peace of Münster (1644–1648)	270
Conclusion	286

Concluding Remarks to Part I   289

Part II 1648–1688

7 The Dutch Army under Johan de Witt and William III (1648–1688) 301

The long shadow of the assault on Amsterdam (1650)	301
The Dutch army under Johan de Witt (1653–1672)	306
The appointment and quality of Dutch officers	308
'Redress of the militia': attempts to restore the Dutch army's fighting strength	317
The development of the new Dutch army under William III (1672–1688)	325
The new Dutch army: revision of the system of *solliciteurs-militair* and government support for recruiting and maintaining companies	330
The disciplining of Dutch officers	342
William III and the restoration of the Dutch army's morale	345

The birth of the Republic's standing army	352
Holland's financing of the Republic's war effort during the 'Guerre de Hollande' (1672–1678)	355

8   The Conduct of War (1650–1688) — 361

The magazine system	362
'Le principal des armées': the provisioning of the Dutch troops	363
Sutlers	373
The impact of the magazine system on the conduct of war	374
Field operations	378
Siege warfare	384
The significance of the siege of Maastricht in 1673	384
The recapture of Grave in 1674 and the unsuccessful siege of Maastricht in 1676	386
The New Netherlandish fortification system	392
The weaponry and tactics of the Dutch troops	396

9   War on Two Fronts against England and Münster: The Dutch Army Falls Short (1650–1667) — 405

The Dutch army's fragmentation – mounting tensions with the bishop of Münster (1652–1657)	405
Expedition to the Dijlerschans (1664)	410
War with Münster and the Second Anglo-Dutch War (1664–1667)	415
Conclusion	425

10 The Dawn of Large-Scale Land-Based Warfare: The War of Devolution and the 'Guerre de Hollande' (1667–1674) — 429

The War of Devolution: France threatens to overrun the Spanish Netherlands (1667–1668)	429
The build-up to the 'Guerre de Hollande' (1669 to May 1672)	433
The attack on the Republic (May–June 1672)	438
Behind the Holland Water Line (June–September 1672)	442
The failed assault on Naarden and the battle of Woerden (September–October 1672)	448
The expedition to Charleroi (November–December 1672)	453
Luxembourg threatens to cross the Holland Water Line (November–December 1672)	456
Louis XIV captures Maastricht – the Dutch counter-offensive (1673)	459
The end of the 'Guerre de Hollande': the peace treaties of Westminster and Cologne (February–April 1674)	467
Conclusion	468

11 **War in the Spanish Netherlands: The Republic is Still Ill-Equipped for the New, Large-Scale Manner of Warfare (1674–1678)** 471

The Republic, Spain and the emperor wage war in the Spanish Netherlands together, but success remains elusive (1674) 471
The siege of Grave – Turenne's winter campaign (July–December 1674) 482
Another disappointing year for the allies (1675) 484
France's spring offensive (January–June 1676) 487
William III's unsuccessful attempt to recapture Maastricht (July–December 1676) 493
The French resume their offensive (January–May 1677) 498
The allied counter-offensive founders (June–December 1677) 503
The French demonstrate their superiority once again – the Peace of Nijmegen (1678) 506
Conclusion 511

Concluding Remarks to Part II 515

Appendices 525
I Effective strength of the Republic's field army (1591–1646) 525
II Important Dutch siege operations (1591–1646) and Spinola's sieges of Ostend (1601–1604) and Breda (1624–1625) 528
III Fifty-seven Dutch infantry regiments mustered on 20 January and other dates in 1676 530
IV Five Dutch infantry regiments mustered on various dates in 1676; Two infantry companies mustered on 19 March 1677 532
V Dutch infantry regiments in the field army mustered on 9 July 1677; Dutch cavalry regiments and dragoons mustered in the field army on 9 July 1677 532
VI The strength of the field armies in the Spanish Netherlands (1674–1678) 534

Bibliography 535
Index of Personal Names and Institutions 559
Index of Alliances, Peace Treaties, Land and Sea Battles, Rivers and Canals, Forts, Towns and Villages 571

Illustrations

1.	Maurits (1567–1625), count of Nassau, prince of Orange from 1618, commander-in-chief of the Dutch army from 1590 to 1625.	4
2.	Willem Lodewijk (1560–1620), count of Nassau, stadholder and captain-general of Friesland, Groningen and Drenthe.	5
3.	*Arte et Marte* (By scholarship and war), the ideal propagated by Justus Lipsius.	6
4.	Military punishments.	56
5.	Firing squad in the French army.	57
6.	Dutch rondache or sword-and-bucklerman.	88
7.	Dutch rondache or sword-and-bucklerman.	89
8.	Dutch soldiers with targes.	90
9.	Dutch infantry equipment.	92
10.	Matchlock.	93
11.	Snaphance or firelock.	95
12.	Heavy cavalry.	98
13.	Wheel-lock.	99
14.	A Dutch officer instructing a musketeer.	102
15.	Pike evolutions in the Dutch army.	103
16.	Johann VII (1561–1623), count of Nassau-Siegen.	104
17.	The countermarch as explained in Willem Lodewijk's letter to Maurits, Groningen 8/18 December 1594.	106
18.	Tactical deployment of the Frisian regiment in 1594.	107
19.	Tactical deployment of the Frisian regiment on 6/16 August 1595.	109
20.	The conversion, c. 1670.	110
21a.	Dutch field and siege artillery.	114
21b.	Undercarriage of a Dutch 12-pounder cannon.	115
22.	Battle array of the Dutch army in the Jülich campaign of 1610.	124
23.	The *trace italienne*.	133
24.	Plan view and profile section of the Old Netherlandish system of fortification.	134
25.	The Spanish siege of Bergen op Zoom in 1622.	136
26.	Battle of Turnhout in 1597.	164
27.	Battle order of the Dutch and Spanish armies prior to the battle of Nieuwpoort (1600).	168
28.	Maurits of Nassau (1567–1625).	170
29.	Albert, archduke of Austria (1559–1621), governor-general (1596–1598) and joint sovereign ruler of the Spanish Netherlands (1599–1621).	172

30.	The siege of Ostend, 1601–1604.	174
31.	Ostend's southwestern defensive works during the siege of 1601–1604.	175
32.	Ernst Casimir (1573–1632), count of Nassau-Dietz, stadholder of Friesland, Groningen and Drenthe, Dutch field-marshal.	210
33.	Frederik Hendrik (1584–1647), prince of Orange-Nassau, captain- and admiral-general of the Union.	211
34.	The besieging of Groenlo in 1627 by Frederik Hendrik and Ernst Casimir.	216
35.	A skirmish between Dutch and Spanish troopers, c. 1635.	233
36a.	Willem, count of Nassau-Siegen (1592–1642), Dutch field-marshal.	257
36b.	The fortifications of Antwerp in 1624.	258
37.	Looting of a village in the Netherlands.	295
38.	Frederik Magnus von Salm-Neufville (1607–1673), Wald- and Rhinegrave, Dutch major-general.	310
39.	A Dutch cavalry officer.	320
40.	William III (1650–1702), prince of Orange, captain-general of the Union from 1672.	326
41.	Gaspar Fagel (1634–1688), Grand Pensionary of Holland, 1672–1688.	327
42.	Georg Friedrich, count of Waldeck and Culemborg (1620–1692), Dutch field-marshal.	328
43.	Dutch recruiting scene.	335
44.	Field hospital.	350
45.	Tombstone of Moses *alias* Antonio Alvares Machado (†1706) and his wife, Rachel Ximenes Cardoso.	366
46.	A plan sketched by field deputy Everard van Weede-Dijkveld during the siege of Maastricht in 1676.	388
47.	Dutch grenadier's cap.	390
48.	Menno, baron van Coehoorn (1641–1704), fortifications engineer, artillerist and siege expert.	393
49.	French musketeer.	398
50.	Flintlock.	400
51.	Plug bayonet.	402
52.	Ring bayonet.	402
53.	Detail of ring bayonet.	402
54.	Willem Frederik (1613–1664), count of Nassau-Dietz, stadholder and captain-general of Friesland.	413
55.	Johan Maurits (1604–1679), count of Nassau-Siegen, commander of the Dutch army in the war with Münster (1665/6).	418
56.	Henri de La Tour d'Auvergne (1611–1675), vicomte de Turenne, French *maréchal*.	435
57.	Siege and recapture of Naarden by the Dutch army on 13 September 1673.	463
58.	The recapture of Naarden by the Dutch army on 13 September 1673.	464

59.	Battle of Seneffe, 11 August 1674.	478
60.	Godard van Reede-Ginkel (1644–1703), Dutch general of horse.	480
61.	Louis XIV (1638–1715), king of France (1643–1715), his brother Philippe, duc d'Orléans (1640–1701), Louis 'le Grand Dauphin' (1661–1711), and François Michel Le Tellier (1639–1691), marquis de Louvois.	490
62.	William III (1650–1702), captain- and admiral-general of the Union.	492

Foreword

The king of Spain has since Ferdinand and Isabel determinedly striven for the hegemony of Europe. The foundations have been lain ... though without being master of these lands it is impossible for them to achieve. We are situated between Germany, France and England, and they shall therefore never abandon their intention towards and against these lands.

Such was the considered judgement of the Dutch Republic's Council of State in December 1636.[1] The strategic location of the Low Countries meant that this region was one of the most important theatres of conflict in Europe for many centuries. From the start of their revolt against their sovereign lord, King Philip II of Spain, the rebellious Dutch provinces stood at the heart of the struggle for supremacy in Europe, first as a main prize for the contending powers and then, from the 1590s, as a belligerent in their own right. From the late seventeenth to the mid-eighteenth century, the Republic of the Seven United Provinces was considered the guardian of the European balance of power. The formation of the Dutch state was the outcome of eighty years of war, and after being recognised as an independent power in 1648 the Dutch Republic still had to rely on military means for its survival. The Republic's ability to withstand mighty opponents for more than one and a half centuries can be attributed to two military revolutions.

Pivotal to this study are the nature and scope of the changes in the organisation, financing and tactics of the Dutch army achieved in the period 1588 to 1688 and their impact on the conduct of land-based warfare – simultaneous developments in the navy are considered in passing. The premise of this study is that the effect and influence of these two military revolutions were unequal, because of the nature of the relationship between the nascent state and its army. A *tactical* military revolution was effected during the final decade of the sixteenth century, making a superbly drilled and highly disciplined army available to the Republic. The Dutch army's opportunities for growth were limited, however, by the fact that the government wished to keep its direct involvement with the troops to a minimum, and the knowledge and battle experience gained at war were swiftly forgotten during peacetime. This situation lasted until a revolution in military *organisation* was achieved between 1667 and 1688. The threat posed

---

[1] NA, RAZH, AJC 48, Advice of the Council of State to the Delegated Councillors of Holland, The Hague, 16 December 1636.

by the France of Louis XIV compelled other European states and the Republic in particular to fundamentally reform their armies. The 1670s and 1680s saw the birth of the Republic's standing army, a military force composed of professionals with organisational and command structures that were maintained intact during peacetime.

Preface to the English Edition

This book is a translation of my study on the Dutch army: *'Deser landen crijchsvolck'. Het Staatse leger en de militaire revoluties 1588–1688*, published in Dutch by Uitgeverij Bert Bakker in 2006. I am grateful to the Netherlands Organisation for Scientific Research (NWO) for its generosity in funding this English translation.

The translation of a volume of this scope and substance requires a translator ready to immerse himself in the subject matter and work in close consultation with the author. Andrew May has acquitted himself in his task with great commitment and I should like to convey my gratitude for his conscientious and meticulous work. He, in turn, would like to thank Rowan Hewison for his ever-astute commentary on the English copy.

The translation of a published work brings with it the temptation to rewrite the text, which I have largely resisted, though I have naturally seized the opportunity to make a few corrections and provide elucidations for international audiences.

Here I would also like to thank Louis Ph. Sloos, Curator/Librarian at the Royal Netherlands Army Museum in Delft, for his generosity in providing prints as well as paintings for this edition, and lastly I would like to express my gratitude to Jan Piet Puype, former Chief Curator at the same museum, for permission to use his detailed drawings of a matchlock, wheellock, firelock and flintlock.

Acknowledgements

This study was part of the 'War and Society in the Golden Age' project at the University of Amsterdam (UvA), which ran from 2001 to 2006 and was funded by the Netherlands Organisation for Scientific Research (NWO). Besides this post-doctoral study from my own hand the project encompassed several articles by Dr Marjolein 't Hart, focusing on the impact of war on Dutch society from 1570 to 1680, as well as three dissertations. Erik Swart investigated the emergence of the armed forces of the rebellious Dutch in the period 1572 to 1590, Peter Decauwer examined the siege of 's-Hertogenbosch in 1629, and Griet Vermeesch focused on the impact of warfare on the fortified towns of Gorinchem and Doesburg between 1572 and 1680. Overall supervision of the project rested with Henk van Nierop, Professor of Modern History and Director of the Amsterdam Centre for the Study of the Golden Age.

I would like to thank Herman Amersfoort, Professor of Dutch Military History at the Dutch Defence Academy in Breda and at the UvA, for his critical reading and commentary on the manuscript. I would also like to thank Dr Leo Adriaenssen, Professor Jeroen Duindam, Dr Michiel de Jong, Dr Paul Knevel and Dr John Stapleton for their perceptive and constructive commentaries. I am profoundly grateful to Her Majesty Queen Beatrix of the Netherlands for allowing me access to the abundance of material in the Koninklijk Huisarchief (Royal Archives) at The Hague, where I conducted a considerable portion of the research for this volume. I would also like to express my thanks to the archivists Charlotte Eymael, Dr Marijke Bruggeman and Hélène de Muij-Fleurke, whose assistance enabled me to consult the archives of the House of Orange-Nassau efficiently. A similar word of thanks is owed to Arie-Pieter van Nienes, former archivist at the Friesland Historical and Literary Centre (Tresoar) in Leeuwarden, for his help in consulting the archives of the stadholders of Friesland. My research was completed prior to the finalisation of the reclassification of these archives both in Leeuwarden and The Hague, so I have used the old inventory numbers. For further information on this process see A.P. van Nienes and M. Bruggeman, *Archieven van de Friese stadhouders. Inventarissen van de archieven van de Friese stadhouders van Willem Lodewijk tot en met Willem V, 1584–1795* (Hilversum, The Hague and Leeuwarden 2002). With the aid of the concordance it should not prove difficult to determine the revised numbering. I was able to draw on the rich collection of portraits of Dutch officers held by the Netherlands Institute of Military History in The Hague (NIMH), for which I would like to express my gratitude to P.H. Kamphuis, Director of the NIMH. I am also grateful to the staff of the Nationaal Archief (National Archives) and the Koninklijke Bibliotheek (National Library of the Netherlands), both in The Hague, as well as the staff of the Provincial archives in Gelderland, Groningen, Overijssel, Utrecht and Zeeland, and of Amsterdam City Archives. I am truly appreciative of their professionalism.

Last but not least I wish to thank my wife, Marjolein, for her unwavering support throughout this project. I dedicate this book to her and to my two sons, Ewout and Marijn.

Olaf van Nimwegen, September 2009

Abbreviations

Repositories

GA	Gelders Archief (Archives of Gelderland), Arnhem
GAA	Gemeentearchief van Amsterdam (Amsterdam City Archives)
GrA	Groninger Archieven (Archives of the Province of Groningen), Groningen
HCO	Historisch Centrum Overijssel (Overijssel History Centre), Zwolle
HUA	Het Utrechts Archief (Archives of the Province of Utrecht), Utrecht
KB	Koninklijke Bibliotheek (Royal Library), The Hague
KHA	Koninklijk Huisarchief (Royal Archives), The Hague
NA	Nationaal Archief (National Archives), The Hague
RAZH	Rijksarchief in Zuid-Holland (State Archives in South Holland), The Hague
ZA	Zeeuws Archief (Archives of Zeeland), Middelburg

Archives

AGF	Archief Gaspar Fagel (Gaspar Fagel Archives)
AGRH	Archief Gecommitteerde Raden van Holland (Archives of the Delegated Councillors of Holland)
AHGC	Archief Heren en Graven van Culemborg (Archives of the Lords and Counts of Culemborg)
AHK	Archief van de Hoge Krijgsraad (Archives of the General Court Martial)
AJC	Archief Jacob Cats (Jacob Cats Archives)
AJvO	Archief Johan van Oldenbarnevelt (Johan van Oldenbarnevelt Archives)
AJdW	Archief Johan de Witt (Johan de Witt Archives)
AR	Archief Rekenkamer (Archives of the Audit Office), Zeeland
ASF	Archief Staten van Friesland (Archives of the States of Friesland)
ASH	Archief Staten van Holland (Archives of the States of Holland)
ASO	Archief Staten van Overijssel (Archives of the States of Overijssel)
ASSO	Archief Staten van Stad en Ommelanden (Archives of the States of Groningen)
ASU	Archief Staten van Utrecht (Archives of the States of Utrecht)
CG	Collectie Goldberg (Goldberg Collection)
CvdH	Collectie van der Hoop (Van der Hoop Collection)
CvLS	Collectie van Limburg Stirum (Van Limburg-Stirum Collection)
FavdC	Familiearchief Van der Capellen (Van der Capellen Family Archives)
FAEVC	Familiearchief Eysinga-Vegelin van Claerbergen (Eysinga-Vegelin van Claerbergen Family Archives)

FAF	Familiearchief Fagel (Fagel Family Archives)
FAH	Familiearchief Hop (Hop Family Archives)
FAHvV	Familiearchief Hoeufft van Velsen (Hoeufft van Velsen Family Archives)
FAvS	Familiearchief van Slingelandt De Vrij Temminck (Van Slingelandt De Vrij Temminck Family Archives)
FH	Financie van Holland (Treasury of Holland)
FSA	Fries Stadhouderlijk Archief (Archives of the Stadholders of Friesland)
HAA	Huisarchief Amerongen (Amerongen Family Archives)
RvS	Archief van de Raad van State (Archives of the Council of State)
SG	Archief van de Staten-Generaal (Archives of the States-General)
SHS	Archief van de Stadhouderlijke Secretarie (Archives of the Stadholder's Office)

Published sources

Archives	G. Groen van Prinsterer, *Archives ou correspondance inédite de la Maison d'Orange-Nassau*
CWB	N. Japikse, *Correspondentie van Willem III en Hans Willem Bentinck*
Duyck	L. Mulder, *Journaal van Anthonis Duyck*
RGP	N. Japikse, *Resolutiën der Staten-Generaal van 1576 tot 1609*, Rijksgeschiedkundige Publicatiën

Notes

Dates
In the sixteenth and seventeenth centuries, both the Julian and the Gregorian calendars were in use in Europe. The difference between Old Style and New Style dates was at this time ten days. All the dates used in the book are New Style, with a few exceptions when both dates are given as OS/NS, for example 4/14 November 1677.

Currency
The principal money of account in the Dutch Republic was the guilder or florin of twenty stivers (*stuivers*); the rix-dollar (*rijksdaalder*) had a value of fifty stivers (two-and-a-half guilders), and the *dukaton* had a value of sixty stivers (three guilders).

Holland and the Netherlands
The Netherlands or Low Countries signifies the whole of the territory that approximates to the modern-day Benelux. Throughout this study Holland refers only to the province of that name, while the Dutch Republic is used to refer to the Republic of the United Netherlands. The Netherlandish provinces that continued to form part of the Spanish empire are referred to as the Spanish Netherlands or southern Netherlands.

Personal names and place names
Personal names of emperors and monarchs have been anglicised. Many towns in modern Belgium have names which can be rendered in Dutch or French. The form most familiar in English has, where possible, been preferred, but giving the Dutch or French alternatives parenthetically on the first mention in each chapter.

Weights and measures
The States of Holland and the States-General decreed around 1600 that in all matters pertaining to fortifications and weaponry the Rhineland foot (31.4cm) would be the standard measurement and the Amsterdam pound (494g) the standard weight, though the standard weight for military 'ammunition' bread was the Brabant pound (469g). The linear measurement used by Dutch troops in the field, both for manoeuvres and for determining firing distances, was the pace. The 'common pace' or 'common stride' measured one-fifth of a Rhineland rod (3.77m) or two-and-a-half feet (c. 75cm).

N
0
25
50 km
OOST-FRIESLAND
Emden
Delfzijl
Leeuwarden
Groningen
Leerort
Dijlerschans
Bourtange
Steenwijk
Eems
Enkhuizen
Coevorden
Hasselt
Kampen
Zwolle
Lingen
Haarlem
Amsterdam
Elburg
Hattem
Ootmarsum
Weesp
Muiden
Almelo
Oldenzaal
IJssel
Naarden
Harderwijk
Deventer
TWENTE
Leiden
Alphen aan de Rijn
VELUWE
Lochem
Bodegraven
Woerden
Utrecht
Amersfoort
Zutphen
Den Haag
Nieuwerbrug
Borculo
Delft
Goejanverwellesluis
Wijk bij Duurstede
Groenlo
Gouda
Arnhem
Doesburg
Rijn
DE GRAAFSCHAP
Rotterdam
Schoonhoven
Doetinchem
Bredevoort
STICHT MUNSTER
Den Briel
Waal
Schenkenschans
Gorinchem
Bocholt
Nijmegen
Emmerik
Dordrecht
Bommel
Kleef
Rees
Grave
Willemstad
Geertruidenberg
Den Bosch
Gennep
Wesel
Breda
Büderich
Middelburg
Gelder
Maas
Rijnberk
Orsoy
MARK
Vlissingen
Bergen op Zoom
Meurs
OPPER-
Wachtendonk
IJzendijke
1597
Venlo
Oostende
Sluis
Turnhout
Philippine
Hulst
GELRE
Nieuwpoort
Sas van Gent
Antwerpen
Weert
Brugge
Herentals
Düsseldorf
1600
Roermond
Duinkerken
Veurne
Diksmuide
Lier
BRABANT
Fort Mardyck
Gent
KEUR-
VLAANDEREN
Mechelen
BERG
Gravelines
Sint-Winoksbergen
Rijn
Calais
Dijle
Demer
VORSTEN-
Dendermonde
PRINS-
Leie
Aarschot
Diest
GULIK
1677
Ieper
Leuven
DOM
Mont-Cassel
Aalst
BISDOM
Menen
Schelde
Dender
Tienen
Gulik
KEULEN
Keulen
Kortrijk
Oudenaarde
Maastricht
Brussel
Saint-Omer
Armentières
Ath
LUIK
Aken
Aire
Saint-Venant
Rijsel (Lille)
Dijle
Bonn
Doornik
Lillers
1678
1674
Limbourg
Béthune
Seneffe
Luik
Lens
Saint-Ghislain
Maas
St. Denis
Namen
Hoei
Hesdin
Condé
Bergen (Mons)
Douai
Sambre
Charleroi
Valenciennes
Arras
Bouchain
Maubeuge
Cambrai
Le Quesnoy
Dinant
HENEGOUWEN
Landrecies
Maas
Amiens
1643
Rocroi
Saint-Quentin
Charleville

Introduction
The Notion of a Military Revolution in the Early Modern Era

An historiographical overview of the debate

The seventeenth century occupies a special place in the history of the Netherlands. During this 'Golden Age' the Republic of the United Netherlands was integrated into the European constellation of states as a sovereign country, international trade grew at an unprecedented rate and the arts flourished.[1] The position that the Republic had achieved by 1648 in Europe and beyond was the outcome of eighty years of war. Only a quarter of a century later, in 1672, the destruction of the Republic as a sovereign state was averted by the Holland Water Line, a defensive system that used controlled inundation of the countryside, and by the Republic's army and navy. The 'Forty Years' War' (1672–1712) against the France of Louis XIV, the Sun King, confirmed the Republic's status as a great power and positioned it as a defender of the European balance of power. Until the mid-eighteenth century, the Republic would fulfil a pivotal role in the Old System, as the defensive alliance of Great Britain, Austria and the Republic was known. Thereafter the Republic's star waned until it became a second-rank power.[2]

The fleet has always received pre-eminent attention in the historiography of the Netherlands. The navy protected commerce, the lifeblood of the Republic, and achieved resounding successes against the English and French fleets during the second and third Anglo-Dutch Wars (1665–1667 and 1672–1674). In contrast to the land-based forces, the fleet was regarded as quintessentially Dutch. While many Dutch soldiers were recruited abroad, the ships' crews were commonly regarded as originating from the territory of the Republic. While this may well be true with respect to the admirals and naval officers, the ordinary sailors were a mix of nationalities: Northern and Southern Netherlanders, Germans, Frenchmen, Scotsmen, Englishmen and Scandinavians.[3] The same held true for

---

[1] Maarten Prak, *Gouden Eeuw. Het raadsel van de Republiek* (Nijmegen 2002), pp. 7–11.
[2] Olaf van Nimwegen, *De Republiek der Verenigde Nederlanden als grote mogendheid. Buitenlandse politiek en oorlogvoering in de eerste helft van de achttiende eeuw en in het bijzonder tijdens de Oostenrijkse Successieoorlog (1740–1748)* (Amsterdam 2002).
[3] Jaap R. Bruijn, *Varend verleden. De Nederlandse oorlogsvloot in de zeventiende en achttiende eeuw* (n.p., 1998), pp. 71–3.

the army; the only difference from the navy was that the army's high command and officer corps were decidedly international. This was inevitable given the size of the army. While the fleet counted approximately 11,000 crewmen in 1642,[4] the effective strength of the Republic's army was 60,000.[5] Given the territory's population of just one and a half million it was impossible to recruit even a majority of officers from within the Republic's borders, never mind the full complement.

A number of studies on the eighteenth century have appeared in recent years, augmenting our understanding of the Dutch army of that era,[6] but for the seventeenth century one still has to revert to old military-operational studies,[7] as well as to the multivolume work written by Colonel F.J.G. ten Raa and Lieutenant-General F. de Bas, *Het Staatsche leger 1568–1795*, of which volumes I to V were published between 1911 and 1921, while volumes VI and VII appeared posthumously in 1940 and 1950.[8] In structure and content these works do not meet the requirements of modern historiography. Broader contexts are absent and there is a paucity of political, financial and social background to military affairs. This deficiency has in part been remedied by the 1969 book *Het leger in de zeventiende eeuw* (The army in the seventeenth century) by C.M. and J.W.M. Schulten, several articles by the noted military historian J.W. Wijn,[9] and studies by Marjolein 't Hart and Eduard Dormans of the Republic's government finances in the seventeenth and eighteenth centuries.[10] Many aspects are beyond the scope of these studies or remain unexplored. It is striking, however, that there is no question

---

[4] Ibid., p. 73.
[5] NA, RAZH, AJC 32, 'Rapport van de heeren gecommitteert bij haer Ed. Groot Mo. op 't stuck van de mesnage waervan de besoigne is begonnen den xi.en october 1635'.
[6] J.W. Wijn, *Het Staatsche leger*, VIII, 'Het tijdperk van de Spaanse Successieoorlog 1702–1715', 3 vols (The Hague 1956–1964); H.L. Zwitzer, 'De militie van den Staat'. *Het leger van de Republiek der Verenigde Nederlanden* (Amsterdam 1991); Olaf van Nimwegen, *De subsistentie van het leger. Logistiek en strategie van het Geallieerde en met name het Staatse leger tijdens de Spaanse Successieoorlog in de Nederlanden en het Heilige Roomse Rijk (1701–1712)* (Amsterdam 1995); and Van Nimwegen, *De Republiek als grote mogendheid*.
[7] See, for example, J. Bosscha, *Neerlands heldendaden te land van de vroegste tijden af tot op onze dagen*, 4 vols, revised and improved edn (Leeuwarden 1872); W.J. Knoop, *Krijgs- en geschiedkundige beschouwingen over Willem den Derde* (Schiedam 1895); J.P. de Bordes, *De verdediging van Nederland in 1629* (Utrecht 1856); J.W. van Sypesteyn and J.P. de Bordes, *De verdediging van Nederland in 1672 en 1673*, 2 vols (The Hague 1850); C.A. van Sypesteyn, *Het merkwaardig beleg van Ostende 5 juli 1601–22 september 1604* (The Hague 1887); J.J. van den Hoek, *De veldtocht van prins Maurits in 1597* (The Hague 1914); W.E. van Dam van Isselt, 'Onze Duitsche bondgenooten tijdens prins Maurits' veldtocht van 1599', *BVGO*, 5th series, V (The Hague 1918), pp. 23–77.
[8] Volume VIII of *Het Staatsche leger* was written by J.W. Wijn and deviates from the other seven volumes in quality as well as structure. See n. 6 above.
[9] J.W. Wijn, 'Military Forces and Warfare 1610–48', in J.P. Cooper (ed.), *The New Cambridge Modern History*, IV (Cambridge 1970), pp. 202–25; and 'Onder het vaandel', in J. Romein et al. (eds), *De Tachtigjarige Oorlog* (Amsterdam 1941), pp. 111–31.
[10] Marjolein C. 't Hart, *The Making of a Bourgeois State. War, Politics and Finance during the Dutch Revolt* (Manchester and New York 1993). This study primarily tackles the first half of

of such historiographical neglect of the Dutch army in the final decade of the sixteenth century, a great many military-historical studies having been devoted to the period 1590–1600.

Wijn gained his doctorate in 1934 for his study of 'Het krijgswezen in den tijd van prins Maurits' (The military system in the age of Prince Maurits),[11] and the 1941 dissertation by the German historian Werner Hahlweg, 'Die Heeresreform der Oranier', defends the hypothesis that 'the army reform of the Oranges' was based on the study of Roman and Greek military organisation and warfare, with its emphasis on drill, exercise and discipline, and laid the basis for the modern army.[12] In 1585 the States of Holland and Zeeland appointed Maurits (1567–1625), count of Nassau, as their stadholder. A younger son of William the Silent, prince of Orange, who had been assassinated the year before, Maurits's election to the office of stadholder or provincial governor afforded him considerable political, administrative and judicial powers. In 1590 he was elected to this office in Overijssel and Utrecht, and the following year in Gelderland. Maurits, Captain-General of Holland and Zeeland since 1587, was in that same year assigned the command of all the troops of the Republic with the exception of those in the northern provinces. Maurits's cousin, Willem Lodewijk (1560–1620), had been Stadholder and Captain-General of Friesland and Groningen's Ommelands (literally the circumjacent countryside) since 1584, and from 1593 also of the sparsely populated region of Drenthe. The city of Groningen proper remained in Spanish hands until its reduction in 1594. Together the two cousins were in command of all the Republic's troops.

In the 1950s and 1960s, the German historian Gerhard Oestreich and, in particular, his British colleague Michael Roberts attributed a significance to the military reforms of the Nassaus that extended far beyond the purely military sphere. Oestreich subscribed to Hahlweg's thesis, but he believed that the military developments of the late sixteenth century were the product of the revival of Classical Roman Stoicism. The political and military publications of the classical philologist Justus Lipsius (1547–1606), whose lectures Maurits had attended in 1583 and 1584 at Leiden University, emphasised the importance of drill, exercise

---

the seventeenth century. Eduard H.M. Dormans, *Het tekort. Staatsschuld in de tijd der Republiek* (Amsterdam 1991).

[11] Barry Harold Nickle, 'The Military Reforms of Prince Maurice of Orange', Ph.D. diss., University of Delaware (1975), is essentially a complement to Wijn's work. Michiel A.G. de Jong, '"Staet van Oorlog". Wapenbedrijf en militaire hervormingen in de Republiek der Verenigde Nederlanden (1585–1621)', Ph.D. diss., Leiden University (2002), provides a detailed overview of the organisation, scale and financing of arms production in the Republic at the time of Maurits.

[12] Werner Hahlweg, *Die Heeresreform der Oranier und die Antike. Studien zur Geschichte des Kriegswesens der Niederlande, Deutschlands, Frankreichs, Englands, Italiens, Spaniens und der Schweiz vom Jahre 1589 bis zum Dreissigjährigen Kriege* (Berlin 1941). See also Hahlweg, 'Wilhelm Ludwig von Nassau und das Cannae-Problem', *Nassauische Annalen*, LXXI (1960), 237–42.

1. Maurits (1567–1625), count of Nassau, prince of Orange from 1618, commander-in-chief of the Dutch army from 1590 to 1625. *Afbeeldinghe ende beschrijvinghe van alle de veldslagen* (Amsterdam 1616). (Royal Netherlands Army Museum, Delft, 00112024/092)

2. Willem Lodewijk (1560–1620), count of Nassau, stadholder and captain-general of Friesland, Groningen and Drenthe. *Afbeeldinghe ende beschrijvinghe van alle de veldslagen* (Amsterdam 1616). (Royal Netherlands Army Museum, Delft, 00112024/015)

3. *Arte et Marte* (By scholarship and war), the ideal propagated by Justus Lipsius. Coloured pen-drawing (1607) by Captain Jacob Wijts (†1643). (KB, 133 M 86)

and strict discipline (*tucht en orde*) among the troops, after the Ancient Roman model. 'All these innovations, which brought about an organisational-tactical revolution in the art of war, but of course also had a profound impact on the internal organisation of the armies, had until this point been regarded as the essence of the reforms of the Oranges.' In Oestreich's view Lipsius's ambitions extended even further. Drill and exercise were intended to produce a new kind of soldier; armies would be composed of civilised officers and soldiers instead of gangs of *soldateska*, rough mercenaries who spared neither civilian lives nor property.[13]

Roberts took this even further than Oestreich.[14] In Roberts's view, the military reforms of the Nassaus led to the birth of the standing army and the modern state. In his opinion, the well-drilled and highly disciplined professional soldiers of the Dutch Republic could operate successfully in smaller units, in contrast to the German *Landsknechte* and the Spanish hirelings of the sixteenth century, who could only fight in extremely deep and unwieldy formations. The high degree of proficiency required for complex manoeuvres in small formations on the battlefield made it undesirable to disband the troops after the conclusion of the campaign. Even during the winter months, when hostilities were generally at a standstill, the soldiers had to be retained in service.

The Eighty Years' War (1568–1648) was chiefly characterised by sieges, which is why, according to Roberts, the offensive potential of the military reforms of the Nassaus was not fully realised until the reign of Gustavus II Adolphus (1594–1632), king of Sweden, who came to power in 1611. During the Thirty Years' War (1618–1648) he insisted on the efficacy of decisive pitched battles, a strategy that required sizeable field armies. The resulting increase in the scale of warfare had great financial consequences and compelled the government to become more closely involved with the armed forces, the outcome of which was a massive increase in the impact of warfare on society. 'The transformation in the scale of war led inevitably to an increase in the authority of the state. ... This development, and the new style of warfare itself, called for new administrative methods and standards; and the new administration was from the beginning centralized and royal.'[15] Roberts grouped this raft of developments together under the term 'military revolution', which apparently reached its completion in 1660, the start of the personal reign of Louis XIV (1638–1715), king of France.

Partly influenced by and partly in reaction to Roberts and Oestreich, Hahlweg elaborated his ideas about the significance of the military reforms of the Nassaus

---

[13] Gerhard Oestreich, 'Der römische Stoizismus und die oranische Heeresreform', *Historische Zeitschrift*, CLXXVI (1953), 17–43, esp. p. 27 (quote).
[14] Michael Roberts, 'The Military Revolution, 1560–1660', reprinted in Clifford J. Rogers (ed.), *The Military Revolution Debate. Readings on the Military Transformation of Early Modern Europe* (Boulder, San Francisco and Oxford 1995), pp. 13–35.
[15] Ibid., p. 20.

in several articles.[16] He acknowledged that they were in essence not limited to the introduction of drill or the adoption and practical application of the intellectual legacy of Classical Antiquity and the Byzantine Empire. '[The military reform] is much more a completely transformational or intellectual process that includes more or less all spheres of the military system and warfare.'[17] For him the reforms consisted of seven components: 1. systematised drill and training of soldiers; 2. the establishment of a modern general staff; 3. the building of a supply and maintenance apparatus; 4. the moulding of a professional officer corps (*wissenschaftlich herangebildeten Offizierskorps*); 5. the practical application of natural sciences (pyrotechnics) for military ends; 6. modern command structures (*zahlreiche Befehlshaber, systemisierte Hierarchie*); and 7. high mobility and flexibility in tactical manoeuvres.[18] According to Hahlweg, all these changes were achieved between 1590 and 1600. He explains the unprecedented tempo at which these developments occurred as being due to the nature of the Eighty Years' War which, in his view, was a 'total war of resistance' (*totale[r] Wiederstandskrieg*) that required the deployment of all the 'vigour and strength of the nation in a temporary struggle for existence [*Existenzkampf*]'.[19]

The picture of the military reforms put in place by the Nassaus as sketched by Hahlweg seems, on the face of it, to justify his conclusion that the developments of the last decade of the sixteenth century were more than worthy of the epithet 'military revolution'. To my mind, however, his line of argument is dubious. In the first place it is remarkable that, contrary to Hahlweg's assertions, the military reforms of the Nassaus did not coincide with the *Existenzkampf* phase of the Eighty Years' War. The first twenty years of the Revolt can justifiably be described as a life-and-death struggle,[20] but in the final decade of the sixteenth century the Spaniards had allowed the pressure on the rebellious provinces to slacken. Civil war had broken out in France in 1589. A year later, Philip II of Spain (1527–1598) ordered his commander-in-chief in the Low Countries, Alexander Farnese (1545–1592), duke of Parma, to intervene immediately to support the French Catholic League. For the king of Spain, the war in the Netherlands

---

[16] Hahlweg, 'Die Oranische Heeresreform. Ihr Weiterwirken und die Befreiung und Etablierung der Niederlande. Studien und Betrachtungen', *Nassauische Annalen*, LXXX (1969), 137–57; 'Aspekte und Probleme der Reform des niederländischen Kriegswesens unter Prinz Moritz von Oranien', *BMGN*, LXXXVI (1971), 161–77; *Die Heeresreform der Oranier. Das Kriegsbuch des Grafen Johann von Nassau-Siegen* (Wiesbaden 1973), introduction, pp. 1–54.
[17] Hahlweg, 'Oranische Heeresreform', p. 139.
[18] Hahlweg, 'Aspekte und Probleme', p. 164.
[19] Hahlweg, *Heeresreform der Oranier*, p. 9.
[20] In November and December 1572 and in August 1575 the Spaniards massacred the inhabitants of Zutphen, Naarden and Oudewater, respectively; in July 1573 they put a large part of the garrison of the captured town of Haarlem to the sword. See Henk van Nierop, *Het verraad van het Noorderkwartier. Oorlog, terreur en recht in de Nederlandse Opstand* (Amsterdam 1999), pp. 82–3, 101 and 103–4.

took on a secondary importance for the time being.[21] This favourable circumstance for the Republic presented the rebels with an opportunity to extend their area of control, which in my opinion allowed Maurits and Willem Lodewijk to experiment with various new tactical formations without taking any grave risks. When the Spaniards once again directed their greatest forces against the Dutch from 1598, the Republic's hour of peril had passed. With the exception of the large-scale Spanish incursions of 1605 and 1629, two fronts were drawn – a southern front (Flanders, Brabant and the River Meuse) and an eastern front (Overijssel and Gelderland) – along which the struggle took place.

The absence of a struggle for survival after about 1589 is, in my view, the most important reason for the influence of the military reforms of the Nassaus remaining limited to the tactical sphere. Hahlweg is correct that between 1590 and 1600 the Dutch army's fighting strength was increased by the constant drilling and exercising of the soldiers and the improvement in the manoeuvrability of the combat units achieved by reducing the size of the tactical formations. His assumption that in tandem with this an officer training programme and a new command structure with a clearly defined hierarchy were introduced is, however, incorrect. Nor was there any question of the development of a logistical apparatus to support the military operations. It is telling that Hahlweg makes no mention of a new relationship between state and army when he enumerates the components of the military reforms of the Nassaus. In *Richelieu's Army* (2001), British historian David Parrott's comprehensive study of the French army during the first half of the seventeenth century, Parrott argues that it was not within the power of the early modern state to instigate a programme of far-reaching reforms of its own volition. Structural changes only came about in the face of a foreign threat or attack.[22] It is therefore no coincidence that, in the case of the Republic's substantial expansion of its armed forces, the adjustment of the hierarchy of the officer corps, reform of the organisational structure and development of a logistical system were ratcheted up from 1672, when the Republic was, after all, embroiled in a struggle for survival against the France of the Sun King.[23]

The British historian Geoffrey Parker has since 1972 been developing an important new perspective on the notion of a military revolution, resulting in several publications.[24] He has demonstrated that Roberts's assertion (and implic-

---

[21] Geoffrey Parker, *The Dutch Revolt* (London 1977), pp. 225–7; Jonathan Israel, *The Dutch Republic. Its Rise, Greatness, and Fall 1477–1806* (Oxford 1995), p. 253, writes: 'It cannot be denied that the spectacular military achievements of the Republic between 1590 and 1597 were possible only because Spain was distracted by the struggle in France.'
[22] David Parrott, *Richelieu's Army: War, Government and Society in France, 1624–1642* (Cambridge 2001), pp. 110–11.
[23] Hahlweg states that the French attack of 1672 plunged Holland (the Republic) 'into the second major struggle for existence in its history'. See 'Oranische Heeresreform', p. 150.
[24] Geoffrey Parker, *The Army of Flanders and the Spanish Road 1567–1659. The Logistics of Spanish Victory and Defeat in the Low Countries' Wars* (1972; rev. edn, Cambridge 1990); *The Military Revolution. Military Innovation and the Rise of the West, 1500–1800*, 2nd edn

itly also Hahlweg's) that the Spanish troops could not match the prowess of the Dutch army because, unlike their adversaries, the Spanish had apparently failed to keep pace with recent developments, requires some qualification. 'The simple fact is that, wherever a situation of permanent or semi-permanent war existed ... one finds, not surprisingly, standing armies, greater professionalism among the troops, improvements in military organization, and certain tactical innovations', Parker writes.[25] No less significant is Parker's proposition that the start of the military revolution must be antedated to 1520, the year in which the development of a new fortification system was achieved. The *trace italienne* or bastion system once again shifted the centre of gravity in the conduct of war from attack to defence. In the 1490s the deployment of mobile siege artillery had transformed the besieging of towns into short-lived affairs. High stone walls proved extremely vulnerable to iron cannonballs. However, by introducing thick earthen walls and erecting projecting artillery platforms, called bastions, from circa 1520 sieges once again became prolonged undertakings. 'Wherever they [artillery fortifications] existed, they made battles irrelevant – and therefore unusual.'[26]

This 'transformation of the art of defensive warfare' was, according to Parker, the driving force behind the expansion of armies in the seventeenth century, rather than the offensive possibilities presented by the military reforms of the Nassaus, as asserted by Roberts.[27] The extremely costly cavalry could, after all, play no part in sieges and pitched battles were rare, so the infantry became increasingly important, both for assaults on fortified strongholds and for their defence. The bastion system also meant that the perimeter of towns and cities expanded, which not only required more defenders but also bigger besieging armies to keep the stronger garrisons within their own gates. Furthermore, while one's own field army was occupied with a siege, the security of one's own towns had to be safeguarded, requiring thousands of garrison troops. Lastly, Parker argues that army expansion compelled the government to become more closely involved with the armed forces: troops had to be mustered frequently and victualled on a regular basis from food depots (*étapes*) established along their marching routes.[28]

Though Parker's emphasis on the importance of the *trace italienne* complements the views of Roberts and Hahlweg on a significant point, he fails to provide any convincing evidence that an all-embracing military revolution occurred between 1520 and 1660. It is beyond question that the bastion system had a major impact on the conduct of war in the early modern era, but Parker's assertion that 'a town defended by the *trace italienne* could only be captured, as a

---

(Cambridge 1996); and 'The "Military Revolution 1560–1660" – A Myth?' (1979) reprinted in Rogers (ed.), *The Military Revolution Debate*, pp. 37–54.
[25] Parker, 'The "Military Revolution 1560–1660" – A Myth?', p. 40.
[26] Ibid., p. 43.
[27] Parker, *Army of Flanders*, pp. 6–7.
[28] Parker, 'The "Military Revolution 1560–1660" – A Myth?', pp. 42–6; *The Military Revolution*, p. 14.

rule, by a total blockade',[29] does not amount to proof of the impregnable nature of the bastion system; it rather indicates that the techniques for laying siege to fortified towns had not yet found an adequate solution to the new system of defence. One might also query Parker's linking of the *trace italienne* with army expansion. The American historian Bert Hall rightly points out that bigger armies and the *trace italienne* 'mesh well in only one case', namely war in the Low Countries.[30] Moreover, the example Parker employs as evidence that the *trace italienne* led to unprecedented military growth paints a distorted picture. 'Thus although the siege of 's-Hertogenbosch [in 1629] itself tied down only 25,000 men, the need to defend the numerous fortified centres of the Republic itself required an increase in Dutch army size from 71,443 in February 1629, to 77,193 in April, and to 128,877 in July.'[31] Parker fails to mention that the Dutch military effort during the entire Eighty Years' War reached its zenith in 1629 or that this army expansion was in response to an attack by the Spanish-Imperial army on the Veluwe and in the province of Utrecht, and that these extra troops were, as far as possible, disbanded as soon as the threat had abated. Thus it was not so much the bastion system that forced the Republic to expand its army in 1629, but the exigency of raising a second mobile force to protect the Republic's own borders against a Spanish counterattack during the siege of 's-Hertogenbosch.

It is true, however, that the Spanish army was a huge force in the sixteenth century and first half of the seventeenth century, at least 200,000 strong around 1590 and 300,000 strong around 1630 (both strengths on paper). Parker is also right to draw attention to the fact that the Spanish government actively clothed and fed its troops. The Spanish example cannot, however, be used as a model for the other European armies. Given that Spain had to engage in a war on several fronts in regions that were geographically remote, its army had to be expanded to an unprecedented size to tackle different adversaries simultaneously. Unlike France and the Dutch Republic, Spain could not make use of internal supply lines to establish a local military dominance by rapid troop movements over land or by river. Furthermore, the increasingly parlous state of the Spanish coffers made it increasingly difficult for the Spanish government to pay its troops. To prevent mutinies, Spanish soldiers therefore received their basic necessities of food and clothing in kind. The remainder of their wages could then be paid out – in full or in part – in cash, at least occasionally.[32]

The expansion of the Spanish army forced Spain's adversaries to reinforce their armed forces as well. 'Threat provoked response; innovation spawned imitation. Once Spain had entered onto a path of escalating army size, Spain's foes had to counter her gambit somehow, and in the end they had no better choice

---

[29] Parker, *Army of Flanders*, p. 8.
[30] Bert S. Hall, *Weapons and Warfare in Renaissance Europe: Gunpowder, Technology, and Tactics* (Baltimore and London 1997), pp. 207 and 209.
[31] Parker, *The Military Revolution*, p. 14.
[32] Parker, *Army of Flanders*, pp. 160–3.

than to match the increased sizes as best they could', writes Hall.[33] But did this escalated war effort also prompt a structural change in the organisation of the land-based forces and a modified relationship between state and army? David Parrott demonstrates that in France this was not the case. On the contrary, in its war with Spain from 1635 to 1659, the French government had to make increasing demands on the officers' credit. As far as possible the French authorities shifted the costs of retention of the companies to the captains. As a consequence the French army had an effective strength of no more than 80,000 men, in contrast to its strength on paper of 120,000.[34] The phenomenal growth of the French army did not begin until 1661; it expanded to an effective strength of no fewer than 250,000 men in 1678 and 340,000 men around 1700.[35] According to Parrott, the reason Louis XIV could maintain three to four times as many troops as his father must be sought in the altered relations between state and army rather than in demographic shifts. The population of France around 1630 was, after all, approximately the same as around 1700. After 1659 the French government became increasingly involved with the army, primarily in the care and welfare of troops. In France, however, this development was not the outcome of a struggle for survival, but of the creeping realisation that the Spanish-Austrian-Habsburg hegemony could only be combatted successfully if the French military capacity was fully developed. The French army's huge losses between 1635 and 1659 were in fact largely to blame on starvation and lack of money. 'The critical factors in determining success and – more often – failure [during the war with Spain] were far more frequently the inadequacies and breakdown of general administration, finance and supply', writes Parrott.[36] The German historian Bernhard Kroener had already reached the conclusion that, between 1635 and 1640, the French field army was losing no less than 30 per cent of its strength per annum, primarily through disease and desertion.[37] The military expansion of the late seventeenth century was not limited to France. The Sun King's urge to expand his realm's boundaries forced France's neighbours to reinforce their armies as well. As a result, during the War of the Spanish Succession (1702–1712) there were between 900,000 and 1,000,000 soldiers serving in the field and in garrisons. The Dutch army attained its greatest strength during this war: an effective strength of more than 100,000 men. However, between 1667 and 1712 it was not only the total manpower of the armed forces that increased; even more spectacular was the growth of the field armies, that is the troops assembled for military

[33] Hall, *Weapons and Warfare*, p. 209.
[34] Parrott, *Richelieu's Army*, p. 220.
[35] John A. Lynn, 'Recalculating French Army Growth during the *Grand Siècle*, 1610–1715', in Rogers (ed.), *The Military Revolution Debate*, pp. 117–47, esp. 125.
[36] Parrott, *Richelieu's Army*, pp. 83 (quote), 222, 434–61.
[37] Bernhard Kroener, 'Die Entwicklung der Truppenstärken in den französischen Armeen zwischen 1635 und 1661', in *Forschungen und Quellen zur Geschichte des Dreissigjährigen Krieges* (Aschendorff and Münster 1981), pp. 163–220, esp. 172.

operations, in contrast to the troops who remained in garrisons.[38] During the first half of the seventeenth century, the field armies in the Netherlandish theatre of war were usually 20,000 to 25,000 strong. By the Dutch War (1672–1678) they had already grown to between 50,000 and 60,000 men, and by the Nine Years' War (1688–1697) they had expanded to 100,000. For the first six years of the War of the Spanish Succession the field armies were approximately 70,000 strong, but from 1708 they totalled more than 120,000 men. By the War of the Austrian Succession (1740–1748) their strength was about 70,000 to 80,000 men and sometimes reached 100,000.[39]

On the basis of the spectacular growth of the armies between 1660 and 1712, the British historian Jeremy Black draws the conclusion that Roberts's interpretation of the military revolution (1560–1660) is untenable. Black agrees with Parker that the development and introduction of the bastion system greatly influenced the conduct of war in the early modern era, but he rejects the thesis that tactical changes and army expansion in the late sixteenth century and the first half of the seventeenth century led to state formation. According to Black, from a military viewpoint this period could in fact be termed static. The weaponry hardly evolved and he sees no noteworthy changes, even in tactics. In his view, a tactical revolution did not occur until about 1700, when the pike and matchlock musket were replaced by flintlock firearms with bayonets. These new weapons made the infantry wholly dominant on the battlefield and the Europeans could stand their ground in the rest of the world against adversaries who were much stronger numerically, which for Black is the crucial point. 'The period from 1660 onwards, up to the outbreak of the French Revolutionary Wars, saw the victory of armies emphasizing the concentrated firepower of disciplined infantry and their supporting artillery over more mobile forces [especially those of the Ottoman Empire and the Moguls in India] that stressed the use of shock-power in attack.'[40]

Black argues that the expansion of European armies was only possible after the cessation of the religious and civil wars of the sixteenth and seventeenth centuries. The restoration of domestic peace apparently made it possible for governments to reassert their authority and tighten their control of the military. 'By setting the decisive changes, in terms of army size, weaponry and organization, in the post-1660 period, rather than the Roberts century, it can be argued that the more stable domestic political circumstances of most states in the period were the cause, and not the consequence, of these changes.' In conclusion, Black identifies three military revolutions: the first around 1500 brought about by the introduction of the *trace italienne*; a second between 1660 and 1712 characterised

---

[38] G. Perjés, 'Army Provisioning, Logistics and Strategy in the Second Half of the 17th Century', *Acta Historica Academiae Scientiarum Hungaricae*, XVI (Budapest 1970), 1–51, esp. p. 1.
[39] Van Nimwegen, *Subsistentie*, p. 9; and *De Republiek als grote mogendheid*, p. 128.
[40] Jeremy Black, *European Warfare 1660–1815* (New Haven and London 1994), p. 15.

by spectacular army growth and the introduction of the flintlock musket with bayonet; and a third between 1792 and 1815, the era of the Revolutionary and Napoleonic Wars that marked the advent of mass armies.[41]

Black is right to draw attention to developments between 1660 and 1712, but his assertion that the conduct of war in the period 1560–1660 was characterised by stasis goes much too far. After all, he himself acknowledges that European victories over non-Europeans in the eighteenth and nineteenth centuries must in part be attributed to superior weaponry, but also and to a much greater degree to improved discipline and proficiency. The constant drilling and exercising of troops was certainly one of the key aspects of the military reforms of the Nassaus. Black's emphasis on the role of the restoration of domestic stability in the second military revolution is applicable only to France; the driving force behind the expansion of the armies of the Dutch Republic, Austria and, from 1689, England was the escalation of the French war effort.

The basic tenets of this study

The aim of this study is to steer the debate about the military revolution in a new direction by an analysis of the moulding and deployment of the Dutch army in the period 1588–1688. One would be justified in questioning whether it is meaningful to refer to *the* military revolution when this concept covers a period of 140 years (1520–1660). This rather seems to indicate an evolutionary process in which developments followed one another in swift or not so swift succession.[42] Making reference to *the* military revolution reduces 'revolution' – in the sense of a radical break with an existing situation achieved in a relatively short time – to a hollow, meaningless term. Were there then no fundamental changes in military organisation and tactics in the early modern period, such that relations between the state and the armed forces were structurally altered and the impact of war on society substantially increased? The answer to this question can only be in the negative. The conduct of war did indeed alter radically between 1500 and 1700, but summarising developments during this period as *the* military revolution is, in my opinion, of little benefit and does not contribute to a better grasp of what actually changed and what significance should be ascribed to those changes. Instead I would argue that there were several military revolutions of varying import. The effect of this succession of military revolutions on warfare in general and the relationship between state and army in particular was highly variable.

This book defends the argument that the military reforms of the Nassaus led to a tactical revolution around 1600. Their reforms had no influence on military structures and nor did they result in army expansion; this required an organi-

---

[41] Ibid., pp. 7–20, 32, 89 and 92 (quote).
[42] Clifford J. Rogers, 'The Military Revolution of the Hundred Years War', in Rogers (ed.), *The Military Revolution Debate*, pp. 55–93, esp. 76–7.

sational revolution, which occurred in the Republic between 1667 and 1688. The Dutch fleet had undergone a similar development some fifteen years earlier. The first Anglo-Dutch War (1652–1654) demonstrated that armed merchant vessels were no match for purpose-built men-of-war. Two fleet-building programmes were intended to provide the Republic with a true battle fleet. In February and December 1653 the States-General ordered the construction of a total of sixty warships. As a consequence of the States-General's resolution of 5 January 1654, which stated that, after the conclusion of the peace, none of the new warships could be sold without the unanimous agreement of the provinces, the Republic had a standing fleet at its disposal.[43]

The great weight that contemporaries attached to the military reforms of the Nassaus is evident from the *Ordres van batailjen gepractiseert in de legers der Vereenighde Nederlanden onder het beleydt van ... Mauritius en ... Frederick Hendrick* (Orders of battle practised in the armies of the United Netherlands under the generalship of ... Maurits and ... Frederik Hendrik).[44] The compiler who enlarged upon and completed this military manual, which was published on the eve of the Year of Disaster (1672), boasted that 'the high school of war has resided here [in the Republic], where kings, princes, counts and lords have attended and from our princes, who are most excellent professors of war, have learnt this science.' However, the author was forced to add with regret that the expertise gained had by 1672 already largely been lost again, because 'the disciples [of Maurits and Frederik Hendrik] due to ... death have mostly passed away or, during this time of peace, have grown old and been weakened by old age, as to make any practical use of [them]'.[45] Captain-Lieutenant Johan Boxel, author of the drill manual *Vertoogh van de krijghsoeffeninge* (Exposition of the exercise of war) published in 1670, also considered it necessary to impress upon the States of Holland that, in view of the French threat, there was a serious need to drill the Dutch troops. Drill (*Wapenoeffeninge*) was the best teacher of battle skills. 'The conduct of war is the bulwark that counters enemies, in which, through God's merciful blessings, the Republic has succeeded so well that, after a war of eighty years, it has won a glorious peace.'[46] Both authors were therefore warning their readers that the high level of proficiency which the Dutch troops had gained under Maurits, Willem Lodewijk and Frederik Hendrik had not lasted. In the Republic of the first half of the seventeenth century, the conduct of war was seen as a personal responsibility of military men, namely the captains of foot and of

---

[43] Bruijn, *Varend verleden*, pp. 92–7.
[44] *Ordres van batailjen* (Amsterdam 1672) was based on material by the engineer Johan le Hon, killed in action before Maastricht in 1632, and was expanded upon by his son, the engineer and regimental quartermaster Christoffel le Hon.
[45] *Ordres van batailjen*, fol. 9v.
[46] Johan Boxel, *Vertoogh van de krijghsoeffeninge soo in 't particulier van musquet en spies, als in 't generael van een corpus of gros der compagniën te voet van de guardes* (The Hague 1670). See also Hahlweg, 'Oranische Heeresreform', p. 142 n. 16.

horse, who were the proprietors of infantry and cavalry companies, respectively. They had to maintain the units at strength and train recruits for the profession of soldiery. The task of government in all this was limited to furnishing the necessary financial resources – though the officers were expected to use their own lines of credit if the wages were late in arriving – and to formulating guidelines for the armament and strength of the companies and the verification of their observance. In this respect the Dutch army was no different from the French army prior to 1667.[47] As early as 1618, during the Twelve Years' Truce (1609–1621), Maurits, Willem Lodewijk and Frederik Hendrik complained that the proficiency of the Dutch troops left much to be desired.[48] For as long as the relationship between state and army remained unchanged and there was no structural reform of the armed forces, war continued to be the only true nursery of soldiers. A number of years of peace or truce was demonstrably detrimental to the proficiency and readiness of the troops with almost immediate effect.

Besides the government's inclination to keep its involvement with the army as indirect as possible, the improvised character of warfare in the sixteenth century and the first half of the seventeenth century was also responsible for the lack of structural military reforms. In short, the state had at that time a preference for *ad hoc* solutions and endeavoured to keep fixed costs associated with the military enterprise to a minimum. Illustrative of this is the decision reached by the States-General in December 1586, 'to reduce the armed forces to such a small number, proportioned as befits the state of the finances', so that it could henceforth be financed from provincial contributions on a monthly basis.[49] The costs of the Republic's defence were shared among the member provinces according to their financial wherewithal as agreed in the Union of Utrecht of 1579. Starting in 1588, each province was assigned a proportionally fixed quota of the army's wages and other military expenses. The unanimous consent of all the provinces was required for the redistribution of the quotas. This financial arrangement was known as the 'repartition system'. Only when circumstances necessitated a greater war effort did the States-General temporarily take more troops into service. As soon as the threat had subsided these men were, as far as possible, discharged again. Until the middle of the seventeenth century the regents preferred such interim solutions. Taking financial measures that would make it possible to fund a military escalation, potentially shortening the war, was not even considered.

---

[47] Parrott, *Richelieu's Army*, pp. 348–9.
[48] NA, SHS 1449, 'Ordre bij sijne Ex.cie [Maurits], sijne gen. Graeff Willem Lodewijck ..., de heere prince Henrick Fred. ... ende den Raet van State volgens de resolutie der ... Staten-Generael van den 2.e may 1616 geraempt om deser landen crijchsvolck ... tot derselver landen dienst bequamer te maecken ende te houden als 'tselve tot noch toe is geweest', The Hague, 5 December 1618.
[49] NA, CvdH 123, Notes by Adriaan van der Hoop (1701–1767), clerk of the Council of State from 1737 to 1748, regarding the States-General resolution of 4 December 1586.

The second key proposition in this study is that the French show of strength from 1667 onwards forced the Republic to reform its army structurally. The French invasion of 1672 provided the impetus that led to the formation of the Dutch standing army. It was, of course, impossible for the States-General to wholly eliminate the discrepancy between the paper and effective strengths of the units, for the simple reason that soldiers were killed in action, taken ill or deserted. However, thanks to the government subsequently providing financial support for the captains to keep their companies at the prescribed strength, the gravest forms of fraud could be eradicated and a professional officers corps could gradually take shape. At the same time, the increase in the scale of warfare necessitated the introduction of special logistical facilities, in the form of bread depots equipped with mills and ovens. Foraging locally to feed field armies of 30,000 or more was an impossibility in view of seventeenth-century demographics. Following France's example, the Republic introduced the 'magazine system' of staples for provisioning troops in the theatre of operations. In the second half of the seventeenth century, France was a guiding light in military organisation and logistics, and she likewise set the tone in the conduct of siege warfare. The impact of the systematised besieging of strongholds devised by the French master of siegecraft and fortifications engineer Sébastien le Prestre (1633–1707), seigneur de Vauban, was that only towns protected by extensive and well-maintained fortifications as well as sizeable garrisons could sustain a lengthy defence. The War of Devolution (1667–1668) and even more the Year of Disaster heralded the era of large-scale warfare. After the Peace of Nijmegen (1678) it was vitally important that the Dutch should preserve the knowledge and experience gained during those seven years of strife and preserve regimental structures intact. The Republic could not afford to become locked into another struggle with France wholly unprepared. The future security of the Republic against France could only be guaranteed by maintaining a core army and exercising the troops regularly during peacetime.

This study's point of departure is that there was indeed a tactical revolution around 1600. The reform of the French army in the 1660s coupled with the introduction of a new logistical system and the development of improved siege techniques led to an organisational revolution in the conduct of war. France's neighbours, and the Republic above all, were faced with the choice of swiftly adapting to this new situation or tasting defeat. The tactical revolution was thus embedded in a more wide-ranging organisational reform. Together they led to the birth of the standing army, a spectacular scaling-up of warfare and ever-greater governmental involvement with the armed forces. Not until the Revolutionary and Napoleonic Wars would the conduct of war once again undergo changes that were as sweeping as those of around 1520 and 1600, and those between 1667 and 1688.

The structure of this study

In view of the basic premises of the research it was self-evident that the structure of the book should proceed from a chronological divide: Part I covers the period 1588–1648, while Part II covers the period 1648–1688. Part I is composed of three thematic and three chronological chapters, while Part II is composed of two thematic and three chronological chapters. The choice of a combination of a thematic approach and one that traces historical developments demands some clarification. The organisation, payment, financing, armament, tactics, the nature of military operations and the logistics of the Dutch army are tackled in the five thematic chapters. The examination of all these aspects in turn makes it possible to conduct a detailed investigation of the tactical and organisational military reforms. The transformation of the military enterprise in the period 1588–1688 did not, however, take place in isolation; a guiding principle in this study is that a serious foreign threat was a prerequisite of military reforms. Furthermore, domestic political relations, the relative strength of the warring parties and unforeseen military events in the theatre of war imposed limitations on the operational freedom of the military commanders. The exploration of this matter requires a chronological approach. An analysis of the course of the Eighty Years' War from 1588, the war with Münster (1665–1666) and the Dutch War (1672–1678), which was the first trial of strength between the Republic and Louis XIV, makes it possible to place the organisational and tactical developments in context.

This study is largely based on original research into primary sources. This might come as a surprise, given that the seventeenth century has been subjected to greater scrutiny than any other period in the history of the Netherlands. As noted, this applies less to the military history and the military-historical studies that are already extant, which are usually based exclusively on published sources and literature. This study draws on the rich documentary sources of the Koninklijk Huisarchief (Royal Archives), the Nationaal Archief (National Archives), the Koninklijke Bibliotheek (National Library of the Netherlands), the States archives of the provinces of Friesland, Gelderland, Groningen, Overijssel, Utrecht and Zeeland, and Amsterdam City Archives. A comprehensive survey of all the records consulted is provided as an appendix.

PART I

1588–1648

♦ 1 ♦

The Organisation and Remuneration of the Dutch Army (1588–1648)

'Those upon whom, next to God, one most depends in the battle array are the *doppelsoldner*, of whom one would do well to have many at one's disposal.'[1] In these somewhat pedantic terms, Johann VII (1561–1623), 'the Middle', count of Nassau-Siegen, a younger brother of Willem Lodewijk, captured the essence of the art of warfare since the late fifteenth century. While the might of the armies of medieval knights had resided in a relatively small number of heavily armoured warriors on steeds, the Burgundian War (1474–1477) and the Italian Wars (1494–1559) demonstrated that foot-soldiers operating in extremely deep formations (*Gewalthaufen*) and armed with five-metre-long pikes (the above-mentioned *doppelsoldner*[2]), halberds and two-handed swords were capable of successfully withstanding a cavalry charge and even of breaching the enemy's battle array. The Swiss and, in imitation of them, the German mercenaries known in German as *Landsknechte*, and in English as 'lansquenets', relied on solidarity, an *esprit de corps* and, not least, battlefield discipline to bring them victory.

With the raising of two bands of lansquenets, each 3,000 to 4,000 strong, between 1481 and 1486, Maximilian I (1459–1519), king of the Romans (i.e. emperor-elect) from 1486 to 1493 and subsequently Holy Roman Emperor until his death, lay the foundations for the military system that would endure until the end of the eighteenth century. If it proved impossible to raise enough men by means of proclamations (*Aufgebote*), the summoning up of vassals and their serfs, then rulers and governing bodies had to turn to mercenaries. The enlist-

---

[1] Hahlweg, *Heeresreform der Oranier*, p. 262.
[2] The *doppelsoldner* or *dobbelsoldner* were originally deployed in the front rank, i.e. the most dangerous position, and by way of compensation they received double pay. They wore a cuirass and were armed with a two-handed sword. Over the course of the sixteenth century, 'dobbelsoldner' became an epithet for pikemen, though by this time there was no question of them being paid twice as much as other infantry. Georg Ortenburg, *Waffe und Waffengebrauch im Zeitalter der Landsknechte* (Koblenz 1984), p. 88; Christian Beaufort-Spontin, *Harnisch und Waffe Europas. Die militärische Ausrüstung im 17. Jahrhundert* (Munich 1982), pp. 98–9.

ment of lansquenets involved striking a deal with a private individual, a military enterpriser who, for an agreed sum of money, delivered a contractually specified number of troops, over whom he retained overall command as colonel. As regimental commander he had the authority to appoint the captains of companies up to 500 men strong. The captain, in turn, appointed the company's lower-ranking officers.[3]

The officers of the Dutch army

In the seventeenth century, all military personnel who held a function (*officium*) were designated officers, including the sergeants, corporals, drummers, company clerk, surgeon and provost in infantry companies, and, in the cavalry, the quartermaster, trumpeters and farrier. These under-officers were known as the minor, common or lesser officers, the term non-commissioned officer (NCO) being coined only later. Command of each company was vested in the three chief officers: the captain, the lieutenant and the ensign in the infantry, and the captain of horse, or rittmaster, the lieutenant and the cornet in the cavalry. From 1588 until the end of the seventeenth century, all Dutch infantry companies, no matter whether they were 89, 113 or 200 strong, had twelve or thirteen officers: three major officers, two sergeants, three corporals, two drummers, a clerk and a surgeon. From 1599 to 1668 each company also had its own provost and, until 1599, companies of 200 and 150 men included an additional musician, a piper. A troop of horse had eight officers: three chief officers, a quartermaster, two trumpeters, a clerk and a farrier.[4]

The various responsibilities and duties of the officers are described in detail in *The Principles Of The Art Militarie, Practised in the Warres of the United Netherlands, under the commaund of His Highnesse the Prince of Orange our Captaine General*, first published in English in 1637.[5] Its author, Henry Hexham (c. 1585–c. 1650), was an Englishman who for forty-two years served as a captain and quartermaster in the Dutch army.[6] The clerk of a company was expected to be 'an honest, and a sufficient man' to whom the captain could entrust his company's financial affairs. What this entailed becomes clear from the instruc-

---

[3] Siegfried Fiedler, *Kriegswesen und Kriegführung im Zeitalter der Landsknechte* (Koblenz 1985), pp. 59, 62, 64 and 66.

[4] HCO, ASO 1457, Council of State (hereafter RvS), The Hague, 8 October 1588, enclosure dated 19 August 1588; *Recueil … betreffende de saaken van den oorlog*, I, no. 2, 'Placaat op het stuk van de monsteringe', 4 February 1599, with the addendum 'Lijste van een compagnie voetvolks van [135] hoofden', 6 February 1599. On the composition of companies of varying strengths see: NA, RvS 2287 and NA, Archief Adriaan Bogaers 46.

[5] I have used Hexham's own Dutch translation of this work: *Principii ofte de eerste gronden van de oorloghskonste gelijck se in dese Vereenichde Nederlanden ghepractiseert wort, onder het gouvernement van sijn hoogheyt mijnheer den prince van Orangien* (The Hague 1642).

[6] Hahlweg, 'Die Oranische Heeresreform', p. 144; Ten Raa, *Het Staatsche leger*, IV, p. 60 n. 1.

tions drafted by Floris II van Pallandt (1577–1639), count of Culemborg, for the clerk of his company. He was to keep an account of payments to the soldiers and other expenditures in a cashbook, and 'likewise to keep pertinent note of all the company's soldiers who desert or who die, recording the day and the hour, name and surname, respectively'. Hexham's military manual states that besides having to be proficient in playing their instruments the two drummers were expected to speak several languages, 'because often he may be sent unto the enemy, for the ransoming of prisoners'. Each of the three corporals was responsible for one of the company's three sections. It was their task to instruct fresh recruits in the use of their arms. The highest-ranking minor officer was the sergeant. He was expected to possess the three qualities of being 'a wise man, a man of spirit, and a man of courage, for a good sergeant is a great help to his captain'. Besides maintaining discipline, the sergeants ensured that the soldiers kept their rank and file when marching. Being entrusted with the banner, the ideal ensign 'ought to be a generous, able young man, above all things to be careful of his honour, and reputation'. After all, the colours were entrusted to him. Besides serving as a point of identification during battle the colours had great symbolic value; its loss meant a serious disgrace. In battle the ensign therefore had to protect the colours with his life, and 'rather than to lose them he ought to make them his winding sheet'. The lieutenant was the captain's deputy, and it was the captain to whom the government granted a commission to raise and maintain a company.[7] The 'election' or choice of captain was therefore a matter of great importance.

The commissioning of captains and senior officers was a sensitive matter in the sixteenth and seventeenth centuries, since civilians placed their lives and chattels in the hands of the mercenaries to whom they entrusted the defence of their towns and cities. Since 1588 the payment of most of the Republic's troops had, for political and financial reasons, been devolved to the provinces using a distribution formula, known as the 'repartition system'.[8] Repartition did not mean that the Dutch army was fragmented into as many small provincial armies – the troops remained 'soldiery of the Generality' – but it did result in the provincial States, their 'paymasters', exercising considerable influence over them. As early as 1589, Holland considered the appointment of company commanders, lieutenants and ensigns or cornets to be a provincial prerogative. In March of that year, Johan van Oldenbarnevelt (1547–1619), Advocate or chairman of the States of Holland since 1586, 'sustained' that the nomination of a captain of foot or of horse fell to the 'province to which the aforesaid [company] is repartitioned'.[9]

---

[7] Hexham, *Principii*, pp. 2–4; GA, AHGC 763A, 'Instructie [from Count Floris II of Culemborg] voor den schrijver van onse compaignie voetvolck Samuel van de Waeter', The Hague, 24 September 1625.
[8] For the following see Simon van Slingelandt, *Staatkundige geschriften*, 4 vols (Amsterdam 1784–1785), IV, 'Historische verhandeling van het gesag over de militie van den Staat', pp. 13–66.
[9] Ibid., p. 35.

The other provinces subscribed to this standpoint of the States of Holland. This development constituted a break with the past, since in 1581 the States-General had empowered William of Orange to appoint all officers in its name. After his assassination in 1584, this privilege was transferred to his son Maurits and the Council of State (*Raad van State*), who were jointly authorised to raise extra troops, providing such military reinforcement could be financed from the contributions the provinces had consented to for that year. However, Robert Dudley (1531–1588), earl of Leicester, who was appointed governor- and captain-general of the Dutch Republic in 1585,[10] took many more troops into service than could be paid from the available resources, thereby sparking mutinies. The experience with Leicester led to the introduction of the above-mentioned system of provincial quotas following his return to England in December 1587. Thereafter the Council of State continued to be charged with the 'disposition in the affairs of war and over the soldiery',[11] but only in the executive sense. For example, it was allowed to order the raising of troops only with the prior permission of the provinces, which now also determined who was eligible for an officer's commission in consultation with the stadholder.

Either the stadholder, in his capacity as provincial captain-general, or the provincial States 'recommended' a new captain of foot or horse to the Council of State, which subsequently issued the commission. The Council of State continued to appoint officers of any rank higher than colonel directly – the reason for this was that the authority of generals extended over all troops, irrespective of the province which financed them – but only with the States-General's stamp of approval. The procedure described only applied for the appointment of officers in garrisons, since Maurits, as commander-in-chief, and Frederik Hendrik after him, reserved the right to immediately replace field officers, company commanders and lower-ranking officers who fell in action or died as a result of accidents or sickness during the campaign. Consultation with the provincial States and the States-General was bypassed in such cases.[12]

Aspiring officers usually began their careers as volunteers in a colonel's company. In June 1604, Ernst Casimir (1573–1632), count of Nassau-Dietz, who was serving as the colonel of a regiment of Germans in Dutch service at the time, entreated his elder brother, Johann VII, to send him from Nassau a few 'noble spirits' (*gentils espricts*) who were eager to learn the art of war: 'I would be able to promote them according to their merit, should the posts of ensigns, lieutenants or captains fall vacant in my regiment.'[13] More or less simultaneously, on the insistence of his father, Johann VI, Willem Lodewijk asked Maurits to assign

---

[10] See pp. 152.
[11] Van Slingelandt, *Staatkundige geschriften*, IV, p. 66.
[12] NA, RAZH, ASH 37, Resolution of the States of Holland (hereafter Res. SH), 12 March 1603.
[13] *Archives ou correspondance inédite de la Maison d'Orange-Nassau*, ed. G. Groen van Prinsterer, 2nd series, II (Utrecht 1858), no. 316.

the captaincy of the first company to become available to one of his cousins (not mentioned by name), so that he might become proficient in the art of war. Willem Lodewijk did not, however, consider a company of horse appropriate, 'for the infantry is the true training-school of young gentlemen'.[14] This was how Johan Maurits (1604–1679), count of Nassau-Siegen, a younger son of Johann VII, began his career. In 1618 and 1619 he served as a pikeman in the Frisian Guards of Willem Lodewijk. In 1620 he accompanied Frederik Hendrik to the Palatinate as a rank-and-file trooper and his promotion to ensign followed later that year. In 1624 he received his commission as captain, whereafter his career progressed swiftly: in 1626 he became a lieutenant-colonel and three years later a colonel. He ended his career as a field-marshal.[15]

Those who lacked patrons as powerful as those of Johan Maurits were reliant on a long record of service and bravery for their commission and career. Not even a member of the Nassau family could be given preferential treatment at the expense of older and more experienced officers, though the right connections were still essential for someone who wanted to rise through the ranks of the Dutch army swiftly. Willem Lodewijk apologised to Maurits that he had not assigned a company in his own regiment to the above-mentioned cousin, pointing out that there were several candidates for each vacant captaincy who 'could not be curbed because of their merits or [are] nobles of the land who, through the solicitations of their family to the States [of Friesland], have even prevented me placing my said nephew before them.'[16] Officers maintained close contact with the provincial States, thereby safeguarding their interests via their family ties with the regents, the ruling oligarchy. In December 1605, for example, the Drost (sheriff) of Drenthe and this region's councillors assigned the captaincy of a company to the ensign rather than the unit's lieutenant. They defended this decision by pointing out that, besides his proven bravery, the ensign was the 'son of a nobleman of this region ... God-fearing, chaste, sober, level-headed, and sympathetic towards his soldiers, also better qualified for the captaincy than the aforementioned lieutenant'. This lieutenant had risen through the ranks and it was therefore only right, the Drost reasoned, that he 'on this occasion ought still to be contented with the lieutenancy'.[17]

Maurits also preferred officers to be noblemen. In 1615, when the States of Friesland refused to appoint a prominent member of the Murray clan as ensign in a Scottish company – they preferred to promote the sergeant – Maurits dug

---

[14] KHA, A22-IX-E-215, Willem Lodewijk to Maurits, 30 January [1604], minute.
[15] NA, RAZH, AJdW 2718-2, 'Memorie waerbij can worden gesien dat prins [Johan] Maurits van Nassau van slecht soldaet aff totte hoochste charges toe den Staet ... nu boven vijffendertich iaeren heeft gedient' (Memorandum from which it can be seen that Prince [Johan] Maurits of Nassau, from being merely a soldier to ranking amongst the highest charges, has now served the State ... for more than thirty-five years).
[16] KHA, A22-IX-E-215, Willem Lodewijk to Maurits, 30 January [1604], minute.
[17] NA, SG 4912-I, Drost and representatives of the region of Drenthe, Groningen, 16 December 1605.

in his heels. He informed Willem Lodewijk that this sergeant 'is nought but a vulgar man and of no quality'. Maurits pointed out that the Scottish companies were in a sorry state and that their improvement could only be expected when they were commanded by officers 'who are gentlemen and persons of quality, who would have credit and authority among the soldatesque'. Murray enjoyed the necessary respect among his men, according to Maurits, and through his family connections he would also be able to ensure his company was replenished with fine new soldiers.[18] However, it was not only the sergeant's low social status to which Maurits objected; he simply did not trust the recommendation of his captain, because it was known that in the apportioning of offices that fell vacant in the Scottish companies the deciding factor was usually not quality but the amount of money the candidates were prepared to pay.[19] Here Maurits was broaching a delicate subject: the sale of 'charges' or offices.

An ideal company commander had to be able to wear two hats comfortably. On the one hand he had to serve as an example to the troops and lead them bravely in battle, which required courage, a sense of duty and a 'chaste' life, in other words he must not drink too much. On the other hand, he had to be capable of holding his company together, for which good connections and ample financial resources were a necessity. For example, a company commander always had to have between 600 and 900 guilders in cash at his disposal, 'to be used if the funds [i.e. the soldiers' wages] should be delayed for too long.'[20] Captains of foot and horse were therefore both soldiers and entrepreneurs. This made it well-nigh impossible to consider military quality alone and also hampered the generals and colonels – to their great annoyance – in taking action against officers who were guilty of reprehensible behaviour, ranging from drunkenness, extorting civilians and prolonged absence from the company, to fraud with muster-rolls. In November 1606, Justinus of Nassau (1559–1631), governor of Breda, informed the Council of State in The Hague about the dereliction of duty of one Captain Bothwel, who

> not only lately, with the enemy being so close to this town, had the impudence to neglect his [command of the] main guard, but has done ... likewise many times before.... Also, he has recently availed himself, on taking furlough of only eight days in Holland, of remaining away from his company for two months, and on his return he did not even come to speak to me, and five or six days thereafter once again ... rode off to Bergen op Zoom, where he spent eight or ten days, having neither my consent nor even having requested it.[21]

---

[18] KHA, A22-IX-A1-443, Maurits to Willem Lodewijk, 10 June 1615, with a letter to the States of Friesland of the same date as an addendum.
[19] KHA, A22-IX-A1-444, Maurits to Willem Lodewijk, 16 June 1615.
[20] GA, AHGC 768, Lieutenant Adolff van Padborch to Count Floris II of Culemborg, Straelen, 1 August 1632, and Count Floris II to Van Padborch, 's Heerenberg, 21 August 1632.
[21] NA, SG 4914, Justinus van Nassau to the SG, Breda, 3 November 1606. See also SG 4913, Van Dijck (commissary of the musters) to the SG, Breda, 9 July 1606.

On 5 December 1618, Maurits, Willem Lodewijk and Frederik Hendrik, who was commander of the cavalry at the time, introduced a raft of measures in conjunction with the Council of State, 'intended to make this country's soldiery, on horse as well as on foot, more proficient in the service of these selfsame lands and to maintain them [to this higher standard] as has been the case thus far'.[22] The provinces still had to approve these instructions, but this was no more than a formality because of the altered political relations in the Republic. Van Oldenbarnevelt had been arrested three months earlier, on 19 August, whereupon Maurits assumed political leadership of the Republic alongside the overall military command he already exercised. The unmistakable objective of the 'Ordre' of 5 December was to curtail the influence of the provincial States in the appointment of officers, but it was also intended to counter the most serious abuses in the Dutch army and improve the quality of its officers. The first proposal of Maurits, Willem Lodewijk and Frederik Hendrik was to dismiss all the cavalry officers up to the rank of lieutenant who, through old age and mutilation, were no longer capable of active service, 'on condition of assigning to them a reasonable maintenance', namely a pension ranging from sixteen guilders per *heremaand* (a pay-month of forty-two days) for a corporal to fifty guilders for a lieutenant, 'and thereagainst to engage other skilled officers'. This was less of an issue for the infantry, since older or invalid infantry officers could perform garrison duties, but the mounted arms required more vigorous officers. On the battlefield a cavalryman had to be capable of exercising optimum control of his steed, and troopers also served as escorts for convoys or undertook long-distance forays, which meant having to spend hours or even days in the saddle.

With respect to the appointment of new company commanders, the 'Ordre' of 1618 stipulated that the filling of rittmasterships and captaincies which 'fell vacant' during the campaign would, as was traditional, remain the privilege of the commander-in-chief, but Maurits and Willem Lodewijk wanted henceforth to have the final say in all such appointments to ensure that only experienced and dutiful candidates attained the rank of captain. The provincial States proposed three candidates who had to have served the States-General for a minimum of four years, but 'the lieutenant and cornet [or ensign] of the same company were likewise considered ... to be nominated', so there were five candidates to choose from in all. The two captains-general made the final decision: 'Thus in the conferment of the rittmasterships or captaincies serious and particular attention

---

[22] NA, SHS 1449, 'Ordre bij sijne Ex.cie [Maurits], sijn gen. graeff Willem Lodewijk van Nassauw, stadthouder &c., de heere prince Henrick Fred. van Nassauw &c. ende den Raet van State volgens de resolutie der Ho. Mo. Heeren Staten-Generael van den 2e may 1616 geraempt om deser landen crijchsvolck, soo te peerde als te voete, tot derselver landen dienst bequamer te maecken ende te houden als 'tselve tot noch toe is geweest', The Hague, 5 December 1618. Another copy is located in GA, AHGC 753. See also Wijn, *Krijgswezen*, pp. 72–3.

shall be paid to those whose good services and courageous deeds make them recommendable.'

This procedure applied only to officers of the Dutch companies; the captaincies of foreign companies (French, Scottish, English and German) would be granted by Maurits and Willem Lodewijk, in the case of a captain of horse, in consultation with Frederik Hendrik, who was general of the cavalry, and for a captain of foot in consultation with the colonels. The colonels, in turn, appointed the new lieutenants and ensigns in consultation with the captains, after receiving the consent of the captains-general. For Dutch companies, the captain drew up a list of candidate lieutenants he deemed suitable and presented it to his 'paymaster' province. The provincial States then proceeded to nominate three men 'in addition to whom the ensign will still always count as being nominated'. The captain-general chose the new lieutenant from among these four nominees. The appointment of new ensigns and cornets proceeded in a similar manner. Only candidates who had served a minimum of three years in the Dutch army could be appointed to one of these three ranks, and in case of 'equality in skill' then a 'native' was to be selected above a foreign candidate. The appointment of the ranks below that of ensign, the non-commissioned offices, remained the privilege of the captains. Lastly, the 'Ordre' included a ban on the selling of captaincies and other 'military offices … unless permission was granted'.

The 'Ordre' of 1618 marked an important step towards professionalisation of the Republic's officer corps, but this was just a beginning. It remained impossible to tackle fraud, insubordination and dereliction of duty with an iron fist. The 'Ordre' was primarily intended to have a preventative effect, because once a company commander had been appointed it was very difficult to dismiss him, even after 1618. Though Maurits and Willem Lodewijk could order the cashiering of officers, this was a double-edged sword. At the end of the 1605 campaign, the Council of State was of the opinion 'that the list of all [officers] who are in service should be properly examined in order to cassate those whom one has found to be lacking in courage or competence'.[23] Maurits and Willem Lodewijk were wary of resorting to such a measure, since it could have serious consequences for the very survival of the companies. Though Dutch soldiers were engaged for the duration of a war and not just for a single campaign, as had once been the case with the lansquenets,[24] there was still nothing resembling a close affiliation between army and government during the first half of the seventeenth century. The mutual loyalty between rank and file and that between men and officers was based on camaraderie and the shared forbearance in the face of all manner of danger and hardship. National allegiance played a subsidiary role, although loyalty to one's birthplace or clan could indeed carry influence. In September 1631, for example, a Dutch captain in Spanish service informed the

---

[23] NA, SG 4911, Extract res. RvS, 17 December 1605.
[24] Fritz Redlich, *The German Military Enterprise and His Workforce. A Study in European Economic and Social History*, 2 vols (Wiesbaden 1964 and 1965), I, p. 461.

States-General in The Hague about a surprise attack planned by the Spaniards on Woudrichem and Gorinchem, 'stating to have been present at all their secret councils, but because it concerned his paternal town of Gorinchem (and seeing as his father was still a burgher there) his conscience obliged him to divulge such information and have it conveyed here'.[25] This was exceptional. For most soldiers and most especially those mercenaries serving in foreign lands, the ties with the company commander weighed more heavily. The dismissal of a captain could therefore lead to the unit's collapse, especially when a replacement could not be found expeditiously. In 1606, Maurits had therefore advised the States-General to retain the most competent captains of a disbanded regiment in service, 'for insofar as the ... captains are dismissed altogether, every one of the aforesaid soldiers will want to leave'.[26] Cashiering was usually a last resort, and action was taken against only the most serious offenders, in the hope that this would deter other officers.[27]

In February 1640 Captain Parfoureux was summarily dismissed from Dutch service. Instead of the 120 men inscribed, the prosecutor had discovered that the captain's company had for the last three to four years numbered sixty men at most. The sergeants explained that to their knowledge there were:

> no other soldiers, [and] that of the remaining ones named some had either died or deserted or had been discharged from the company and have had their names inscribed on the muster-roll all the same for the last three, four and five years, together with other workmen and burghers who appear at the musters in return for a small fee.

Charges were brought against Parfoureux, but he got away with it because he was in France at the time.[28]

Besides fraud, after 1618 absence without leave was common among officers, even during the campaign,[29] and the sale of officers' commissions continued to cause problems. Company commanders circumvented the ban by requesting 'gifts' from their successor. A captain or rittmaster was permitted to relinquish his company and recommend the new company commander. In exchange for this nomination, the departing commander asked for pecuniary compensation from his successor. Frederik Hendrik and the States of Holland attempted to call a halt to such abuses in 1628 by ordering that 'no rittmasters nor captains ...

---

[25] KHA, A23-VII-C-1059, Johan van Veltdriel, one of Friesland's deputies to the SG, to Ernst Casimir, The Hague, 5 September 1631.
[26] NA, SG 4914, Maurits to the SG, Arnhem, 22 November 1606.
[27] RGP 71, Secret res. SG, 19 September 1598 (no. 167).
[28] Robert Jaspar van der Capellen (ed.), *Gedenkschriften van jonkheer Alexander van der Capellen, heere van Aartsbergen, Boedelhoff en Mervelt*, 2 vols (Utrecht 1777–1778), II, pp. 24–5.
[29] NA, SG 4971, Frederik Hendrik to the SG, before Breda, 27 August 1637; KHA, A24-IV-E-2, RvS to all captains, of foot and of horse, and field officers, The Hague, 30 December 1639.

should be allowed to sell their offices ... but dying or having died, they should in accordance with the law of the Land be generously conferred without the new captain being burdened with any onus other than [value of] the weaponry'. Selling other ranks was also forbidden, and nor should 'prospective officers be pressed ... to render any recognition to the colonels, lieutenant-colonels or others'.[30] Nine years later, in 1637, the Council of State felt compelled to reiterate the prohibition on the sale of offices, since it was still going on under the guise of 'honourings'. Henceforth, besides swearing an oath of allegiance to the Republic, all 'military officers, great and small' had to declare under oath that they had 'not acquired their office by purchase' when accepting their commissions.[31]

The raising of companies and regiments

During the Eighty Years' War, the composition and strength of the Dutch army varied greatly. Extra troops were commonly recruited at the start of a new campaign to make a major operation feasible and, after 1621, the escalating war effort necessitated taking many more troops onto the payroll and retaining them while hostilities lasted. For the raising of companies and entire regiments, the States-General or the Council of State entered into contracts with private individuals. The 'capitulation', as such contracts were known, specified where a stated number of troops should be recruited, the length of their contract, who was permitted to appoint officers, when the companies had to be complete, and where they would subsequently report for muster. Terms were also made about the pay, the level of the 'marching money' (*loopgeld*), the travel allowance and the required weaponry. In June 1604 the States-General entered into a contract with Joost, count of Limburg Stirum, 'for the raising of ten-, twelve-, fifteen-hundred or, at most, two-thousand German foot soldiers'. To protect the domestic labour market for soldiers, Count Joost was compelled to recruit Germans who lived outside the Republic's borders, and he and his officers were expressly forbidden to engage soldiers who were already serving the United Netherlands. Debauching or luring away serving troops was an attractive form of recruitment, providing officers with battle-ready soldiers and making it possible for them to raise full-strength companies swiftly. The captain offered the 'debauched' the protection of registration on the muster-roll under an assumed name. This form of corruption was extremely grave for two reasons: the strengthening of the forces was illusory and such debauching had a serious financial impact on the commanders of the companies from which men absconded.

Captains were not allowed to promise recruits more pay than was specified in the pay-lists, but when Count Joost of Limburg Stirum complained that he could not recruit any German soldiers for the standard wages in the Republic he

---

[30] NA, RAZH, FAH 5, Extract res. SH, 15 March 1628.
[31] KHA, A24-IV-E-1, RvS to Hendrik Casimir I, The Hague, 16 February 1637.

received permission from The Hague to offer the higher German rate, on condition that, should the States-General decide to extend their engagement after three months, these troops 'ought to be satisfied with such pay as is observed for the Netherlandish soldiers therein'. If the soldiers declined to accept this lower rate of pay, they were free to request a discharge. The States-General granted the colonel permission to appoint captains and lieutenants, as was the norm for a newly formed regiment, provided that they were 'persons well-qualified and with battle experience'. Count Joost had to assemble 1,000 men at the musterground no later than six weeks after signing the contract. The remaining 200, 500 or 1,000 men were to be recruited on the same terms, but if the companies to which they belonged were not up to full strength after six weeks then these men were distributed among the other companies. The States-General fixed the level of travelling money at two rix-dollars per head.[32] This sum was intended as compensation for the travel expenses between the place of recruitment and the muster-ground, the rendezvous for new recruits. Regular pay began only once the company was complete and the recruits had been approved by a commissary of the musters from the Council of State. Until that time, company commanders had to foot the bill for the upkeep of the recruits.

Travelling money was in theory given only to captains and rittmasters who levied their troops outside the Republic's territory. However, when the military situation necessitated a heightened recruitment effort, the conditions for enlistment could be relaxed in a manner favourable to the company commanders. In 1631, for example, the States-General decided to temporarily enlist 6,000 Germans divided into two regiments to protect the eastern frontier. Walraven, baron van Gendt (c. 1580–1644), colonel of one of these two new regiments, was granted permission to recruit 'both within and outwith the land'. Walraven van Gendt or his captains received travelling money of six guilders for each soldier irrespective of whether they delivered them in a town in Gelderland or in the adjoining German duchy of Cleves. As usual, the captains were required to provide board and lodging for the recruits at their own expense until the muster, but to encourage them to make haste with the recruitment drive they received a pledge that they would be recompensed five stivers per head per day for the men's upkeep, over and above the travelling money, as soon as they had assembled fifty or more soldiers.[33]

From the end of the sixteenth century through to the middle of the seventeenth, the travelling money for Dutch and German foot-soldiers invariably amounted to between three and five guilders.[34] A rittmaster received ten to four-

---

[32] NA, Tweede Afdeling, CvLS LN 25, 'Capitulatie over 't lichten van 2000 man tot dienst van den Staet der Vereenigde Nederlanden met graef Joost opgericht', 22 June 1604.
[33] NA, SG 4958, Capitulation entered into by Frederik Hendrik and the field deputies with Walraven, baron van Gendt, for the recruitment of 3,009 German infantry, 12 April 1631. Gerard Erentreiter was contracted to recruit a further 3,000 Germans that same day.
[34] NA, SG 4960, Field deputies to the SG, Liège, 12 June 1632.

teen guilders as 'riding money' (*aenrijdtgelt*), the travel expenses for each cuirassier and twelve guilders for each less heavily armoured arquebusier (dragoon).[35] The distance from the place of recruitment to the muster-ground was decisive in calculating the travelling money. Captain Mathijs Egberts Knoop set out for the Holy Roman Empire in 1602 to raise 1,200 men. For each German soldier he received two rix-dollars 'and for each genuine Swabian half a rix-dollar more'.[36] The travelling money for a Walloon was six guilders, while for Englishmen, Scots and Frenchmen it was eight guilders per head, 'on condition that the French captains shall get their recruits so deep within France that they cannot return so hastily as do those who are recruited on the frontiers of these lands'. The Swiss surpassed them all at nine guilders per soldier.[37] The granting of travelling money meant that the commissary of the musters had to be especially vigilant, as it was tempting for the captains to raise recruits closer to home. In January 1615, Maurits informed Willem Lodewijk that, during the muster of an English company garrisoned in Friesland, it had come to light that the men were 'mostly Netherlanders'.[38] Fraud with travelling money was so prevalent because the company commanders received no compensation for the costs of recruitment apart from this indemnification towards the travel expenses.

The government took no account of developments in the military labour market nor was it prepared to remunerate the costs that company commanders incurred for the replacement of men who had fallen or deserted. Until the second half of the seventeenth century, captains and rittmasters were expected 'to keep [their companies] complete without cost to the Land'. Only in exceptional circumstances, such as an epidemic or plague, after an extremely bloody siege, or when a unit's paper strength was increased, was there any deviation from this standpoint.[39] In January 1605 the States-General agreed to grant travelling money to the captains of the Dutch and German companies in order to bring their units up to full strength, on condition they raised their recruits in batches outside the Republic's territory. The Council of State informed the company commanders that this exception had been decided upon 'in view of the weakness of many different companies caused by the number of deaths that, over the last year [1604] more than at other times, has run rampant, both within Ostend [besieged by the Spaniards] and in the [Dutch] army before Sluis'. At one and a half rix-dollars instead of two, the level of the travelling money was,

---

[35] RGP 71, Res. SG, 5 January 1599 (no. 238); *Journaal van Anthonis Duyck, advokaat-fiscaal bij den Raad van State (1591–1597, 1600–1602)*, ed. Lodewijk Mulder, 3 vols (The Hague and Arnhem 1862–1866), III, p. 321.
[36] RGP 92, Secret res. SG, 11 March 1602 (no. 150).
[37] RGP 101, Res. SG, 20 December 1605 (no. 108); NA, SG 4960, Field deputy Cornelis van Terestein to the SG, Liège, 13 July 1632.
[38] KHA, A22-IX-A1-434, Maurits to Willem Lodewijk, The Hague, 3 January 1615.
[39] NA, SG 4953, RvS to SG, The Hague, 22 June 1629, Advice concerning 'travelling money for the recruits'. See also SG 4953, Field deputies to the SG, before 's-Hertogenbosch, 8 June 1629.

however, a quarter lower than usual, and the Council of State also emphatically pointed out that captains whose companies were not at least 90 per cent of their full complement on 1 March 1605 would have to repay the travelling money received.[40] This measure was resorted to again in December that year.[41] In these two instances, travelling money effectively served as a contribution towards the recruitment costs. Though such an insignificant sum hardly amounted to financial compensation, in June 1629 the Council of State nevertheless warned that the States-General should not make a habit of granting travelling money for bringing the companies up to the prescribed strength (*ordinaris getal*). Only in exceptional circumstances like those mentioned above did the Council of State consider financial support for the captains desirable. In all other instances the captains had to gather recruits at their own expense, which, according to the Council of State, they could manage without difficulty 'from the pay of those who, from time to time, fall in action, die or desert'. The Council of State impressed upon the States-General that deviation from this rule would actually discourage captains from keeping their companies at full strength, 'in which case they would draw the pay for those who have deserted, have been slain or have died, and enjoy travelling money for those who they enlist in their place, yes, even the hope of enjoying so much travelling money could give cause for wastage of the companies'.[42]

A melting-pot of nationalities

Many nationalities served in the Dutch army: Netherlanders, Germans, Englishmen, Scotsmen, Frenchmen and sometimes also Swiss and Swedes. Foreign troops made up about half the numbers.[43] The denominational affilia-

---

[40] Tresoar, FSA 17, RvS to Ernst Casimir, The Hague, 15 January 1605. In December 1634, the captains who had been instructed to dispatch ten men each to Maastricht received the order to bring their companies to the prescribed strengths. Since they were not to blame for the depletion of the units, they received travelling money of five guilders for each new recruit. KHA, A24-IV-E-2, RvS to Hendrik Casimir I, The Hague, 20 December 1634.
[41] Tresoar, FSA 17, RvS to Ernst Casimir, The Hague, 27 December 1605; RGP 101, Res. SG, 20 December 1605 (no. 108).
[42] NA, SG 4953, RvS to SG, The Hague, 22 June 1629, Advice concerning 'travelling money for the recruits'.
[43] NA, SG 4910, exh. 24 February 1605, documents the composition of the Dutch army in 1605, namely 235 infantry companies, including 21 companies of Frenchmen, 55 companies of Englishmen and 27 companies of Scotsmen; the Germans are not mentioned separately. Ten Raa, *Het Staatsche leger*, IV, p. 221, gives the proportion of nationalities, based on the paper strengths in 1635, as follows: 75 companies of Englishmen (9,550 men), 30 companies of Scots (3,870 men), 70 companies of Frenchmen (8,980 men), 20 companies of Walloons (2,530 men), 43 companies of Germans (6,760 men), and 181 companies of Dutchmen (28,355 men). Only the troops accounted for in the three military lists known as the 'States of War' (*Staten van Oorlog*) are mentioned here. See below, pp. 71 and 78.

tion of the men was no impediment to their enlistment. Even Catholics served in the Dutch army. In Articles I and II of the 'Articulbrief ofte ordonnantie op de discipline militair' (Letter of articles or the ordinance on military discipline) of 13 August 1590 – the document that provided the basis for the enforcement of discipline in the Dutch army until 1795 – the soldiers were generally forbidden to mock 'the name of the Lord' and the 'word of God or the servants of the Church', but that was all.[44] Access to a Dutch encampment was reserved for Protestant preachers; the Catholic soldiers and cavaliers could visit priests and attend Mass in nearby villages.

The greatest advantage of recruiting soldiers from afar was that it reduced the risk of 'swift desertion'.[45] The likelihood that a Scot or an Englishman, never mind a Swiss, would find his own way home was, after all, much smaller than in the case of Netherlanders and their neighbours the Germans. Hence when granting the aforementioned travelling money in December 1605, the States-General did not want any reimbursement to be available for soldiers recruited in nearby Bremen, Oldenburg, Emden and Münster.[46] The slimmer chances of desertion among English, Scottish and French soldiers was the main reason Frederik Hendrik impressed upon the States-General in June 1629 and July 1632 that these companies should be brought up to full strength and that the captains should be granted travelling money for doing so. According to Frederik Hendrik it was 'unreasonable ... while the captains are poorly paid, that they should still be responsible for the reinforcement of companies without travelling money'. In 1629 the payments amounted to 25,600 guilders (1,200 Frenchmen and 2,000 Englishmen at the rate of eight guilders) and in 1632 to a total of 40,000 guilders (1,500 Frenchmen, 2,000 Englishmen and 1,500 Scots at eight guilders).[47]

Besides reducing the likelihood of desertion, there were three other reasons why Maurits and Willem Lodewijk considered it advantageous to take foreign troops into service. First, because they did not consider it possible 'to raise elite soldiers who are all ready for battle in such multitude' within the Republic. In August 1596 they had therefore proposed to the States-General to henceforth permanently maintain four foreign regiments (Englishmen, Scots, Germans and Frenchmen), so that 'one shall always be able to field a goodly army of skilled men'.[48] The second and third reasons why Maurits and Willem Lodewijk consid-

---

[44] The complete *Articulbrief* is reproduced in facsimile in M.L. Dorreboom, 'Gelijk hij gecondemneert word mits deezen'. Militaire strafrechtspleging bij het krijgsvolk te lande, 1700–1795 (Amsterdam 2000), pp. 307–12, esp. 308.
[45] NA, SG 4911, RvS to the SG, The Hague, 30 December 1605.
[46] NA, SG 4911, RvS to the SG, The Hague, 30 December 1605; Tresoar, FSA 17, RvS to Ernst Casimir, The Hague, 27 December 1605.
[47] NA, SG 4953, Frederik Hendrik to the SG, before 's-Hertogenbosch, 8 (first quote) and 16 June 1629; Field deputies to the SG, before 's-Hertogenbosch, 8 June (second quote), 17 July 1629; SG 4954, Field deputies to the SG, 27 July 1629; NA, SG 4960, RvS to the SG, The Hague, 15 July 1632.
[48] Duyck, II, Appendix II.

ered this necessary were that 'each nation will strive all the more to do its best, and through diversity of the nations the lands [i.e. the Dutch provinces] will have less to fear from mutiny or otherwise'.[49] For example, in the event of the English threatening to mutiny, the Dutch, French, Scots and Germans could be used to bring them back into line. Oddly, this method of preventing mutinies failed to work in the Spanish army, despite the Spanish practice of intentionally assembling their tactical units from a diversity of nations.[50] There was, all the same, a drawback to the Dutch method. The rivalry between the different nations could easily get out of hand, resulting in massive brawls. Article XXXIX of the above-mentioned 'Articulbrief' was intended to prevent this, stating that those who, during a quarrel or a fight, 'shall call on his nation to assist, or raise gatherings, shall be hanged and strangled'.[51] Despite this article's firmness of tone there were still almighty brawls in the Dutch army encampment in 1594, 1600 and 1603. Thereafter they no longer occurred on such a grand scale.

In June 1594 several drunken Germans and Englishmen had a falling out. Colonel Georg Eberhard, count of Solms (1568–1602), and the English general, Sir Francis Vere (1560–1609), had to intervene in order to restore peace. One German and three Englishmen were killed, and many more were injured.[52] In April 1600, a wager between a Frenchman and a German degenerated into a great 'tumult'. The Frenchman wanted to walk away without paying and this prompted a scuffle during which both parties drew their swords. Ten or twelve Frenchmen dashed to the aid of their compatriot, then Germans and Frisians entered the fray. Eventually a total of 500 to 600 men were involved. When calm was at last restored at least six men had been killed. Ernst Casimir, to whose regiment the Germans belonged, was, however, convinced that the French had suffered many more dead, but dared not admit this openly. With a measure of pride he told Willem Lodewijk that the number of wounded Frenchmen was certainly thirty or forty, including two captains. In his renowned journal, the advocate-fiscal Anthonis Duyck (c. 1560–1629) mentions just one fatality and ten wounded on the French side, with three dead and six or seven wounded among the Frisians.[53]

The last major fight between the different nations in the Dutch army occurred on 5 August 1603. For reasons that remain unclear, French and English soldiers became involved in a scuffle. Maurits was forced to interrupt his evening meal in order to part the two groups, with the aid of Léonidas de Béthune, a French

---

[49] RGP 71, 169 n. 3.
[50] Parker, *Army of Flanders*, p. 198.
[51] Dorreboom, 'Gelijk hij gecondemneert word mits deezen', p. 310.
[52] Duyck, I, p. 426.
[53] KHA, A22-IX-A6, Ernst Casimir to Willem Lodewijk, n.p., n.d., though the letter must have been written on 15 April 1600. Ernst Casimir began his letter: 'Three days since a great misfortune has, as it were, befallen our camp due to gambling.' See also Duyck, II, p. 565, which mentions this same incident taking place on 12 April.

colonel, but it was no easy task: 'There are some dead and several injured on each side, including seigneur de Béthune, [who] in separating them received various injuries, whereof some are so perilous that it is feared it will be difficult [for him] to recover.' Maurits informed the States-General that, in order to prevent 'such quarrels and unrest' between the nations, he had established watch-posts between the various quarters, but they had not withstood the 'surging masses and the fury'.[54]

The recruitment of foreign troops presented few problems until the end of the Twelve Years' Truce. Besides the States-General being permitted to openly raise forces in the lands of their allies (France and England), they could also recruit within the Holy Roman Empire, the Habsburg emperor having no objection to this. After England and Spain concluded peace in August 1604, James I (1566–1625), king of Scotland from 1567 and also of England from 1603, allowed the recruitment of soldiers for both Spain and the Republic.[55] For The Hague this presented a dilemma. Since 1587 the Republic's policy had been to take no prisoners at sea. Sailors and soldiers from captured Spanish ships were simply thrown overboard, euphemistically referred to as the 'washing of feet'. The States-General had taken this decision because they saw no other means of countering the pernicious privateering by Southern Netherlanders. The rationale was that this draconian measure was the only way to deter Northern Netherlandish seafarers from choosing to sail for the more lucrative Spanish privateers.[56] The execution of English troops in Spanish pay would, however, have strained relations between The Hague and London. When the Dutch fleet intercepted a troopship with seventy Englishmen on board before the Flemish coast in June 1605, Maurits spared the lives of the prisoners. He advised the States-General to distribute the forty-five or so Englishmen who had declared they wished to enter into Dutch service among the English companies paid by the Republic, and send the rest home, 'and that one gives them notice that in all the harbours and cities of England they happen to pass through they publicly declare that here no quarter shall be granted to those who are captured at sea, from whatever nation they might be'. Their lives had been spared this one time because of the 'friendship and alliance' with England.[57] The outbreak of the Thirty Years' War in 1618 led to a serious narrowing down of recruitment options for the Dutch Republic. The Holy Roman Emperor forbade the Calvinist Dutch free access to the German soldiers markets, and the Protestant German princes needed troops themselves. Recruitment had therefore to take place 'in secret or silence without the beating of drums, with great peril, difficulty and costs'.[58] The struggle between Catholics

---

[54] NA, SG 4906, Maurits to the SG, Geertruidenberg, 5 August 1603.
[55] Parker, *Dutch Revolt*, p. 236.
[56] Bruijn, *Varend verleden*, pp. 79–80.
[57] NA, SG 4910, Maurits to the SG, Watervliet, 26 June 1605.
[58] NA, SG 4947, 'Requeste voor Hendrich Ludwich van Hatzfeldt, heer van Wildenbergh, coronnel', discussed on 2 July 1625. He had recruited a regiment of 3,000 foot-soldiers.

and Huguenots that concurrently flared up again in France in the 1620s hampered the enlistment of Calvinist French troops. Until La Rochelle, the stronghold of the French Calvinists, had been conquered, it was 'strictly' forbidden to transport soldiers to the Republic via French harbours. Paris feared that otherwise, under this pretence, reinforcements would be dispatched to the besieged city. 'As a consequence the ... colonels and captains [of the French troops in Dutch service] cannot come by one single man but by stealthy means', Maurits reported to the States-General.[59] La Rochelle fell in October 1628. The Danish and later Swedish intervention in the Thirty Years' War presented the Republic with an opportunity to tap alternative sources of troops. In 1629, during the siege of 's-Hertogenbosch, the States-General took more than 2,600 Swedes into service for the duration of the campaign,[60] and following the death of King Gustavus II Adolphus of Sweden at the battle of Lützen in November 1632, the market for soldiers was flooded with thousands of Protestant troops. In September 1633 the Republic turned this to its advantage, temporarily reinforcing its relatively weak cavalry with more than 4,700 Swedish-Hessian troopers.[61]

Special forms of recruitment: *waardgelders*, Spanish mutineers and military enterprisers

One advantage of taking soldiers into service temporarily was that during the winter months, when 'the war ... actually ceased altogether',[62] no wages had to be paid, but this was counterbalanced by two significant disadvantages: there was no guarantee it would be possible to raise troops for the new season's campaign and the cost of engaging troops on temporary contracts was higher than that of soldiers who were taken into service permanently. Outstanding wages had to be paid out when their term of engagement came to an end. Moreover, such troops insisted on higher pay, to be able to support themselves until their next engagement.[63]

Additional troops for the field army could also be obtained by freeing up garrison troops. This is where the *waardgelders* – 'or soldiers on guard duty in the towns'[64] – stepped in. According to Hugo de Groot (1583–1645), the only

---

[59] NA, SG 4941, Maurits to the SG, 21 September 1622.
[60] KHA, A23-VII-Db1, Julius van Eysinga, Goosen Schaffer and Rembt Jensema to Ernst Casimir, Groningen, 2 August 1629.
[61] GAA, Missives of Amsterdam's deputies to the States of Holland 71 (microfilm 7548), The Hague, 1 September 1633.
[62] Carl von Clausewitz, *Vom Kriege*, 'Vollständige Ausgabe im Urtext mit historisch-kritischer Würdigung von Dr. Werner Hahlweg', 16th edn (Bonn 1952), p. 471.
[63] Duyck, I, p. 372, states that the German levy of 1594 had to be paid every thirty-two days, 'as high as or higher than all the other soldiers every forty-eight days, because they were engaged for just three months'.
[64] NA, RAZH, AJC 51, Notes about *waardgelders*.

difference between members of the civic militias and the *waardgelders* was that the former 'serve for nothing and the *waardgelders* for money, to relieve the militiamen'.[65] Willem Lodewijk had little truck with *waardgelders*. In early 1598, when the States-General formulated a plan to reduce the manpower of the infantry companies, trimming those of 200 men down to 160 and those of 150 to 120, he informed Maurits that, in his opinion, it was wiser to do without the *waardgelders* and maintain the companies at their existing strengths with the money thus saved. In the initial draft of the letter, Willem Lodewijk had written that the *waardgelders* 'to speak the truth are of little service ... and seem to provide occasion for the gentlemen of Holland to be less careful about maintaining their companies at full strength'. On revising his letter, however, rather than casting this serious aspersion he thought it better to write that the States of Friesland considered it greatly preferable 'to garner the aforesaid sum by cassating the *waardgelders*, by which the Common Cause would without comparison be less damaged than by the cassation and loss of so many fine soldiers'.[66] The Council of State shared this low opinion of *waardgelders*, and in 1633 it impressed upon the States-General that these men, often hastily assembled, were both 'young and old, [and] in the state they arrive many of them have never handled a weapon or are even capable or aware of how to do this, but only join up [so that they] can remain idle and still get paid'.[67]

The objections of Willem Lodewijk and the Council of State notwithstanding, *waardgelders* were used throughout the Eighty Years' War for the guarding of towns and cities away from the frontiers. In 1628 the States-General decided to expand the Dutch army with fifty companies of foot (10,000 strong initially, reduced to 7,500 from 1632) rather than with *waardgelders*, but these men too were soon required in the field, so the *waardgelders*, usually to the number of 6,000 men, were needed after all.[68] The garrison troops received a daily wage of seven stivers,[69] two stivers more than the daily wage of ordinary soldiers. The *waardgelders*' higher wage was justified by their having no source of income during the winter months, though this had the undesired effect of making it attractive for soldiers to have themselves 'debauched' before leaving the garrisons. As far back as April 1602, the States-General had therefore forbidden that, for the *waardgelders*, 'any men shall be drawn from companies serving the Land, other than with the full knowledge and consent of the captains, and only in order to be employed as officers of the aforesaid companies [of *waardgelders*]'.[70]

---

[65] NA, RvS 1907-I, Notes about *waardgelders*.
[66] KHA, A22-IX-E-86, Willem Lodewijk to Maurits, Leeuwarden, 25 February 1598, minute.
[67] NA, SG 4964, RvS to the SG, The Hague, 5 December 1633.
[68] RGP 62, Res. SG, 1 May 1596 (no. 189), mentions 6,000 to 7,000 *waardgelders*; RGP 92, Res. SG, 8 April 1602 (no. 22), mentions 6,000; RGP 101, Res. RvS, 1 June 1606 (no. 98), mentions 4,600; and NA, SG 4975, 'Verdeelinge van[de] comp[ag]ni[e]ën waertgelders bestaende in ses duysent man', 6 April 1640, mentions 6,000 *waardgelders*.
[69] RGP 92, Res. SG, 8 April 1602 (no. 22).
[70] Duyck, III, p. 338 n. 1.

Whether this ban was effective is doubtful, since the post of a *waardgelder* was an attractive one: besides earning more, he did not have to sleep in the open air or serve in a water-filled trench.

*

In 1602 the Republic was presented with an unforeseen opportunity to levy a couple of thousand experienced Spanish troops. The mutiny at Hoogstraten began on 1 September 1602 and was to last until 18 May 1604. The Spanish army had a tradition of mutinies: between 1572 and 1607 there were no fewer than forty-five, of which twenty-one broke out after 1596. As ever, the root cause of the Hoogstraten mutiny was pay arrears. Soldiers usually entered into service for the duration of a war, which in practice meant they served for life and could only exact outstanding pay by means of mutinies. The chance that they would still be alive when the time came for them to be discharged was, after all, negligible, given the duration of most sixteenth- and seventeenth-century wars.[71] The mutineers of 1602 employed tried and tested means to lend weight to their demands. Their first concern was to establish a secure base for themselves as well as their wives and children. Initially they hoped to be able to hold out in Hamont for as long as it took for the Spanish government in Brussels to comply with their demands, but on hearing that Francisco de Mendoza (1545–1623), Admiral of Aragon, Spain's second in command in the Netherlands at the time, was advancing with 3,700 men to crush them, the mutineers, between 1,000 and 1,800 strong, fled to the castle of Hoogstraten, less than twenty kilometres south of Dutch-controlled Breda. Besides leaving them in peace, the States-General in The Hague ensured they were supplied with food, munitions, tools and construction materials from Breda, so that they would be able to withstand an extended siege. It was, after all, in the Republic's interest that the mutiny should be long and become as difficult to put down as possible. This ruse worked, because by 1603 the ranks of the 'Esquadron', as the mutineers called themselves, had swelled to between 8,500 and 9,500: 3,500 'fighting' men, 1,000 boys, and between 4,000 and 5,000 women and children.[72]

Mendoza left the mutineers undisturbed until the summer of 1603, but then he advanced on Hoogstraten with between 12,000 and 13,000 men. This prompted the 'Esquadron' to ask for protection from the Dutch army. Maurits promised the mutineers that, if the 'common' enemy were to appear before Hoogstraten, he would advance with the Dutch troops to relieve the town. The mutineers, in turn, promised Maurits that they would then leave behind 600 men in the castle and proceed to Breda with the others 'to join the troops of His Excellency'.[73] Both parties were true to their word. In early August 1603 they joined forces to

---

[71] Parker, *Army of Flanders*, pp. 183 and 185.
[72] NA, SG 4906, Maurits to the SG, 5 September 1603.
[73] KHA, A22-IX-A6-30, Ernst Casimir to Willem Lodewijk, n.p., 29 May 1603.

prevent Hoogstraten being taken by the Spanish army. All the same, the 'Electo et Consiglio', the elected captain and the council of the mutineers, no longer felt safe there after this episode. They petitioned the States-General to assign them a stronghold 'under oath that they will preserve it for use of the United Provinces, so that from there they might collect their payments and contribution'. In exchange for this they would be prepared to be deployed as if they were Dutch troops, with the exception of deployment overseas. Maurits advised that the States-General agree to this, as it was a unique opportunity to acquire 1,200 cavalry and 2,000 foot-soldiers, 'experienced warriors without cost to the Land'.[74]

The States-General agreed that Wachtendonk, ten kilometres east of Venlo, would be assigned to the 'Esquadron', at least 'until they have received their pay from the king of Spain'. The mutineers were made to promise they would leave Wachtendonk's inhabitants in peace and would not interfere with Calvinist worship. As far as their personal religious observance was concerned, 'they will practise it as they see fit'.[75] The mutineers were not content with Wachtendonk, a town too small to accommodate between 8,500 and 9,500 people and more than 1,300 horses. Nor could its location have met with their approval: Wachtendonk was surrounded by Spanish garrisons, in Venlo, Roermond, Gelder and Straelen.[76] The mutineers wanted Rheinberg as a base, but the States of Holland categorically refused to allocate this important stronghold to the 'Esquadron' – Rheinberg was the key to Dutch trade via the Rhine[77] – so they eventually had to be satisfied with Grave. One piquant detail is that this town had been captured from the Spaniards only a year earlier (September 1602).

To ensure that the mutineers would leave Grave again, Maurits selected eight hostages, two men from each nation represented in the 'Esquadron', namely Spaniards, Italians, Germans and Frenchmen/Walloons.[78] In April 1604 the mutineers carried out a raid in Spanish Brabant and Hainault together with a body of Dutch cavalry. In the interim, however, the negotiations between representatives of the mutineers and the Spanish government in Brussels had reached such an advanced stage that for the former it was no longer attractive to cause too much damage. In mid-May 1604 a settlement was reached with the mutineers. In exchange for rehabilitation, payment of an advance on the outstanding pay, handing over of hostages and the allocation of Roermond as a place of

---

[74] NA, SG 4906, Maurits to the SG, Hoogstraten, 12 August 1603 (quote) and 24 August 1603.
[75] NA, SG 4906, 'Poincts et articules sur lesquels l'on est resolu de prester la ville de Wachtendoncq [the town's name struck out] à l'Esquadron, Electo et Conseil', Vught, 1 September 1603.
[76] NA, SG 4906, Field deputies to the SG, 4 September 1603; Maurits to the SG, 5 September 1603.
[77] NA, SG 4906, RvS, The Hague, 13 September 1603; RGP 92, Res. SG, 4 October 1603 (no. 68).
[78] NA, SG 4906, Joachim van Hardenbroeck and Kamminga to the SG, Vught, 16 October 1603; RGP 92, Res. SG, 10 October 1603 (no. 71).

refuge, they returned to service under the Spanish flag.[79] In accordance with the contract concluded with the Republic, the former mutineers surrendered Grave to the States-General. On 7 June 1604 the 'Esquadron' left for Roermond, to the great relief of Grave's inhabitants. Because of a shortage of stables, the mutineers had stabled their horses in private houses, causing considerable damage. The floor of the house of burgomaster Kerst Lievens proved to be incapable of supporting the weight of so many horses, 'so that it collapsed, filling the cellar with horses'.[80]

*

In 1622 the States-General entered into a new collaborative agreement with troops who had not been recruited at its behest. The scale of this undertaking was, however, of a wholly different order than that of 1602. Ernst, count of Mansfeld (1580–1626), and Christian, duke of Brunswick-Wolfenbüttel (1599–1626), offered the Republic the services of 7,000 cavalry and 12,000 foot-soldiers.[81] Mansfeld and Brunswick were military enterprisers, which meant they did not raise a mere company or regiment, but entire armies over which they retained personal command.[82] In 1621 they had raised troops for Frederick V (1596–1632), Elector-Palatine, who was elected king of Bohemia in 1619. However, against the Austrian Habsburgs supported by Spain, the Winter King, as he was known, had not a shadow of a chance and he fled to the Republic in 1621. Mansfeld and Brunswick tried to turn the tables, but the following year they also fled to the Republic with their troops.[83] In early September 1622 they arrived in the vicinity of Breda. Their arrival may well have raised hopes of the swift relief of Bergen op Zoom – the Spaniards had been besieging this stronghold since July of that year – but the States-General were not unequivocally pleased with this assistance, because Mansfeld's and Brunswick's troops had a terrible reputation. Maurits had received reports that, during their march through Luxembourg, they 'are reputed to have slain … five thousand peasants'.[84] This was certainly an exaggeration, but to what degree was unknown. Mansfeld's and Brunswick's forces were, moreover, severely battle-spent. On 29 August 1622, while on their way to the Netherlands, they had fought against the Spaniards in the battle of Fleurus. Though they claimed victory, their forces were 'extraordinarily reduced and depleted' because of the long march and the heavy fighting; the horses were

---

[79] L.M.G. Kooperberg, 'Een muiterij in den Spaanschen tijd. De muiters van Hoogstraten (1602–1604)', *BVGO*, 5th series, V (1918), 113–72, esp. pp. 168–9.
[80] NA, SG 4907, Eco Bonerde to the SG, Grave, 13 January 1604 (quote); Gabriel Seveyns, Grave, 9 June 1604.
[81] GA, AHGC 581, Ernst Casimir to Count Floris II of Culemborg, The Hague, 21 June 1622.
[82] Redlich, *German Military Enterpriser*, I, p. 159.
[83] Geoffrey Parker (ed.), *The Thirty Years' War*, 2nd edn (London and New York 1997), pp. 46, 51, 52, 56, 58 and 60.
[84] NA, SG 4941, Field deputies to the SG, 's Gravenweert, 19 August 1622.

exhausted and much weaponry had been lost.[85] While the original strength of Mansfeld's and Brunswick's forces was some 19,000 men, in September 1622 they had been whittled down to some 4,000 cavalry and between 3,000 and 4,000 infantry.[86]

Before the Republic could draw any advantage from Mansfeld's and Brunswick's troops they would first have to be paid and supplied with food and new weaponry. Mansfeld declared that he needed 2,000 muskets and 2,000 pikes. The availability of large stockpiles of weapons in the Republic – especially in Amsterdam, which, as the 'arsenal of the world', was pivotal in the arms trade – made this possible in short order.[87] The firm of Louis de Geer (1587–1652) delivered all the weapons required in just two days.[88] Maurits then wanted to head out to relieve Bergen op Zoom as soon as possible, but Mansfeld cautioned him that this would be impossible 'before I give them [the troops] some money'.[89] An appeal had to be made to the burghers of Amsterdam to raise even these funds. A few 'notable' Amsterdam merchants were prepared to provide 240,000 guilders, on condition that the States of Holland guaranteed the loan. A subsidy of 50,000 guilders per month that Venice owed in accordance with its defensive treaty with the Republic of 31 December 1619 was set aside for its repayment.[90] In early October 1622 everything was in place, and Maurits advanced together with Mansfeld and Brunswick to relieve Bergen op Zoom. The Spaniards wanted to avoid a battle, so the objective was achieved, but then a solution had to be found for Mansfeld's and Brunswick's troops.

The States-General wanted rid of this undisciplined band of men as soon as possible, but paying them off would require a great deal of money, because the men would demand their outstanding wages. In other words, Mansfeld and Brunswick would have to be persuaded to leave the Republic's territory with all their troops voluntarily. Brunswick left of his own accord – he was hoping to reconquer Bohemia – but Mansfeld exerted pressure on the States-General to offer him an attractive solution. Otherwise, or so he threatened, he was intending to leave his troops to their own devices and leave for Venice himself 'and that in that case Your High Mightinesses would be permitted to retain as many ... of his troops in service as would be judged to be of use by Your High Mightinesses'.[91] The spectre of thousands of Mansfeld's scrounging and looting soldiers overrun-

---

[85] NA, SG 4941, Justinus van Nassau to the SG, Breda, 2 September 1622, transcript.
[86] Van der Capellen, *Gedenkschriften*, I, pp. 69–72, 77, 106. Mansfeld claimed that he still had between 10,000 and 11,000 men under him. See NA, SG 4941, Field deputies to the SG, Geertuidenberg, 9 September 1622.
[87] De Jong, 'Staet van Oorlog', pp. 170–8.
[88] NA, SG 4941, N. van der Meer to the SG, Haarlem, 6 September 1622.
[89] NA, SG 4941, Maurits to the SG, 's Gravenweert, 10 September 1622, with a letter from Ernst von Mansfeld to Maurits, 6 September [1622].
[90] NA, SG 4941, Philips Doubleth to the SG, Amsterdam, 16 September 1622. On the treaty see: Ten Raa, *Het Staatsche leger*, III, pp. 311, 312.
[91] NA, SG 4941, Field deputies to the SG, Roosendaal, 16 October 1622.

ning the countryside made the States-General decide to shift the problem onto its German neighbours. Mansfeld received permission to enter the counties of Bentheim and East Friesland, and in late October 1622 he marched there with approximately 7,000 men.[92]

Mansfeld was still there the following year, and he was joined in East Friesland by Brunswick together with the remnants of his army in August 1623. The States-General deplored the damage caused by Mansfeld's and Brunswick's troops, but the security of the Republic required that for the meantime they should remain in East Friesland in order to prevent this region being occupied by the Spaniards or Imperialists.[93] From September 1623, Ernst Casimir, stadholder of Friesland since the death of his brother Willem Lodewijk in 1620, provided Mansfeld's and Brunswick's troops with 2,500 eight-pound loaves of bread and one hundred barrels of beer every day, sufficient victuals for 10,000 men.[94] However, Ernst Casimir was becoming increasingly concerned about the damage that the brutal behaviour of the troops of Mansfeld and Brunswick was causing to the reputation of the Republic in the neighbouring German territories.[95] He complained to the influential Gelderland nobleman and politician, Count Floris II of Culemborg, that the 'misery increases more and more, that soldiers and peasants are dying in droves from hunger and affliction every day, not to mention the pestilence that still rages in the county of East Friesland'.[96] In February 1624, the East Frisians were at last delivered from Mansfeld's and Brunswick's troops. Ernst Casimir wrote with relief to Count Floris II:

> Mansfeld has at last had to dismiss all his men, so too milordliness Duke Christian, who together were still 4,300 horse and 3,000 foot strong ... having paid to their army the sum of one hundred and sixty-five [thousand] guilders, the rest will be paid [to Mansfeld and Brunswick] in The Hague, to the amount of three times one hundred thousand guilders.[97]

Though the direct collaboration between the Republic and Mansfeld was terminated in 1624, the States-General were not rid of him yet. By order of King James I of England, Mansfeld raised a new army of 12,000 men, with which he took up a position on the Lower Rhine in 1625.[98] The condition of Mansfeld's men was degenerating rapidly due to a lack of money and provisions, and by late June 1625 there were only 4,000 infantry and between 600 and 700 cavalry remaining. Mansfeld petitioned the Republic to assume responsibility for the food supplies. As surety he offered weapons to the value of 50,000 guilders and he pledged his own silverware to guarantee payment for beer. He eventu-

---

[92] Van der Capellen, *Gedenkschriften*, I, pp. 109–12.
[93] Tresoar, FSA 17, SG to Ernst Casimir, The Hague, 7 September 1623.
[94] Tresoar, FSA 17, SG to Ernst Casimir, The Hague, 11 September 1623.
[95] GA, AHGC 581, Ernst Casimir to Count Floris II of Culemborg, Delfzijl, 8 October 1623.
[96] GA, AHGC 581, same to same, Delfzijl, 3 December 1623.
[97] GA, AHGC 581, same to same, Leeuwarden, 3 February 1624.
[98] Parker, *The Thirty Years' War*, p. 68.

ally received the undertaking that bread would be supplied to a value of 6,000 guilders, gaining him a few days to go to The Hague for deliberations with the king of Bohemia.[99] Despite his promise to return to his troops swiftly, Mansfeld was still in The Hague at the end of July 1625. To Rutger Huygen and Edzard Jacob Clant van Stedum (1584–1648), who oversaw the deliveries of provender as deputies of the Council of State, the future looked grim. Due to Mansfeld's continued absence 'and because of the lack of money things are now starting to get out of hand. They plunder the people, in contravention of the *sauvegardes*, taking all their cattle on both sides of the Rhine.' A *sauvegarde* was a warrant proving that a 'fire-tax' had been exacted in lieu of pillaging and fire-raising, buying the farmers and villagers the right to be left unscathed. However, Mansfeld's officers were powerless and even ran the risk of 'being handed over to the enemy' by their own soldiers: 'In sum, all discipline and respect is gone.' Approximately 1,000 men had already deserted over the preceding weeks, according to Huygen and Clant.[100]

About four weeks later, Mansfeld at last returned to his army, but this barely improved the situation: plundering continued unabated and the Dutch soldiers seized this opportunity to go looting themselves, 'even serve as guides [for Mansfeld's troops] and pretend to belong to Mansfeld's army'.[101] It was early October 1625 before a solution was found: Mansfeld and his army transferred into Danish service.[102] The infantry (2,400 healthy soldiers and 600 sick) were transported by river to Amsterdam and from there shipped to Bremen. The cavalry, 600 horse, travelled by land.[103] In April 1626 Mansfeld suffered defeat against the Imperial army under Wallenstein in the battle of Dessau Bridge. On 29 November that year an illness brought an end to his turbulent life.

The experiences with Mansfeld and Brunswick demonstrated that for the Republic there were more disadvantages than advantages attached to the use of military enterprisers. The States-General and the provincial authorities could maintain control of such enterprisers when they merely needed to recruit companies and regiments, but when it came to raising entire armies that was an impossibility. In 1625 it was beyond dispute that the experiment with military enterprisers had failed and should never be repeated. From now on, when an extra military effort was needed there was no alternative but to reinforce the Republic's own army. This could be achieved in part by strengthening the existing units, but establishing new companies and regiments was the only means of achieving a substantial expansion.

---

[99] NA, SG 4947, Rutger Huygen and Edzard Jacob Clant van Stedum to the SG, Rees, 30 June and 3 July 1625.
[100] NA, SG 4947, same to the SG, Rees, 13, 20 and 23 (quote) July 1625.
[101] NA, SG 4947, same to the SG, Rees, 5 August 1625.
[102] Parker, *The Thirty Years' War*, p. 69.
[103] NA, SG 4947, Rutger Huygen and Edzard Jacob Clant van Stedum to the SG, Rees, 29 September 1625; Antwerpen and J. Witzen to the SG, Amsterdam, 20 October 1625.

The size of the Dutch army: the difference between paper and effective strengths

In the sixteenth century and the first half of the seventeenth century there was a marked discrepancy between the prescribed or paper strength of armies and their actual or effective numbers. The Dutch army was no exception. The Republic's captains and rittmasters were in practice only obliged to have brought their companies to full strength at the *outset* of the campaign. A tally of the losses suffered *during* the campaign was kept by means of musters. The prime intention was not to make the officers enlist new recruits, but rather to prevent more pay being distributed than was due to the number of men actually present. The provincial States remitted full pay only after the company had been brought back to full strength at the commander's personal expense. It was therefore to a captain's advantage to include more soldiers on the muster-roll at the outset of the campaign than were actually present. In late March or early April, when recruitment had to be completed, they could then claim the remittance of a company at full strength. The calculation of wages was based on this muster-roll until the next muster. If a subsequent muster showed that the company's strength had decreased, then the company commanders could ascribe this decrease to the consequences of action, sickness and desertion. It was impossible to determine the extent to which non-existent soldiers were included among the losses, so the captains and rittmasters could not be forced to repay wages they were not entitled to receive. The Council of State branded this behaviour fraudulent and in formal terms that was correct, but most captains and rittmasters regarded this as a legitimate way of conducting business. The government, in turn, neglected to distribute the pay on time or in full, besides which the musters were called irregularly and often at long intervals, which resulted in the captains and rittmasters having to pay recruits who had arrived at the rendezvous after the most recent muster out of their own pockets for weeks or even months.[104] They could not abandon them to their fate because that would constitute a breach of contract between the company commander and the recruit. This meant the captains and rittmasters were 'forced ... against their will to steal' from the government.[105]

The Council of State attributed pretty much the entire difference between the paper and effective strengths of companies to fraud. The Dutch army was therefore one-third weaker than the payrolls suggested.[106] In his journal, Duyck fulminates against the 'excessive avarice' of the captains who kept their companies 'more than a quarter and almost a third weaker' than was stated on the muster-rolls, while 'the provinces pay the soldiery in accordance with the musters or

---

[104] In 1626, the first muster after the start of the campaign was not called until October. NA, SG 12548.180, SG to the field deputies, The Hague, 3 October 1626.
[105] NA, Tweede Afdeling, CG 305, no. 36.
[106] RGP 62, Res. SG, 22 March 1597 (no. 135).

thereabouts'.[107] The judgement of the Council of State and Duyck is doubtless tainted by frustration with the hopeless struggle to quash deception in any guise. The practicalities of waging war also make it untenable to blame the enfeeblement of the companies on the fraudulent practices of the officers alone. Duyck's allegation takes no account whatsoever of losses caused by fighting and disease. In June 1604, Maurits impressed upon the field deputies 'that the army can never be kept in the field for three or four months without being enfeebled by a great portion, or at least one-third or one-fourth part of the soldiery, due to the sick, deserters, dead and injured'.[108] This demonstrates that Maurits also took account of a difference between paper and effective strengths of 25 to 30 per cent. This seems to justify the conclusion that fraud in the muster-rolls and the seriousness of losses due to combat, disease and desertion were *jointly* responsible for the difference between the army's actual and paper strengths. If a company became too weak for active duty then the unit was sent to a garrison in order to replenish itself, a fresh company filling the place that fell vacant if necessary. This combination of factors meant that the army in the field was much stronger at the start of the campaign than at its end.

Another factor that complicates efforts to determine the army's effective strength is the familiar habit of enlisting extra troops temporarily, whether to make a specific military operation feasible or to be able to cope with unforeseen circumstances. This makes it well-nigh impossible to determine the aggregate effective strength of the Dutch army for each year, though the field army is an exception here, since its strength can be ascertained fairly accurately from lists of effective strengths on different dates (see Appendix I). Using an army overview based on muster-rolls it can be determined with reasonable certainty that in December 1587 the Dutch army was actually 25,000 strong.[109] Fifteen years later, in the summer of 1602, it had an effective strength of 31,000 men,[110] and in 1608 approximately 49,000 men.[111] After 1621 the Dutch army expanded swiftly and in 1629 briefly peaked at 120,000 men on paper and perhaps 80,000 to 90,000 men in reality.[112] In the 1630s and 1640s, its effective strength was approximately 60,000 men.[113] Compared with the actual size of the French army in those same

---

[107] Duyck, II, p. 176. See also I, p. 241; II, p. 148.
[108] NA, SG 4908, Otto Roeck and Ferdinand Heman to the SG, before Sluis, 6 June 1604 (quote); Duyck, I, p. 241; II, pp. 148 and 176.
[109] NA, RAZH, AJvO 2942A, 'Staet van het crijchsvolck tegenwoordich in dienste van de Vereenichde Provintiën wesende', 31 December 1587.
[110] NA, RAZH, AJvO 2813, 'Staet van alle 't crijchsvolck soe te peerde als te voete in 's Lands dienst sijnde, haere respective sterckte en[de] jegenwoordige betalingen derzelven', summer 1602.
[111] Ten Raa, *Het Staatsche leger*, II, pp. 148, 368–9.
[112] NA, Tweede Afdeling, CG 305, nos 30a, 30b and 30c.
[113] NA, RAZH, AJC 32, Report of 11 October 1635.

years, an estimated 80,000 men,[114] the war effort of the Dutch Republic was impressive indeed.

Muster and direct payment: prerequisites for efficient military management

In 1588 the States-General affirmed in a new instruction the right of the Council of State to muster all Dutch troops in accordance with the placard of 10 January 1587. The most important proviso in this instruction was that all companies had to be mustered in the same place at the same day and hour, otherwise the captains and rittmasters would be able to borrow troops from one another in order to make their units seem complete. Together with the muster-roll the officers had to present a list with the tally and whereabouts of sick and wounded men, so that these could be visited and counted 'by one or more trusted persons' at the same time as the muster. The same procedure was followed for soldiers who were on watch and therefore could not attend the muster. During the inspection, the muster commissary noted down the weaponry possessed by each soldier, where he came from and how long he had been serving in the company. The muster commissary was not permitted to 'pass muster' for absent troops unless the captain and the lieutenant swore under oath that the soldiers in question were absent on furlough 'for a short time'. This was limited to a maximum of four men. If a subsequent muster revealed that the absent soldiers had still not returned, then the company commander had to reimburse the pay received. After the inspection the muster commissaries sealed the muster-rolls and sent them together with a written report to the Council of State 'so that the pay ordinances can be amended accordingly'.[115]

The revised 'Placard on the matter of the muster for the prevention of all frauds in keeping the companies complete' of 4 February 1599[116] provided a more precise formulation of the 1587 document. Article III, for example, obliged infantry and cavalry from then on to be in possession of weapons and equipment as prescribed in an annex to the placard, namely the 'Ordre op de waapeninge' (Rules and regulations for armaments) of 1597. A system of fines, ranging from half a guilder for a missing morion to ten guilders for a cuirassier who had no pack-horse, was intended to ensure that troops were correctly armed and equipped. The same article prohibited the captains and rittmasters from mixing 'any burghers, peasants, sutlers, freebooters, soldiers from other companies … or

---

[114] Parrott, *Richelieu's Army*, p. 220.
[115] Tresoar, ASF 2985, 'Instructie memorial van wegen sijner Ex.cie waernae de gecomiteerde ende commissarisen van de aenstaende monsteringe hen zullen hebben te reguleren', The Hague, 30 April 1587.
[116] *Recueil … betreffende de saaken van den oorlog*, I, no. 2, 'Placaat op het stuk van de monsteringe tot voorkoominge van alle frauden in het compleet houden van de compagni[e]ën'.

others' among their company during the inspection. The Council of State threatened both the officers and these *passe-volants* with corporal and capital punishments. A *passe-volant* was anyone who pretended to be a soldier to make the company's tally complete. If someone admitted to fraudulent practices during the muster and turned himself in to the Council of State within a year – with the exception of muster commissaries, rittmasters and captains – he would not only be forgiven the delict but could count on a reward of fifty guilders (Article IV).

To be able to combat desertion and fraud even more effectively, the captains and rittmasters were henceforth forbidden to recruit in frontier towns and in places where their companies had been garrisoned, or to enlist farmers or peasants living within a one-mile radius (Article VII). Article VI empowered each province's Delegated Councillors or Delegated States (*Gecommitteerde Raden* or *Gedeputeerde Staten*, as the executive bodies responsible for day-to-day government in the provinces were called) to have troops mustered by its own commissaries anywhere in the Republic, 'including those engaged at the expense of the Generality or repartitioned to another province, providing that, in conducting the said muster they shall secretly advise the Council of State'. This article was of great importance to Holland in particular. While the taxpayers of Holland financed the upkeep of more than half the Dutch army, most of its own troops were quartered outside the province. It only made sense to muster Holland's troops in, for instance, the garrisons in Gelderland if Holland's commissaries were authorised to muster all the soldiers in the towns concerned simultaneously. Otherwise the companies repartitioned to Holland could easily be brought up to full strength using soldiers who were repartitioned to, for example, Gelderland or Utrecht. In practice, however, Holland made scant use of this right until the second half of the seventeenth century.[117]

In the final decade of the sixteenth century, musters were called with great regularity and were primarily intended to track down and punish officers who were committing fraud.[118] This was a logical consequence of the decision reached in December 1586,[119] which decreed that a smaller but better paid army should be maintained instead of a larger but poorly remunerated military force, thus preventing mutinies and reducing the difference between paper and effective

---

[117] NA, CvdH 107, Adriaan van der Hoop, notes regarding the muster.
[118] Res. SG, 9 October 1598 (RGP 71, no. 172), is an order addressed to Maurits, Willem Lodewijk and the field deputies: '[T]o conduct an exact review of all the cavalry and foot-soldiers ... [in order to then] immediately punish (by cassation at least), as an example to others, those rittmasters and captains who are found to have most seriously defrauded the Generality in ratio to the last payment they received for their horsemen and foot-soldiers, without exemption and status of anyone, and that to such a number as His Excellency [i.e. Prince Maurits] and [Willem] L[odewijk] deem fit to cause sufficient fright and as shall be deemed of service to the Land.' See also RGP 57, Res. SG, 28 January 1594 (no. 95); RGP 62, Res. SG, 25 January 1597 (no. 192), and annotations by Van Cuyck dated 21 February 1597 (no. 204); RGP 92, Res. SG, 20 September 1602.
[119] See p. 69.

strengths to a minimum. This first expectation transpired but the second did not, as we have seen.

In February 1596 the Council of State therefore published its advice about the measures it considered necessary to effect a more efficient management of the troops. First and foremost the Council of State advised increasing the pay, 'as it is evident that in these expensive times a soldier cannot provide for himself on the Land's wage, being a wage set ... fourteen years ago, since which time all the victuals have risen in price by almost half'. The Council of State proposed paying them the same wage every forty-two days (a *heremaand*) instead of every forty-eight days, the standard pay-month at that time, which represented a pay rise of about 15 per cent. The Council of State's rationale was that bringing the pay more in line with current price levels would not only ensure that the officers and soldiers could better provide for themselves but would also deprive them of any justification for perpetrating fraud. The Council of State calculated that the funds necessary for the pay increase could in large part be found by dismissing about 15 per cent of the men of each infantry company and 10 per cent of each cavalry company. An infantry company of 150 men would have a complement of 130 men after such a reduction. The Council of State reassured the States-General that 'the Land will be at no disadvantage in the tally of heads, because of the very great abuses ... in the musters'. The Council of State concluded its advice with the comment that this investment would be amply recovered if they were simultaneously to switch to direct payment by treasurers employed by the Generality, the federal institutions of the Republic. Payment had until now been distributed via the company commanders, but paying the wages to each soldier individually from then on would make it possible to eradicate fraud completely.[120] According to Duyck this would yield annual savings of an estimated 800,000 guilders, which was twice the additional expenditure needed to cover the increase in pay.[121]

The provinces agreed to raising the pay, but they rejected the Council of State's proposal to devolve payment to the treasurers of the Generality, which would have necessitated the subdivision of the Republic's territory into seventeen pay-districts. A number of treasurers under the supervision of a commissary would be responsible for distributing the wages in each district. While this could gain the approval of the provinces, they still had insuperable objections to the argument posited by the Council of State that for practical reasons it was impossible to have individual payment administered by the provincial treasurers. According to the Council of State, this would be feasible only if all the troops repartitioned to a particular province were quartered within its borders, which was never the case. The Frisian companies, for example, were billeted 'so far from the others ... as from Zutphen or Groningen to Ostend'. The Council of State therefore

---

[120] NA, SG 4883, RvS to SG, The Hague, 19 February 1596.
[121] Duyck, II, pp. 148, 209, 265–7 footnote and 446.

argued that it was necessary for the provinces to remit the pay directly to treasurers appointed by the Generality.[122] For the provincial States this was not open to discussion, because it would mean ceding their direct control of the troops to the Council of State. The States-General consequently decided to shorten the pay-month to 42 days, but 'for the present' not to switch to individual payment,[123] a decision that made it impossible to follow the muster regulations to the letter.

The placard of 1599 prescribed at least twelve musters per annum, but in practice this did not happen. After all, so long as payment was not properly organised the officers could not be required to keep their companies at full strength. Maurits had two further reasons for considering it inadvisable to muster the men too often. First, a muster-call could result in extra money having to be paid to the soldiers, and if this were not immediately available then great commotion would result. Understandably, the officers and soldiers were of the opinion that, if they were called to account, then the government ought to pay the outstanding wages and bonuses for work performed during sieges. When the States-General ordered the mustering of the siege army before Sluis in June 1604, the field deputies retorted that so long as the provinces sent no money Maurits considered it 'inadvisable at this juncture'.[124] The second risk associated with calling musters was much more serious: it could lead to a weakening of the army. To hedge against the payroll being amended downward in accordance with the new muster-roll, many captains would dismiss several soldiers, and these were usually the veterans because they drew the highest pay. Ernst Casimir refused to muster the troops under his command for this very reason in July 1605, 'seeing that after the completed muster they [the captains] will surely licence [i.e. dismiss] a few soldiers, and therefore our army would be weakened by a half-thousand men or more'.[125] The military command therefore preferred a review to gain insight into the number of troops under their command. In contrast to a muster no disciplinary or financial consequences attached to such a review for the company commanders, thus averting turmoil among the rank and file.

The situation with regard to musters did not improve at all after the Twelve Years' Truce. In August 1623, the Council of State promulgated a 'Placard on the matter of the musters' that was formulated even more rigidly,[126] but the commotion this caused among the soldiery was so great that it remained 'unenacted'. Article V of this proclamation specified that fraud ascertained at the muster would invariably result in dismissal 'without hope of pardon or of ever again being allowed to assume the position of rittmaster or captain'. Article III, in which the

---

[122] RGP 62, Res. SG, 8 January 1597 (no. 119a).
[123] RGP 62, Res. SG, 17 March and 2 April 1597 (nos. 132 and 138).
[124] NA, SG 4908, Ferdinand Heman and Otto Roeck to the SG, before Sluis, 18 June 1604.
[125] NA, SG 4911, Henrik van Brienen, J. van Duvenvoirde and Otto Roeck to the SG, Rheinberg, 29 July 1605. See also Duyck, I, pp. 611, 618 and 619.
[126] 'Placaat op het stuck van de monsteringe', *Recueil ... betreffende de saaken van den oorlog*, I, no. 3, The Hague, 17 August 1623.

commanders were ordered to keep their companies 'constantly complete', was occasion for equally serious disquiet. Both articles were unacceptable to the officers and unworkable in practice, since there was no question of 'it being possible to conduct the muster precisely alongside tardy or incomplete payment'.[127] In the 1630s and 1640s, Holland endeavoured to organise the payment of the troops in a more efficient manner, but in spite of this the credit of the officers and that of their private financiers, the *solliciteurs-militair*, remained the mainstay on which the Republic's war effort depended until 1672.

Company management

The prime concern of the captains and rittmasters was to ensure the survival of their companies, on which they depended for their livelihood. This meant their numbers could not fall too far below the full complement and their weapons and equipment had to be in a good to fair state. The *Landsknechte* used to enter the service of their paymaster with their own weapons and equipment, but by the end of the sixteenth century this was no longer the norm, and company commanders had to provide the armaments. Weapons and equipment acquired for the company were considered the captain's property, though he docked the expenditure from the pay of his men in three monthly instalments.[128] The officers did not, however, enjoy complete freedom in the choice of weapons. In 1593, when the States-General entered into a contract with Ernst, count of Solms, for the raising of an infantry regiment of approximately 2,000 men, they not only made sure that the capitulation specified that half of each company had to be comprised of pikemen and the other half of musketeers and calivermen; they also obliged the captains to take delivery of the body armour for their men at the rendezvous.[129] Their request to be allowed to supply this armour themselves was refused, 'because experience has repeatedly taught us that if the lieutenant-colonel and captains assume responsibility for the armaments of the men, this generally results in deplorable inadequacy, great disservice and costs to the Land'.[130] Besides cost savings, an additional advantage of the government issuing weapons and equipment was, of course, that the armaments of the Dutch army were rendered more uniform.

Maurits, Willem Lodewijk and Frederik Hendrik in particular were constantly drumming home that the companies had to be complete, well clothed, correctly

---

[127] NA, CvdH 107, Simon van Slingelandt, 'Memorie dienende tot informatie op het stuk van de monstering'. See also his *Staatkundige Geschriften*, IV, p. 217.
[128] RGP 57, Res. SG, 6 October 1593 (no. 107); RGP 62, Res. SG, 8 January 1597 (no. 119a); RGP 92, Res. SG, 11 May 1602 (no. 162).
[129] NA, RAZH, AJvO 2875, 'Solmsen regiments'; RGP 57, Res. SG, 6 October 1593 (no. 107).
[130] RGP 57, Res. SG, 7 April 1594 (no. 112).

armed and drilled every day, every other day or at the very least every week, and not only in the use of their weapons but in fighting in formations at company and batallion level as well.[131] It was the duty of the colonel, as chief of the regiment, to ensure the observance of these orders.[132]

Captains and rittmasters who were also colonels or held civic office, for example in the provincial States or in the States-General, delegated responsibility for their company to the lieutenant. Count Floris II of Culemborg was captain of a company of horse and a company of foot, but his political activities at both provincial and Generality levels prevented him from taking personal command of his companies, never mind being able to serve in both military posts simultaneously. In May 1636 he entered into a contract with Lieutenant Adolph van Padborch to assume command of his infantry company of 150 men. As captain-lieutenant, Van Padborch took responsibility for ensuring that the company would be comprised of 'fine and skilled' soldiers who were provided with fine weapons and clothing. He also had to 'furnish [the company] with money'. This meant that he had to collect the pay ordinances from the province to which the company was repartitioned – in this case Holland – and cash them.[133] For a complete company of 150 men, the pay amounted to 2,014 guilders per *heremaand*, the pay-month of 42 days. After deducting the one-hundredth penny and 71 guilders for transaction costs, 1,923 guilders remained. Van Padborch paid out more than 80 per cent of this to the officers and soldiers, and 180 guilders (30 guilders more than the usual captain's fee) was destined for Count Floris II as the company's proprietor. After deducting his personal fee of 45 guilders, Van Padborch was left with approximately 100 guilders, with which he had to defray all the company's maintenance costs, such as the repair of weapons and equipment, the purchase of new clothing – 'leather jerkins and overcoats' – and the enlistment of new recruits.[134] This last responsibility was the cause of greatest concern to the captains and their deputies, since a company lost a quarter to a third of its strength each year, making it necessary to raise twenty, thirty or even more men each winter to make good the shortfall.[135]

Until around 1680 pay was not uniform for all rank-and-file soldiers, the most experienced receiving a bonus. From 1599 to 1609 the majority of musketeers and

---

[131] KHA, A24-28 and 131, Frederik Hendrik to Hendrik Casimir I, Panderen, 1 November 1635, 6 January 1640; GA, AHGC 768, Adolph van Padborch to Count Floris II of Culemborg, Druynen, 29 August 1631.
[132] KHA, A24-IV-E-2, RvS to Hendrik Casimir I, The Hague, 5 February 1637, transcript; KHA, A25-VII-AII-9, Frederik Hendrik to Willem Frederik, The Hague, 18 February 1644.
[133] GA, AHGC 769, Contract between Count Floris II of Culemborg and Adolph van Padborch, The Hague, 19 May 1636.
[134] GA, AHGC 769, 'Staet van complete betaelinge van eenen maendt soldts voor sijn[e]r gen[ade] compaignie infanterie'.
[135] ZA, AR C 312–314, 322–324, 332, 333 and 335 include the muster-rolls of forty-six companies repartitioned to Zeeland from the years 1603–1606; GA, AHGC 769 contains seven muster-rolls from 1631 and 1632.

pikemen earned eleven and a half or twelve guilders per *heremaand*. Calivermen, armed with matchlock firearms that were smaller in calibre than those of the musketeers, received nine and a half guilders per *heremaand*. The pikemen who stood in the unit's front line, the most dangerous position, received an additional one to six guilders, and the most highly skilled musketeers and calivermen received a bonus of one guilder and of ten stivers, respectively.[136] The company commanders were obliged to distribute the full pay on the 'issue date', the last day of a *heremaand*, but in practice this did not happen. Experience had taught them that it was not sensible to distribute the wages to the soldiers in one go, because they 'usually ... are not wise enough to manage so much money'. The temptation to go and live it up in grand style was too great. Moreover, a one-off payment of the full wages increased the likelihood of desertion. The soldiers could, after all, 'with those ready monies ... manage ... to leave for their homeland and elsewhere'.[137] It was therefore better to advance the soldiers a portion of their pay every week or every eight to nine days. This was called the 'loan', an advance that was usually set at five stivers per day. Per *heremaand* of forty-two days the advance therefore amounted to ten and a half guilders per soldier.[138] The captain set aside the remainder of the wages for the company's upkeep. As one might expect, the captain was intent on building up a reserve from which he could cover as much of the expense of enlisting new recruits as possible.

The captains of Dutch companies were assigned a recruitment area within the Republic. The recruitment process is described in detail in the archives of Count Floris II of Culemborg.[139] On 23 November 1635, the ensign Johan Catz left Wijk bij Duurstede for Utrecht accompanied by the *capitaine des armes*, the sergeant who was charged with supervising the company's weaponry.[140] From 24 to 27 November, Catz had the drum sounded in Utrecht, and for four guilders he hired several people who 'searched out and rounded up' suitable recruits for him. The yield after four days of enlisting amounted to twenty recruits. As we have seen, the captains were not allowed to offer higher pay than was established in the payrolls, but they were at liberty to decide the level of the *handgeld*, a bounty paid on enlistment. This enabled captains to snatch recruits away from one another. Catz gave half the recruits a bounty of 2-10 (i.e. 2 guilders and 10 stivers), two soldiers received 3-4, another 3-15 and one even insisted on 5 guilders, whereas two received 2 guilders and four just 1-5 or 1-10. These four were probably young recruits with no military experience whatsoever. The

---

[136] The composition of a company of 135 men was as follows: 13 officers, 45 pikemen (one at the rate of 18 guilders, one at 16, one at 15, two at 14, five at 13, fifteen at 12 and twenty at 11½), 30 musketeers (five at the rate of 13 guilders, thirteen at 12, twelve at 11½) and 44 calivermen (twelve at the rate of 10 guilders, thirty-two at 9½). Ten Raa, *Het Staatsche leger*, II, p. 335.
[137] NA, RAZH, ASH 1354f, 'Consideratiën over de hooftelijcke betal[ing]e anno 1651'.
[138] GA, AHGC 769, 'Differente form van betalinge gebruyckt bij die capiteynen'.
[139] GA, AHGC 763, Declaration of ensign Johan Catz.
[140] Wijn, *Krijgswezen*, p. 41.

four men who commanded the highest bounty must have been veterans. The remaining twelve recruits were probably mature men who would make useful soldiers. In all, Catz had to spend 49 guilders and 13 stivers on bounties. From Catz's declaration it is evident that the beer flowed freely during the recruitment drive, because during those four days in Utrecht his accommodation expenses, 'including that which the soldiers drank when they were enlisted', amounted to no less than thirty-six guilders. The new soldiers would receive their first advance as soon as they reached Wijk bij Duurstede, the assembly point for the recruits. Until such time (3 December 1635), Catz had to pay them a daily allowance of more than five stivers for food and drink. Besides these major expenses, Catz owed the drummer one guilder for every day he had sounded the drum (four guilders in all), the journey to Utrecht had cost Catz and the sergeant three guilders, and the latter had also had to make a round trip via The Hague and Wijk bij Duurstede to collect money (his travel expenses came to seven guilders). Catz had spent a total of 132 guilders.

On 28 November 1635, Catz headed back to Wijk bij Duurstede with the recruits. Seven soldiers took to their heels en route, most notably the soldier who had received five guilders for signing up. Desertion was always highest among 'newly recruited' soldiers.[141] The domestic labour market also made desertion tempting. Experienced soldiers were sought-after manpower for dike-reeves and foremen, since siegework had made them expert diggers.[142] Catz recruited another ten men in Wijk bij Duurstede. In early January 1636, the twenty-three recruits sailed for Emmerich, where the company was garrisoned. By that point, the total costs, including the first month's pay, amounted to 373 guilders. The bounties and the daily allowance or retention fee were the captain's personal responsibility. The company commander could, however, declare the advances at the provincial paymaster's office, subject to the muster-roll being approved. Catz had enlisted only thirty men, but captains sometimes had to gather forty, fifty, even seventy or more recruits.[143]

The risk of desertion was, as noted, less serious with foreign soldiers, but was certainly not excluded. A thousand English recruits who landed at Ostend in July 1601, for example, had been 'press-ganged ... and lifted from all the prisons'. Deserting from a city under siege was no simple matter and the English were also easy to recognise from their red jackets.[144] Netherlandish, German and French soldiers did not wear uniform clothing at that time and could therefore desert

---

[141] NA, SG 4910, Maurits to the SG, Watervliet, 16 July 1605, PS.
[142] NA, SG 4967, Proclamation of the SG, The Hague, 2 August 1635. Dike-reeves and foremen were forbidden to employ soldiers on penalty of a fine of 100 guilders for each soldier as well as everything he had earned.
[143] See, for example, ZA, AR C 312, 322 and 332, with muster-rolls of the companies of Balthazar de Ghistelle and Magnus; AR C 313, 323, 324, 333, muster-rolls of the companies of Joost van Chantraine; NA, Tweede Afdeling, CG 305, no. 20, muster-rolls of the companies of Dupuis.
[144] Philippe Fleming, *Oostende vermaerde, gheweldighe, lanckdurighe ende bloedighe beleg-*

more easily. French soldiers who were in the service of the Dutch Republic were sometimes exhorted to desert by priests, who refused to grant them absolution 'before they remove themselves from the service of the Land on account of them being employed against the king of Spain'.[145] For Catholics, the king of Spain was 'the champion of the true faith'. Because desertion caused the captains such serious financial damage, they did everything possible to call a halt to this evil. In May 1632, Adolph van Padborch informed Count Floris II of Culemborg that two deserters from the company had that very day been punished: one was hanged and the other was 'strappadoed' (*gestropadeert*, after the Spanish *stroppa da corda*), a harsh corporal punishment involving one's hands being tied behind one's back, then being hoisted up on a pulley and allowed to fall with a jerk. The names of fifteen deserters who were still at large were nailed to the scaffold.[146]

The death penalty for desertion placed the company commanders and the military leadership in a dilemma: its deterrent effect might dissuade others from deserting, but the punishment also burdened the captains and rittmasters with the expense of finding a replacement, while the government lost a trained soldier. They had to be more circumspect about how they treated older, experienced soldiers, even if they were guilty of desertion,[147] as they were a great asset, especially in spring and autumn, 'because such men can better tolerate the cold and the frost than those newly recruited ... who are used to the good times and a better life'.[148] During the winter of 1624–1625, the Dutch army largely remained in the field in connection with the Spanish siege of Breda. In February 1625, Ernst Casimir wrote to Count Floris II of Culemborg from the Dutch encampment: 'The poor soldiers are naked and bare, with rainy weather they stand everywhere to over their shoes in mud.'[149] Sometimes a general amnesty for all deserters was proclaimed during the campaign. Deserters had to report to their companies within a given time.[150] Combatting desertion on campaign was the responsibility of the provost-marshal, who had *stokknechten*, literally 'servants with sticks', and an executioner at his disposal.

---

heringhe, bestorminghe ende stoute aenvallen ... in de jaren 1601, 1602, 1603 ende 1604 (The Hague 1621), p. 78.

[145] NA, SG 4966, RvS to SG, The Hague, 10 May 1635, appendix to Extract res. SG, 4 May 1635.

[146] GA, AHGC 768, Adolph van Padborch to Count Floris II of Culemborg, 12 May 1632 (quote); NA, CvdH 149, Overview of military punishments. For the etymology of the Dutch *stropaderen* see Wijn, *Krijgswezen*, p. 112.

[147] In July 1634, Frederik Hendrik entreated the States of Utrecht to ensure that all the deserters 'should be zealously sought by the officers of the towns and countryside and, once found, shall be brought here to this army under strict security in order to be rejoined with their companies'. HUA, ASU 278-4, Nijmegen, 12 July 1634.

[148] Tresoar, FSA 30, Willem Frederik to the Delegated States of Friesland, Oisterwijk, 8 October 1642.

[149] GA, AHGC 581, Ernst Casimir to Count Floris II of Culemborg, Roosendaal, 12 February 1625.

[150] NA, SG 4967, Proclamation of the SG, The Hague, 2 August 1635.

4. Military punishments, c. 1630. The *stroppa da corda* is depicted in the centre, the wooden horse (see p. 347) on the left. Jacques Callot, *De droeve ellendigheden van den oorloogh* (Amsterdam). (Royal Netherlands Army Museum, Delft, 0011678/10)

5. Firing squad in the French army, c. 1630. Jacques Callot, *De droeve ellendigheden van den oorloogh* (Amsterdam). (Royal Netherlands Army Museum, Delft, 00116878/12)

Though the infantry increasingly dominated warfare from the late fifteenth century, the cavalry enjoyed much greater prestige until the early twentieth century. The costs associated with the mounted arms were, however, extremely high. A complete suit of armour for an arquebusier cost twenty guilders and that for a cuirassier cost thirty guilders. A musketeer could be armed and equipped for twelve guilders.[151] The wages for a company of 100 cuirassiers and 81 servants amounted to 4,167 guilders per *heremaand*,[152] more than twice the cost of two infantry companies of 150 men. The servants were called 'bidets' because they were mounted on small horses. They were responsible for transporting the personal effects of the cuirassiers and for collecting the forage or gathering it in the vicinity, rather than the heavily armoured cuirassiers having to do this for themselves, thus sparing their horses. More lightly armoured, the arquebusiers did not need packhorses.

The greatest debit item for the cavalry was not the raising of recruits – desertion was rare among the cavalry and the chances of being killed in battle were much smaller for the mounted arms than for the infantry[153] – but the replacement of horses that were lame, sick or had perished. The steeds were not only highly vulnerable but also extremely expensive. In the second half of the seventeenth century, between 120 and 130 guilders had to be paid for a cavalry horse.[154] If a horse was lost towards the end of a campaign, then the rittmaster was allowed to wait three months before purchasing a new animal. Until then the 'dis-mounted' cavalryman received half his pay; the rittmaster kept the rest. The rittmaster used this money and a contribution from his own pocket and from every other horseman in the company to buy a new mount. The contribution of the ordinary troopers was also intended to encourage them to ensure 'that others treat their horses well'.[155] For the same reason, Simon Stevin (1548–1620), the army's quartermaster-general from 1604, advised that the horses should always be tethered with their heads facing the entrance of the hut in which the horsemen are sleeping, 'because in this way every one of them can easily keep an eye on the

---

[151] NA, RvS 2287, 'Lij[s]te tot wat prijse de heeren Staten allerley behoeften geduerende den oorlooge ingecocht hebben' (1590–1607).
[152] NA, RvS 2287, 'Ordre op de wapenen van de compagni[e]ën ruyteren curassiers', gives the composition and payment of a company of cuirassiers as follows: a rittmaster at 250 guilders with six armed lackeys at 25 guilders each, a lieutenant at 80 guilders with four horses at 25 guilders, a cornet at 70 guilders with three horses at 25 guilders, a quartermaster with two horses at 25 guilders, two trumpeters at 40 guilders, a quartermaster-sergeant (*fourrier*) at 30 guilders, a blacksmith at 30 guilders and 81 cuirassiers at 30 guilders, each with a 'packhorse' (*bagagiepeert*) at 10 guilders, plus an extra allowance of 12 guilders for three corporals.
[153] GA, AHGC 759, Dirck van Noordinghen to Count Floris II of Culemborg, The Hague, 24 June 1628, appendix; NA, Tweede Afdeling, CvLS LM 23, Muster-roll, Wesel, 16 December 1641.
[154] HUA, HAA 2732, Godard van Reede-Ginkel to his father, near Ghent, 26 April 1677; NA, RAZH, AGRH 3027, Resolution of the Delegated Councillors of Holland, 8 May 1677; NA, Collectie De Jonge van Ellemeet 115, Extract res. SG, 27 July 1690.
[155] NA, CvdH 102, Notes by Adriaan van der Hoop regarding the cavalry.

oats he is giving his horse and that it is not taken away by his neighbours.'[156] An offence of a more serious nature than the stealing of oats was the sale of well-trained horses, which was common practice among cavalrymen. In the regulations of December 1618, Maurits, Willem Lodewijk and Frederik Hendrik ordered the rittmasters to pay careful attention, 'since it has been discovered that many cavalrymen sell their mounts once they are well trained and purchase young horses again in their place.'[157] The use of *passe-volants* during the muster was less common among the cavalry than among the infantry, but in December 1606 the muster commissaries discovered that the Scottish rittmaster, Archibald Arskin, had not only tried to deceive them with 'many borrowed' horses, but he and his troops had 'set many borrowed young men, yes even children, on their troopers' packhorses and other borrowed horses during muster'. It also came to light that Arskin had paid his cavalrymen only nine weeks' wages over the preceding twenty-two weeks.[158]

Until the middle of the seventeenth century it was normal for soldiers to be accompanied by wives and children on campaign. Soldiers' wives washed clothes, prepared food and cared for their sick or wounded husbands. The life of the soldiers' wives and children was precarious and tough. In August 1622, during the siege of Bergen op Zoom, a Walloon in Spanish service fled to the beleaguered city 'in full armour, with his housewife and a three-year-old child'. The Spanish besieging army was famine-stricken.[159] The Spanish army as well as other armies that marched across the Holy Roman Empire during the Thirty Years' War were accompanied by a mass of army-followers.[160] Maurits, Willem Lodewijk and Frederik Hendrik, by contrast, tried to limit the camp-followers to servants and the indispensable sutlers and victuallers, the independent tradespeople who sold food and clothing. A throng of thousands of women and children not only restricted the army's mobility, but was a cause of serious nuisance to the surrounding area.

In July 1591 the Dutch field army was just under 8,500 strong, but the army train of women, children, servants and peddlers swelled its number to more than 12,000.[161] Feeding these people did not present any problems so long as the army remained close to major towns it controlled, but in 1602, when The Hague resolved to launch an incursion deep inside enemy territory, Maurits forbade

---

[156] Simon Stevin, *Castrametatio dat is legermeting* (Rotterdam 1617), facsimile with commentary and a parallel English translation as *Castrametatio, that is the Marking out of Army Camps*, in *The Principal Works of Simon Stevin*, ed. W.H. Schukking et al. (Amsterdam 1964), IV, 'The Art of War', pp. 261–397, esp. 285.
[157] NA, SHS 1449, 'Ordre op 't stuck van de militie', The Hague, 5 December 1618.
[158] NA, SG 4914, 'Pointen die tot last van den ritm[eeste]re Archibald Arskin wordden gebracht', 22 December 1606.
[159] NA, SG 4941, N. van der Meer to the SG, Bergen op Zoom, 3 August 1622.
[160] Tresoar, FSA 30, Willem Frederik to the Delegates States of Friesland [Botbergen], 8 August 1642.
[161] Duyck, I, pp. 41–2.

the soldiers' wives from accompanying the troops.[162] Willem Lodewijk concurred with this decision, but he pointed out to Maurits that while the soldiers were in the field someone had to provide for their wives and children. He therefore recommended billeting them somewhere where they could await the return of their husbands,[163] but this solution gave rise to another problem. The inhabitants of towns and cities were wary of providing board and lodging to soldiers' wives. For as long as the troops were quartered in garrisons, the Council of State paid billet-money for board and lodgings (*logies- en serviesgeld*) on a monthly basis, ranging from one guilder and four stivers for a foot-soldier and one guilder and sixteen stivers for a cavalier with his horse, to six guilders for a captain and six guilders and sixteen stivers for a rittmaster. The officers used this money to rent quarters from civilians. Soldiers or cavalrymen were lodged four or six men to a room and had to make do with one bed between them; an exception was made for the married soldiers. To prevent any argument about settling the bill, the money for lodgings was not paid to the 'billeted' soldiers, 'but to those who provide them with lodgings.'[164] Payment for lodgings ceased as soon as the troops left the town. Soldiers' wives and children who stayed behind therefore had to manage without this allowance. In response to Maurits's recommendation, the States-General decided to switch to allocating them half of the billet-money 'during the time that they were not allowed to accompany their husbands'.[165] This was a means of ensuring that the 'poor and shabby housewives' would not be forced to turn to the local poorhouses. As the States of Utrecht observed, these already had enough on their hands with the 'great mass of their own ordinary poor'. Nevertheless, there was always room for the wives of sick soldiers or those who had just given birth.[166]

Soldiers and troopers entered into service for the duration of a war, unless agreed otherwise at their enlistment. In practice this meant that they served as soldiers for decades, if not for their entire lives. In 1609, with the commencement of the Twelve Years' Truce, thousands of soldiers were discharged from Dutch service; this did not happen again until after the conclusion of the Eighty Years' War in 1648. There were no pension provisions for elderly servicemen,

---

[162] Fredrich van Vervou, *Enige gedenckweerdige geschiedenissen tot narichtinge der nakomelingen, sommarischer wijze beschreven*, published by the Friesch Genootschap (Leeuwarden 1841), p. 121.
[163] KHA, A22-IX-E-168, Willem Lodewijk to Maurits, 28 January 1602, minute.
[164] NA, SG 4963, RvS to the SG, The Hague, 19 November 1595, 'Ordre dienende op de logeringe van het crijchsvolck ende betalinge van de logysgelden in de frontiersteden'. On the garrison's departure from Emmerich in August 1634 there was uproar among the locals about the failure to pay for the lodgings, whereupon the soldiers plundered their lodgings and a burgomaster's house, 'for which at long last some were arrested and a cavalry corporal has been hanged, as an example to others'. See: NA, SG 4965, Field deputies to the SG, Nijmegen, 22 August 1634.
[165] NA, SG 4941, Field deputies to the SG, 's Gravenweert, 22 August 1622.
[166] NA, SG 4960, States of Utrecht to the SG, Utrecht, 9 June 1632.

so captains and rittmasters sometimes retained decrepit soldiers in service. The quartermaster of Count Floris II of Culemborg's company of cuirassiers, for example, was eighty years old.[167] Nor, as a rule, did company commanders and paymasters abandon to their fate the younger soldiers and cavaliers who were permanently injured in action. A 'List of those kept in pay by the companies of Friesland',[168] compiled between October and December 1606, gives an impression of the various categories of invalids they provided for – the *geappoincteerden*. For each of the nineteen companies in the Frisian regiment at that time, the names of two to four aged or invalid soldiers are listed, and often also the names of the widows and offspring of deceased captains, lieutenants and ensigns. Besides veterans – such as Corporal Syrck Gerbrants van Worckum, 'a broken man, about 70 years of age', Jan Dircx van Hegam, 'an old, broken soldier who has served more than 30 years', and Borchard van Munder, 'a soldier aged between 70 and 80 years' – the list mentions many soldiers who had lost limbs. Claes Veghes, for example, 'is missing both his legs', Dirck Bogerts van Hoxter 'has had one arm shot off close to the shoulder', Thonys Ruyter van Wagevelt had 'lost one of his legs within Ostend', and Pieter Fijt had been 'shot by a musket-ball in the thickest part of his leg and the ball cannot be found and has left him in great pain'. The list also mentions two soldiers with symptoms of probable 'shell-shock': Haye Hettes was 'tormented by an evil spirit' and Court Onger was 'out of his mind'. The *geappoincteerden* were registered on the muster-roll and therefore continued to receive their regular pay. Those who were 'not completely lame or crippled' had to provide the training for recruits, and they also performed guard duties in towns and at other places away from the Republic's frontiers.[169]

Prisoners of war

In the early years of the Revolt the Spaniards regarded the Dutch troops as rebels and gave them no quarter. Spanish soldiers were equally uncertain of their lives if they fell into the hands of the insurgents. This situation improved as the struggle developed into a regular war. Senior officers certainly had the best chances of being spared in the heat of battle, simply because they were worth a fortune alive. Ernst Casimir, for example, was taken prisoner by the Spaniards in September 1595 but was released that same month on payment of a ransom of 10,000 guilders.[170] Company commanders, lower-ranking officers and men who were taken prisoner could purchase their freedom for an individually negotiated

---

[167] GA, AHGC 760, Lieutenant Alexander Schimmelpenninck van der Oye to Count Floris II of Culemborg, Arnhem, 15 July 1636.
[168] KHA, A22-VIII-5, 'Lijste van de geappoincteerde staende op de compaigni[e]ën van Vrieslandt', October–December 1606.
[169] Van der Capellen, *Gedenkschriften*, I, p. 53.
[170] Duyck, I, p. 672.

ransom. After the Dutch army captured Bredevoort in 1597, the advocate-fiscal, Anthonis Duyck, and Olivier van den Tempel (1540–1603), head of military justice in the Dutch field army, negotiated with each Spanish soldier individually to determine the level of his ransom 'and usually had one after the other promise 20, 25 or 30 guilders as ransom',[171] which was equivalent to two to three months' pay.[172] This method worked well so long as the warring factions attached equal importance to the speedy exchange of prisoners. Otherwise sky-high ransoms could be demanded, and if release took a long time the prisoners of war also faced the risk of having to go deeply into debt in order to avoid starvation.

Captured soldiers were usually transported to walled towns in the interior and gaoled by the local provost, who for a fee had to supply them with straw, fuel for warmth and food. Until 1600 there were no guidelines regulating the level of the 'provost's perquisite', comprising a gaoler's fee and a charge for provisions. In October 1599, the Spanish army's second-in-command in the Low Countries, Mendoza, proposed to The Hague that they codify the ransom and the provost's perquisite in a cartel in order to protect the troops from abuses,

> seeing as arguments arise daily about the individuals' ransoms ... and about the expense of provisions and otherwise that one claims from the prisoners, excessiveness that they will never have the means to satisfy [i.e. recompense] and are constrained to remain in prison for a long time, to their total ruin and in the interests of those who have taken them prisoner.

Mendoza proposed imposing a ceiling of one month's pay on the ransom for the rank and file and under-officers. Lieutenants and ensigns would have to pay 60 guilders for their release, cornets 150 guilders, cavalry lieutenants 200 guilders, infantry captains 600 guilders, and rittmasters and lieutenant-colonels 1,000 guilders. With regard to the cost of provisions, the provosts on either side would 'not be permitted to charge more than ten stivers' per diem for common soldiers, fifteen stivers for horsemen and one guilder for officers up to the rank of captain and rittmaster, while colonels and 'other gentlemen of higher quality shall be treated as they themselves state and desire'. It was forbidden to charge the soldiers, troopers and minor officers more than a one-off contribution of one guilder for the gaoler's fee for the duration of their imprisonment, while officers had to pay two guilders.[173] The Republic adopted Mendoza's proposal, but by the

---

[171] Duyck, I, p. 382.
[172] Between 1590 and 1634, a rank-and-file Spanish soldier earned 3 escudos (7.5 guilders) per pay-month of thirty or thirty-one days. Parker, *Army of Flanders*, pp. 158 and 163 n. 1.
[173] NA, SG 12548.211, Mendoza, Grotelith, 29 October 1599 (first quote), and the 'Lijste waernaer de prevosten alle crijchsgevangenen nyet alleen in de leghers maer oick in alle garnisoenen innegebracht zullen behoiren te tracteren en[de] dezelve teercosten te schatten' (List according to which the provosts shall be expected to treat all prisoners of war, not only in the armies but also held at all the garrisons, and how to calculate the costs of provisions for the same), drawn up by Francisco de Mendoza, Admiral of Aragon, 29 October 1599, transcript (second quote). See also Parker, *Army of Flanders*, pp. 169–70.

following year the States-General suspended the agreement. During the battle of Nieuwpoort (1600), the Admiral of Aragon and hundreds of other Spanish officers were taken prisoner by the Dutch forces, and The Hague exploited this opportunity to demand the release, 'without ransom or costs', of all the Dutch soldiers and sailors who were in Spanish hands. The States-General promised to release all Spanish prisoners of war as well, on condition that 'their expenses and ransom are reasonably paid [by them]'. However, Mendoza himself would be allowed to leave only after agreement was reached about how they would treat each other's prisoners of war in the future. The Spanish commander assented to the agreement in January 1601.[174] The 'general quarter' for the exchange of Spanish and Dutch prisoners of war, in essence a more comprehensive version of the 1599 cartel with some changes to the details, was signed on 14 May 1602 after almost a year and a half of negotiations.[175] This time it took the personnel of the artillery and supply trains into consideration as well: ransom was set at 10 guilders for a waggoner, 15 guilders for a cannoneer, 70 guilders for a pyrotechnician and 100 guilders for a commissary of the victuals, to mention just a few. Soldiers' wives and children aged twelve years or younger could not be taken prisoner. The conclusion of the cartel, as the formal agreement for the exchange and treatment of prisoners of war was known, was as important for the company commanders as for the government, since the captains and rittmasters were obliged to assume responsibility for payment of the ransom, the gaoler's fee and the charge for provisions.[176] Prisoners of war were not removed from the pay ordinances but this was scant compensation, as a captain had to pay five stivers from his own pocket for every day a rank-and-file soldier was held prisoner. The cost of provisions amounted to ten stivers per day, which was double the daily advance on their pay. The captains and rittmasters could hardly be expected to bear these extra costs for an extended period, so the cartel of 1602 stated that prisoners had to be released within '48 hours' of payment of the ransom.

The general quarter remained in force until 1648 and usually functioned well. In August 1603, a ship with twelve sick and wounded Dutch soldiers from Ostend fell into the hands of the Spaniards. According to the Spanish commanders the cartel only applied on land – strictly speaking this interpretation was correct – and they therefore had them put to death at sea, as was customary. When Maurits received news of this he immediately gave the order to execute about twice as many Spanish prisoners of war.[177] Hereafter both parties upheld the agreements for many years, but in 1638 the Spaniards suspended the cartel for six months. In June that year there was a fierce battle at Kallo, a village near Antwerp,

---

[174] Duyck, II, p. 720; III, pp. 17–20, 25–6.
[175] Duyck, III, pp. 359–62.
[176] GA, AHGC 760, Lieutenant Alexander Schimmelpenninck van der Oye to Count Floris II of Culemborg, Arnhem, 8 July 1636.
[177] Fleming, *Oostende*, p. 405.

in which more than 2,000 Dutch troops were taken prisoner.[178] The Republic wanted to purchase their freedom as quickly as possible, but the governor of Antwerp refused to issue a passport to the Republic's commissary, a certain Ruysch, who was authorised to conclude agreements regarding the ransom. The Spaniard claimed that at the launch of the Spanish assault the Dutch troops had yelled that they 'wanted to know of no quarter' and, moreover, a passport could be issued only by the Governor-General in Brussels, 'to whom he hardly dares speak of the matter, all the more because at [Fort] Liefkenshoek, having promised quarter, they [the Dutch] had massacred a Spanish captain of high birth along with two soldiers in cold blood'.[179] Only many months later, after Frederik Hendrik had personally intervened in the affair, did the Governor-General agree to release the Dutch prisoners of war on payment of a ransom including the gaoler's fee and costs for provisions amounting to no less than 150,000 guilders. Because the cartel had been suspended by the Spaniards, the provinces assumed responsibility for paying the ransom, but the company commanders would have to find the costs of provisions and the gaoler's fee. The captains raised objections to this, as they were not to blame for the paying of the ransom being delayed so long. The Council of State concurred. In an opinion of 30 January 1642 the body recognised

> that it was not in the power of the officers to secure the release of their soldiers, the enemy insisting that they were not ransomable, and consequently it seems unreasonable that during these disputes between state and state an officer should be expected to pay ten stivers a day to have his soldiers provided with food for such a remarkably long time instead of the [usual] advance of five stivers.

The Council of State therefore proposed withholding five stivers against the pay ordinances for each day a soldier spent in captivity while the provinces would be expected to pay the other half plus the ransoms. This at last resolved the 'Kallo affair', which had dragged on for three and a half years.[180]

The *solliciteurs-militair*

The *solliciteurs-militair* were an indispensable cog in the payment machine of the Dutch army. These 'agents' were private financiers who, for a monthly salary supplemented where necessary by interest payments, advanced the pay to the company commanders, since the provinces seldom distributed the wages on time.[181] The system of *solliciteurs-militair* meant the Republic could fall back on

---

[178] HUA, ASU 314-6, Godard van Reede-Amerongen, Bergen op Zoom, at 11 a.m., 23 June 1638; NA, SG 4974, Extract res. SG, 28 December 1638.
[179] NA, SG 4973, Field deputies to the SG, Bergen op Zoom, evening of 30 June 1638.
[180] NA, SG 4979, Extract res. RvS, 30 January 1642.
[181] Zwitzer, *Militie van den Staat*, pp. 91–9.

a dual financial buffer, namely the credit of officers and of private financiers. Conversely, if there were hitches with the payment of wages in the Spanish or French armies then any outstanding amount had to be offset in full by the officers.[182] The notion that the Dutch soldiers always received their pay on time and in full is a fallacy, though the situation was much better than in other European armies because of the *solliciteurs*. The best evidence of this is that major mutinies failed to materialise after 1589. There were still tensions, but these usually affected soldiers who could not find a *solliciteur* or whose company commander had died without arranging a successor.

In 1606 the Council of State warned the States-General that there was no money available at the army camp near Wesel to pay the soldiers their wages and this was threatening to degenerate into a dangerous situation. The 'grumbling' soldiers had already put 'their heads together'.[183] The 'decayed and utterly ruined' officers and horsemen in the company of Rittmaster Johan van Bawijr, lord of Franckenberg, complained in January 1638 that they had not been paid for a whole year. In order to keep themselves, their horses, wives and children alive they had been forced to spend their last resources or to pawn 'whatever goods they possessed in the world'.[184] These cavalrymen continued to wait resignedly, but a Frisian infantry company in 's-Hertogenbosch was less ready to exercise patience. In June that year they set out 'fully armed [and] with great tempestuousness for the commander's house', where they 'entreated' payment.[185]

Problems arose among foreign troops more often than among the indigenous companies. In August 1602, for example, there was dire poverty among the English soldiery, 'who are consumed by hunger and want'.[186] Foreign officers had to go to greater pains than native and German officers to acquire credit, because the *solliciteurs* were wary of soliciting for a company without surety; it was not inconceivable that a captain or rittmaster would take to his heels with the money advanced by a *solliciteur*. For non-native officers there were few obstacles to fleeing to foreign parts, and if an officer had neither family nor property in the Republic then he could only offer his company's weapons as collateral. These had an average assessed value of 2,000 guilders for an infantry company of 150 men and 2,500 guilders for a company of 200 men.[187] These amounts were almost equal to one month's pay: 2,014 and 2,612 guilders, respectively.

---

[182] Parrott, *Richelieu's Army*, pp. 348–9; Parker, *Army of Flanders*, pp. 160–1.
[183] NA, SG 4914, RvS to the SG, before Wesel, 16 September 1606.
[184] NA, SG 4972, 'Requeste voor de gesamentl[ijke] officieren & ruyteren van[de] ritm[eeste]r Franquenburch', a company repartitioned to Gelderland, 30 January 1637 [ought to be 1638].
[185] NA, SG 4972, Field deputies to the SG, at Schans Ter Voorn, evening of 4 June 1638.
[186] NA, SG 4902, Gerrit Coren to the SG, before Grave, 17 August 1602 (quote), Maurits to the SG, before Grave, 19 August 1602.
[187] HUA, ASU 278-4, Frederik Hendrik to the States of Utrecht, The Hague, 18 July 1636; KHA, A24-IV-H2, Hendrik van Goor to Hendrik Casimir I, n.p., n.d. [probably August 1638].

The captains and rittmasters could themselves choose the *solliciteur-militair* with whom they wished to strike a deal. The provincial States did not draw up directives pertaining to this until 1673. The contract between a *solliciteur* and a company commander stated that the former would collect the pay ordinances at the provincial treasurer's office and would redeem them for cash. This sounds simpler than it actually was. The *solliciteur* often had to bribe the treasurer's clerks with 'venerations' before they would issue the pay ordinances on time and redeem them in full.[188] Besides dealing with such purely financial business, the *solliciteur-militair* had to represent all the other interests of the officers in The Hague and elsewhere, such as when the Council of State raised objections to closing (i.e. approving) a muster-roll. In this respect he was no different from the dozens of normal solicitors who congregated around the Binnenhof – the hub of government at The Hague – professional and well-connected intermediaries who knew how to tread the corridors of power and were well-versed in the titulature and usages.[189] Unless a petition was submitted and formulated in the proper manner it would not even be taken into consideration.

A company commander sent his own clerk to the office of the *solliciteur* every month to collect the wages. This meant that the *solliciteurs* for an infantry company always had to have 2,000 to 2,500 guilders available in cash, while those contracted to a company of cuirassiers needed about 4,000 guilders. However, most *solliciteurs* took care of more than one company and therefore had to have access to tens of thousands of guilders in cash. As recompense for his services the *solliciteur* received a monthly salary,[190] though this fee and the rate of interest charged varied. Dirck van Noordinghen, *solliciteur* of the company of cuirassiers of Count Floris II of Culemborg, for example, undertook to serve the unit for a salary of 100 guilders per *heremaand* in July 1624. In February 1626 his salary was raised to 130 guilders per month on condition that he henceforth pay out the wages precisely on the due date.[191] Cathelyna Maes, the female *solliciteur* of Count Floris II's infantry company, received a monthly salary of 120 guilders, for which she had to pay the wages 'in advance on the day each month begins ... provided that his grace shall have each month's wages collected in The Hague and shall bring them to the company at his own expense and peril'.[192]

---

[188] Paul Knevel, *Het Haagse bureau. Zeventiende-eeuwse ambtenaren tussen staatsbelang en eigenbelang* (Amsterdam 2001), p. 162.
[189] Ibid., p. 167.
[190] GA, AHGC 769, Contract between Count Floris II of Culemborg and Dirck van Noordinghen, The Hague, 26 July 1624.
[191] GA, AHGC 769, Addendum to the contract between Count Floris II of Culemborg and Dirck van Noordinghen of 26 July 1624, Culemborg, 21 February 1626.
[192] GA, AHGC 769, Contract between Count Floris II of Culemborg and Cathelyna Maes, widow of Jacob van Duynen, 6 January 1631.

Van Noordinghen's salary was reduced to 110 guilders in August 1627,[193] but the ever-greater arrears in the distribution of wages prompted him to sharpen his terms, as he informed Count Floris II in January 1629: '[T]he payment of the soldiery repartitioned to Holland is falling so far behind that I have usually distributed three months' wages and oftentimes four months' wages to your grace's company, amounting to 16,000 guilders in capital, before I have received a single stiver thereagainst from the Land.' Furthermore, the 'venerations' he had to pay to the clerks of the treasurer's office cost him more than 150 guilders per annum. The two other rittmasters with whom he had a contract had already agreed henceforth to remunerate him at 130 guilders per month instead of 120. He expected Count Floris II would agree to the same.[194] Two years later, in 1631, the 'extraordinarily poor payment practices' of Holland – arrears in payment of army wages ran to at least four, five or sometimes even six months – necessitated increasing his fee to 160 guilders.[195] Over the years that followed, the situation failed to improve.

In April 1632, Van Noordinghen had advanced 18,483 guilders to the company of cuirassiers of Count Floris II. 'I am so tired of solicitation that it is unbelievable', the exasperated *solliciteur* complained.[196] In June of that year he signalled his desire to cease 'the servicing of all the companies'.[197] Count Floris II then entered into a contract with Arnold Jordan Rampers, who negotatiated a salary of 240 guilders per *heremaand*.[198] Rampers soon found himself in financial difficulties all the same. In June 1635, Lieutenant Johan van Welderen apologised to Count Floris II of Culemborg for the fact that he had not written earlier, underscoring 'the great occupation I had in order to obtain some money for your grace's company, because there was such poverty among the cavalrymen and they were all so denuded of means that they could barely leave the town, yet [I] have at long last received money in dribs and drabs from the *solliciteur*'.[199] In February 1636, Count Floris II re-established his collaboration with Van Noordinghen, who declared himself ready to advance the company's pay for four successive months, always fourteen days after the due date. However, in the event of his not being able to cash one of the four pay ordinances at the treasurer's office after

---

[193] GA, AHGC 760, Contract between Count Floris II of Culemborg and Dirck van Noordinghen, The Hague, 17 August 1627.
[194] GA, AHGC 759, Dirck van Noordinghen to Count Floris II of Culemborg, The Hague, 5 January 1629, with two letters from fellow *solliciteurs* as addenda.
[195] GA, AHGC 759, same to same, The Hague, 12 October 1631.
[196] GA, AHGC 759, same to Tobias van Eyck, adviser to Count Floris II, The Hague, 27 April 1632.
[197] GA, AHGC 759, same to Willem van Langen, adviser to Count Floris II, The Hague, 16 June 1632.
[198] GA, AHGC 759, Contract between Count Floris II of Culemborg and Arnold Jordan Rampers, The Hague, 27 April 1635.
[199] GA, AHGC 770, Lieutenant Johan van Welderen to Count Floris II of Culemborg, Valkenburg, 2 June 1635.

the fourth month, Van Noordinghen was not obliged to advance pay for a fifth month unless Count Floris II paid him interest of 1 per cent per *heremaand* (i.e. 8.67 per cent annualised) over and above his monthly salary of 240 guilders. The payment of interest would be suspended as soon as one of the four ordinances was redeemed for cash.[200] This demonstrates that in the space of barely twelve years (1624–1635), the fees of *solliciteurs* had more than doubled, from 100 guilders to 240 guilders per *heremaand*.

The problems Van Noordinghen had to contend with were common to all the *solliciteurs-militair*. In October 1634, Willem Rooclaes, the former *solliciteur* of one Captain Read, informed the States-General that he was still owed 9,491 guilders in wages from the period 13 December 1632 to 11 July 1633.[201] In 1639 the *solliciteurs* employed by the companies from Holland that had been repartitioned to that province's South Quarter submitted a joint petition to the States of Holland. They pointed out that they had advanced millions of guilders – the wages for a single *heremaand* of forty-two days amounted to more than 600,000 guilders[202] – without being able to foresee or believe, 'it being beyond all precedent', that the pay ordinances 'currently assigned to the respective Comptoirs of Holland remain unpaid for three, four years and longer'. The *solliciteurs* had continued to advance money in the expectation that they would be remunerated swiftly, 'whereas now, quite to the contrary, some are sorrowfully discouraged and have even died through this long delay, others are starting to wither and have had to absent themselves in order to escape the threats of their creditors to bring lawsuits against them, of being condemned and executed [i.e. declared bankrupt]'.[203] The situation was threatening to spiral out of control. In January 1643, Holland owed more than three million guilders in pay arrears,[204] while all the provinces together owed more than five million guilders.[205] This was not only disastrous for the creditworthiness of the *solliciteurs*; it placed the captains and rittmasters in great peril. A year earlier, for example, an officer had informed Frederik Hendrik that his *solliciteur* had gone bankrupt, his company losing

---

[200] GA, AHGC 760, Contract between Count Floris II of Culemborg and Dirck van Noordinghen, The Hague, 10 February 1636.
[201] NA, SG 4965, 'Requeste' from Willem Rooclaes, 9 October 1634.
[202] NA, RAZH, AJC 52, 'Staet van een maend solts van[de] compagni[e]ën staende op de repartitie van Holland. Betaelt werdende op ordonnantie van[de] Ed. Moo. heeren Gecommitt[eerd]e Raeden in Zuyt-Holland'.
[203] NA, RAZH, ASH 1354B*, 'Requeste van wegen de gemeene solliciteurs van[de] Zuyt-Hollandtsche comp[agnie]ën ruyteren ende knechten 1639'.
[204] NA, RAZH, ASH 1293-II, 'Staet van 't geene aen de naevolgende compagni[e]ën tot in dese lopende maent van january 1643 noch te betaelen staet', and ASH 75, Res. SH, 8 May 1643.
[205] NA, RAZH, AJC 32, 'Pointen van mesnage voorgeslagen bij de heeren Gecommitteerden octobris 1635'.

10,000 guilders as a consequence.[206] The States of Holland were certainly not blind to the financial disarray, and from the 1630s they made frantic attempts to put on a firm footing the financing of Holland's troops, who constituted more than half the Republic's entire army, some 52,000 men on paper.[207]

'This great and cankerous malady of negotiation': financing the Republic's war effort and the question of army reduction

Under the governor-generalship (1586–1587) of the earl of Leicester, the number of troops on the Republic's payroll was substantially increased, but this expansion was implemented without consulting the provinces. The day after Leicester returned to England on 4 December 1586 to consult with Elizabeth I, the States of Holland under the leadership of Johan van Oldenbarnevelt presented a proposal to the Council of State to dismiss sixty-five companies of foot and several of horse from Dutch service.[208] The Hollanders wanted the Council of State to draw up 'a proper account of all the soldiery that one will be able and allowed to maintain with the Land's means, cashiering the excess men in order to prevent all further desertion'.[209] In May that year the Council of State had estimated it would be possible to defend the Republic with a minimum of 26,000 foot-soldiers and 2,050 cavalrymen.[210] The States-General thought this number excessive and agreed to 19,000 foot and 1,500 horse. This meant that, besides disbanding the specified companies of foot and of horse, a further 4,000 infantrymen and 850 cavalrymen would have to be discharged.[211] These reductions slashed the total pay bill for the provinces from more than 450,000 guilders to about 200,000 guilders per month (2.4 million guilders per annum).[212] These costs were shared by the four rebellious provinces still remaining in 1586, according to their financial wherewithal: Holland assumed responsibility for 64.25 per cent, Zeeland for 15.81 per cent, Utrecht for 6.64 per cent and Friesland for 13.29 per cent. The intention was to eradicate the discrepancy between

---

[206] HUA, ASU 278-4, Frederik Hendrik to the States of Utrecht, The Hague, 25 February 1642.
[207] NA, RAZH, AJC 52, 'Staet van[de] soldije van ruyteren en[de] knechten in de naevolgen[de] jaeren tot laste van[de] provincie Holland gestelt'.
[208] Jan den Tex, *Oldenbarnevelt*, 4 vols and a separate index (Haarlem and Groningen 1960–1972), I, pp. 322–3.
[209] NA, FAF 1005, Extract res. SG, 8 December 1586.
[210] Tresoar, ASF 3025, 'Overgebracht bij de heeren Meetkercke ende Valck van wegen den Raedt van State', 9 May 1586.
[211] Tresoar, ASF 1352, 'Staet van het getal van de ruyteren en[de] soldaten die … voortaen zullen gehouden worrdden', 23 January 1588, reviewed and updated on 27 and 28 May 1588; NA, RAZH, AJvO 2942A, 'Staet van het crijchsvolck', 31 December 1587.
[212] NA, CvdH 123, Res. SG, 4 December 1586; HUA, ASU 657, 'Staet sommier van de petitiën bij den Raedt van State gedaen tot onderstant van den oorloge sedert den jare 1586 totten jaere 1637'.

the paper and effective strengths of the small military force that the Republic retained in service. In practice this was unachievable, as we have seen. From 1599 the costs of war were shared among seven provinces – Gelderland, Groningen and Overijssel, besides the four already mentioned – and their allotted quotas were recalculated. From 1617 to 1792, Holland's contribution to defence expenditure amounted to a good 58 per cent.

A major advantage of the repartition system was that army administration was shared among seven provinces, which the severely limited size of the federal administration made desirable. The Council of State, to which the supervision of national defence was assigned by the States-General, had too few staff to oversee the payment, recruitment and upkeep of the Dutch army. The 'Councillors of State', who besides the stadholders included twelve normal members, of which Holland provided three, Gelderland, Zeeland and Friesland two apiece, and Utrecht, Overijssel and Groningen one each, were supported by only twenty or so staff. The Council of State's most important administrative staff were the treasurer-general, the secretary and the Union's receiver-general. The chronic understaffing forced the administrators and clerks to hire assistants at their personal expense, but they could still barely manage the workload and such a set-up was hardly conducive to the running of an efficient bureaucracy.[213] The repartition system meant that responsibility for the Dutch army was devolved to the Delegated Councillors in the seven provinces (see p. 48). There was no serious danger that this solution would undermine the cohesion of the Dutch army until the mid-seventeenth century. The two stadholders and the fact that Holland paid for more than half the troops meant that the army could function as an entity and did not disintegrate into seven provincial armies.

The management and financing of the Dutch navy were organised differently from the army. The Boards of Admiralty or Admiralty Colleges were responsible for war at sea and had access to their own sources of income: besides the duties on imports and exports there was the sale of the licences permitting trade with the enemy. From 1586, both these taxes were levied at a uniform rate by representatives of the admiralties in all the provinces. In 1596 there were five Boards of Admiralty: three in Holland (one in Rotterdam, one in Amsterdam, and one seated alternately in Enkhuizen or Hoorn), one in Zeeland, and one in Friesland. This arrangement would remain unchanged until the demise of the Republic in 1795. The States-General appointed the members, but the majority always came from the province or region where the admiralty was based. The admiralties had a threefold brief. They were above all responsible for shipbuilding and the equipping and maintenance of the fleet; they were a court of law (passing judgment in, for example, conflicts about privateering and imposing penalties when duties and licences were evaded); and lastly, they collected taxes. There were far

---

[213] A. Th. van Deursen, 'De Raad van State onder de Republiek 1588–1795', in *Raad van State 450 jaar* (The Hague 1981), pp. 47–91, esp. 49, 55 and 60–1.

fewer people serving in the Dutch navy than in the army. The naval historian J.R. Bruijn estimated the number of sailors employed by the admiralties at just 8,500 in 1628 and 11,000 in 1642. Only the crews of the blockade ships before the Flemish coast were taken into service for an indefinite period; other seamen served from spring to early autumn.[214] While land-based warfare was seasonal too, the majority of troops remained in service during the winter.

The repartition system determined the distribution of the costs for the troops, but to be able to employ them for a military operation the Council of State had to petition the provinces every year to approve the release of the necessary funds. Some historians have misunderstood the 'State of War' (*Staat van Oorlog*) as a budget for annual defence expenditure,[215] which was the case only after 1650. Prior to that year the State of War was purely an overview of the apportionment of military costs among the provinces according to the quotas. No part of it could be modified without the sanction of all the provinces. As long as the State of War remained unchanged there was no need for it to be re-approved every year. It was regarded as 'a repartition of the approved costs, which the Council of State reviewed and redressed when a change arose in the quotas or in the burdens'.[216] This explains why the States of War were recalculated only fourteen times between 1586 and 1648 (including the introduction of two supplements in 1626 and 1627).[217]

The General Petition drawn up annually by the Council of State was the war budget proper, asking the provinces to sanction the outlay for a military campaign, known as *legerlasten*, and to make available the pecuniary means to maintain and improve fortifications, found guns, assume responsibility for the payment of *waardgelders* and, if required, raise extra regiments to make a specific military operation feasible. If circumstances making extra military expenditure necessary arose during the course of the campaign, then the Council of State submitted supplementary petitions. The provinces approved the General Petition and such 'suppletory' petitions in full or in part, but they were also at liberty to reject these requests outright. If the Council of State proposed recruiting additional troops these could only be transferred to the State of War with the consent of the provinces. If the provinces refused to approve the petitions then these unrepartitioned troops had to be paid from the States-General's revenues,[218] which were primarily taxes levied in the Generality Lands and income from the fire-tax exacted as protection against pillage and fire-raising. The Generality Lands included States Brabant, States Flanders, the Land of Overmaze, Westerwolde and Wedde (in

---

[214] Bruijn, *Varend verleden*, pp. 16–19 and 73.
[215] See also Van Deursen, 'Raad van State', pp. 77–81, and Zwitzer, *De militie van den Staat*, pp. 73–4.
[216] Van Slingelandt, *Staatkundige geschriften*, III, p. 95.
[217] NA, SG 4981, 'Redenen die sijnne hoocheyt & den Raet van State hebben bewooge om den ouden Staet van Oorloge de anno 1621 te redresseeren', exh. 16 December 1644.
[218] NA, SG 4921, Delegated States of Friesland to the SG, Leeuwarden, 19 June 1610.

East Groningen), which were territories conquered from the Spanish that were governed by the States-General directly. The States-General could also borrow money, but its creditworthiness was not very robust: it borrowed almost 4.9 million guilders between 1596 and 1617, and 8.2 million guilders between 1618 and 1648, 'almost all being raised through Holland's intervention and on the basis of its credit'.[219] In 1637, annual interest of 418,000 guilders had to be paid on the 11 million guilders the States-General had amassed in debt.[220]

In 1586 the States-General considered a monthly bill of 450,000 guilders for military wages irresponsibly high. In 1628 the military costs accounted for in the three States of War (including the two supplements of 1626 and 1627) were double that amount: 931,414 guilders per month.[221] In 1595 the States of Friesland had indicated that 'in order to alleviate its great burden somewhat' it had ordered the captains of the Frisian regiment to refrain from enlisting any new soldiers.[222] However, with the reinforcement of the Dutch army in 1599, the Dunkirk campaign in 1600 and the exhausting struggle to hold Ostend (1601–1604) in particular, followed by the onslaught of a major Spanish offensive in 1605 and 1606, the Council of State was compelled to ask for even more money from the provinces. In late 1601 the Council of State calculated that the costs of war already exceeded those of 1598 by approximately 6.5 million guilders.[223] The military situation forced the Council of State to issue supplementary petitions for an average of 1.9 million guilders per annum, over and above the State of War, which already amounted to almost 5 million guilders in 1599, 5.77 million guilders in 1600 to 1604, and 7.32 million guilders in 1605 to 1607.

The provinces usually assented to the extra sums requested, but this did not mean that they always actually converted their authorisations into cash. The Generality was therefore forced to borrow enough to cover the shortfall for the defaulting provinces. Between 1601 and 1616 it borrowed 718,500 guilders, primarily for Zeeland.[224] This was not a huge amount but it was a serious matter nonetheless. After all, if a province refused to bear a burden or, much worse, failed to meet commitments then it immediately undermined the zeal of other member provinces to actually provide the promised resources. In January 1637 delegates from the Council of State impressed upon the States of Friesland that they were 'withholding an excessive sum of monies from its allies [i.e. the other provinces]', and in doing so were responsible for the other provinces refusing,

---

[219] NA, CvdH 28, 'Staet in 't corte … van de capitalen die door ordre van de Generaliteyt op interest genegotieert sijn … 't sedert den 11.en january 1596 tot den 5.en april 1617 soo ten behouve van de General[itei]t als voor de defecten van de provinciën'.

[220] NA, SG 4971 'Staet sommier van[de] pennin[gen] op interest gelicht ende tegenwoordich loopende ten Comptoire van den Ontfanger-Generael', exh. 28 October 1637.

[221] NA, SG 4955, RvS to the SG, 'General Petition', The Hague, 17 November 1629.

[222] RGP 57, Res. SG, 5 February 1595 (no. 160).

[223] NA, SG 4901, 'Memorie van de lasten die bij de Vereenichde Nederlanden alsnu meer gedragen moeten worddden als voor den jaere xcviii [1598]'.

[224] NA, CvdH 28, 'Staet in 't corte'.

already for two years, to approve the financial contributions requested by the Council of State.²²⁵ Though the States-General were at liberty to use military means to exact from a province those commitments it could not shirk, such as those that derived from the State of War, the provincial States were all too aware that this was a double-edged sword: constraint might be turned against them at some other juncture. Deputing, the dispatch of a delegation from the States-General or the Council of State, was in effect the most strenuous means of coercion available to the federal government in The Hague in the seventeenth and eighteenth centuries.²²⁶

The escalating war effort placed increasing pressure on Holland to take the financial strain on behalf of the Republic. Until the expiry of the Twelve Years' Truce, Holland had to a large extent been able to cover war expenses from tax revenues. In 1622, Holland had an estimated 671,000 inhabitants; thirty years later this had increased to 765,000, approximately half the Republic's entire population.²²⁷ Holland had been divided into a North Quarter and a South Quarter since 1573 due to the vicissitudes of war. Seven of the eighteen towns and cities of Holland lay in the North Quarter, the remaining eleven in the South Quarter. In financial wherewithal there was no comparison between the two quarters, the South Quarter assuming responsibility for 80 to 90 per cent of the war burden.²²⁸ Amsterdam, Leiden, Haarlem, Rotterdam and Dordrecht, five of Holland's six biggest cities, lay within the South Quarter; the sixth biggest city, Enkhuizen, was in the North Quarter.

The receivers were responsible for tax collection, divided among eleven local receivers' offices or 'comptoirs': the receiver-general of Holland was based in The Hague, the province's North Quarter had its own comptoir, and the nine others were in Dordrecht, Haarlem, Delft, Leiden, Amsterdam, Gouda, Rotterdam, Gorinchem and Den Briel (Schiedam and Schoonhoven fell under this office). The receiver-general collected the tax on the ownership of houses and land (*verponding*) in both quarters. The revenues from this constituted approximately 19.5 per cent of the 'ordinary' tax revenues. The municipal receivers were responsible for the collection of the allocated 'common means' (*gemeene middelen*), primarily taxes on life's basic necessities, and the 'collective means' (*collectieve middelen*), which were levied on juridical proceedings.

The ordinary revenues of Holland were insufficient to cover the costs of war. Initially Holland's budget deficit was limited: between 1574 and 1599 the province's burden of debt grew by just 3.6 million guilders.²²⁹ From 1599, however,

---

225 Tresoar, FAEVC 547, 'Propositie van den Raet van Staete', 14 January 1637, transcript.
226 Van Nimwegen, *De Republiek als grote mogendheid*, p. 81.
227 't Hart, *Making of a Bourgeois State*, p. 138.
228 NA, RAZH, AJC 25, 'Repartitie van 100 pond [guilders] over d'ontfangers van[de] steden'; AJC 22, 'Staet van[de] lasten in Zuyt-Holl[and]d [en in 'Noort-Holland'] daertegens 't incomen [1634]'.
229 NA, RAZH, FH 806, 'Recapitulatiën der schulden ZQ'.

Holland's burden of debt started to rise sharply. In that year expenditure (5.78 million guilders) outstripped revenue (4.63 million guilders) by 1.15 million guilders.[230] In order to cover the shortfall the States of Holland decided to impose a wealth tax. A two-hundredth penny tax (0.5 per cent) was imposed on all property, movable and immovable, valued at 3,000 guilders or more, 'on condition that those who wear clothes entirely of silk or velvet (even though these are not valued at three thousand pounds) shall also be taxed at fifteen guilders'. Collection of this capital levy would take place in four instalments, namely in April and July 1599 and in April and July 1600.[231] Until the 1690s, property taxes or forced loans continued to serve as the standard financial instruments to raise extra income if there was a sudden need to ratchet up the war effort or at least to maintain it at current levels.[232]

The basis for the capital loans was set out in a register (*kohier*) that distributed the imposed assessments among the towns with voting rights (i.e. represented in the States of Holland) and The Hague. Amsterdam was responsible for no less than a quarter of the sum to be raised.[233] The manner in which a levy was collected was the responsibility of the local comptoirs.[234] They initially endeavoured to raise the money required by issuing voluntary loans, but often the military situation was too urgent for them to wait until such loans were fully subscribed.[235] In 1625 the States of Holland once again resorted to imposing a two-hundredth penny tax against the issue of redeemable long-term debentures (*losrenten*). Everyone who paid the assessment within two months would receive interest of 3 per cent over the drawn sum for six years and thereafter the full interest rate of 6.25 per cent.[236] The receipts from this one-off levy were estimated at 1.66 million guilders.[237] In 1630 the two-hundredth penny tax raised 1.2 million guilders. In September 1635 Holland decided 'in this predicament, seeing as the finances fall short in every respect', to borrow 300,000 guilders against the anticipated receipts from this levy.[238]

The extra tax receipts were not insubstantial, but they were still insufficient to cover the shortfall; there was no other option than to raise large sums of money on private money markets. In March 1626, for example, the States of Holland

---

[230] Dormans, *Het tekort*, p. 25.
[231] NA, RAZH, AGF, Extract res. SH, 27 February 1599.
[232] Dormans, *Het tekort*, p. 27.
[233] NA, RAZH, FAH 9, 'In C guld. betalen de navolgende steden [and The Hague] als volcht'.
[234] 't Hart, *Making of a Bourgeois State*, p. 176.
[235] J.M.F. Fritschy, *De patriotten en de financiën van de Bataafse Republiek. Hollands krediet en de smalle marges voor een nieuw beleid (1795–1801)* (The Hague 1988), pp. 37–8.
[236] D. Houtzager, *Hollands lijf- en losrentenleningen vóór 1672* (Schiedam 1950), p. 139.
[237] NA, RAZH, FAH 9, 'Staet van den tweehondersten penn[in]k van den iaer 1625'.
[238] NA, RAZH, AJC 15, 'Staet van 't incomen soo ordinaris als extraordinaris voor den jaere 1635', 10 October 1635, 'Lasten en[de] incomen a.o 1630'; GAA, Missives of Amsterdam's deputies to the States of Holland 71 (microfilm 7548), The Hague, 13 September 1635.

informed the North Quarter's Delegated Councillors that, in order to avoid 'confusion' among the troops, some two million guilders had to be borrowed, either 'furnished by the towns against interest [i.e. by issuing bonds] or against redeemable annuities and life annuities'.[239] The States of Holland preferred to issue life annuities (*lijfrenten*), because even though the interest rate was 4 to 5 per cent higher than for the other two forms of loan the principal lapsed on the death of the creditor. Nevertheless, the bulk of the loans were issued against redeemable annuities (*losrenten*). Until 1606 the interest on such loans was 8.33 per cent, and from 1608 to 1640 it stood at 6.25 per cent. The least economical credit vehicle from the government's perspective was the issuing of bonds (*obligaties*), because a broker's fee or commission of 1 per cent (reduced after 1605 to 0.5 per cent) had to be paid over and above the interest.[240] For the subscribers, bonds were an attractive investment because they could be traded freely on the Amsterdam bourse.[241]

Despite the wealth of the inhabitants of Holland, the States of this province were wary of financing a war with long-term loans. After all, it meant that a greater portion of each year's revenues would have to be reserved for interest payments, 'whereby the existing means would at some point be completely exhausted, in such manner that all these revenues shall be consumed by the payment of annuities and interests'. And anyhow it was 'unprecedented ... to wage war based on negotiations and credit alone, which in an instant, through some accident or bad practices, would likely falter and no longer be available'.[242] When the States of Holland adopted this stance in October 1640, the province's burden of debt had already swelled by tens of millions of guilders: between 1621 and 1634 it had borrowed 40.23 million guilders, chiefly in redeemable annuities and bonds.[243]

There had been no shortage of measures taken to reduce the annual deficits, but they had been inadequate. In 1626, for example, the States of Holland had decided to impose a one-thousandth penny tax, a property tax of 0.1 per cent, which raised 340,000 guilders in the province's South Quarter. Holland deposited the revenues from this levy in a fund specifically intended for the payment of the interest on a loan of 2 million guilders.[244] In addition, in 1632 the assessment register for the tax on immovable property was recalculated and adapted to the altered demographic circumstances; the old register dated from as far back as 1584. This measure doubled the revenue from the *verponding* to 2.4 million guil-

---

[239] NA, CvdH 24, States of Holland to the Delegated Councillors of the North Quarter, The Hague, 28 March 1626.
[240] Houtzager, *Hollands lijf- en losrentenleningen*, pp. 5, 7, 8, 10, 53, 55, 56 and 58.
[241] 't Hart, *Making of a Bourgeois State*, pp. 176 and 179.
[242] NA, RAZH, ASH 73, Res. SH 16, 17 October 1640.
[243] NA, RAZH, AJC 18, 'Penningen op intrest tot laste van Holland genegotieert in de naevolgende jaeren'.
[244] NA, CvdH 25, 'Staet van den 1000en penn. over de respective steden van Hollandt & de dorpen onder deselve resorteeren[de] geheven in de jaren 1621 & 1654'.

ders per annum.[245] In all, Holland now had approximately 10 million guilders available to it from ordinary revenue, which was more than twice as much as in 1599. This was supplemented by temporary extraordinary revenues, such as the two-hundredth and one-thousandth penny taxes, but in spite of this the province's spending continued to outstrip its income by more than 5 million guilders per annum.[246] Holland's share of the war burden (its quota in the three States of War, in the wages of the other troops and in the petitions) amounted to 9.28 million guilders in 1630, 11 million guilders in 1634, 12.36 million guilders in 1635, and 10.24 million guilders in 1640.[247] By 1632 the total debt of the South Quarter had risen to approximately 44.44 million guilders.[248] The calls to economise on military expenditure were plangent.

Holland's escalating debt was a cause of consternation to the Hollanders but was also of serious concern to the regents of other provinces.[249] Political tensions in the province were escalating in step with the financial problems. 'It goes with the people of Holland as with those of the Tower of Babel; they cannot understand one another', quipped Tobias van Eyck, adviser to Count Floris II of Culemborg.[250] The forcing up of taxes exacerbated the aversion to increased or new military expenditure, among citizens of Amsterdam in particular. After all, the big city had to contribute the lion's share and Amsterdam's burghers were therefore of the opinion that the land-based war should not become any more expensive than was strictly necessary, a standpoint shared by a growing majority throughout Holland. In September 1633, while the States of Holland had already impressed upon Frederik Hendrik that they would indeed provide him with the means to continue that year's campaign, in the same breath they noted that this was 'without howbeit committing the Land to any further costs or entering into any extraordinary exploits other than with great circumspection'.[251] The Republic had been on the offensive since 1629, and an aggressive war on a large scale was extremely costly. Campaign expenditure had until 1607 amounted to between 500,000 and 600,000 guilders per annum. From 1621 to 1628 each campaign

---

[245] NA, RAZH, AJC 15, 'Staet van 't incomen soo ordinaris als extraordinaris voor den jaere 1635', 10 October 1635; Dormans, *Het tekort*, p. 25; Fritschy, *De patriotten*, p. 36.
[246] 't Hart, *Making of a Bourgeois State*, p. 164.
[247] NA, RAZH, AJC 23, 'Lasten en[de] incomen a.o 1630', 'Lasten en[de] incomen voor a.o 1634' and 'Staet van[de] lasten en[de] incomsten 1635'; AJC 84, 'Voor den jaere 1640'.
[248] The debt was structured as follows: almost 37.31 million guilders was borrowed against *losrenten* and *obligaties*, the remaining 7.13 million guilders against *lijfrenten*. See: NA, RAZH, FH 806, 'Memorie ofte verhandeling van hetgeene omtrent het stuk van de finantie van … Holland … van tijd tot tijd is voorgevallen', 1755, probably drafted by Pieter Steyn, Grand Pensionary of Holland, appendix 1. A facsimile of this appendix can be found in Houtzager, *Hollands lijf- en losrenteleningen*, between pp. 38 and 39.
[249] Van der Capellen, *Gedenkschriften*, I, p. 506.
[250] GA, AHGC 737, Tobias van Eyck to Count Floris II of Culemborg, The Hague, 3 April 1631.
[251] GAA, Missives of Amsterdam's deputies to the States of Holland 71 (microfilm 7548), [The Hague, n.d.], received 23 September 1633.

cost between 800,000 and 1 million guilders, but then the operational costs skyrocketed, to 1.8 million guilders in 1629, a peak of 3 million guilders in 1632, 2 million guilders in 1633 and 1635, and 1.5 million guilders in 1634. In 1636 and 1637 campaign costs were limited to 1 million guilders, but thereafter they rose again, attaining an average of 1.66 million guilders per annum between 1640 and 1644.[252]

In December 1634 Holland's Delegated Councillors sounded the financial alarm bells. They warned that the overstretched finances were common knowledge in Brussels, so 'were this course to be pursued any longer the comptoirs of the Land must necessarily fall into impotence and irreparable confusion'. Circumstances were already so pressing that several of the most important comptoirs had left the ordinances of the 'soldatesque' unpaid for one and a half and even two years, 'to the great disreputation of the Land and the considerable detriment of many private parties', the *solliciteurs-militair* first and foremost. The reputation and creditworthiness of these comptoirs could only be upheld by borrowing large sums of money. The only hope of ameliorating this worrisome state of affairs was by increasing the ordinary revenues or, more importantly, by reducing the defence expenditure, given that 'this great and cankerous malady of negotiation [i.e. issuing debt] has so weakened the treasury that no [other] remedy is a match for it or powerful enough to restore it and help it back to its feet'. Moreover, loans were susceptible to fraud. It was common knowledge that some receivers used tax revenues to subscribe to a loan with their 'own' money.[253] The Delegated Councillors therefore proposed a total of thirteen measures to lighten Holland's financial burden, the most important of which was the conversion of the interest on all redeemable annuities and bonds from 6.25 to 5 per cent, a new imposition of the two-hundredth penny tax and a raising of the tax on the milling of grain.[254] However, the decision to lower the interest rate could not actually be implemented until 28 April 1640. Creditors who were unwilling to accept the reduced rate of interest could request the reimbursement of the principal.[255]

Frederik Hendrik resolutely rejected army reduction because it would have thwarted his military plans. In April 1634, France had pledged to assume responsibility for a portion of the Republic's war expenses, and the following year the collaboration between the States-General and the French king was widened into an offensive alliance with the aim of conquering the Spanish Netherlands and dividing it among themselves. A sizeable army was needed to be able to execute

---

[252] HUA, ASU 657, 'Staet sommier'; NA, SG 4982 and NA, RAZH, ASH 1293-II, RvS to the SG, The Hague, 13 June 1645, overview of army costs 1640–1644.
[253] NA, RAZH, AJC 32, 'Pointen van consideratiën tot redres van de confusiën der finantiën van Hollant ende West-Vrieslandt', November 1638.
[254] NA, RAZH, AJC 31, 'Advys G[ecommitteerde] R[aden] ontrent de finantie 19 dec. 1634'. See also NA, RAZH, ASH 73, Res. SH 16, 17 October 1640.
[255] Houtzager, *Hollands lijf- en losrenteleningen*, pp. 58 and 61–3.

this ambitious plan. The campaign of 1635 was, however, far from a success and in October the Hollanders therefore considered the possibility of 'redacting' the size of the Republic's army 'to such count of cavaliers and foot-soldiers as is ... included in the three States of War'. Including the troops extraneous to those in the States of War, the States army's strength on paper was 85,000 at this time. Seeing as some 62,000 men were included in the three States of War this meant that 23,000 would have to be discharged. Holland wanted to achieve this reduction by disbanding all the unrepartitioned troops and by dismissing an average of one-sixth of the men from the infantry companies included in the three States of War and a similar proportion from the fifty infantry companies raised in 1628 in lieu of *waardgelders*. According to the Hollanders this retrenchment would not be detrimental to the effective strength of the Dutch army because more than a quarter of the current 80,000 or more men existed only on paper. The reduction would make it possible henceforth to pay the remaining 62,000 men on time and in full, and captains would therefore have no reason to keep their companies below their prescribed complement.[256] There was a lot to say for this proposal but it was not without risk, because the objective could only be achieved if the companies were mustered regularly and punctiliously from then on and if there was certainty that the wages would be paid in full and on time. Otherwise the strength of the Dutch army would swiftly drop below 60,000.

Between 1635 and 1643, the financial experts of Holland's treasury tabled a series of proposals to streamline the payment of the soldiers. The fees of the *solliciteurs*, for example, could be paid by allowing the captains to retain five to eight fewer men per company than the paper strength prescribed. A captain would have to use the money thus saved to bring his company up to the prescribed strength. Implementing this measure would mean that the Republic had 2,000 fewer men in service than was currently projected in the States of War: the Dutch army would have an effective strength of 60,000. Individual payment was revived as a point of discussion, but the province's Delegated Councillors still considered this undesirable, because Holland would then no longer be permitted to be in default in the paying of its troops for a single day.[257]

Another proposal was that company commanders would only be allowed to change their *solliciteur* with permission from the States of Holland as soon as he had advanced two months' pay. This measure was intended to discourage captains from changing their *solliciteurs* so often, thereby reducing the risk that an untrustworthy company commander would leave the *solliciteur* with unpaid bills. In exchange for this guarantee the *solliciteurs* would from then on be obliged to advance a maximum of two forty-two-day pay-months for a reduced salary of 100 guilders per month for a company of cuirassiers, 76 guilders for a company

---

[256] NA, RAZH, AJC 32, 'Rapport', 11 October 1635; AJC 86, 'Lijste van alle de compaig[nie] ën soo ruyteren als knechten jegenwoordigh [1635] in 's Landts dienst sijnde'.
[257] NA, RAZH, AJC 32, 'Pointen van mesnage voorgeslagen bij de heeren Gecommitteerden octobris 1635'.

of arquebusiers and 66, 54 and 46 guilders for infantry companies of 200, 150 and 120 men, respectively. Company commanders would be permitted to deduct these fees from the wages of their men. In return, the captains and rittmasters would, if necessary, be required to advance one month's pay 'from their own means or on the basis of their credit'. The *solliciteurs* would have no reason to complain either, according to the plan's author, as this arrangement was also to their advantage. He calculated that the *solliciteur*'s fee for an infantry company of 150 men would amount to 468 guilders per annum (9 guilders per week). After deducting interest at 7 per cent from 3,987 guilders and 14 stivers, the sum of the two full pay-months that the *solliciteur* would have to advance over the year, he had almost 189 guilders remaining.[258] Part of this would have to be used as remuneration for his services, but the rest could be regarded as profit. Because the *solliciteurs* had to advance a maximum of two pay-months, the interest they charged over the advanced wages would be limited to the specified 7 per cent, when otherwise they would have charged a full 12 per cent. Many *solliciteurs* found it necessary to borrow money from wealthy people themselves.[259]

For all the planning, an army reduction was out of the question before a solution had been found for payment of the outstanding wages, an issue that threatened to defeat the object of the whole operation. Resorting to dismissal without at the same time paying the outstanding wages was an inconceivable move. For the army reduction of 1609, the company commanders had received an order 'to give to all the soldiers who ... are to be discharged full settlement of their services up to the day of discharge, and thereabove to issue each of them a dollar of 30 stivers, for which you [the captain] shall once again be properly reimbursed by your paymasters'.[260] In 1640, Holland owed the troops approximately three million guilders in pay arrears,[261] but even if Holland were to succeed in paying off this debt completely it could not guarantee that it would henceforth manage to pay the remaining troops on time every month. Frederik Hendrik justifiably refused to endorse a reduction of the Dutch army on the basis of such shaky arguments. He and the Council of State thought it was an illusion to think that the companies would ever meet the prescribed strengths. He warned that the proposed reduction would render the Republic's army too small to be deployable in the field.[262] In December 1636, ten members of the Council of State attended the meeting of the States of Holland in order to lend weight

---

[258] NA, Tweede Afdeling, CG 305, no. 32. This was the net amount after deduction of the one-hundredth penny tax.
[259] Ten Raa, *Het Staatsche leger*, IV, p. 180.
[260] HUA, HAA 4120, RvS to Jacob Wijts, The Hague, 22 May 1609.
[261] NA, Tweede Afdeling, CG 305, no. 3 and no. 36; NA, RAZH, AJC 84, 'Voor den jaere 1640'.
[262] NA, RAZH, ASH 68, Res. SH, 21 and 22 December 1635; ASH 69, Res. SH, 20 and 28 February 1636; ASH 70, Res. SH, 19 December 1637; NA, RAZH, AJC 87, 'Besettinge van de garnisoenen soo deselve wesen sullen het leger te velde sijnde'.

to Frederik Hendrik's arguments. They pointed out that the alliance with the French disallowed army reduction, that the peace negotiations with Spain would have to be conducted from a position of strength, and that such army cutbacks would expose the Republic to a Spanish-Imperial invasion.[263]

Leaving everything as it stood was equally impossible. Frederik Hendrik managed for several years to resist the reduction on military, political and primarily financial grounds, but in 1640 a clerk of Holland's treasury, one Van de Broucke, tabled a proposal that refuted the financial objections, thus clearing the way for the army reduction. In a memorandum he pointed out that, seeing as one comptoir paid the troops more reliably than the next, they had to ensure 'the distribution of the troops between the comptoirs in such manner that they are paid on an equal footing ... and then draw up an overview of the shortfall in the payment of the troops and, on establishing this, to work out the necessary means to cover the shortfall'.[264] The arrears were greatest at the comptoir of the receiver-general: the forty-three infantry companies repartitioned to it were owed an average of fifteen pay-months of forty-two days (more than a year and a half), and the cavalry as much as seventeen pay-months (almost two years). At the remaining offices in Holland's South Quarter the pay arrears ranged from just one or two pay-months at the comptoirs in Dordrecht, Haarlem and Amsterdam (to which a total of seventy-three infantry companies were repartitioned), to four or five pay-months in Delft and Den Briel (forty-two infantry companies), six pay-months in Gouda (ten infantry companies), seven pay-months in Leiden (twenty-five infantry companies) and ten pay-months in Gorinchem (nine infantry companies). Only the companies repartitioned to Rotterdam's comptoir were 'paid monthly'. In January 1643 the infantry repartitioned to Holland made claim to a total of 2.3 million guilders in pay arrears and the cavalry some 1.1 million guilders.[265]

The States of Holland set about remedying this problem in accordance with Van de Broucke's proposal. Frederik Hendrik and the Council of State endeavoured to obstruct this for as long as possible using the above-mentioned arguments,[266] but on 21 January 1643 the States of Holland carried a resolution to reduce the troops as of 1 March.[267] After the reduction, the number of soldiers repartitioned to Holland would still be 35,780 men (29,900 foot-soldiers, 3,095 cuirassiers, 500 arquebusiers and 2,195 *bidets*). The wages of this

---

[263] NA, RAZH, ASH 69, Res. SH, 16 December 1636; NA, RAZH, AJC 48, Advice of the RvS, The Hague, 16 December 1636.
[264] NA, RAZH, AJC 82, 'Memorie ofte consideratie van menage', drafted by clerk Van de Broucke 1640, point 12.
[265] NA, RAZH, ASH 1293-II, 'Staet van[de] comp[agnie]ën en[de] haere 't achterheyt 1643'; ASH 76, Res. SH, 8 May 1643.
[266] NA, RAZH, ASH 73, Res. SH, 9, 10, 16 and 17 October 1640; ASH 74, Res. SH, 2 February 1641.
[267] NA, RAZH, ASH 76.

force amounted to 4,596,521 guilders per annum, a decrease of almost 2 million guilders compared with the former wage bill.[268] Each of the eleven comptoirs had to assume responsibility for part of this sum, the assigned amount being geared to an office's tax revenues 'according to the wherewithal and resources of the offices in question'.[269] The revised repartition departed markedly from the ratios that were normally applied for the apportionment of the provincial contributions to the costs of the army (see p. 82).

With its decree of 21 January 1643, Holland was formally acting in contravention of the ban on the dismissal of soldiers without Union-wide consent,[270] but the Hollanders could counter this accusation by pointing out that it was an army reduction only on paper. The new strength of the Dutch army was, after all, equal to its old effective strength. Moreover, the other provinces applauded the diminution of their financial burdens. Friesland had been complaining for years that it could not raise its contribution to the war budget, failing to pay its quotas in full or not until months or even years after they were due.[271] Confronted with this *fait accompli*, Frederik Hendrik and the Council of State could do little but accept it. The Council of State subsequently presented a draft for a new, consolidated State of War with a total headcount of 60,430, composed of 53,480 infantry and 6,950 cavalry. The pay package for a year would then amount to 8.18 million guilders, a reduction of almost 3 million guilders.[272]

The provinces were satisfied with the proposed army strength, since it corresponded with their wishes, but they could not agree among themselves about the replacement of the three States of War with a single new document,

> for the reason that the soldiers included in the State of War from the year 1621 have not been repartitioned between the provinces in accordance with each one's quota in the costs of war, but that the one province has been burdened to a greater extent with the named soldiery than another, these being charged with other expenses instead [of soldiers' pay].

The effect of this was that provinces which, for example, contributed more to the maintenance of fortifications than their quota prescribed would gain less from

---

[268] The pay projected in the three States of War amounted to 11,177,088 guilders and 12 stivers. Holland's quota amounted to 6,515,640 guilders and 18 stivers. See: NA, RAZH, AJC 23, 'Staet van[de] lasten en[de] incomsten 1635'.
[269] NA, RAZH, ASH 1293-II, 'Voorslach tot beter egaliteyt van betalinge aen de militie te doen', 1643; ASH 76, Res. SH, 29 April 1643.
[270] Van Slingelandt, *Staatkundige geschriften*, IV, pp. 150–1.
[271] Tresoar, FAEVC 547, 'Propositie van den Raet van Staete [to the States of Friesland]', 14 January 1637.
[272] NA, RvS 1251, 'Staet ende repartitie van het crijchsvolck ende andere lasten van der oirloghe', 1643; NA, RAZH, FAvS 3, 'Nieuwe Staet van Oorloge geformeert & aen de provinciën gesonden in den jaere 1643'.

the reduction than provinces such as Holland, which proportionately paid too many soldiers.[273]

Table 1. Repartition of the pay bill among Holland's comptoirs after the army reduction of 1643

Comptoir	Share based on the repartition (%)	Share in wage payments after the reduction (%)	In guilders per annum
Receiver-General	19.5	12.88	592,075
Dordrecht	8	1.37	62,987
Haarlem	8	5.41	248,756
Delft	8	11.94	549,091
Leiden	8	8.87	408,073
Amsterdam	14	23.63	1,086,232
Gouda	5	3.74	171,957
Rotterdam	5	4.91	225,894
Gorinchem	2	2.3	106,118
Den Briel	2	1.83	84,306
North Quarter	20.5	23.08	1,061,032
	100.0%	(99.96%)	4,596,521

Source: NA, RAZH, AJC 27, 'Repartitie van betaellinge over de naevolgende comptoiren'.

In early February 1643 the Council of State sent commissaries to the garrisons to properly supervise the reduction. They had to draw up lists of 'the most notable characteristics of the best and most highly skilled soldiers in order to retain them in service'. On 1 March 1643 the companies of foot were reduced from 200 men to 150, those of 150 to 120, and those of 120 to 100.[274] For the payment of the outstanding wages of the cashiered troops, Holland decided to charge a two-hundredth penny property tax, 'and should it fall short [the rest] shall be negotiated [i.e. borrowed]'.[275] The army reduction of 1643 did not exclude there being any discrepancy between the paper and effective strengths of the companies through until 1648, but it had been reduced considerably. It was much more important that this measure averted a serious financial crisis, though it was the unrepartitioned soldiers who would now bear the brunt.

The position of the unrepartitioned companies had always been worse than that of the repartitioned soldiery, but from 1621 things went from bad to worse

---

[273] NA, SG 4981, 'Redenen die sijne Hoocheydt & den Raet van State hebben bewooge om den ouden Staet van Oorloge de anno 1621 te redresseeren', 16 December 1644 (quote); Van Slingelandt, *Staatkundige geschriften*, III, p. 96.

[274] NA, RAZH, FAvS 237, 'The Council of State ... has deemed it desirable hereby to request and commit ... [name unspecified] to report in the towns and places noted in the margin and from there to report the following ...', The Hague, 1 February 1643. See also NA, SG 12548.251, 'Voorslach van den Raedt van State ... op 't stuck van de reductie van 't volck van oorloch te voet', The Hague, 16 January 1643.

[275] KHA, A25-VII-C-256, Johan van Veltdriel to Willem Frederik, The Hague, 5 April 1643.

with the payment of their wages. In 1633 the number of unrepartitioned soldiers was 19,000 men on paper. Two years later this had shrunk, primarily through desertion, to just under 14,000 men and in 1643 to 11,500 men.[276] The unrepartitioned soldiers were the closing entry on the provincial budgets, meaning that even if they could find a *solliciteur* he would have access to hardly any credit.[277] From 1634, some of these troops were paid from the subsidies that France was obliged to provide because of its alliance with the Republic,[278] but Paris transferred the annual subsidy irregularly and incompletely. The provinces were not prepared to make up the difference or advance the pay. France should have transferred a total of 9 million guilders between 1637 and 1643, but the amount actually received by the States-General was just shy of 6 million guilders.[279] That is an average of 850,000 guilders per annum, little more than half the amount that was needed: the wages of the unrepartitioned soldiers ran to 181,835 guilders per *heremaand* and approximately 1.57 million guilders per annum.[280] In August 1643 the unrepartitioned cavalrymen complained that over the last six years they had received no more than an average of nine rix-dollars per month from their rittmasters and even that was only 'in dribs and drabs', and were 'therefore still ten months' wages behindhand'. They were close to despair and no longer knew how they could provide for their wives and children. If they did not receive their money soon then they would be forced 'by poverty to sell their horses and personally take to the roads as beggars'.[281]

There may well have been sympathy for the dire straits of the unrepartitioned companies in the provincial States, but they failed to dip into their coffers. As mentioned, the States of Holland wanted to completely disband all the unrepartitioned troops, but Frederik Hendrik prevented that. A compromise was reached in March 1644: the States-General decided to reduce the unrepartitioned troops 'to such number that they can be sustained from the subsidy of France'. This meant that their tally had to be reduced to 5,760 men,[282] but this did not settle the matter since the resources to pay the outstanding pay ordinances still had

---

[276] NA, SG 4964, RvS to the SG, The Hague, 5 December 1633; NA, RAZH, AJC 45, 'Compagni[e]ën buyten de Staeten van[de] Oorloch'; NA, SG 4967, 'Staet van 'tgene de logisgelden bij raminge sullen comen te beloopen over 't jaer 1636'.
[277] NA, SG 4967, Field deputies to the SG, Arnhem, 9 November 1635, appendix; RvS to the SG, The Hague, 8, 19 and 28 November 1635; Exh. 6 December 1635, 'Staet van de betalinge in 600.000 gl. over 3 maenden voor de ongerepartieerde trouppes des jaers 1635'; SG 4970, Field deputies to the SG, near Rammekens, evening of 16 July 1637.
[278] NA, SG 4966, RvS to the SG, The Hague, 7 April 1635.
[279] Tresoar, FSA 26, 'Staet van den ontfanck ... over het gelt secours bij ... Vranckrijck ... belooft, mitsgaders van de betalingen daeruyt gedaen'.
[280] NA, SG 4971, 'Staet van een maent solts verschenen 4 juli 1637 voor 't ongerepartieerde crijchsvolk'; NA, Tweede Afdeling, CG 305, nr. 44, 'Staet van een maent soltz voor 't ongerepartieert chrichsvolck verschenen den 15e augusty 1637'.
[281] NA, SG 4980, Field deputies to the SG, Assenede, 1 August 1643.
[282] NA, SG 4981, 'Sommieren staet van 't ongerepartieerde crijschvolck te peert & te voet', exh. 1 March 1644.

to be found.[283] In 1644 Johan van Veltdriel, one of Friesland's two deputies to the States-General, warned Willem Frederik (1613–1664), stadholder of Friesland since 1640, that should the unrepartitioned troops not be afforded redress there would be the devil to pay, 'for these people are desperate and because of their terrible sufferings know not what to do'. He was afraid of mutiny and the surrender of towns and cities to the enemy.[284] On 1 July 1647 the States-General eventually decided to distribute the remaining unrepartitioned troops among the provinces. This arrangement was short-lived, because they were soon encouraged to enter the employ of the Dutch West India Company, whereupon the companies to which they belonged were disbanded.[285]

---

[283] NA, SG 4981, Minute of Res. SG, 25 March 1644.
[284] KHA, A25-VII-C-256, Johan van Veltdriel to Willem Frederik, The Hague, 18 and 23 April 1644.
[285] Ten Raa, *Het Staatsche leger*, IV, pp. 160–1.

◆ 2 ◆

The Dutch Army and the Revolution in Infantry Tactics (1592–1618)

In the early modern era, experience in war was the soldier's only true training ground. Military academies for officers and training units in which recruits received basic instruction before being dispatched to fight emerged only gradually towards the end of the eighteenth century. No fundamental changes were made in the organisation of the Dutch army during the late sixteenth century and the first half of the seventeenth century, as was the case with the military forces of other European states. The way troops were recruited and maintained in 1648 differed little from sixteenth-century methods, but to conclude that military affairs had remained static in the meantime would be mistaken: between 1592 and 1618 there were such radical tactical innovations that 'revolutionary' would be a fitting predicate. The new, more scientific approach to the art of war was marked by theoretical discussion, experiments with a diversity of tactical formations using 'tin soldiers',[1] and eventually exercises with actual soldiers, thus establishing the basis for the systematic exercising and drilling of troops as a prerequisite for optimising the use of firearms on the battlefield.

The types of soldier and their weaponry

One of the great virtues of Maurits and Willem Lodewijk was their active concern with the weaponry, exercising, drilling and tactical deployment of the States-General's troops. It was of the utmost importance that the companies should be drilled and armed in the same way, so that the foot-soldiers and cavalrymen could be deployed in identical tactical formations. On 9 August 1596 Maurits and Willem Lodewijk informed the States-General that the Dutch cavalry and infantry 'are armed and equipped extremely poorly'. In order to ameliorate this situation they drafted a memorandum which described the weaponry and equip-

---

[1] Le Hon, *Ordres van batailjen*, fol. 26v.

ment for each type of soldier and horseman in detail.[2] Rather than focusing on the quality of the weapons used and the equipment, they levelled their critique at the proportion of pikes, halberds and swords to firearms and, above all, at the lack of uniformity across the various companies.

There had been previous attempts to reduce the great diversity in composition and armament of the Republic's troops by specifying fixed percentages of the various weapons per company, but this had failed to win the support of the captains. In August 1588 the Council of State had drawn up a list, in consultation with Field-Marshal Joost de Zoete, lord of Villers (†March 1589), 'of those weapons ... with which the company's foot soldiers shall henceforth be armed and [accordingly] paid'.[3] This order dictated that approximately half of every infantry company had to be provided with firearms and the rest with polearms and swords, though not in a simple two-way split, there being two types of firearm and four types of polearm and sword. The prescribed composition of a company of 150 men (13 officers, 3 servants and 134 soldiers) was 18 musketeers (13 per cent), 52 calivermen (39 per cent), 45 pikemen with corselets (34 per cent) and 3 sword-and-bucklermen (2 per cent), 12 halberdiers (9 per cent), and 4 soldiers armed with two-handed broadswords (3 per cent). The company commanders thought the percentage of firearms too low and were dismissive of the number of pike prescribed.

Willem Lodewijk and Maurits concurred with the critique of the officers, as is evident from the composition of the Frisian regiment and of the Solms regiment established in the county of Nassau in early 1594 on the orders of the States-General. Willem Lodewijk's regiment served as a model for the rest of the Republic's army. The overviews of their composition reveal that neither of these regiments included sword-and-bucklermen and the proportion of halberdiers was much lower than prescribed by the 'Ordre' of 1588, while the proportion of soldiers armed with pike or musket was markedly higher.

Sword-and-bucklermen or rondaches (*rondassiers*) were armed with a small, round shield known as a rondache or buckler and a short sword. Their specialism was attacking beneath and between the metres-long pikes when opposing units of pikemen were engaged in a push of pike, thus wreaking chaos in the enemy's battle order. Soldiers with two-handed broadswords served a similar purpose, namely breaking the pikes of the opponent with powerful blows. Halberdiers were also meant to make short shrift of the pikemen. For a long time Maurits was intrigued by the potential of soldiers armed after the Roman manner with

---

[2] This memorandum is identical to the 'Ordre van 't voetvolck' (Rules and regulations for the infantry) submitted to the States-General on 6 November 1597 (NA, SG 4887). See also Ten Raa, *Het Staatsche leger*, II, pp. 337–9.
[3] HCO, ASO 1457, RvS to the States of Overijssel, The Hague, 8 October 1588, with a 'Lijste van die wapenen' as an appendix, The Hague, 19 August 1588.

Table 2. Composition of the Frisian regiment for the 1592, 1594 and 1595 campaigns (rank and file)

Date	Pike	Musket	Caliver	Halberd	Broadsword	Total (100%)
1592	971 (42%)	384 (16%)	887 (38%)	91 (4%)	–	2,333 men
1594	694 (40%)	288 (17%)	684 (40%)	56 (3%)	–	1,722 men
23 July 1595	980 (41%)	425 (18%)	920 (39%)	45 (2%)	5 (0.2%)	2,375 men
15 Aug. 1595	859 (40%)	385 (18%)	864 (40%)	54 (2.5%)	4 (0.2%)	2,166 men

Sources: KHA, A24-IV-H10, Battle array of 1594; Tresoar, FSA 5, Battle arrays of 1592 and of 23 July and 15 August 1595.

Table 3. Composition of the 'Solms regiment' in early 1594 (rank and file)

Pike	Musket	Caliver	Halberd	Total (100%)
698 (35%)	351 (18%)	877 (44%)	67 (3%)	1,993 men

Source: NA, RAZH, AJvO 2875.

swords and large shields, known as targes, to break up formations of pike,[4] though he was fully aware that troops of this type were consigned to the past. For him the priority was no longer the hand-to-hand fray but the superiority of firearms. Werner Hahlweg has rightly pointed out that Classical Antiquity was an important source of inspiration for Maurits and Willem Lodewijk, though they did not unquestioningly adopt the Roman or Greek methods of warfare.[5] Maurits and Willem Lodewijk considered pikemen indispensable in lending solidity to the battle array, but breaking through the enemy lines was no longer their chief purpose; from now on their main task was to provide protection for soldiers bearing firearms. The sword-and-buckler and broadswords disappeared from the Dutch army formation around 1595 and halberdiers were replaced by pikemen in 1599.[6] The only type of soldier that continued to bear halberds until the end of the eighteenth century was the sergeant, as 'the symbol of his authority'.[7]

---

[4] Duyck, I, p. 635. His journal entry for 6 August 1595 states: 'His Excellency had long ago ordered the manufacture of large shields or targes in the Roman manner in order to see whether one could break a battalion of pikes with them, which he had on several occasions put to the test at The Hague and found to work to good effect. Wherefore today in camp he had the same [technique] tried out against the English soldiers, who fight well with pikes, and achieved the same result, for the targes broke through all the pikes.' This experiment was repeated on 27 August and was a resounding success once again (see Ducyk, I, p. 649).
[5] Hahlweg, 'Oranische Heeresreform', p. 141.
[6] KHA, A22-IX-A1-139, Maurits to Willem Lodewijk in the encampment at Aert, 17 April 1599.
[7] Hexham, *Principii*, fol. 3.

6. Dutch rondache or sword-and-bucklerman. Adam van Breen, *Le maniement d'armes de Nassau* (The Hague 1618). (Royal Netherlands Army Museum, Delft, 00116642/21)

7. Dutch rondache or sword-and-bucklerman. Adam van Breen, *Le maniement d'armes de Nassau* (The Hague 1618). (Royal Netherlands Army Museum, Delft, 00116642/22)

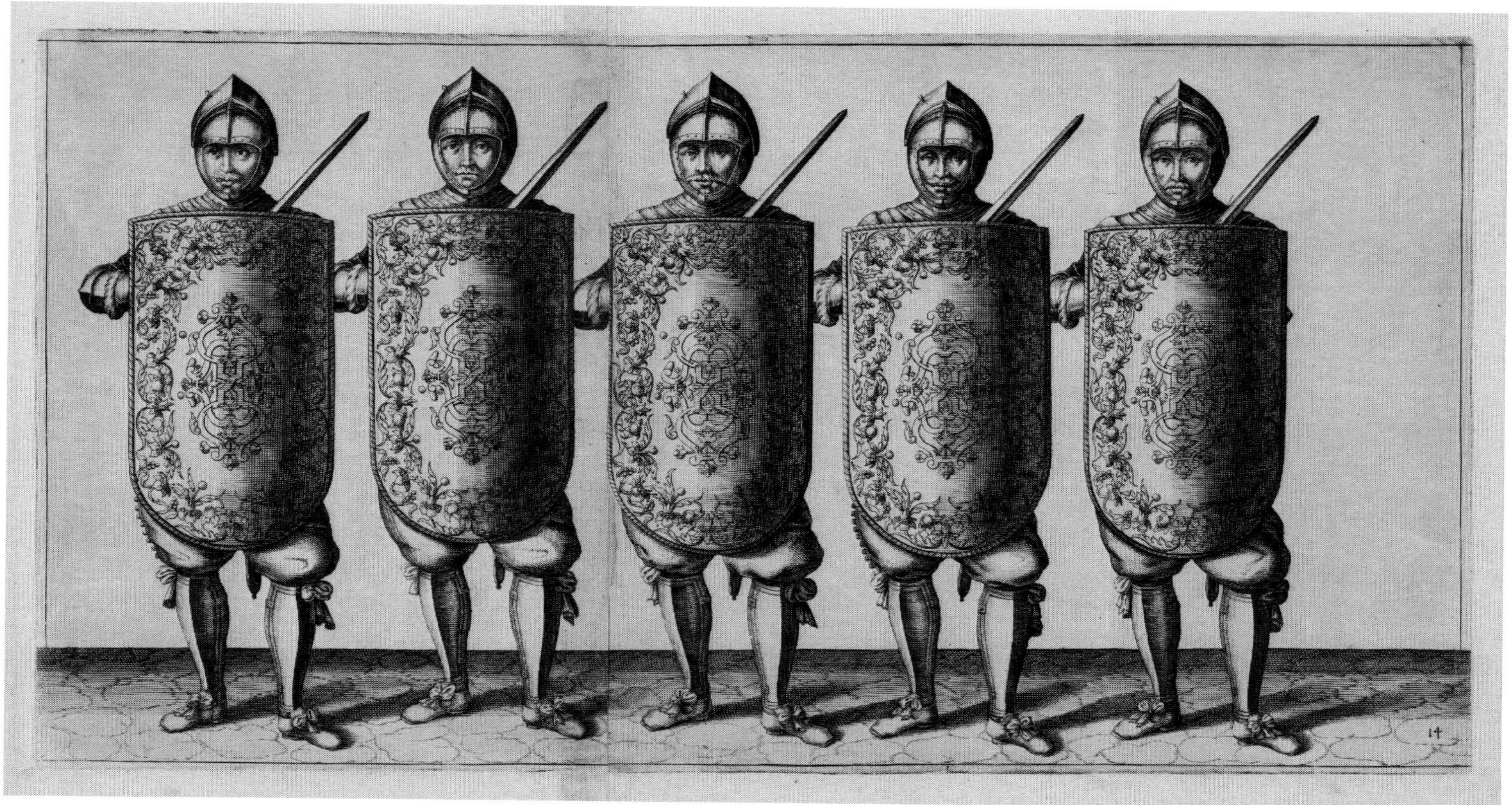

8. Dutch soldiers with targes. Adam van Breen, *Le maniement d'armes de Nassau* (The Hague 1618). (Royal Netherlands Army Museum, Delft, 0011642/46)

Maurits and Willem Lodewijk issued a revised 'Ordre op de waapeninge van het voetvolk' (Regulations for the arming of the infantry) in February 1599, which took into account the changes in weaponry and precisely stipulated the ratio of the different weapons in each company. A company of 135 men – 13 officers, 3 servants and 119 soldiers – served as a benchmark of the proportions of arms which all other companies, whether of greater or lesser number, had to match. Each company of infantrymen would henceforth consist only of pikemen (38 per cent), musketeers (25 per cent) and calivermen (37 per cent).[8] The captains had to arm 'the tallest and most capable' recruits with pikes. A pike was an ash pole fitted with an iron point, initially eighteen feet long (c. 5.5m), later shortened to fifteen feet (c. 4.5m). If it came to light during an inspection that a pikeman had shortened his pike then he was fined one guilder and the pike was summarily broken. Besides this primary weapon the pikemen were armed with a rapier. Their heads were protected by a visorless helmet known as a morion, and the neck by a gorget, while a cuirass covered the chest and back. The pikemen in the front ranks, approximately one-quarter of the unit, were also protected by arm-guards, which were iron arm-guards down to the elbow, and tassets, which were thigh-plates for the protection of the abdomen.[9] A pikeman's armour, including pike and rapier, weighed an average of 27 pounds (c. 13.5kg).[10]

Well-set men with 'good legges' were most suitable as musketeers, 'yes, such as may be able to endure both hardship and labour'. Musketeers kept watch in the towns, served on the walls or in the trenches during sieges, and on the battlefield they stood directly alongside the pike. A musketeer was armed with a firearm with an average length of 150 centimetres and a calibre of ten 'tight-fitting' balls to the pound or twelve 'rolling' balls to the pound. This meant that the shot had to weigh 41.16 grams (a twelfth of an Amsterdam pound), while the bore of the barrel had to be the diameter of a lead ball of 49.4 grams (a calibre of 20mm).[11] This 'windage' was necessary to make possible extended use of the weapon, because after a few shots had been fired the barrel became so soiled with gunpowder residue that it was no longer possible to load perfectly fitting balls. The length and weight of the musket was the reason why musketeers had to use a forked musket-rest known as a 'furket' when firing. The nominal range of a musket ball was 300 paces (c. 225m), but the likelihood of a marksman hitting a target at such a distance was negligible because of the required windage. Accuracy improved at a range of approximately 130 paces (c. 100m), but only at

---

[8] Recueil ... betreffende de saaken van den oorlog, I, no. 2, pp. 17–19, 22.
[9] J.P. Puype and A.A. Wiekart, Van Maurits naar Munster. Tactiek en triomf van het Staatse leger / From Prince Maurice to the Peace of Westphalia. Tactics and triumphs of the Dutch army (Delft 1998). This exhibition catalogue, published by the Army Museum in Delft, presents many fine examples of such weapons and armour.
[10] Boxel, Krijghsoeffeninge, vol. 3, pp. 4–5.
[11] Puype, From Prince Maurits to the Peace of Westphalia, pp. 139–43.

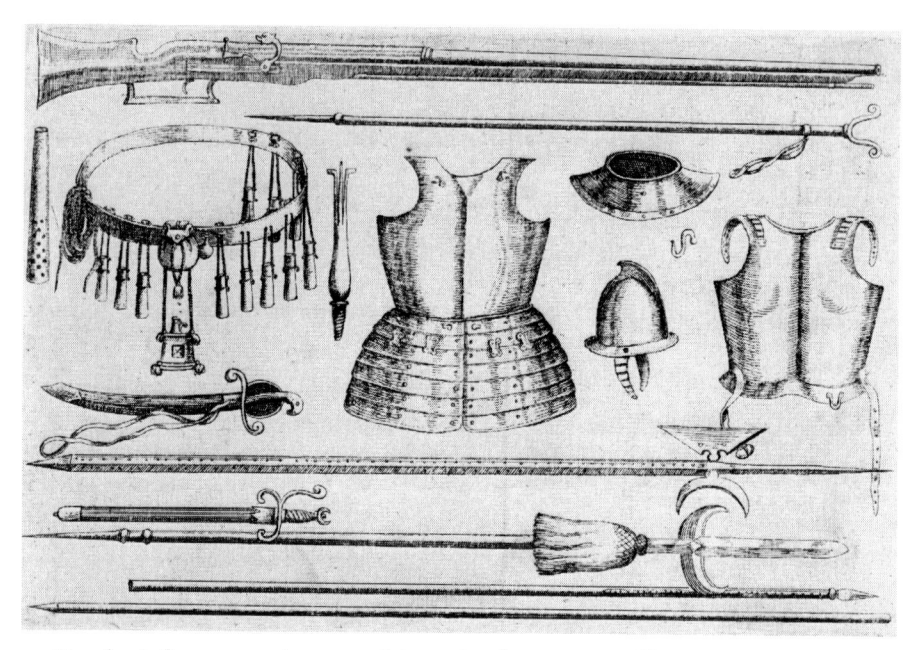

9. Dutch infantry equipment. Johan Jacobi von Wallhausen, *L'art militaire pour l'infanterie* (Franeker [1615]). (Royal Netherlands Army Museum, Delft, 00102287/002)

a distance of 60 to 65 paces (c. 45 to 50m) or less did musket fire become really effective.[12]

The firing mechanism of the matchlock musket was simple. On pulling the trigger a cock holding a length of smouldering slow-match was forced down into a pan filled with fine priming powder. Via the touch-hole, a small opening in the barrel, this ignited the main charge. After firing the musketeer removed the match from the cock and began reloading his weapon, making sure not to hold the match too close to his powder containers, which were small wooden flasks, usually twelve in number, and contained a pre-measured charge of gunpowder sufficient for a single shot. These were attached to a broad strap hung across the chest known as a 'bandolier'. A musketeer's equipment weighed about 23.75 pounds (just under 12kg) in all, which was lighter than a pikeman's equipment, 'yet it encumbers more than that of a pikeman', as Captain-Lieutenant Johan Boxel noted.[13] After all, the pikeman bore the bulk of his kit's weight as body armour, while the musketeer had to carry approximately seven kilograms

---

[12] Jacques François de Chastenet, marquis de Puységur, *Art de la guerre, par principes et par règles*, 2 vols (Paris reprint 1749), I, p. 323; Louis de Gaya, *Traité des armes* (Paris 1678; facsimile edn with an introduction by Charles Ffoulkes, Oxford 1911), p. 22; Wijn, *Het Staatsche leger*, VIII, iii, p. 352; Van Nimwegen, *De Republiek als grote mogendheid*, p. 116.

[13] Boxel, *Krijghsoeffeninge*, vol. 3, pp. 4–5.

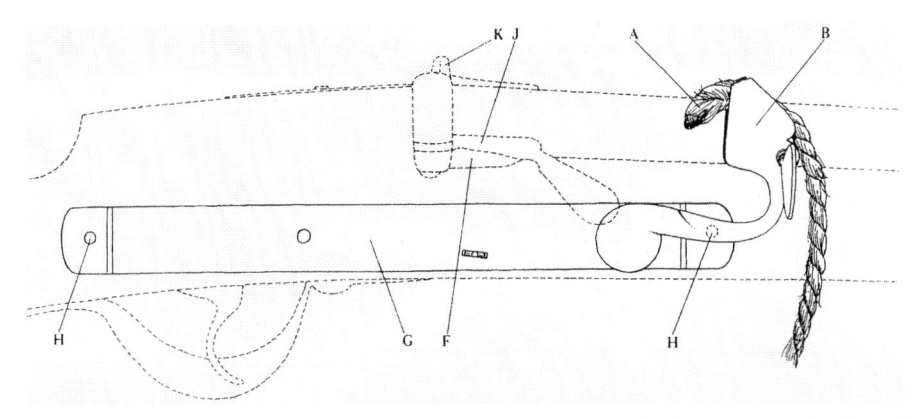

10. Matchlock (line drawing by Jan Piet Puype, former chief curator at the Royal Netherlands Army Museum, Delft).
Key: A. slow-match; B. cock; F. pan; G. lockplate; H. lock screws; J. pan-cover.

(musket and furket) in his hands.[14] It is therefore hardly surprising that many musketeers tried to lighten their firearm by shortening the barrel; even the fine of two guilders (equal to eight days' pay) failed to deter the soldiers. Six years after the introduction of the 1599 'Ordre', the Council of State felt it necessary to reiterate to the colonels that the musketeers had to be correctly armed, 'no longer allowing the bearing of any shorter muskets, seeing that they [i.e. the musketeers] are commonly shortening and sawing them down for their comfort'.[15]

Besides the musketeers, an infantry unit's '*simpele schutten*' – the arquebusiers – also bore firearms, namely the caliver or arquebus (*roer*), which like the musket was fitted with a matchlock mechanism. The calibre of this type of gun was twenty 'tight-fitting' balls to the pound (17.4mm) and it fired twenty-four 'rolling' balls to the pound. On average a caliver weighed just 3.8 kilograms,[16] making a rest unnecessary. Despite the caliver being lighter and cheaper (a complete caliver cost seven guilders compared to twelve guilders for a musket with furket),[17] the captains were no advocates of its widespread deployment, because the caliver's ball had less stopping-power than the heavier musket ball, a factor of great importance in an age when many foot-soldiers and cavalrymen wore armour.[18]

---

[14] Around 1600 the weight of 'the standard Netherlandish matchlock musket … [was] approximately 7 kilogrammes'. See J.P. Puype, 'Hervorming en uitstraling. Tactiek en wapens van het Staatse leger tot de Vrede van Munster en hun invloed in andere Europese landen', in Jacques Dane (ed.), *1648 Vrede van Munster. Feit en verbeelding* (Zwolle n.d.), pp. 47–81, esp. 53.
[15] Tresoar, FSA 17, RvS to Ernst Casimir, The Hague, 27 December 1605.
[16] Wijn, *Krijgswezen*, p. 146.
[17] NA, RvS 2287, 'Lij[s]te' of the price of weapons 1590–1607.
[18] Hall, *Weapons and Warfare*, pp. 177 and 179.

As we have seen, Maurits and Willem Lodewijk paid heed to the captains' objections to the caliver by increasing the proportion of soldiers armed with muskets to one-quarter of each company, but their hope that this would foster 'equality of arms' across all regiments remained unachieved. Though the captains were content with the increase in the number of musketeers, they still felt that 37 per cent calivermen was too high a proportion and would have preferred more pikemen. Less than two years after the introduction of the 'Ordre' of 1599 even the Frisian companies included appreciably fewer calivermen than was prescribed. In July 1601 the Frisian regiment numbered 2,826 men, subdivided into 1,146 pikemen (40 per cent), 700 musketeers (25 per cent) and 980 calivermen (35 per cent). Five months later this regiment was composed of 42 per cent pikemen, 27 per cent musketeers and only 31 per cent calivermen, which was 6 per cent less than prescribed in the 1599 'Ordre'.[19] The deviation was even more extreme among the foreign troops in Dutch service; by around 1600 there was not a single caliver to be found in the English companies.[20]

Maurits disapproved of such variations in company composition, because they made it impossible to use the same tactical formation for all the battalions. He therefore insisted that the captains should obey the regulations regarding the composition of their companies and, moreover, that they arm their troops with muskets and calivers that corresponded with the models specially manufactured for this purpose in Dordrecht by order of the Council of State.[21] This had little effect, because it was almost impossible to maintain strict oversight of compliance with the 1599 'Ordre' when most company commanders were still obliged to purchase the weapons themselves. From the muster-rolls of forty-seven companies repartitioned to Zeeland for the years 1604 to 1606 it appears there was no more than an average of one, two or three calivermen in each company.[22] The muster-rolls from 1598, 1599 and 1602 for twenty-four companies repartitioned to other provinces record an average of 20 to 30 per cent calivermen instead of the prescribed 37 per cent. In most companies one also finds 'several firelocks', an average of four men, despite Maurits having 'expressly' forbidden this kind of weapon.[23]

---

[19] Tresoar, FSA 5, 'Omtrent den 15 july [1601] aldus gestaen' and 'Ordre gemaect den 16 9.bris 1601'.
[20] NA, SG 4900, Michiel Everwijn to the SG, Ostend, 14 September 1601, appendix 'Le nombre et force des compaignies Angloyses présentement à Ostend'.
[21] On 17 April 1599 Maurits wrote to Willem Lodewijk: 'Observe at all times that the companies are equipped in conformity to the uniform arms, namely the musketeers all with muskets, the arquebusiers all with arquebuses [i.e. calivers] and the pikemen all with pikes. And also take pike instead of halberds and partizans.' A partizan was a polearm with a leaf-shaped point, approximately eight feet long. KHA, A22-IX-A1-139, camp at Aert. De Jong, *Staet van oorlog*, p. 18, mentions that five model muskets and five model calivers were manufactured in Dordrecht.
[22] ZA, AR C 312–314, 322–324, 332–333, 335 1e grossa 1e summa I.
[23] NA, RAZH, AJvO 3008, 'Lijste van[de] monsterrollen van[de] Hollandsche compaignyen tot Oostende den xiiii may 1599 gemonstert'; AJvO 2954, 'Sommiere gestaltenis der

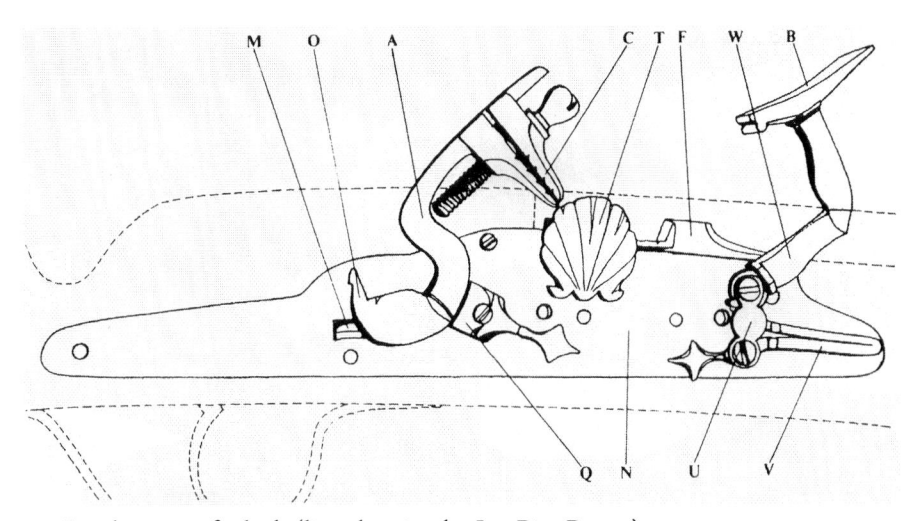

11. Snaphance or firelock (line drawing by Jan Piet Puype).
Key: A. cock; B. steel; C. jaws for holding a piece of pyrites; F. pan-cover; T. side-fence; V. steel spring; W. arm.

A 'firelock' or 'snaphance' (*vierroer*, *vuyrroer* or *snaphaan*) was a firearm with a snaphance lock. With this type of mechanism it was not a slow match that ignited the priming powder but the spark from an artificial flint (pyrites) striking against a steel. This meant that a snaphance, unlike a musket, was always ready to fire. However, this major advantage was negated by two drawbacks that made the weapon suitable only for specialists. In the first place, the snaphance mechanism required great care and maintenance: the pan cover had to slide open at precisely the instant the trigger was pulled. In later flintlocks the cover of the priming-pan and the steel were combined in a single unit called the battery, but with the snaphance lock they were still two separate components. Secondly, most snaphances had a rifled barrel. The spiral of tapering grooves caused the projectile to rotate, thus stabilising the ball during its trajectory. However, this was to the detriment of the reloading time, because to achieve this effect the ball had to be forced into the grooves, which required the loading of balls of a larger calibre than the barrel. The long intervals between each shot made the snaphance unsuitable for use on the battlefield.[24]

---

comp[agnie]ën gemonstert den xvii.n en[de] xviii.n nov.bvris 1598 tot Bergen op ten Zoom en[de] in den lande van der Tholen', a report which mentions the precise number of men bearing snaphances; NA, SG 4903, Maximiliaan Hornes to the SG, Heusden, 6 July 1602, appendix.
[24] In 1624 the States-General ordered the establishment of four companies of snaphances. These were incorporated into a special regiment under the command of Johan van Wijnbergen in 1632. Ten Raa, *Het Staatsche leger*, IV, pp. 224–5.

Calivers were formally abolished in the English as well as the French infantry companies in Dutch service in 1605.[25] Four years later, at the start of the Twelve Years' Truce, they were abolished in the rest of the Dutch army. In May 1609, the Council of State ordered the captains 'to reduce your company as soon as you are handed this letter ... immediately dismissing and removing the most unsuitable [men]'. The Council clarified this decree in a postscript: 'We mean that insofar as you have any calivermen among your company, you shall have to dismiss these first and foremost, being the worst or most unsuitable.'[26] J.W. Wijn was under the impression that this coincided with 'the introduction of lighter muskets, making the rest redundant, effectively merging the two categories.'[27] There is no evidence for this whatsoever, but quite the converse: the ordinances concerning weaponry of 1618, 1623 and 1639 actually ratified that all musketeers had to be equipped with a matchlock musket and a rest, in accordance with the 'Ordre' of 1599.[28] Lighter muskets had been available since 1604,[29] but Maurits and later also Frederik Hendrik did not venture to introduce them, probably fearing that the reduction in calibre necessary to achieve the reduction in weight would be overly detrimental to the ball's penetrative force. The furket remained part of the Dutch musketeer's standard kit until the last quarter of the seventeenth century.[30]

After 1609 the Dutch infantry consisted exclusively of pikemen and musketeers. By this time the infantry was therefore using only one type of firearm, though not all musketeers were equipped with the same model of musket. Calibres ranged from 19 to 20.5 millimetres and the barrel was often 5 to 15 centimetres shorter than the prescribed length of 125.6 centimetres (4 Rhineland feet).[31] This situation did not improve until 1627, two years after Maurits's death, when in October the States of Holland took the historic decision that henceforth all the companies repartitioned to this province

> shall have to collect [their new weapons] from the arsenal in Delft at the prices charged by the Land, and [the cost of] these weapons shall be docked from the respective companies over six pay-months, with the order that at the muster atten-

---

[25] NA, SG 4911, Extract res. RvS, 17 December 1605; RvS, The Hague, 30 December 1605; RGP 101, Res. SG, 10 December 1605 (no. 107).
[26] HUA, HAA 4120, RvS to Captain Jacob Wijts (†1643).
[27] Wijn, *Krijgswezen*, p. 145.
[28] NA, SHS 1449, 'Ordre' of 5 December 1618; Ten Raa, *Het Staatsche leger*, III, p. 288; IV, p. 352.
[29] In September 1604, Pieter Thonisz. and Jan Claesz. Wageman, gunsmiths in Dordrecht, demonstrated 'a new model of ... long calivers with the length of muskets to the great comfort and convenience of soldiers who shall fire these muskets without rests, the same as they have done so far with the common hand-calivers'. NA, SG 4909, Maurits to the SG, before Sluis, 1 September 1604, appendix 'Aen zijne princel[ijke] Ex.cie'.
[30] See p. 397.
[31] NA, SHS 1449, 'Ordre', The Hague, 5 December 1618; Puype, *From Prince Maurice to the Peace of Westphalia*, pp. 139–43.

tion shall be paid to whether the weapons of the soldiers are of the calibre of the Land in order to bring all the ... companies ... to uniformity of weapons ... and to avoid the inconveniences caused by calibre and balls not matching.[32]

*

The Dutch cavalry was initially composed of lancers, cuirassiers and mounted arquebusiers. Lancers were armed with a lance approximately four metres long. A lancer had to be an outstanding horseman, seeing as he made his attack at a full gallop. This limited the employability of lancers, who could only develop their strength – an attack at speed – on flat, hard ground. Cuirassiers, on the other hand, could be deployed both offensively and defensively on terrain that was more difficult to negotiate, and their style of combat required less practice and horses of lesser quality. Cuirassiers attacked at only a trot. In January 1597 the Dutch lancers were transformed into cuirassiers. This change was effected almost simultaneously in the Spanish army.[33]

The 'Ordre' of 1596 (repeated in the 1599 'Ordre') prescribed that these cuirassiers had to ride 'strong, stallion-like' horses and be furnished with 'bullet-proof' cuirasses, a visored helmet, arm-guards, a bridle gauntlet, a short sword fit for cutting and thrusting, and a pair of wheel-lock pistols. As with the snaphance lock, with a wheel-lock mechanism it was sparks from an artificial flint (iron pyrites) that ignited the gunpowder. Maurits allowed the cavalry to use this type of firearm because it was impossible to use a matchlock pistol on horseback. The match scared the animals and it was difficult to reload the pistol while holding the smouldering match between one's fingers on a nervous horse. To fire a wheel-lock the cock with the flint had to be brought into contact with a small wheel with a number of sharp teeth. Pulling the trigger released a spring that made the wheel spin rapidly, and the shower of sparks ignited the priming powder in the pan. The wheel-lock mechanism was even more intricate than the snaphance lock: the winding of the spring was especially critical.

In each company of one hundred cuirassiers, twenty-five of the best horsemen were armoured with heavier cuirasses and with knee-plates. To compensate for the extra weight they were not required to carry their baggage on the back of their own steeds. This was the task of the '*bidets*', servants mounted on small packhorses (*bidet* being the French for a nag) who were also responsible for gathering forage. These pages were expected to participate in battle,[34] but in practice were 'usually a hindrance and detrimental when one has to fight, because of the running and fleeing of the boys'. Simon Stevin therefore advocated replacing the *bidets* with dragoons, 'these being foot-soldiers on horseback'. These lightly

---

[32] NA, RAZH, ASH 60, Res. SH, 6 October 1627; HUA, HAA 4120, Delegated Councillors of Holland to Captain Jacob Wijts, The Hague, 3 December 1627 (quote).
[33] Wijn, *Krijgswezen*, pp. 158–9.
[34] NA, RAZH, AJvO 2876, Contract for the raising of a regiment of 1,000 horse, 17 January 1599 (quote); Duyck, II, p. 208.

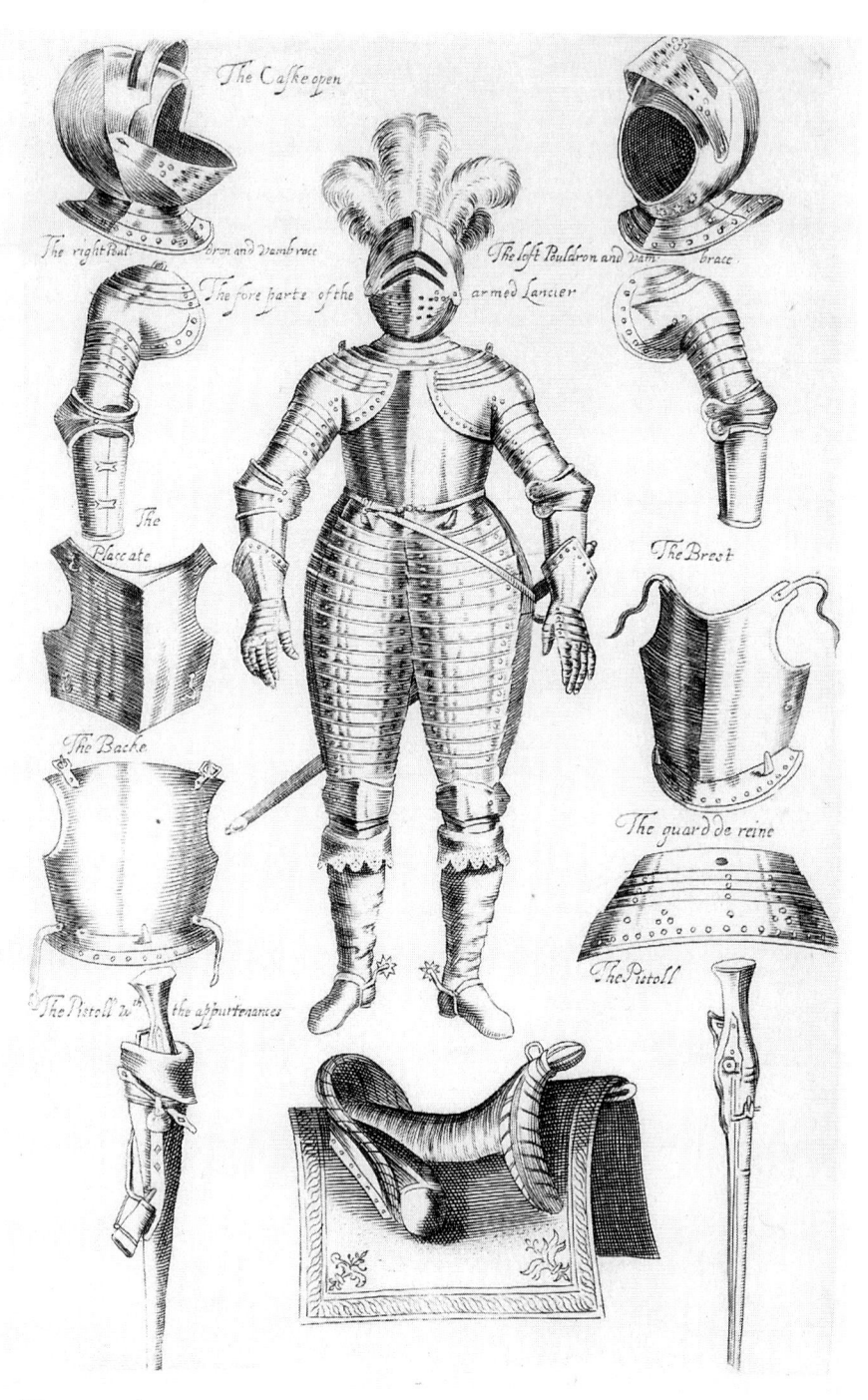

12. Heavy cavalry. Henry Hexham, *Principii ofte de eerste gronden van de oorloghskonste* (The Hague 1642). (KB, 604-B-27)

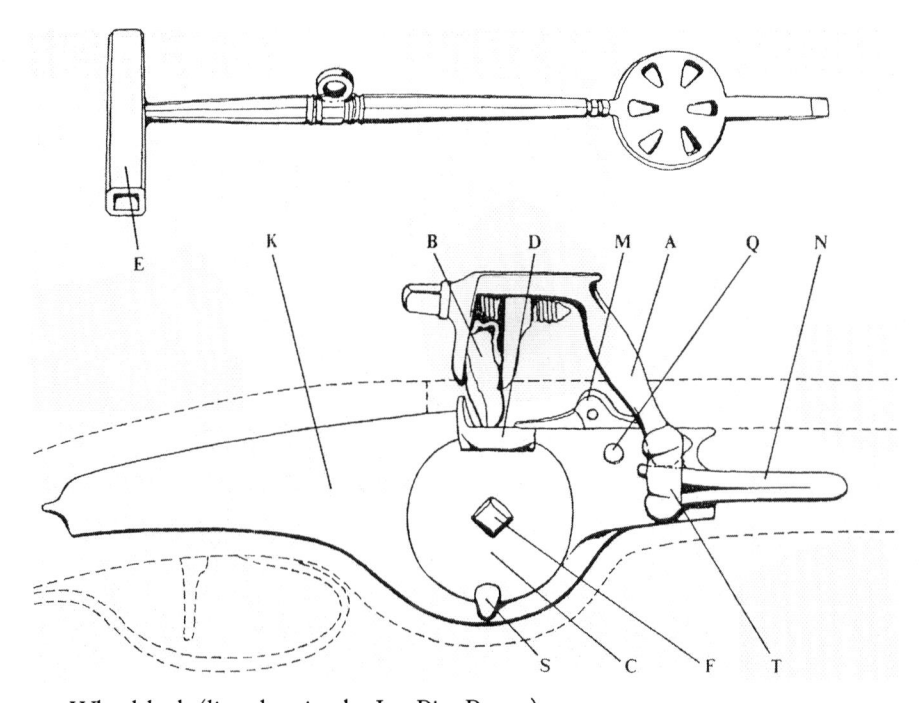

13. Wheel-lock (line drawing by Jan Piet Puype).
Key: A. cock; B. pyrites; C. wheel; D. pan; E. spanner and key; F. spindle; K. lockplate; M. pan-cover; N. cock-spring.

armoured troops could transport the baggage of the cuirassiers and fetch forage for the horses just as well.[35]

Besides being a mathematician and engineer, Stevin was a castrometer or 'camp-measurer' and in January 1604, as noted, he received his commission as Quartermaster-General. He managed the logistics for the Dutch field army but advised Maurits on other military matters as well. Stevin's recommendation to establish regiments of dragoons remained unheeded until the second half of the seventeenth century, but their task was in part already performed by the arquebusiers. These were mounted infantry equipped with a visorless helmet (morion), a cuirass, a sword and a wheel-lock carbine. A carbine was a firearm with a length of 'three big men's feet' (c. 90cm) and a calibre of 17 millimetres.[36] The relatively short barrel made it possible to load and fire a carbine while in the saddle.

---

[35] KB, HS 128 A-9II, 'Eenighe stucken der crijchconst beschreven deur Simon Stevin', fol. 94.
[36] *Recueil ... betreffende de saaken van den oorlog*, I, no. 2, appendix. See also Puype, *From Prince Maurice to the Peace of Westphalia*, p. 146.

The tactical revolution: Dutch infantry tactics and drill

Maurits and Willem Lodewijk failed in their attempts to fully standardise Dutch weaponry, which was achieved later under Frederik Hendrik, but they did succeed in reforming the moulding and tactical deployment of the troops in accordance with their personal insights. The theoretical formulation behind the reforms was chiefly the work of Willem Lodewijk and Johann VII, one of his younger brothers, as Maurits was more a man of deeds.[37] The problem the Republic faced was the superiority of the Spanish troops in battle in the open field. In ambushes or when ensconced behind ramparts the Dutch troops were a match for the Spaniards, but in open battle they were at a disadvantage. Maurits and Willem Lodewijk strove to compensate for this in two ways: by drilling and exercising the troops and, during battle, by dissipating the thrust of an enemy assault across various relatively small units. This spreading of risk meant that when one unit took to its heels this did not automatically result in the overthrow of the whole army. Maurits and Willem Lodewijk no longer divided the field army into just three parts, namely the vanguard, battle and rearguard, which was the traditional battle array of the bands of *Landsknechte* and initially of the Spaniards, too (the Spanish term *tercio* originally meant one-third of the field army), but subdivided these three roughly equal combat formations into units of 800 to 900 men each, reduced a few years later to between 500 and 600 men. Each of these 'battalions', as they were known from 1592, could operate independently. Following the example of the Romans, the battalions were positioned three lines deep in echelon, aligned in a chequer-wise pattern rather than directly behind one another. The main advantage of this order of battle was that the troops in the front line could be relieved or reinforced by the battalions disposed further to the rear without this leading to disorder.

Maurits and Willem Lodewijk were sticklers for ensuring that all the troops were serried in rank and file in like manner, so that several companies could operate as a unit when combined into a battalion. This was of the utmost importance, as the company was the only fixed military formation until the second half of the seventeenth century. Regiments or 'colonelships' were of practical signifi-

---

[37] Kees Schulten, 'Prins Maurits (1567–1625), legerhervormer en vernieuwer van de krijgskunde, of trendvolger?', *Armamentaria*, XXXV (2000), 7–22, esp. pp. 15 and 17; Nickle, 'Military Reforms of Prince Maurice', pp. 147–8; Hahlweg, *Heeresreform*, p. 34, states in no uncertain terms that Willem Lodewijk was 'the ever thoughtful and untiringly creative mind of the military reformers'. E.H. Waterbolk's assessment is more nuanced, highlighting the difference between Willem Lodewijk's 'interests [being] oriented more towards the Classical authors, and the more mathematical bias of Maurits, nourished by the ingenuity of Simon Stevin'. See his 'Willem Lodewijk als opvoeder', in *Omtrekkende bewegingen. Opstellen aangeboden aan de schrijver bij zijn tachtigste verjaardag* (Hilversum 1995), pp. 160–78, esp. 170 (quote), and 'Met Willem Lodewijk aan tafel 17.3.1560 – 13.7.1620', in *Verspreide opstellen aangeboden aan de schrijver bij zijn aftreden als hoogleraar aan de Rijksuniversiteit Groningen* (Amsterdam 1981), pp. 296–315, esp. 303–4, 310 and 315.

cance only during the campaign. The colonels insisted that the captains replaced losses, maintained the weapons and drilled the troops, but there was no question of direct supervision of the everyday management of each company. Shortly before the start of a new campaign, Maurits, Willem Lodewijk and Frederik Hendrik notified the colonels of the regimental strengths they required. The colonels then drew up an inventory of the current state of the companies under their command and reported this to The Hague or to the Frisian court in Leeuwarden. Based on these particulars, Maurits, Willem Lodewijk and Frederik Hendrik designated the companies which would serve in that year's campaign.[38] During the winter months the companies were scattered across many garrisons; maintaining the regimental structure was not even a consideration. This meant that the troops could not exercise at battalion level until they were assembled at the rendezvous. That is why Maurits and Willem Lodewijk attached great importance to the constant drilling of troops on campaign.

In July 1592 they utilised the period of calm after their conquest of Steenwijk to range the infantry (5,875 men) in battle array and drill the men in 'turning, wheeling, retreating and advancing ... without breaking formation'.[39] The battle formation of the Frisian regiment at that time is documented in detail. In 1592 the Frisians were divided into three battalions numbering 794, 882 and 905 men. The pike stood eleven, twelve or thirteen ranks deep in the middle of each battalion. The musketeers were ranged to the left and right of the pike and the calivermen stood alongside the musket. In the first battalion the musketeers stood fifteen ranks deep and the calivermen sixteen ranks deep, in the second battalion they stood fourteen and thirteen ranks deep, respectively, and in the third battalion they stood fourteen and twelve ranks deep. The pike were divided into blocks four men across (except for the third battalion, which had one extra pikeman per rank), while soldiers with firearms fought in blocks that were five men across. The total width of the front line of these battalions was 58, 68 and 75 men, respectively.[40]

---

[38] In March 1645, Colonel Eustachius Puchler sent a list of his regiment's companies to Constantijn Huygens, secretary to Frederik Hendrik, 'from which His Highness is to choose as many and whichever companies it would please His Highness to take on campaign this coming summer, only I bid that Your Honour do me the courtesy of arranging the associated business with His Highness, so that ... [Captain] Billoue shall for this summer alone be permitted to remain with his company in garrison, because he has informed me that because of recruitments by [the elector of] Brandenburg he has lost many of his best soldiers and that he has twice sent out recruiters but did not gain more than one man.... Instead of taking ... Billoue, I therefore ask whether it would please His Highness to take Captain Berenson's company, which is in excellent shape and in good order and has fine and well-clothed soldiers ... on campaign this summer'. KHA, G1-3, The Hague, 19 March 1645. See also Puchler's letter of 10 May 1646 from Schenkenschans.
[39] Duyck, I, p. 104; Pieter Bor Chistiaensz., *De Nederlandsche historien*, 4 vols (Amsterdam 1679–1684), III, p. 630.
[40] Tresoar, FSA 5, Formation of the Frisian regiment on 8/18 July 1592. Three days earlier (5/15 July) the Frisians were ranged in a similar battle array.

14. A Dutch officer instructing a musketeer according to the drill manual, *Wapenhandelinghe van roers, musquetten ende spiessen*, published in 1607. P. von Isselburg, *Die Drillkunst* (Nuremberg 1664). (Royal Netherlands Army Museum, Delft, 00106621/1)

Troops who were trained to handle their weapons in the same way could, self-evidently, more readily fight side by side. Maurits and Willem Lodewijk devoted attention to this as well, though they felt no need to set down the method followed in writing, as they did not have to work with companies made up exclusively of fresh recruits and could therefore focus on standardising the exercise of troops who were for the most part experienced. First published in 1607, the renowned drill manual for caliver, musket and pike, *Wapenhandelinghe van roers, musquetten ende spiessen*,[41] was not authored by Maurits and Willem Lodewijk but by Johann VII, who had served in the Low Countries in 1592 and 1593. He later led the Swedish troops against the Poles in Livonia (1601–1602). Armed with such practical experience he subsequently endeavoured to establish a 'Militia Force' (*Landesverteidigung*) for the county of Nassau. Being too poor to raise a sizeable professional army, the county's core defence had to be provided

[41] This first Dutch edition has been published in facsimile with an introduction by J.B. Kist as *The Exercise of Armes: A Commentary* (Lochem 1971). Soon after its initial publication the manual was translated into all major European languages and was even published in polyglot editions.

15. Pike evolutions in the Dutch army. Johan Jacobi von Wallhausen, *L'art militaire pour l'infanterie* (Franeker [1615]). (Royal Netherlands Army Museum, Delft, 00102287/005)

by the inhabitants themselves. In order to instil the rudiments of the art of war into these inexperienced soldiers, Johann VII produced a drill manual in which he described every motion with musket, caliver and pike, and illustrated them with drawings, which were subsequently artistically engraved by Jacob de Gheyn. He based this drill on practices he had observed in the Dutch army. Johann VII also turned his mind to how soldiers should be led as a group in battle, but his ideas were elaborated only in notes for personal use.[42]

In the Spanish and French armies recruits were taught by veteran soldiers, a method of instruction that dated back to the age of the bands of *Landsknechte*. Under Maurits and Willem Lodewijk the Dutch company commanders were still entrusted with the instruction of young, inexperienced soldiers, but they no longer allowed captains to do this according to their personal insights; the corporals were to 'instruct with gentle words, not with beating, swearing and scolding'.[43] They were above all not to 'suffer the old soldiers to mock or jeer the

---

[42] Hahlweg, *Heeresreform*, pp. 3–5, 21 and 41; Kist, *Exercise of Armes*, pp. 4–5 and 13–15.
[43] Le Hon, *Ordres van batailjen*, fol. 33v.

16. Johann VII (1561–1623), count of Nassau-Siegen. Jacobus Kok, *Vaderlandsch Woordenboek*, late eighteenth century. (Royal Netherlands Army Museum, Delft, 00146410)

younger if they do not do their postures as they ought, as every man in every science and profession must have a time of learning before he can be perfect'.[44] The notion that Dutch officers had to drill their troops with the *Wapenhandelinghe* in hand is a stubborn misconception. This drill manual was intended solely for individual instruction of 'young or untrained soldiers'.[45] It was not intended for groups of soldiers who had already undergone basic training, though it was often being used with such groups seventy years after its publication. In 1679, Captain Louis Paen complained that the drill manuals were being

> misused by many officers, who practise it with a great troop standing in ranks and files, for a soldier should understand the correct use of the musket before he is ranged in ranks and files. Therefore, when a troop stands in ranks and files no other command should be used after the musketeers have readied themselves than

---

[44] Hexham, *Principii*, fols 2–3.
[45] Boxel, *Vertoogh van de krijghsoeffeninge*, title-page of the first of the three parts.

present and then *give fire*, so that the soldiers might give due consideration to the necessary skill.[46]

Ranging troops in battle formation was no easy task in the sixteenth and seventeenth centuries. Each battalion was composed of men equipped with polearms or firearms. The muskets and calivers had the advantage of being able to join battle at a distance, but the sheer inaccuracy of gunfire and most especially the time required to reload meant that a successful deployment of firearms was possible only when several shots were discharged simultaneously and each subsequent volley followed after no more than a short interval. Otherwise the opponent had the opportunity to regroup or throw themselves at the adversary. Under battle conditions it was possible to discharge one, sometimes two shots per minute with a musket or caliver.[47] Prior to 1594 the records reveal nothing about the way in which the Dutch musketeers and calivermen were expected to discharge their weapons simultaneously as a hail of fire. It was in December 1594 that Willem Lodewijk first informed Maurits about the method he had devised to make it possible to fire continuous volleys:

> [N]amely that as soon as the first rank has fired simultaneously it steps back *per evolutionem et versum* [i.e. makes an about-turn and returns to the rear of the block]; the second [rank] steps forward or stands still and shoots simultaneously, then marches back; the third and the following do the same. Thus before the last rank has fired the first has reloaded.

Willem Lodewijk explained what he had in mind using a diagram. He subdivided the soldiers with firearms into blocks numbering nine men across by five ranks deep. After the musketeers or calivermen had fired together by rank they were to make an about-turn to the right and march to the rear between the files.[48]

It is highly unlikely that the countermarch, as this firing method was known, was used in such a form in practice. When loading a musket or caliver a soldier needed at least three feet of space to manoeuvre on either side. During the loading process he had to swing his firearm around and move it from his right side to his left while simultaneously making sure that his smouldering match did not ignite another soldier's gunpowder. Moreover, Willem Lodewijk's proposal required a 'street' measuring three feet across to be kept free between each file, so that soldiers who had fired could return to the rear of the column, so the files stood a total of six feet apart. In the field, such an open formation presented an

---

[46] Louis Paen, *Den korten weg tot de Nederlandsche militaire exercitie. Inhoudende eenige consideratien tot het manuael, soo van musquet, picq als andere noodige evolutiën, &c.* (Leeuwarden 1679).
[47] Hall, *Weapons and Warfare*, p. 149.
[48] Hahlweg, *Heeresreform*, p. 610; Geoffrey Parker, 'From the House of Orange to the House of Bush: 400 Years of "Revolutions in Military Affairs"', *Militaire Spectator*, CLXXII, 4 (2003), 177–93, esp. pp. 180–1.

17. The countermarch as explained in Willem Lodewijk's letter to Maurits, Groningen 8/18 December 1594. (KHA, A22-IX-E-79)

easy target for the cavalry, who could exploit the spaces to penetrate the unit speedily. Based on a hitherto unknown sketch of the Frisian regiment's battle array preserved in the Royal Archives (Koninklijk Huisarchief) at The Hague,[49] it is plausible that Willem Lodewijk tried out his ideas at the drill ground in the winter of 1594 and the spring of 1595, which made him realise that a modified tactical formation was preferable. Willem Lodewijk himself had doubts about the practicality of the new firing method, witness the warning to Maurits in his letter of December 1594: 'If your Excellency wants to joke about it [i.e. the countermarch], let that be in private and amongst friends.' Furthermore, Willem Lodewijk did not want this manner of shooting to be adopted by the colonels of the other regiments until he was wholly certain of his case.[50]

[49] KHA, A24-IV-H10.
[50] Parker, 'House of Orange', p. 181, concludes from Willem Lodewijk's plea for secrecy ('so that monsieur Vere [commander of the English troops in the Dutch army] and the other colonels do not imitate it'), that he was so sure of the 'destructive potential' of the salvoes that he wanted to keep it secret from the other troops in Dutch service. This interpretation is in my view incorrect for two reasons: in the first place because Willem Lodewijk did not raise any objections to all the Dutch troops as well as the English auxiliary troops being drilled

18. Tactical deployment of the Frisian regiment in 1594. For an explanation see the text. (KHA, A24-IV-H10)

The sketch in the Royal Archives bears no date, but by reconciling the dates on which captains received their commissions or transferred charge of their companies it is possible to deduce the date fairly accurately. Among the captains mentioned in the sketch there are two (Hans van Oestheim and L. Huygens) who received their commissions on 15 February 1594, while two others (Jacques de Vries and Jan Yvens) relinquished charge of their companies on 9 May 1595.[51] The sketch can therefore be dated to between February 1594 and May 1595. The division of the regiment into two battalions matches the formation during the 1594 campaign,[52] while the number of musketeers and calivermen per rank more or less tallies with the diagram in Willem Lodewijk's letter of December 1594.

The two battalions depicted are 800 strong (314 pike, 36 halberd, 144 musket and 306 caliver) and 922 strong (380 pike, 20 halberd, 144 musket and 378 caliver). In the usual manner the pike stand in the middle of the units in seven and eight blocks, respectively, each of which is five files wide and eight ranks deep (except

and exercised in the same way, and in the second place because it would have been impossible to keep the countermarch secret once the field army had gathered, it then being possible for everyone to see the Frisian troops practising their drill.

[51] Tresoar, Nadere Toegang 5.17, 'Persoonnamen- en zaaknamenindex op de commissie- en instructieboeken (1502), 1587–1808', and 5.18, part 1, 'Lijsten van door Friesland tot en met 1723 aangestelde officieren (gebaseerd op gegevens uit de Statenresoluties en uit commissie- en instructieboeken)'.

[52] Duyck, I, pp. 379 and 381; II, p. 677.

for the two outermost blocks, each of which has an additional rank of pike[53]). To the left and right of the pikemen stand blocks of musketeers, each of which is eight files wide and nine ranks deep. The calivermen are positioned on the flanks: in the first battalion they are divided into four blocks, each eight or nine files wide and nine ranks deep, and in the second battalion they are divided into six blocks, each seven files wide and nine ranks deep. Two ranks of pike support the musketeers and a rank of halberdiers supports the calivermen. The battalions therefore have an average depth of ten ranks. This is twice the number depicted in the formation in Willem Lodewijk's letter of December 1594, but there is still an obvious reduction compared with the depth of the formation in 1592, when it had been fourteen or fifteen ranks for the musketeers and twelve, thirteen or even sixteen ranks for the calivermen. The front of the first battalion in the sketch extended 405 feet (c. 127m): 300 feet for the musketeers and calivermen (50 men x 6 feet) and 105 feet for the pikemen (35 x 3 feet). The front of the second battalion extended 474 feet (c. 148m).

In the summer of 1595 Willem Lodewijk presented another firing tactic for the infantry. In the presence of Maurits and the Dutch army's senior officers, the Frisian troops fired in salvo according to Willem Lodewijk's newly devised method, which was adopted by all the regiments in Dutch service shortly thereafter.[54] In August 1595 the Frisian regiment was composed of three battalions of 680, 724 and 762 men, in total 2,166 strong. The pikemen were arrayed in the middle of the battle formation, which was nothing new. The major change involved the musketeers and calivermen, who no longer made an about-turn individually after firing a salvo but made a right turn as a rank and marched in file to the flank of the block, and thence to the rear of the unit. The blocks were therefore separated from each other by a street of six feet, 'so that once it has fired the front rank can march through it to the rear of its unit to get ready again and can there properly prepare itself for firing by the time it has once again become the front rank', to quote Simon Stevin.[55] Willem Lodewijk's original solution for achieving a continuous hail of gunfire was in principle preserved, but the front of each battalion could be reduced considerably, because the soldiers now marched to the rear via the streets between the blocks rather than between the individual files. By simultaneously reducing the number of soldiers in each block of musket and caliver to five or six men per rank it was possible to increase the rate of fire;

---

[53] N.B. In the second battalion the ranks of the two outermost blocks of pike were six men across instead of five.
[54] Tresoar, FSA 5, Battle formations of 13 July and 5 August 1595. See also Duyck, I, pp. 636, 637 and 664. Duyck also mentions (pp. 683–4) that in October 1595 Maurits serried all the infantry regiments in battle array and, besides having them perform all kinds of manoeuvres, also had them 'advance towards each other as if they were going to shoot in order to practise this same thing'. The formation of the Frisian regiment for this exercise was also recorded. See Tresoar, FSA 5, Formation of 7/17 October 1595 at Bislich.
[55] KB, HS 128-A-18, 'Formen van slachorden (soowel ten deel als in 't geheel) van 't leger'. A French version of the same text is to be found in KHA, A14-IX-2, 'Ordres de batailles'.

19. Tactical deployment of the Frisian regiment on 6/16 August 1595 (Tresoar, FSA 5). The sketch shows the formation of the Frisian regiment in three battalions. In the first battalion the centre is formed by six blocks of pike, while the other two battalions have five. The pikemen are standing ten ranks deep, the outer blocks twelve, and a block of musketeers stands on either side of the block of pike. To the left and right are two wings of calivermen of three blocks each. Each block of pikemen, musketeers and calivermen is five men wide.

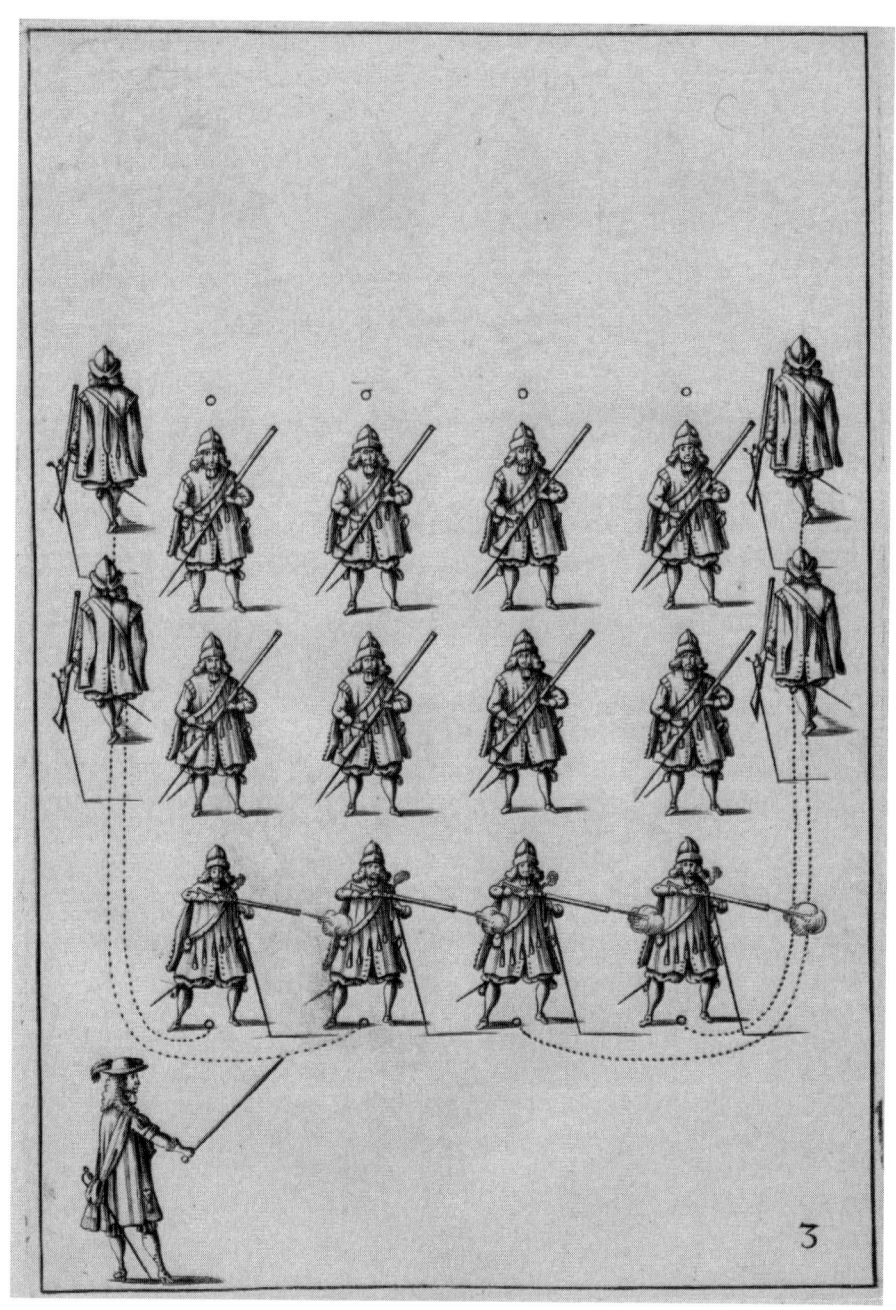

20. The conversion, c. 1670. Johan Boxel, *Vertoogh van de krijghs-oeffeninge* (The Hague 1670). (Royal Netherlands Army Museum, Delft 00118853/77)

the troops who had fired could clear the front of the battalion more quickly so the following rank could loose its salvo sooner.

After the abolition of the caliver in 1609 a model battalion of the Dutch army consisted of 250 pikemen and 240 musketeers divided into five blocks of pike, each five men across and ten men deep, and six blocks of musket, each four men across and ten men deep. Such a unit had a front of only 183 feet (c. 57m): 49 x 3 feet plus six streets of 6 feet. After each salvo the rank that had fired split itself 'into two parts, one half [marching] to the rear via the right-hand side and the other half via the left; this moves them out of the way of the other musketeers sooner'. This variation on the countermarch was called the 'conversion'.[56] But Maurits and Willem Lodewijk were not yet satisfied with this formation. It may have provided a satisfactory solution to making continuous volleys of musketfire possible, but in close combat it was less suitable, 'given that in the clash of the battle orders the musketeers must pull back'. Musketeers were no match for armoured pikemen or halberdiers in close combat, but this was not the sole disadvantage of this formation. During the battle of Nieuwpoort (1600) it became evident that the pikemen were unable to provide adequate cover for the musketeers and calivermen when they were subjected to a cavalry charge, 'insofar as the pikemen must serve as the breastwork of the musketeers and that with their being in two parts, to the right as well as to the left side [of the pikes] ... if they were charged by cavalry they [could] not retreat behind a group of pikes without confusion'.[57]

At first Maurits and Willem Lodewijk did not venture to radically alter the tried and tested infantry formation, because 'the slightest alteration overwhelms the common soldier',[58] but when the war with Spain was suspended for twelve years in 1609 they seized the small-scale War of the Jülich Succession (1609–1610 and 1614) that followed the death of the childless Duke Johann Wilhelm as an opportunity to improve the tactical formation: 'And when one subsequently devoted further consideration to the matter ... [one] found that it was better to remove all the musketeers away from the flanks of the pikemen and to arrange them behind their pikes ... and that thereby the whole battle order gained greater security, being serried closer together.'[59] When they had to fire, all the musketeers advanced and formed a closed line in front of the pikemen.

This new tactical formation was first employed during the Jülich campaign of 1610. Soon thereafter it became standard practice to combine three battalions into a brigade. This made it possible to fire salvoes with seventy-two musketeers at once (three times twenty-four musketeers per battalion). In the rules

---

[56] KHA, A23-VII-Db-O, 'De woorden van commandement waerdoor de capiteynen hunne soldaten gebieden ende exerceren', Leeuwarden 1630.
[57] Le Hon, *Ordres van batailjen*, fol. 6v.
[58] NA, CvdH 124, Memorandum by Lieutenant-General Daniël de Savornin (1669–1739).
[59] KB, HS 128-A-18, Stevin, 'Formen van slachorden', fols 5v and 6r (quote).

and regulations of 1618 the essence of the new tactic was formulated as follows: 'Exercise of musketeers. The two front ranks make ready, present, give fire (and so on until all the ranks have discharged).'[60] It was also possible to have two front ranks fire simultaneously, a coordinated salvo by 144 men, as described by Stevin: 'If one wants to have the two front ranks fire simultaneously one should have the musketeers in the front rank either crouch or kneel and have the second rank shoot over their heads in order to inflict greater damage on the enemy in the same amount of time.'[61] Geoffrey Parker draws the conclusion that Willem Lodewijk's original proposal from December 1594 had some two decades later been transformed 'into a production line of death'.[62] Volley fire was to dominate land-based warfare until the mid-nineteenth century.

Michael Roberts maintains that the new tactics of the Nassaus required more highly trained units as well as a higher proportion of officers. This was supposedly the reason why Maurits and Willem Lodewijk reduced the number of men per company while the number of officers remained constant.[63] This is based on a misconception, because both men were advocates of large companies. In February 1601 Maurits informed his cousin that he would comply with his request to leave several Frisian companies behind in garrison during the forthcoming campaign, notwithstanding that, as Willem Lodewijk knew all too well, companies of 200 men 'are of greater service than those of 113'.[64] Maurits was opposed to small companies because through losses and casualties they were too quickly rendered unfit for service in the field. A company of 150 or 200 men had greater resilience.

---

[60] NA, SHS 1449, 'Ordre', The Hague, 5 December 1618.

[61] KB, HS 128-A-9I, fol. 45 and verso. Simon Stevin discusses three different forms of the conversion in the same manuscript: 'If one wants to have the musketeers fire while the battle array remains in the same place, then once the front rank has fired and has moved away [towards the rear] one shall *have the whole battle array advance* until the current front rank comes to where the departed one was standing.
'But if one wants to fire while advancing towards the enemy, then once the front rank that has fired has moved out of the way one shall have the battle array move forward as far as time and other circumstances permit.
'And if one wants to fire while drawing back from or retreating for the enemy, once the front rank that has fired has moved out of the way one shall leave the battle array standing and have the men go to the rear constantly, so that with each departing rank the battle array then draws back or yields as far from the enemy as the ranks are standing from one another, the distance of which one can decide depending on whether the retreat be allowed to proceed slowly or must proceed quickly.'

[62] Parker, 'House of Orange', p. 184.

[63] Michael Roberts, 'The Military Revolution', p. 14. See also Parker, *Military Revolution*, p. 20.

[64] *Archives*, 2nd series, II, no. 230, Maurits to Willem Lodewijk, The Hague, 19 May 1601.

Cavalry and artillery

Maurits and Willem Lodewijk devoted scant attention to mounted arms. Apart from abolishing lancers they left everything as it was. There is a straightforward explanation for this: the terrain in the Northern Netherlands rarely lent itself to charges on horseback. The basic tactical group for the cavalry was the 'squadron', which consisted of three companies comprising 225 horse at full strength. Each company formed a block measuring fifteen horses across and five ranks deep; each horse occupied a space measuring three by five feet, so a company's front was forty-five feet across. The blocks were separated from each other by a fifty-foot street, 'through which the companies can wheel, for otherwise they cannot turn as required'. A squadron therefore had a front of 235 feet (c. 74m).[65]

The cuirassiers and arquebusiers (dragoons) were trained to advance towards the enemy at a trot, fire their pistols and carbines, and then fall back in order to reload their weapons. This manoeuvre was called the *caracole* and was an effective tactic against pikemen. A head-on charge against a block of pike had no chance of success unless the cavalry reached the unit it was attacking before the pikemen had lowered their pike, as occurred in January 1597, when the Dutch cavalry surprised a Spanish column near Turnhout and managed 'to get under their pikes before they … were lowered'.[66] The *caracole* was less effective against musketeers, because the musket's greater range meant they could inflict much more damage on the cuirassiers than the cuirassiers could visit on the musketeers with their pistols. Instead of performing the *caracole*, the cavalry could therefore better await the moment when the infantry fell into disarray or exposed its flanks. The attacking potential of the mounted arm was rediscovered by King Gustavus II Adolphus of Sweden, who launched his cavalry attacks at high speed with *armes blanches*, that is, steel in hand. He employed this same tactic in confrontations with the enemy cavalry. Being protected by cuirasses, a pistol-ball was effective only when it struck the unprotected thighs or face of the enemy trooper. 'And some are of the opinion', noted Hexham, 'that a horseman ought not to shoot before he has set his pistol under his enemy's armour or to some part of his body that is not armour-clad.' And should this prove impossible then the horseman had to aim for the head or chest of the horse of his opponent.[67]

The Dutch army's artillery played no significant part in open battle until the second half of the seventeenth century. This required cannon that could provide short-range artillery support for the infantry, but Maurits saw little value in 6- or 3-pounder field-pieces, the two calibres most suitable for this task because they were light enough to be moved around on the battlefield and could follow the troops in their attack. Even 12-pound pieces failed to meet with Maurits's approval. Count Johann VII of Nassau-Siegen commented that 12-pounders

---

[65] KB, HS 128-A-18, Simon Stevin, 'Formen van slachorden', fol. IV.
[66] Duyck, II, p. 217.
[67] Hexham, *Principii*, fol. 56.

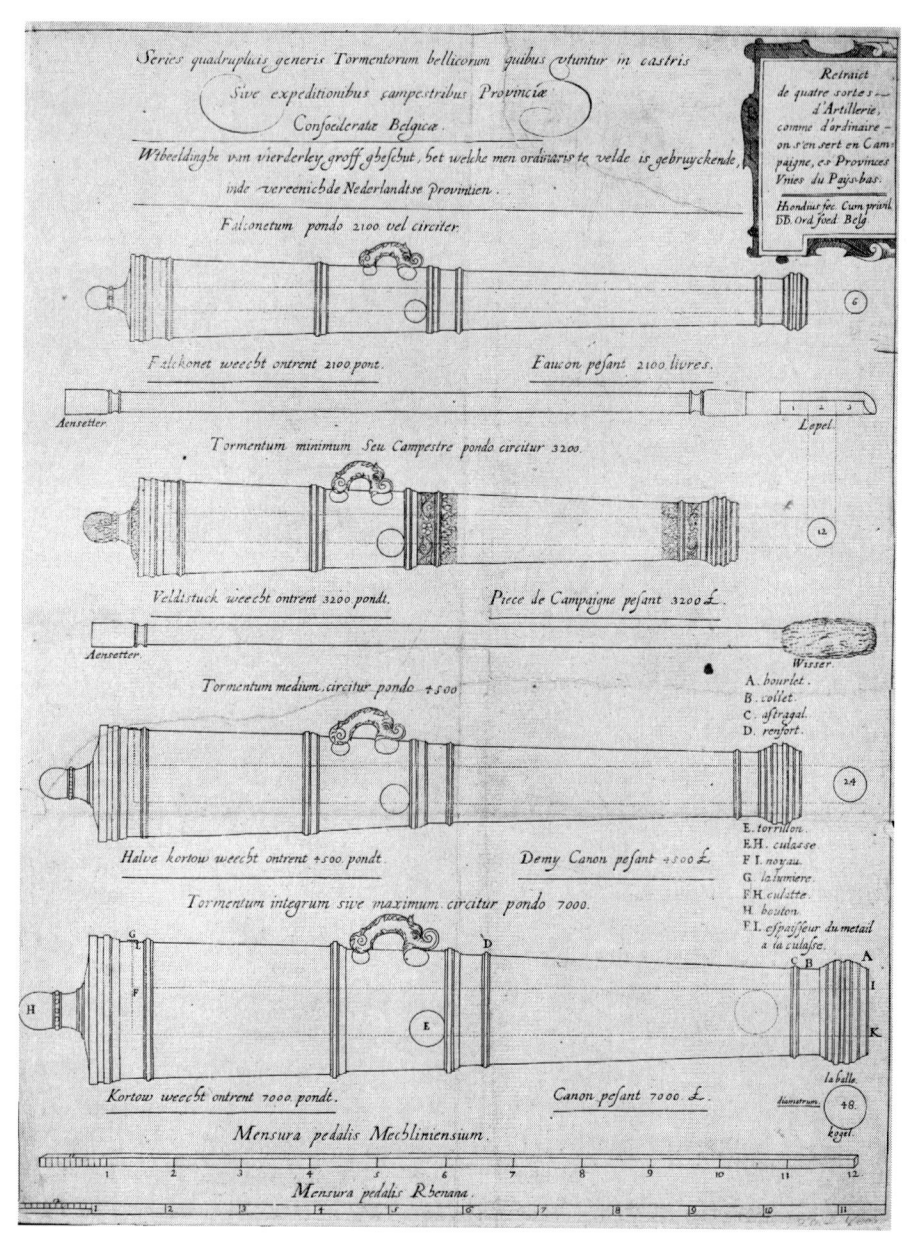

21a. Dutch field and siege artillery, first half of the seventeenth century. Henricus Hondius, *Korte beschrijvinge ende afbeeldinge van de generale regelen der fortificatie* (The Hague 1624). (Royal Netherlands Army Museum, Delft, 00102269/0001)

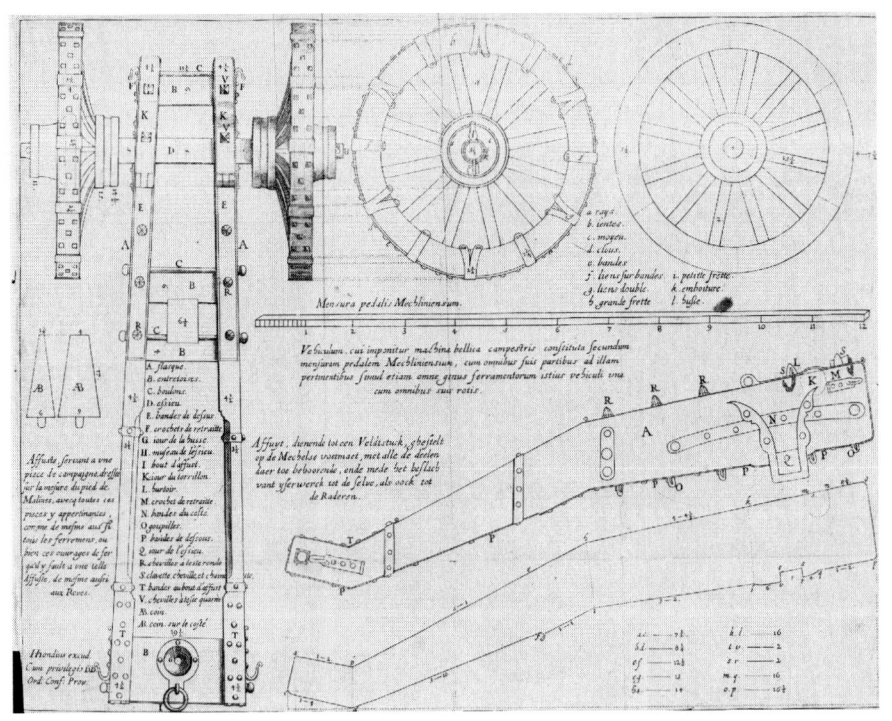

21b. Undercarriage of a Dutch 12-pounder cannon. Henricus Hondius, *Korte beschrijvinge ende afbeeldinge van de generale regelen der fortificatie* (The Hague 1624). (Royal Netherlands Army Museum, Delft, 00102269/011)

'are considered worthless by those knowledgeable of war, and do not cause much more damage and dread than a musket'. The whole-cannon (*hele kartouw*) and demi-cannon (*halve kartouw*) fired iron balls weighing 48 and 24 pounds, respectively, and in Maurits's view these were the only useful calibre. He held the 24-pounders in particularly high esteem, 'seeing as they not only instil a great terror, but when properly aimed and manned by good cannoneers they do great damage and effectively prevent the enemy from acting as he pleases in the battlefield'.[68] However, the 48- and 24-pound cannon were so heavy – their barrels alone weighing 7,500 and 4,500 pounds – that they could be used only from fixed positions. The role of the artillery was therefore confined to ushering in the battle proper. The pieces were usually assembled into one big battery and placed to the fore of the front line, so firing had to cease as soon as the troops advanced to avoid hitting one's own units.

Unlike his half-brother, Frederik Hendrik was not dismissive of cannon of a calibre smaller than 24 pounds. The gargantuan whole-cannon was phased out from the Dutch field-train under his command – they were from then on

---

[68] Hahlweg, *Heeresreform*, pp. 395–6.

used only for sieges – and he took along several 6-pounders 'belonging to him personally' when on campaign,[69] even though 12-pounders were the backbone of the Dutch artillery at the time. This calibre of cannon was designated a field-piece, but they were in fact too heavy to be re-positioned during battle: the barrel weighed approximately 3,200 pounds, and together with the gun carriage, limber and loading tools the piece weighed more than 5,600 pounds (c. 2,700kg) in all. In 1642 and 1643 the Dutch artillery-train included thirty-six 12-pounders and six 24-pounders.[70]

[69] F.H.W. Kuypers, *Geschiedenis der Nederlandsche artillerie*, II (Nijmegen 1871), p. 200.
[70] Tresoar, FAEVC 713, 'Ordre de bataille comme il a este ordonné par monseigneur le prince d'Orange dans le fort de Voorn le 2e de juin 1642'; *Gloria Parendi. Dagboeken van Willem Frederik stadhouder van Friesland, Groningen en Drenthe 1643–1649, 1651–1654*, transcription J. Visser and ed. G.N. van der Plaats (The Hague 1995), p. 10.

• 3 •

Field Operations (1590–1648)

The conduct of warfare

Ultimate authority over Dutch troops lay with the States-General and the provincial States, the bodies that dealt with affairs of war and peace, but for reasons of secrecy these many-headed assemblies were unsuitable for the determination of operational objectives, let alone strategy; military decision-making was a matter for more intimate circles.[1] For more than a quarter of a century Johan van Oldenbarnevelt had the greatest say. In a memorandum from around 1620, Joris de Bye, comptroller-general of the Union from 1588 to 1628, wrote that, following the earl of Leicester's departure, Maurits and Van Oldenbarnevelt had agreed a division of responsibilities. As commander-in-chief the stadholder retained control of the troops and led the campaigns, while the Advocate of Holland assumed responsibility for 'the politics and the finances in particular'. There was, however, no question of equality; Van Oldenbarnevelt mapped out the political path and raised the finances necessary for the implementation of the military plan and thus had the final say in matters of strategy. It was he who devised the 'exploits of war'.

At first this did not lead to tensions between Van Oldenbarnevelt and the military command. Maurits still had much to learn and as stadholder of Friesland Willem Lodewijk wielded autonomous command in the north of the Republic.[2] He remained Maurits's mentor in tactics as well as strategy. In April 1593 Maurits entreated Willem Lodewijk to take part in that year's campaign, 'because for me it would be an extreme burden to be alone in an army without any assistance of counsel'.[3] Even Van Oldenbarnevelt turned to Willem Lodewijk for advice in military matters,[4] though he by no means felt obliged to comply

---

[1] G. de Bruin, *Geheimhouding en verraad. De geheimhouding van staatszaken ten tijde van de Republiek (1600–1750)* (The Hague 1991), pp. 53–4.
[2] KHA, A22-IX-A1-30, Maurits to Willem Lodewijk, before Geertruidenberg, 21 May 1593.
[3] KHA, A22-IX-A1-27, Maurits to Willem Lodewijk, Zwolle, 13 April 1593.
[4] A.J. Veenendaal Sr, *Johan van Oldenbarnevelt. Bescheiden betreffende zijn staatkundig beleid en zijn familie*, vol. II (The Hague 1962), no. 6, Willem Lodewijk, 29 March 1602.

with such advice when it did not suit his personal plans. From 1600 this arrangement placed an increasing strain on relations between Van Oldenbarnevelt and the two stadholders. Despite Maurits having by then established a formidable military reputation, Van Oldenbarnevelt continued to interfere directly in the 'principality of the war', such as manning garrisons and moving troops, and he did not shy from forcing through decisions concerning military operations against the will of Maurits and Willem Lodewijk.[5]

Following Van Oldenbarnevelt's arrest in 1618 and his execution the following year, Maurits was able to mould both the military and political decision-making to his personal liking. Frederik Hendrik managed to consolidate the military authority of the princes of Orange even further through his appointment on 23 April 1625 as Captain- and Admiral-General of the Union, offices that his half-brother, Maurits, had failed to obtain. As overall commander, Frederik Hendrik ranked above his Frisian cousins, who were captains-general at the provincial level. Frederik Hendrik dealt with Ernst Casimir on an equal footing. A field-marshal since 1607, Ernst Casimir had succeeded to the stadholderate of Friesland following the death of his elder brother Willem Lodewijk in 1620, and from 1625 he was also stadholder of Groningen and Drenthe. Frederik Hendrik's relationship with Ernst Casimir's two sons was, however, quite the reverse. He treated Hendrik Casimir I (1612–1640), stadholder of the Republic's three northern provinces from 1632 to 1640, as a subordinate, while Willem Frederik (1613–1664), stadholder of Friesland from 1640, was prevented from wielding any autonomous military command until Frederik Hendrik's death.

Frederik Hendrik could to all intents and purposes formulate a campaign plan according to his personal insights.[6] Though he was obliged to do this in consultation with a States-General committee that dealt with foreign, military and financial affairs known as the *secrete besogne*, he in fact had considerable influence over the selection of the committee's members, usually eight in number: two from Holland and one from each of the other six provinces. These deputies were empowered 'without report or consultation to reach such resolution as they deem necessary in the best interests of the Republic'.[7] This meant they were allowed to make autonomous decisions without consulting the full assembly of the States-General or the provincial States; a majority of votes was sufficient to validate a decision. Members of the *secrete besogne* also accompanied Frederik Hendrik on campaign, which was nothing new, since field deputies had accompanied the army under Maurits, providing him with support in 'word and deed' as well as arranging all manner of business of which 'they shall be instructed

---

[5] Fruin, 'Gedenkschrift van Joris de Bye', pp. 439 and 455. See also A.Th. van Deursen, *Maurits van Nassau. De winnaar die faalde*, 4th edn (Amsterdam 2002), pp. 171–2, 194 and 195; Den Tex, *Oldenbarnevelt*, II, pp. 221, 442 and 456.

[6] S. Groenveld, *Verlopend getij. De Nederlandse Republiek en de Engelse burgeroorlog 1640–1646* (Dieren 1984), pp. 77 and 80.

[7] NA, SG 4562, Secret res. SG, 11 September 1626.

by memorandum'. For example, they oversaw the musters together with deputies from the Council of State, and they ensured the provisioning of the troops and the supply of ammunition during sieges.[8] Under Frederik Hendrik such field deputies performed similar duties but were in addition authorised 'to take decisions without consultation with respect to the ... military expedition' in all matters that arose in the field.[9] At the headquarters a decision could also be promulgated without a unanimous vote being required.

While there were good relations between the commander-in-chief and the States of Holland this system worked well, but this ceased to be the case after 1632. Frederik Hendrik's power was based on his influence on the leading regents in the provinces. This élite chose its delegates to the States-General by rotation and therefore also provided the members of the *secrete besogne*. For Holland, however, this approach proved ineffectual, because the province's regents were so numerous they were always sending different delegates to The Hague and it was therefore not within the stadholder's powers to ensure that only compliant delegates from Holland occupied the seats on the Generality committees.[10]

Sieges dominated warfare in the early modern era, particularly in northern Italy and the Low Countries, two densely populated regions with many fortified towns. Administration, trade and industry were concentrated in towns, so their conquest yielded great political and economic advantage. As a town dominated the surrounding countryside, 'contributions' or 'fire-taxes' could be levied in the wide environs. These war contributions were imposed on the population in areas governed by the enemy. In September 1632 the field deputy Cornelis van Terestein (1579–1643) informed the States-General about the taking of the town of Limbourg: 'Here it was understood by the most capable for a great victory, not because of the place's strength but because of the contributions and other considerations. All the time I have abbots, prelates, monks, also nobles and private individuals [i.e. farmers and villagers] coming to visit me in order to come under contribution.'[11] This contribution bought them a safeguard against plunder and pillage.

Besides their political and financial significance, towns were of great military import. Garrisons could thwart an enemy advance for a long time, and though an enemy force could bypass a town this entailed the risk of supply lines being severed. The majority of towns were situated alongside waterways, along which armies transported their siege artillery; a garrison still had to be neutralised, even when the army of the invader had nothing to fear from it in a strictly military sense. There was no advantage to be gained from bypassing a town, for without

---

[8] NA, RAZH, FAvS 239, Extract res. SG, 13 July 1600, appendix 'Memorie voor deze vijf gedeputeerden te velde'.
[9] NA, RAZH, FAvS 239, 'Extract uyt de commissie voor de heren gedeputeerden om sijn Excell. [Frederik Hendrik] te velde t'assisteren', 4 May 1635.
[10] Groenveld, *Verlopend getij*, pp. 83–4.
[11] NA, SG 4961, Cornelis van Terestein to the SG, Liège, 10 September 1632.

artillery the advance would inevitably grind to a halt at the next stronghold. Hence both the Dutch and the Spanish attached great importance to fortified towns. Occasionally fortifications of towns that were difficult to defend were demolished to prevent the enemy being able to use them as bases to launch attacks. For example, Maurits ordered the dismantling of the defensive works of Enschede and Ootmarsum in 1597, and those of Oldenzaal in 1626.[12]

There is a stark contrast between the importance attributed to pitched battles during the early modern era and in the nineteenth and twentieth centuries. In the early modern era they were seen as a means of opening the door to further conquests or of checking an enemy offensive and not as the object of a military operation. The fear of losing a pitched battle generally prompted Dutch commanders to proceed with extreme caution. Though Maurits, Willem Lodewijk and Frederik Hendrik could be commended for never suffering a defeat in open battle – unlike Stadholder William III – it must immediately be noted that they were spared this because they avoided every risk, with the adverse consequence that their strategic options were severely limited. The battle of Nieuwpoort (2 July 1600), Maurits's most renowned feat of arms, was a victory reluctantly gained. Just once, in July 1602, did Maurits and Willem Lodewijk attempt to draw the Spanish into a pitched battle. The reason for this was that they saw no other means of giving the campaign a successful turn, but the Spaniards refused to be drawn.[13] According to the Gelderland politician Alexander van der Capellen (1592–1656), the Twelve Years' Truce caused the Dutch officers' taste for combat to flag even further. 'The Truce and the comfort corrupt our soldiers so seriously that they hardly ever think about doing harm to the enemy, but only how they might live long and draw good pay', he sneered in 1624.[14] Frederik Hendrik's caution assumed exaggerated forms in his later campaigns, prompting a Dutch colonel to share his concerns with Willem Frederik about such reluctance to leave anything to chance:

> [T]here are hardly any officers, whether of foot or of horse, who have seen any event in the field, but only sieges, where one is solidly entrenched and out of danger of being attacked, which is a wholly different thing to fighting in the field, where one must act well and pay heed to all occurrences and events and not be neglectful.[15]

Frederik Hendrik's reputation as a great captain was so severely at issue that in 1638 François van Aerssen (1572–1641), lord of Sommelsdijk, a confidant of the stadholder, felt it necessary to point out to a French field-marshal that the prince had to proceed with such caution because the Dutch army 'is largely composed of foreigners, whom once broken … would not know how to repair

---

[12] Duyck, II, p. 402; NA, SG 4949, Clant van Lyclema to the SG, Deventer, 10 August 1626.
[13] Duyck, III, pp. 412–13.
[14] Van der Capellen, *Gedenkschriften*, I, p. 290, see also p. 414.
[15] Visser, *Dagboeken van Willem Frederik*, p. 74.

themselves [i.e. find recruits] so quickly'.[16] The reluctance of Maurits and Frederik Hendrik to waste troops in risky engagements was, of course, praiseworthy, but it was not always prudent. Disease and desertion were, as noted, the reason for an army losing a great part of its strength every year, so it was sometimes better to imperil the lives of the troops in order to achieve a military goal rather than lose them later without having made any use of them. 'It is remarkable that our men ... having suffered no fatigue, are so seriously tormented by sickness, death, desertion ... that we would not have been more consumed by such great loss from a battle or siege', noted Van der Capellen in his diary at the end of the 1624 campaign. Van der Capellen thought Maurits and Frederik Hendrik might occasionally venture a greater risk, like truly great captains such as the Spanish general, Ambrogio Spinola (1569–1630). 'Spinola, knowing that the field armies are subject to these inconveniences [i.e. sickness and desertion], in particular his Walloons and Englishmen ... uses them as swiftly as he gets them, as if he were laying them on the butcher's slab'.[17]

When none of the belligerents enjoyed a numerical superiority, a pitched battle was often the only means of breaking a military stalemate. Maurits and Willem Lodewijk were initially spared confrontation with this problem. Their first four campaigns (1591–1594) were among the most successful in the Eighty Years' War, but they were aware that the results achieved were largely due to the weakness of the Spaniards. In August 1596 they informed the States-General that they considered almost twice as many field troops were necessary to be able to match the enemy in the future, 'especially if the enemy were to wage war in two quarters again'.[18] They cautioned that a field army of approximately 6,000 foot and 1,500 horse would no longer be adequate; 12,000 men, or 10,000 at the very least, were required. If necessary this military force could be split into two separate armies. The course of the war meant that only a few years later even this increased strength no longer sufficed. In 1602, Maurits and Willem Lodewijk set out on campaign with approximately 24,000 men. Frederik Hendrik had an average of 20,000 to 25,000 men under his command. The Spanish and French field armies were of similar size.[19] Appendix I provides an overview of the strength of the Dutch field army from 1591 to 1646.

The explanation for the steep increase in the number of Dutch field troops after 1600 must be sought in the transformation of the theatre of war. Maurits and Willem Lodewijk could at first wage war via internal lines of communica-

---

[16] *Archives*, 2nd series, III, no. 534, François van Aerssen-Sommelsdijk to *maréchal* Gaspar de Coligny, duc de Châtillon, The Hague, 10 April 1638.
[17] Van der Capellen, *Gedenkschriften*, I, p. 332.
[18] Duyck, II, Appendix II.
[19] HUA, ASU 314-6, Godard van Reede-Amerongen, before Breda, 5 August 1637; NA, SG 6766, Tieleman Aquilius, agent of the States-General to the French field army in the Spanish Netherlands, before Aire, 4 July 1641, and at Vervins, 13 July 1642; SG 6769, Willem van Lier to the SG, Paris, 20 May 1645; Parrott, *Richelieu's Army*, pp. 190, 203, 205–10 and 220.

tion. They were able to move troops rapidly from north to south and from west to east, and vice versa, via the waterways. The great advantage in this was that a local superiority could be achieved with relatively few men. The Spaniards, on the other hand, were forced to travel great distances over land. After 1600 hostilities were chiefly focused in Brabant and Flanders, the heart of the Southern Netherlands, and the roles were reversed: it was not the Spaniards but the Dutch troops who had to operate far from their bases. Maurits, Willem Lodewijk and Frederik Hendrik hoped to deter their Spanish adversary from putting up any resistance to the Dutch advance by raising as strong a military force as possible, because they remained wary of allowing events to lead to a 'hazardous battle' even though they were in command of over 20,000, 25,000 or occasionally even 30,000 men.[20] Their tendency to avoid any risk was one of the causes of the strategic stalemate in which the war in the Low Countries was mired after the reduction of Maastricht in 1632; the other reason was the Republic's vulnerability to an attack from the east. Spanish troops could easily launch incursions via the Rhine into Gelderland, Overijssel and even the province of Utrecht. The need to protect the eastern front meant that approximately 12,000 troops had to be left behind there in order to defend the Republic's borders. The field army that remained, some 20,000 to 25,000 strong, was insufficient to wage an offensive war. Such numbers were too small to successfully attack an entrenched opponent, which was a prerequisite for being able to force a pitched battle and to lay siege to Antwerp, the gateway to Brabant and Flanders.

According to Willem Lodewijk, 'the enemy ... has learnt so much from [the battle of] Nieuwpoort ... that he will only face us in such an advantageous [position] where he can receive us [i.e. fight] gloriously'.[21] The southern as well as the northern Netherlands were ideally suited to a defensive war: rivers, streams, woodland and marshes offered countless opportunities to establish strong positions.[22] Antwerp was therefore indispensable for an assault on the Spanish Netherlands from the north: control of this city made it possible to use the rivers Scheldt, Leie, Dijle and Demer. A siege of Antwerp was, however, an extremely taxing undertaking, because its investment required two armies, one on the Flanders bank and one on the Brabant bank of the River Scheldt, both of which had to be strong enough to withstand a Spanish relief attempt, requiring a force of 30,000 to 35,000 men in all.[23]

---

[20] NA, SG 4949, Frederik Hendrik to the SG, Millingen, 19 September 1626.
[21] Veenendaal, *Oldenbarnevelt*, II, no. 6, Willem Lodewijk, 29 March 1602.
[22] Jamel Ostwald, 'The "Decisive" Battle of Ramillies, 1706: Prerequisites for Decisiveness in Early Modern Warfare', *Journal of Military History*, LXIV (July 2000), 649–77, esp. p. 660.
[23] NA, SG 4562, Secret res. SG, 8 April 1631.

The campaign and the logistical organisation of the Dutch army

The campaign plan for the coming year was outlined during the winter. Once the operational goal was decided – usually the reduction of a particular town – preparations for the campaign could begin. Preparing the train demanded most effort. The Dutch army included the troops and the ordnance, but the majority of the artillery personnel, the waggoners, the draught horses, the provisions and baggage waggons and the transport ships had to be hired anew for each campaign. This was the Council of State's responsibility. In September 1605 the Council calculated that 672 waggons, 314 draught horses and 200 transport ships were needed for Maurits to be able to move the Dutch army swiftly.[24] In July 1627 the munitions, provisions and baggage of the Dutch field army were transported on 1,012 waggons,[25] and four years later some 894 waggons and 232 ships were needed.[26] After the conclusion of the 1634 campaign, the Council of State informed the States-General that, besides 'many' ships, some 1,250 waggons and 800 draught horses had been hired, the former at a rate of three guilders a day and the latter at one guilder.[27]

Maurits, Willem Lodewijk and Frederik Hendrik rarely launched military operations before late May or early June. The reason for this was that it allowed them to take advantage of the fresh, vitamin-rich grass essential to restoring the strength of the horses after their extended sojourn in stables. After the horses had spent a few weeks in the meadow, the captains and rittmasters received an order to proceed to the rendezvous with their companies. On arrival at this assembly point the companies were merged into battalions and regiments and then divided among the three 'hosts': the vanguard, the main battle (*bataille*), and the rearguard. The three hosts switched names every day, 'according to the change in their marching in the van or to the rear', otherwise the same troops would always be the last to arrive at the encampment and would have to make do with the least enviable places. The artillery and the munition waggons were positioned with the vanguard, so that they were immediately at hand when combat was called for. The baggage waggons, on the other hand, travelled between the main battle and the rearguard, the safest place. If the enemy was to the rear of the army then this order was reversed: the baggage behind the vanguard and the artillery and munitions with the rearguard.

Contrary to what their designations might lead one to expect, the vanguard, main battle and rearguard were not the first, second and third line of the battle

---

[24] NA, SG 4911, RvS to the SG, Deventer, 13 September 1605, appendix.
[25] NA, SG 4951, 'Staet van[de] verdeelinghe van de legherwaghens jegenwoordich te velde zijnde', 25 July 1627.
[26] NA, SG 4959, 'Staet in 't corte van de verdeelinge van de legerwagens gemonstert den 7.en july 1631'.
[27] NA, SG 4965, 'Memorie van 'tgeene 't leger in 't jaer 1634 bij raminge heeft gecost ende daer beneffens vuyt de legerpenningen is bet[aald] geworden', 3 November 1634.

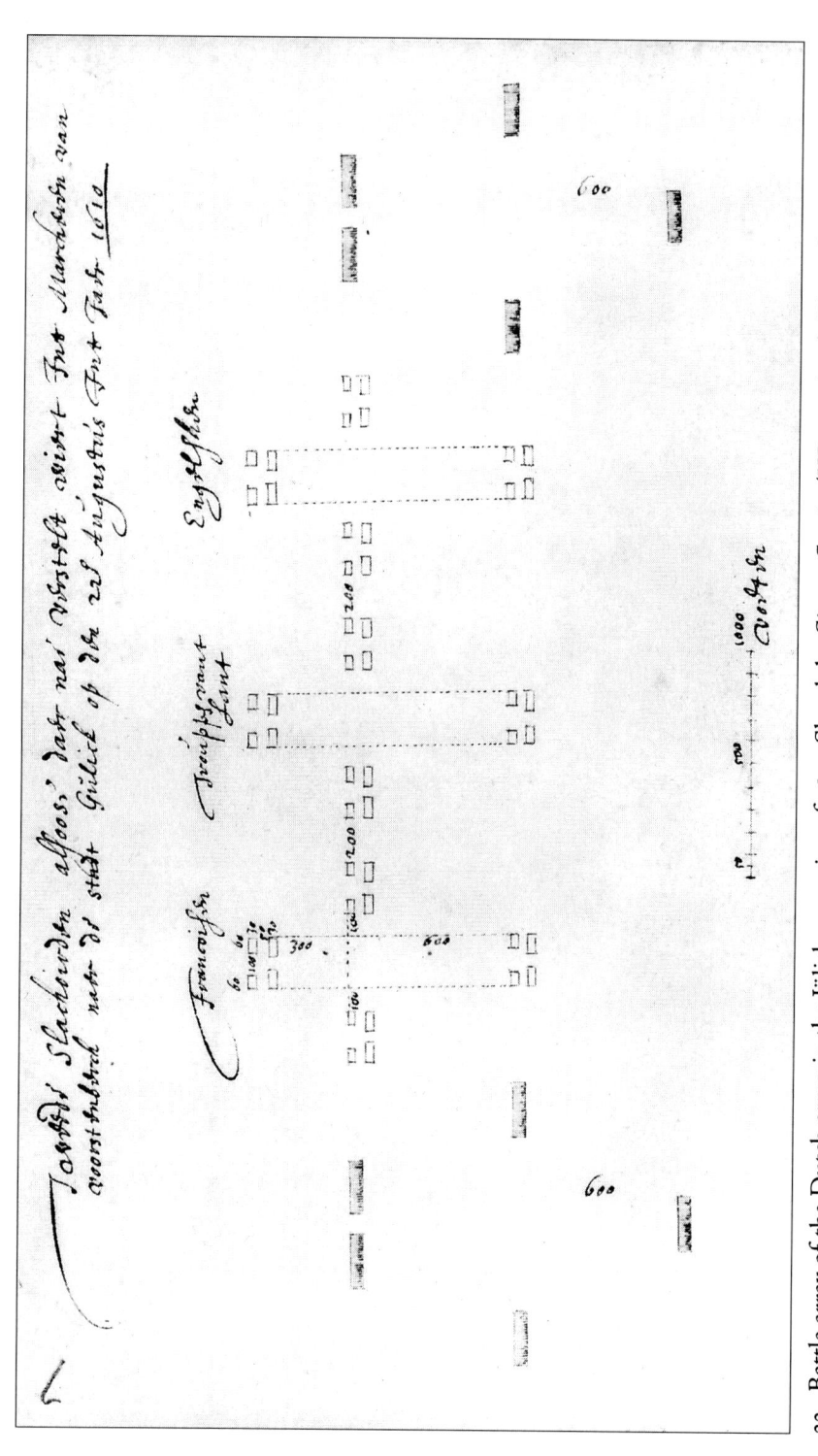

22. Battle array of the Dutch army in the Jülich campaign of 1610. Sketch by Simon Stevin (KB, 128-A-19). The infantry regiments are arrayed in the centre and the cavalry on either flank.

order. According to Simon Stevin this was unfeasible, because the regiments of each host would then be 'spread too widely from one another to be managed properly by a single commander under whose orders they stand'. The troops refused to follow orders from any commander other than the one in charge of their host. Stevin informs us that with the Dutch army being composed of different nations this was important:

> [For] if the main battle, which is possibly of another nation or countryfolk, yea possibly natural enemies of the foremost [i.e. the first battle line] (as happens on occasion), [and] the second battle line were to go to the aid and rescue of the first, then it would be of concern that such different nations would not provide proper care to save one another. It certainly does not seem to be safe enough to allow it to come to this, as one might if the first and second battle line are of one and the same nation and stand under orders of a single head.

It was therefore advisable, Stevin continues, to arrange each host in a formation that was three lines deep: the main battle in the centre of the battle array and the vanguard and rearguard on either flank. The cavalry was divided in two and positioned on the left and right flank of the battle order.[28]

Prior to the Napoleonic Era it was usual for the various parts of the army to remain close together during the march. If the enemy was close by then they marched in battle array. The quartermasters were responsible for mapping out the line of march, but there was a distinct lack of organisation *en route*. 'One must also be aware that this army undertakes such short daily journeys that it can (at most) cover no more than two leagues [11 to 12 kilometres] in one day, even though one begins to march at about two or three o'clock in the morning', noted Fredrich van Vervou (1550–1621), steward to Willem Lodewijk, regarding the campaign of 1602.[29] In the sixteenth and seventeenth centuries troops did not march in step, so each column eventually fragmented into small groups of soldiers. Despite the short distances covered daily, a heatwave during the summer could take a heavy toll on the troops. On 10 July 1602, Duyck recorded in his journal that another forty soldiers had fallen dead by the wayside because of the heat that day, and 'a further 5 or 6,000 people were left lying in the corn on the way',[30] too exhausted to keep on walking.

As soon as the troops arrived at a place where they would remain for some time they started building huts with straw roofs. For the sake of convenience they used the roofs of the farmhouses in the vicinity. In his *Castrametatio, dat is legermeting* (*Castrametatio, that is the Marking out of Army Camps*),[31] published in 1617, Simon Stevin describes the Dutch encampment that Maurits and

---

[28] KB, HS 128-A-18, Simon Stevin, 'Van de oirden der slachoirden', fol. 2v (quote); KB, HS 128-A-9II, fol. 93, 'De manier van reysen eens legers te verclaren'.
[29] Vervou, *Enige gedenckweerdige geschiedenissen*, p. 131.
[30] Duyck, III, p. 414.
[31] Schukking (ed.), *The Principal Works of Simon Stevin*, presents the facsimile with a parallel English translation and commentary. See vol. IV, *The Art of War*, pp. 261–397.

Willem Lodewijk established before Jülich in 1610 in detail. Maurits and Willem Lodewijk strove to follow the Roman model in this regard as well, but given that the strengths of the companies and regiments were not of 'a similar constitution', which had been the case with Roman legions, concessions were necessary. The headquarters, the artillery and the ammunition supplies were positioned in the middle of the Dutch camp, the most secure place. The various regiments set up camp round about, resulting in a large rectangle. The camp was protected against a surprise attack by an earthen wall with a ditch measuring eight feet wide and six feet deep to the fore of it. The soldiers were obliged to work on entrenching their own quarters for no extra pay but had to be paid separately for all other tasks, which was highly lucrative for them: as workmen the soldiers earned a daily wage of no less than ten stivers, which was double their daily advance. Stevin disapproved of this policy, since many soldiers were only interested in money, 'and there are many who have not once in their lives held a shovel or spade in their hands, in particular the French, who instead of working spend most of the time laughing and playing, for one Frisian or other hardworking man can do more in a day than four Frenchmen, which I have learnt from experience.'[32]

Under the supervision of the field deputies, the commissary of the victuals (*commis van de vivres*) and the provost-general, a market square was set up within the camp where the sutlers could proffer their wares to the soldiers. Only tradespeople who had been granted a licence by the commissary of the victuals were allowed to 'suttle', and they were obliged to use weights and measures issued by the provost-general for the weighing of their merchandise. If it came to light that a vendor had cheated the soldiers by using 'completely false measure' then the provost ordered all his goods to be seized and sold them, 'one half to the profit of the poor and the other half to the regiment'. The sutler himself was handed over to the advocate-general 'to be arbitrarily punished'.[33] In 1632 the rules for suttling were tightened and limits were imposed on the number of traders per company. In previous campaigns it had too often transpired that the 'great crowd of victuallers' that followed the Dutch army had caused serious nuisance because of 'the considerable disorderliness perpetrated by these people'. From then on only those sutlers who had received a licence from the colonel were allowed to attend upon a company, and their number was limited to a maximum of two for a standard infantry company and three for a larger colonel's company. The sutlers were obliged to follow the troops everywhere for the duration of

---

[32] NA, RvS 2287, Instructions for the artillery. The anonymous compiler was in all probability Simon Stevin. In terms of content it is largely the same as 'Beschrijvinge van[de] officieren ende offitiën der Grootmoegende Heeren Staeten-General ... bij de artillerie ende munitie van oorloghe te velde gedient hebende' (KHA, A13-IX-6), the manuscript which Henricus Hondius used for his *Korte beschrijvinge ende afbeeldinge van de generale regelen der fortificatie* (The Hague 1624).

[33] *Groot Placaetboeck*, II (The Hague 1664), p. 186, 'Placaet raeckende alle legerpersoonen', 7 May 1631, art. XVII–XIX, XXIII–XXVI.

the campaign, for which they had to equip themselves with a robust waggon or cart. In exchange they enjoyed the exclusive right to set up stalls to the rear of the company quarters in the camp. Farmers and hawkers who came to the army camp to proffer their wares had to register with the provost-general, whereupon they were assigned a spot on the general marketplace.[34]

Soldiers' rations consisted primarily of bread, beer, cheese, butter, bacon and salt herring. Market prices in the nearby towns served as the benchmark for the price of the foodstuffs. To encourage the supply of foodstuffs, the field deputies could pronounce exemption from duties, which meant that all goods could be transported to the army camp without being subject to tolls or other levies.[35] Traders who were attacked by the enemy or by pillaging and plundering soldiers *en route* and managed to escape with their lives were sometimes awarded compensation for some of the damages suffered.[36] If the road to the army camp became too dangerous to travel alone, the sutlers were assembled into convoys of a few hundred waggons and brought to their destination under military escort.[37]

Providing the troops with bread demanded the greatest organisational effort, because during the summer months its storage life was limited to six days, eight at the very most; while in the autumn it remained edible for a day or two longer.[38] The baking and distribution of bread was the responsibility of the commissary of the victuals. Dutch soldiers bought fresh bread every day, unless their commanders ordered them to stock up for three to six days at once, so that the army could continue marching for a while without delay. If the supplies had to last longer than six days then each company was assigned a waggon on which the extra provisions were loaded. Part of these usually consisted of rusk, a rye bread that was re-fired to keep longer.[39] When the Dutch army operated near its own or neutral towns the bread was produced by local bakers and transported to the camp by waggon or ship, either by the bakers themselves or by sutlers. In 1627, for example, the army before Groenlo was supplied from Deventer, Arnhem and Doesburg, and two years later the bread for the besiegers of 's-Hertogenbosch was baked in Heusden.[40] During the siege of Jülich in 1610, the commissary of the victuals, one Nicasius Kien, initially baked the bread using flour he had stockpiled for the army, but it could be produced much more cheaply using locally grown grain, 'because there is an abundance of grain here in the

---

[34] Ibid., pp. 361–2, 'Ordonnantiën voor de soetelaers 't leger volgende', 2 March 1632, revised 1 July 1637.
[35] NA, SG 4971, Field deputies to the SG, Ginneken, evening of 5 August 1637.
[36] Duyck, III, p. 354 n. 1, Res. SG, 14 May 1602.
[37] NA, SG 4949, Ernst Casimir and the field deputies to Frederik Hendrik, before Oldenzaal, 25 July 1626, transcript; SG 4951, Field deputies to the SG, Zutphen, 9 August 1627.
[38] Van Nimwegen, *Subsistentie*, p. 11.
[39] Duyck, I, p. 394; NA, SG 4982, Field deputies to the SG, Sas van Gent, 4 July, before the Nieuwerhavense Gat, 9 August 1645.
[40] NA, SG 4951, Field deputies to the SG, Zutphen, 6 August 1627; SG 4953, Field deputies to the SG, Crevecoeur, 3 May 1629.

countryside, so the farmers are threshing with great diligence and the grain is being milled in two watermills situated here on the River Ruhr'. On realising this, Kien 'immediately stopped baking' with flour from the army's stockpile.[41] Under such favourable conditions a small 'ammunition-loaf' of three pounds, which was sufficient for two days, was supposed to cost two stivers, but if there was any shortage the price could increase to two or even two-and-a-half stivers per pound.[42] A 'shortage of proviant' during the siege of Coevorden in 1592 so severely inflated the price of bread that most Dutch soldiers could not afford it, and 'oftentimes had to be contented with a drink of water'.[43] The Spanish government cared better for its troops in this respect. Spanish soldiers were, moreover, protected against exorbitant food prices. 'For the enemy, the ammunition-bread always [remains] ... at one price', Maurits reported in 1622. Spanish troops never had to pay more than three stivers for a loaf of three pounds.[44]

The supply of foodstuffs became truly problematic when an army penetrated deep into hostile territory. In 1600, when Maurits advanced along the Flemish coast to Dunkirk with a military force of about 12,000 men, the States-General tried to guarantee the supply of bread by ordering a huge quantity to be baked and sending it ahead to Ostend by ship. This measure did not achieve the desired outcome, because even though part of the shipment was distributed among the soldiers, 'the greatest portion (because it could not remain fresh for long) was thrown overboard, at great cost to the Land'.[45] There were grave consequences. After the battle of Nieuwpoort, the Dutch army was left without food 'because all the ships had departed and during the battle the men had thrown away the vivres distributed to them'.[46] Despite achieving victory there was no option but to set out on the journey home. This experience made it obvious to Maurits that a successful campaign in the Southern Netherlands was only feasible if the logistics were properly organised.

In 1602, when on Van Oldenbarnevelt's insistence it was decided to launch an attack into Spanish Brabant in the hope of forcing the Spaniards to break up the siege of Ostend, Maurits ensured that the provisions necessary to supply 20,000 men with bread on a daily basis were calculated precisely.[47] After all, they could not depend on the necessary mills and ovens being available in enemy territory. The defending party often rendered windmills and watermills in the countryside inoperable by removing the axles and tearing down the sails. Sometimes they

---

[41] NA, SG 4921, Nicasius Kien to the SG, before Jülich, 10 August 1610.
[42] Vervou, *Enige gedenckweerdige geschiedenissen*, p. 131.
[43] Tresoar, FSA 321, Captains of the Frisian regiment to the States of Friesland, 1592.
[44] NA, SG 4941, Maurits to the States of Zeeland, 16 August 1622, transcript; Parker, *Army of Flanders*, p. 163.
[45] KHA, A13-IX-6, 'Beschrijvinge', chapter on 'Vivres'.
[46] Duyck, II, p. 680.
[47] KHA, A13-IX-6, 'Beschrijvinge', chapter on 'Vivres', with lists.

even resorted to breaking the millstones or razed the whole structure.[48] In 1602 the Dutch army therefore took along its own mills and ovens, so that it would always be possible to bake sufficient bread. Six horse-driven mills and twenty iron field-ovens had to guarantee the supply of the Dutch army's daily bread. With a horse-powered mill it was possible for eight animals and two millers to mill one last of corn per day. A single last was sufficient for an average of 900 'ammunition-loaves' of six pounds and each ammunition-loaf was sufficient for four soldiers' portions of one and a half pounds. A field-oven was six feet long, four and a half feet wide, and twelve or thirteen inches in height. Before using them for baking, these iron ovens had to be covered with clay or loam. 'When baking long loaves of six pounds in weight such an oven can easily bake five times, namely taking six hours for the first bake, and for the other four bakes, which will be hotter, it takes a good four hours each.' With a field-oven of this type it was possible to bake 2,000 pounds of bread in twenty-four hours. The capacity of twenty ovens was therefore more than sufficient for the 30,000 pounds of bread required per day. It required a total of twelve millers to grind the corn, forty masons to set the ovens up and seventy-two bakers to operate them. The transportation of all the necessary materials, including baking equipment, corn measures and breadbins, required 150 waggons, including twenty waggons laden with reserve parts to be able to repair twelve windmills while on the road. Distribution of the ammunition loaves to the troops was supervised by the commissary of the victuals. The company commanders had to sign for the loaves and the cost of the bread supplied was deducted from the pay ordinances based on these receipts.[49]

Despite all the preparations, the logistics during the 1602 campaign ran completely amok. The problem was not so much a lack of sufficient milling and baking capacity, but the availability of grain. It was impossible to transport grain on waggons for the whole duration of the campaign. Much greater quantities of grain could be transported by ship, but this was not an option at the time: Antwerp blocked access to the River Scheldt, so Brabant could only be entered from the east. Before setting out on the campaign, Maurits therefore ordered the milling of 100 lasts of rye and had the flour loaded onto waggons in tuns. This quantity was intended as a reserve that could provide the Dutch army with bread for twenty days in case of an unforeseen delay, but the flour and grain for everyday use would have to be bought or gathered *in situ*. To reduce the risk involved in this, the States-General had ordered the stockpiling of a large quantity of corn in Tongeren (Tongres) and Sint-Truiden (Saint-Trond), which were places under Spanish control, using a local merchant as a front. The plan was that the Dutch troops would stock up with bread for a whole ten days at

---

[48] NA, SG 4941, Justinus van Nassau to the RvS, Breda, 10 August 1622; SG 4954, H. van Eck to the SG, Wageningen, 5 September 1629; KHA, A23-VII-C-564, Jehan Foutlau, commander of the garrison at 's Gravenweert, to Ernst Casimir, 27 July 1629.
[49] KHA, A13-IX-6, 'Beschrijvinge', chapter on 'Vivres', with lists.

the start of the march and would be able to get by on this until these two places were reached.[50] Once the army had re-stocked with provisions the march would continue to Louvain, which would have to serve as a base for the onward march. Willem Lodewijk had warned Van Oldenbarnevelt that the Spaniards could easily disrupt the supply lines between the Dutch army and the Republic, and the food supplies for the Dutch troops could not be guaranteed unless they took this major town. By subsequently occupying Aarschot, Herentals and Hoogstraten it would be possible to establish a new supply line with Breda.[51]

Maurits and Willem Lodewijk set out on the march to Louvain on 22 June 1602. Their 24,000-strong army was followed by a train of more than 3,000 waggons carrying baggage and victuals. Yet mere days after the start of the journey it became evident that it would be impossible to reach Tongeren and Sint-Truiden without first distributing fresh bread, because the English troops had sold their bread to the local population *en route*,[52] and as a result they 'are at the end of their vivres sooner than the others'.[53] This meant new bread had to be baked before they could proceed, but the baking capacity required was unavailable in the immediate vicinity. In Maaseik, the nearest town, there were only four bread ovens. Though Maurits gave the order to make ready ten or so field-ovens,[54] the resulting loss of time could no longer be made up. The Dutch army could not resume its advance until 2 July 1602. It reached Tongeren two days later, but by then it had missed the window of opportunity to press on to Louvain; in the meantime the Spaniards had established a strong position near Tienen (Tirlemont), blocking the line of march. Following consultation with Willem Lodewijk, the English general, Sir Francis Vere and the field deputies, Maurits decided to press on to Sint-Truiden all the same, in the hope that the Spaniards would meet him to protect this small town. On 7 July 1602 the Dutch army reached Sint-Truiden without incident, but the storehouses there turned out to contain no more than sixteen lasts of corn, sufficient for just three days. Moreover, the Spaniards had remained in their positions at Tienen. On 10 July, Maurits therefore gave the order to withdraw to the River Meuse.[55] The invasion of Brabant was scuppered. Frederik Hendrik made a fresh attempt to invade the Spanish Netherlands from the east in 1635, but this also failed. Louvain had proven to be beyond reach yet again.

The campaigns of 1600, 1602 and 1635 were exceptional; the Dutch army usually operated at a short distance from its bases. In March 1602, Willem Lodewijk had already 'frankly' informed Van Oldenbarnevelt that he could

---

[50] Duyck, III, pp. 384 and 388.
[51] Veenendaal, *Oldenbarnevelt*, II, no. 6, Willem Lodewijk to Van Oldenbarnevelt, 29 March 1602.
[52] Duyck, III, p. 396.
[53] NA, SG 4903, Field deputies to the SG, Aldeneik (a monastery near Maaseik), 1 July 1602.
[54] KHA, A22-IX-A1-221a, Maurits to Willem Lodewijk, Aldeneik, 27 June 1602.
[55] Duyck, III, pp. 408–14.

not comprehend how one could support an army of more than 20,000 men 'at a two-day journey from our frontiers (even though the season of the year was so far advanced that one could grind the corn with hand-mills and quern-mills[56]) without it [the army] consuming and destroying itself within 14 days or 3 weeks'.[57] Willem Lodewijk's prediction may well have been more pessimistic than the reality, but by August 1602 the Dutch army was still a couple of thousand men weaker than at the start of the expedition in June.[58] Frederik Hendrik continued to amass stockpiles of rye and set up field-ovens at regular intervals during his campaigns, but only during siege operations. In August 1629 he gave the order to purchase 400 lasts of rye flour 'as speedily as possible' and have it transported to the siege camp before 's-Hertogenbosch. Three years later, during the siege of Maastricht, the bread for the Dutch troops was baked in Liège, but the field deputies purchased an additional 300 lasts of rye and had it milled as quickly as possible. In 1637 Frederik Hendrik gave the order to establish a stock of flour complete with ovens in Terheiden, a small town at a short distance from Breda, the town to which he was laying siege. The stockpile, some 300 lasts of rye flour, was sufficient to feed the Dutch siege army of 24,000 men for a month and a half.[59] He thereby prevented the Spaniards being able to force him to abandon this siege by cutting off supplies to the Dutch army.[60]

Hunger was calamitous for an army. Because of the minimal nutritional value of the food and the monotonous diet – vegetables were hardly ever eaten – armies were particularly susceptible to infectious diseases. In October 1632 the field deputies warned The Hague 'that diseases in the army are increasingly prevalent'. New cases of pestilence and 'bloody flux' (dysentery) were skyrocketing, 'due to which every day a great number of soldiers and more than prudence allows us to mention ... collapse. There are many companies of horse and of foot who have twenty, thirty and more sick.'[61] In armies of the early modern era the hygiene and medical assistance were poor. There were no other measures besides the prohibition to do one's 'easement' anywhere in the camp but for 'the place ordained' and the requirement to bury the entrails of slaughtered animals outside the camp perimeter.[62] Sick and wounded soldiers were usually lodged in municipal hospices for a fee of four stivers per day. The Spaniards had a military

---

[56] Three men were needed to operate a 'quern' or hand-mill, 'namely two to turn the mill and one to attach and detach the sack, also to attend to the corn and flour. And should the quern have to be turned continually then it would be necessary to refresh the aforementioned three men with a similar number from time to time, amounting to six men for each quern, which one would be permitted to draw from the regiments or companies.' With four querns it was possible to mill one last of corn per day. See NA, RAZH, AJvO 2953, Memorandum.
[57] Veenendaal, *Oldenbarnevelt*, II, no. 6, Willem Lodewijk, 29 March 1602.
[58] Duyck, III, pp. 389–90 and 431–2.
[59] NA, SG 4971, Field deputies to the SG, Ginneken, 1 and 5 August 1637.
[60] NA, SG 4960, Field deputies to the SG, Liège, 12 June 1632.
[61] NA, SG 4961, Field deputies to the SG, Maastricht, 26 October 1632.
[62] *Groot Placaetboeck*, II, pp. 185–6, art. XI and XXI.

hospital with 330 beds in Mechelen (Malines),[63] but it was the last quarter of the seventeenth century before such facilities were available for Dutch troops. The hospices could cope with a limited influx of sick and wounded soldiers, but they were not geared to cope with an epidemic or a bloody battle. Alexander van der Capellen thought it a disgrace

> that we do not provide the soldiers who leave the army in ill health, seeing as they have risked their lives for us and contracted the diseases in our service, with shelter and good care ... that one leaves them lying in the churches in straw, where there are neither windows nor beds or any conveniences, where the women lie alongside the men and ... where the women must deliver their children alongside and in view of all the men.[64]

There were no special vehicles for the transportation of the wounded from battlefield to hospice. Wounded soldiers were simply loaded onto supply waggons or transported by cargo ship. Light injuries could be treated effectively, but when bones in arms or legs were shattered the only thing that could save the patient from death was amputation of the limb. Amputations were the most common operation, especially during sieges; in the initial months of the siege of Ostend alone, the arms and legs of more than 500 wounded defenders were sawn off. One eye-witness noted that the casualties were 'treated somewhat carelessly by the surgeons, which was to be lamented, but in the initial confusion it was impossible to establish the order that needs required.'[65] Because of their mass, cannon-balls smashed limbs to smithereens. Musket-balls caused less serious injuries, but a hit to the abdomen or chest was usually fatal because the simultaneous introduction of dirt into the wound caused infection.

Fortifications and siege warfare

At the outbreak of the Revolt only a few towns and strongholds in the Low Countries were fortified using low, thick ramparts with bastions and ditches, according to the latest insights.[66] This situation altered completely within a few years. By the end of the sixteenth century, the *trace italienne* was to be found throughout the Low Countries, albeit in a form adapted to local topography.[67] Instead of sheer defensive works revetted with stone, both the Dutch rebels and the Spaniards constructed bastions and ramparts solely of earth. This construc-

---

[63] Parker, *Army of Flanders*, p. 167.
[64] Van der Capellen, *Gedenkschriften*, I, p. 119.
[65] Fleming, *Oostende*, p. 135.
[66] The fort of Rammekens near Vlissingen is a fine extant example.
[67] For the following see Wijn, *Krijgswezen*, pp. 252–76; Christopher Duffy, *Siege Warfare. The Fortress in the Early Modern World 1494–1660* (London 1979); Olaf van Nimwegen, 'Maurits van Nassau and Siege Warfare (1590–1597)', in Marco van der Hoeven (ed.), *Exercise of Arms. Warfare in the Netherlands, 1568–1648* (Leiden 1997), pp. 113–31, esp. 118–20.

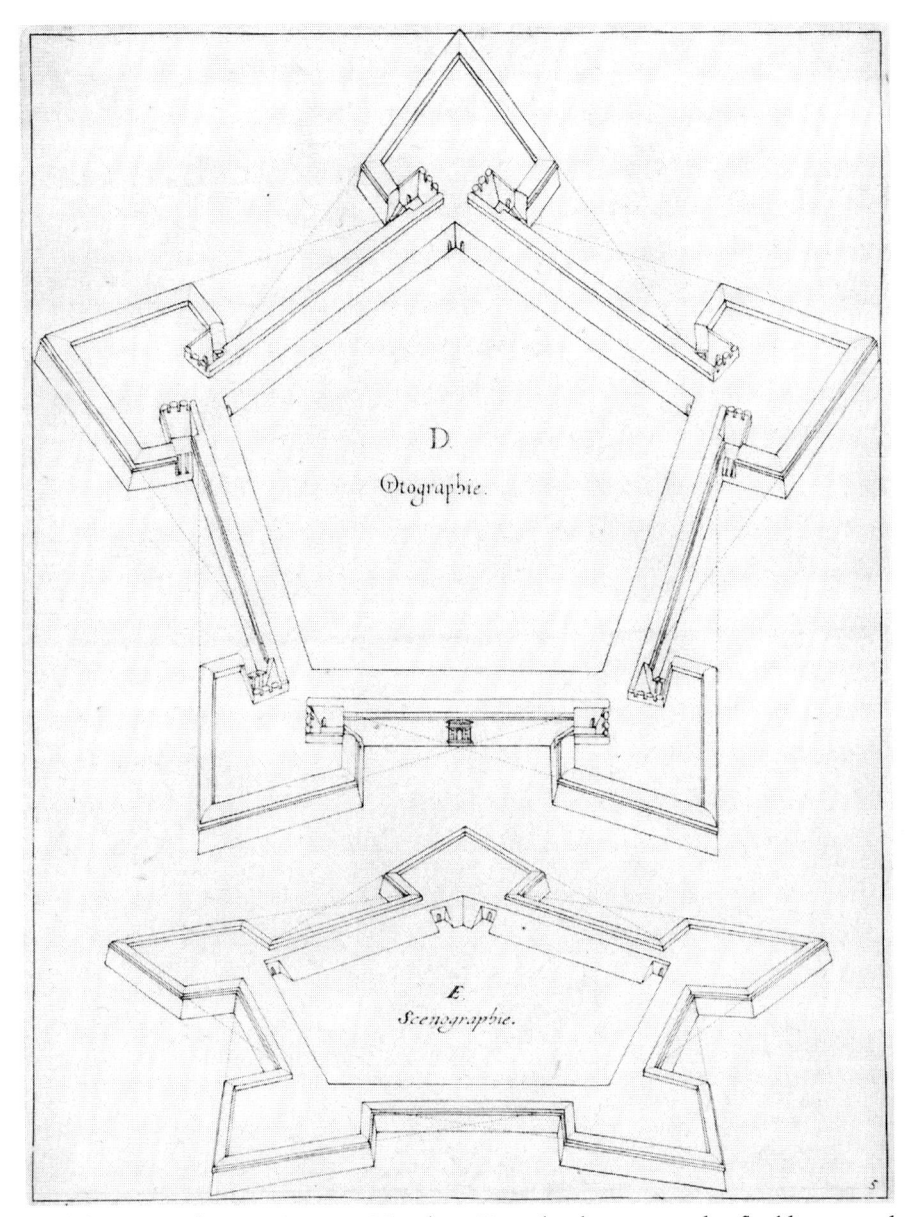

23. The *trace italienne*. Henricus Hondius, *Korte beschrijvinge ende afbeeldinge van de generale regelen der fortificatie* (The Hague 1624). (KB, 2108-A-2)

24. Plan view and profile section of the Old Netherlandish System of fortification. Hondius, *Korte beschrijvinge ende afbeeldinge van de generale regelen der fortificatie* (The Hague 1624) (KB 2108-A-2). From left to right, the section shows the glacis, the covered way, the ditch, the fausse-braye and the main rampart.

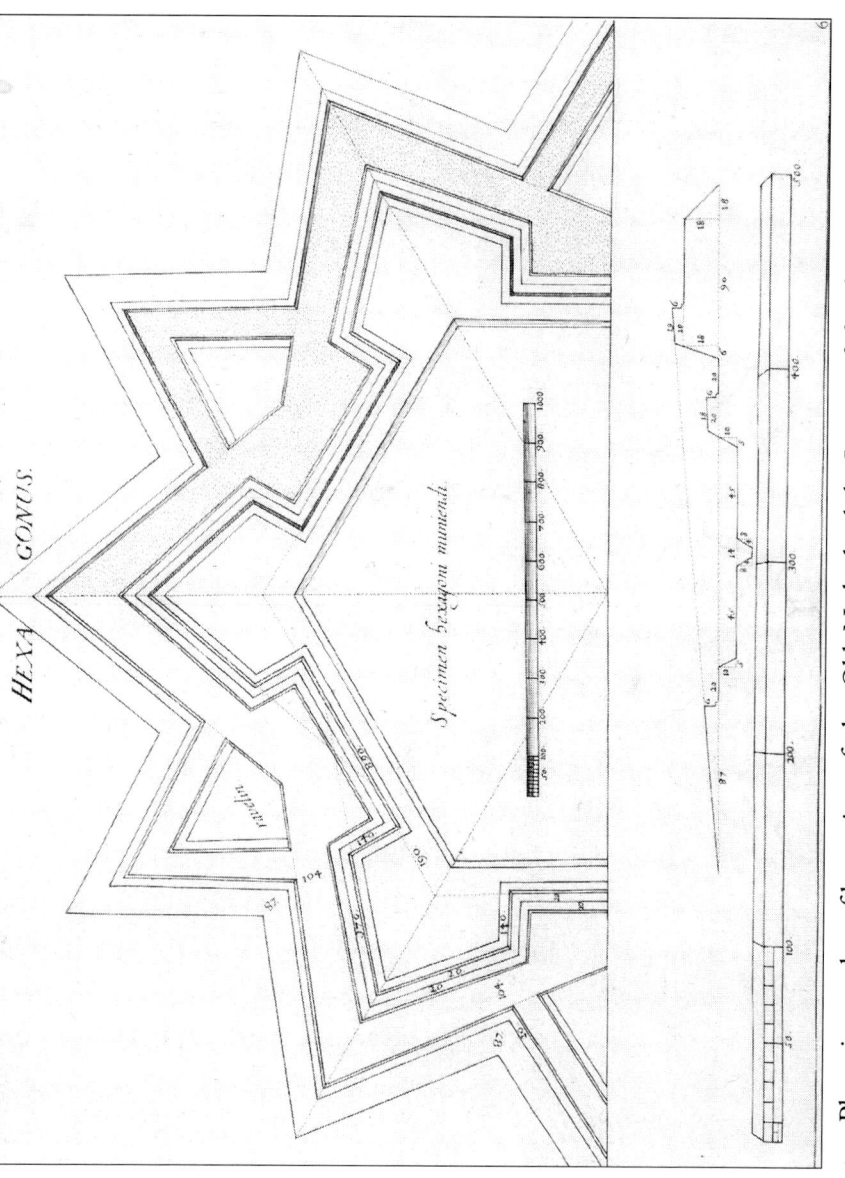

tion method was much less expensive and could be realised swiftly. A wet ditch was intended to prevent the attacker attempting to take the stronghold by storm. The addition of outworks afforded protection in the form of horizontal depth rather than vertical height. Characteristic features of the 'Old Netherlandish System', as this fortification method came to be known, were the bastions set at an interval equivalent to the range of a musket shot – 300 paces or 225 metres[68] – a fausse-braye, a wet ditch with ravelins, a continuous covered way along the outer edge of the ditch, and hornworks.

Bastions were the mainstay of the defences. A bastion is a five-sided structure comprised of two outward-looking 'faces' that meet in a point (the 'salient') and two flanks that connect it to the main wall. The faces could accommodate several pieces of artillery so that an approaching assailant could be fired on from a distance, while the flanks made it possible for the defenders to enfilade the faces of adjacent bastions and the curtain, the section of rampart between two bastions. The fausse-braye is a breastwork running along the foot of the main wall from which musketeers could defend the ditch. Ravelins are diamond-shaped works that were primarily intended to be able to cover the curtain and to support the adjacent bastions with outflanking fire from cannon and musket. The bastions, in turn, enfilade the ravelins, and these were lower than the main rampart, which therefore dominated them.

The 'covered way' made it possible for the garrison to defend from the outer edge of the ditch. This outwork is formed by a continuous pathway that runs parallel to the ditch. The covered way was protected from view by the 'glacis', an extended parapet with a depth of fifty to sixty-five paces that is 'the height of a man, sloping down to the outside … until it gradually disappears into the field.'[69] A palisade was placed just behind the crown of the glacis, a fence of pointed stakes that projected slightly above the ground. The covered way gave the garrison three important advantages. First, from this covered position it was possible to launch sorties to the trenches of the besieger. Secondly, the crown of the glacis obstructed the attacker's view of the foot of the main wall, so they could only start breaching the rampart with cannon-fire after gaining control of the covered way. Thirdly, this outwork meant the garrison was not crowded together in the fortress proper, thus reducing the likelihood of diseases and the impact of bombardments. The hornworks were the last component of the Old Netherlandish System and consisted of two demi-bastions joined to the covered way by long wings.

Until 1600 or so, most towns and cities were protected only by bastions and ravelins. The turning point came during the siege of Ostend (1601–1604), which was to a large extent dominated by the struggle for the outworks. In early

---

[68] 'One reckons that a musket shoots 300 paces level … the pace reckoned at 2 1/2 feet.' See Wijn, *Het Staatsche leger*, VIII, iii, p. 351, with Pier Willem van Sytzama, 'Militair Memorie-Boeck', as an appendix.
[69] Wijn, *Krijgswezen*, p. 273.

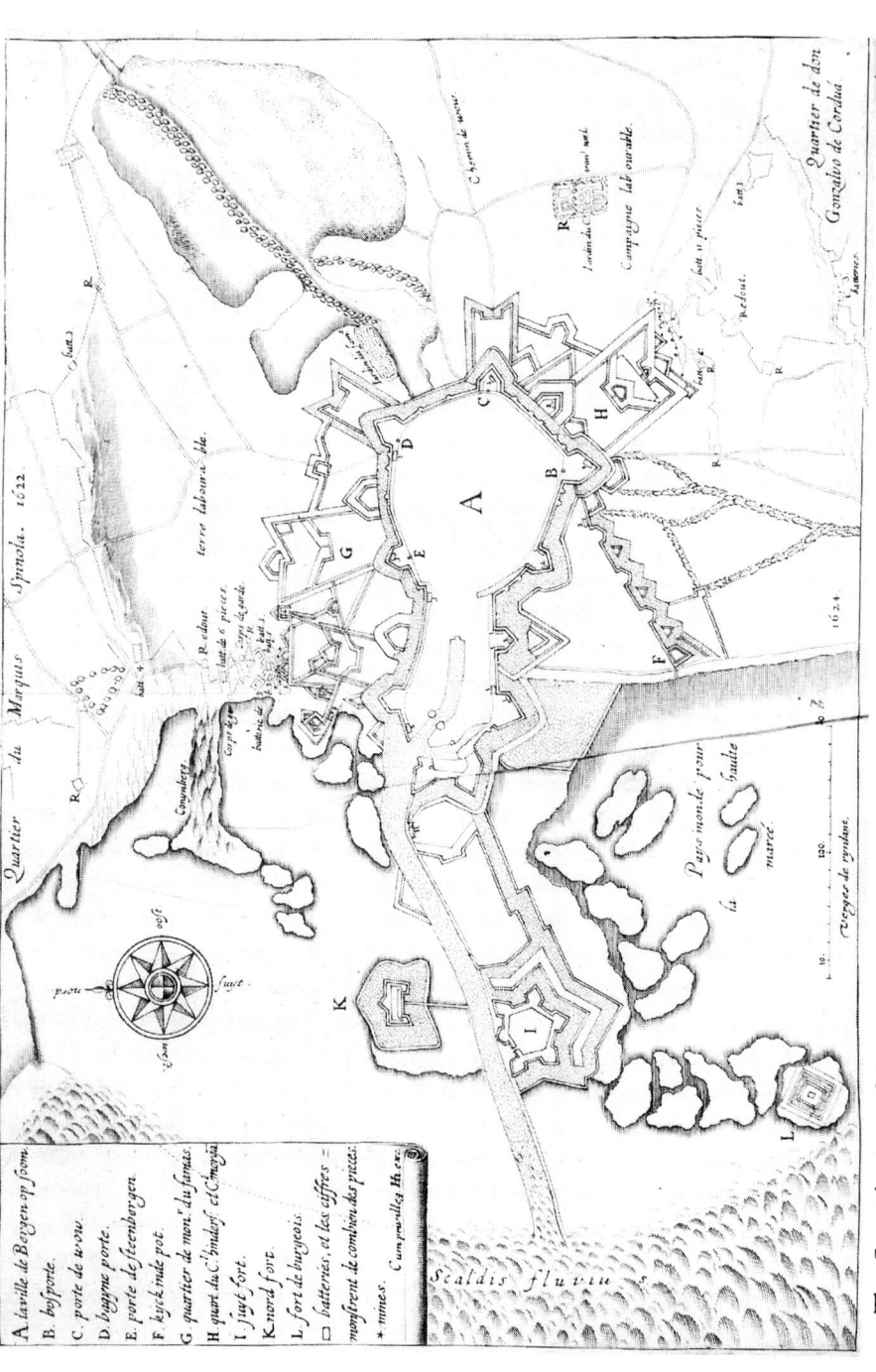

25. The Spanish siege of Bergen op Zoom in 1622. Clearly visible are the hornworks, which were often used in the Old Netherlandish system. Hondius, *Korte beschrijvinge ende afbeeldinge van de generale regelen der fortificatie* (The Hague 1624). (KB, 2108-A-2)

September 1602, when Maurits congratulated the States-General on the reduction of Grave, he added that the Spanish garrison 'has long expected the siege and [Grave] is therefore well furnished with outworks, from which your Honours [the States-General] may easily surmise that such cities cannot be carried so easily'.[70] It was soon no longer the storming of the breach in the enceinte that was the pivotal event during a siege, but the conquest of the covered way. In 1605 Maurits therefore insisted that the small town of IJzendijke should be reinforced with several ravelins so that the defence of the covered way could be conducted with greater tenacity. He drew the States-General's attention to the fact that this investment would be amply rewarded, 'for it would be difficult and costly (as your Noble Mightinesses can imagine) to come to its defence with an army every time the enemy should make preparations to violently attack these parts'.[71] In an entry in his 1645 journal, Willem Frederik articulated a widely held view: 'I would also risk my men in the outworks with sorties, alarms and mining, because if one is chased into the ditch [and] the counterscarp [i.e. the covered way] is lost, it is done and over for those within'.[72] The breach batteries could then be positioned on the edge of the ditch, so it was only a question of time before the main wall was ready for storming.

The advantage with earthen defence structures was that they could be constructed more quickly and less expensively than bastions and walls revetted in stone, though maintenance was more costly.[73] The risk of subsidence and crumbling called for regular inspection of earthen defences and their repair where necessary. Another disadvantage was that they were easy to scale. Ladders were essential to scale the *trace italienne* with its sheer stone walls, but were unnecessary for climbing up grass-covered earthen ramparts, which were always raised at an angle of forty-five degrees. The only means of preventing an assault by storm was by placing thousands of 'storm-poles', a palisade of pointed wooden stakes measuring seven to nine feet long that were set into the earthen rampart horizontally in an extremely dense configuration just beneath the breastwork.[74] The fraising of the works, as the placing of storm-poles was known, was a labour-intensive and costly affair. In 1670, no fewer than 30,000 stakes were needed 'to fraise [Maastricht] properly ... each storm-pole seven feet long, 15 to 16 inches thick, which would amount to a cost of six Holland stivers per piece'.[75]

The Council of State and the provincial States devoted the necessary attention to towns and forts on the front line, such as Maastricht, but the fortifica-

---

[70] NA, SG 4904, Maurits to the SG, before Grave, 9 September 1602.
[71] NA, SG 4910, Maurits to the SG, Watervliet, 7 June 1605.
[72] Visser, *Dagboeken van Willem Frederik*, pp. 180–1.
[73] Guillaume le Blond, *Elémens des fortifications*, 5th, expanded edn (Paris 1764), pp. 166–7; Duffy, *Siege Warfare*, p. 93.
[74] Le Blond, *Elémens des fortifications*, pp. 10–11.
[75] NA, RAZH, FAvS 21, Jacob Pieck and Hendrik van Raesfelt to the RvS, Maastricht, 26 October 1670.

tions of towns that lay further inland or had for a while not been subject to any threat were often in a dilapidated state.[76] On the enemy's approach, the outworks had to be raised 'in all haste',[77] repairs made to the enceinte, storm-poles planted and palisades positioned,[78] but if the enemy push proceeded swiftly then the necessary repairs and tasks could often no longer be completed in time. It was impossible to fraise the defences and bolster them with palisades on a permanent basis, because of the huge costs; the timber rotted away, so the stakes had to be replaced at regular intervals. A wet ditch was therefore essential to protecting an earthen stronghold against a surprise attack, which was why extra vigilance was required during periods of frost, when the garrison commanders had to break the ice continually and as an extra precaution poured water down the ramparts, resulting in a thin layer of ice that rendered them extremely slippery.[79]

Sieges during the Middle Ages had essentially been blockades. The town was invested until starvation or disease forced the defenders to surrender. At the end of the fifteenth century this changed abruptly, due to the development of mobile siege artillery, which made it possible to make a sizeable breach swiftly. However, the introduction of the bastion system barely a quarter of a century later meant that sieges once again dragged on for weeks or even months. Though the new scientific method for designing geometric defence systems certainly deserves most credit for this, it is not the only explanation for the capture of a fortified town costing such great effort: insufficient coordination in the assault was also a factor. Maurits, Willem Lodewijk and Frederik Hendrik left the day-to-day running of siege operations to engineers and the master-general of the artillery. The former supervised the digging of trenches and the raising of sconces, while the latter was in charge of the ordnance. The authority and responsibilities of the master-general and other artillery personnel were set out in an order in 1599.[80] This was a means of avoiding many misunderstandings with the engineers, but it was still a serious shortcoming that there was no overall commander who could coordinate the digging of approaches and the artillery bombardment. Neither artillerists nor engineers were considered part of the army proper. They had their own hierarchy and took no orders from soldiers.

Engineers were an extremely rare commodity at first. Jacob Kemp had to single-handedly direct the siege of Geertruidenberg in 1593. Maurits therefore asked Willem Lodewijk to second one of his Frisian engineers to him, because he feared that without this extra assistance he could not succeed in bringing

---

[76] NA, SG 4910, Maurits to the SG, Wouw, 25 May 1605; SG 4913, Maurits to the SG, Deventer, 18 July 1606; SG 4977, RvS to the SG, The Hague, 31 August 1641.
[77] NA, SG 4913, Field deputies to the RvS, Deventer, 19 July 1606.
[78] NA, SG 4910, 'Aengaende de staet Rhijnberck', 1 April 1605.
[79] NA, RAZH, FAvS 21, Johan Maurits van Nassau-Siegen to Govert van Slingelandt, Wesel, 10 December 1671, with addendum.
[80] *Groot Placaetboeck*, II, pp. 326–50.

the venture to a successful conclusion.[81] The job of an engineer was extremely dangerous, seeing as they had to be present in the trenches. In 1595, for example, Kemp took a ball through his head during the siege of Groenlo. The Council of State exhorted the States-General to train new engineers. Simon Stevin therefore devised an engineering syllabus which was taught at the University of Leiden from 1600. Besides theory, a great deal of attention was devoted to practical skills. On completing their studies the fresh engineers set out to join the field army or to a fortress under construction in order to gain hands-on experience.[82] This school meant that the Republic had a permanent body of engineers at its disposal. In 1631 there were seven 'ordinary' engineers engaged on a permanent basis serving in the field, alongside nine 'extraordinary' or temporary engineers.[83]

To avoid being delayed at each castle or fort, in the sixteenth and seventeenth centuries it was standard practice to give no quarter to a garrison which had continued to resist against better judgement. In October 1595, for example, the English general, Sir Francis Vere, was forced to bring three demi-cannon into position before the castle of Weert. The following day the defenders announced that they wanted to surrender, to which Vere retorted: '[T]hey all must hang, because they had awaited the arrival of the artillery for such a dog-hole of a place … and [Vere] therefore wanted the 26 men in the castle to draw straws and hang the half of them that drew the short straw.' The life of one of these thirteen unfortunates was to be spared if he 'hanged the others, which he did.'[84]

A 'formal' siege cost an enormous amount of money. The siege army established various quarters beyond reach of the stronghold's artillery (c. 1.5km). The soldiers dug entrenchments around these encampments to protect themselves against a surprise attack. Once this task was completed, the field deputies contracted out the realisation of the lines of contra- and circumvallation. This was a double ring that interconnected the various quarters and made it possible for the besieger to contain the garrison while simultaneously being prepared to counter any attack from the outside by the enemy's relief force. Until the second half of the seventeenth century field armies were too small to leave the investment to a siege corps and be ready to check the opponent's relief army with the remainder, known as the 'army of observation'. The line of circumvallation gained the besieger the time to concentrate his troops where the relief army was endeavouring to break through the encirclement. The lines of contra- and circumvallation made it practically impossible to relieve a beleaguered stronghold. Maurits demonstrated this in 1593 when he recaptured Geertruidenberg

---

[81] KHA, A22-IX-A1-28, Maurits to Willem Lodewijk, before Geertruidenberg, 1 May 1593.
[82] Mulder, *Journaal van Anthonis Duyck*, I, pp. lxxviii–lxxxix; F. Westra, 'Nederlandse ingenieurs en de fortificatiewerken in het eerste tijdperk van de Tachtigjarige Oorlog, 1573–1604', Ph.D. diss., Rijksuniversiteit Groningen (1992), pp. 49, 54 and 82–4.
[83] NA, SG 4959, 'Lijste van[de] officieren soo van[de] treynen van de artillerie, munitie van oorloge, de vivres ende fortificatie dewelcke … in den jaere 1631 te velde gebruyckt werden'.
[84] Duyck, I, p. 687.

right under the nose of the Spanish field army. Willem Lodewijk praised his cousin on this splendid victory by drawing a comparison with Julius Caesar's siege of Alesia (52 BC).[85]

The outer ring could be very long: the length of the circumvallation of Groenlo in 1627 was a three-hour walk (15km), but the circumvallation of 's-Hertogenbosch (1629) was unmatched, extending for 30 to 35 kilometres.[86] The outer ring was sometimes reinforced by digging a dry ditch. In 1637, during the siege of Breda, Frederik Hendrik ordered the digging of a ditch that was sixteen feet wide and eight feet deep, set some twenty to thirty feet in front of the line of circumvallation. A couple of thousand peasants from Holland were drummed up to perform this task. This hardly proved to be a success, because the farmers, 'of whom only about 1,300 have come across from Holland, have no chief or commander with them, behave themselves very poorly, spending most of the time boozing and sleeping'.[87] The soldiers therefore did most of the digging themselves for a daily wage.

A siege officially began with the opening up of the trenches at approximately 250 metres from the covered way, outside the maximum range of a musket-ball. Each soldier had to 'make a hole and heap up the earth towards the town, in such manner that whoever works most assiduously is the first to be out of danger.... And thus to make a continuous, straight trench.' When digging the 'approaches', as the system of trenches used to approach the invested town was known, it was necessary to ensure that they could not be enfiladed. The trenches were protected from the defender's sorties by the construction at intervals of small redoubts (*corps de garde*). A siege tactic frequently used by Maurits and Frederik Hendrik was to approach the stronghold from three or four sides simultaneously, which left the defenders in the dark about the intended target of the main assault. There was, however, another reason for doing this: each 'nation' of the Dutch army was assigned its own approach so that the Netherlanders/Germans, English/Scots and French would vie with each other to reach the ditch first.

When they had advanced to within approximately 60 to 65 paces (c. 45 to 50m) of the covered way, the distance at which musketfire was really effective, 'one begins sapping and these saps are contracted out by the rod [c. 3.7m], to wit, three feet deep and three feet wide, and a rod of sapping like this costs an average of six guilders'. The sap was widened to six feet over the ensuing days.[88] Soldiers in Dutch service were obliged to risk their lives only in open battle, and otherwise they were not prepared to imperil themselves without the prospect of a pecuniary reward. 'Our soldiers [are] neither willing nor accus-

---

[85] Van Nimwegen, 'Maurits van Nassau and Siege Warfare', pp. 117–18.
[86] NA, SG 4951, Field deputies to the SG, before Groenlo, 23 July 1627, and Frederik Hendrik to the SG, before Groenlo, 31 July 1627; SG 4953, Frederik Hendrik to the SG, Vught, 5 May 1629.
[87] NA, SG 4970 and 4971, Field deputies to the SG, before Breda, 27 July and 1 August 1637.
[88] KHA, A13-IX-6, 'Beschrijvinge'.

tomed ... to working without receiving prompt payment', Maurits reminded the States-General in 1622.[89] This meant that the construction of emplacements for the artillery made up of gabions, which were baskets filled with earth, and the bundling of branches into fascines had to be contracted out. For batteries and redoubts which had to be realised in extremely dangerous spots, the contractors charged between twenty-five and twenty-eight guilders per Rhenish rod, sometime even more.[90] Sieges therefore required a substantial reserve of cash. In June 1632 the field deputies implored the States-General to send money to the army before Maastricht immediately, 'at first certainly no less than 300,000 guilders, [for] the circumference of the works is great and the approaches are proving costly because of the enemy's continual firing with cannon'.[91] Three years earlier, the costs of the siege of 's-Hertogenbosch had amounted to more than 200,000 guilders per month.[92]

During the first phase of the siege the task of the siege guns was to silence the defender's artillery, though the cannonade was often aimed at the town itself, in the hope of stirring up a revolt against the garrison. In the wake of the siege of Steenwijk in 1592 there was not a single house 'which had not been shot through several times', and in 1601, after suffering the third siege in the space of five years, Rheinberg was also 'severely battered'.[93] The inhabitants of neither Steenwijk nor Rheinberg had rebelled, but the Spanish had greater success with the siege of Venlo in 1637. On 24 September they set the town ablaze, whereupon the burghers, who had been supplied with weapons to assist in the defence of the town, 'gathered into a crowd and, while our soldiers were busied by the enemy in the outworks ... sought to take control of the person of the governor, of the market, the arsenal and lastly of a gateway'. The burghers forced the governor to clear the covered way and open negotiations with the besiegers. Venlo capitulated the following day.[94]

The two most frequently used siege cannons were the whole- and demi-cannon. A complete 24-pounder weighed about 7,300 pounds (3,600kg) and required seventeen draught horses to haul it, while no fewer than twenty-one draught horses were needed to shift a 48-pounder. In December 1605 Maurits advised the States-General to found four 'battery pieces' each year for six years, so that the Republic would have 'forty whole- and [forty] demi-cannons, and

---

[89] NA, SG 4941, Maurits to the SG, Emmerich, 21 July 1622 (quote); NA, SG 4900, Field deputies to the SG, before Rheinberg, 25 July 1601; SG 4903, Field deputies to the SG, before Grave, 4 August 1602.
[90] NA, SG 4908 Field deputies to the SG, before Sluis, 21 June 1604.
[91] NA, SG 4960, Field deputies to the SG, before Maastricht, 23 June 1632.
[92] NA, SG 4953, Field deputies to the SG, Crevecoeur, 9 May 1629.
[93] Duyck, I, p. 102; NA, SG 4900, Maurits to the SG, before Rheinberg, 1 August 1601.
[94] NA, SG 4971, Frederik Hendrik to the SG, before Breda, 2 September 1637, with an appendix, Jan de Zeghers, sergeant-major of Venlo, to Frederik Hendrik, Grave, 28 August 1637, transcript.

twenty each of the other field-pieces' at its disposal.[95] However, no start was made on this project until the Twelve Years' Truce. In 1610 the States-General ordered the making of the casts for six whole-cannon, twelve demi-cannon and six 12-pounders.[96] The founding of artillery of any other calibre was forbidden from then on, which was no more than a formalisation of the existing situation, given that the Dutch field artillery had already been restricted to these calibres for two decades.[97] The decree of 1610 meant the Republic had sufficient artillery at its disposal to assemble a mighty siege train every year. Cannons were subject to considerable wear and tear. The great heat that was generated on firing wore away the touch-hole, which could deform the barrel and even burst. The gun carriages suffered most: the recoil was so forceful that a 24-pounder would roll back some five to six metres after each round, while a 12-pounder had a recoil of some one and a half to two metres.[98]

After 1621 the Dutch artillery grew considerably. In October 1624 the artillery train counted seventy-two pieces 'both small and large', in 1629 Frederik Hendrik had 116 cannon brought into position near 's-Hertogenbosch,[99] and in 1632 he took eighty-three pieces of artillery on his campaign along the River Meuse.[100] These figures do not reflect only whole- and half-cannons and 12-pounders; they also include 6- and 3-pounders, as well as breech-loader chamber-pieces, a type of cannon that weighed less than a muzzle-loading gun but was less robust. The artillery before 's-Hertogenbosch consisted of seven whole- and twenty-eight demi-cannon, eight 12-pounders and three 6-pounders as well as seventy chamber-pieces (six demi-cannon, sixteen 12-pounders, twenty-four 6-pounders and twenty-four 3-pounders).[101]

During sieges, a few mortar-pieces that hurled a projectile weighing a hundred pounds were used alongside the cannon. The mortar was still being developed and was not very effective. The difficulty was to ensure that the bomb, a hollow iron sphere filled with gunpowder and combustible materials, exploded at the right moment. This relied on the experience of the 'fire-workers' or 'bombardiers', the specialists who operated the mortars. The powder in the bomb was ignited by means of a wooden fuse, so the fire-worker had to estimate the distance to the target and then cut the fuse to such a length that the projectile would explode in the air at the right moment. A complicating factor was that the bomb's reach was determined by the strength of the powder charge that launched it from the

---

[95] NA, SG 4911, RvS to the SG, The Hague, 30 December 1605.
[96] Kuypers, *Geschiedenis van de Nederlandsche artillerie*, II, pp. 198–9; Ten Raa, *Het Staatsche leger*, II, pp. 176–7.
[97] In 1598 the Dutch artillery train consisted of sixteen whole- and sixteen demi-cannon, ten 12-pound field-pieces and five mortars. See Hahlweg, *Heeresreform*, pp. 369–70.
[98] NA, SHS 1454, Experiments with ordnance on 16 March and 19 April 1621 using the standard powder-charges of 12 pounds for a 24-pounder piece and 6 pounds for a 12-pounder.
[99] Duffy, *Siege Warfare*, p. 102.
[100] Ten Raa, *Het Staatsche leger*, IV, p. 59.
[101] Kuypers, *Geschiedenis van de Nederlandsche artillerie*, II, p. 230.

mortar. During the siege of Groningen in 1594, the master pyrotechnician Jan Bovi attempted to lob four 'grenades' (*graenaeden*) into a ravelin, but 'two were thrown too far and the other two burst before they came down, causing peril to some of our own soldiers', Duyck wrote in his journal.[102]

The defenders did not allow the besiegers to proceed without harassment. The narrow front of the attacking force as they approached the town presented the garrison with an ideal opportunity to make sorties in which they could also deploy their cavalry. Edged weapons such as half-pikes, halberds and swords were the arms most suitable for such sorties, being best for skirmishes in the confines of the trenches and, moreover, were an advantage in rainy weather, when it was 'impossible to keep any matches burning in the trenches',[103] rendering the musketeers defenceless. Besides the element of surprise, a sortie's success depended on the number of soldiers who could be spared. With garrisons of just a couple of hundred or, at most, a thousand men it was impossible to undertake effective action against the besieger. The ease with which Maurits and Willem Lodewijk wrested fifteen towns from Spanish control between 1591 and 1597 was largely thanks to the small garrisons. Only a few pieces of artillery were employed during these sieges, with the exception of the siege of Steenwijk (1592), where, in the space of three weeks (13 June–3 July 1592), the Dutch artillery fired no fewer than 29,000 rounds. Johann VII, who was present at the siege, was astounded by the violence done 'by the heavy artillery'.[104] Nevertheless, Steenwijk pales into insignificance in the light of the siege of Ostend (1601–1604).

There was a Dutch garrison of about 4,000 men in Ostend, and during hostilities these were refreshed by rotation via the North Sea. This was no luxury, because an estimated '1,000 healthy soldiers were needed every month to replace the injured, dead and sick'.[105] Between July 1601 and June 1604, a total of 151 Dutch infantry companies served in Ostend, 'alongside the English troops, without mentioning into how many companies these were divided, to the figure of 2,800'.[106] Ostend's defenders shot their way through 2,000 pounds of musket powder each day and the cannon unleashed an average of 300 balls each day.[107] When Ostend was at long last surrendered on 20 September 1604, after a siege lasting more than three years, the Spanish besiegers had lost an estimated 40,000 men.[108] The losses on the Dutch side are unknown, but going by the 1,000 dead,

---

[102] Duyck, I, p. 445.
[103] Duyck, I, pp. 408 and 410–11.
[104] Van Nimwegen, 'Maurits van Nassau and Siege Warfare', p. 116.
[105] HUA, HAA 5075, 'Instructie voor … joncker Pieter de Sedlintsky', The Hague, 26 August 1601, addenda.
[106] NA, RvS 18961, 'Memorie van het getal der militie die geduyrende het belegh van Ostende … tot secours in de stadt sijn gesonden'.
[107] HUA, HAA 5075, 'Instructie voor … joncker Pieter de Sedlintsky', The Hague, 26 August 1601, addenda; NA, SG 4900, Deputies in Middelburg to the SG, 17 September 1601, addenda; SG 4908, Nicasius Kien to the SG, Ostend, 17 June 1604.
[108] Duffy, *Siege Warfare*, p. 88.

wounded and sick each month that records mention, the total would not have been much lower. The siege of Ostend was exceptional in every respect, but the emphasis on an aggressive defence from the outworks had an enduring influence on the tactics of siege warfare. Garrisons of a thousand men or less were consigned to the past, on the Dutch as well as the Spanish side. After 1600, garrisons of between 2,000 and 3,000 men were billeted in key frontier towns such as Sluis, Breda, 's-Hertogenbosch and Rheinberg (see Appendix II).

Gaining control of the covered way ushered in the final phase of the siege. While the breach batteries attempted to reduce the foot of the enceinte to rubble by means of salvoes, the engineers started to build a dam or a bridge across the ditch. Once again, volunteers were called on to perform this extremely dangerous task for a fee. As soon as the far side of the ditch had been reached, preparations could be made to storm the stronghold. The breach had to be scaleable, so if the breach batteries had not yet achieved that goal – and with the cavalier way in which the artillerists handled their guns that was often the case – then the miners and sappers had to be called in. These specialists dug tunnels that extended beneath the rampart and bastions under attack. They then set the props ablaze, causing the tunnel to collapse along with the fortifications above. Sometimes kegs of gunpowder were placed at the end of the tunnel and ignited. The defenders would make every effort to defend a ravelin, but they did not usually wait around for an attack on the enceinte itself. After the loss of this last line of defence there was no place of refuge, and according to the rules of war the attackers were under no obligation to give quarter to opponents who had persisted until it came to a storm assault. Maurits summoned the town to surrender as soon as the breach was scaleable. As a rule the governor then flew white banners and sounded the drum, which advertised that he wished to surrender the stronghold subject to terms. Maurits was compelled to give the order to launch a storm assault only once in his long career. On 9 October 1597 he made preparations for the storming of Bredevoort, but even before the assault began the Spanish troops abandoned their posts and pleaded for mercy. Maurits spared the garrison and the town's inhabitants, but as punishment he allowed the Dutch soldiers to plunder the town into the evening,[109] but this was exceptional. Maurits usually punished garrisons for an overly stubborn defence by stripping the companies of their weapons, colours and horses, and by making the captains and rittmasters swear that they would desist from fighting against the Republic for three to six months.

After the resumption of the Eighty Years' War in 1621, sieges increasingly became ritualised undertakings. Once towns were invested Frederik Hendrik demanded their capitulation, at which the Spanish governor would respond that he could not comply prior to a breach being shot in the enceinte. This was followed by the opening of the trenches, the readying of the artillery and the

---

[109] Duyck, I, p. 379.

assault on the covered way. After the ditch had been crossed, the batteries had played upon the enceinte, and the miners and sappers had 'lodged' themselves in the rampart, Frederik Hendrik dispatched 'his trumpeter to the governor ... in order, in the circumstance of him having seen that our [men] have made so much progress, to sound out whether his Honour [would be prepared] to capitulate, having now sufficiently demonstrated his valour and the duty of an honourable man'.[110] Even on the extremely rare occasions that this failed to prompt capitulation, an assault by storm no longer meant that everyone was put to the sword. On the night of 10 to 11 November 1645 the Dutch troops stormed Fort Sint-Andries, and 'despite the said fort having defended itself with unbearable and unseemly stubbornness, only six to seven men therein have been slain and the rest ... were given quarter'.[111] Regrettably this trend was not apparent throughout Europe. In 1631 the troops of the German Catholic League sacked the 'old, great and wonderful town' of Magdeburg. The carnage was horrendous; there were reports that no fewer than 20,000 to 30,000 men, women and children were killed. Edzart Jacob Clant, a Groningen deputy to the States-General, wrote to Stadholder Ernst Casimir that this deed was 'so cruel as one has not heard of in many years and of which there are few or no instances in Germany'.[112] In the struggle between Spain and the Republic such occurrences had been consigned to the past more than fifty years earlier.

The sieges in the Low Countries were concluded with the signing of a contract by both parties known as the capitulation, which set out the conditions of the town's surrender in detail. If the defence had been brave then the garrison troops marched out through the breach with colours flying, drums rolling, trumpets blazing, matches smouldering, with a bullet in their mouths and the cavalrymen on their steeds. As an additional mark of honour the governor was often allowed to take a pair of small cannon and a small supply of munitions with him.[113] On the other hand, if the defenders had taken longer to capitulate than convention dictated then their colours and weapons were confiscated and they had to leave the town with drums silent. Garrisons were not taken away as prisoners of war. A separate agreement was reached with the inhabitants of the town, wherein the most important stipulations related to the appointment of magistrates and the allocation of churches to Catholics. The Oldenzaal capitulation treaty of 1626, for example, determined that the 'town and burghers shall retain their old privileges ... but on this occasion [the States-General] will appoint such magistrate as they deem will be of best service to the town'.[114]

---

[110] NA, SG 4982, Field deputies to the SG, before Hulst, 2 November 1645.
[111] NA, SG 4982, Field deputies to the SG, before Hulst, 11 November 1645.
[112] KHA, A23-VII-C-342, Edzart Jacob Clant to Ernst Casimir, The Hague, 5 June 1631.
[113] NA, SG 4951, Capitulation of Groenlo, 19 August 1627.
[114] NA, SG 4949, Ernst Casimir and the field deputies to Frederik Hendrik, before Oldenzaal, 25 July 1626, transcript with addenda.

The war's impact on the countryside: fire-tax, contribution and plundering

There was no love lost between peasants and soldiers. The troops treated the rural population with contempt, while the farmers saw a potential thief or worse in each and every soldier.[115] Soldiers frequently perpetrated 'extortionings'. Officers, for instance, used hunting as a front to extract money from villagers. The inhabitants were forced to purchase hares, rabbits and partridges at extremely high prices, but that was only the half of it: the officers also forced the farmers to care for their hunting dogs, 'and if the hounds are stolen they want their value recompensed by the same farmer, [to a sum] as high as they deem appropriate, yea even manage to incite people to steal such hounds'.[116] Countryfolk were placed in an extremely difficult position when opposing forces operated in the same area for a long time. When the Spaniards initiated the siege of Breda in 1624, the Dutch army took up positions in the vicinity. The farmers found themselves caught between the hammer and the anvil, because while the besiegers were exacting food from them the States-General promulgated a ban on complying with this. Ernst Casimir felt compassion for the rural population: 'The poor farmer has nothing left. They have lost all their worldly possessions and are still greatly oppressed every day by the enemy and by our armies, since it [is] impossible to serve two masters well at one and the same time.'[117] Just two years earlier the farmers had found themselves in a similar quandary during the Spanish siege of Bergen op Zoom, when Dutch soldiers had extorted money from the farmers with the excuse that, in contravention of the edict, they had supplied food to the Spaniards. 'The poor folk [were] sorely burdened, and subjected to extortion by one [group of soldiers] after the other', Maurits lamented, 'in such manner that as soon as they have given something to one [soldier] another ... is at the door.'[118]

No matter how serious the above-mentioned abuses, from the end of the sixteenth century the misconduct of Dutch and Spanish soldiers did not usually go beyond extortion. Maurits and Willem Lodewijk threatened plundering soldiers with death,[119] and Spinola also imposed a 'discipline regimen mightily'.[120] The situation was much more gruesome in the Land of Berg, where in 1605 the farmers beat to death all the deserters from the Spanish army who they 'were

---

[115] Ronald G. Asch, '"Wo der soldat hinkömbt, da ist alles sein": Military Violence and Atrocities in the Thirty Years War Re-examined', *German History. The Journal of the German History Society*, XVIII, 3 (2000), 291–309, esp. pp. 300–2.

[116] NA, SG 4958, RvS to the SG, The Hague, 28 March 1631, with the 'Placcaet tegens de jagers', 27 March 1631, as an appendix.

[117] GA, AHGC 581, Ernst Casimir to Count Floris II of Culemborg, Roosendaal, 12 February 1625.

[118] NA, SG 4941, Maurits to the SG, Roosendaal, 5 October 1622.

[119] KHA, A22-IX-A1-222, Maurits to Willem Lodewijk, [Aldeneik], 1 July 1602.

[120] NA, SG 4910, Field deputies to the SG, Rheinberg, 25 July 1605.

able to entrap in the hills'.[121] In the 1630s and 1640s the war took a callous turn within the Low Countries once again, but only in those provinces bordering France, where the French plundered most mercilessly. In September 1641, for example, they torched more than thirty villages in Flanders and in the outskirts of Lille they razed 500 houses.[122] The French did not even eschew ransacking churches and manor houses for which contribution had been paid and which should therefore have been spared such looting.[123] It should come as no surprise that the French were profoundly hated in the Spanish Netherlands.

In May 1640 Johan Euskercken (†1642), secretary to the Republic's ambassador in Paris, apologised for being unable to carry out the order of the States-General to visit the French army:

> [I]t shall be impossible for me to catch up with it [i.e. the French army] without considerable danger to my life, for the 'forest Croats', as one calls them, as well as the farmers are killing everyone they come across … owing to the fact that the recruits who are marching in numbers to the respective [French] armies are perpetrating such disorder and mischief with all manner of malice that the farmers have withdrawn into the woods and attack all passers-by, both great and small.[124]

The 'forest Croats' were Habsburg soldiers from the border with the Ottoman Empire renowned for their brutal guerrilla warfare. In October 1645 the farmers in the Southern Netherlands beat to death 'many hundreds' of French soldiers who were on their way to Menen (Menin), in revenge for 'the land … [having been] all but plundered bare [by the French], the booty being extremely [great], principally of horses and cattle'. A year later, Tieleman Aquilius, the States-General's agent to the French army, reported to The Hague that the shortage of food had forced the French to quit the environs of Courtrai: 'There is such fear on all sides in the land that [the population] has totally abandoned all the villages between the Bruges waterway, the River Leie and the River Scheldt, so all supplies must come from Artois.'[125]

Unlike France, the Dutch Republic and Spain adhered to the negotiated contribution treaties punctiliously. This was not ethically motivated, but because both factions knew that a violation could easily be avenged, the small, densely populated theatre of war providing plenty of opportunities to do this. Moreover, both The Hague and Brussels hoped to persuade the populace to take sides and it was therefore not in their interest to force them into the arms of the opponent.[126] The Spanish governor imposed war contributions in Overijssel and Gelderland,

---

[121] NA, SG 4911, Field deputies to the SG, Rheinberg, 30 July 1605.
[122] NA, SG 4978, Field deputies to the SG, Assenede, 17 September 1641.
[123] NA, SG 4984, Field deputies to the SG, Lokeren, 30 July 1646.
[124] NA, SG 6766, Johan Euskercken to the SG, Paris, 26 May 1640.
[125] NA, SG 6769, Tieleman Aquilius, Menin, 8 October 1645, and Courtrai, 10 July 1646.
[126] Asch, '"Wo der soldat hinkömbt, da ist alles sein"', p. 307.

while the States-General exacted them in Opper-Gelre, Flanders and Brabant. Each year the Council of State petitioned the States-General to agree to the 'continuation of the imposition of contributions ... as high and as far as these can be implemented and executed by the army of these Lands'.[127] Here the term 'contributions' refers to the collection of the contribution proper as well as to fire-tax. Both terms refer to the levying of fees within enemy territory, but they are not interchangeable. The contribution was a war tax that was collected with the cooperation of the local authorities,[128] unlike a fire-tax, which was money demanded under threat of the plunder and pillage of houses. The payment of the contribution was hardly voluntary – when the area under contribution failed to fulfil its obligations houses were ransacked and prominent persons taken hostage until the levy was paid[129] – but its imposition was nevertheless less onerous and damaging than imposition of a fire-tax.

In 1602, for example, the States-General decided to exact a fire-tax across a large part of the Spanish Netherlands, 'calculating the fire-tax [of Spanish Brabant] at [the equivalent of] 10 months of the contribution currently ... paid by the willing villages', while Flanders was assessed to the sum of 2.4 million guilders.[130] Villages under contribution paid the annually imposed war tax in instalments throughout the year, while places that were fire-taxed had to produce the whole sum in one go, which was often accompanied by rampant violence. Van Oldenbarnevelt gave the deputies who accompanied the army to Brabant in 1602 the task of burning down a few houses in 'numerous' villages as soon as the Dutch army entered hostile territory 'in order to set an example and foment fear'.[131] To encourage the troops to do their very best, Maurits was authorised to share a quarter of the fire-tax revenue among the 'colonels, cavalrymen, captains and other officers of the army' as a reward.[132] An area placed under contribution,

---

[127] Van Slingelandt, *Staatkundige geschriften*, III, p. 192.
[128] On 14 October 1645 the field deputies wrote: 'Today we were visited by three deputies from the Land of Waes, informing us that [they] were charged by this Land to conclude with their High Mightinesses of the Republic [payment of] a monthly contribution .... They say that the ... Land of Waes is comprised of twenty-five parish villages.' NA, SG 4982, to the SG, before Hulst.
[129] In 1638 several cavalrymen from the garrison of Maastricht carried out a raid into the land of Namur 'for the collection of the contributions'. They returned with four hostages, including two 'ecclesiastical women' from the abbey of Marche les Dames. As a reward for the successful execution of this dangerous mission the troopers received a princely sum of 5,000 to 6,000 guilders. NA, SG 4973, Field deputies to the SG, Maastricht, 24 December 1638; SG 4974, RvS to the SG, The Hague, 3 January 1639.
[130] Duyck, III, p. 375.
[131] NA, RAZH, AJvO 2985, 'Memorie van eenige poincten daerop in de aenstaen[de] expeditie bij den gecommitteerden wten heeren Staten-G[e]n[er]ael & Raden van State sal dienen gelet', 1602, minute.
[132] RGP 92, Secret res. SG, 1 June 1602 (no. 33).

on the other hand, was indemnified against plunder and pillage by *sauvegardes*, a written guarantee that people, houses and goods would be left untouched. Soldiers billeted at country houses, monasteries, farmsteads and fields, to guard them, afforded extra protection as 'live' *sauvegardes*.[133]

The advantage of a contribution treaty was that war damage remained limited, but the drawback was that a large portion of the tax revenues flowed into the enemy's coffers. In December 1605, Willem Lodewijk warned Maurits that if troops were not dispatched to his stadholderates forthwith he would not be able to prevent Groningen's rural Ommelands from 'submitting themselves to the *sauvegarde* of the enemy', thus siphoning off 300,000 guilders in tax receipts.[134] The stadholder of Friesland pointed out that the Spaniards could undertake predatory raids from Lingen and Oldenzaal with an estimated 2,000 infantrymen and 300 cavalry.[135] Maurits agreed with his cousin that the farmers could hardly be required to refuse to pay the contribution unless they could rely on sufficient troops being available to protect the countryside from the imposition of fire-tax, 'for otherwise the *courreurs* [the Spanish raiders] would advance and always take risks in order to take prisoners and impose the contribution on the countryfolk'.[136] However, Maurits could not offer Willem Lodewijk any military support, because at that juncture he needed all his troops to deter Spinola from further conquests.

The warring factions were at liberty to exact contributions in cash or in kind. When the States of Zeeland lobbied to impose a ban on supplying victuals to the Spanish siege army encamped before Bergen op Zoom in 1622, Maurits refused to comply, because the Spaniards would have interpreted this as a breach of the contribution treaty, which 'will not only be the utter ruin of the ... inhabitants [of States Brabant] ... but would also give the enemy cause to denounce similar prohibitions for the inhabitants of Gelderland and Overijssel and on our other frontiers'.[137] This would most certainly hinder the food supply to Dutch garrisons. Maurits acknowledged that the Spaniards benefited from contributions in kind, but this was counterbalanced by the countryside being spared and the farmers having to relinquish only part of their harvest to the enemy, when otherwise all the crops 'should surely fall into the hands of the enemy'.[138] Fire-taxes were still imposed after 1621, but only in areas that lay further inland and

---

[133] NA, SG 4941, Maurits to the SG, 's Gravenweert, 16 August 1622, appendix, Maurits to the States of Zeeland, 16 August 1622, transcript.
[134] KHA, A22-IX-E-250 and 251, Willem Lodewijk to Maurits, n.p., 5 December 1605 (quote), and Groningen, 11 December 1605, minute.
[135] NA, SG 4912, Willem Lodewijk to the SG, Groningen, 22 March 1606.
[136] KHA, A22-IX-A1-338, Maurits to Willem Lodewijk, The Hague, 20 April 1606.
[137] NA, SG 4941, Maurits to the SG, 's Gravenweert, 16 August 1622.
[138] NA, SG 4941, Maurits to the SG, 's Gravenweert, 16 August 1622, appendix, Maurits to the States of Zeeland, 16 August 1622, transcript.

normally had little to fear from the enemy. In 1629, for example, the Spanish and Imperial troops imposed a fire-tax of 600,000 guilders on the inhabitants of the Veluwe.[139]

---

[139] NA, SG 4954, Field deputies to the SG, Arnhem, 9 August 1629, and the States of Gelderland to the SG, Arnhem, 11 August 1629.

♦ 4 ♦

The Dutch Offensive and the Spanish Counter-Offensive (1590–1609)

By the mid-1580s the end of the Revolt seemed to be in the offing. In 1579, the duke of Parma, freshly appointed as governor-general of the Spanish Netherlands, launched a major counter-offensive. He concluded his victory march with the recapture of Antwerp on 17 August 1585.[1] By this time, the only towns in the Southern Netherlands still controlled by the rebels were Ostend and Sluis, and the Spaniards were also achieving major triumphs in the Northern Netherlands. The stadholder of Friesland, Groningen, Drenthe and Overijssel, Georges van Lalaing (c. 1550–1581), count of Rennenberg, had withdrawn from the Union of Utrecht in 1580. The Frisians and the inhabitants of the Ommelands, Groningen's rural environs, remained loyal to the Revolt, but Groningen, Delfzijl and Oldenzaal switched their allegiance to Philip II of Spain. Two years later, Francisco Verdugo (1537–1595), Rennenberg's successor as stadholder in Groningen, Drenthe and Overijssel, managed to capture Steenwijk and Coevorden. Zutphen opened its gates to the Spaniards in 1583, and on 10 July 1584 the Spanish delivered the crowning blow by assassinating William of Orange. The successful attack on the stadholder of Holland, Zeeland and Utrecht, and since 1580 also of Friesland, was a major political coup, robbing the Dutch rebels of their leader.[2] The only native candidate who might have laid claim to the leadership was Maurits, but at barely seventeen years of age he was still too young to assume overall military command. He could only serve 'as a reserve for future times'.[3] This left the rebel forces without a commander-in-chief. Nijmegen, a town that was in grave danger of being besieged by the Spaniards, chose autonomously to make advances to the governor-general. The reconciliation with Parma took place in April 1585.[4]

---

[1] Parker, *The Dutch Revolt*, pp. 210–12.
[2] Van Deursen, *Maurits*, p. 22.
[3] Fruin, 'Gedenkschrift van Joris de Bye', p. 425.
[4] Van Deursen, *Maurits*, p. 21.

The critical situation forced the Dutch rebels to choose between two evils 'and to accept the lesser, namely that in order to escape the threat of the enemy one would, under reasonable conditions, transfer the lands to a powerful neighbouring prince, by whom they would be protected against all violence'.[5] Henry III (1551–1589), king of France, did not dare offend Philip II and declined the offer, whereupon the rebels made advances to the English monarch, Queen Elizabeth I (1533–1603). She was equally loath to openly challenge the king of Spain, though she was prepared to send a relief force, or *secours*, numbering more than 7,000 men. She asked a considerable price for this military assistance. The rebel provinces would have to accept her favourite, the earl of Leicester, as governor-general and, moreover, permit English garrisons in Den Briel (Brill), Vlissingen (Flushing) and the adjacent Fort Rammekens. These 'cautionary towns' meant that the queen of England could exert her influence in Holland and Zeeland. The rebels had little choice but to agree to these terms, which were elaborated in the Treaty of Nonesuch (20 August 1585).[6]

Leicester's appointment did not correspond to the expectations of the Dutch. As mentioned, he ignored his orders and took on many more troops than could be paid from the financial resources apportioned each year by the provinces.[7] When he returned to London for consultation at the end of the 1586 campaign, the unpaid soldiers resorted to plundering. Holland had seen enough. On Van Oldenbarnevelt's suggestion, the Hollanders decided to dismiss a large number of troops and drastically curtail Leicester's powers as well. On 24 January 1587 the States of Holland and Zeeland appointed Maurits as their captain-general.[8] In and of itself this was not unusual: Willem Lodewijk had been captain-general of Friesland since 1584, and Count Adolf of Nieuwenaar and Meurs (c. 1545–1589) held this rank in Gelderland, Utrecht and Overijssel. However, thirteen days after Maurits's appointment, the States of Holland passed a resolution that left no shadow of a doubt as to their intention to deprive Leicester of supreme command over the Dutch troops. In a resolution adopted on 6 February 1587 they declared that 'whosoever pays their wages', within the province of Holland there was nobody, 'not even a governor-general', permitted to give orders to the troops, this being the preserve of the stadholder of Holland as captain-general of the province.[9] The immediate cause for this decision was the betrayal of Sir William Stanley, the English governor of Deventer, who eight days earlier had sold the town entrusted to him to the Spaniards. Almost simultaneously, another English officer, Rowland York, surrendered the redoubt before Zutphen to the enemy.[10]

---

[5] Fruin, 'Gedenkschrift van Joris de Bye', pp. 415–17.
[6] Israel, *The Dutch Republic*, pp. 219–20; Parker, *The Dutch Revolt*, pp. 217–18.
[7] See pp. 24 and 69.
[8] Den Tex, *Oldenbarnevelt*, I, pp. 322–3 and 325.
[9] Van Slingelandt, *Staatkundige geschriften*, IV, p. 114.
[10] Van Deursen, *Maurits*, pp. 36–7.

During the summer of 1587 the military prospects for the Dutch rebels deteriorated even further. Parma laid siege to Sluis, prompting Leicester to return from England immediately. By relieving Sluis he hoped to be able to restore his position in the rebellious provinces, but nothing came of this plan 'because the Land's soldiery was not strong enough to face the enemy in the open field'.[11] Sluis fell on 5 August. It was evident that Leicester's position was untenable unless he succeeded in seizing power in Holland. However, his surprise attack on Leiden was discovered in time and his plans to occupy Enkhuizen and Hoorn, two important ports in West Friesland, also failed. Immediately hereafter, on 16 December 1587, Leicester returned to England for the second time, this time for good. The disarray in the rebel army assumed alarming forms. Many officers feared they would be punished for their support of Leicester and the troops were concerned they would be left unpaid.[12] The States-General tried to restore calm by introducing the previously discussed 'repartition system' and enacting a revised oath of allegiance. Henceforth the soldiers had to swear allegiance to the States-General, to their paymasters, to the States of the province where they were quartered, and lastly to the regents of the towns where they were billeted.[13] The combination of the new form of military financing and the new oath of allegiance transformed the former rebel forces into the States-General's army, making 1588 the founding year of both the Dutch Republic and her army.

Maurits was ordered to bring the recalcitrant troops to order, but he could not prevent the Dutch-German garrison of Geertruidenberg rising in mutiny.[14] The town's governor, the English officer John Wingfield, chose the side of the mutineers and made overtures to Parma. If Geertruidenberg had opened its gates to the Spaniards and, furthermore, the governor-general of the Spanish Netherlands had managed to reduce Bergen op Zoom, then he would have been able to attack the geographical heart of the Dutch Republic – Holland, Zeeland and Utrecht – from two sides simultaneously. The Spaniards already had bridge-heads on the River IJssel, namely Deventer and Zutphen, but developments on the international stage prevented Parma being able to gain an advantage from the weakness of the Dutch.

In 1588 everything had to be set aside for Philip II's plan to invade England. Parma was ordered to keep his main army in readiness at the Flemish harbours in order to set sail for England as soon as the 'Invincible Armada' arrived from Spain. As everyone knows, this came to nothing: the battle fleet was destroyed by the English. With the invasion sunk, Parma immediately ordered his troops

---

[11] Fruin, 'Gedenkschrift van Joris de Bye', p. 427.
[12] Den Tex, *Oldenbarnevelt*, I, pp. 391–2.
[13] Van Slingelandt, *Staatkundige geschriften*, IV, p. 20 (res. SG, 1 June 1588, and res. SH, 14 September 1588); Wijn, *Krijgswezen*, p. 19. Israel, *The Dutch Republic*, p. 229, is mistaken in dating the introduction of a new oath of allegiance for the army as early as 1587, namely prior to Leicester's definitive departure and before the introduction of the repartition system.
[14] Ten Raa, *Het Staatsche leger*, II, p. 8.

to disembark; he would endeavour to execute his original campaign plan. In September 1588 he laid siege to Bergen op Zoom. The lateness of the season and the impracticability of fully investing this coastal town forced Parma to abandon the operation in early November. The following year he seemed to have better luck. On 10 April 1589 the mutineers surrendered Geertruidenberg to the Spaniards. The following summer the Spanish army invaded the Bommelerwaard, an isle between the rivers Waal and Meuse, but a mutiny by the *tercio* of Lombardy forced Parma to break off the incursion for the time being. In the interim, on 1 August 1589, Henry III had been murdered in France, an event which had major repercussions for the war in the Low Countries.

The only candidate with a legitimate claim to the French throne was Henri de Bourbon (1553–1610), king of Navarre, who was a Huguenot. For Madrid this was unacceptable, so Philip II ordered Parma to march into France with a substantial army to support the Catholic League, an alliance of French Catholics, in their struggle against Henri de Navarre. For the time being the war in the Low Countries was of secondary importance to Madrid.[15] This placed Verdugo in an awkward position, as this decision resulted in the military-strategic advantage in the Northern Netherlands shifting to the Dutch rebels. The Spanish stadholder had to defend an elongated line of towns, while the Dutch army could operate from a central position. Parma's successes had unintentionally resulted in the limited military strength of the Dutch Republic being concentrated in Holland, Utrecht and Zeeland rather than being fragmented, handing the rebels the advantage of being able to decide the time and place of attack; they could therefore establish a local military preponderance while Verdugo was forced to divide his troops among dozens of garrisons. The course of the major rivers was also to the rebels' advantage. Dutch troops could rapidly be transported from Holland and Zeeland to the east via the rivers Waal and Rhine, and a landing in States Flanders (the part of Flanders known today as Zeeuws-Vlaanderen) could be organised and executed relatively quickly. Initially the rebels did not dare venture beyond their heartland, but when there was some degree of certainty that the Spanish intervention in France was no temporary affair – Parma took Paris on 19 September 1590 – the States-General decided to go on the offensive.

Ten successful years (1590–1600)

In March 1590 eighty Dutch soldiers managed to take Breda by surprise. This was a glorious feat, but it was unlikely that a similar opportunity would soon present itself again. On 1 December 1590, when submitting the General Petition for the coming year to the States General, the Council of State acknowledged that 'for a while now the enemy has endured his principal violence in

---

[15] Parker, *The Dutch Revolt*, pp. 225–7, and *Army of Flanders*, p. 245.

France, whereby the pressure [i.e. military threat] has not been so very heavy [on the Dutch Republic]'. However, the Council of State immediately added the caveat that there was no assurance this would be the case the year thereafter, and that without the States-General having a substantial field army at their behest it would be impossible for the provinces to check the Spaniards. The Council cautioned that, even if this occasion did not arise, the States-General still had to ensure that enough troops could be mobilised for field service in 1591, so that 'in the event of being able to do the enemy any substantial damage ... not to let it pass without reaping advantage from it'. In May 1588 the strength of the Dutch army was established at 19,000 infantrymen and 1,500 cavalrymen. The garrisoning of all the towns and forts in the Republic as well as of Ostend required about 14,800 men in all, leaving only 5,500 men for field-service.[16] This prompted the Council of State to impress upon the provinces that they had to bring the companies in their pay to full strength and to entreat them to lend their stamp of approval to the temporary employment of 300 cavalry and 3,000 infantry.[17] The provinces consented to the hiring of between 300 and 400 horse and 2,400 foot for a period of four months.[18] In 1591 the Republic could at last field an army of 9,000 infantry and 1,500 cavalry with Maurits as commander.[19] Now that the manpower had been taken care of, the strategy for the coming campaign could be determined.

The Republic could launch an offensive on three sides: towards the south (Geertruidenberg, 's-Hertogenbosch, Grave and Hulst), to the east (the towns along the River IJssel and Nijmegen), and to the north (Steenwijk, Coevorden and Groningen).[20] An incursion into Brabant was out of the question because the Spanish were far too strong there and, moreover, it precluded working in conjunction with the Frisians. In view of the supply lines a push towards Groningen was not to be recommended, seeing as the advance would have to pass by the enemy strongholds in Overijssel. The choice therefore fell on the east. The recapture of Deventer, Zutphen and Nijmegen would give Utrecht and Holland a buffer zone. A further advantage of this operation was that Verdugo could then be trapped in a pincer movement: from the west by Holland's and Utrecht's troops, and from the north by the Frisians.

Maurits's first great campaign went extremely well. Willem Lodewijk's presence within the army ensured that the campaign plan was executed swiftly and purposefully. The towns on the River IJssel fell in quick succession; Zutphen capitulated on 30 May 1591 after a three-day siege, while the garrison at Deventer abandoned its defence after a week (10 June). On Willem Lodewijk's advice, the

---

[16] Tresoar, ASF 1352, 'Staet van het getal van de ruyteren en[de] soldaten', 23 January 1588, reviewed and corrected on 27 and 28 May 1588.
[17] RGP 55, Petition of the RvS of 1 December 1590 (no. 266).
[18] RGP 55, Res. SG, 7 February and 19 March 1591 (nos. 114 and 146).
[19] Duyck, I, p. 16.
[20] Ten Raa, *Het Staatsche leger*, II, p. 17.

Dutch army then headed north. Verdugo managed to ready Groningen's defences in time, but he could not prevent the fall of the port of Delfzijl. Maurits and Willem Lodewijk then set their sights on Steenwijk, but on the day the army arrived before this important stronghold, they received an appeal for help from the governor of Fort Knodsenburg. Parma had unexpectedly appeared before Nijmegen and had then sent troops across the River Waal to invest the fort opposite the town. Maurits left for Arnhem with the troops under his command (about 5,700 foot and 1,400 horse), while Willem Lodewijk pulled back to Friesland to keep an eye on Verdugo. Once troop reinforcements had arrived, Maurits advanced on Knodsenburg with almost 8,500 men. The Spanish force, an estimated 7,000 strong, did not await the arrival of the Dutch army but retreated back across the River Waal.[21]

After the Dutch army had relieved Fort Knodsenburg, a decision had to made about how then to deploy it. Dordrecht's regents insisted on laying siege to Nijmegen, so that ships with merchandise from Holland could sail up the River Waal to the Rhine. The States of Holland and the States of Gelderland backed this proposal.[22] Parma quit the environs of Nijmegen in early August 1591 and once again headed for France with his army. Nijmegen could now be invested, but Maurits hesitated. Almost all the senior officers thought the army had been on campaign long enough and that another siege action could in any case only be contemplated after the captains and rittmasters had been given time to replenish their companies. The cavalry had suffered most terribly from the persistent rain. The rittmasters complained that if they could not shelter their horses in stables shortly then they would all be lost to disease. The commander-in-chief, still aged only twenty-three, could put up scant resistance to the older and much more experienced officers without the backing of his cousin. Having waited for more than two weeks, Van Oldenbarnevelt's patience was exhausted and on 17 August 1591 he arrived at the Dutch army's headquarters. After he had tried to talk Maurits round for a few hours he returned to The Hague, but only, according to Duyck, when 'he had done so much that a resolution was reached to seize the town of Nijmegen'. Under pressure from the officers, Maurits changed his mind again almost immediately, and on 21 August preparations were made for the army to disband. 'That same day the Advocate of Holland returned to the army', Duyck records in his journal, 'on whose arrival the aforesaid resolution of dispersing was again called into question with such arguments that his Excellency has once again started to vacillate.' The officers, however, continued to insist on deferment, in order to give their troops the time to 'refresh'. Maurits yielded to this pressure and the army eventually disbanded on 23 August 1591.[23]

However, this did not mean the campaign was completely over, because in mid-September, on the insistence of the States of Zeeland, Maurits assembled some

[21] Duyck, I, pp. 10–39.
[22] Den Tex, *Oldenbarnevelt*, II, p. 136.
[23] Duyck, I, pp. 44–8.

of the Dutch troops and laid siege to Hulst. For the feeble garrison of fewer than 300 men there was no hope of relief and it therefore put up little resistance. The town capitulated on 24 September, after a siege of just five days, whereupon the idea of taking Nijmegen was broached once again. Willem Lodewijk dispatched eight Frisian companies to help with this siege. Maurits invested Nijmegen on 16 October 1591 with approximately 10,000 men and, after a mere five days, the 300 defenders surrendered. The unexpectedly swift capitulation was the result of disagreement between the burghers and the garrison.[24]

The 1591 campaign had exceeded the wildest expectations, but Maurits, Willem Lodewijk and the Council of State warned the States-General that they should not draw the conclusion that a smaller military force would suffice for the following year.[25] It was, after all, self-evident that Verdugo would take precautionary measures to prevent the loss of more towns. Steenwijk was on the campaign agenda in 1592. The reduction of this fortress would mean the Spaniards losing their grip on the northern part of Overijssel, while the southern part of Friesland would have less to fear from Spanish incursions. It would also severely disrupt the Spanish supply lines between Groningen and the eastern parts of Overijssel and Gelderland that were still under Spanish control, namely Twente and the Achterhoek.

Maurits and Willem Lodewijk invested Steenwijk on 28 May 1592. They anticipated being able to compel its defenders to surrender by means of an overwhelming play of fire from a battery of sixteen whole-cannon and twenty-nine demi-cannon, but this proved to be a miscalculation. The cannon began the barrage on 13 June. More than 5,000 rounds were fired, but to little avail. The earthen ramparts were reinforced with plaited osier 'whereby they would not collapse'. This meant there was no alternative but to approach the town with saps and render it indefensible by undermining the walls.[26] This was an extremely arduous task, because the garrison of about 1,100 men under the Walloon lieutenant-colonel Antoine de Cocquiel (c. 1545–1614) put up a brave defence. It took until 3 July before the mines were prepared. The plan was to storm the wall as soon as these mines had achieved their devastating effect, but events turned out differently. Cocquiel discovered that the mines had been primed with explosives and pulled his troops from the wall in time, 'and after the mines [i.e. powder kegs] had achieved their effect, presented themselves in the same place again', according to Johann VII, who was an eye-witness.[27] Unsuspecting, Willem Lodewijk's regiment stormed the breach and, as a result, 'a great number of soldiers, on the breach as well as thereabouts, were shot dead and injured'.[28] The Spaniards repelled the assault. According to Duyck there were thirty-two dead

---

[24] Duyck, I, pp. 51–64.
[25] RGP 55, Res. SG, 5 November 1591 (no. 187).
[26] Duyck, I, pp. 73–82.
[27] Hahlweg, *Heeresreform der Oranier*, pp. 689–91.
[28] Tresoar, FSA 321, Petition from the joint Frisian captains, November 1592.

and many wounded on the Dutch side. A second mine was ignited at the same time as the first, but instead of damaging the fortifications this explosion threw 'all the earth over our own soldiers', burying 100 Dutch troops alive, if we are to believe Duyck, but as many as 300 men according to Johann VII.[29] Some of them were hauled in a wounded state from beneath the scattered earth, but there were also many fatalities. Though the assaults were repulsed, they still achieved the desired outcome, causing heavy losses among the garrison and exhausting its stocks of gunpowder. That same evening Cocquiel announced that he was ready to surrender Steenwijk. Maurits and Willem Lodewijk were furious about the obstinate defence and therefore had little inclination to be lenient. The garrison were allowed to leave, but with drums silent and without colours or arms, and the soldiers were also obliged to swear 'not to serve on this side of the Rhine for half a year'.[30]

Once the walls of Steenwijk had been repaired, the Dutch army continued onward to Coevorden, the key to the control of Drenthe, where a garrison of about 600 men was billeted under the command of Count Frederik van den Bergh (1559–1618), stadholder of Upper Gelderland. Maurits and Willem Lodewijk arrived in the vicinity of this small town on 26 July 1592. Besides boasting sophisticated defensive works, Coevorden's situation in the midst of a quagmire made it a robust stronghold, which presented an array of problems for provisioning the besiegers, the closest town from which victuals could be fetched being Zwolle. Food convoys arrived intermittently because of the great distance to be covered. The Dutch army's fragile lines of communication presented Verdugo with the opportunity, even with the limited number of troops available to him, to mount an attempt to relieve Coevorden. He gathered about 5,000 men, with whom he approached the beleaguered city via the county of Bentheim, thereby cutting off the supply lines to the Dutch siege army from Zwolle. Maurits and Willem Lodewijk had borne this danger in mind, leaving the road to Meppel 'open and unused until now'. On 4 September 1592 they dispatched a great convoy to this town to collect victuals.[31] However, the road was unable to withstand hundreds of waggons and was soon so severely damaged that for waggons it was no longer passable. As a result the food available to the siege army was too expensive for the soldiers to afford, 'who often, lacking bread, have had to be content with a draught of water'.[32]

Verdugo appreciated that providing only indirect assistance to the garrison would be insufficient. Frederik van den Bergh warned him that he would not be able to hold the town for much longer. Almost every day a dog carrying letters from Van den Bergh dashed across the siegeworks to Verdugo's headquarters and subsequently returned to Coevorden. The besiegers cannot have

---

[29] Duyck, I, p. 98; Hahlweg, *Heeresreform der Oranier*, p. 689.
[30] Duyck, I, p. 100.
[31] Duyck, I, pp. 109, 119 and 129–30.
[32] Tresoar, FSA 321, Petition from the joint Frisian captains, November 1592.

been very observant, because 'they did not know of it until, after the conquest of the stronghold, the beleaguered men themselves pointed it out', according to Johann VII.[33] Verdugo ordered a surprise attack on the Dutch encampment at dawn on 7 September. The Spaniards wore white shirts over their clothes to prevent them attacking their own in the confusion. The attempt to break up the siege of Coevorden failed. After a struggle lasting more than an hour, Verdugo called off the assault. The Spaniards lost about 200 men, while Dutch losses amounted to only three dead and a few wounded. Van den Bergh held out for a further four days, but on 11 September 1592 he ordered the trumpet be sounded as a signal that he wanted to negotiate the town's surrender. Maurits and Willem Lodewijk were relieved that at long last the siege was over and granted favourable terms. The garrison was allowed to depart with full military honours and could head wherever it desired.[34]

The sieges of Steenwijk and Coevorden meant the Dutch army was too enfeebled to undertake any other major operation that year. However, Paul Choart (†1607), seigneur de Buzanval, who served as Henri de Navarre's ambassador to The Hague, impressed upon the States-General that they should not yet scatter the troops across the garrisons, as this would allow the Spaniards a free hand to send reinforcements to France. Van Oldenbarnevelt pledged Buzanval his cooperation, because he was convinced that the Republic could persist in the struggle against Spain only with French assistance. For the time being they could expect scant help from Henri de Navarre, but Van Oldenbarnevelt assumed that the Huguenot successor to the French throne would emerge as the spearhead of the anti-Habsburg alliance in Europe once he had managed to establish his authority throughout France.[35] Maurits and Willem Lodewijk pitched a camp at Zevenaar 'to keep the enemy in suspense so that he does not head for France'. In late October 1592, the campaign season already long over, the Dutch army dispersed to its winter quarters.[36]

Within the Republic there was agreement that the war should again be conducted aggressively in 1593, but opinion was divided about where such an offensive should be directed. Gelderland's regents insisted on the besieging of Groenlo, while the people of Overijssel were champions of laying siege to Oldenzaal. Both places served as bases for the Spaniards to collect contributions. As ever, the Frisians had their eye on Groningen. By reducing all the surrounding Spanish sconces, Willem Lodewijk tried to isolate this major town as far as possible,[37] but a siege was the only means by which the rebels could truly seize control of Groningen. For the people of Holland, however, the first priority

---

[33] Hahlweg, *Heeresreform der Oranier*, p. 693.
[34] Duyck, I, pp. 136–7.
[35] Den Tex, *Oldenbarnevelt*, II, pp. 65, 77 and 87.
[36] Duyck, I, pp. 141–7.
[37] G. Overdiep, *De Groninger schansenkrijg. De strategie van graaf Willem Lodewijk. Drente als strijdtoneel. 1589–1594* (Groningen 1970), pp. 35, 38 and 39.

was to recapture Geertruidenberg. The campaigns of 1591 and 1592 had, after all, primarily served the interests of the eastern provinces and, moreover, the circumstances were now opportune to attack this town, which had previously belonged to Holland. Parma had died in early December 1592, and it was to be expected that it would be a long time before the confusion this caused in the high command of the Spanish army would be resolved.[38]

On 28 March 1593, Maurits surrounded Geertruidenberg with an army approximately 7,000 strong.[39] This was the first time he had assumed autonomous command of a sizeable military operation. Willem Lodewijk, his mentor, had remained in Friesland to lead the defence of his stadholderates. Geertruidenberg's garrison, about 1,000 strong, put up a fierce resistance, especially the soldiers who had participated in the perfidy of 1589, when they sold out to the Spaniards. The States-General had promulgated a placard with the order to hang every 'Bergverkoper' (i.e. the men who had 'sold out' on Geertruidenberg) who was taken prisoner,[40] so these men had nothing to lose. One month into the siege the Dutch troops had made little progress, which caused Maurits grave concern. He had just one engineer available to him and everything indicated that he would still have to withstand a strong relief army as well. Maurits tried to remain confident. 'Our camp is very well entrenched', he wrote to Willem Lodewijk, 'and on the main approach roads able to endure the tests of the cannon.'[41] His perception of the situation a few weeks later was somewhat bleaker.

Count Peter Ernst of Mansfeld (1517–1604), Parma's replacement as governor-general of the Spanish Netherlands, reached Oosterhout in late May 1593 with between 9,000 and 10,000 men.[42] Maurits urged Willem Lodewijk to send him 1,000 men as reinforcements. He was aware that this would make it more difficult for Willem Lodewijk to ward off Verdugo, so in exchange for this assistance he assured his cousin that 'if after this siege I might be of assistance to you in your quarter, then I would be very willing to employ myself there'.[43] Willem Lodewijk could comply with Maurits's request only in part, since he could spare no more than four Frisian infantry companies (about 600 men). The Frisians joined the siege army on 15 June.[44] Though they were fewer in number than Maurits had requested, they still proved to be precisely what was needed, because there were skirmishes with Mansfeld's troops almost daily. Around this time the Dutch were at last starting to make swifter progress with the siegeworks. After eighty-one days they were in a position to start traversing the ditch. The assault targeted a ravelin and the main rampart. On 24 June 1593 Maurits ordered the storming

---

[38] Parker, *The Dutch Revolt*, p. 230.
[39] Hahlweg, *Heeresreform der Oranier*, p. 694; Duyck, I, p. 241.
[40] Ten Raa, *Het Staatsche leger*, II, p. 9.
[41] KHA, A22-IX-A1-28, Maurits to Willem Lodewijk, before Geertruidenberg, 1 May 1593.
[42] Duyck, I, p. 201.
[43] KHA, A22-IX-A1-30, Maurits to Willem Lodewijk, before Geertruidenberg, 21 May 1593.
[44] KHA, A22-IX-A1-35, Maurits to Willem Lodewijk, before Geertruidenberg, 16 June 1593.

of the ravelin. The garrison's commander, Gesan, was killed that same day. The prospect of having to withstand a full-scale assault without a leader made the defenders decide to give up the fight. The signing of the capitulation took place the following morning. The garrison was allowed to withdraw but without colours flying, and three of the 'Bergverkopers' were hanged. Maurits assured the civilians they would be 'treated like all other inhabitants of towns that stand under the Generality'.[45] The reduction of Geertruidenberg established Maurits's reputation as a general, the triumph being wholly due to his personal perseverance. His self-reliance was severely tested by the absence of Willem Lodewijk, but he had persevered.[46] Little of importance happened during the rest of the 1593 campaign. Mansfeld and Maurits kept a watchful eye on each other, but there was no confrontation.

In 1594 the focus of the war in the Low Countries shifted back to the north. The States-General instructed Maurits and Willem Lodewijk to seize the town of Groningen. For this sizeable operation the Dutch army was temporarily reinforced with 2,600 German infantrymen and 260 cavalrymen, making a total of 9,500 foot and close to 1,900 horse available for field service. Prior to investing Groningen, Maurits and Willem Lodewijk decided to march to the relief of Coevorden, which Verdugo was blockading with approximately 4,400 men. The Spanish general fled before the arrival of the Dutch force. Once Coevorden had been replenished with victuals and munitions, the Dutch force pushed onward to Groningen, arriving there on 22 May 1594. Groningen was a large town, but the garrison numbered a mere 700 men and the inhabitants were divided into two camps. The commoners were deeply attached to their Catholic faith, while the burghers had grave concerns about their town's economic decline and saw greater advantage in an affiliation to the Republic.[47] After the Dutch troops had stormed the ravelin before the Eastern Gate, the civil militiamen were no longer prepared to persevere with the town's defence. On 22 July 1594, Groningen opened its gates for the Republic's army. The capitulation stipulated that the city would be reintegrated into the Union as a full member, but in exchange for this the city's regents had to be reconciled with the States of the Ommelands, accept Willem Lodewijk as stadholder, and agree that only the Reformed faith would be professed within the town walls, but 'under condition that one shall not inquire into anyone's conscience', thereby assuring religious liberty. The Spanish garrison was allowed a free withdrawal providing the men agreed not to serve on the right bank of the Rhine for three months.[48]

---

[45] Duyck, I, pp. 225, 235–9 and 242.
[46] Van Deursen, *Maurits*, p. 124, maintains that Maurits already ranked among the great generals by the close of the 1591 campaign: 'His renown as a general was established in a single year.' This was, in my view, two years too early, for the reasons mentioned.
[47] Ibid., p. 137.
[48] Duyck, I, pp. 460–3.

In early August 1594 the Dutch troops left for the garrisons in order to allow the captains and rittmasters to bring their companies up to full strength. While the hostilities were at a temporary standstill, the deputies of the States-General and the Council of State turned their minds to what important task the Dutch army might undertake before winter set in. They chose to order Maurits to lay siege to Groenlo, the stronghold from which the Spaniards were holding the county of Zutphen under contribution. For Maurits this decision was less than satisfactory, as he was of the opinion that he had too few troops available to undertake this operation. Only if Willem Lodewijk were to support him did he consider this siege viable. 'If you do not come I will be all alone and without a sufficient number of companies', Maurits informed his cousin.[49] The stadholder of Friesland advised Maurits not to undertake this operation. In his view Groenlo opened no pathways to further conquests – the small town did not stand on the banks of a river – and he anticipated that this siege operation would entail a great many problems, especially so late in the year, when it would be impossible to find straw for the soldiers' huts. Willem Lodewijk thought it would be better to lay siege to Lingen rather than Groenlo. The reduction of Lingen would force the Spanish to abandon Twente altogether. According to Willem Lodewijk there were also logistical arguments in favour of this operation: food and munitions could be conveyed via Emden without difficulty, and he impressed upon his cousin that Holland would have no cause for concern with the costs of this undertaking, for 'the gentlemen [i.e. the States] of Friesland and the Ommelands will bear all the expenses'. Willem Lodewijk was convinced that this operation would take only ten days. The only thing he asked of Holland was to make four demi-cannon available to him – without ammunition, which Friesland would provide – together with 3,000 infantrymen and the entire Dutch cavalry. If The Hague rejected this proposal then Maurits could depend on thirteen Frisian companies setting out for Groenlo.[50] The States-General stuck to their original decision. In accordance with their orders, Maurits gathered the Dutch troops at Arnhem and Doesburg in early October 1594. However, at more or less the same time, King Henry IV of France entreated The Hague to make a Dutch relief force available to him; in exchange he promised to declare war on Spain.

The then Henri de Navarre had in July 1593 dealt his adversaries a heavy political blow by converting to Catholicism. In February 1594 he was crowned king and in March he made his triumphal entry into Paris, thus incontrovertibly establishing his sovereignty.[51] Van Oldenbarnevelt readily agreed with Henry IV's request and arranged for twenty-two infantry companies, originally intended for the assault on Groenlo, to leave for France immediately. He then insisted that Maurits should go ahead with the siege irrespective of this reduction in his

---

[49] KHA, A22-IX-A1-77a, Maurits to Willem Lodewijk, The Hague, 14 September 1594.
[50] KHA, A22-IX-E-74, Willem Lodewijk to Maurits, Groningen, 19 September 1594, minute.
[51] Parker, *The Dutch Revolt*, p. 231.

manpower, but Maurits refused and called off the operation.[52] France declared war on Spain on 17 January 1595.

At first the French declaration of war was of little advantage to the Republic. Maurits and Willem Lodewijk hoped to make use of the circumstance that Spain was now forced to wage a war on two fronts in the Low Countries to at last reduce Groenlo. However, on 17 July 1595, barely a week after they had invested this town, the approach of a Spanish relief army that was an estimated 6,000 to 7,000 strong forced them to raise the siege. The lines of communication with the towns along the River IJssel were under threat and, furthermore, the strength of the Dutch army (8,800 men) was insufficient to guard Groenlo's line of contravallation and its more extensive line of circumvallation simultaneously. The retreat was chaotic and resulted in the loss of many pieces of siege equipment. Maurits and Willem Lodewijk spent the rest of the summer and autumn of 1595 improving the discipline and combat skills of the Dutch troops. In mid-September another Dutch auxiliary force headed for France, this time to assist with the relief of Cambrai, but in early October this stronghold fell into Spanish hands. A couple of weeks later the Dutch army disbanded to its winter quarters.[53]

The 1596 campaign was also a disappointment for the Republic. On 18 February a new governor-general arrived in Brussels, namely Cardinal Albert (1559–1621), archduke of Austria. Besides his administrative expertise he brought along substantial reinforcements, approximately 8,000 Spanish and Italian veterans.[54] He deployed these troops immediately. First he captured Calais and in early July 1596 he invested Hulst, where there was a sizeable garrison of 3,700 to 3,800 men under the command of Georg Eberhard, count of Solms (1568–1602). He could not expect any assistance from Maurits, because Elizabeth I had recalled 2,200 men from the English relief force in the Low Countries for an expedition to Cadiz, leaving barely 5,000 Dutch troops for field service.[55] The behaviour of the English queen did, however, have an opportune effect: in the Republic it brought about a growing awareness that while alliances were necessary they were no replacement for autonomous military strength.

On 9 August 1596 Maurits and Willem Lodewijk presented a memorandum to the States-General in which they warned that as long as the Republic was unable to deploy 12,000 or, at the very least, 10,000 men for field service, further Spanish successes could not be precluded, 'especially if the enemy were to wage war in two quarters again',[56] as had been the case prior to 1590. Albert's arrival made this danger real. The States-General took the advice of the two stadholders and issued orders to reinforce the Dutch army with two new infantry regiments,

[52] Den Tex, *Oldenbarnevelt*, II, pp. 96–7; Van Deursen, *Maurits*, p. 139.
[53] Duyck, I, pp. 603–86.
[54] Parker, *Army of Flanders*, p. 278.
[55] Duyck, II, pp. 119–20; Ten Raa, *Het Staatsche leger*, II, p. 40; Van Deursen, *Maurits*, p. 153.
[56] Duyck, II, p. 461, Appendix ii.

26. Battle of Turnhout in 1597. Fictional depiction engraved c. 1690–1700. (Royal Netherlands Army Museum, Delft, 00121746)

one composed of Germans and one of Huguenots, and to temporarily engage 6,000 *waardgelders*, which would make forty to fifty Dutch companies available for field service. Together with an English and a Scottish regiment that were already in Dutch employ it would then be possible to take the requisite 10,000 to 12,000 troops on campaign.[57] This decision had no effect on the siege of Hulst – the governor surrendered the town on 18 August 1596 – but its significance was to become evident at a future date. On 31 October 1596 the Republic joined an offensive and defensive alliance forged four months earlier between France and England, the Treaty of Greenwich.[58] For the States-General this great diplomatic success constituted an important incentive to assert their rights and thus convert the *de facto* recognition of the Republic into a *de jure* legitimisation.

Anno 1597 began with a spectacular Dutch victory at Turnhout (24 January). Some 800 Dutch cavalrymen under Maurits's personal command surprised a Spanish force, consisting of 4,000 infantrymen – 'all of them veterans' – and 500 cavalrymen, which was on its way from Turnhout to Herentals. 'There it was evident how the cavalry can operate among disordered infantry and how

---

[57] Ibid.; Ten Raa, *Het Staatsche leger*, II, p. 41.
[58] Den Tex, *Oldenbarnevelt*, II, pp. 176 and 186–7.

each blow and shot took a human life, because in less than a quarter of an hour they killed more than 2,000 people of this army', wrote Duyck. All thirty-seven colours of this elite force fell into Dutch hands. At a cost of only seven dead and a few wounded on the Dutch side, the Spaniards suffered 2,000 dead and some 500 to 700 men, most of them seriously wounded, were taken as prisoners of war.[59] This eradicated the danger that the Spaniards would go on the offensive against the Dutch, all the more because they were waging war successfully against the French. Amiens fell into Spanish hands by means of a surprise attack on 11 March 1597 and Henry IV undertook everything in his power to undo this disgrace. For the Republic the French-Spanish struggle presented an ideal opportunity to launch an offensive; for their part the Spaniards had to make every effort to retain Amiens, leaving them with even fewer troops to defend the remaining Spanish strongholds in the Northern Netherlands.[60]

In July 1597 Maurits and Willem Lodewijk marched to the Rhine with approximately 8,500 men. The objective was Rheinberg, a fortress of great military and economic consequence. Its reduction was important for Gelderland because it would increase the isolation of the Spanish bases in the Achterhoek. Holland attached great importance to opening the lines of communication with Cologne, so that trade with the German hinterland would be free of stiff Spanish tolls.[61] The operation went well. The Spanish garrison, by then a mere 850 or so strong, capitulated on 20 August, after a siege of just twelve days. Rheinberg's swift surrender was primarily due to unrest among the defending garrison, 'who were unpaid and did not want to fight'.[62] Maurits and Willem Lodewijk subsequently captured the small town of Meurs slightly further south. The Gelderlanders wanted the army to continue north to oust the Spaniards from the county of Zutphen. The States-General consented and on 11 September the Dutch army appeared before Groenlo. By then its effective strength was about 7,400 men, some 1,400 fewer than in July 1595, when Maurits had first stood before this town and suffered a serious setback. The Dutch commander-in-chief had, however, learnt from his mistakes: this time, instead of dividing the army into two quarters, he kept the bulk of the troops together and managed to beset the northern and eastern fronts of Groenlo 'with just a few sconces'.[63] By omitting a line of circumvallation he avoided the troops being spread so thinly that they would be unable to repel an incoming attack. On this occasion Verdugo did not show himself, so the besiegers could pursue their goal undisturbed. On 25 September Maurits sent his trumpeter to the beleaguered town to summon its defenders (still about 1,000 strong) to surrender. If they obeyed then they could

---

[59] On the battle at Turnhout see Duyck, II, pp. 214–19, and Van den Hoek, *De veldtocht van prins Maurits in 1597*, pp. 13–28.
[60] Den Tex, *Oldenbarnevelt*, II, pp. 192–3.
[61] Van den Hoek, *De veldtocht van prins Maurits in 1597*, pp. 53–4.
[62] Duyck, II, p. 325.
[63] Duyck, II, p. 348.

count on favourable terms, but otherwise, Maurits threatened, he would launch an assault on Groenlo and put everyone to the sword. The Spaniards capitulated the following day. The Dutch army proceeded to Bredevoort. Maurits once again had his men make ready for a storm assault. Initially it seemed the 300 Spanish defenders wanted to allow it to come to this, but panic broke out within this small town once the Dutch troops had assumed their starting positions. The garrison fled from the ramparts to the castle and on 9 October 1597 surrendered unconditionally to Maurits.[64]

The unexpectedly swift reconquest of the Achterhoek meant there was time to polish off the Spaniards in Twente during this campaign season. Maurits demanded Enschede's surrender on 18 October 1597, under duress 'that he would break the heads of them all if he had to fire a single shot with the artillery'. A mere 108 strong, the garrison chose to make the best of a bad situation and hastily evacuated the town. The Dutch troops then laid siege to Oldenzaal and Ootmarsum simultaneously. The latter had a garrison of 120 men and fell on 21 October. Approximately 400 men were garrisoned in Oldenzaal, but after four days they also capitulated. This string of successes was crowned with the capture of Lingen on 12 November.[65]

*

In 1597 the 'garden of the Republic' had at last been ring-fenced, the borders of the Union of Utrecht (1579) restored. Retaining what had been captured was all that mattered now, because it was unlikely the Spaniards would resign themselves to such losses. Van Oldenbarnevelt hoped that Henry IV would be prepared to join a concerted campaign in the Southern Netherlands in 1598, but this hope was dashed. On 19 September 1597 the French had recaptured Amiens and the king of France readily agreed to a Spanish peace offer. Henry IV assured The Hague that he would continue to support the Republic furtively, but he no longer deemed an open confrontation with Spain to be in France's interests. On 2 May 1598 Paris and Madrid concluded the Peace of Vervins. This left the Republic with but one ally, namely England, though they could hardly expect much help from Elizabeth I.[66]

The negative consequences of the Spanish-French peace soon made themselves felt. In mid-October 1598 the Spaniards recaptured Rheinberg under their new second-in-command in the Low Countries, Mendoza. They then made an incursion into the Achterhoek and took Doetinchem on 8 November. The Spanish army established its winter quarters in these environs and in the bishopric of Münster, representing a constant threat to Gelderland and Overijssel.[67] There was growing concern in The Hague that Mendoza would continue his offen-

[64] Duyck, II, pp. 379–81. See also p. 62.
[65] Duyck, II, pp. 391–400, 409 and 430–1.
[66] Den Tex, *Oldenbarnevelt*, II, pp. 289, 294, 320 and 329–33.
[67] Ten Raa, *Het Staatsche leger*, II, pp. 48–50.

sive northwards in 1599, thereby driving a wedge between Holland, Zeeland and Utrecht on the one side and Friesland and Groningen on the other. Based on Spanish muster-rolls acquired by spies, Van Oldenbarnevelt came to the grim conclusion that Mendoza had approximately 16,000 infantry and 1,600 cavalry under his command, while Maurits could muster only 8,400 men to oppose them.[68] The Peace of Vervins presented the States-General with the opportunity to enlist a few thousand disbanded French soldiers from Henry IV, but in March 1599 these had still not arrived. Maurits feared the worst, because so long as the Spaniards were numerically superior Mendoza would be able to divide his force 'in order to assail us not only in the Betuwe but also in the Veluwe.'[69] Nevertheless, a Spanish two-pronged offensive between the rivers Waal and Rhine and across the IJssel failed to materialise. Mendoza probably did not dare to push further into the territory of the Republic because it would overstretch his supply lines. Instead he invaded the isle of Bommelerwaard with about 12,000 men in mid-May 1599 and laid siege to Zaltbommel. The operation was not a success, because Maurits managed to prevent the town being cut off from the outside world by building a pontoon bridge across the River Waal. After about a month Mendoza abandoned his assault. Shortly thereafter he was beset by a series of mutinies that totally crippled the Spanish war effort. Willem Lodewijk took advantage of this to recapture Doetinchem on 25 August 1599.[70]

The chaos in the Spanish camp led Van Oldenbarnevelt to believe that the time was ripe to transfer the focal point of the theatre of war to the Southern Netherlands. The plan was to push through along the coast to Dunkirk, the home port of the Flemish privateers who inflicted serious damage on Holland's and Zeeland's merchant and fishing fleets. The destruction of this pirates' nest would serve an important economic objective, but no less significant was that it would gain the Republic access to a second coastal base besides Ostend for launching 'raids' into Flanders. This would substantially increase revenue from contributions and fire-taxes, thus alleviating the burden on the Republic's federal coffers. A military operation deep inside enemy territory that was reliant on maritime lines of communication was not without peril, but under these particular circumstances, notably the rash of mutinies in the Spanish army, Van Oldenbarnevelt considered it to be an acceptable risk.[71]

Maurits did not share this assessment. Even after Holland had consented to employing 3,000 extra men, making it possible to deploy 12,000 men for

---

[68] NA, RAZH, AJvO 3053, 'Estat de liste des gens de guerre qui sont au service du roy d'Espaigne et de archiduc Albert selon la cognoissance que nous en avons ce 20 de décember 1598', based on muster-rolls from August 1598; Bor, *Nederlandsche historiën*, IV, p. 482. Ten Raa (*Het Staatsche leger*, II, p. 48) as well as Van Deursen (*Maurits*, pp. 168 and 169) are mistaken when they ascribe a strength of 25,000 men to the Spanish field army.
[69] KHA, A22-IX-A1-124a, Maurits to Willem Lodewijk, Arnhem, 8 March 1599.
[70] Ten Raa, *Het Staatsche leger*, II, p. 52; Parker, *Army of Flanders*, p. 249.
[71] Den Tex, *Oldenbarnevelt*, II, pp. 356–61.

27. Battle order of the Dutch (left) and Spanish (right) armies prior to the battle of Nieuwpoort (1600). Engraving by Floris Balthasarsz. van Berckenrode, published by Henricus Hondius, c. 1610. (Royal Netherlands Army Museum, Delft, 00012408)

field operations, Maurits still had his doubts, and these were exacerbated by his having to manage without Willem Lodewijk's counsel or assistance on this daring expedition. The stadholder of Friesland was needed for the protection of the Republic's eastern borders against Spanish attack, while the main Dutch force was in Flanders. In view of Maurits's doubts, Van Oldenbarnevelt and the other deputies from the States-General decided to accompany the Dutch army on campaign, and 'thereby maintain control of it in such manner that this expedition will be directed to Dunkirk and diverted nowhere else, as well as to be on hand in the event of any difficulties and, where possible, to bring the contributions from Flanders onto established lines and to impose a high fire-tax on all the villages'.[72]

The 1600 campaign did not achieve the desired outcome. The mutinous Spanish troops suspended their 'strike actions'[73] and rallied under the colours in the nick of time. The renowned battle in the dunes near Nieuwpoort took place on 2 July 1600, presenting the threat that was precisely what Maurits had always feared: the obliteration of the Dutch field army. The Dutch troops found themselves in a situation that was indeed awkward – the Spaniards blocked the line of retreat to Ostend, so defeat would be tantamount to annihilation – but a Spanish victory was not a foregone conclusion, in fact quite the contrary. Both armies were just about equal in strength (each numbering some 10,000 infantry and 1,200 cavalry), but the Dutch troops received artillery support from warships that were cruising just off the coast, plus they had the advantage of the tactical reforms that had been introduced in the Dutch army. The strength of the Spaniards lay in their fighting spirit and high morale, but in discipline and stamina they were no match for the Dutch troops.

The battle of Nieuwpoort was joined at around half past three in the afternoon. For a long time the battle wavered, but then the Dutch troops started to bend before the Spanish attack, which was conducted with 'exceptional courage'. Only a small number of Dutch soldiers and cavalry were seized by panic and took to their heels, 'but nevertheless there was a general yielding of all the men, abandoning dune after dune and position after position'. It seemed that victory would be Mendoza's and Albert's, but the attacking drive of their men proved to be a drawback: the Spanish infantry had moved so far forward that its flanks were left unprotected. Maurits saw his chance to decide the battle. He had kept a few companies of horse in reserve and now these fresh troopers went on the offensive. The Dutch cavalrymen hit the Spaniards in the flank and scattered them. The Spanish army's retreat began at around seven o'clock in the evening. Both parties had sustained heavy losses. The Dutch army suffered 1,000 fatalities and 700 wounded, but on the Spanish side there were 3,000 or so fatalities

---

[72] Duyck, II, pp. 612, 614–15 and 637 (quote).
[73] Parker, *Army of Flanders*, p. 205.

28. Maurits of Nassau (1567–1625), commander-in-chief of the Dutch army. Fleming, *Oostende vermaerde, gheweldighe, lanckdurighe ende bloedighe belegheringhe* (The Hague 1621). (Royal Netherlands Army Museum, Delft, 00112009/013)

and a further 600 Spaniards were taken prisoner, including Mendoza.[74] After the battle of Nieuwpoort the Dutch army was too enfeebled to continue the campaign and provisioning was presenting serious problems. On 15 July 1600 they began the withdrawal to Ostend, where the Dutch troops boarded ships to return to the Republic.

---

[74] Duyck, II, pp. 671–9 (quote). The battle is treated in detail by J.P. Puype, 'Victory at Nieuwpoort, 2 July 1600', in Van der Hoeven (ed.), *Exercise of Arms*, pp. 69–112.

The struggle of attrition for Ostend (1601–1604)

The year 1600 was a turning point in the Eighty Years' War. The battle of Nieuwpoort demonstrated that the Dutch troops were equal to the Spaniards in open battle, but it also raised the question of whether placing the Republic's army at risk in such a manner could ever be justified again. The outcome of a battle was, after all, influenced by all manner of uncontrollable factors. Between 1590 and 1597 the Republic had succeeded in consolidating its territorial basis appreciably, but its domain was still very small. Under these circumstances a lost battle could be calamitous. Even if the majority of Dutch troops managed to escape with their lives, the enemy would for a while be able to continue his invasion unhampered and trample the recaptured provinces of Gelderland and Overijssel, 'before one would be able to redress [i.e. replace] the defeated and scattered troops'.[75] Maurits was of the opinion that the Republic could not risk a second battle of Nieuwpoort, a view wholly endorsed by Willem Lodewijk.[76] Maurits was prepared to give battle again only when he was assured of a clear-cut numerical superiority, when the enemy positions were not overly strong, and when the withdrawal of his own army was secure.

Van Oldenbarnevelt concurred with both generals that the decision to fight a pitched battle should not be taken lightly, but he was not convinced that the Republic was sufficiently equipped to successfully pursue a 'strategy of attrition' (*Ermattungs-Strategie*).[77] Despite the Advocate of Holland's misgivings, the siege of Ostend that began on 5 July 1601 would draw the Republic ever deeper into the quagmire of a war of attrition. Voluntarily surrendering Ostend was unthinkable. In view of future operations in Flanders this stronghold was critically important, but this was not the chief motivation. The defence of Ostend soon became a question of prestige, 'given that … the ruining of the enemy's reputation and authority relies on its preservation, since the eyes of all the neighbouring states and lands are turned to it'.[78] The Spanish government in Brussels was confronted with the same problem as the States-General in The Hague. After the battle of Nieuwpoort, even the Spaniards could muster little enthusiasm for another showdown in the open field. The recapture of Ostend was meant to efface the memories of the lost battle. As soon as this last foothold of the Dutch rebels in Flanders was destroyed, the two archdukes, as Albert and Isabella were known after marrying in 1599, wanted to resume the attack on the Dutch Republic.

In May 1598 Philip II ceded the Spanish Netherlands to his daughter Isabella (1566–1633) and her betrothed, Archduke Albert. They would rule over this

---

[75] Fruin, 'Gedenkschrift van Joris de Bye', p. 459.
[76] *Archives*, 2nd series, ii, no. 231, Willem Lodewijk to Maurits, 24 May 1601.
[77] Hans Delbrück, *Geschichte der Kriegskunst im Rahmen der politischen Geschichte*, IV (Berlin 1920), pp. 334–5.
[78] HUA, HAA 5075, 'Instructie voor … Pieter de Sedlintsky', The Hague, 26 August 1601.

29. Albert, archduke of Austria (1559–1621), governor-general (1596–1598) and joint sovereign ruler of the Spanish Netherlands (1599–1621) with his wife, Isabella (1566–1633), daughter of King Philip II of Spain. *Afbeeldinghe ende beschrijvinghe van alle de veldslagen* (Amsterdam 1616). (Royal Netherlands Army Museum, Delft, 00112024/021)

territory as 'joint sovereigns', though Madrid retained the final say in political and military affairs. If their marriage was childless or one of them died then the Spanish Netherlands would revert to the Spanish crown. They were married in May 1599 in Spain. Philip II had already died (in September 1598) and his son Philip III (1578–1621) had succeeded him to the Spanish throne. Isabella accompanied Albert when he returned to the Low Countries in August 1599.[79]

[79] John Lynch, *Spain under the Habsburgs*, 2nd edn, 2 vols (Oxford 1981 and 1986), I, pp. 355–6.

Ostend was an impoverished fishing town with barely 3,000 inhabitants, but with the construction of all kinds of retrenchments outside its walls the Dutch had transformed it into a substantial stronghold with a garrison about 4,500 strong. It therefore closely resembled a fortified army camp.[80] Besides its extensive defensive works, Ostend's strength was derived from its geographical situation. Dutch troop reinforcements, munitions and food supplies could be imported via a natural harbour known as the 'New Harbour' or the 'Gully' (*Geul*) on its northeast flank. Quicksand and the unremitting tides made it extremely difficult for a besieger to approach Ostend from that angle. This natural obstacle was not the only difficulty which had to be overcome to reach the harbour; to effectively prevent ships putting in at Ostend the assailant would have to capture a detached bastion, known as the 'Spanish ravelin', and disable the artillery on the main rampart. The Spanish ravelin stood on the opposite side of the Gully and was linked to the fort by a bridge. Until this structure had been captured and the artillery behind it silenced it would be possible for the defenders to continue bombarding the besieger's batteries and dams to pieces, providing, that is, they were not simply washed away by the sea. The severing of Ostend's lifeline would therefore require a gargantuan effort on the part of the Spanish, all the more because the Dutch fleet were sailing back and forth in front of the harbour entrance and the besiegers therefore had to endure cannonades from the sea. For all these reasons Albert decided to direct the main Spanish assault at the southwestern defences. At least this side was approachable, but it presented the disadvantage that the greatest care and attention had been devoted to the defensive works there.

Colonel Charles van der Noot was governor of Ostend at the start of the siege. On 12 July 1601 he gave the order to undertake a sortie to the Spanish trenches 'in order to exercise our soldiers somewhat'. No fewer than 800 to 900 Dutch troops were involved in this operation, 'but because they [i.e. the besiegers] lie very securely and inaccessibly entrenched [i.e. high in the dunes] it was impossible to gain any advantage from it'. Van der Noot broke off the fight after an hour of skirmishes and ordered his troops to withdraw to the town. 'I cannot ascertain', he wrote to the States-General, 'that one would be able, other than by pouncing upon their men with the might of superior numbers, to cause him to leave his trenches because of the high and strong entrenchment in the dunes.'[81] In other words, he needed more troops. At The Hague they had in the meantime come to the same conclusion and taken the decision to double the strength of the garrison to approximately 8,000 men. The forty-seven-year-old English general, Sir Francis Vere, arrived in the beleaguered town along with the first reinforcements on 15 July. Van der Noot remained at his post as governor, but the States-General had assigned overall charge of the defence to Vere. He

---

[80] Van Sypesteyn, *Beleg van Ostende*, pp. 6–9.
[81] NA, SG 4900, Charles van der Noot to the SG, Ostend, 14 July 1601.

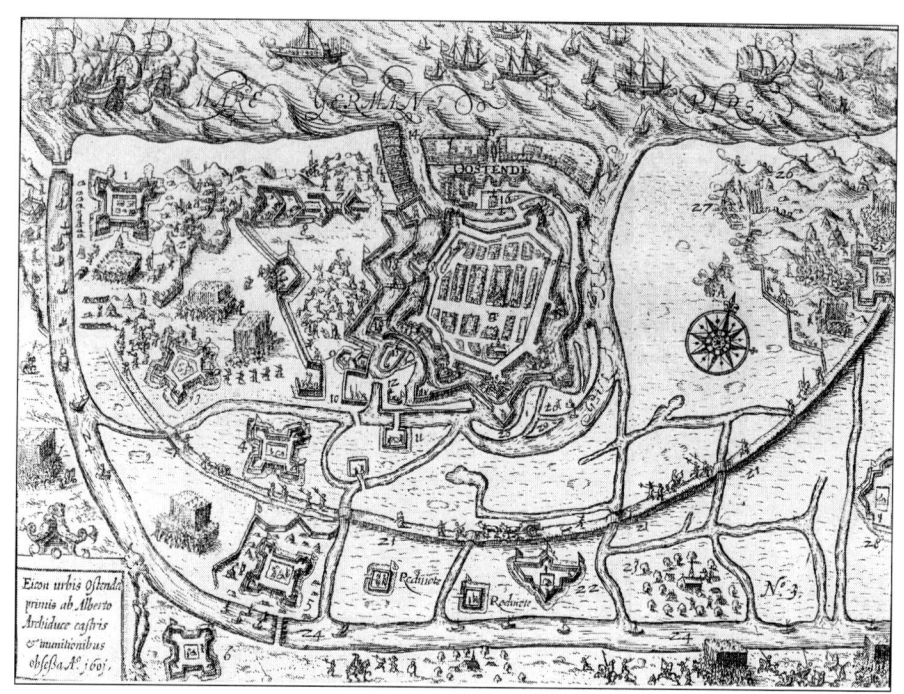

30. The siege of Ostend, 1601–1604. Illustration in Fleming, *Oostende vermaerde, gheweldighe, lanckdurighe ende bloedighe belegheringhe* (1621) (Utrecht University, Special Collections, S.qu. 1036). The *Geul* (Gully), or New Harbour, is depicted to the right of the town. Missing from this plan is the Spanish ravelin, an outwork which stood on the far side of the Geul in front of the Spanish bulwark (the bastion to the bottom right).

had orders to defend Ostend 'like an army', namely by means of an active defence from the outworks.[82]

The Hague had decided to appoint Vere instead of Van der Noot or another capable Dutch colonel as commander-in-chief in Ostend for two reasons: Vere's presence ensured that Elizabeth I raised no objections to troops of the English expeditionary force serving in the beleaguered town and, moreover, the English general was extremely driven. By pursuing an energetic defence he hoped to eclipse Maurits as the Republic's most renowned general. It therefore hardly comes as a surprise that Maurits was not favourably disposed towards Vere's appointment, all the more because his rival was constantly pressing for extra troops to be sent there. This request could only be complied with at the expense of the strength of the field army, potentially placing Maurits in an awkward position. He had been laying siege to Rheinberg since 13 June 1601 and he could not exclude the possibility that the Spaniards would come to the aid of this town as

[82] Duyck, III, p. 89 n. 1.

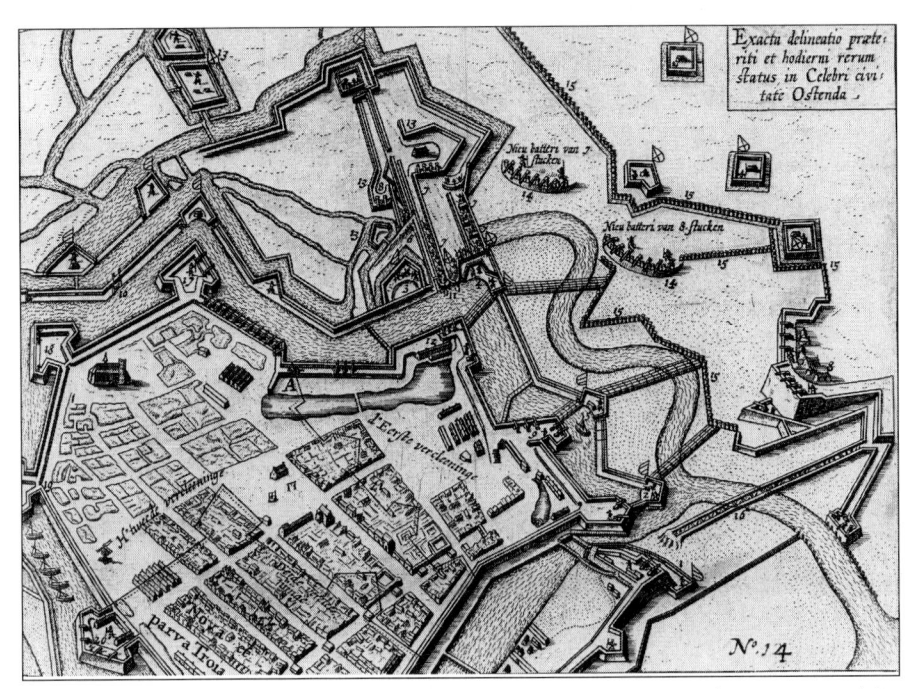

31. Ostend's southwestern defensive works during the siege of 1601–1604. The orientation of the drawing is with south at the top. Fleming, *Oostende vermaerde, gheweldighe, lanckdurighe ende bloedighe belegheringhe* (1621) (Utrecht University, Special Collections, S.qu. 1036). The Polder is depicted just above the centre of the plan with the Polder ravelin (no. 3). To the right of this stands the Southwest ravelin (no. 4) and behind it the Southwest bulwark (no. 12). Alongside this stand the West ravelin (no. 5), the West bulwark (no. 9), the Porc-Épic or 'Porcupine' (no. 2) and the Helmond bastion. The Old Harbour and the Sandhill fort (no. 1) can be seen to the bottom right. The plan also depicts the outlines of the retrenchments or reduits within the walls.

soon as the reinforcements they were expecting from Italy – an estimated 6,000 or so men, but actually as many as 8,000 – had arrived in the Low Countries. At the head of this military force stood Ambrogio Spinola, the future major opponent of Maurits and Willem Lodewijk.[83]

In mid-July 1601, on the States-General's insistence, Maurits eventually allowed twenty English companies, one-fifth of his infantry, to leave for Ostend. This reduction in strength would have no adverse consequences, because a Spanish attempt to relieve Rheinberg failed to materialise and the Spanish

---

[83] NA, SG 4900, Maurits to the SG, before Rheinberg, 23 July 1601, appendix, 'L'ordre que les trouppes du roy d'Espaigne tiennent allant trouver l'Archeduc ... et le nombre'; *Archives*, 2nd series, ii, no. 230, Maurits to Willem Lodewijk, The Hague, 19 May 1601; Parker, *Army of Flanders*, p. 278.

garrison capitulated on 30 July. Maurits now had a free hand, which immediately raised the question of how Ostend's defenders might best be assisted. Maurits and Willem Lodewijk agreed that an 'advertised diversion' was the best tactic for drawing the Spaniards away from Ostend. Willem Lodewijk had long been a champion of laying siege to 's-Hertogenbosch. Hulst and Grave would be easier to capture, but he doubted whether Albert attached enough significance to these two towns to raise the siege of Ostend. If the Republic were to attack Sluis that would certainly be the case – from this port the Spanish galleys made the Scheldt estuary unsafe and threatened Zeeland – but Willem Lodewijk considered this operation too risky, 'because it [Sluis] is so close to Ostend I find it is subject to much greater difficulties, such as the risk of a battle'.[84] A second battle of Nieuwpoort had to be avoided at all costs.

In early August 1601, Vere pressed for the sending of even more reinforcements. This time he asked for 2,000 men, which would swell the garrison of Ostend to 8,000, as prescribed by the States-General. Consenting to this would, however, have been tantamount to disbanding the field army, because it had already been necessary to leave behind a garrison of about twenty companies in Rheinberg.[85] Taking the extra troops for Ostend into account, there would be barely forty companies remaining for field service. Maurits made it clear to the States-General that they had to make a choice: either Ostend should be left to defend itself, 'from now on assigning all our forces to that end, in order to reinforce and refresh the garrison of Ostend every time the situation requires it, or one tries to make the enemy raise [the siege of] Ostend by means of some diversion'. Maurits declared that he and Willem Lodewijk were also prepared to agree to implementing both measures, but that they would first need more troops to be made available to them, because no operation of consequence could be undertaken with an army of just 7,000 men. Maurits then broached the prospect of besieging 's-Hertogenbosch, whereby Albert would almost certainly be forced to interrupt the assault on Ostend, but he saw 'no prospect ... of forcing ['s-Hertogenbosch] with so few men'.[86] Seeing that, under the given circumstances, Maurits did not consider the siege of 's-Hertogenbosch to be a viable proposition, the States-General instructed him to ship the above-mentioned 2,000-strong reinforcement to Ostend and to return to The Hague for further deliberations.[87]

The situation in Ostend failed to improve despite the arrival of substantial reinforcements. Vere was suddenly seized by doubts about whether he could

---

[84] *Archives*, 2nd series, ii, no. 222, Willem Lodewijk to Maurits, Leeuwarden, 25 February 1601.
[85] NA, SG 4900, Maurits to the SG, before Rheinberg, 1 August 1601.
[86] NA, SG 4900, Maurits to the SG, received 11 August 1601, addendum, 'Memorie van 'tgene de gedeputeerde van de Raden van State alhier in 't leger geweest hebbende zullen hebben te verclaeren aen mijnheeren de Generale Staten der Vereenichde Provintiën'.
[87] NA, SG 4900, Maurits to the SG, Rheinberg, 13 August 1601; Duyck, III, pp. 128–9.

keep this stronghold out of Spanish hands if there was to be no assault on 's-Hertogenbosch. Moreover, on 14 August 1601 he was seriously wounded, so he had to be transferred to Zeeland to convalesce. The critical situation ultimately forced the States-General to agree to the besieging of 's-Hertogenbosch and they ordered the levying of 6,000 extra troops on a temporary basis.[88] The States-General also decided to send Major-General Pieter Sedlnitzky (†1610), baron of Soltenitz, to Ostend in order to garner better intelligence about the local situation and to encourage the town's garrison to persevere in the town's defence for all they were worth, urging them to 'defend [it] foot by foot, to the utmost'.[89] This called for the digging of countermines underneath the ravelins and bastions that were threatened, 'thus, should the enemy want to mine these ravelins and bulwarks, to better find their mines and obstruct them, indeed be able to fight in those mines and to thwart him'.[90] The States-General were aware that they were asking huge sacrifices from their officers and soldiers, so Sedlnitzky was also to convey the States-General's assurance to the garrison that they would do everything 'that shall be necessary for the preservation of their persons and the place, which they [i.e. the States-General] do not regard as a town but as an army that is being besieged by another'. The defenders could depend on their being sent sufficient munitions to fire 300 cannon-ball and about 30,000 shots with muskets and calivers every day,[91] leaving no doubt that the struggle for Ostend was being conducted as a war of attrition.

At The Hague they estimated that '1,000 healthy soldiers were needed every month to replace the injured, dead and sick' in Ostend. Army organisation made it impossible to send recruits every month – the replacement of casualties was, after all, the private responsibility of the captains. It was therefore decided to relieve the companies with fresh units every couple of months. Having the Dutch troops serve in Ostend by rotation would make it possible to maintain the garrison at a constant effective strength of about 4,000 men. According to Maurits this was sufficient to pursue an active defence,[92] and he even advised against a larger garrison. Food supplies could easily be shipped into Ostend from Holland and Zeeland in the summer – over the course of 1601 no fewer than 554 ships entered the harbour – but as soon as the autumn gales began to blow, the town would be cut off from the outside world for several months and would therefore have to survive on its amassed stocks of food. Furthermore, Ostend was

---

[88] RGP 85, Res. SG, 24 and 25 August 1601 (no. 69).
[89] HUA, HAA 5075, 'Instructie voor ... Pieter de Sedlintsky', The Hague, 26 August 1601.
[90] Ibid., addendum to the 'Instructie': 'Memorial' from Maurits and the States-General for the garrison of Ostend, The Hague, 27 August 1601, transcript.
[91] Ibid., addenda to the 'Instructie': the 'Memorial', a 'Liste van 'tghene binnen Oostenden sal gesonden werden boven all 'tgene datter gesonden is en[de] noch onderweghen is' and a 'Liste van 't geschut en[de] ammonitie daertoe behoorende die binnen Oostende sal gesonden worden'.
[92] Ibid., addendum to the 'Instructie' entitled 'Volcht den memoriael van 'tgene dat noch binnen Ostende nodich te bestellen'.

by no means geared to accommodating 8,000 soldiers. Even at half this strength the troops were 'lodged thirty to fifty to a room' and there was insufficient straw for mattresses.[93] The number of sick skyrocketed by the day, as did the number of dead and wounded as a result of intense Spanish artillery fire. In the overpopulated stronghold almost every shot made its mark. In September 1601 there were 4,633 English troops among the garrison: 3,659 'able-bodied' men and 974 sick and wounded.[94] Just over two months later the effective strength of the English contingent had decreased to just 1,141 men, in addition to 700 sick and wounded. The garrison's other troops – Dutchmen, Germans, Frenchmen and Scots – numbered 2,719 'able-bodied' men and 1,005 sick and wounded at this time.[95] In order to alleviate this perilous situation, Maurits ordered the construction of thirty-three captain's quarters and 198 soldiers' huts in the outworks. These shelters had to be covered with a thick layer of earth so they could withstand a cannonball strike. Each of the soldiers' barracks accommodated twenty men – two soldiers per box-bed – so a total of more than 4,000 men could be accommodated in these huts.[96]

Sedlnitzky returned from Ostend on 18 September 1601 and reported his findings to Maurits and Vere in Middelburg. His assessment was that the town 'was indeed defensible', but the officers lacked confidence that they would be able to maintain the town's defence during the winter. They therefore considered it a matter of great urgency: the sooner a 'diversion' was effected to 'draw the enemy away from the place' the better. Vere, who had now recovered from his injuries, left for Ostend that night,[97] while Maurits proceeded to The Hague to make preparations for the march on 's-Hertogenbosch. In the night of 1/2 November, Maurits and Willem Lodewijk appeared before 's-Hertogenbosch with seventy-three infantry companies and thirty-three cavalry companies. The Dutch army remained encamped before this town for three weeks. 'Our artillery fired on the town a great deal, here and there on the defences [i.e. the fortifications]', noted Duyck in his journal. However, the hope that this would prompt the inhabitants of 's-Hertogenbosch to rise against the garrison was in vain. Willem Lodewijk harboured not one jot of confidence that this operation could be turned into a success. The Dutch army was too small to invest 's-Hertogenbosch completely, which meant that fresh Spanish troops, sometimes hundreds at a time, were regularly able to reach the town. Moreover, as frost set in, the digging of trenches and the raising of redoubts and batteries became extremely arduous.[98] On 23 November 1601, Willem Lodewijk informed Maurits that in his view they

---

[93] Duyck, II, p. 728 n. 1, Governor Maximiliaan of Cruyningen to the SG, 22 August 1600.
[94] NA, SG 4900, Michiel Everwijn to the SG, Ostend, 14 September 1601, annex.
[95] NA, RAZH, AJvO 3008, 'Sterckte van alle de compaigni[e]ën nu ter tijdt binnen de stat Ostende volgende de rollen van de capiteinen overgelevert de 24.en novembris 1601'.
[96] NA, SG 4900, Johan Biel to the SG, Nijmegen, 29 September 1601, annex.
[97] Duyck, III, pp. 157 (quote), 159 and 172.
[98] Duyck, III, pp. 193 (quote), 203–4 and 208.

had already done everything possible for the year to draw the Spaniards away from Ostend and that the lateness of the season did not permit them to keep the Dutch troops in the field any longer.[99] Maurits concurred and the Dutch army's departure followed three days later. Maurits subsequently informed the States-General that it was high time they made preparations to replace Ostend's entire garrison with about 4,000 fresh troops, 'for in our opinion the town shall be adequately manned with fifty companies'.[100]

Vere was by now close to despair. The besiegers were preparing for a full-scale storm assault with an estimated 6,000 to 7,000 men and, according to Vere, his garrison was so drastically enfeebled by heavy bombardments, sickness and tiring guard duties that he did not think it possible to defend the outworks against these superior numbers. It was, however, inconceivable that they should abandon the outer defences voluntarily, 'since this would undoubtedly have resulted in the loss of the town'.[101] On 26 December 1601, Vere surprised Maurits with the announcement that the critical situation had left him with no other choice but to have recourse to a risky ruse. Three days earlier (23 December) he had informed the Spaniards that he was ready to parley about the surrender of Ostend. Vere was aware that such a step could be construed as treason and he had therefore given his word of honour to all the captains that these negotiations were only intended 'to amuse [i.e. distract] the enemy for a while, until he should receive succour from the States'.[102] Vere kept his word: on the same day he wrote his letter to Maurits an initial convoy (400 men) of the 4,000 relief troops arrived, whereupon he ordered the parleys with the Spaniards to be broken off immediately.[103] A week or so later Vere sounded the alarm anew. The situation in Ostend was perilous and he feared for the worst if thousands of extra troops were not sent there quickly. The only chance of saving Ostend for the Republic, in his view, was if the garrison were to be reinforced to the tally of no fewer than 10,000 men.[104]

The dreaded Spanish storm assault began at about seven o'clock in the evening on 7 January 1602. By launching an assault via the Old Harbour – it was low tide – Albert hoped to be able to overrun the Sandhill fort and the Porc-Épic (Porcupine), a ravelin located on the seaward side of the town, and thereby wholly invest Ostend. The venture ended in a bloodbath. The defenders opened the sluices, allowing water from the ditch to stream through the Old Harbour to the sea, which simply washed away the Spaniards or isolated them from one another, making them easy prey for the garrison. The cannon on the ramparts

---

[99] *Archives*, 2nd series, ii, no. 249, Willem Lodewijk to Maurits, before 's-Hertogenbosch, 23 November 1601.
[100] NA, SG 4901, Maurits to the SG, Gorinchem, 30 November 1601.
[101] *Archives*, 2nd series, II, no. 251, Francis Vere to Maurits, Ostend, 26 December 1601.
[102] Duyck, III, pp. 233–4 (quote); Van Sypesteyn, *Beleg van Ostende*, p. 45.
[103] *Archives*, 2nd series, II, no. 251, Francis Vere to Maurits, Ostend, 26 December 1601.
[104] *Archives*, 2nd series, II, no. 253, Francis Vere to Maurits, Ostend, 4 January 1602.

were, moreover, loaded with canister-shot – tin boxes filled with musket-balls – which caused heavy casualties among the closely packed assailants. The Spanish suffered a total of 2,500 dead and wounded.[105]

Paradoxically this success meant that Vere had created an impossible situation for himself. At The Hague there was no doubt that he had acted in good faith in December 1601, but this did not diminish the commotion in the Republic. The betrayal of Deventer, the redoubt at Zutphen and Geertruidenberg were still fresh in people's minds. The news about the repulsion of the major storm assault was, of course, received with elation in the Republic, but the ease with which this had been achieved raised the question of how this could be reconciled with Vere's complaints in recent months. How much credibility ought to be attached to his repeated calls for the sending of reinforcements? Vere was apparently incapable of coping with the responsibilities of his command and he therefore painted a bleaker picture of the situation than was actually the case. Willem Lodewijk's verdict was damning, deploring that a fine colonel wished to play the general.[106] The stadholder of Friesland restated his view that Ostend could only be saved by a 'diversion'; further reinforcement of the garrison was senseless. Ostend was, after all, too small to accommodate the 10,000 men that Vere considered necessary and the Spanish siegeworks were too strong to attack them frontally. By complying with Vere's call to substantially expand the garrison there would, moreover, be too few troops remaining to assemble a sizeable field army. And had the failed siege of 's-Hertogenbosch not sufficiently demonstrated that the Spaniards would not be drawn away from their positions before Ostend by a mere pinprick?[107] Vere travelled to The Hague in early March 1602 to rebuff Willem Lodewijk's critique. He stated that he could hold Ostend with 7,000 men, 3,000 less than he had previously stated, but to no avail. The States-General decided to replace the old garrison with eighty fresh companies (c. 5,500 men) and to charge the nobleman Frederik van Dorp (c. 1547–1612) with the command of the stronghold. Vere was reassigned to the field army.

*

The failed assault on 's-Hertogenbosch convinced The Hague that Ostend could be relieved only by launching a sizeable incursion into Brabant. The infantry and cavalry companies were reinforced by a total of 10,000 men and a further 2,000 German cavalrymen and 6,000 *waardgelders* were contracted, placing Maurits in command of a field army numbering no fewer than 24,000 men in 1602. Never before had the Republic assembled an army of such size,[108] and Van Oldenbarn-

---

[105] Van Sypesteyn, *Beleg van Ostende*, pp. 51–4.
[106] *Archives*, 2nd series, II, no. 250, Willem Lodewijk to Maurits, Leeuwarden, 26 December 1601.
[107] *Archives*, 2nd series, II, no. 269, Willem Lodewijk to his father, Count Johann VI of Nassau, 20 July 1602.
[108] Duyck, III, pp. 293, 317–18 and 320–1.

evelt had high expectations for the 1602 campaign. In a detailed memorandum he explained precisely what he expected of the Dutch commander-in-chief. Maurits would have to enter Brabant from the east, 'and taking into account the undoing of the enemy's forces will completely or partially achieve the objective [i.e. the relief of Ostend], the task shall [then] be to aim to achieve that on all occasions, whether it be the enemy that presents himself there [to fight] or that some appropriate opportunity to achieve this arises [during the campaign]'. In other words, Van Oldenbarnevelt wanted Maurits to angle specifically for a battle. A Spanish defeat would leave Albert no other choice than to raise the siege. However, if Albert avoided any contest in the open field, then Maurits had to head straight for Ostend or lay siege to Dunkirk, 'the conquest of which must undoubtedly bring about the relief of the town of Ostend'. If none of these alternatives proved feasible, then as a last resort Maurits would have to switch to 'the general ruination and devastation and destruction of beasts and crops' in Brabant. Lastly, Van Oldenbarnevelt underscored how this campaign was costing a great deal of money and that a great deal was expected of Maurits.[109]

Maurits was hardly disposed towards Van Oldenbarnevelt's call to give battle. He would have preferred to lay siege to a town within easy reach of the Republic's borders. Maurits had little confidence in his ability to change the Advocate of Holland's mind,[110] but if Willem Lodewijk were to approach him then they might persuade him.[111] The stadholder of Friesland was wholly in agreement with his cousin. He formulated a lengthy memorandum and sent this to Van Oldenbarnevelt in the middle of March 1602. Alongside an historical exposition about the logistical problems an invading force would face in the Southern Netherlands, Willem Lodewijk made it clear that he was convinced Albert would not be prepared to join battle. By establishing a succession of strong positions he would easily be able to delay the Dutch advance into Brabant *ad infinitum*.[112] Van Oldenbarnevelt stuck by his original plan. On the basis of intelligence gathered by spies he knew that Albert would be able to call up more than 28,000 infantry and 5,000 cavalry for that summer's field operations,[113] meaning his army would

[109] NA, RAZH, AJvO 2985, 'Memorie van eenige poincten daerop in de aenstaen[de] expeditie bij den gecommitteerden wten heeren Staten-G.nael ... & Raden van State sal dienen gelet', minute taken by Van Oldenbarnevelt.
[110] Van Deursen, *Maurits*, p. 194, underscores how Van Oldenbarnevelt and Maurits were headstrong men, each convinced that he was in the right: 'They lacked the ability to prevail upon one another and were just as unwilling to submit to the will of the other.'
[111] *Archives*, 2nd series, II, no. 256, Maurits to Willem Lodewijk, The Hague, 14 February 1602.
[112] Veenendaal, *Van Oldenbarnevelt*, II, no. 6, Willem Lodewijk to Van Oldenbarnevelt, 29 March 1602. There is a French translation of this memorandum addressed to Maurits (KHA, A22-VIII-4, 'Graeff Willems advys over 't ontsett van Oostende ende den tocht in Brabant 1602').
[113] NA, RAZH, AJvO 3053, 'Liste de trouppes q[ue] l'archiduq Albert faict estat de mettre en campagne sur la fin de may 1602'.

be strong enough to continue the siege of Ostend with robust determination and field a covering force, too. It was therefore of the utmost importance to steal the initiative from the Spaniards and move into Brabant with the Dutch army as soon as possible. From a logistical perspective, besieging a town close by one's own frontiers would certainly be advisable, but this would be to little avail if it was not to Ostend's advantage.

On 3 June 1602 the States-General adopted a secret resolution that was in line with Van Oldenbarnevelt's ideas in which they determined that the Dutch army would make an incursion into Brabant with the aim of seeking out and 'smashing' the enemy's main army.[114] Four days later the troops intended for the offensive were mustered at Elten and Schenkenschans. The Dutch cavalry numbered 5,400 men (not counting 1,000 or so *bidets*) and the infantry some 18,800 men. This army of 24,000 or so men was divided into three groups: Willem Lodewijk took command of 7,600 men, Ernst Casimir of 8,100, and Vere of 8,400.[115] Maurits was in supreme command. The 1602 campaign proved to be a dismal failure, as we have seen.[116] On 8 July the Dutch army presented itself in full battle order before the Spanish positions at Sint-Truiden (Saint-Trond), but Mendoza, who had been released from Dutch captivity a short while earlier, kept his 16,000 to 17,000 troops safe behind their entrenchments. This might not have been very honourable, but it was certainly highly effective. Duyck wrote that the Dutch army was therefore forced 'to turn about without reaping any benefit from Brabant or towards the relief of Ostend and to consider all its [i.e. the States-General's] extraordinary costs to have been in vain'.[117] In order to gain some benefit from this massive military exertion, on 18 July Maurits laid siege to Grave, a small but resilient fortress on the River Meuse. Willem Lodewijk initially feared that Mendoza would come to the aid of Grave's defenders, but on 1 September a few thousand Spanish soldiers mutinied.[118] Grave capitulated on 18 September, after a siege of sixty-three days. The taking of this town marked the conclusion of the 1602 campaign. After the Dutch troops had passed in review on 21 September, the German cavalrymen were dismissed and Maurits divided the rest of the army across the garrisons.

The 1602 campaign had unequivocally shown that, as long as Spain was in a position to mobilise a siege army as well as a covering army, the Republic had insufficient resources to force Brussels to abandon the siege of Ostend. In 1602 the Dutch field army had been more than twice as strong as in the ten previous years, but an effective invasion of Brabant would require a much higher number of troops. Between 1590 and 1600, Maurits and Willem Lodewijk had in

---

[114] RGP 92, Secret res. SG, 3 June 1602 (no. 35).
[115] Van Vervou, *Enige gedenckweerdige geschiedenissen*, pp. 125–7; RAZH, AJvO 2954, 'Staet sommier van[de] monsteringe gedaen den xvii.en juny 1602'.
[116] See pp. 128–30.
[117] Duyck, III, pp. 412–13.
[118] On the Hoogstraten mutiny, see pp. 39–41.

large measure been able to pursue their strategies undisturbed. The war against Henry IV was a higher priority for Spain, so the Republic had been able to achieve important successes without too great an effort. Defeating scattered and often isolated opponents was, however, quite a different kettle of fish compared to attacking an enemy who could deploy his military might within an easily defensible area. After 1600 the Spaniards enjoyed the additional advantage of the interior lines, so they could quickly transfer troops from the siege army before Ostend to the field army in Brabant, and vice versa. The military force available to Maurits in 1602 was without doubt of impressive proportions, but even with 24,000 men it was impossible to induce a reluctant and well-entrenched adversary of 16,000 to 17,000 men to join battle. This called for thousands more soldiers. The Republic and Spain had been embroiled in a war of attrition since 1601 and neither of the belligerents was strong enough to force the issue militarily. Brussels could continue with the siege of Ostend unhindered, but the Spaniards could not prevent the Republic bringing fresh troops, food supplies and munitions into the beleaguered town. The strategic impasse remained unbroken.

Thirty-six Dutch infantry companies left for Ostend in November 1602.[119] These fresh troops were sorely needed there. The town may have been spared any major assault since January, but the losses were no less severe. The Spaniards endeavoured to prevent ships entering the harbour by means of vigorous cannonade, and thus blockade the town on its seaward side. Repairing damage to the fortifications under such conditions was an extremely perilous chore and resulted in many casualties. During the summer of 1602 there was also a new outbreak of the pestilence that had claimed many victims a year earlier. In August, of the erstwhile garrison of seventy-one companies, 'certainly a third ... is infected [and] could not be employed for any duties, though the vehement expiration was [by then] considerably alleviated'.[120]

*

In 1603 it took great effort to get the campaign off the ground. It was mid-January before Maurits at last received permission to draw up a list of the 100 to 120 infantry companies he wished to deploy in the campaign.[121] He was therefore seriously concerned about whether he would be in a position to bring together a field army for that year's campaign 'as soon as need would require'.[122] In the middle of April news reached The Hague that, after bloody fighting, the Spaniards had taken Ostend's outermost line of defence, the 'Polder' situated to the south of the town.[123] The town's defence was continued from the ravelins to the rear – especially the 'Polder Ravelin' – and from the main wall, but this

[119] Duyck, III, p. 510.
[120] Fleming, *Oostende*, p. 280.
[121] RGP 92, Res. SG, 23 January 1603 (no. 173).
[122] KHA, A22-IX-A1-265, Maurits to Willem Lodewijk, The Hague, 16 January 1603.
[123] RGP 92, Res. SG, 15 April 1603 (no. 18).

Spanish success smashed any illusion that the archdukes were tired of the siege. Having captured the Polder the Spaniards could hold Ostend under direct fire, and with the defenders crammed even closer together owing to the capture of this outwork their number of sick also rose. Losses were indeed rising fast. At the end of June 1603 the effective strength of Ostend's garrison was 3,800 men, but by early September the complement of 'healthy' troops had been reduced to 2,550 'fighting men' while the tally of wounded and sick had reached more than 1,400.[124] In the meantime Maurits had set out on campaign with approximately 14,000 men. He proposed to The Hague that he might make a renewed attempt to capture 's-Hertogenbosch. He cannot have meant this terribly seriously, because his army was not up to the task. The States-General did indeed reject this plan, because 'in addition the sobriety [i.e. limitations] of the Land's finances must be duly considered, to defray the great costs of such a siege'.[125] The Republic's finances had still not recovered from the massive blood-letting a year earlier. Nothing of significance occurred for the rest of the 1603 campaign.

From July 1601 to December 1603 the Spaniards had directed their main assault at Ostend's southwestern front. The taking of the Polder outwork had been an important success, but thereafter the Spaniards had failed to make any progress, despite employing intense artillery and musket fire. Albert therefore decided to switch tactics and endeavour to render the Gully (New Harbour) inaccessible after all. Pompeo Targone (1575–c. 1630), an expert on siegecraft seconded by Pope Clemens VIII (1536–1605), devised all manner of ingenious structures and contraptions to help the besiegers seize control of the so-called Spanish Ravelin and, by extension, dominate the harbour. His designs included a great bridge for storm assaults that was conveyed underneath an enormous carriage drawn by forty horses. In February 1604 this 'hell-waggon' was ready, but the Dutch cannoneers managed to smash one of the four wheels, forcing the Spaniards to abandon their assault. Targone's other inventions, including a gigantic rolling gabion to provide cover for the Spanish soldiers and a floating battery, were as dismal a failure, and his plan to seal off the Gully by raising a dam was also a flop. However, Targone's activities were not completely fruitless. The simultaneous threat to the southwestern and eastern fronts demanded the utmost from the garrison. There was no time to rest between watches and the psychological pressure was enormous: no place in the town was safe from the Spanish barrage.[126] Shortly thereafter, Spinola's efforts ratcheted up the intensity of the siege of Ostend even further.

---

[124] Fleming, *Oostende*, pp. 395–6; NA, SG 4906, 'Verscheyden lijsten van comp[ag]ni[e]ën binnen Oostende', received 11 September 1603.
[125] RGP 92, Res. SG, 11 August 1603 (no. 49).
[126] Jan Jansz. Orlers and Henrick van Haestens, *Den Nassauschen laurencrans* (Leiden 1610; facsimile Amsterdam 1979), pp. 182–3; Duffy, *Siege Warfare*, p. 86; Anna E.C. Simoni, *The Ostend Story: Early Tales of the Great Siege and the Mediating Role of Henrick van Haestens* ('t Goy-Houten 2003), pp. 163–70.

Spinola, scion of a Genoese family of bankers, had entered into an agreement with Philip III to finance the siege of Ostend. He would ask for pecuniary settlement only when the town had been reduced. This munificent offer had its price: in exchange Spinola wanted supreme command over the entire operation.[127] Following careful study of the military situation and having sought advice from Italian engineers in his entourage, Spinola came to the conclusion that it made no sense to persist with the assault on the Spanish Ravelin. He argued that Ostend's defenders could only be forced to surrender by wearing them down, which required the launching of large-scale storm assaults.[128] The assaults would probably cost the lives of many Spanish troops, but by comparison the defender's losses would not be much smaller. There was, moreover, no alternative. So long as the town could not be sealed off from the outside world, bleeding the opponent dry was the only means of achieving its reduction. Spinola thought like a banker rather than a soldier. While generals of the early modern era were usually as sparing as possible with their troops, Spinola did not baulk at laying them on the 'butcher's slab' if this brought him closer to the intended objective. This was the only way to recoup the investment in troops. After all, armies were constantly afflicted by disease and desertion, and Spinola therefore considered it better to send troops into the firing line rather than lose them without having gained any advantage from them.[129]

In April 1604 the Spaniards captured the Polder Ravelin and the West Ravelin and could then proceed with the assault on the main rampart. The Dutch defenders put up a valiant fight. Behind the threatened enceinte they raised a line with bastions and began constructing a 'reduit' to the rear of this. This last place of refuge was dubbed 'New Troy'. A shortage of earth forced the defenders to resort to a gruesome solution. On the proposal of the nobleman Jacob van der Meer (†1604), the third governor to be charged with the high command in Ostend in as many weeks – one of his predecessors was killed in action in late March, the other seriously wounded in early April 1604 – the council of war decided that the bodies of casualties, Dutch as well as Spanish, would be used for constructing the line and the redoubt. For this unpleasant and perilous task the troops received a bonus of fourteen stivers for each corpse they delivered, over and above their basic pay of fifteen stivers a day.[130] There was not much time to realise the new defences, because 'even though we to some extent repair the damage to the outworks during the night, during the day they are damaged

---

[127] Van Deursen, *Maurits*, p. 194; Parker, *The Dutch Revolt*, p. 236.
[128] Van Sypesteyn, *Beleg van Ostende*, pp. 70–1, 74, 80, 87 and 90; Duffy, *Siege Warfare*, pp. 86–8.
[129] See p. 121.
[130] Van Sypesteyn, *Beleg van Ostende*, pp. 90–1.

once again by his [i.e. the besieger's] batteries of more than forty pieces, [and they are] preparing even more batteries to dominate our flanks'.[131]

In the Republic there was growing alarm about Ostend. The valour of the defenders was beyond question, but the Spaniards were gaining more and more ground. The fall of Ostend now seemed inevitable and this raised the question of how much money and how many more troops would have to be sacrificed for its defence. By July 1603 this operation had already cost the Republic more than 2.67 million guilders,[132] and tens of thousands of lives had been lost. Among the provincial States and the captains there was increasing reluctance to allow their companies to serve in Ostend.[133] In order to put in place a fair distribution of the burden, Maurits and the Council of State drew up a list of all the infantry on the Republic's payroll, 326 companies in all. Over the course of 1604 the garrison of Ostend was to be refreshed five times. The garrison would on average be sixty-five companies strong and each tour of duty would last about ten weeks.[134] This standing order dispelled the unrest among the captains to some extent. Officials in The Hague were in the meantime desperately seeking a stronghold that might compensate for the loss of Ostend. In January 1604 Maurits had already assembled 3,600 infantry and the entire cavalry for a surprise assault on Maastricht, but in the early evening, when he was within seven to eight kilometres of this town, the guides lost their way. The tired troops did not arrive before Maastricht until shortly before four o'clock the following morning, when the operation had to be abandoned.[135] Waiting for a new window of opportunity to present itself was out of the question, because the soldiers had brought too little food and there was none to be found in the vicinity. '[W]e have ourselves seen that the peasants roundabout are taking flight, so soon as they learn that any soldiers are taking to the field', Maurits wrote to the States-General.[136]

The capture of Maastricht would certainly have been an important success for the Republic, but for Holland and Zeeland it was of little strategic significance, as it would not increase the security of merchant and fishing fleets. The more imminent the capitulation of Ostend, the greater Van Oldenbarnevelt's concern about the security of Holland's southern flank. This concern was fuelled by a lack of clarity about the stance of the king of England. Elizabeth I had died

---

[131] NA, SG 4907, Governor Pieter van Ghistelles, esquire (killed in action on 21 March 1604) and the joint colonels and captains of the garrison to the SG, Ostend, 12 March 1604.
[132] NA, RAZH, AJvO 3001, 'Staet in 't corte van de oncosten van Osteyn[de] gevallen zedert den v.en july 1601 beginne van[de] belegeringe tot in julio 1603'.
[133] KHA, A22-IX-A1-267, Maurits to Willem Lodewijk, The Hague, 11 February 1603.
[134] KHA, A22-IX-A1-282, Maurits to Willem Lodewijk, The Hague, 29 December 1603, appendix, 'Liste van de verdeelinge van de regimenten ende andere comp[ag]ni[e]ën die onder geen regimenten en staen, ende bij wat ordre deselve voortaen binnen Oostende sullen gesonden worden, te weten op elcke veranderinge het vijfde part'.
[135] KHA, A22-IX-A1-283, Maurits to Willem Lodewijk, The Hague, 17 January 1604.
[136] NA, SG 4907, Maurits to the SG, Groot Linden, 12 January 1604.

in March 1603, and was succeeded by King James VI of Scotland, who also became King James I of England. Van Oldenbarnevelt feared that, in exchange for a Spanish-English peace treaty, James I would devolve to Spain those Dutch coastal towns given to England as surety in 1585. This would re-open the lines of communication between Antwerp and the North Sea.[137] Van Oldenbarnevelt believed the capture of Sluis would minimise this risk, and Willem Lodewijk agreed wholeheartedly, as he assured his father:

> Then the taking of the galleys [stationed in Sluis], the securing of the province of Zeeland, the [conquest of] the most important and best harbour in these lands [i.e. States Flanders], a useful and strong foothold in Flanders, not only for exacting contributions from the countryside but also for prosecuting the war on enemy soil, will make it easy to forget the loss of Ostend.[138]

The States-General ordered the levying of an additional 5,000 men and the bringing of the companies intended for field service to full strength, so that Maurits would have a sizeable force of about 19,000 men for the highly important operation of taking Sluis. However, events in Ostend compelled Maurits to open the campaign before enlistment was complete. In early May 1604, Governor Jacob van der Meer warned The Hague that his garrison was close to exhaustion, though the besieger, 'under the favour of his batteries, is working with greater assiduity, by day as well as by night, without us being able to prevent him doing so'. The defenders were working on the redoubt with might and main, but they needed another two to three weeks to complete it. Van der Meer was unsure whether he could sustain the defence of the main rampart for that long.[139] On 23 May 1604 Maurits laid siege to Sluis. The quality of the Dutch army left much to be desired because of the haste with which this operation had to be undertaken. The infantry was weak, particularly the companies from Zeeland and Holland, which were 'but 50 men strong, and some even thereunder'.[140] Moreover, the size of the Spanish garrison (3,000 to 4,000 men) and the sheer extent of the fortifications forced Maurits to spread his troops over a great many redoubts, 'yea, as many as sixty'.[141] By the start of July, the siege of Sluis had made scant progress. The wide ditches made it necessary to construct two extremely costly pontoon bridges with a length of no less than 350 and 400 feet. The field deputies wrote to The Hague that for financial reasons it was probably better to starve the garrison into submission, but that the situation in Ostend did not allow time for this.[142]

[137] Den Tex, *Oldenbarnevelt*, II, pp. 499–500.
[138] *Archives*, 2nd series, II, no. 315, Willem Lodewijk to Count Johann VI of Nassau, before Sluis, 22 May 1604.
[139] NA, SG 4907, Governor Jacob van der Meer, lord of Berendrecht, and the joint colonels and captains of the garrison to the SG, Ostend, 7 May 1604.
[140] NA, SG 4908, Field deputies to the SG, before Sluis, 8 June 1604.
[141] NA, SG 4908, Field deputies to the SG, before Sluis, 8 and 19 June (quote) 1604.
[142] NA, SG 4908, Field deputies to the SG, before Sluis, 1 and 4 July 1604.

On 29 May 1604 the Spanish had seized control of Ostend's Porc-Épic ravelin and on 17 June they had lodged themselves in a section of the main rampart, the Southwest bulwark. A simultaneous storming of the West bulwark was repelled by the Dutch, but at an extremely high price. During the struggle the garrison had lost no fewer than 1,200 men, about a third of its total strength.[143] On 22 July a convoy carrying 800 men departed for Ostend from Zeeland.[144] This was some compensation for the losses suffered, but it was obvious to everyone that the siege was in the final phase. Now there was no doubt about the outcome Spinola dared to undertake an attempt to relieve Sluis. On 25 July he appeared with 7,000 to 8,000 men before the Dutch circumvallation,[145] but this proved to be too strong for a storm assault. On 17 August, after a pause of three weeks, Spinola attempted to force his way onto the island of Cadzand, thus hoping to sever the Dutch army's lines of communication with Zeeland, but Willem Lodewijk managed to prevent this.[146] Sluis capitulated three days later. Van Oldenbarnevelt, who had arrived to size up the situation in person, wrote to The Hague in relieved tone: 'One must praise and thank the Lord God and His Excellency [Maurits] for the great effort, attention and assiduity. The costs are extremely great, but are well spent.'[147]

With this operation successfully wrapped up, the relief of Ostend was once again on the agenda. The garrison was still courageously standing its ground, thus confounding expectations. Van Oldenbarnevelt and his fellow field deputies therefore urged Maurits and Willem Lodewijk to come to Ostend's aid directly. According to the muster-rolls for 23 August 1604, the Dutch field army numbered almost 18,000 men. 'However, His Excellency and also Count Willem [Lodewijk] object to it [i.e. the relief attempt] as before, by reason of the enemy being positioned everywhere roundabout to his advantage.'[148] Once again it was Willem Lodewijk who elaborated the objections in a memorandum. He pointed out that the Spaniards could bar the Dutch army's advance to Ostend with ease by taking up strong positions. 'And that one ought therefore not to break up this army on a vain and idle hope, seeing as the enemy is lodging itself in this quarter, shall deny our army all means of retreat and victuals, without it being possible [for us], because of his strong situation, to force him by means of battle.'[149] The die was cast: Ostend was deemed lost.

---

[143] Van Sypesteyn, *Beleg van Ostende*, pp. 97–8; NA, RAZH, AJvO 3008, 'Lijste van het volck in Ostende in martio 1604', 'Lijste van 't garnisoen binnen Oostende in junio 1604'.
[144] NA, SG 4908, Field deputies to the SG, before Sluis, 22 July 1604.
[145] NA, SG 4908, Field deputies to the SG, before Sluis, 2 August 1604; SG 4909, Maurits to the SG, at the house 'ter Reede', 3 August 1604.
[146] Orlers, *Nassauschen laurencrans*, p. 203.
[147] NA, SG 4908, Johan van Oldenbarnevelt to the SG, before Sluis, 20 August 1604.
[148] NA, SG 4909, Field deputies, before Sluis, 28 August 1604.
[149] KHA, A13-XIA-36, 'Graeff Wilhems advys op 't onsett van Oostende', with the army by Sluis, 11 September 1604.

After the Spaniards had captured the Helmond bastion and the Sandhill fort on 13 September, Daniël de Hertaing (†1625), seigneur de Marquette, who from 24 June 1604 served as the ninth governor of Ostend since the start of the siege, decided to start preparations for the garrison's evacuation. On 20 September 1604 he surrendered Ostend. Two days later the garrison, more than 3,500 strong, marched out with full military honours, bringing one of the longest and bloodiest sieges in history to a close. The Spaniards assumed control of a town that was totally devastated and empty of people.[150]

Spinola on the offensive (1605–1606)

The end of the siege of Ostend gave cause for the two belligerents to reassess their strategies. The 1602 campaign had made it evident that there were serious shortcomings attached to a Dutch attack via Brabant. It was possible to mount predatory incursions into Flanders from the bases in Zeeland, but access to the River Scheldt was essential for an effective invasion of the Spanish Netherlands, because otherwise the Dutch could not transport any siege artillery. However, the Dutch army was too small to be able to besiege the city of Antwerp. For the Spaniards the possibilities for offensive action were more opportune, since Spinola could make use of the Rhine to attack Gelderland and Overijssel and the German princes would be loath to refuse passage to the Spanish army. In January 1605 Maurits urged the provinces to ensure that the captains had brought their companies up to full strength before 1 March 1605, 'in order that we might be the first to set out on campaign and be ahead of the enemy as much as possible'. He feared for the worst if they failed to make this pre-emptive move, because by all accounts the Spaniards would be operating with two armies in the Low Countries in 1605,[151] as soon as the reinforcements Brussels was expecting from Italy and the Iberian peninsula arrived.[152] On 28 August 1604, England and Spain had concluded a peace. The English navy no longer posed a threat to the Spanish maritime routes, so troop transports direct to the Low Countries could be resumed.[153]

Maurits was almost certain that Spinola would attempt 'something' in the Achterhoek – the fortifications of Bredevoort, Groenlo, Doesburg and Doetinchem were in a dilapidated state – but he could not rule out an attack on Bergen op Zoom, Breda or Geertruidenberg.[154] In order to thwart Spinola's plans, in early June 1605 Maurits landed at IJzendijke in States Flanders with

---

[150] Orlers, *Nassauschen laurencrans*, p. 186.
[151] KHA, A22-IX-A1-302, Maurits to Willem Lodewijk, The Hague, 13 January 1605.
[152] This force was 10,000 strong: 4,000 Spaniards, of which 1,200 were transported from Spain by sea, and 6,000 Italians. See Parker, *Army of Flanders*, p. 279.
[153] Parker, *Dutch Revolt*, p. 236.
[154] NA, SG 4910, Maurits to the SG, Wouw, 25 and 29 May 1605.

23,400 men,[155] then marched onward to Watervliet. From this position the Dutch army threatened Sas van Gent and Damme, but Maurits had little hope of being able to lay siege to these two places, 'noting that the enemy has a great portion of his men stationed in the Land of Waas and can very swiftly transfer those who are lying on the Brabant side, by favour of the bridge that he [Spinola] has had constructed across the River Scheldt'.[156] This is indeed what happened, after which the belligerent armies maintained a close watch on each other from their entrenched camps. It was then a question of waiting for the moment when the Spaniards had assembled their second field army.[157] The suspense was broken at the end of June.

On 2 July 1605 the Dutch headquarters received reports that Spinola had headed east with Spain's main army and had crossed the River Meuse. Maurits dispatched Ernst Casimir to Dordrecht with 4,000 men that same evening, and from there they were to sail up the River Waal 'with the order to shadow the enemy and obstruct him in his attacks'.[158] A couple of days later they received news that Spinola was heading towards Rheinberg with about 7,000 infantrymen and twelve cavalry companies. Maurits promptly sent reinforcements to assist Ernst Casimir: eleven cavalry companies under the command of his half-brother Frederik Hendrik, and eighteen infantry companies.[159] Willem van Beveren (1556–1631), one of the field deputies, left for The Hague at the same time, where he conveyed Maurits's message to the States-General that he could not send any more troops to the eastern frontier, because it would then be impossible for him to match the Spanish army in the Land of Waas. He also warned that, if the army were to withdraw from Watervliet before IJzendijke's fortifications had been strengthened, then the Spaniards would 'likely' attack this small town. If the main Dutch force were to remain in Flanders then Maurits could not vouch for Rheinberg's safety. In other words, a choice had to be made between two evils: 'That therefore the … lords, the States, will in their wisdom be so kind to discuss which of the enemy's designs is most injurious to the Land and in which place the greatest forces are therefore needed, considering his Excellency finds himself concerned about undertaking something without express orders from their Noble Mightinesses.'[160] The States-General ordered Maurits to head for the Rhine with all his troops.[161]

Maurits delayed his departure from Watervliet for as long as possible, because he could not be certain that Spinola was really planning to attack Rheinberg

---

[155] NA, SG 4910, Field deputies to the SG, Bergen op Zoom, 29 May 1605.
[156] NA, SG 4910, Maurits to the SG, Wouw, 29 May 1605.
[157] *Archives*, 2nd series, II, no. 327, Willem Lodewijk to his father, Count Johann VI of Nassau, Watervliet, 7 June 1605.
[158] NA, SG 4910, Maurits to the SG, Watervliet, 29 June (quote) and 2 July 1605.
[159] NA, SG 4910, Maurits to the SG, Watervliet, 5 July 1605.
[160] NA, SG 4910, 'Instructie [van Maurits] voor de heere Beveren, gedeputeert van mijnheeren de Generale Staten', Watervliet, 8 July 1605, transcript.
[161] NA, SG 4910, Maurits to the SG, Watervliet, 16 July 1605.

and he also doubted whether the Spanish commander would dare to cross the River IJssel. Then, after all, Ernst Casimir would be able to follow him and block the line of retreat.[162] The States-General were hearing alarming news from Rheinberg. Spinola's army was initially estimated at between 7,000 and 9,000 infantry and the cavalry 'closer to 3 than 2,000 horse', but a couple of days later the 'informant' reported that the Spaniards numbered between 16,000 and 17,000 men.[163] This prompted Maurits to set out for the River IJssel at the end of July 1605 with sixty-one infantry companies and six cavalry companies, leaving behind fifty infantry companies to cover IJzendijke.[164] He reached Deventer on 10 August. Spinola had placed Oldenzaal under siege two days earlier and its garrison (two companies) had capitulated by the following day. The Spaniards then marched on Lingen. Ernst Casimir's and Frederik Hendrik's troops joined up with the army of Maurits and Willem Lodewijk on 11 August. The news that Oldenzaal had fallen and that Spinola was marching on Lingen reached the Dutch headquarters that same day.[165] Maurits immediately convened a council of war about 'what is to be done'. No names are specified in the minutes of the meeting, but 'some' were of the opinion that the Dutch army had to limit itself to the defence of the River IJssel, Groningen and Emden, while 'others' were opposed to this.

> That in doing this one would, as may be imagined, have to give up one quarter or the other and would have to surrender Lingen if it is not relieved, with the risk of having to give up many other places as well ... thereby diminishing the contributions severely, and the hearts of the peasants and soldiers, seeing no imminent relief, are becoming seriously discouraged.

This brought the discussion to the pivotal question: was the relief of Lingen worth 'hazarding' a battle? The war council did not venture to take a decision about this; The Hague would have to do that.[166] The fall of Lingen on 19 August 1605 rendered this question academic.

The loss of Lingen led to serious disquiet in Groningen and Drenthe. Willem Lodewijk insisted on securing Coevorden, but the field deputies warned the States-General that if the Dutch army headed there then the Spaniards would be able to capture some other town, such as Doesburg. This made reaching a

---

[162] NA, SG 4910, Maurits to the SG, Watervliet, 16 and 17 July 1605.
[163] NA, SG 4910, Field deputies to the SG, Rheinberg, 25 July 1605; SG 4911, same to same, 29 and 30 July 1605.
[164] NA, SG 4910, 'Comp[ag]ni[e]ën die tot Isendijck sullen blijven' and 'Comp[ag]ni[e]ën die met zijne Ex.tie opwaerts sullen trecken'; both lists are dated 31 July 1605.
[165] NA, SG 4911, Maurits to the SG, Deventer, 11 August 1605.
[166] NA, SG 4911, Maurits, Willem Lodewijk and the field deputies to the SG, Deventer, 12 August 1605, with an instruction for Hendrik van Brienen (1540–1620) 'to transport himself in all diligence to The Hague' as an addendum.

decision extremely difficult.[167] Maurits eventually gave the order to march to Coevorden. Scouts had reported that Spinola was amassing huge stocks of food, 'such that it is most obvious that the first thing that he shall want to undertake is Coevorden'. This fortress was surrounded by marshes, so for their provisions the besiegers would be wholly reliant on what they brought along themselves. For this same reason Maurits did not consider it wise to wait until Spinola had actually invested Coevorden. It would certainly not be difficult to cut through the Spanish army's supply lines, but this was counterbalanced by the implausibility of Spinola launching this operation before he had amassed as much food as his troops would need for the duration of the siege.[168] Maurits marched to the threatened town with 12,000 to 13,000 men on 30 August. In Deventer, Zutphen, Zwolle, Rheinberg, Bredevoort and Groenlo he had left behind garrisons with a total strength of 8,100 men.[169] Spinola abandoned the idea of besieging Coevorden. In mid-September the Spaniards drew back to the Rhine, crossed this river and laid siege to Wachtendonk. This town fell into Spanish hands on 28 October 1605. The Dutch and the Spanish troops took up their winter quarters in late November.[170]

*

Maurits travelled to The Hague as soon as the 1605 campaign was concluded. He pointed out to the States-General that Spinola's successes were threatening to clip the wings of the Republic. He was being forced to assign more and more Dutch troops to garrison duties, but the Spaniards could be deterred from further conquests only by the Republic deploying as large an army as possible. It was therefore crucial, according to Maurits, that the captains brought their companies to their full prescribed strengths as soon as possible: an estimated 12,000 recruits were needed to achieve this. But even this would not be sufficient, he warned. The States-General would also have to order the recruitment of an additional 6,000 infantry and 2,000 cavalry, initially for six months. Without these reinforcements it would, according to Maurits, be impossible to field an army of any import for the 1606 campaign. Otherwise, after subtracting the troops who would have to perform garrison duties during the summer months – 258 infantry companies in all – there would be just 101 companies remaining for field service.[171]

---

[167] NA, SG 4911, Field deputies to the SG, Deventer, 26 August 1605; KHA, A22-IX-E-249, Willem Lodewijk to Maurits, 27 August 1605, minute.
[168] NA, SG 4911, Field deputies to the SG, Deventer, 30 August 1605.
[169] NA, RAZH, AJvO 2956, 'Monsteringe den xxvi augusti 1605 in 't leger voor Deventer gedaen'.
[170] Ten Raa, *Het Staatsche leger*, II, p. 80.
[171] NA, RAZH, AJvO 460, 'Lijste van[de] besettinge voor den somer 1606'. The same list is to be found in KHA, A22-IX-A1-327, Maurits to Willem Lodewijk, The Hague, 3 January 1606.

Maurits informed Willem Lodewijk in confidence that, if it were his decision, he would prefer to block Spinola at the Rhine, though he thought the chances of this proving feasible were slim. To achieve this it would be necessary to bring the Dutch army up to strength in early spring. Maurits impressed upon his cousin that it was therefore of the utmost importance to billet a military force of 5,000 men at Rheinberg by the middle of March 1606 to hamper the Spanish advance and, if the States-General were also to quickly agree to the recruitment of the aforementioned 8,000 men, he expected his army would be strong enough to protect the Achterhoek against Spanish attack over the summer.[172] Maurits thought he could count on the full cooperation of Friesland and Groningen for the execution of his plan. As soon as he was assured of a bridgehead on the Rhine, Spinola would be able to push onward into the Achterhoek but also into Twente. With Oldenzaal and Lingen as bases he would then be able to launch an assault on Coevorden or Bourtange. For Maurits it came as a very unwelcome surprise that Friesland's and Groningen's delegates to the States-General wanted to know nothing whatsoever of his proposal to reinforce the Republic's army. 'Instead of helping to bring about the adoption of such a good resolution, the provincial deputies of your stadholderates here at the assembly of the States-General have been more contrary than anyone', he wrote to the stadholder of Friesland acerbically, 'by which I was extremely astonished.'[173] At the root of this lack of cooperation lay the discord among the provinces regarding the sharing of the costs of the troop reinforcements.[174]

Willem Lodewijk shared Maurits's concerns, but he advised his cousin against leading the Dutch army into a campaign so early in the year and he also rejected his proposal to have 5,000 men, more than a third of all the available field troops, commence digging in at Rheinberg by the middle of March. The soldiers would suffer greatly from the cold and the rain, and during the summer, when they were most needed, they would be useless to him. It would, of course, have been preferable if the Republic could rob the Spaniards of the initiative by means of an offensive along the Rhine, but Willem Lodewijk feared it would be impossible to raise the necessary reinforcements, either on time or in their entirety. He did not believe, moreover, that Spinola would open the campaign before June. He warned Maurits that, if the provinces were to see their troops ravished by disease before the enemy had even set out on campaign, they would hold him accountable, and they would also be displeased about the high outlays they had been required to pay for the supply of oats. Maurits ought not to allow the Gelderlanders to hound him 'for the love of places so small', such as Lochem, Bredevoort, Borculo and Groenlo. As a compromise Willem Lodewijk proposed billeting strong garrisons in the towns on Gelderland's frontiers, 'so that in such an unlooked-for instance, at the first warning one would be able to thrust the

---

172 KHA, A22-IX-A1-328a, Maurits to Willem Lodewijk, The Hague, 25 January 1606.
173 KHA, A22-IX-A1-328a, Maurits to Willem Lodewijk, The Hague, 25 January 1606.
174 Ten Raa, *Het Staatsche leger*, II, p. 82.

men forward, before the enemy is in the field'. If the body of men intended for Rheinberg was assembled in late April or early May 1606 it would be early enough, according to Willem Lodewijk.[175]

Maurits did not agree with his cousin, and at the start of June he informed Willem Lodewijk that the provinces had levied twelve infantry companies and forty-four companies of *waardgelders*, so he now had 122 companies of foot at his behest. If Willem Lodewijk were to add as many Frisian and Groningen troops as he could spare, Maurits expected to be able to check Spinola's progress at the Rhine.[176] However, the Frisian stadholder responded that, far from being able to spare troops, he actually needed reinforcements himself, 'because the enemy, [by] joining his troops from the Rhine with those from Lingen and Oldenzaal, can always field 10,000 foot-soldiers and 1,500 horse, whereas I will not be able to man my garrisons, not to mention thwart any incursion'.[177] Maurits did not comply with this request. All he promised was that he would come to Willem Lodewijk's aid if the Spaniards pushed northward. He did not consider this move very likely, because a corn agent for the Spanish army had confided to him that 'the expedition of the enemy ... [would] be towards the IJssel'. From a Spanish deserter he had also heard that Spinola's army numbered 10,000 foot and 2,000 horse, and that there was a rumour the Spanish general had set his sights on Zwolle or Deventer.[178] A second Spanish force (7,000 to 8,000 men) under the command of Charles Bonaventure de Longueval (1571–1621), comte de Bucquoy, would simultaneously invade the Betuwe. Maurits had therefore decided to remain in the vicinity of the towns on the River IJssel with his main body of men, and in addition he ordered the construction of entrenchments and redoubts along this river and the River Waal, 'at such distances that the signals could be properly sent and received'.[179] These security measures were intended to make it possible for him to rally his troops at the point under threat in good time. The attention that Maurits devoted to the defence of the IJssel line and the Waal meant there was little danger of the Spaniards penetrating into the Veluwe or the Betuwe during this campaign, but it meant the garrisons in the Achterhoek and along the Rhine were abandoned to their fate. This was, however, unavoidable, because the munitions depots in Zwolle, Nijmegen, Deventer and Hasselt were quite bare, so these towns were incapable of enduring a siege.[180]

---

[175] KHA, A22-IX-E-258, Willem Lodewijk to Maurits, Groningen, 3 February [1606], minute.
[176] KHA, A22-IX-A1-344, Maurits to Willem Lodewijk, The Hague, 7 June 1606.
[177] Tresoar, FSA 3, Willem Lodewijk to the SG, [Groningen], 6 July 1606, transcript (quote); KHA, A22-IX-E-276, Willem Lodewijk to Maurits, [Groningen], 6 July 1606, minute.
[178] KHA, A22-IX-A1-351, Maurits to Willem Lodewijk, Arnhem, 10 July, with a letter from an anonymous corn merchant to Maurits as an annex; KHA, A22-IX-A1-353, 12 July, with the 'Rapport d'un soldat Esp.l qui sert venu rendre dehors l'armée de l'ennemy' as an annex; KHA, A22-IX-A1-357, 16 July 1606.
[179] NA, RvS 548, Missive from the RvS to the SG, 7 December 1671.
[180] NA, SG 4913, Maurits to the SG, Zutphen, 23 July 1606.

By the end of July 1606, of the 122 companies intended for the campaign army Maurits had managed to assemble a mere thirty-nine companies at Zutphen, the rest remaining scattered across the threatened fortresses and in the Betuwe.[181]

The Spanish offensive in the Achterhoek began on 20 July 1606 with the investment of Lochem, where just one company of *waardgelders* was garrisoned. This small town capitulated after a siege of three days.[182] It was Groenlo's turn next, and Maurits decided to come to the aid of its defenders. Spanish deserters had assured him that Spinola's army was seriously weakened. It reportedly amounted to just 12,900 infantrymen and twenty-nine cavalry companies, prompting Maurits to write to Willem Lodewijk on 7 August, 'that it is [therefore] nowhere near as strong as one estimated it to be. I am resolved, on condition that I could deploy a hundred companies of infantry on the campaign, to rescue the said town.' In order to assemble the desired military force of about 12,000 men it was necessary for Willem Lodewijk to participate in this operation with ten of his companies.[183] He agreed to this, whereupon a start could be made with the preparations. On 15 August the Dutch army left Zutphen and headed for Doesburg. Maurits and Willem Lodewijk were planning 'to effect the intended exploit' the following day, but shortly after midday they received news that Groenlo had fallen on 14 August and that its garrison (with an effective strength of 1,100 men) had arrived at Zutphen. Groenlo's governor, Colonel Diederik van Dorth, who had previously served in Ostend, reported that the Spanish had breached its bastions in three places, 'and that it was not in his powers to contend the place any longer because of the unwillingness of the soldiers.... They let it be advertised that if he did not negotiate a capitulation, they themselves would sign the accord.'[184]

After the taking of Groenlo it was logical that Spinola would march onward to Rheinberg. Maurits ordered Frederik Hendrik to escort fourteen infantry companies and two cavalry companies to the endangered fortress under cover of the entire cavalry. This expanded Rheinberg's garrison to no less than fifty infantry companies and two cavalry companies.[185] With a garrison of this size a tenacious defence could be depended upon. Spinola, together with part of Bucquoy's army, laid siege to Rheinberg on 22 August 1606. Now that the threat to the IJssel towns and the Betuwe had abated, Maurits could at last turn his mind to mounting a counter-offensive. Following consultations with deputies from the Council of State and with Willem Lodewijk he decided to advance to

---

[181] NA, SG 4913, Maurits to the SG, Zutphen, 27 July 1606.
[182] NA, SG 4913, Field deputies to the SG, Deventer, 21 July 1606; Maurits to the SG, Zutphen, 23 July 1606.
[183] KHA, A22-IX-A1-372, Maurits to Willem Lodewijk, Zutphen, 7 August 1606, with a 'Liste van de regimenten die met kennisse van sijn Ex.cie in 't leger van den vijandt zijn' as an appendix.
[184] NA, SG 4913, Deputies from the RvS to the SG, Doesburg, 16 August 1606.
[185] NA, SG 4913, Maurits to the SG, Doesburg, 21 August, and Neder-Elten, 25 August 1606.

the Rhine with eighty-four companies of foot and 'to go and encamp so close to the enemy as shall be opportune to see and observe all occasions of advantage that one might achieve over him for the relief of Rheinberg'.[186]

The Dutch army established positions near Wesel, but nothing came of the intention to relieve Rheinberg. On reflection, Maurits and Willem Lodewijk considered the terrain too advantageous for the enemy, which was also too strong numerically. A diversionary manoeuvre in the direction of Groenlo or Lingen was, in their view, equally impossible because it would allow Spinola the opportunity to execute his 'principal design' after all: the crossing of the IJssel or Waal. Rheinberg therefore had to be considered lost. However, this was not the only thing that was causing the Dutch headquarters serious concern; the coffers of the field army were utterly empty, 'which is causing our soldiers to desert in serious numbers because of hunger'.[187] The field deputies feared mutiny: 'It must above all be ensured that, for want of payment, the army does not fall into alteration [i.e. mutiny], so that it might be used as a means (whatsoever might become of Rheinberg) to repel and thwart the enemy's further intentions towards other important towns.'[188] The soldiers were especially angry about not being paid for their days of digging to entrench the camp by Wesel. Maurits loaned 2,000 guilders to the field deputies, who topped this up with as much money as possible from their own pockets and those of third parties.[189] Rheinberg capitulated on 2 October 1606.

In mid-October the Spanish army was hit by yet another mutiny.[190] Maurits took advantage of the disarray in the Spanish camp to recapture Lochem. On 29 October the Dutch siege artillery opened fire and the garrison of about 400 men surrendered after just six salvoes.[191] The Dutch army then laid siege to Groenlo. Its garrison of approximately 2,000 men defended valiantly and Spinola, who had now squared up with the mutineers,[192] advanced to relieve the beleaguered stronghold. Maurits did not await the arrival of the main body of Spaniards. On 10 November he abandoned the siege and returned to Doesburg.[193] This marked the conclusion of the 1606 campaign.

Hostilities are suspended for twelve years (1607–1609)

The Republic's military prospects at the close of the 1606 campaign were plain dismal. Spinola's capture of Rheinberg and Groenlo had secured the lines of

---

[186] NA, SG 4913, Deputies from the RvS to the SG, 's Gravenweert, 26 August 1606.
[187] NA, SG 4914, same to the SG, by Wesel, 16 September 1606.
[188] NA, SG 4914, same to the SG, by Wesel, 9 September 1606.
[189] NA, SG 4914, same to the SG, by Wesel, 17 September 1606.
[190] NA, SG 4914, Justinus van Nassau to the SG, Breda, 18 and 20 October 1606.
[191] NA, SG 4914, Maurits to the SG, Ruurlo, 29 October 1606.
[192] NA, SG 4914, Justinus van Nassau to the SG, Breda, 26 October 1606.
[193] NA, SG 4914, Maurits to the SG, Doesburg, 15 November 1606.

communication with Oldenzaal and Lingen, placing him in a strong position to resume the offensive in 1607. In addition, from here he could exact a fire-tax from the Achterhoek and from Twente. The need to protect the Betuwe, the IJssel towns and the northern strongholds of Coevorden and Bourtange forced Maurits and Willem Lodewijk to post strong garrisons everywhere. As a consequence, in the summer of 1607 no fewer than 311 of the 367 infantry companies in Dutch service would have to be used for garrison duties – fifty-three more than the previous year – leaving just fifty-six for field service.[194] With a military force of such meagre size it would be impossible to prevent the loss of more Dutch strongholds. Only a substantial expansion of the Dutch army or the engineering of a peace treaty with Madrid could save the Republic from further setbacks. Van Oldenbarnevelt preferred the latter solution or, if necessary, a truce.[195] The attritional struggle for Ostend, followed by the loss of Oldenzaal, Lingen, Groenlo and Rheinberg, had convinced him that continuation of the war was beyond the powers of the Republic. Thanks to the Peace of Vervins (1598) and the Peace of London (1604), Spain's hands were now free to settle the score with the Dutch rebels.[196] Henry IV may well have continued to support The Hague in secret, but as long as he left the Spanish supply lines (the 'Spanish Road') from Italy undisturbed and did not assemble an army on France's northern border, then Brussels could continue to combat the Republic with two armies. The States-General could expect nothing from the quarter of James I, who even allowed Philip III to recruit troops for the Spanish army in England.

Despite Spain's fine military prospects, in Brussels and Madrid the mood was also propitious for a peace treaty. Spain's overstretched finances necessitated a termination, or at least a suspension, of the struggle with the Republic. Continuing the Spanish offensive would require an even greater military effort, because once he had crossed the IJssel or the Waal Spinola would have to safeguard his supply lines by leaving behind strong garrisons *en route*. Moreover, on 11 December 1606 yet another large-scale mutiny broke out, and this one would last for almost a year. More than 4,000 Spanish troops joined the mutiny and ensconced themselves in Diest.[197] However, it was no simple matter for Spain to open negotiations with the rebellious Dutch, all the more because there was no certainty it would be possible to find a majority in favour of peace within the Republic. The position of the Dutch Catholics presented the greatest stumbling block, because Madrid would be unable to recognise the autonomy of the rebellious provinces without the guarantee that the rights of Catholics would be restored. Within the Republic there was therefore widespread suspicion among

---

[194] KHA, A22-IX-E-299, 'Staet van de comp[ag]ni[e]ën in dienst van 't Landt wesende', 27 November 1606.
[195] Den Tex, *Oldenbarnevelt*, II, p. 538.
[196] Van Deursen, *Maurits*, p. 202.
[197] Parker, *The Dutch Revolt*, p. 238; *Army of Flanders*, pp. 250 and 292; Jonathan I. Israel, *The Dutch Republic and the Hispanic World 1606–1661* (Oxford 1982), p. 10.

the regents that the only objective of a Spanish peace proposal was to lull the provinces into a false sense of security. All the Spaniards had to do was await the moment when the majority of Dutch troops had been disbanded to resume hostilities and deliver the *coup de grâce*. Maurits shared this distrust. Van Oldenbarnevelt was equally unsure of the good intentions of Madrid and Brussels, but he felt that the defensive alliance concluded on 23 January 1608 between The Hague and Paris offered sufficient surety against such skulduggery. This pact would come into force as soon as the peace between the Republic and Spain was ratified. Hereafter Maurits no longer opposed a peace settlement, but he wanted nothing to do with a truce, because this would mean the most important war objective had not been achieved: the recognition of the Republic as an independent nation.[198]

Spain and the Republic concluded the Twelve Years' Truce on 9 April 1609. Though no peace had been brokered, the Republic could be satisfied with the result: Philip III and the archdukes had, *nota bene*, declared that they were entering into this truce 'with the Illustrious Lords, the States-General of the United Provinces of the Netherlands, these being considered in character to be free [i.e. independent] states, provinces and countries, against which they make no claim'.[199] In the terms there was no mention of the position of Catholics, the opening of the River Scheldt and the ban on Northern Netherlandish merchants sailing to the East and West Indies, which were issues Spain held dear. The River Scheldt remained closed, which meant that goods intended for Antwerp, Ghent or Bruges had to be brought ashore at one of Zeeland's ports before being traded or transhipped. Brussels resigned itself to this situation for the time being, primarily because this economic setback would largely be compensated by the anticipated increase in trade via the Flemish seaports, which would be freely accessible again after the lifting of the blockade by the Dutch fleet.[200] The armistice applied only in Europe; in Asia and America the struggle would continue, at Amsterdam's insistence.[201]

Conclusion

When one surveys the period 1590–1609 one is immediately struck by the contrast between pre- and post-1600. In the final decade of the sixteenth century the Republic was in a sorry state, territorially and militarily, yet it was during these years that Maurits and Willem Lodewijk achieved their greatest triumphs.

---

[198] Van Deursen, *Maurits*, pp. 203 and 209.
[199] Fruin, 'Gedenkschrift van Joris de Bye', p. 442.
[200] Jan Hendrik Kluiver, *De souvereine en independente staat Zeeland. De politiek van de provincie Zeeland inzake vredesonderhandelingen met Spanje tijdens de Tachtigjarige Oorlog tegen de achtergrond van de positie van Zeeland in de Republiek* (Middelburg 1998), pp. 124 and 127.
[201] Parker, *The Dutch Revolt*, p. 239; Israel, *The Dutch Republic*, pp. 30–1 and 40.

In the first decade of the new century the Seven Provinces were delivered from the Spanish enemy (until 1605, at least) and the stadholders were in command of a field army that was twice as strong as in the 1590s, but instead of reaping the benefits of this escalated war effort the military successes failed to materialise. The Republic's great military exertion in 1602 failed to elicit the raising of the siege of Ostend. The conquest of Sluis in 1604 was a significant boost, but the loss of Oldenzaal, Lingen, Groenlo and Rheinberg caused the defence of the eastern frontier to falter. Even the wonderful victory at Nieuwpoort yielded the Republic only a negative outcome: the army was intact but the plan to capture Dunkirk had to be abandoned.

The Dutch historian A.Th. van Deursen expressed the opinion that Maurits had reached his zenith as a general in 1600 and that after the reduction of Sluis in 1604 his reputation was based on earlier triumphs alone.[202] Is this critique justified? Van Deursen acknowledges that the siege of Ostend was a huge trial of strength and that the struggle between Maurits and Spinola was unequal: 'Maurits' military force was not great in number [in 1605]. It would be his stock complaint over the ensuing years: he had to face that mighty army of Spinola with a handful of men.'[203] Van Deursen failed to realise that the pre- and post-1600 circumstances were so different that any comparison between Maurits's military exploits in the years 1591–1599 and 1600–1606 is impossible. The Spanish intervention (1590–1598) in the French civil war had presented the Dutch rebels with the opportunity to achieve successes that, in view of the balance of power, they would never have been able to depend on otherwise. It was to the credit of Maurits, Willem Lodewijk and Van Oldenbarnevelt that they took full advantage of the opportunity presented. The Peace of Vervins brought a temporary cessation to the ongoing struggle between France and Spain. It simultaneously marked the end of the Republic's triumphal march. It would, however, be incorrect to regard the French-Spanish peace as the sole reason for this. In 1597 Maurits and Willem Lodewijk had closed the gates of the Republic's 'garden': the Union of Utrecht was restored. The Dutch offensive had in that year reached the 'culminating point of victory' (*Kulminationspunkt des Sieges*), to use Clausewitz's characterisation.[204] Nothing more could be done with the military resources available.

The Republic was ill-equipped for the war of attrition that raged from 1601 to 1604 for Ostend. This siege was responsible for the loss of an estimated 40,000 troops in Dutch service. For the captains a tour of duty in Ostend spelled financial disaster. By the time they were relieved most companies were only forty or fifty strong. Losses this dire could not be redressed in a single year. The States-General were aware of this and therefore allowed the captains to replenish their companies to a strength of sixty, seventy or seventy-five men 'and no higher',

---

[202] Van Deursen, *Maurits*, pp. 192–4.
[203] Ibid., p. 197.
[204] Clausewitz, *Vom Kriege*, p. 833.

which was approximately half their strength on paper.[205] For want of government support, nothing more could be asked of the company commanders. The structure of the Dutch army prior to the second half of the seventeenth century made it unsuitable for a 'strategy of attrition' (*Ermattungs-Strategie*). The 1605 and 1606 campaigns tested the Dutch defences severely. Spinola was a general with great qualities, but he was certainly not the superior of Maurits and Willem Lodewijk. The defensive war obliged Maurits and Willem Lodewijk to man more than seventy towns, forts and redoubts with garrisons, so there were few troops remaining for the field army. Under such circumstances the negotiation of a truce was the most sensible option, though it failed to resolve the issue of the Dutch army's inadequate size. Following the resumption of hostilities in 1621 this would narrow down the Republic's strategic options even further.

[205] RGP 92, Res. SG, 16 November 1602 (no. 183).

✦ 5 ✦

The Republic Escalates Her War Effort (1610–1634)

The Republic intervenes in the Jülich War of Succession – internal strife in the Republic (1610–1621)

In 1609 the Dutch army was 30,000 strong, a reduction of approximately 20,000 men. Fifty or so infantry companies had been disbanded and the size of the remaining units reduced. The security of the Republic's borders could be adequately assured with the remaining manpower, as the archdukes had already decided to effect a much more drastic reduction of the Spanish army in the Low Countries: it had been slashed from 49,000 to 15,000 men.[1] International tensions ensured that the proficiency of the Dutch troops was, moreover, kept up to standard. The last duke of Jülich, Johann Wilhelm (born 1562), had died in March 1609, a month before the signing of the Twelve Years' Truce. Besides Jülich his possessions included the duchies of Cleves and Berg, the counties of Mark and Ravensberg, and the Ravenstein seigniory in Brabant. The strategic position of these territories, located on both banks of the Rhine and adjacent to the eastern border of the Northern and the Southern Netherlands, made the distribution of the legacy a matter of European concern. Those who had the strongest claim to the succession were Johann Sigismund (1572–1619), elector of Brandenburg since 1608 and husband to a niece of Johann Wilhelm, and Wolfgang Wilhelm (1581–1653), count of Palatine-Neuburg, a nephew of the deceased duke. In July 1609 they agreed, in the Treaty of Dortmund, to govern the territories jointly for the time being. However, with both claimants being Lutheran, Rudolf II (1552–1612), Holy Roman Emperor from 1576, could hardly approve of this compromise. The emperor ordered Jülich's occupation by approximately

---

[1] Parker, *Army of Flanders*, pp. 271–2.

2,000 men commanded by his brother, Archduke Leopold (1586–1632), bishop of Strasbourg and Passau.[2]

In The Hague and Paris this development was cause for consternation. The States-General warned Vienna that they would support the claims of the elector of Brandenburg and the count of Palatine-Neuburg militarily. King Henry IV of France did the same and it seemed he would immediately suit the action to the word. He began making preparations to deploy no fewer than 42,000 men (an effective force of 29,000 men).[3] Van Oldenbarnevelt was unfavourably disposed towards the prospect of a large-scale French intervention: Spain would probably no longer be able to stand aloof and the outbreak of a Spanish-French war would mean the end of the Twelve Years' Truce. The Advocate of Holland felt that the Jülich dispute ought to remain a local conflict.[4] The murder of Henry IV on 14 May 1610 defused the situation. The heir to the French throne, Louis XIII, was a mere nine years old and Nicolas de Neufville (1542–1617), marquis de Villeroy, minister for foreign affairs and the *de facto* leader of the French government, was of the opinion that without a powerful king France could not allow herself to become involved in a war against the Habsburgs. Maria de Medici (1573–1642), queen-regent of France, did indeed send troops to the Holy Roman Empire, but the size of the French intervention force was cut to less than a quarter of the originally estimated strength and the operational objective was limited to dislodging the Imperialists from Jülich in association with the Republic. This was precisely what Van Oldenbarnevelt wanted.[5]

In July 1610 Maurits set out on the march to Jülich with 136 companies of foot and thirty-six of horse.[6] He took the route along the Rhine, so that the siege artillery and munitions could be transported by ship. On 18 July the Dutch troops reached Xanten. Maurits sent word to The Hague:

> We shall remain here tomorrow as well and wait until the … ammunition has passed by Rheinberg, even though the [Spanish] governor there … let it be known that he shall allow this ammunition to pass freely and unhindered, in case he should perchance receive other tidings and orders from Brussels to refuse us passage in the meantime.

Opposition from the archdukes failed to materialise and three days later all the ships had sailed past Rheinberg 'without any difficulty'.[7] On 29 July 1610 the Dutch army appeared before Jülich, where Maurits encountered Christian von

---

[2] Israel, *The Dutch Republic*, p. 21; Parker, *The Thirty Years' War*, pp. 24 and 27; Ten Raa, *Het Staatsche leger*, III, pp. 4–6.
[3] Parrott, *Richelieu's Army*, p. 183 n. 49; André Corvisier, 'La paix nécessaire mais incertaine, 1598–1635', in *Histoire militaire de la France*, I, pp. 331–51, esp. 342.
[4] Den Tex, *Oldenbarnevelt*, III, pp. 100–1.
[5] Van Deursen, *Maurits*, pp. 235–7; Den Tex, *Oldenbarnevelt*, III, p. 104.
[6] Stevin, *Castrametatio*, in Schukking (ed.), *The Principal Works of Simon Stevin*, IV: *The Art of War*, pp. 298–307.
[7] NA, SG 4921, Maurits to the SG, Fürstenberg near Xanten, 18 (quote) and 21 July 1610.

Anhalt (1568–1630), commander of a small army raised by order of the elector of Brandenburg and the count of Palatine-Neuburg, but the French army of approximately 9,000 men under the command of *maréchal* Claude, baron de La Chastre (1526–1614), was still nowhere to be seen. Maurits received news on 14 July that four days earlier the French were near Limbach in the Sauerland, 'but on the map we cannot ascertain the position of the aforesaid place'.[8]

The siege of Jülich went well. By the middle of August 1610 all the outworks were in Dutch hands. *Maréchal* La Chastre eventually arrived on 17 August and two weeks later the Imperialists surrendered Jülich. Maurits granted the garrison a free withdrawal. About 1,650 men, plus 150 sick and wounded, marched out on 2 September; Maurits estimated that during the siege the defenders had suffered 150 fatalities.[9] A garrison paid by both Johann Sigismund and Wolfgang Wilhelm, the two 'possessing' princes, was billeted in the town of Jülich, but the castle's garrison was Dutch and Frederik van Pithan, a Dutch army major, was appointed as governor of Jülich. Van Pithan was to defend Jülich 'for the common profit and service' of the two potentates and, not least, of the Republic.[10] Maurits and Chastre broke up their encampments in mid-September, marking the end of the 1610 campaign.

New problems arose around the Jülich legacy three years later. Elector Johann Sigismund converted to Calvinism, while Count Wolfgang Wilhelm married a sister of Maximilian, duke of Bavaria (1573–1651), head of the Catholic League of German princes established in 1609. In May 1614 Wolfgang Wilhelm drove the Brandenburgian troops out of Düsseldorf, whereupon he demonstratively attended Mass there, prompting Van Pithan to relieve the Palatine troops of their duties in Jülich and send them away. By April 1614 the two archdukes had pronounced that should The Hague side with Brandenburg then Wolfgang Wilhelm could depend on Spanish military support. Unlike four years earlier, Albert and Isabella did not remain above the fray this time. In 1614 Brussels dared to pursue a policy of confrontation, since now no French intervention was to be expected. The French queen-regent and Villeroy were keen to establish closer relations with Spain, to be better able to tackle internal difficulties. Spinola was instructed to raise an army.[11]

The Spanish preparations for war gave Maurits serious cause for concern. In the middle of June he warned Willem Lodewijk that the Spaniards already had 9,800 men ready for field service and that they would soon be joined by a further 13,200 men.[12] A month later there could have been no shadow of a doubt that Spinola would set out on campaign in early August 1614, given that the Spanish

---

[8] NA, SG 4921, Maurits to the SG, 's Gravenweert, 15 July 1610.
[9] NA, SG 4922, Maurits to the SG, before Jülich, 1 and 3 September 1610.
[10] Ten Raa, *Het Staatsche leger*, III, p. 17.
[11] Den Tex, *Oldenbarnevelt*, III, pp. 104 and 116.
[12] KHA, A22-IX-A1-414, Maurits to Willem Lodewijk, The Hague, 15 June 1614, with the 'Estat de l'armée des Archiduqz juing 1614' as an appendix.

troops had hired 1,200 waggons for the conveyance of their baggage, victuals and munitions. Maurits reinforced the garrison of Jülich (seven companies strong) with an additional 2,000 men and dispatched sufficient food supplies and munitions for a protracted siege. He hereby hoped to gain sufficient time to assemble a relief army. The prospects did not, however, bode well for this, because no fewer than 228 of the Dutch army's 352 infantry companies were needed for garrison duties. 'You yourself can judge that 124 companies (which are at the moment so feeble) is a small number to be deployed on campaign', Maurits lamented to Willem Lodewijk.[13] Maurits told his cousin that the majority of infantry companies numbered just seventy men, so 'we [shall be] entering the campaign with a meagre army and therefore consider it urgently necessary to gather together as many companies as is feasible'. Willem Lodewijk would in any case have to march with the majority of the Frisian companies, each of them being 100 strong.[14] By drawing additional troops from towns that were not under serious threat Maurits expected to be able to raise an army composed of 136 infantry companies and forty cavalry companies.[15]

In the latter half of August 1614, Spinola gathered about 15,000 men near Maastricht and used them to occupy Aix-la-Chapelle (Aachen) and thereafter Wesel (5 September), two towns with garrisons from Brandenburg.[16] He left Jülich undisturbed. Maurits then marched on Rees with an estimated 18,000 men. Spinola subsequently established a position near Xanten, whereupon he opened negotiations with Maurits about a neutrality pact. He explained that the two archdukes were prepared to withdraw from Wesel and the other places occupied by Spanish troops in Jülich, 'provided my lords the States-General want to promise ... [that they] shall not come back with their army hereafter ... into the lands of the possessing princes to occupy any places there', Maurits wrote to Willem Lodewijk. 'We already consider these to be trifles and that they are seeking nothing else but to delay us', he continued, with regard to reinforcing the defences of Emmerich, Rees and Jülich.[17] The parties ultimately agreed a provisional partition of the Jülich estate. In the Treaty of Xanten (12 November 1614) Jülich and Berg were allocated to Count Wolfgang Wilhelm, while Cleves, Mark, Ravensberg and Ravenstein were assigned to Elector Johann Sigismund. The accord was not implemented immediately, the mutual distrust between the parties being too great; nevertheless confrontations between Spanish and Dutch

---

[13] KHA, A22-IX-A1-417, Maurits to Willem Lodewijk, The Hague, 15 July 1614 (quote), and KHA, A22-IX-A1-418, The Hague, 17 July 1614, with 'Besettinge van[de] garnisoenen' as an appendix.
[14] KHA, A22-IX-A1-419, same to same, The Hague, 24 July 1614.
[15] NA, SG 4929, 'Liste van de comp[ag]ni[e]ën die men dit jaer 1614 te velde soude connen gebruycken', 19 July 1614.
[16] KHA, A22-IX-A1-423, Maurits to Willem Lodewijk, The Hague, 13 August 1614, with an overview of the strength of the Spanish field army as an appendix. See also Parker, *The Thirty Years' War*, p. 32.
[17] KHA, A22-IX-A1-439, Maurits to Willem Lodewijk, The Hague, 19 March 1615.

troops failed to materialise. During the winter of 1614 to 1615 a total of about seventy Dutch infantry companies were quartered in Jülich, Cleves and Mark.[18] Looking ahead, Maurits considered this buffer essential, for when the Twelve Years' Truce expired it would be advantageous to ensuring the security of the Betuwe and the towns along the River IJssel. The Dutch troops could, after all, sever the lines of communication between the Spaniards and their bases in the Achterhoek and Twente. Spinola wanted to retain Wesel, situated in the duchy of Cleves, for similar reasons.

Direct hostilities between Spain and the Republic did not materialise in 1615 either. Nevertheless, in April 1616 Spinola tightened his control of the disputed territories by occupying Soest,[19] a town in the easternmost part of the county of Mark. The capture of Soest did not pose any immediate threat to the Republic, but for Maurits Spinola's action represented additional proof of Madrid's hostile intentions. Maurits did not consider the 'cold war' of 1614 to 1616 to be in the Republic's interests, as it gave Spinola the opportunity to reinforce the Spanish position on the eastern flank of the Republic even further, so that in 1621, when the Twelve Years' Truce expired, he would be able to resume the offensive halted in 1606 with vigour. Maurits therefore believed it would be better for the Republic to revoke the Truce as soon as possible. Van Oldenbarnevelt did not share this viewpoint; he still regarded the 1609 arrangement as the best chance of brokering a peace with Spain.[20]

Besides this difference of opinion regarding war and peace, in these same years the Advocate of Holland and the commander-in-chief came to stand at the counterpoles of a religious conflict. For Van Oldenbarnevelt the crux of the theological dispute was not which of the two Dutch Calvinist movements was right – the Remonstrants (Arminians) or the staunchly Calvinist Counter-Remonstrants – but who should be allowed to decide the matter. In his opinion the provincial States also had the final say in ecclesiastical affairs, not the synod.[21] This view was not shared by all members of the States of Holland: the municipal governments of Amsterdam, Enkhuizen, Edam, Purmerend and Dordrecht were Counter-Remonstrant at the time. The States of Zeeland, Groningen and Friesland were also of the opinion that a national synod ought to settle the religious conflict. Utrecht and Overijssel, on the other hand, agreed with Van Oldenbarnevelt, while opinion in Gelderland was divided.[22] Van Oldenbarnevelt wanted Maurits to use troops to bring the Counter-Remonstrants into

---

[18] KHA, A22-IX-A1-434, same to same, The Hague, 3 January 1615, with a 'Liste van de besettinghe van de garnisoenen in den lande van Gulich, Cleve en[de] van der Marck' as an appendix.
[19] KHA, A22-IX-A1-423, same to same, The Hague, 5 and 13 April 1616.
[20] Den Tex, *Oldenbarnevelt*, III, pp. 99 and 121.
[21] Van Deursen, *Maurits*, p. 231.
[22] Simon Groenveld, 'Evidente factiën in den Staet'. *Sociaal-politieke verhoudingen in de 17ᵉ-eeuwse Republiek der Verenigde Nederlanden* (Hilversum 1990), pp. 15 and 20.

line if necessary, but he refused to comply with this. The conflict intensified. On 4 August 1617 a majority of the States of Holland voted for a resolution which specified that: 1. a national synod is incompatible with provincial sovereignty; 2. the towns represented in the States have the right to recruit their own garrison troops (*waardgelders*) in order to maintain order; and 3. all the Dutch troops paid by Holland or billeted in a town in Holland are obliged to obey the orders of the States. For Maurits this 'Sharp Resolution' was unacceptable. After all, it constituted a corrosion of his stadholderate and captain-generalship.[23] Van Oldenbarnevelt had already endeavoured to curtail Maurits's military power in 1610, when he had vainly put forward Frederik Hendrik to lead the expedition to Jülich.[24] Maurits resolved to effect a *coup d'état*. Having eliminated the Arminian factions in Gelderland and Overijssel, in July 1618 he seized control of Utrecht and dismissed the *waardgelders* the city had enlisted. He then advanced into Holland, had Van Oldenbarnevelt arrested, and in the majority of towns and cities he purged the town councils (*vroedschappen*): the Remonstrants were removed from municipal government and replaced by members of the Counter-Remonstrant faction.[25] A special court imposed a death sentence on Van Oldenbarnevelt for high treason, which was carried out on 13 May 1619.

The beheading of Van Oldenbarnevelt made Maurits the undisputed leader of the Republic. Politically there was no longer anything standing in the way of resuming the war with Spain. The Counter-Remonstrants wanted nothing more than to resume the struggle against the Catholics. Financially, however, the situation was less favourable to breaking the Truce. Anthonis Duyck, who was to be appointed as Grand Pensionary of Holland on 22 January 1621, had complained about this some three weeks earlier:

> The great changes in the town councils are to our serious disadvantage. The new [regents] are inexperienced and in addition pusillanimous, fearing to do anything that might displease the community and that they by doing so will be cast into discredit once more. The deposed [regents] are bold, feeding and reinforcing that fear in the novices, which causes us great difficulty, [while] the Arminians are also tremendously stirring trouble.[26]

The fear for disturbances meant there was little enthusiasm among the Counter-Remonstrant faction for allowing new taxes, when these were necessary to be able to resume the struggle with Spain with vigour.[27] This was made even more urgent by events that in the meantime had taken place within the Holy Roman Empire, which would have a great effect on the war in the Low Countries.

---

[23] Van Deursen, *Maurits*, pp. 255–6, 258 and 260.
[24] Den Tex, *Oldenbarnevelt*, III, pp. 105–6.
[25] Van Deursen, *Maurits*, pp. 264–5.
[26] *Archives*, 2nd series, II, no. 467, Anthonis Duyck to Ernst Casimir, The Hague, 31 December 1620.
[27] Jonathan Israel, *Empires and Entrepots. The Dutch, the Spanish Monarchy and the Jews, 1585–1713* (London 1990), pp. 77–8.

In 1618 the Protestant nobles in Bohemia had rebelled against the Habsburgs. Philip III decided to lend his Austrian relatives military support to quash the rebels. The States of Bohemia, in turn, called upon the help of the German Protestant rulers and offered Frederick V, the Elector-Palatine, the crown of their kingdom. Hereafter the hostilities swiftly expanded across the German lands. The Catholic princes, united in the Catholic League, affiliated themselves with the emperor. In 1620 Spinola invaded the Palatinate at the head of approximately 20,000 men, in order that the emperor and the Catholic League could focus all their efforts on subduing Bohemia. On 8 November 1620 the Protestants lost the battle on White Mountain near Prague, whereupon Frederick V fled to the Republic.[28]

War is resumed: Spinola goes on the offensive again (1621–1625)

In 1621 the Dutch army was once again brought to its wartime strength by recruiting upward of 11,000 men and enlisting 4,000 *waardgelders*. Over the summer the Dutch field army established positions between Emmerich and Rees. By establishing this forward position Maurits could protect the Betuwe and the towns along the River IJssel, but he could not prevent the Spaniards surrounding Jülich on 5 September 1621. After a blockade of five months the food supplies were exhausted and Governor Frederik van Pithan was forced to capitulate. Jülich was evacuated on 2 February 1622.[29] This Spanish success confirmed Maurits in his view that the Spaniards would launch an attack on the IJssel and Waal line during the summer of 1622. However, Spinola took up Parma's old plan from 1588 and in late July 1622 he laid siege to Bergen op Zoom. This stronghold was the key to Zeeland, 'because the island of Tholen lies so close that one must only wade up to two feet deep in that direction'.[30] The Spanish siege army was an estimated 20,000 strong,[31] which was much stronger than the force the Republic could commit to the campaign.[32] Spinola was, nevertheless, as unsuccessful in severing communications between Bergen op Zoom and Zeeland as Parma had been earlier. Food, munitions and fresh troops could therefore be brought into the besieged town without hindrance.[33] The Spanish siege army's supply lines, by contrast, were seriously disrupted by

---

[28] Parker, *The Thirty Years' War*, pp. 44–52 and 56.
[29] Ten Raa, *Het Staatsche leger*, III, pp. 73–4, 78, 84 and 91.
[30] Ten Raa, *Het Staatsche leger*, II, appendix XVI, p. 398.
[31] NA, SG 4941, N. van der Meer to the SG, Bergen op Zoom, 29 July 1622.
[32] In July 1622 Maurits had 132 infantry companies available to him; he had been forced to leave behind no fewer than 231 infantry companies and twenty-six companies of *waardgelders* in the garrisons. NA, RvS 2061-II, 'Lijste van de compaigni[e]ën die sijne excellentie te velde sal brengen' and 'Besettinge van de garnisoenen als men te velde sal wesen', 12 July 1622.
[33] NA, SG 4941, Maurits to the SG, 's Gravenweert, 21 August 1622.

raids carried out by Breda's garrison. Spinola was therefore forced to provide the convoys between Antwerp and Bergen op Zoom with an escort of twenty mounted companies and 700 to 800 musketeers.[34]

Despite the provisioning difficulties faced by the Spanish siege army and the open communications with Zeeland, the field deputies of the States-General in Bergen op Zoom were not convinced that the siege would end well for the Republic. The Dutch garrison had a fair size on paper but appearances were deceptive, because most of the seventy-two infantry companies were undermanned, 'given that some were dead, had deserted [or] were injured and many were sick'. Around this time Spinola received reinforcements of no fewer than 125 infantry companies and twenty-eight cavalry companies. These troops were led by Fernández de Córdoba (1585–1635), commander of the Spanish army in the Palatinate. On 29 August he had done battle with the Protestant army commanders, Ernst von Mansfeld and Duke Christian of Brunswick, close by Fleurus, a hamlet to the west of Namur, whereafter the three armies had continued on their march to the Republic.[35] According to Spanish deserters who had fled to Bergen op Zoom, Córdoba's army was still approximately 14,000 strong. The deputies of the States-General in Bergen op Zoom did not believe there were so many, 'yet a great multitude of soldiers has augmented [the siege army], along with twelve whole- and demi-cannon and two small artillery pieces, consequently we have to expect an attack on two or three places at any time'.[36] It did not come to this, however, because following the arrival of Mansfeld's and Brunswick's troops Maurits considered his force strong enough to relieve Bergen op Zoom. Spinola did not await Maurits's arrival. On 2 October 1622 he abandoned the siege. The Spanish siege army had suffered massive losses: approximately 6,500 Spaniards were killed in action, an estimated 8,000 or more sick and wounded were lying in the hospices of Antwerp and Brussels, and no fewer than 2,500 Spanish deserters had fled to Bergen op Zoom.[37] News of Spinola's withdrawal was received with jubilation in the Republic, but there was also criticism of Maurits. The Gelderland regent and the province's delegate to the States-General, Alexander van der Capellen, wondered why the Dutch commander-in-chief had not taken advantage of the siege of Bergen op Zoom to capture 's-Hertogenbosch or Wesel. Van der Capellen could find but one explanation for this, namely 'the fear of the Hollanders'. As long as Spinola continued to pose a threat to Geertruidenberg the States of Holland wanted Maurits to keep his hands free to be able to pursue him at a moment's notice.[38]

---

[34] NA, SG 4941, Justinus van Nassau to the SG, Breda, 9 September 1622.
[35] See pp. 41–2.
[36] NA, SG 4941, Field deputies to the SG, Bergen op Zoom, 10 September 1622.
[37] NA, SG 4941, Gijsbert van Hertevelt to the SG, Roosendaal, 12 October 1622; Van der Capellen, *Gedenkschriften*, I, p. 95; Ten Raa, *Het Staatsche leger*, III, p. 95.
[38] Van der Capellen, *Gedenkschriften*, I, p. 95.

The Spanish defeat at Bergen op Zoom dampened the enthusiasm in Madrid for the pursuit of an offensive strategy in the Low Countries.[39] Spinola took the view that the Republic could be brought to its knees only by a war of attrition – the successes in the years 1604–1606 seemed to prove that – but the attack on Bergen op Zoom and the subsequent siege of Breda demonstrated that the price the Spaniards had to pay to achieve this bore no relation to the losses inflicted on the Republic. On 28 August 1624 Spinola invested Breda with about 18,000 men, a choice that was controversial. Breda was not situated on a river and control of the town did not open any direct path to further conquests, so Breda's strategic significance was limited.[40] In the wake of the massive losses the Spaniards had suffered before Bergen op Zoom, Spinola decided to proceed more calmly. No storm assaults but starvation would have to force Justinus van Nassau, the governor of Breda, to surrender.[41] 'The general opinion of the officers in the [Spanish] army is that, in view of the multitude of soldiers which is within Breda [c. 4,000 men[42]], there will be a shortage of [provisions] there within three or four months, whereby they hope to achieve their intention.'[43] This proved to be a miscalculation and the garrison held out for a good nine months. However, fame was the only reward that Justinus van Nassau received for his indomitability, because during the months-long blockade he received no outside help whatsoever. Maurits was seriously ill, so the forty-year-old Frederik Hendrik assumed command of the Dutch army from his half-brother, but he was lacking in experience. He may well have been a brave cavalry commander, but he had never taken command of an army. In early October 1624, Frederik Hendrik established a camp near Made with 180 companies of foot and twenty-eight of horse, only a few kilometres to the north of the beleaguered town of Breda, but he did nothing more than observe the Spanish positions.[44]

Maurits died on 23 April 1625, aged fifty-eight. The following day the States-General assigned supreme command over the army and the fleet to Frederik Hendrik. For the first time since Leicester, a captain- and admiral-general of the Union stood at the head of the Republic's land- and sea-based forces. Gelderland, Holland, Zeeland, Utrecht and Overijssel chose Frederik Hendrik as stadholder, but Groningen and Drenthe preferred Ernst Casimir, stadholder of Friesland. The collaboration between Frederik Hendrik and Ernst Casimir displays many similarities to that between Maurits and Willem Lodewijk. Ernst Casimir was ten years older than the stadholder of Holland and had participated in many military operations. In 1607 he was promoted to the rank of field-marshal. The stad-

---

[39] Israel, *The Dutch Republic and the Hispanic World*, pp. 102–3.
[40] Ibid., pp. 102–7.
[41] Ten Raa, *Het Staatsche leger*, III, pp. 124 and 137.
[42] NA, SG 4946, Field deputies to the SG, Waalwijk, 6 June 1625.
[43] NA, SG 4945, Phillippe de Zoete de Lake, lord of Villers, governor of Willemstad, to the SG, 20 September 1624.
[44] NA, SG 4945, Field deputies to the SG, Geertruidenberg, 2 October 1624.

32. Ernst Casimir (1573–1632), count of Nassau-Dietz, stadholder of Friesland, Groningen and Drenthe, Dutch field-marshal. (Royal Netherlands Army Museum, Delft, 0112024/082)

holder of Friesland may well have been second-in-command of the Dutch army, but he was certainly not Frederik Hendrik's inferior. Quite the contrary: Ernst Casimir undertook the most difficult missions, while Frederik Hendrik with the bulk of the troops kept an eye on the main enemy force. Frederik Hendrik's first year as supreme commander did not provide him with any triumphs. At the start of June 1625, Justinus van Nassau surrendered Breda. Spinola granted the garrison, approximately 3,000 healthy soldiers and 800 sick,[45] a free withdrawal. Nothing important occurred during the rest of that year.

[45] NA, SG 4946, Field deputies to the SG, Waalwijk, 6 June 1625.

33. Frederik Hendrik (1584–1647), prince of Orange-Nassau, captain- and admiral-general of the Union. Oil painting, artist unknown, second half of the nineteenth century, after a painting (c. 1620) by M.J. van Miervelt. (Royal Netherlands Army Museum, Delft, 0053/050710)

The Dutch counterattack tentatively gathers momentum (1626–1628)

Since the resumption of hostilities against the Republic, Spinola had twice made a grave strategic error, first of all by wasting thousands of soldiers in bloody attacks on Bergen op Zoom, the Republic's strongest fortress, and subsequently by failing to invest Breda until the end of August. He had indeed limited himself to a blockade at the time, but the losses through disease and desertion had been alarmingly high because the Spanish strike force had been obliged to remain in the field for the entire winter of 1624/5. The fact that the losses in the Dutch camp were not much smaller was but scant consolation. Ernst Casimir tellingly expressed the suffering of the troops in a letter of 12 February 1625 to Count Floris II of Culemborg:

> It is disagreeable to be in the field so long in this wintertime, and to witness the great misery of the poor soldiers.... Without fire the watch duties are exhausting in wintertime. The poor soldiers are naked [i.e. their clothes are in rags], in rainy weather standing everywhere in mud to over their shoes. Hay and straw can no longer be come by, neither for fodder nor to lie on.[46]

The experiences of the campaigns of 1622 to 1625 prompted the young king of Spain, Philip IV (1605–1665), who had succeeded his deceased father in 1621, to decide to heed the advice of his chief minister, Gaspar de Guzmán (1587–1645), duke of Olivarez, and limit the war in the Low Countries to a *guerra defensiva*. Governess-General Isabella – Albert had also died in 1621 – reconciled herself to this situation, but her commander-in-chief would not accept it. Spinola was therefore suspended from his duties and the command over the Spanish army in the Low Countries was temporarily assigned to Count Hendrik van den Bergh (1573–1638), stadholder of Upper Gelderland. According to Olivarez, Spanish interests would be better served by challenging France. In 1624 the French had taken control of a number of passes in the Alps and therefore constituted a serious threat to the Spanish possessions in northern Italy. Olivarez was, moreover, of the opinion that the Republic could only be subdued with help from the Austrian Habsburgs.[47] For the moment, however, Ferdinand II (1578–1637), emperor since 1619, had plenty on his hands dealing with the German Protestants, who were receiving assistance from the king of Denmark, Christian IV (1577–1648). The Thirty Years' War was increasingly becoming a Europe-wide conflict.[48]

To judge by events since 1621, Frederik Hendrik had reached the opposite conclusion to the Spanish court: he wanted to go on the offensive. Besides the

---

[46] GA, AHGC 581, Ernst Casimir to Count Floris II of Culemborg, Roosendaal, 12 February 1625.
[47] Israel, *The Dutch Republic and the Hispanic World*, pp. 103, 109 and 162–3.
[48] Parker, *The Thirty Years' War*, pp. 63, 66–8 and 93–4.

old adage, *'guerre defensive, guerre consumptive',*[49] he could posit the sound argument that the Republic would never be able to exact a peace agreement from Spain unless she demonstrated her military might. Frederik Hendrik could count on the Remonstrant factions in the Republic supporting this viewpoint, given that they had sustained serious economic setbacks from the resumption of the struggle with Spain. Particularly in Amsterdam, where the Remonstrants had gained full control of city government in 1622, there was a stark contrast between the commercial interests of the Arminians and the Counter-Remonstrants. The latter invested heavily in trade with the East and West Indies and therefore benefited from a long-lasting conflict with Spain to strengthen their overseas positions further, while the former were largely dependent on cargo trade with European destinations for their income. As long as war between the Republic and Spain continued, the trade in staple goods was seriously complicated.[50] The fisheries also suffered a great deal from the strife with Spain flaring up again, especially after a new admiralty had been established at Dunkirk in 1626, an admiralty that was wont to issue many letters of marque. In the summer of 1626, five privateers from Dunkirk surprised a fishing fleet from Holland, sinking eighteen herring-busses, 'and many people, who by the drawing of lots were singled out', were thrown overboard and drowned. There was great panic among the fishermen: 700 to 800 skippers fled to the English coast 'to escape the cruelty of the Dunkirkers'.[51]

However, before a Dutch counter-offensive could be contemplated the army's finances had to be straightened out. Frederik Hendrik's first concern as commander-in-chief was the elimination of the arrears in pay for the troops. In 1623 Holland already owed more than 1 million guilders in pay arrears.[52] Frederik Hendrik and the Council of State advised the States of Holland to allocate a slice of the provincial revenues for the army alone.[53] For the regents of Holland this overstepped the mark, though in March 1626 they did decide to float a loan of 2 million guilders to remedy the 'confusion' in the payment of wages.[54]

The Dutch counter-offensive was undertaken with caution. On 24 July 1626 Ernst Casimir invested Oldenzaal, while Frederik Hendrik took up a position near Isselburg with his main force. From Oldenzaal the Spaniards were imposing a fire-tax on Twente. The garrison of this small town was about 1,000 strong

---

[49] Waterbolk, 'Willem Lodewijk als opvoeder', p. 169.
[50] Johan E. Elias, *Geschiedenis van het Amsterdamsche regentenpatriciaat* (2nd rev. edn; The Hague 1923), pp. 36–7, 45–6 and 86–7; Israel, *Empires and Entrepots,* p. 65.
[51] NA, SG 12548.180, Jacob van Brouchoven to his fellow field deputies, The Hague, 25 September 1626 (quote); Adri P. van Vliet, 'De Staatse vloot in de Tachtigjarige Oorlog', in Jaap R. Bruijn and Cees B. Wels (eds), *Met man en macht. De militaire geschiedenis van Nederland 1550–2000* (Amsterdam 2003), pp. 44–62, esp. 59–61; Groenveld, *Evidente factiën,* p. 28.
[52] Ten Raa, *Het Staatsche leger,* III, pp. 106–7.
[53] J.J. Poelhekke, *Frederik Hendrik prins van Oranje. Een biografisch drieluik* (Zutphen 1978), p. 126.
[54] See pp. 74–5.

but Ernst Casimir expected little resistance, 'firmly trusting that Your Excellency [Frederik Hendrik] shall be graciously pleased ... to ensure that no force which shall be able to hamper us shall, unforeseen, be at our throats'.[55] Oldenzaal fell on 1 August, after a siege of nine days. Frederik Hendrik and Ernst Casimir subsequently agreed that the latter and his troops would keep an eye on the Spanish army under Hendrik van den Bergh – with an estimated strength of 11,000 to 12,000 infantrymen and 35 or 36 cavalry companies – while the former would depart for Flanders with the main force in order to ascertain 'whether we shall be able to obtain something against the town of Hulst by means of a siege'.[56] On 29 August 1626 the Dutch vanguard attempted to land at Kieldrecht, but the Spaniards were on the alert and managed to beat them back with cannon fire.[57] Frederik Hendrik therefore decided to return to the eastern frontier and explore the possibility of besieging Groenlo or Lingen.

Following deliberations with Ernst Casimir, the field deputies and the senior army officers Frederik Hendrik came to the conclusion that either operation would involve irresponsibly high risks. Jacob van Brouchoven (1577–1642), one of Holland's field deputies, travelled to The Hague to give an explanation. He reported to the States-General that the army under Hendrik van den Bergh boasted more cavalry than initially thought – more than sixty companies instead of thirty-five or thirty-six – 'and in addition, being able to gather even more men, would not want to stay idle'. There was a real danger that Hendrik van den Bergh would exploit his numerical superiority to force Frederik Hendrik into joining a 'hazardous battle' or to compel him to 'draw all the [Dutch] horses within the retrenchment [i.e. circumvallation] to await him there, which would lead to a lack of forage, the vivres could be cut off and other mischiefs could be caused, such that one would be forced to opt for a shameful retreat'.[58] The deputies to the States-General were convinced by these arguments. 'I am well aware that many [of them] have expected some fine and great things of our army this summer,' the field deputy Van Brouchoven wrote to his colleagues in the army headquarters after this meeting, 'yet I do not understand that someone's policy or actions are in any way whatsoever being held culpable or calumniated.'[59] The 1626 campaign still had a sting in its tail for Frederik Hendrik: at the break of day on 3 October, Hendrik van den Bergh surprised the ten Dutch cavalry companies who were meant to be guarding the Kalkar Inlet, a key crossing-point on the Rhine, with fifty companies of horse and 300 soldiers armed with firelocks. The Dutch caval-

---

[55] NA, SG 4949, Ernst Casimir and the field deputies to Frederik Hendrik, before Oldenzaal, 25 July 1626.
[56] NA, Frederik Hendrik to the SG, Isselburg, 21 August 1626, on our ship before de Kille, 26 August 1626 (quote).
[57] NA, SG 4949, same to same, aboard a Dutch ship before Bergen op Zoom, 30 August 1626.
[58] NA, SG 4562, Secret res. SG, 23 September 1626.
[59] NA, SG 12548.180, Jacob van Brouchoven to his fellow field deputies, The Hague, 25 September 1626.

rymen offered meagre resistance, having removed their armour and stabled the horses, 'not thinking that any enemy would attack them so late [in the season]'. The raid was over by about eight o'clock in the morning: an unknown number of Dutch cavalrymen were taken prisoner and approximately 400 horses were seized by the Spaniards as loot.[60]

In 1627 Frederik Hendrik revived the plan to recapture Groenlo, but he warned the provinces that he could achieve this only if he were able to assemble a substantial military force. He was thinking of 168 infantry companies – ultimately no fewer than 190 were assembled[61] – and fifty-five cavalry companies. Some 8,000 *waardgelders* would have to be enlisted in order to achieve this.[62] The provincial States granted their consent. On 20 July 1627 the Dutch army appeared before Groenlo, where an estimated 1,360 men were garrisoned.[63] Maurits had forgone the construction of a line of circumvallation during the 1597 siege, but that was impossible this time because the terrain around Groenlo was 'everywhere so dry and accessible' that a relief army could approach from all sides. There was no other option but to interconnect the quarters by means of defensive lines and redoubts. Frederik Hendrik refused to open the trenches 'before these works are constructed'.[64] By early August the digging activities were largely complete.[65] Frederik Hendrik's precautionary measures were not excessive, as was demonstrated a short time later, when Hendrik van den Bergh marched on Groenlo and in the night of 15/16 August ordered a surprise attack by 1,500 men, including 600 armed with firelocks, on Ernst Casimir's quarters, 'but withdrew with the loss of nine waggons laden with corpses'.[66] The Spanish defenders capitulated three days later and the garrison left on 20 August, at that point counting approximately 950 infantrymen and a company of horse.[67]

With Groenlo captured the States-General felt enough had been achieved that year, 'considering the scarcity of money against the mass of debts and payments to be expected here after the disbanding of the army, which are still running higher and higher by the day'. The field deputies were instructed to confront Frederik Hendrik with the difficult financial situation and then submit to him, if he had no plans to undertake further operations with the army during this campaign, 'whether it would not therefore be advisable to relieve the Land', namely by dismissing the 8,000 *waardgelders* as well as 2,000 Frenchmen and

---

[60] NA, SG 4949, Frederik Hendrik to the SG, Vijnen, 3 October 1626 (quote); Field deputies to the SG, Vijnen, 3 October 1626.
[61] NA, SG 4951, Field deputies to the SG, before Groenlo, 14 August 1627.
[62] Ten Raa, *Het Staatsche leger*, IV, p. 12.
[63] NA, SG 4951, Field deputies to the SG, before Groenlo, 21 July 1627.
[64] NA, SG 4951, same to same, before Groenlo, 23 July 1627.
[65] NA, SG 4951, Frederik Hendrik to the SG, before Groenlo, 31 July 1627.
[66] KHA, A14-IX-2, Note on a plan of the siege of Groenlo in 1627.
[67] NA, SG 4951, Frederik Hendrik to the SG, near Groenlo, 20 August 1627; Field deputies to the SG, near Groenlo, 21 August 1627.

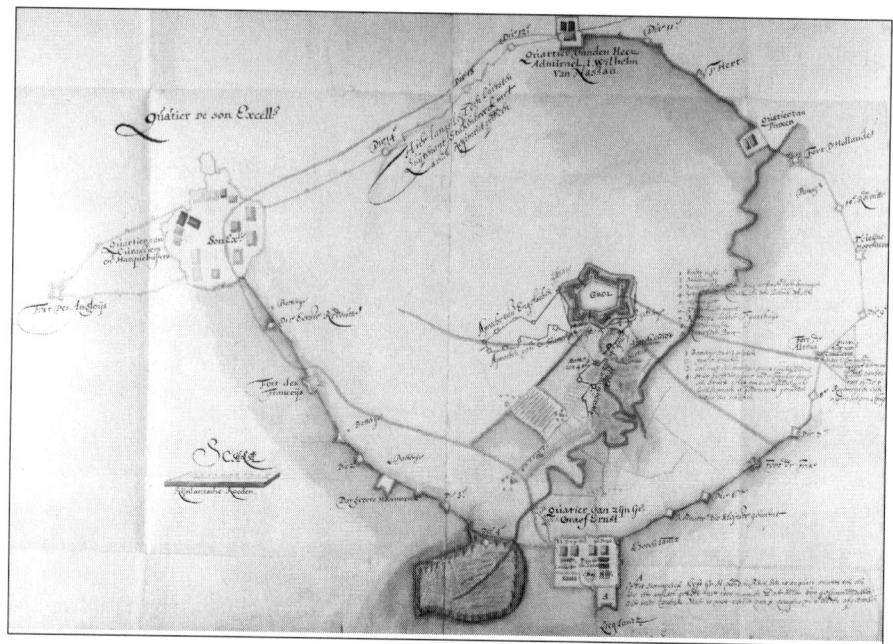

34. The besieging of Groenlo in 1627 by Frederik Hendrik and Ernst Casimir, clearly showing the line of circumvallation and the three *attaques*. (KHA, A14-IX-2)

1,400 cavalry,[68] troops who had been taken into service temporarily in 1625 'solely for the extraordinary urgency of the besieging of Breda'.[69] The field deputies and Frederik Hendrik discussed this matter on 13 September 1627. The Dutch commander-in-chief wanted to hear nothing of an army reduction, pointing out the proximity of Hendrik van den Bergh's army, which counted 158 infantry companies and seventy cavalry companies. Disbanding the *waardgelders*, the French and the above-mentioned cavalrymen would weaken the Dutch field army by no less than 11,400 men. Frederik Hendrik feared the gravest consequences, because the campaign season was still far from over. It would give Hendrik van den Bergh a free hand for a month and a half, making it possible for him to besiege any town he desired 'without one being able to prevent him doing this'. According to Frederik Hendrik there was, moreover, enough money reserved to retain the *waardgelders* in service until late October or early November 1627.[70] At the end of September, Frederik Hendrik dispersed the Dutch troops across the towns along the rivers IJssel and Waal. In the event of an emergency he could use them to assemble a field corps.[71]

[68] Ten Raa, *Het Staatsche leger*, III, p. 133.
[69] NA, SG 4951, Letter from the SG to the field deputies, 8 September 1627, minute.
[70] NA, SG 4951, Field deputies to the SG, near Groenlo, 13 September 1627.
[71] NA, SG 4951, Frederik Hendrik to the SG, near Groenlo, 25 September 1627.

The turn of events within the Holy Roman Empire meant that in 1628 the Dutch army had to be expanded by fifty companies, each 200 men strong. In 1626 the Imperial troops under the command of Albrecht Wenzel Eusebius von Wallenstein (1583–1634) as well as the Catholic League's forces under Jean t'Serclaes (1559–1632), count of Tilly, had won great victories over the Danes and the German Protestants. Christian IV hastily retreated to Denmark: Holstein, Schleswig and Jutland were lost. In December 1627 troops from the Catholic League and the Imperial army were encamped in East Friesland. In the Republic this raised the fearful spectre that the king of Spain 'shall endeavour to raid these lands with the assistance of the soldiers of the popish League'.[72] There was, however, little danger of this happening, as Madrid was wholly preoccupied with the war in Italy. The duke of Mantua, the last of the House of Gonzaga, had died in December 1627. Charles, duke of Nevers (1580–1637), had the strongest claim to the legacy, but Madrid found him unacceptable because he was French. This provoked the War of the Mantuan Succession (1628–1631). The war in Italy drained the greatest portion of Spanish receipts, and to make matters worse the entire Spanish treasure fleet, heavily laden with silver, was lost in September 1628, having been surprised by Admiral Piet Heyn (1577–1629) in a bay near Cuba.[73] The prospects for a Dutch offensive had not been so propitious since 1597. The States-General consented to the besieging of 's-Hertogenbosch. The capture of this important Brabant town would deliver Holland, Gelderland and Utrecht from Spanish raids, and no less importantly give the States-General lordship over the Meierij, the sizeable territory belonging to 's-Hertogenbosch.

The great Dutch offensive: 's-Hertogenbosch and the Spanish-Imperial incursion into the Veluwe – the siege of Maastricht (1629–1632)

According to an anonymous author writing in 1608, 's-Hertogenbosch was a substantial and 'more by nature than by art [i.e. manmade means] a very secure town, lying in the morasses formed by the [River] Dieze'.[74] It required a siege army of at least 25,000 men to wholly encircle 's-Hertogenbosch. In early 1629 the States-General approved a substantial but temporary expansion of the Dutch army: besides enlisting 6,000 *waardgelders* they ordered the recruitment of 12,000 extra troops. Although 'the new levy of 12,000 men was nowhere near complete',[75] it enabled Frederik Hendrik to mobilise no fewer than 280 infantry companies. The Dutch field army, including 4,000 to 5,000 cavalrymen, was 28,000 to 29,000 strong. On 1 May 1629 Frederik Hendrik ordered the invest-

---

72 Ten Raa, *Het Staatsche leger*, IV, p. 21.
73 Israel, *The Dutch Republic and the Hispanic World*, p. 172; Lynch, *Spain*, II, pp. 82 and 84; Parker, *The Thirty Years' War*, pp. 95–6.
74 Ten Raa, *Het Staatsche leger*, II, Appendix XVI, p. 404.
75 NA, SG 4953, Field deputies to the SG, before 's-Hertogenbosch, 19 May 1629.

ment of 's-Hertogenbosch. The garrison, under the command of Governor Anthonie Schetz, baron of Grobbendonk, was not very substantial – 2,500 to 3,500 strong – but the food stores were amply stocked and 4,000 to 5,000 bellicose burghers fought alongside the Spaniards. 'There are also 80 artillery pieces and sufficient gunpowder and ammunition for them, so we are informed', the field deputies reported.[76] During the initial weeks the besiegers were preoccupied with the construction of the quarters and, first and foremost, the line of circumvallation, which was exceptionally long, 'because the forts built outside the town [by the Spaniards] jut out so widely'.[77] After the line had been completed the siege proper could begin. However, attention soon turned to events in the east of the Republic.

Over the course of June 1629 alarming reports reached The Hague about the Spanish and Imperial preparations along the eastern border. Everything pointed to an imminent attack on the towns along the River IJssel or into the Betuwe, as all the bakers in Wesel and Rheinberg had been ordered to bake bread for the Spanish and Imperial troops. In addition, three large barges laden with flour lay ready in Neuss 'and great quantities of rye are being brought thereto from the quarters of Upper Gelderland by waggon'. Furthermore, in Cologne the Spanish-Imperial forces had purchased sufficient grain for 25,000 men, and 10,000 Imperial troops were expected to arrive at any moment in Berg and Mark.[78] Brussels was indeed making ready for a concerted Spanish-Imperial attack on the Republic. The peace that had been concluded with Denmark at Lübeck on 22 May 1629 made it possible for Ferdinand II to do his Spanish cousins a favour in return for their earlier assistance in his struggle against the Protestants in Bohemia and the Palatinate.[79] The planned invasion was not intended to bring the Republic to its knees, which would require more than a single campaign, but the Spaniards hoped that the incursion would cause such great panic that Frederik Hendrik would be forced to raise the siege of 's-Hertogenbosch, and perhaps it would even lead to a renewal of the Truce. It was of great importance to the king of Spain to retain control of 's-Hertogenbosch: its loss would be a heavy blow to the prestige of the Spanish monarchy, and Isabella was therefore authorised by Philip IV to proffer the Republic a truce of thirty-four years on the same terms as the Truce of 1609–1621.[80]

In mid-July 1629 Spanish troops marched to Veghel via Boxtel, which indicated a possible siege of Grave. Frederik Hendrik remained level-headed. The

---

[76] NA, SG 4953, same to same, Fort Crevecoeur, 1 May 1629.
[77] NA, SG 4953, same to same, Fort Crevecoeur, 3 and 9 May 1629; Frederik Hendrik to the SG, Vught, 5 May 1629 (quote).
[78] NA, SG 4953, J. Hessell to the SG, Emmerich, 21 June 1629, with 'Verteyckenunge van 't keysers volck te peert & te voet, soo in de Bergische landen en[de] graefschap Marck geleyt sullen worden' as an appendix.
[79] Parker, *The Thirty Years' War*, p. 71.
[80] Israel, *Empires and Entrepots*, p. 43.

garrison of this fortified town had already been increased to 4,000 men, so he saw no cause for concern.[81] A week later, however, he received news that in the night of 22/23 July a Spanish vanguard had crossed the River IJssel at Westervoort, a small town just to the east of Arnhem. Major-General Herman Otto, count of Limburg Stirum (c. 1592–1644), the commander responsible for the security of the line along the rivers IJssel and Waal, made a 'great effort' to force the Spaniards back across the river, but they had by then entrenched themselves so effectively that each attack was repelled. Hendrik van den Bergh followed up with the main force at the end of July – 15,000 to 16,000 Spaniards and approximately 8,000 Imperial troops with twenty to thirty pieces of artillery[82] – with which he occupied Dieren (31 July) and proceeded to build a bridge across the River IJssel at Brummen, a village about seven kilometres southwest of Zutphen, to establish a secure link with Wesel. This was followed by more than a week of inactivity, the sluggishness of the Spanish advance affording Frederik Hendrik the opportunity to take countermeasures. Ernst Casimir left for Arnhem with fifty companies of foot and eight of horse. Together with the troops already there, the field-marshal would have 130 infantry companies and thirty cavalry companies available to him 'in order to prevent the enemy from penetrating further into the Veluwe or, this not being possible, that at least the state of the Land might be preserved from confusion to the extent that this is in any way feasible.'[83] To prevent the Spaniards and Imperialists advancing beyond the Veluwe, the States of Holland decided to arm 5,000 burghers and Friesland and Groningen ordered the recruitment of 3,000 *waardgelders*. The States-General also entered into contracts with various colonels to provide battle-ready regiments for a period of two or three months. Not only Spain but also the Republic profited from the end of the war between the emperor and Denmark. The Peace of Lübeck left thousands of Danish, German, Swedish, Scottish, English and French soldiers without work. The Republic managed to recruit a total of about 13,000 experienced troops.[84] All were not immediately deployable, of course, since their transportation and preparing them for battle would take several weeks. It is therefore a question of great importance why Hendrik van den Bergh and Count Ernesto Montecuccoli (c. 1580–1633), commander of the Imperial troops and uncle of the later general of great repute, Raimondo (1609–1680), failed to take advantage of their head start to push on to Utrecht or to lay siege to Deventer, Zutphen or Doesburg immediately, before these towns' garrisons were reinforced. Why did they allow the Republic the time to take countermeasures? On 31 July the garrisons of the three threatened towns on the River IJssel were brought to suffi-

---

[81] NA, SG 4953, Frederik Hendrik to the SG, before 's-Hertogenbosch, 17 July 1629.
[82] KHA, A23-VII-C-564, Jehan Foutlau, commander of 's Gravenweert, to Ernst Casimir, 27 July 1629; Ten Raa, *Het Staatsche leger*, IV, p. 37.
[83] NA, SG 4953, Frederik Hendrik to the SG, before 's-Hertogenbosch, 25 July 1629.
[84] NA, Tweede Afdeling, CG 305, no. 30c, 'Staet in 't corte van ruyteren ende knechten anno 1629 in 's Lants dienst geweest sijnde'.

cient strength to be able to repel a storm assault. By that time there were twelve companies and 400 men from Emden quartered in Doesburg, while Zutphen and Deventer had garrisons of fourteen companies apiece.[85]

In 1629 the Spanish and Imperial generals faced a complex logistical problem. It was not the forcing of the IJssel line but supplying food to the troops on the Veluwe that made the invasion of the Republic a military venture to which numerous difficulties were attached. Food supplies had to be organised before the assault could be executed. The Spanish-Imperial army's main depot was located in Wesel, but this town's milling and baking capacity was inadequate to be able to meet the daily bread requirements of all the troops so some food had to be requisitioned locally. However, the poor reputation of the Imperial troops caused Gelderland's countryfolk to take flight *en masse*,[86] and in addition Ernst Casimir had threatened to have anyone who supplied food to the enemy 'shot dead immediately'.[87] Hendrik van den Bergh ordered the repair of two damaged watermills in Bocholt in order to guarantee supplies,[88] but this was time-consuming and the Spanish-Imperial troops had not brought along enough food to wait for this. The Spanish commander-in-chief therefore ordered the inhabitants of Gelder, Stralen, Venlo and Roermond to bake as much bread as possible, but this created yet another problem: the limited shelf life of the bread. After all, there was no possibility of using barges to transport the bread to Wesel and from there to the Spanish-Imperial army along the River IJssel, so everything had to be loaded onto waggons. Hendrik van den Bergh hoped to overcome this difficulty by baking each loaf twice, effectively transforming it into rusk, 'so that it should remain good for longer'.[89]

The 'long-expected convoy' with bread had still not reached the Spanish-Imperial army at the start of August 1629. The field deputies with Ernst Casimir's army were astonished that 'those soldiers can still be kept together' in spite of the hunger in the enemy camp.[90] Frederik Hendrik was therefore furious when he heard not only that the farmers who had fled the Veluwe were returning home and supplying food to the Spaniards, but that 'the bailiffs themselves are returning landward [i.e. to the countryside], trading with the enemy and

---

[85] NA, SG 4954, Field deputies to the SG, Arnhem, 31 July 1629.
[86] In 1632 the fear caused by the Imperial forces among the rural population was so great that 'up to two hours walk around Pappenheim's troops ... there [were] no farmers to be found'. NA, SG 4961, Alexander van de Capellen and Frederik, baron of Schwartzenberg, to the SG, Wesel, 11 September 1632. Pappenheim was an Imperial general who arrived in the Low Countries with his army in August 1632.
[87] KHA, A23-VII-Da5, Deputies of the county of Zutphen to the field deputies in Arnhem, Zutphen, 30 July 1629.
[88] NA, SG 4954, H. van Eck to the SG, Wageningen, 5 August 1629.
[89] NA, SG 4953, Hendrik van den Bergh to the magistrates of Gelder, Stralen, Venlo and Roermond, Zeventer, 28 July 1629. This letter was intercepted by Dutch troops.
[90] NA, SG 4954, Field deputies to the SG, Arnhem, 7 August 1629.

supplying food to his army'.[91] The great convoy from Wesel eventually arrived in the second week of August, 'so it can with certainty be assumed that he [Hendrik van den Bergh] will no longer waste time by standing still, but shall undertake some march at the speediest', according to the States-General's deputies in Arnhem. They dreaded Zutphen being besieged or an advance on Amersfoort.[92] Ernesto Montecuccoli captured Amersfoort without a struggle on 14 August. Van den Bergh stayed behind with his Spanish troops to guard the bridgehead on the River IJssel.

The Imperialist occupation of Amersfoort sowed panic in Utrecht. The city's magistrate had little confidence that a garrison of 3,000 men was sufficient to be able to withstand an assault. There was increasing pressure on Frederik Hendrik to raise the siege of 's-Hertogenbosch and use his main army to drive the enemy out of Amersfoort and the Veluwe. The Union's captain-general summarily dismissed this plan. According to him there was a garrison of almost 4,000 men in Utrecht and more troops were on their way, so the city was not in danger. He also considered Zutphen's garrison to be sufficiently strong: 'In any case we are not of the opinion that Your High Mightinesses would approve of us denuding this army of more men, because for the advancement of our approaches, which have now reached as far as the town moats, [we] ourselves require more men, all the more because the enemy is gathering near Herentals.'[93]

Frederik Hendrik was right about the city of Utrecht and the towns along the River IJssel facing no immediate threat, but this did not alter the fact that the situation was extremely perturbing. The enemy had, after all, penetrated into the heart of the Republic and was already imposing a fire-tax of 600,000 guilders on the Veluwe.[94] Ernst Casimir had too few soldiers available to him to be able to attack Hendrik van den Bergh directly, so the only way to force the Spanish-Imperial troops to leave the Republic's soil was by severing their supply lines. It was Otto van Gendt (c. 1580–1640), lord of Dieden, the colonel who

---

[91] NA, SG 4954, Frederik Hendrik, before 's-Hertogenbosch, 6 August 1629. To provide a whitewash, the deputies of the county of Zutphen wrote to the members of the States-General and the Council of State in Arnhem: 'Since we fear that once the enemy has been warned of this [i.e. the ban on supplying food to the Spanish-Imperial army], in the same way [he] shall likewise forbid all supply to this side's fortified towns on pain of similar punishment, which shall then result in a great disservice to the aforesaid towns, because it shall not be possible satisfactorily to provision them and, moreover, due to such an interdict the crops will be left standing in the countryside and actually accrue to the profit of the enemy, being its master [i.e. having it in his power to harvest it], we have therefore found it necessary … to request commander Winbergen [in Zutphen] to supersede his duties for the aforesaid for a day or two in order in the meantime to send Your Noble Mightinesses this [our letter] in order that we … may receive your further intention and command in this matter.' KHA, A23-VII-Da5, Zutphen, 30 July 1629.
[92] NA, SG 4954, Field deputies to the SG, Arnhem, 9 and 10 (quote) August 1629.
[93] NA, SG 4954, Frederik Hendrik to the SG, before 's-Hertogenbosch, 14 August 1629.
[94] NA, SG 4954, Field deputies to the SG, Arnhem, 9 August 1629; States of Gelderland to the SG, Arnhem, 11 August 1629.

was commanding officer in the Upper Betuwe, who extricated Frederik Hendrik from this thorny position. He assembled 2,500 soldiers armed with firelocks from the neighbouring towns and launched a surprise attack on Wesel at about three o'clock in the morning on 19 August 1629. The garrison of sixteen companies put up hardly any resistance. Van Gendt had the governor, the captains and other officers imprisoned, but released the common soldiers – approximately 800 men – that same day, fearing he would be unable to retain the town otherwise. There was no discipline whatsoever among the assembled Dutch troops, who cared only about 'looting the town'. He therefore insisted that Ernst Casimir and the deputies in Arnhem should send him eight or ten complete companies immediately. Four or five companies were already *en route* from the garrisons of Rees and Emmerich.[95] In Wesel's warehouses the Dutch troops found more than 2,700 *malder* of rye and buckwheat, enough grain for approximately 110,000 six-pound loaves, which would have been enough to feed the Spanish-Imperial army with bread for two and a half weeks. Besides this great quantity of proviant the spoils consisted of six whole-cannon and fourteen demi-cannon, twenty-five pieces of smaller calibre and three mortars.[96]

The reduction of Wesel heralded the end of the Spanish-Imperial invasion. Captain Reinier van Goltstein, commander of Hees, reported to The Hague on 21 August 1629 that four 'well-mounted' Imperial cuirassiers with six horses had that day arrived in Hees and 'are requesting passage and [permission] to sell their horses'. They told him that Montecuccoli had left Amersfoort that morning and had begun the withdrawal to the IJssel.[97] Hendrik van den Bergh returned to Bocholt with the Spanish troops in early September, commencing the march back to Spanish Brabant from there on September 10. Montecuccoli left behind a small force to guard the bridge across the IJssel and headed for the Holy Roman Empire with the bulk of the Imperial force. The last of the Imperial troops left the Veluwe in October, but they no longer posed any threat whatsoever.[98] In the meantime, on 14 September, 's-Hertogenbosch had fallen.

The Spanish-Imperial attack had transformed the 1629 campaign into a battle of prestige that was splendidly won by the Republic. The Republic had demonstrated that it had access to sufficient financial reserves to simultaneously bring a major siege to a successful conclusion and withstand a sizeable enemy counterattack, all without foreign assistance. This erased the memories of the military setbacks of 1605–1606 and 1624–1625 in one fell swoop. The joy about the

---

[95] KHA, A23-VII-C-602, Otto baron van Gent to Ernst Casimir, Wesel, 19 August 1629; NA, SG 4954, Field deputies to the SG, Arnhem, 20 August 1629; Otto van Gent to the field deputies, Wesel, 19 August 1629.
[96] NA, SG 4955, Field deputies to the SG, n.p., n.d., received 2 September 1629, with 'Staet van het coorren soo hier bevonden is in de stadt Wesel den 21e augusty 1629' as an appendix.
[97] NA, SG 4954, Reinier van Goltstein to the SG, Hees, 21 August 1629.
[98] NA, SG 4955, Frederik Hendrik to the SG, before 's-Hertogenbosch, 7 September 1629; Ernst Casimir to the SG, Arnhem, 13 September 1629; Field deputies to the SG, Arnhem, 14 September 1629.

triumph of 1629 was, however, short-lived. The regents were all too aware that the Republic could not afford a financial exertion of such proportions again.[99] In 1629 the land-based war had cost no less than 18 to 19 million guilders.[100] The prospect of a speedy final victory was, however, absent. The capture of 's-Hertogenbosch was an important political success, but its military-strategic significance was limited. It is true that Heusden and the Bommelerwaard were no longer in danger and that the Spanish garrison in Breda had been isolated, but the reduction of 's-Hertogenbosch failed to break the military stalemate that had prevailed in the Low Countries since 1606. Bringing a swift end to the Eighty Years' War would still only be possible at the negotiation table. This prompted many regents to question whether it would not therefore be wiser to convert the accumulated military glory into a peace settlement with Spain that same winter. Over the preceding months Brussels had repeatedly shown its willingness to negotiate. The Hague had not responded to this seriously at the time – while the Spanish-Imperial troops were still in the Veluwe the Republic's position at the negotiation table was, after all, weak – but now that the enemy had evacuated Gelderland and 's-Hertogenbosch had fallen the Republic had the best cards in hand. Exploratory discussions were opened in Roosendaal.

The States of Overijssel, Gelderland and Utrecht pronounced their support for the renewal of a truce with the Spanish Netherlands. The leading regents in Amsterdam, Rotterdam and Dordrecht shared this view. The political stance of Amsterdam was increasingly dictated by the Bicker family, with Andries (1586–1652) at its head. The business interests of the Bickers were primarily in the European sphere of trade. In religious affairs, Andries Bicker, like Van Oldenbarnevelt before him, believed that the Counter-Remonstrants had to resign themselves to decisions reached by government. If they continued to resist then the city government had every right to take action, as in January 1629, when the strictly Calvinist preacher, Adriaan Jorissen Smout or Smoutsius (c. 1580–1646), was banished from Amsterdam.[101] Haarlem and Leiden were, by contrast, outspoken opponents of a peace deal with Brussels. Dominated by Counter-Remonstrants, the governments of these two towns feared that a truce would undermine their political and economic positions. Zeeland, Friesland and Groningen also wished to continue the struggle. Thus three provinces were in favour of opening truce negotiations, while three were emphatically against, and Holland was too divided on this issue to be able to adopt a provincial standpoint. Frederik Hendrik was in favour of a truce, but he had no intention of using his position as stadholder to impose this view on the States of Holland,[102] because by choosing sides he

---

99 Van der Capellen, *Gedenkschriften*, I, pp. 506–7.
100 GA, AHGC 754, State of the war expenses in 1629; NA, CG 305, 'Lasten die gevallen sijn in den jare 1629'.
101 Elias, *Het Amsterdamsche regentenpatriciaat*, pp. 93, 95–7, 114 and 119–20.
102 Groenveld, *Evidente factiën*, p. 30; Israel, *Empires and Entrepots*, pp. 45–51 and 56, and *The Dutch Republic and the Hispanic World*, pp. 231–2.

would lose much of his authority. It was by cooperating with one provincial faction and then the other that the stadholder and his 'court faction' could influence the decision-making at meetings of the States.[103] In addition, developments in Europe and South America made a swift conclusion of the truce negotiations in Roosendaal less urgent, even undesirable.

In February 1629 France had intervened in the Mantuan War of Succession and in December of that year Armand Jean Duplessis (1585–1642), *duc de* Richelieu – Louis XIII's chief minister since 1624 – had it intimated in The Hague that the king of France was prepared to invade the Spanish Netherlands together with the Republic. By entangling Brussels in a war on two fronts The Hague would be able to deploy its army in the Southern Netherlands without running the risk of incurring such huge expenses as in 1629. It would, after all, force Isabella to devote all her military manpower to defence, leaving her with no troops for an attack on the Republic's eastern borders. For the Republic, too, the advantages of continuing the war overseas seemed to outweigh the disadvantages. In February 1630 troops from the West India Company captured Pernambuco (Recife) on the northeast coast of Brazil, and Madrid made its retrocession a precondition for a truce.[104] Under such circumstances it was extremely unlikely that the discussions in Roosendaal would lead to anything.

In the same month that Pernambuco fell into Dutch hands the States of Zeeland pressed 'very hard' for a campaign in Flanders, 'for which, already contrary to their habit, they have the money ready in The Hague, something which we, the Imperialists being so close to us, consider perilous for our provinces', Friesland's deputies to the States-General wrote to Ernst Casimir.[105] The Frisians informed Frederik Hendrik that the northern provinces would prefer the Dutch army to lay siege to Lingen, to which the commander-in-chief responded 'that he was of the opinion to attempt the other [option] first, but that should he encounter any difficulty in this, to have the men descend [i.e. sail down river] to Deventer by barge'. By 'any difficulty' Frederik Hendrik was referring to the differences of opinion in Holland. The champions of a truce were specifically refusing to consent to the hiring of 6,000 *waardgelders* and they were equally ill-disposed to furnishing the pay for 6,500 men recruited in 1629 who, unlike the other troops taken on temporarily, had not yet been disbanded – they were in the meantime being retained at the expense of Cleves, Berg and Mark.[106] A few months later these 6,500 men were reduced to forty-nine companies of foot and two of horse with an effective strength of 5,500 men. Lastly, there was the issue of the fifty infantry companies established in 1628, which Frederik Hendrik

---

[103] Groenveld, *Evidente factiën*, pp. 36–7.
[104] Israel, *Empires and Entrepots*, pp. 54–5, and *The Dutch Republic and the Hispanic World*, p. 238.
[105] KHA, A23-VII-C-555, Julius van Eysinga and Johan van Veltdriel to Ernst Casimir, The Hague, 6 February 1630.
[106] KHA, A23-VII-C-556, Julius van Eysinga to Ernst Casimir, The Hague, 16 March 1630.

wanted to bring to their full strength of 10,000 troops by recruiting 5,000 extra men. The commander-in-chief argued that if the provinces agreed to the enlistment of the *waardgelders* and the extra 5,000 men and, in addition, made funds available for the mobilisation of the force in the duchy of Jülich's territories, then he could be confident about undertaking a campaign of conquest in the Spanish Netherlands. There would then be sufficient troops available to safeguard the eastern frontier during the summer of 1630.

Frederik Hendrik's portrayal of the state of affairs was, however, rosier than one could deduce from reports from France and the Spanish Netherlands. It was even highly doubtful whether an invasion of the Spanish Netherlands in 1630 would have any chance of success, because Richelieu had watered down his offer for an offensive alliance: he no longer wanted to go beyond furnishing an annual subsidy of 1 million guilders. This subsidy treaty was signed on 17 June 1630 for a term of seven years.[107] France's financial support stood the Republic in good stead, but it could not compensate for the French assault on the southern frontier of the Spanish Netherlands failing to materialise. The consequences of the French decision were noticeable almost immediately. Now that Brussels no longer needed to take into account a war on two fronts, the bulk of the Spanish troops could be quartered in and near Antwerp. 'The enemy is making himself very strong in Antwerp', a correspondent warned Count Floris II of Culemborg in early July 1630.[108] Without possession of Antwerp, an invasion of the Spanish Netherlands from the north was a well-nigh impossible undertaking, because there would then be no possibility of using the rivers Scheldt, Leie, Dijle and Demer, waterways which were vital for the transportation of artillery and provisions. Spanish Brabant could, of course, be invaded from the east, but the 1602 campaign had made it clear that this presented great logistical disadvantages. With French military support unforthcoming, Frederik Hendrik's plan 'to offensively attack [the Spaniards] in several places' in 1630 was scrapped.[109] Nevertheless, in July the discussions in Roosendaal were broken off. This was lamented in Brussels, but Olivarez shed no tears about this; he wished to negotiate with the Republic only from a position of strength.[110]

Richelieu's stance made it obvious to Frederik Hendrik that he needed to find an operational objective in the Spanish Netherlands which the Republic would be able to achieve autonomously. Four possibilities presented themselves: a campaign along the River Meuse, laying siege to Hulst, besieging Bruges or an attack on Dunkirk. Frederik Hendrik's preference was for the destruction of this

---

[107] Ten Raa, *Het Staatsche leger*, IV, p. 44.
[108] GA, AHGC 737, Tobias van Eyck, adviser to Count Floris II of Culemborg, The Hague, 8 July 1630.
[109] KHA, A23-VII-C-340, Edzard Jacob Clant van Stedum to Ernst Casimir, Groningen, 23 February 1630.
[110] René Vermeir, *In staat van oorlog. Filips IV en de Zuidelijke Nederlanden 1629–1648* (Maastricht 2001), pp. 18 and 41.

major Spanish naval base and privateers' nest, as he would be able to count on the undivided support of the Hollanders. On 8 April 1631 he tabled a proposal to undertake a campaign to Dunkirk or Bruges in the *secrete besogne*, but he informed the seven members of this secret committee for military affairs who were present that 'for these designs a greater number of soldiers ... [would be] necessary than is currently in the service of Their High Mightinesses [the States-General], bearing in mind that approval of this design would require fielding two armies'. He needed a main body of 30,000 infantry and about 4,000 cavalry 'with which to go on the offensive' and a smaller covering army on the Rhine of 10,000 foot and 1,800 to 2,000 horse 'for the defence of the Land'. The *secrete besogne* agreed to Frederik Hendrik's proposal and for its implementation acquiesced in the raising of three new regiments, each 3,000 strong. Ultimately two of these regiments were enlisted and the French annual subsidy of 1 million guilders was earmarked for the payment of these 6,000 troops.[111] The ease with which Frederik Hendrik's proposal was approved ought to come as no surprise, as he was empowered to select the members of the *secrete besognes* as he saw fit. The delegates from Gelderland, Friesland and Groningen – Baron Arnold van Randwijck (1574–1641), Julius van Eysinga (†1649) and Goosen Schaffer (1601–1637), respectively – were reassured by Frederik Hendrik's concern for the eastern frontiers. So long as troops were available to protect their provinces during the summer months they had no objections to an offensive in the Spanish Netherlands. Represented by Simon van Beaumont (1574–1654), the States of Zeeland had lobbied for an incursion into Flanders in 1630. This meant the selection of the secret committee's members from Holland was of decisive importance. It is surprising that besides Nicolaes van den Bouchorst (†1641), lord of Noordwijk and Wimmenum, who was a strict Calvinist and from 1619 served as the standing representative of Holland's Knighthood at the States-General, Frederik Hendrik chose Dirk Jacobsz. Bas (1569–1637) from Amsterdam and Willem van Beveren (1556–1631) from Dordrecht. Bas had been ejected from Amsterdam's city council by Maurits in 1618, but four years later he had already regained his seat. He was one of the leaders of the Arminian faction in Amsterdam.[112] Van Beveren was a highly experienced regent who had personally witnessed numerous military operations by Maurits as a field deputy. He also belonged to the Remonstrant faction, but was spared during the purge of Remonstrant magistrates (*wetsverzetting*) in 1618.[113] Frederik Hendrik's choice was, however, less surprising than it might initially seem. The Remonstrant faction did indeed zealously champion

---

[111] NA, SG 4562, Secret res. SG, 8 April 1631. Contracts were concluded with Walraven baron van Gendt and Gerard Erentreiter for the raising of two regiments, each composed of 3,000 'German' infantrymen, on 12 April. See SG 4958, Contracts.
[112] Elias, *Het Amsterdamsche regentenpatriciaat*, pp. 80 and 87; Israel, *Empires and Entrepots*, pp. 81 and 84.
[113] *Nieuw Nederlandsch biografisch woordenboek*, 10 vols (reprint, Amsterdam 1974), III, pp. 113–14.

the renewal of a truce, but at the same time the cargo trade in European waters was most severely affected by the activities of Dunkirk's privateers and, as noted, in the main it was Remonstrant merchants who sustained the greatest losses.

Frederik Hendrik urged the provincial States to consent to the secret resolution of 8 April 1631 as swiftly as possible, because there was no time to be lost with its implementation, in the knowledge that Brussels was expecting the arrival of substantial troop reinforcements. Some 1,200 men from Spain had already arrived in Dunkirk in the middle of March and in Italy preparations were underway to transfer thousands of soldiers to the Low Countries as soon as the peace negotiations with France about the Mantuan succession were concluded. The Treaty of Cherasco was signed in April 1631. More than 11,000 men under the command of Alvarez de Bazán, marquès de Santa Cruz, headed north from Lombardy.[114] The Dutch war preparations were in the meantime making little headway, as Count Floris II of Culemborg was informed by a correspondent from The Hague:

> The greatest difficulty is that the synod of the North Quarter [of Holland] has pronounced that [the city council of] Amsterdam shall have no authority in ecclesiastical affairs and that they shall once again engage Smoutsius [the clergyman banished in January 1629], which causes great alarm in the assembly [of the States of Holland].... His Excellency [Frederik Hendrik] is greatly troubled by these matters, concerned that setting out on campaign shall thereby be prevented.[115]

Tensions ran so high that Amsterdam's burgomasters threatened to enlist 2,000 to 3,000 soldiers in order to bring the Counter-Remonstrants in their city into line. The States of Holland eventually consented to the readying of the field army, but without dipping into their coffers, seeing as 'those [regents] from Enkhuizen and Gouda [two Counter-Remonstrant bastions] are holding back everyone, the negotiation of the 200th penny [tax] and the redress of the tax on land and houses'.[116] The pressure on the Hollanders to at last reach an agreement was by now increasing by the day. On 16 April 1631 a 'whole mob' of fishermen's wives from Maassluis and other fishing ports gathered before the assembly hall of the States of Holland 'because of the Dunkirkers who lie before the [mouth of the] River Maas and here in view of Scheveningen and are hanging about so that the fishermen do not dare put out to sea'.[117] Two weeks later Frederik Hendrik was at the end of his tether. On 30 April he asked the members of the secret committee whether they still wished to proceed with the plan put forward. Their

---

[114] GA, AHGC 737, Tobias van Eyck to Count Floris II of Culemborg, The Hague, 28 March 1631; Lynch, *Spain*, II, p. 84; Parker, *Army of Flanders*, p. 279; Vermeir, *In staat van oorlog*, p. 45.
[115] GA, AHGC 737, Tobias van Eyck to Count Floris II of Culemborg, The Hague, 3 April 1631.
[116] GA, AHGC 737, same to same, The Hague, 7 April 1631. See also p. 75.
[117] GA, AHGC 737, same to same, The Hague, 17 April 1631.

answer to this was unanimously in the affirmative.[118] However, the expedition to Dunkirk was not blessed by the gods.

The only chance of an assault on Dunkirk succeeding was if the Spaniards were kept guessing about the objective of the Dutch operation. Otherwise Brussels would be able to reinforce the garrison in due time and take measures to hinder or prevent the flow of food supplies to the Dutch siege army. To Frederik Hendrik's great displeasure he received news from a diversity of sources in the Spanish Netherlands 'that it is everywhere publicly known that Their High Mightinessess [the States-General] are planning to break through into Flanders and are resolved to undertake something against Dunkirk'.[119] The likelihood that they would succeed in destroying the naval base was therefore very slim. Frederik Hendrik remained firmly in favour of a campaign in Flanders, because if it proved impossible to besiege Dunkirk then it would still be possible to lay siege to Bruges. With an army of approximately 200 infantry companies, 1,000 soldiers armed with firelocks and thirty-nine or forty cavalry companies he thought success was assured.

The Dutch field army was assembled in the east in the vicinity of Emmerich in mid-May 1631 in order to wrong-foot Brussels about the thrust of the offensive.[120] On 25 May this force departed for Zeeland by barge. Twenty cavalry companies and 4,000 infantrymen remained behind in the environs of Emmerich to protect the eastern frontier. As soon as the two new infantry regiments had been recruited this covering army would attain the intended strength of 12,000 men.[121] On 30 May the main body landed near IJzendijke and established a position by Watervliet. Frederik Hendrik ordered the reconnoitring of the surroundings from this encampment in order to gain an impression of the enemy's strength. Between 6,000 and 7,000 Spanish troops were gathered near Bruges and a similar number in the Land of Waas.[122]

On 1 June 1631 the Dutch army struck camp and set out for Bruges. The following day the troops crossed the Ghent Canal, so a decision about whether or not to lay siege to Dunkirk brooked no further delay. The majority of the field deputies and officers thought it 'not advisable … to proceed deeper and landwards'. Frederik Hendrik acquiesced and then proposed laying siege to Bruges, but even this plan was no longer deemed feasible 'given that the enemy has already approached close to this place with his whole army, [which is] 60 cornets of cavalry and a great number of infantry strong'.[123] This was not, however, the main reason for calling off the operation. 'There has been great hunger in our

---

[118] NA, SG 4562, Secret res. SG, 30 April 1631.
[119] NA, SG 4962, Secret res. SG, 12 May 1631.
[120] NA, SG 4958, Field deputies to the SG, Emmerich, 21 May 1631.
[121] NA, SG 4958, same to same, Emmerich, 26 May 1631.
[122] NA, SG 4958, same to same, before Rammekens, 29 May, and IJzendijke, 31 May 1629; Frederik Hendrik to the SG, Watervliet, 31 May 1631.
[123] NA, SG 4958, Frederik Hendrik to the SG, Kaprijke, 6 June 1631.

army by reason of the inaccessibility and great distance from which the vivres must come, which one believes to be the greatest reason for the withdrawal', Overijssel's deputy to the States-General, Bernard Sloet, was able to inform his principals.[124] Frederik Hendrik returned to IJzendijke with the Dutch army and embarked the troops. In The Hague this raised the question of what might still be achieved with the army during this campaign. Alexander van der Capellen thought the capture of Breda, Rheinberg or Venlo was not worth the military exertion or expense.[125] In his memoirs he noted:

> I consider this ... too scant a reward for all the great preparations and costs that with this advantage of time (the enemy being in a state of confusion, the Emperor still being engaged together with Spain in Italy and having to use all his might against Sweden alongside the [Catholic] League) could be better employed to cause greater harm to our enemies.[126]

The Treaty of Cherasco was not ratified until 19 June 1631.[127]

On 6 July 1630 a Swedish force commanded by King Gustavus II Adolphus landed in Pomerania. The electors of Brandenburg and Saxony had initially bided their time, but after the sacking of Magdeburg (20 May 1631) by the army of the Catholic League under Tilly they rallied together under the banners of the 'Lion of the North'. The battle of Breitenfeld was joined on 17 September 1631, with Tilly suffering a crushing defeat against Gustavus Adolphus.[128] A couple of days earlier the Spaniards had also been dealt a heavy blow. While deliberations were underway in The Hague, in Brussels it was decided to launch a daring landing in Holland. The plan was to land 6,000 men at Willemstad and then advance on Gorinchem or Woudrichem, where there were only skeleton garrisons. The success of this undertaking depended on strict secrecy, but this constituted as big a problem in the Spanish Netherlands as it did in the Republic. A Dutch captain in Spanish service warned The Hague,[129] so the Dutch fleet was readied to intercept the invasion. The Spaniards suffered a heavy defeat in the naval battle of the Slaak (12 September 1631), with more than 4,000 men and eighty-three of the ninety troop-ships falling into Dutch hands.[130] Despite this triumph Frederik Hendrik did not deem it viable to execute the original operational plan. New Spanish reinforcements from Italy were expected at any moment,[131] and he was

---

[124] HCO, ASO 992, Bernard Sloet to the States of Overijssel (henceforth SvO), The Hague, 10 June 1631.
[125] NA, SG 4562, Secret res. SG, 16 and 17 July 1631.
[126] Van der Capellen, *Gedenkschriften*, I, p. 626.
[127] Parker, *The Thirty Years' War*, p. 113.
[128] Ibid., pp. 103 and 112–13.
[129] KHA, A23-VII-C-1059, Johan van Veltdriel to Ernst Casimir, The Hague, 5 September 1631.
[130] Ten Raa, *Het Staatsche leger*, IV, p. 53.
[131] KHA, A23-VII-C-1057, Johan van Veltdriel to Ernst Casimir, The Hague, 30 August 1631.

concerned that the enemy had set their sights on Bergen op Zoom or a town in States Flanders. Frederik Hendrik had therefore decided to establish a position with the bulk of the Dutch troops between Bergen op Zoom and Steenbergen and to remain there until the end of the campaign season.[132]

Frederik Hendrik was determined to achieve a success in 1632 that would justify the high war expenditure. He could not permit himself to remain passive for the third successive year, so in the secret committee he proposed laying siege to Antwerp.[133] However, shortly after this decision was adopted unforeseen developments meant that taking Maastricht rather than Antwerp became the operational objective of the 1632 campaign. In April and May, there arrived in The Hague 'in secret ... some persons of great note and quality from the other side, who aired their inclination and affection for the advancement of the affairs of this State'.[134] Among these high-placed persons was Hendrik van den Bergh. He made it known that the dissatisfaction with Spanish rule among the nobility of the Spanish Netherlands had become so great that they wished to switch their allegiance.[135] As stadholder of Upper Gelderland he could give the assurance that the garrisons of Venlo, Stralen and Roermond would put up minimal resistance and that the Dutch army would therefore be able to press on to Maastricht swiftly. It would then be possible to move into Brabant. Based on this information the States-General endorsed the besieging of Maastricht. After reducing this stronghold Frederik Hendrik would continue the offensive 'right into the heart of the principal provinces' of the enemy, namely Brabant and Flanders.[136] At the end of May 1632 the troops intended for the field army arrived at Nijmegen. Frederik Hendrik took command of 281 companies of foot and fifty-eight of horse, approximately 28,000 men.

Hendrik van den Bergh had not been exaggerating: the towns of Upper Gelderland did indeed fall like a house of cards. The jubilation about this on the Dutch side was, however, tempered by the death of Ernst Casimir on 2 June 1632; during a reconnaissance of Roermond's fortifications he was fatally struck by a musket-ball. The twenty-year-old Hendrik Casimir I, Ernst Casimir's eldest son, succeeded him as stadholder of Friesland, Groningen and Drenthe, but his political influence was limited and as a military commander he still had to prove himself. The Dutch troops arrived before Maastricht on 10 June. The field deputies pushed on to Liège to purchase food, powder and siege tools, as well as rent ships for a pontoon bridge across the River Meuse. It was also their responsibility

> to assure the magistrate and other members of the government [of Liège] of Your High Mightinesses' good and sincere intention to continue the neutrality, with the

---

[132] NA, SG 4959, Frederik Hendrik to the SG, Drunen, 4 September 1631.
[133] NA, SG 4562, Secret res. SG, 21 March 1632.
[134] NA, SG 4562, Secret res. SG, 19 May 1632.
[135] Israel, *The Dutch Republic and the Hispanic World*, p. 184; Poelhekke, *Frederik Hendrik*, p. 374.
[136] NA, SG 4562, Secret res. SG, 19 May 1632.

request that they would ensure that the towns of Maaseik, Stockem and Weset [Visé], lying below and above Maastricht on the river, cannot be taken by the enemy to hinder the supplies to the [Dutch] army.[137]

The security of the money convoys from Nijmegen required special consideration. Realising the lines of circum- and contravallation, the raising of batteries and the digging of trenches always cost a great deal of money, and the basic wages would also have to be paid. At the start of the campaign the soldiers had received one month's pay,[138] but a new shipment of cash would have to be delivered to the Dutch army camp by the middle of July. The garrisons in Stralen, Venlo and Roermond had to ensure the security of the lines of communication between Maastricht and Nijmegen, and were therefore reinforced with an extra 2,600 men. Assuming all the companies were complete, a total of 5,100 men were garrisoned there.[139]

The siege of Maastricht was plagued by difficulties. The line of circumvallation was very long and because the defenders fired their artillery incessantly the approach trenches could advance but slowly. On 23 June 1632 the approaches were within twenty rods (75m) of the ditch, and 'they would almost be there if one had been able to go in a straight line, [but] the enemy is defending himself bravely with shots from whole- and demi-cannons, also with *drylingen* [i.e. French whole-cannon] firing 36-pound iron balls'. This forced the besiegers to dig their trenches in a zigzag.[140] A setback more serious than the heavy cannonade from the stronghold was the arrival of a Spanish relief army numbering 178 infantry companies and seventy cavalry companies under the command of Santa Cruz. By 27 June the Spaniards had approached to within a short distance of Maastricht. 'So we shall probably have an assault tomorrow or the day after tomorrow', the field deputies surmised. According to some deserters the enemy force was 33,000 strong, though others reported it to be no more than 23,000.[141] The anticipated attack failed to materialise. The Spaniards established a position near Lanaken, a village to the north of Maastricht.

Frederik Hendrik started to become increasingly concerned about his lines of communication with Nijmegen, all the more because there was reason to fear that Brussels would summon the assistance of an Imperial army under the command of Gottfried Heinrich, count of Pappenheim (1594–1632). Frederik Hendrik therefore entreated the field deputies to agree to levy 3,000 men in the bishopric of Liège, so that enough troops could be posted along the right bank of the River Meuse to prevent the Spaniards gaining control of both banks.

---

[137] NA, SG 4960, Field deputies to the SG, before Roermond, 6 June 1632, Liège, 12 June 1632 (quote).
[138] NA, SG 4960, same to same, Nijmegen, 30 May 1632, late in the evening.
[139] NA, SG 4960, same to same, Liège, 12 June 1632, P.S.; RvS to the SG, The Hague, 24 June 1632.
[140] NA, SG 4960, same to same, before Maastricht, 23 June 1632.
[141] NA, SG 4960, same to same, before Maastricht, 27 June 1632.

The deputies agreed to this. 'We are fully aware', they wrote to The Hague in justification, 'that we do not have the right to do such recruitment.' This was normally the exclusive reserve of the States-General and the Council of State, but necessity knows no law, 'for we have not yet noticed that the flocking [of South Netherlandish troops and disaffected nobles] to Count Hendrik van den Bergh is as great as we had believed'. There had thus far been no sign of the uprising in the Southern Netherlands that Van den Bergh had predicted.[142] The States-General approved of the action of the field deputies and also complied with the request from the Union's captain-general to levy 5,000 recruits for the English, French and Scottish companies.[143] The Hague also ordered the enlistment of 6,000 *waardgelders*. The field deputies eventually contracted 2,000 cavalrymen and 5,200 infantrymen, while Hendrik van den Bergh recruited a further 1,000 cavalry and 4,000 infantry in his former stadholderate, all at the Republic's expense.[144]

In late July 1632 the Spanish army was still encamped near Lanaken. By purchasing enormous quantities of flour in Liège the Dutch army was assured of bread for more than a month,[145] but in early August the campaign coffers were running dry.[146] At around the same time Pappenheim's army, approximately 12,500 strong,[147] crossed the Rhine and reached the village of Meerssen to the northeast of Maastricht on 12 August, 'whereby our passage is cut off on one side of the Meuse as well as on the other'. This made it impossible to collect money for the siege army from Nijmegen. The field deputies therefore entreated the States-General 'to think of means whereby we shall be able to get the coins by bill of exchange [in Liège], and that in all haste, in order to be able to keep the work here going'.[148] The Hague had to disappoint the deputies 'because in Liège ... they do not deal in bills of exchange, as well as in view of the scant amount of cash available there'.[149] The critical situation made Frederik Hendrik decide to undertake a bold venture. Despite the great risks involved he gave orders for a convoy to set out from Nijmegen with more than 40,000 guilders for the Frisian companies. The Spaniards kept a close watch on the road to Maastricht and

---

[142] NA, SG 4960, same to same, before Maastricht, 9 July 1632, partly in cipher (quote), and 12 July 1632, late evening; Cornelis van Terestein to the SG, Liège, 13 July 1632.
[143] NA, SG 4960, RvS to the SG, The Hague, 15 July 1632.
[144] NA, SG 4961, 'Staet van vier maenden soldie voor dertich compaigniën sterck 3,000 ruyters ende 12,630 man te voet mit aenvanck september 1632 in dienst gecommen ende tot vuytganck february 1633 te continueren', read during the meeting of the States-General on 17 September 1632.
[145] NA, SG 4961, Cornelis van Terestein to the SG, Liège, 31 July 1632.
[146] NA, SG 4961, Field deputies to the SG, before Maastricht, 2 August 1632.
[147] NA, SG 4961, Otto van Gendt, lord of Dieden, to the SG, Arnhem, 6 August 1632.
[148] NA, SG 4961, Field deputies to the SG, before Maastricht, 13 August 1632, in the evening.
[149] NA, SG 4961, Jan Cornelisz. Geelvinck to the SG, Amsterdam, 18 and 22 August 1632.

35. A skirmish between Dutch and Spanish troopers, c. 1635. Oil painting by Pruisentem. (Royal Netherlands Army Museum, Delft, 056855)

waited in ambush. The Dutch escort was scattered and 'all the money together with two artillery pieces were taken'.[150]

Around the same time, however, the besiegers achieved two important military successes from which they could take heart. On 17 August 1632 Pappenheim ordered a storm assault on the circumvallation, but the Dutch troops stood their ground and repelled Pappenheim's men, inflicting heavy losses (1,500 to 1,600 dead and wounded).[151] Four days later the besiegers exploded a mine beneath Maastricht's main rampart, 'thus making a fair-sized breach in the wall, we immediately ordered an attack be carried out on it by some English troops'. The garrison managed to drive the Englishmen away from the breach, but the following day (22 August), 'under the pretext of both sides wanting to collect the dead, [the defenders] shortly thereafter became engaged in a formal discussion with us', according to a relieved Frederik Hendrik. The capitulation was concluded that same evening and Dutch troops entered Maastricht the following day.[152] The field deputies discovered that the reason the garrison had given up the fight with such unexpected swiftness was because of the shortage of gunpowder. The Spaniards would have been able to persevere with the city's defence for a long time 'if their powder had not dwindled from one thousand to thirty tonnes'.

---

[150] NA, SG 4961, Jacques Saint Hillaires, seigneur de Rignac, governor of Nijmegen, to the SG, Nijmegen, 15 August 1632; Field deputies to the SG, before Maastricht, 21 August 1632 (quote).
[151] NA, SG 4961, Field deputies to the SG, before Maastricht, 21 August 1632.
[152] NA, SG 4961, Frederik Hendrik to the SG, near Maastricht, 23 August 1632.

The garrison, still approximately 1,500 infantrymen and fifty cavalrymen strong, withdrew on 24 August.[153]

Frederik Hendrik remained in Maastricht until the damage to the fortifications was repaired.[154] In early September 1632 Pappenheim left for Saxony with his troops, while the Spaniards took up positions in Brabant. After the departure of the Spanish-Imperial troops the connection with Nijmegen was free once again and the wages for the Dutch troops could at last be collected there. In the middle of September a money transport with a value of no less than 500,000 guilders arrived in the Dutch army camp.[155] In the meantime, on 8 September, Dutch troops had occupied Limbourg and on 16 November they also took control of Orsoy, a fort overlooking the Rhine. This left the Spanish garrison in Rheinberg completely isolated. Hereafter Frederik Hendrik dispersed the Dutch army across the winter quarters.[156] On the same day that Orsoy capitulated, Gustavus Adolphus died at the height of his fame in the battle of Lützen. The death of the champion of the German Protestants made this Swedish triumph a Pyrrhic victory.[157]

The Dutch offensive stalls (1633–1634)

The Meuse campaign had required an expansion of the Dutch army with no fewer than 12,600 infantrymen and 3,000 cavalry, at a cost of more than 258,000 guilders per pay-month of forty-two days. However, in contrast to 1631, the 1632 campaign achieved an outcome that fulfilled the expectations attendant on high war expenditure. Frederik Hendrik insisted that the States-General should retain the extra troops 'temporarily', so that he could continue the offensive in 1633. The provinces consented to this, as there was no prospect of a near-term peace. After the fall of Maastricht, Brussels once again made advances to the Republic, but a diplomatic breakthrough failed to materialise. Isabella had hoped that if the initiative for the peace negotiations came from the States-General of the Spanish Netherlands rather than representatives of Madrid, then the Dutch would be more likely to be prepared to negotiate a new truce, but after five months the discussions were still at a deadlock. Withdrawal of all the Spanish troops from the Low Countries, the quartering of Dutch garrisons in the Flemish seaports and ceding the Meierij of 's-Hertogenbosch to the Republic were out of the ques-

---

[153] NA, SG 4961, Field deputies to the SG, near Maastricht, 24 August 1632.
[154] NA, SG 4961, same to same, near Maastricht, 29 August 1632; Frederik Hendrik to the SG, near Maastricht, 13 September 1632; Alexander van der Capellen and Frederik, baron of Schwartzenberg, to the SG, Wesel, 11 and 30 September 1632.
[155] NA, SG 4961, Frederik Hendrik to the SG, near Maastricht, 13 September 1632; Arent de Bye and L. Clant to the SG, Nijmegen, 15, 21 and 22 September 1632.
[156] NA, SG 4961, Frederik Hendrik to the SG, near Maastricht, 13 September, Herkenbosch, 8 November 1632.
[157] Parker, *The Thirty Years' War*, pp. 116–17.

tion for Brussels, while The Hague refused to talk about the retrocession of Pernambuco. Amsterdam, Rotterdam and Dordrecht were prepared to surrender Dutch territories in Brazil in exchange for peace, but they were alone in this.[158] The discussions with Brussels were suspended in mid-June 1633. However, in order to avoid estranging Holland's peace faction, Frederik Hendrik decided to begin the 1633 campaign by capturing a town that would be of great advantage to the merchants of Dordrecht and Rotterdam, namely Rheinberg. This operational goal could also depend on the approval of the regents of Gelderland and Overijssel, the majority of whom were also in favour of peace. The Spaniards were exacting contributions on the Achterhoek and Twente from Rheinberg.[159]

The siege of Rheinberg went well, with the 1,700 or so defenders holding out for no longer than twenty-two days, surrendering on 2 June 1633.[160] Frederik Hendrik then established a camp near Nijmegen. At The Hague, the French ambassador, Hercule, baron de Charnacé (1588–1637), was in the meantime lobbying for a Dutch incursion into Luxembourg. The king of France was intent on capturing Nancy, the capital of Lorraine. The duke of Lorraine was an ally of Spain, so if the Republic occupied the Spanish troops in the Low Countries and Luxembourg then the siege of Nancy could be undertaken with a high chance of success. Charnacé swore to Frederik Hendrik that if he 'should desire to take the king and seigneur the cardinal [Richelieu] into full confidence they would never abandon him, no matter what might transpire'. Frederik Hendrik did, however, have to unequivocally announce that he wanted to continue the war against Spain. He would, in other words, have to publicly distance himself from the regents who favoured peace.[161] Frederik Hendrik played for time. Before allowing it to boil down to a public rift with the Remonstrant faction in Holland, he wanted to have the guarantee that France would support the Republic militarily in her struggle against Spain, not as an auxiliary of the Dutch but as a full partner: Paris would have to declare war on Madrid. 'Previously one has not only had the king of France as a friend, but [France] has also been in open war against Spain. One knows what advantage these lands enjoyed during that time [1590–1598]', according to the stadholder.[162] To demonstrate his friendship to Louis XIII and Richelieu, Frederik Hendrik was certainly prepared to support them in the reduction of Lorraine. Without waiting for approval from the provincial States, the States-General granted Frederik Hendrik permission to enlist a Swedish-Hessian cavalry corps (an effective force of 4,700 men) for a

---

[158] Israel, *Empires and Entrepots*, p. 94.
[159] Ten Raa, *Het Staatsche leger*, IV, p. 67.
[160] NA, SG 4962, Frederik Hendrik to the SG, near Rheinberg, 3 June 1633; Albert Sonck (1571–1658) to the SG, near Rheinberg, 5 June 1633.
[161] *Archives*, 2nd series, III, no. 493, Hercule, *baron de* Charnacé, to ?, 14 March 1633.
[162] KHA, A14-XI-D1, Collection of notes by Frederik Hendrik, 'Om 't Lant te stellen op een goede voet ende bequam om te resisteeren alle de groote macten so van Spagniën als van de keiser moet mins bedenckens daer wel op wo[r]den gelet', n.d.

few months so that one of the options open to him was a 'cavalry service', namely a large-scale raid deep into enemy territory.[163]

In early September 1633 the Dutch army established a position near Dommelen, a village to the south of Eindhoven, but two weeks later it was still there. Frederik Hendrik had intended to make use of his numerically superior cavalry to effect an incursion into Brabant 'yet to do this with certainty and profit the enemy ought to be drawn into a *bataille* and defeated in order to prevent the vivres being cut off'. However, the new Spanish commander in the Netherlands, Francisco de Moncada (1586–1635), count of Osona and marquis of Aytona, refused to oblige Frederik Hendrik. 'He [Aytona] is always positioning himself in advantageous places, withdrawing from one to the other, so it was not advisable to go and attack him', the field deputies complained. Given that a pitched battle was out of the question they had to try something else. Frederik Hendrik sent Cornelis van Terestein from Holland, Johan de Knuyt (1587–1654) from Zeeland, Pieter van Waltha from Friesland and Edzard Jacob Clant van Stedum from Groningen to The Hague to explain his plans. Via them the Dutch commander-in-chief proposed establishing the winter quarters of the entire field army, including the Swedes and Hessians, in the small towns of Spanish Brabant, 'in order to be at the enemy's throat even earlier in the spring [of 1634]'. If The Hague thought this proposal was too risky – with 'the forces of this State being so far away' the Spaniards would, after all, be able to launch an attack on the Rhine strongholds or those in States Flanders – then the army could instead attempt to capture Antwerp that year, though Frederik Hendrik considered the chances of this undertaking being a success to be very slim. It would be better to attack Breda, but this presented the danger that the Spaniards would in the meantime recapture Maastricht. It was for The Hague to decide what was most sensible under such circumstances. But the States-General would not commit themselves: they approved both the siege of Breda and an advance into the Spanish Netherlands.[164] Frederik Hendrik opted for an invasion. 'As a consequence of this, it has been decided to begin this campaign in God's name, and to that end the army shall tomorrow [29 September 1633] strike camp here', according to the field deputies.[165]

On 2 October the Dutch army reached Lafelt, a hamlet just west of Maastricht, where the Dutch advance came to an abrupt halt: it was logistically impossible to take along the pay for the whole duration of the incursion on waggons, and the military solicitors could not be expected to continue conveying cash once the army had penetrated deep into enemy territory, because the threat of the Spaniards intercepting convoys from Maastricht would be unacceptably great.

---

[163] GAA, Missives of Amsterdam's deputies to the States of Holland to the city council, 71 (microfilm 7548), The Hague, 1 September 1633; Ten Raa, *Het Staatsche leger*, IV, pp. 69 and 294.
[164] NA, SG 4562, Secret res. SG, 22 and 23 September 1633.
[165] NA, SG 4963, Field deputies to the SG, Dommelen, 28 September 1633.

The field deputies had already petitioned The Hague to arrange for someone 'who shall draw the bills of exchange in Amsterdam, because otherwise we shall not be able to acquire any cash [other than] in the manner of merchants'.[166] The field deputies reiterated their appeal on 2 October 1633 and impressed upon the States-General that they should be informed of his name as soon as an Amsterdam merchant had been found, 'for without this we would not be able to draw any bills of exchange and we do not doubt that we will have to do this soon with regard to the Swedish and Hessian troops'.[167] Shortly thereafter these poorly paid cavalrymen resorted to plundering in Liège and its environs. The problems with pay and the disquiet among the auxiliary troops prompted Frederik Hendrik to decide to abandon the incursion. On 14 October he gave the order to retreat. The Swedish-Hessian corps was sent across the Rhine and was subsequently disbanded near Wesel. On 27 October the Dutch troops were dispatched to the garrisons.[168]

After the conclusion of the campaign, the diplomatic discussions with Brussels that had been suspended in June 1633 were resumed, but without success. Frederik Hendrik, who had thus far steered a middle course between the Arminian and Counter-Remonstrant factions, came to the conclusion that he could no longer continue down this path of compromise. In December 1633 he made a final attempt to broker an agreement with both groups. He underscored that if Brussels refused to agree to a peace treaty that could meet with the approval of all the regents in the Republic there was just one solution remaining: the enemy had to be brought to its knees by military means. An offensive war called for retaining the services of the forty-nine companies of foot and two of horse from 1629 as well as the two infantry regiments raised in 1631. Frederik Hendrik assured the Arminian faction that this also served their interests: 'If one wants to attack the enemy forcefully, both on land and for the relief of affairs at sea, one shall surely have need of those [extra] soldiers to be able to go into the field early.' Lending further weight to his argument, he continued:

> That one understands that a defensive war costs as much as an offensive one and that it [i.e. the former] is seriously prejudicial for the Land since this cannot be conducted without substantial losses. Howbeit that in this I refer to the worthy opinion of the noble States that everything which I say in this regard is because I believe that the wellbeing of the Land depends on this. Otherwise I am quite indifferent to whether the men are retained in service or are dismissed.[169]

Frederik Hendrik failed to convince the Arminian faction and a rift with Amsterdam was now inevitable. He then devoted the utmost effort to engineering

---

[166] NA, SG 4963, same to same, Dommelen, 28 September 1633.
[167] NA, SG 4963, same to same, Lafelt, 2 October 1633.
[168] Ten Raa, *Het Staatsche leger*, IV, p. 70.
[169] KHA, A14-XI-D1, 'Reden waerom men behoort de troupes [forty-nine infantry companies and two cavalry companies] die met graef Willem sein geweest alsmede de nieuwe regimenten van Gent ende Eerentruiter [established in 1631] in dienst te houden', December 1633.

an alliance with France, seeing this as the only means of being able to finance the war effort he considered so necessary.[170] In his view an alliance with Paris presented the best opportunities to foreshorten the war. A French declaration of war would, after all, force the Spaniards to divide their forces between two fronts. Frederik Hendrik hoped this would place him in a position to capture Antwerp, which would at last clear the path for a major Dutch offensive in the Southern Netherlands. On 15 April 1634 France and the Republic concluded a 'closer alliance'. Until Louis XIII declared war on Spain he would furnish the Republic with an annual subsidy of 2 million guilders, besides a contribution of 300,000 guilders per annum for the upkeep of a newly established regiment of Frenchmen in Dutch service. In exchange for this financial support the Republic had to promise to conduct the war on land and at sea with all its might and refrain from peace negotiations with Spain. This treaty would remain in force for seven years.[171] Frederik Hendrik had achieved a great diplomatic success. There was still no question of France declaring war on Spain, but it was prospectively only a question of time. Madrid would not stand for France's substantial financial support for the Republic and the invasion of Lorraine with impunity, and Spain demonstrated that she was still a formidable opponent just a short time later.

In July 1634 Aytona neared Maastricht with an army of no fewer than 30,000 men. The town boasted a strong garrison, but this notwithstanding the Dutch governor was seriously concerned, because the Dutch troops were 'discouraged ... by letters coming from below [i.e. down river] which maintain that the people there [i.e. in The Hague] have little concern about the town even were it to be lost, because [its preservation] would only burden the Land with the costs thereof'.[172] Frederik Hendrik was seriously disgruntled when he learnt of this, as he believed that everything humanly possible had to be done to retain Maastricht. He thought there were three ways to achieve this objective: meeting the enemy and joining battle, threatening Breda, Hulst or Bruges, or landing in Flanders with 18,000 men and laying siege to Dunkirk. No matter which of these three options was preferred, the Dutch army would have to enter the campaign with as strong a force as possible. Frederik Hendrik therefore insisted on the recruitment of 6,000 *waardgelders* and the enlistment of 3,000 Hessian cavalrymen, in order that there would be enough troops available to assemble a main army as well as a covering army for the eastern frontier.[173] The States-General issued the order to employ the requested troops. At the end of August 1634 Frederik Hendrik advanced on Breda with approximately 15,000 men,[174] while Count Willem van Nassau-Siegen (1592–1642), as a field-marshal in command of about seventy

---

[170] Israel, *Empires and Entrepots*, pp. 56–63, 82, 91 and 94–5.
[171] Ten Raa, *Het Staatsche leger*, IV, pp. 72–3.
[172] NA, SG 4965, Field deputies to the SG, Nijmegen, 9 and 12 August (quote) 1634.
[173] KHA, A14-XI-D1, 'Proiet pour le secours de Maestrict', Nijmegen, 15 July 1634.
[174] Ten Raa, *Het Staatsche leger*, IV, p. 76.

companies of foot and nine of horse, took up a position near Roermond. As soon as the field-marshal received news that Aytona was heading for Breda he was to advance on Maastricht together with the Hessians in order to break through the encirclement. On his way to Breda, Frederik Hendrik received the unwelcome news that the Hessian cavalry were unavailable. This meant that Count Willem van Nassau-Siegen could not hasten to Maastricht's aid, unless Frederik Hendrik managed to lure away Aytona with the main body of the Spanish army. Frederik Hendrik therefore decided to continue the march to Breda,[175] and on 5 September 1634 the Dutch troops surrounded this stronghold.[176] Frederik Hendrik's plan was a success. 'In the same way our army suddenly arrived before Breda it likewise hastily marched onward from there again', according to Willem Marienburgh, Overijssel's delegate to the States-General.[177] Frederik Hendrik had on 7 September received news that Aytona was approaching 'with most of his army and the troops that he had sent for from Flanders'. The Dutch army then took up positions along the Langstraat, a series of villages along the road between 's-Hertogenbosch and Geertruidenberg.[178] Maastricht was saved. To prevent the Spaniards re-blockading this outlying city during the winter, Frederik Hendrik reinforced its garrison to sixty-six companies of infantry and ten of cavalry.[179]

In the Republic there was great indignation about France's passive stance during the 1634 campaign. In The Hague they had assumed that the king of France 'shall be able to bring and maintain in the field' some 60,000 infantrymen and 7,000 cavalry during the campaign.[180] If several field armies had been established from these men, then the Spaniards would not have dared to lay siege to Maastricht and Frederik Hendrik would have been able to launch an offensive. It was evident that the 'closer alliance' had not provided the advantage that Frederik Hendrik had expected of it. Holland's Grand Pensionary, Adriaen Pauw (1585–1653), and Johan de Knuyt from Zeeland were instructed to devise an offensive and defensive alliance with Paris. Grand Pensionary since 1631, Pauw shared Frederik Hendrik's conviction that the Republic could not manage without French military assistance. Adriaen Pauw was a son of the orthodox Calvinist Reynier Pauw (1564–1636), Amsterdam's most influential burgomaster in the years 1617 to 1619 and one of the delegated judges on the special tribunal which sentenced Van Oldenbarnevelt to death.[181] Adriaen was no friend of the war-hungry faction within Holland, but he was of the opinion that if peace

---

[175] HCO, ASO 992, Willem Marienburgh to the SvO, The Hague, 24 August 1634.
[176] NA, SG 4965, Field deputies to the SG, before Breda, 5 September 1634.
[177] HCO, ASO 992, Willem Marienburgh to the SvO, The Hague, 9 September 1634.
[178] NA, SG 4965, Frederik Hendrik to the SG, Dongen, 8 September 1634.
[179] HUA, ASU 654-8, 'Garnisoen van Maestricht', 16 November 1634; NA, SG 4965, Res. SG, 18 November 1634, minute.
[180] HCO, ASO 992, Willem Marienburgh, The Hague, 26 August 1634.
[181] Elias, *Het Amsterdamsche regentenpatriciaat*, pp. 52, 60–1 and 75–7.

proved unattainable then the Republic had to continue the fight as vigorously as possible, with France as a mighty ally.[182]

The Franco-Dutch alliance was signed on 8 February 1635. Pauw wrote with satisfaction to Count Floris II of Culemborg: 'God be praised that our aforesaid negotiations have ended happily ... and the treaty concluded of so great an affair as has not arisen in our lifetime, this mighty crown undertaking with and alongside their High Mightinesses to enter into the war against the king of Spain to save the oppressed provinces from the Spanish slavery.' Pauw had no doubt that the French would turn their words into deeds as soon as the treaty was ratified, since Louis XIII himself had told the Dutch negotiators *'qu'il faut faire une bonne guerre aux Espagnols'*.[183] The offensive and defensive alliance bound each of the two signatories to make available 25,000 infantry and 5,000 cavalry for a joint campaign of conquest in the Spanish Netherlands. If the Southern Netherlanders revolted against Spain then the king of France would be satisfied with the Flemish seaports, Namur and Thionville, and the Republic with Breda, Gelder and Hulst, while the remnants of the Spanish Netherlands would, following the Swiss example, be transformed into a league of independent cantons. On the other hand, should the inhabitants remain loyal to Philip IV, then Luxembourg, Namur, Hainaut, Artois and West Flanders would fall to France, while Antwerp, Hulst, Mechelen, Ghent and Bruges would fall to the Republic.[184] The month of May was set as the date for the start of the invasion of the Spanish Netherlands.

Conclusion

Because Brussels and The Hague respected each other's strategic interests in the Jülich War of Succession (1610–1616), the confrontation between the two states remained limited to a 'cold war'. However, Van Oldenbarnevelt's execution and the outbreak of the Thirty Years' War made resumption of the struggle inescapable after the Twelve Years' Truce expired in 1621. From 1618 Maurits was both political and military leader of the Republic, but this concentration of power did not provide an impulse for waging an offensive war. Maurits's last four campaigns (1621–1624) were in fact characterised by passivity. The Arminian faction's exclusion from the decision-making process meant that the financial basis for vigorous warfare was lacking. Maurits's declining health and the death of Willem Lodewijk in 1620 made the Dutch commander-in-chief even more cautious than usual. During Spinola's siege of Breda, Maurits displayed no leadership whatsoever. Under Frederik Hendrik the offensive capability of the Republic burgeoned. Unlike his half-brother, during the wrangles about the truce he had

---

[182] Groenveld, *Evidente factiën*, p. 32.
[183] GA, AHGC 744, Adriaen Pauw to Count Floris II of Culemborg, Paris, 28 February 1635.
[184] Israel, *The Dutch Republic*, p. 527; Ten Raa, *Het Staatsche leger*, IV, p. 78.

not sided with the Counter-Remonstrants. Frederik Hendrik could not relate to the intolerance of the strict Calvinists. In the early years of his stadholderate he maintained good relations with the Remonstrant factions. The fruits of this collaboration were the conquest of Oldenzaal, Groenlo, 's-Hertogenbosch and Maastricht.

The Dutch army grew explosively during the years 1628–1632. The growth in troop numbers was not, however, part of a military plan, but the result of circumstances. The ominous situation in the Holy Roman Empire required the formation of fifty new infantry companies in 1628, while the war on two fronts with which the Republic was confronted in 1629 by the Spanish-Imperial invasion necessitated the reinforcement of the Dutch army with tens of thousands of soldiers. After the conclusion of the 1629 campaign these additional troops were, as far as possible, cashiered, but forty-nine infantry companies and two cavalry companies (5,500 men) remained in service. The plan for the assault on Dunkirk in 1631 required the raising of two new infantry regiments (6,000 men), and a further 3,000 cavalrymen and 12,600 infantry, besides 6,000 *waardgelders*, were added to this during the Meuse campaign in 1632. In December 1633 the Dutch army counted almost 90,000 men (on paper): more than 63,000 men on the three 'States of War' and approximately 26,000 men who had been 'temporarily' enlisted in 1628, 1629, 1631 and 1632.[185] In Frederik Hendrik's opinion these extra troops were indispensable and he endeavoured to garner the funds to pay them in every way imaginable. For example, he argued that the forty-nine infantry companies could be used to replace the *waardgelders* in towns. However, the appetite of the captain-general of the Union for extra troops seemed to know no bounds, and in 1634 he insisted on the levying of 6,000 *waardgelders* and the recruitment of 3,000 Hessian cavalrymen. The blockade of Maastricht could not be broken without these 9,000 extra men, he argued at the time.

The unstoppable escalation of the war effort increasingly brought Frederik Hendrik into conflict with the Arminian faction in Holland. After the reduction of 's-Hertogenbosch and Maastricht their cooperation began to show cracks. Frederik Hendrik continued to ask for substantial military outlay, but he was unable to offer the prospect of a speedy final victory. This was the one argument that could have justified this substantial war effort. Moreover, the attitude of the Counter-Remonstrants in Holland thwarted a vigorous waging of war. By linking the imposition of new taxes and revision of the tax on land and property to the reinstatement of the orthodox Calvinist clergyman Smoutsius, previously exiled from Amsterdam, the Counter-Remonstrants were the root cause of the attack on Dunkirk in 1631 having to be forgone. Much more serious, however, was that the religious differences of opinion which had led to the crisis in 1618 were stoked up again. The paradox was that Frederik Hendrik was duly aware that the powers of the Republic were inadequate to bring the Spaniards

---

[185] NA, SG 4964, RvS, The Hague, 5 December 1633.

to their knees, which was precisely why he considered an alliance with France indispensable. However, among the regents favourably disposed to peace, the alliance with France reinforced the impression that the captain-general of the Union wanted to pursue the struggle with Spain to the death. The rift between Frederik Hendrik and Amsterdam in 1633 had grave consequences for the Dutch war effort. As stadholder, Frederik Hendrik could turn the decision-making in the secret committees of the States-General and in the secret preliminary discussions in Holland to his advantage and thus repeatedly confront Amsterdam with a *fait accompli*, but there were no instruments available to force Amsterdam's regents to implement a decision. It was of course impossible for Amsterdam to refuse all cooperation, as this would have resulted in the city losing any influence in Holland or the other provinces and would have damaged its commercial interests, but the only way in which the Amsterdammers could continue to make their voice heard was by using delaying tactics and by threatening to thwart the implementation of resolutions.

✦ 6 ✦

Warfare Hits a Strategic Ceiling (1635–1648)

The Dutch-French invasion of the Spanish Netherlands founders (1635)

Expectations for the 1635 campaign were very high. Cardinal Richelieu made no secret of the fact that he had set himself the objective of superexalting Louis XIII, making him 'the world's most powerful monarch and most esteemed prince'.[1] The only means of achieving this highly ambitious goal was by eliminating the Habsburgs, primarily the dynasty's Spanish branch. Almost 75,000 French troops were available for the war in the Netherlands, the Holy Roman Empire and northern Italy.[2] The biggest French field army, with an effective strength of 29,000 men, was under the command of *maréchals* Gaspar III de Coligny (1584–1646), duc de Châtillon, and Urbain de Maillé (1597–1650), marquis de Brézé,[3] and would invade the Spanish Netherlands in conjunction with the Dutch troops (c. 20,000 men). The combined Dutch-French invasion force numbered approximately 50,000 'combatant heads'.[4] Van Aerssen, lord of Sommelsdijk, a confidant of Frederik Hendrik, believed that with such a great army the intended enterprise would necessarily lead to the desired outcome, without great peril and in a 'short' space of time. 'Three years or less would achieve the effect', he wrote in a letter to the Dutch envoy in Paris, adding the proviso that '[we] properly concert our designs together'. Van Aerssen asserted that to ensure effective concerted action by the Republic and France it was necessary to open the campaign with the besieging of the Spanish naval base of Dunkirk, 'in

---

[1] Richard Bonney, *The King's Debts. Finance and Politics in France 1589–1661* (Oxford 1981), p. 151.
[2] Parrott, *Richelieu's Army*, pp. 193–4.
[3] NA, SG 4966, Frederik Hendrik to the SG, Nijmegen, 22 May 1635, at about nine o'clock in the evening, with a letter from *maréchal* Châtillon to Frederik Hendrik, n.p., n.d., as an appendix. According to Parrott the French field army dispatched to the Spanish Netherlands was 26,500 strong. See *Richelieu's Army*, p. 190.
[4] GA, AHGC 749, Bernard van Welderen to Count Floris II of Culemborg, Nijmegen, 7 June 1635. Israel mentions as many as 60,000 men, but this is certainly 10,000 too many. See Israel, *The Dutch Republic and the Hispanic World*, p. 252.

order to expunge the unwillingness of those [Amsterdam's regents in particular] who do not look favourably on the grandeur of France'.[5]

Misgivings about the alliance with France were, however, not expressed in Holland alone; the States of the county of Zutphen, for example, were 'offended' by Article V, 'as it speaks of the Romish religion and the promise to leave it and the clergy in the state one finds them in towns apportioned to us [by treaty]'. When Alexander van der Capellen raised this point in a conversation with Frederik Hendrik, the latter, with a 'fixed countenance', responded that without this concession Louis XIII would never have endorsed the treaty. Moreover, he continued, had it not been the case that 'in East India we allowed the heathen idolatries and images, of the Chinese as well as of others living in places that stand under our authority there? [By comparison] the popish ceremonies were not so terrible.' And in conclusion Frederik Hendrik pointed out that 'alone ... we [could] not dislodge the Spaniards'.[6] Van der Capellen did not dispute the correctness of this last argument, but he was sceptical whether the French were actually planning to allow it to come to open war with Spain. In a letter of 19 May 1635 to Count Floris II of Culemborg he complained that in The Hague there was still no information about whether 'on the French side any hostility is being perpetrated against the frontiers of Brabant'.[7]

Van der Capellen's question was answered that very same day, when a royal herald carrying Louis XIII's declaration of war to Philip IV arrived in Brussels. Three days later, on 22 May 1635, the French and Spanish joined battle in the vicinity of Huy.[8] The Spaniards were seriously outnumbered – 9,000 men against 29,000 – but the Spanish commander, François Thomas, prince of Savoy (1596–1656), saw no other means of preventing the French and Dutch armies conjoining. The Spaniards suffered a severe setback.[9] After gaining victory, Châtillon and Brézé continued on their trek to Maastricht, the starting point agreed with The Hague for the incursion into the Spanish Netherlands. After the two armies had been conjoined the plan was to march straight for Brussels. In The Hague and Paris they assumed that the reduction of the seat of government in the Spanish Netherlands would result in the collapse of the Spanish

---

[5] *Archives*, 2nd series, III, no. 503, François van Aerssen, lord of Sommelsdijk, to Jean Hoeufft (†1651), the Republic's envoy in Paris, The Hague, 5 June 1634.
[6] NA, Aanwinsten Eerste Afdeling 105, Notes from the memoirs of Alexander van der Capellen, 9 April 1635.
[7] GA, AHGC 671, Alexander van der Capellen to Count Floris II of Culemborg, The Hague, 19 May 1635.
[8] Parrott, *Richelieu's Army*, pp. 109 and 113.
[9] The French *maréchals* estimated the Spanish losses at 4,000 to 5,000 dead and 1,500 prisoners of war. As proof of their 'signal victory', a few days later they presented three guidons, ninety-five colours, twelve 'cornets' (i.e. cavalry standards) and sixteen pieces of artillery to Frederik Hendrik and the Dutch field deputies. See NA, SG 4966, Frederik Hendrik to the SG, Nijmegen, 22 May, at about nine o'clock in the evening, and Gennep, 23 May 1635; Field deputies to the SG, Maastricht, 30 May 1635.

resistance there, whereupon all the towns in the Southern Netherlands would automatically fall into the hands of the allies. On 2 June the French arrived at Maastricht. In the meantime some 350,000 pounds of bread had been baked in Maastricht and at Aix-la-Chapelle for the troops, and in addition Frederik Hendrik ordered the loading of 200,000 pounds of rusk onto waggons. The rusk was already two years old, but was nevertheless 'still as good ... as when it was first baked'. This stockpile was intended to feed the Dutch-French army until it reached Tienen (Tirlemont), and from then on this town would serve as the logistical base for the onward push to Brussels. The bread and rusk supply would be sufficient for nine to ten days at most, but the Spaniards were not expected to put up much resistance in view of the superior Dutch-French numbers. It was estimated that Brussels could still assemble up to 18,000 or 19,000 field troops, as well as 10,000 or so armed peasants, 'because in Flanders and Brabant every third man has been called to arms.'[10] The fighting power of the peasants was negligible, while the morale of the Spanish soldiers had been dented by the defeat at Huy.[11] The mood among the Dutch and French troops was, on the other hand, excellent. The field deputies wrote with satisfaction to The Hague: 'Our army is in very good order, good soldiers and very willing, for they have been given hope that they shall make good spoils, which is the reason why none have ... deserted.'[12]

The prospects for the Spaniards were, however, less gloomy than they seemed on the face of it. On 4 November 1634, Ferdinand of Austria (1609–1641), the Cardinal-Infante, had arrived in Brussels. The appointment of Philip IV's younger brother as governor-general of the Spanish Netherlands was one aspect of the change in strategy decided on in Madrid. The war against the Republic would once again be persecuted aggressively. The Cardinal-Infante had therefore brought along reinforcements of 11,500 troops from Italy,[13] and in June 1635 a further 1,400 to 1,500 Spaniards arrived in Dunkirk.[14] The French declaration of war forced the scrapping of the plan for an offensive against the Republic, but the extra troops sent by Madrid still constituted a welcome reinforcement of the Spanish army in the Netherlands. The consequences of the defeat at Huy therefore remained limited; the French had achieved a tactical triumph, but nothing more. The combined Dutch-French army was indeed much stronger than the military force at the Cardinal-Infante's disposal, but the circumstance that Brabant was highly suitable for a defensive war largely compensated for this

---

[10] GA, AHGC 749, Vincentius Bergeus to the magistrate of Culemborg, Maastricht, 29 May 1635, in the evening.
[11] GA, AHGC 770, Lieutenant Johan van Welderen to Count Floris II of Culemborg, Valkenburg, 2 June 1635.
[12] NA, SG 4966, Field deputies to the SG, Maastricht, 30 May 1635.
[13] Vermeir, *In staat van oorlog*, pp. 105 and 109; Parker, *Army of Flanders*, p. 279.
[14] GA, AHGC 749, A. van Randwijck to Count Floris II of Culemborg, The Hague, 11 June 1635.

drawback. The commander of the Dutch fort of Liefkenshoek on the banks of the River Scheldt sent word to The Hague: 'The enemy shall do all that he can, is intending to thwart His Excellency [Frederik Hendrik] at Tienen.'[15] The basin of the rivers Grote and Kleine Geet and Dijle presented 'fine opportunities for establishing strong positions.

At the start of June 1635 the allied forces set out on their advance to Tienen. On 8 June they were within an hour's march of this town. To Frederik Hendrik's relief the Cardinal-Infante did not await the arrival of the Dutch-French army. He withdrew to Louvain, where his troops established new positions on the far side of the River Dijle. Then Frederik Hendrik ordered Tienen's defenders to open the gates, but they refused to comply. The Dutch commander-in-chief repeated his summons the following evening, but once again it fell on deaf ears, so on the morning of 10 June he ordered the storming of Tienen. The garrison of approximately 1,200 men put up very little resistance.[16] However, what occurred thereafter was a cause of serious embarrassment to Frederik Hendrik. As was usual after a storm assault the soldiers went on the rampage and 'killed those who were found on the streets', but the governor, a captain and 'many women and daughters [were] saved, brought into the church and protected during this time of difficulty'. But they were not safe there for long, for later that day 'mobs from the French army [came] into the town ... forced past the sentries [at the church], shot dead the soldiers among them, took out of the church and carried off those who were found therein'. To make matters worse a fire broke out, reducing most of Tienen to ashes.[17] In his report to the States-General, Frederik Hendrik tried to place the blame for the perpetrated excesses onto the shoulders of Martin de Los Harquos, the Spanish governor. He pointed out that the defenders had been enjoined some four or five times to deliver Tienen 'into our hands on reasonable terms ... which the governor, being a Spaniard, refused, obliging us to storm it'.[18]

According to Frederik Hendrik's biographer, J.J. Poelhekke, from the viewpoint of propaganda the devastation of Tienen was a highly unfortunate episode – hereafter it would be impossible for the people of Brabant to see the Dutch and French troops as their 'liberators' from the 'Spanish yoke'.[19] It is beyond question that Frederik Hendrik deplored what had happened, but not for the reason put forward by Poelhekke. From the outset the 1635 campaign had not, after all, been intended as a campaign of liberation but as a campaign of conquest. A matter of grave concern to the Dutch commander-in-chief was that Tienen's devastation denied the allies an essential logistical base. The field deputies informed The Hague that, due to the fire, the Dutch and French troops 'have been frustrated

---

[15] NA, SG 4966, Commander of Liefkenshoek to the SG, 30 May 1635.
[16] NA, SG 4966, Field deputies to the SG, Hilsem, 10 June 1635.
[17] HCO, ASO 992, Swier van Haersolte (1582–1643) and Ruittenburch to the SvO, The Hague, 16 June 1635.
[18] NA, SG 4966, Frederik Hendrik to the SG, Heylissem, 10 June 1635.
[19] Poelhekke, *Frederik Hendrik*, pp. 443–4.

of all the vivres and ammunition, which was available in great quantity there'. Just 300 *malder* of corn were saved, which was enough to supply the combined army with bread for just one day. The Dutch army's commissioner of the victualling, Nicolaas Kien, left for Diest together with his French colleague to arrange the transportation of provisions from Maastricht via the River Demer. It was evident, however, that the invasion could now be successful only if Frederik Hendrik managed to capture Louvain as swiftly as possible.[20] Without control of this major town it would be impossible to safeguard the supply of provisions during the onward push into Brabant and the 1635 campaign would surely end as ingloriously as that of 1602.

The situation was deteriorating by the day. The poorly paid French soldiers were melting away: by the end of June 1635 the French contingent counted just 17,000 men.[21] The Spaniards were in the meantime industriously reinforcing their positions on the far side of the River Dijle and assistance from the emperor was close at hand as well. Field-Marshal Willem, count of Nassau-Siegen, warned The Hague that General Ottavio, prince of Piccolomini (1599–1656), was heading for the Low Countries with approximately 12,000 Imperial troops.[22] Count Willem van Nassau-Siegen was charged with the defence of the eastern frontier 'around the rivers', namely the Rhine, Waal, Meuse and IJssel, for which he had ninety-five infantry companies and seven cavalry companies, some 8,000 to 8,500 men in all, available to him.[23] There was a grave danger that Piccolomini and his army would establish a position between the allied forces and Maastricht, completely blocking the supply lines. This placed Frederik Hendrik under even greater pressure to advance swiftly on Louvain. A frontal attack on the Spanish army's positions was too hazardous – the Spaniards were by now too securely entrenched to attempt this – but if they managed to out-manoeuvre the Spanish right flank then the Cardinal-Infante would have to abandon his position behind the River Dijle if he wanted to avoid having the allies to his rear.

On 21 June 1635 the allied forces arrived at Overijse – a village sixteen kilometres south of Louvain – crossed the River Dijle there and then marched to Voskapel, a village on the highway between Brussels and Louvain. The Cardinal-Infante did not await their arrival. With the bulk of his troops he took up a new position near Vilvoorde behind the Brussels waterway. He had left behind a garrison of 3,000 men in Louvain. On 25 June the French and Dutch troops laid siege to this town.[24] After a week and a half the trenches were drawing very close to the moat, but there was no hope of a swift surrender, 'because the town has

---

[20] NA, SG 4966, Field deputies to the SG, Roosbeek, 14 June 1635; Frederik Hendrik to the SG, Roosbeek, 14 June 1635.
[21] Parrott, *Richelieu's Army*, p. 190.
[22] NA, SG 4966, Willem van Nassau-Siegen to the SG, Emmerich, 24 June 1635.
[23] NA, SG 4563, Secret res. of the SG, 11 June 1635.
[24] NA, SG 4966, Field deputies to the SG, Overijse, 21 June, Voskapel, 24, 25 and 27 June 1635.

been attacked on just one side, so the enemy has obtained more troops within, on horse as well as on foot, besides ammunition'. To speed up the siege Louvain had not been wholly invested. Frederik Hendrik had speculated that so soon after the bloodbath at Tienen the Spaniards would not dare put up any serious resistance for fear of being stormed, but this proved to be incorrect. Because the Cardinal-Infante also expected the arrival of Piccolomini's army 'any day', which would enable him to advance to relieve Louvain, in the council of war with the field deputies and the French *maréchals* Frederik Hendrik pronounced that he now thought it too risky to invest Louvain on both sides of the River Dijle. He asked the war council what they wished to be done, but before a decision was reached news arrived that the Imperial forces were close by. This prompted the decision to raise the siege of Louvain forthwith and withdraw to Aarschot in order 'to observe the countenance of the enemy'. A couple of days later it became known that the Imperial army had not crossed the River Meuse in its entirety, but that Piccolomini had ridden on ahead with 4,000 to 5,000 cavalrymen, including many of the feared Croats.[25] The enfeeblement of the French army – 'due to the persistent scarcity of vivres' – did not, however, permit a new attempt to capture Louvain in the near term. The French *maréchals* insisted on their troops being allowed to recuperate in the Meijerij of 's-Hertogenbosch, but Frederik Hendrik would hear nothing of it; he decided to head for Roermond, 'thereby to best spare the provinces and to keep them [i.e. the French] at arm's length, as well as on all occasion [i.e. in any circumstance] to be closer to the towns of Maastricht, Roermond and Venlo'.[26]

The Cardinal-Infante and Piccolomini took advantage of the allied withdrawal to block the eastern approach to Brabant. They laid siege to Diest, which capitulated after a few days. They then crossed the River Meuse and continued onward to the duchy of Cleves, where they were joined by the Imperial infantry. The fiasco of the Dutch-French invasion was complete when Fort Schenkenschans was surprised by 500 Spaniards from Gelder on 28 July 1635. The sixty or so Dutch defenders were put to the sword. This unexpected setback forced Frederik Hendrik to head for Nijmegen with haste to prevent the Spanish-Imperial army following up this important success with a foray into Gelderland.[27] At the start of August 1635 the captain-general of the Union commanded the opening of the trenches before Schenkenschans, but he was under no illusion about being able to regain control of the fort quickly, because 'the enemy has the side towards Cleves free, so that he can bring in as many fresh soldiers and necessaries as he wants'. The numerical weakness of the French meant it was impossible to invest

---

[25] NA, SG 4966, same to same, before Louvain, 3 July (quote), Aarschot, 6 July 1635.
[26] NA, SG 4966, Frederik Hendrik to the SG, Goor, 12 July 1635 (quote).
[27] NA, SG 4966, same to same, Nijmegen, 29 July 1635; W. Bergsma (ed.), *Poppo van Burmania. 'Enege gedenckwerdege geschiedenissen'*, entries dated 13/23 July 1635 (KB, Ms 132-B-10).

Schenkenschans on the Cleves side as well.[28] A shortage of money and hunger led to a wave of desertions from the French army, and by October the French military force had been reduced to a third of its original strength.[29] The siege of Schenkenschans continued the whole winter. In February the remnants of the French army – less than 9,000 men[30] – returned to France. The fort eventually fell into Dutch hands on 29 April 1636.[31]

The 1635 campaign had demonstrated that even an army of 50,000 men was no guarantee of success when the logistics were not properly organised. Depending on food supplies that had to be seized in hostile towns for the success of a military operation was the equivalent of building on quicksand, making the operation vulnerable to the slightest setback. So long as an army operated on the frontiers it was possible to supply the troops with bread and other victuals from one's own towns in the vicinity, but this solution was not on hand when fighting deep inside enemy territory, and certainly not when it involved 50,000 men. In his authoritative work, *Art de la guerre, par principes et par règles*, which was published posthumously in 1748, Jacques François de Chastenet (1655–1743), marquis de Puységur, who served as the French army's quartermaster-general during the wars of the Sun King, rightly pointed out that the provisioning of a large army, namely one that is more than 30,000 strong, required thorough study and sound knowledge of the logistics,

> that one cannot acquire but from those who have been charged with this for a long time, and who have acquitted themselves of this [duty by adherence to] rules and principles, which is something rarely found.... Truly such [men] as would carry themselves well with an army of twenty- to thirty-thousand men, would find themselves seriously burdened with a great army, as I have seen happen to many.[32]

The food supply for armies greater than 30,000 men required the prior arrangement of food magazines, because only then was a regular supply of bread guaranteed. Until the second half of the seventeenth century this solution was not even considered by the government of the Republic. After all, it stood by the standpoint that its involvement with the army ought to remain as indirect as possible. This also meant that the company commanders themselves took responsibility for the deliveries of victuals by entering into contracts with sutlers. The 200,000 pounds of rusk which Frederik Hendrik had, as mentioned above, ordered to be loaded onto waggons was intended solely as an emergency supply,

---

[28] NA, SG 4967, Field deputies to the SG, Pannerden, 12 August 1635.
[29] Parrott, *Richelieu's Army*, p. 190.
[30] At the start of December 1635 the French infantry (171 companies) numbered just 8,800 men. HUA, ASU 654-8, received 11 December 1635 from the commissary of the musters, Jacob Groessen, 'Lijste van 't legher 'twelck a.o 1635 bij sijne Co.e Ma.t van Vranckrijck d'Hoo. Mo. Heeren Staten-Generael ... tot secours gesonden is onder 't beleydt van de heeren mareschals de Chastillon en[de] Brézé'.
[31] Ten Raa, *Het Staatsche leger*, V, p. 90.
[32] Puységur, *Art de la guerre*, II, p. 155.

sufficient to feed 50,000 men for four days. But this was not the only problem. The distance from Maastricht to Louvain was too great to be able to provide the troops with fresh bread from the former town on a regular basis. The capture of Tienen was supposed to obviate this problem, but this would have been a big gamble even had its stockpiles of grain not been destroyed by fire, the Spaniards having had plenty of time to carry off the grain or, if need be, even burn it themselves. Frederik Hendrik's plan to attack Louvain from the west was militarily brilliant, but made the problem of provisioning even more acute. Baking bread in Diest seemed to offer consolation, but when the allies arrived at Voskapel it proved to be impossible to deliver a new supply of bread to the allied camp in time, 'because the [waggons with] bread-crates are arriving very slowly, due to the unsuitability of the roads'.[33]

Rather than march straight to Tienen, Frederik Hendrik would have done better first to establish flour stocks and build field-ovens in the towns along the River Demer, depots that could have served him for the onward push into Brabant. Then the allies would not have been dependent on the food stocks in Tienen and the bread deliveries during the siege of Louvain would have been guaranteed. It would not have been difficult to fetch bread and other food from Diest and Tienen. The distance between Diest and Tienen as well as between Tienen and Louvain was after all just a single day's march. During the siege of Louvain a new supply of flour could have been milled in Maastricht in the meantime and then transported to Diest by barge. Once Louvain had been taken, the food stocks in Diest and Tienen could have been transferred to Louvain, whereupon this major town could have served as the base for the assault on Brussels. Seventy years later, in 1705, a Dutch-English army attempted to march into the Spanish Netherlands via the same route as Frederik Hendrik. On this occasion, in preparation for an assault on Brussels, stockpiles of flour were established in Tienen and Diest, from where the allied army could be provided with bread until Louvain was taken.[34] The magazine system would not, however, reach maturity until the 1670s.[35] With this form of victualling the troops were not dependent on local supplies for their basic nourishment (bread). A fresh supply of bread was delivered to the army camp every four days. An army could then operate at between forty and sixty kilometres from its bases without running the risk of starvation. The development and impact of the magazine system is discussed in detail in Chapter 8.

---

[33] NA, SG 4966, Field deputies to the SG, Voskapel, 24 June 1635.
[34] Van Nimwegen, *Subsistentie van het leger*, pp. 171–2.
[35] In the 1640s the French government was already establishing magazines on occasion, in order to facilitate operations in the largely devastated Holy Roman Empire. In the 1650s this also occurred along the border with the Spanish Netherlands. Bernhard Kroener, 'Les routes et les étapes'. *Die Versorgung der französischen Armeen in Nordostfrankreich (1635–1661). Ein Beitrag zur Verwaltungsgeschichte des Ancien Régime* (Münster 1980), pp. 83–5.

Besieging Dunkirk proves impossible – the siege of Breda (1636–1637)

The disappointing course of the 1635 campaign led to a sharp clash between Frederik Hendrik and the States of Holland. The attitude of Paris during the siege of Louvain had, if anything, further reinforced the distaste of Amsterdam, Rotterdam, Dordrecht and Alkmaar for the alliance with France. During this siege, the field deputies had urged Louis XIII, via the French envoy, Charnacé, to create a diversion in Picardy to lure away the Imperial troops under Piccolomini towards the south of the Spanish Netherlands, but instead of giving the undertaking of doing his very best to arrange this, Charnacé had responded that, based on the alliance treaty, his king was not obliged to do this.[36] This reaction seemed to indicate that Richelieu was not intending to attack Spain with all the means available and that he primarily wanted to shift the financial burden of the war in the Low Countries onto the Republic's shoulders. The war effort required of the Republic was, however, already greater than Holland's finances could bear. The Hollanders therefore considered it necessary to make it clear to Frederik Hendrik that things could not continue like this. In December 1635 the members of the committee 'on the matter of thriftiness' proposed to the States of Holland the reduction of the Dutch army from 80,000 men to an effective strength of 60,000, 'on which basis it would be possible to economise a whole fourth part of the whole militia without this, however, resulting in a reduction in the number of heads'. After all, a quarter of the army existed only on paper.[37]

Frederik Hendrik fought the suggested army reduction tooth and nail, because in his view the Republic would then no longer be able to meet the commitment laid down in the treaty of 1635 to field an army of 30,000 men. However, this argument had no effect, because France remained far more seriously in default. Though the French army in the Low Countries had numbered 29,000 men at the start of the 1635 campaign, by June it had been reduced by almost a half and was a mere 9,000 strong towards the end of the campaign. Hunger was much to blame, but no less the failure of salary payments. Otherwise the Dutch army should have dwindled proportionately, which was not the case.

The disagreement between Frederik Hendrik and the Hollanders prevented any Dutch campaigning in 1636.[38] To prevent a repeat of this failure in 1637 Frederik Hendrik sought a rapprochement with the Arminian faction. He proposed dealing with Dunkirk's privateers, a plan that could reliably gain broad support within Holland, as attacks from Dunkirk were devastating the herring fleet; in August 1635 no fewer than 124 herring-busses were captured or sunk by the Dunkirkers and some 975 fishermen taken prisoner.[39] Military considerations

---

[36] NA, SG 4966, Field deputies to the SG, before Louvain, 3 July 1635.
[37] NA, RAZH, ASH 68, Res. SH, 20 December 1635. See p. 78.
[38] GA, AHGC, Extract res. SG, 19 April 1636.
[39] Bruijn, *Varend verleden*, p. 62; Israel, *The Dutch Republic and the Hispanic World*, pp. 264–5.

as well as economic arguments pleaded in favour of an attack on Dunkirk. In September 1636 it was reported to The Hague that no fewer than thirty-eight English ships had safely reached Dunkirk's harbour, with an estimated 3,600 to 4,000 Spanish infantry and a hoard of 1.5 million ducats on board.[40]

In 1634 London and Madrid had entered into an agreement that allowed Spanish soldiers and goods to be shipped to Flemish ports in neutral English merchant vessels. For now it was not in Holland's interest to challenge the English overtly, and a total sea-blockade of the Flemish ports was impossible, so the only means of cutting off the seaborne supplies to the Spanish Netherlands was by capturing Dunkirk.[41] Frederik Hendrik could give the Hollanders the assurance that Paris would lend substantial military and financial support for this undertaking. In the treaty of 10 June 1637 the king of France pledged to send a sizeable military force of 308 infantry companies and seventy cavalry companies to the Spanish Netherlands.[42] Some 4,500 men would provide direct support to the Dutch army with the siege of Dunkirk and, later on, with the siege of Antwerp or Hulst. Louis XIII also promised to resume payment of the subsidy. The subsidy had been halted when France declared war on Spain, in accordance with the 1634 treaty.[43] In 1637 Paris transferred more than 1.1 million guilders.[44] And lastly, the king of France pledged that the French army would open the campaign by besieging Namur, Thionville or Mons, in order to distract the Spaniards away from Dunkirk. However, if the Cardinal-Infante did not take the bait and advanced with the main Spanish force to relieve Dunkirk, then the French army would follow the Spaniards 'and carry out sieges or wreak devastations in the heart of the territory of the common enemy'. After Dunkirk's capture a Dutch garrison would be billeted there 'until the conquests of the Low Countries projected by the treaty of the year 1635 have been carried out according to the tenor of said treaty'.[45] In contradistinction to 1635, the Dutch and French troops would not be merged into a single army. Given the impossibility of feeding a mass of 50,000 men the two forces could better operate separately.

Despite the French pledges the assault on Dunkirk was still an uncertain undertaking, as the only chance of the Dutch succeeding was if Frederik Hendrik managed to invest the town before the Cardinal-Infante had amassed a substantial force in Flanders. It was therefore essential that the Dutch troops should begin their advance on Dunkirk unexpectedly. Due to 'contrary' wind the

---

[40] Israel, *The Dutch Republic and the Hispanic World*, pp. 265–6.
[41] Bruijn, *Varend verleden*, p. 34.
[42] NA, RAZH, Familiearchief Van Wassenaer van Duvenvoorde 2050, Agreement between France and the Republic with regard to the forthcoming campaign, The Hague, 13 May 1637.
[43] See p. 238.
[44] Tresoar, FSA 26, Overview of payments and receipts of the French subsidy in the period 1637–1643.
[45] NA, SG 12587.64, Hercule de Charnacé and the deputies at the SG, The Hague, 10 June 1637.

assembly of the Dutch army at the rendezvous off Fort Rammekens, close to Vlissingen (Flushing), suffered more than a week's delay. It took until 16 July 1637 for all the transport ships to arrive. The opportunity of swiftly advancing to Dunkirk and investing this coastal stronghold before the Cardinal-Infante had assembled a relief army was already lost, because by then 15,000 to 16,000 Spanish troops had been assembled in the Land of Waas.[46] Frederik Hendrik was faced with an awkward predicament. To make the planned operation possible the Hollanders had agreed to the retention in service of the fifty companies temporarily recruited in 1628 so that a force of 24,000 men could have been assembled, but if Frederik Hendrik were to allow this campaign to end without achieving something with such a strong army then he would have been giving the critics of his war policy the ammunition to attack him: for a second time it would show that the French-Dutch alliance was not providing the Republic with what it expected, namely a swift end to the war with Spain. Only the French seemed to be prospering from the 1635 treaty. In July 1637 they laid siege to Landrecies, exploiting the presence of the majority of the Spanish field troops in the Land of Waas. Landrecies fell on 26 July. Richelieu subsequently insisted to the Republic's ambassador that Frederik Hendrik should make a new attempt to reach Dunkirk,[47] but he was already heading for Breda with the Dutch army.[48]

The reduction of Breda was nothing more than a consolation prize. No matter how earnestly Van Aerssen-Sommelsdijk insisted to Frederik Hendrik that laying siege to this town was 'so greatly preferable above all other, that it can cover the heart of the State', and assured him that Louis XIII and Richelieu could hardly reproach the captain-general of the Union because there was little to be done against 'the contrariness of the winds',[49] neither of these arguments could mask the fiasco of failing to push through with the reduction of Dunkirk. The capture of Breda would bolster Frederik Hendrik's reputation as the 'Tamer of Towns', but from a political and military perspective the town's capture would be of little moment. Since the seizure of 's-Hertogenbosch the struggle in the northern part of Brabant had been decided in the Republic's favour. The isolated position of Breda made the town unsuitable as a base for a Spanish assault on the Republic; the possession of Breda was of limited strategic value to The Hague for the same reason. Its capture may well have rid the Republic of a both-

---

[46] GA, FAvdC 70, Alexander van der Capellen to his brother Henrik (†1659), Utrecht, 18 July 1637; NA, SG 4970, Espionage report, Brussels, 8 July 1637.
[47] *Archives*, 2nd series, III, nos. 526 and 528, Jean Hoeufft to François van Aerssen, lord of Sommelsdijk, Paris, 17 and 31 July 1637.
[48] In *Het Staatsche leger*, IV, pp. 95–6, Ten Raa bends over backwards to create the impression that Frederik Hendrik had been planning to lay siege to Breda from the outset: 'According to rumours the Prince was intending to launch an assault on Dunkirk, Ostend or Bruges. The unremittingly unfavourable weather facilitated his plan to lay siege to Breda while the enemy was massing his troops in Flanders.' He fails to mention the treaty of 10 June 1637.
[49] *Archives*, 2nd series, III, no. 527, François van Aerssen, lord of Sommelsdijk, to Frederik Hendrik, The Hague, 26 July 1637.

ersome Spanish outpost, but it would have little impact on the strategic situation in the Low Countries. The Dutch historian J.W. Wijn rightly points out that the natural military-geographical frontier in 'North Brabant' was reached in 1629: major military operations were impossible on this region's poor, sandy soil.[50] The reduction of Dunkirk, by contrast, would have provided the Republic with a gateway into Flanders, besides achieving the destruction of this naval base.

Frederik Hendrik invested Breda on 21 July 1637. The town's garrison was 2,600 to 2,700 strong, but despite this fair-sized defensive force the field deputies had hoped for a swift *dénouement*, because the defenders 'are driving out the poor women and children. [From this] it is presumed that there is no great stockpile of corn and even less of gunpowder in [Breda]. This siege has caught them [the Spaniards] by surprise.'[51] However, the stocks of food proved to be more substantial than supposed, because a month later there was still no prospect of a speedy capitulation. The Cardinal-Infante had in the meantime assembled an estimated 20,000 men.[52] The Dutch field deputies kept a beady eye on the build-up of Spanish troops: 'Whether [he] has now fixed his sights on our army, on pitching some soldiers into the town or on heading somewhere as a diversion, time will have to tell. It is however credible that he shall not abandon so important and dearly gained pearl without prior effort.'[53] The deputies were deceived, because the Cardinal-Infante made no attempt whatsoever to relieve Breda. Instead, in the middle of August he marched to the River Meuse and recaptured Venlo (25 August 1637) and Roermond (3 September 1637), thus severing the lines of communication between the Republic and Maastricht. The Cardinal-Infante granted the Dutch garrisons (thirty-two infantry companies and three cavalry companies in all) a free withdrawal to Grave.[54] Breda did not capitulate until 7 October 1637, after a siege of seventy-nine days. On 10 October the defenders withdrew with full military honours, 'besides their expelled clergymen'. At that point the 'able-bodied and healthy' Spaniards still numbered approximately 1,800 to 2,000. On the Dutch side between 700 and 800 soldiers had lost their lives during the siege.[55] Compared with the massive losses suffered by Spinola

---

[50] Wijn, 'Onder het vaandel', p. 130.
[51] NA, SG 4970, Field deputies to the SG, before Breda, 24 July, in the evening (quote), and 27 July 1637.
[52] NA, SG 4971, Field deputies to the SG, Ginneken, 5 August, in the evening, before Breda, 17 August 1637; HUA, ASU 314-6, Godard van Reede-Amerongen (1593–1641) to the SvU, before Breda, 5 August 1637, at three o'clock in the afternoon.
[53] NA, SG 4971, Field deputies to the SG, Ginneken, 1 August 1637.
[54] NA, SG 4971, same to same, before Breda, 17 August and 11 September 1637; Original capitulations of Venlo and Roermond; Frederik Hendrik to the SG, before Breda, 2 September 1637, with a copy of a letter by Jan de Jegher, sergeant-major of Venlo, to Frederik Hendrik, Grave, 28 August 1637, as an appendix.
[55] NA, SG 4971, Field deputies to the SG, before Breda, 8 October 1637; Frederik Hendrik to the SG, Breda, 11 October 1637; HUA, ASU 314-6, Godard van Reede-Amerongen to the SvU, before Breda, 11 October 1637 (quote).

in 1624–1625, Frederik Hendrik had retaken Breda with a minimal loss of life, but whether the capture of this town compensated for the loss of Venlo and Roermond is debatable. Without these two towns the Dutch could not threaten the Spanish Netherlands from the east, so the Cardinal-Infante could in future employ all his might against them for the defence of Antwerp and Flanders.

Frederik Hendrik has limited success in the east – Antwerp and the major Flemish towns remain beyond his reach (1638–1641)

Once the 1637 campaign had drawn to a close, the Hollanders, under the leadership of their new Grand Pensionary, Jacob Cats (1577–1660), insisted on the disbanding of the fifty infantry companies recruited in 1628. Cats, Pensionary of Dordrecht from 1623 to 1636, was a loyal servant to Frederik Hendrik, but even he could not ignore the financial difficulties Holland was facing. Frederik Hendrik did, however, have two strong trump cards at his disposal, though both were negative, to thwart reduction of the Dutch army that year: first he could argue that France would suspend payment of the recommenced subsidy if the Republic did not once again commit a sizeable army to the campaign, and secondly he could point out that, as a speedy peace was not yet within reach, out of self-interest the Republic had to do everything to capture Antwerp and thus prevent France alone benefiting from the alliance.[56]

On 17 December 1637 the French ambassador and the States-General reached agreement about a new coordinated assault on the Spanish Netherlands. To ensure there was no misunderstanding about what was expected from the two allies, each ally promised to provide a military force with an effective strength of 18,000 to 20,000 infantry and 4,500 to 5,000 cavalry for the struggle against the common enemy in the Spanish Netherlands. Louis XIII also pledged a subsidy of 1.2 million guilders, but on condition that this sum of money would be used exclusively for the support of the unrepartitioned troops in Dutch service. Paris hereby precluded the provinces being able to use this money for the payment of the repartitioned troops and leaving the unrepartitioned soldiers to fend for themselves. Both armies would have to head into the field by 10 April 1638 at the latest. The Republic pledged to attack a town of *grande considération*, such as Dunkirk, Antwerp or Hulst, while the French would once again have to lay siege to Thionville, Namur or Mons and, should that prove impossible, they would have to entice the Spaniards away from Frederik Hendrik's heels by means of a diversion (an attack on Saint-Omer), so that he could execute his plans.[57]

---

[56] NA, RAZH, ASH 70, Res. SH, 19 December 1637.
[57] NA, SG 12587.67, Subsidy treaty between France and the Republic, Paris, 17 December 1637.

On 13 June 1638, Field-Marshal Willem van Nassau-Siegen landed at the Dutch fort of Liefkenshoek with sixty-four companies of foot and four of horse, an effective force of about 5,700 men. He had orders to blockade Antwerp on the Flanders side of the River Scheldt, whereupon Frederik Hendrik would do the same on the Brabant side with the main army. The field-marshal established positions with his troops near Kallo, a village facing Antwerp.[58] He then ordered the digging of entrenchments to secure his position but this proved to be inadequate, because in the night of 20/21 June 1638 the Spaniards managed to break through the Dutch lines. The Dutch troops put up a struggle at first, but when the Spaniards launched a second assault they fled *en masse*. Willem van Nassau-Siegen managed to escape to Liefkenshoek with 1,500 men, but more than 2,000 Dutch solders were taken prisoner and all the cavalry's horses and the entire artillery train of six demi-cannon, six 6-pounders and three 3-pounders were lost.[59] Utrecht's field deputy, Godard van Reede-Amerongen (1593–1641), wrote to his principals about this painful defeat: 'One estimates the dead on our side not to exceed 400 to 500 men. On the enemy side there were more who perished in the first attack, so this flight was caused by the unassuageable terror among our soldiers that they would not have been able to withstand a second assault.'[60]

The repercussions of the defeat at Kallo were grave. Writing from The Hague, a correspondent of Count Floris II of Culemborg lamented the situation: 'Here one is gravely pessimistic about this business of Count Willem, because one considers it certain that the enemy shall bring all his force to bear against it [i.e. the Republic] and thus scupper our plan, the relief of St. Omer being no small cause of this, in time everything will become clear to us.'[61] The French had laid siege to Saint-Omer on 1 June 1638, but in the night of 8/9 June the Spaniards managed to smuggle 1,500 men into the besieged town and on 12 June even more troops arrived there. This prompted the French army commanders to raise the siege.[62] Frederik Hendrik informed Cornelis Musch (1593–1650), *griffier* of the States-General, that in the wake of the defeat at Kallo and the unsuccessful French assault on Saint-Omer he no longer saw any means of undertaking an

---

[58] HUA, ASU 314-6, Godard van Reede-Amerongen to the SvU, Bergen op Zoom, 14 June 1638; NA, SG 4972, Field deputies to the SG, Bergen op Zoom, 14 June 1638.

[59] KHA, A24-75, Frederik Hendrik to Hendrik Casimir I, aboard the *Noordgeest*, 23 June 1638, with a copy of a letter from Willem van Nassau-Siegen to Frederik Hendrik, Fort Kallo, 21 June 1638, four o'clock in the morning, as an appendix; NA, SG 4972, Field deputies to the SG, Bergen op Zoom, 22 June 1638; Frederik Hendrik to the SG, on board the *Noordgeest*, 23 June 1638; HUA, ASU 314-6, Godard van Reede-Amerongen to the SvU, Bergen op Zoom, 23 June 1638, at eleven o'clock in the morning.

[60] HUA, ASU 314-6, Godard van Reede-Amerongen to the SvU, Bergen op Zoom, 5 July 1638, at two o'clock in the afternoon.

[61] GA, AHGC 671, Burgomaster Henrick Nobel to Count Floris II of Culemborg, The Hague, 17 June 1638, in the afternoon.

[62] Parrott, *Richelieu's Army*, p. 128; HUA, ASU 314-6, Tristran de Cuper to the SvU, Middelburg, 23 June 1638.

36a. Willem, count of Nassau-Siegen (1592–1642), Dutch field-marshal. (Collection NIMH)

operation in Brabant or Flanders that year. He therefore wanted to hear from the *secrete besogne* what the States-General wished the Dutch troops to undertake for the remainder of this campaign.[63] Frederik Hendrik was personally considering laying siege to Gennep or Gelder, which would have exposed the Spanish garrisons in Venlo and Roermond to the persistent threat of a Dutch surprise attack. The *secrete besogne* lent its approval to Frederik Hendrik's second suggestion. The Dutch army surrounded Gelder in mid-August 1638,[64] but the prospects for this siege were hardly favourable. The day before the investment a reinforcement of 300 Spanish soldiers had arrived within the stronghold, thus augmenting its garrison – already strong – to an estimated 3,000 infantrymen and a cavalry company. An active defence was possible with a garrison of such proportions, while because of the defeat at Kallo the Dutch army was already reeling from bruising losses. Frederik Hendrik also warned The Hague that the Dutch companies 'here in the field [with me] are becoming weaker and weaker

[63] NA, RAZH, Familiearchief Van Wassenaer van Duvenvoorde 2055, Frederik Hendrik to Cornelis Musch, aboard the *Noordgeest*, 17 July 1638.
[64] KHA, A24-79, -92 and -98, Frederik Hendrik to Hendrik Casimir I, aboard the *Noordgeest*, 30 June, 30 July and 7 August 1638; A24-101, same to same, Klarenbeek, 18 August 1638.

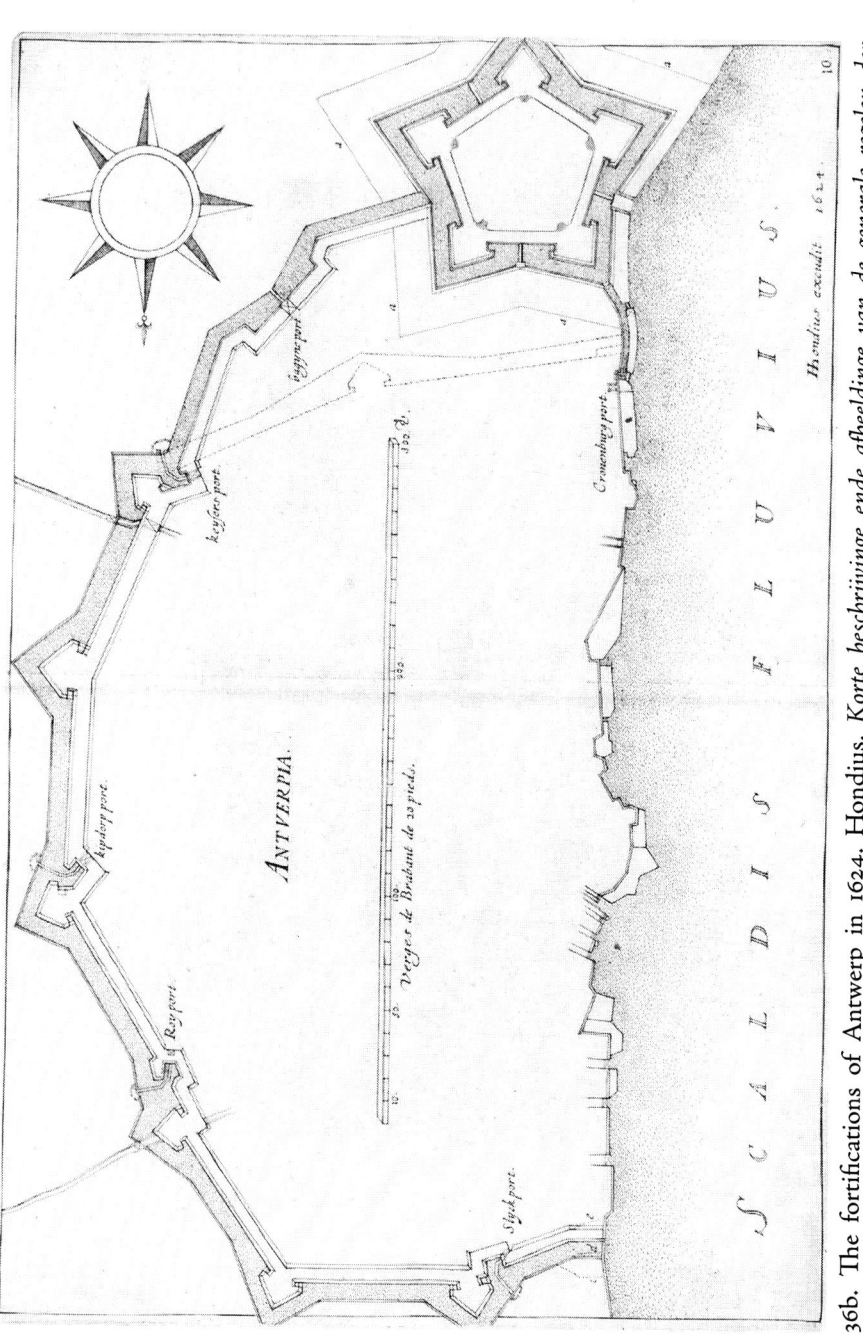

36b. The fortifications of Antwerp in 1624. Hondius, *Korte beschrijvinge ende afbeeldinge van de generale regelen der fortificatie* (1624). (KB, 2108-A-2)

by the day, because of sickness as well as other misfortunes.'[65] After a week and a half the captain-general of the Union decided to raise the siege of Gelder. On 13 October the companies left for the winter quarters in order to recuperate and regain their full complement.[66]

The 1638 campaign had once again demonstrated that so long as the Republic lacked any firm footing in Flanders, Antwerp could not be besieged and nor could the Spanish Netherlands be invaded. The defeat at Kallo was largely the blame of panic among the Dutch soldiers, but the more deep-seated reason for this fiasco must be that the Republic could not attack with superior numbers. About 22,000 field troops had been available to Frederik Hendrik.[67] The Cardinal-Infante had assembled approximately 18,000 men to face the Dutch,[68] while the remaining Spanish field troops and the Imperial supporting army under Piccolomini were being deployed against the French. This meant the Dutch army was about a quarter stronger than the Spanish, a numerical superiority wholly negated by the strategic advantage of access to interior lines enjoyed by the Cardinal-Infante. Via bridges across the River Scheldt near Antwerp he could swiftly transfer troops to and fro between the Brabant and Flanders sides. This made it possible for the governor of Antwerp to attack Willem van Nassau-Siegen's force with success. In a letter the field-marshal sent to Frederik Hendrik during the battle, he informed the commander-in-chief that the Spaniards had attacked the Dutch positions 'with a very great violence … and began that time and again anew up to three, four times'.[69] The lesson to be drawn from the events of 1638 was crystal clear: Antwerp, Ghent and Bruges could not be besieged unless the Cardinal-Infante was obliged to dispatch the majority of his field troops to the border with France by a large-scale French offensive. Since 1635 France had brought strong armies into the field each year, but due to a lack of money and food these evaporated into thin air. In the autumn the Spaniards could undo most of the French conquests,[70] so the Cardinal-Infante accepted losses along the border with France during the summer months and deployed the bulk of his field troops to check the Dutch army. There was a saying in Brussels, as noted by Alexander van der Capellen in his memoirs: 'That which the French win in the summer we shall take back from them again in the winter. And experience has taught us that the French soldiers are more adept at winning a place than retaining it.'[71] There was, nevertheless, a glimmer of hope for the Republic that the military deadlock would at last be broken in 1639.

---

[65] NA, SG 4973, Frederik Hendrik to the SG, before Gelder, 23 August 1638.
[66] Ten Raa, *Het Staatsche leger*, IV, p. 107.
[67] Parrott, *Richelieu's Army*, p. 127.
[68] Vermeir, *In staat van oorlog*, pp. 144–7.
[69] KHA, A24-75, Willem van Nassau-Siegen to Frederik Hendrik, Fort Kallo, 21 June 1638, at four o'clock in the morning, copy.
[70] Parrott, *Richelieu's Army*, p. 129.
[71] Van der Capellen, *Gedenkschriften*, II, p. 117.

The failure of the siege of Saint-Omer was a disgrace for France. To restore Louis XIII's reputation, in 1639 two French field armies were deployed in the Spanish Netherlands. A relative of Richelieu, *maréchal* Charles de la Porte (1602–1664), duc de La Meilleraye, was given the command over the bigger of the two armies (27,500 men on paper[72]) and, in order to leave no shadow of a doubt that France would wage war vigorously that year, the French king decided to participate in person alongside Richelieu in the campaign in the Low Countries.[73] In addition, Dutch spies in Antwerp sent news that the financial straits in the Spanish army were very serious. In the city on the Scheldt clothing for 3,000 to 4,000 men was loaded onto waggons, 'being clothes for the new Spaniards who are coming across, who are expected at Dunkirk with the first wind, and must come, for there is a serious shortage of those Spaniards here, as well as of money, which is sorely wanting'. The Spaniards were owed wages for eleven to twelve pay-months, while the other 'nations' were owed arrears of seventeen to eighteen months. The people of Antwerp feared the worst, for were Holland and Zeeland to put a fleet to sea in order to prevent the transport ships with the fresh Spanish troops putting in at Dunkirk, 'then for us here [in Antwerp] it would be a miserable business'.[74] Despite this information the Dutch blockade fleet was unable to prevent no fewer than 7,000 Spanish troops, according to other reports as many as 10,500, running the blockade and landing in Dunkirk a short time later.[75] This made laying siege to Antwerp an impossibility once again. Nevertheless, Frederik Hendrik hoped to take advantage of the French offensive to invade Flanders via a backdoor. After capturing Hulst he wanted to push onward to Ghent or Bruges, but the hope that this operation would succeed was also swiftly dashed shortly thereafter. At the start of June 1639 the Dutch troops lay ready and waiting in ships at Bergen op Zoom to sail across to Philippine, when news was received that the smaller French field army had on 6 June 1639 been crushed near Thionville by the Imperial forces under Piccolomini. Despite this serious setback Frederik Hendrik decided to march on Hulst all the same, even though the field deputies had low expectations under such circumstances.[76] The Dutch troops landed at Philippine on 18 June. 'Of the enemy', the deputies wrote to The Hague, 'there are current tidings that the Cardinal-Infante is approaching these quarters and Piccolomini to the French before Hesdin'.[77] The main French army was besieging that town.

The arrival of the Spanish army under the Cardinal-Infante precluded Frederik Hendrik being able to invest Hulst. The two armies faced off for a month

---

[72] Kroener, *Entwicklung der Truppenstärken*, p. 203.
[73] Parrott, *Richelieu's Army*, pp. 129 and 136.
[74] NA, SG 4974, 'Uyt Antwerpen den 5 april 1639'.
[75] Parker, *Army of Flanders*, p. 279; Vermeir, *In staat van oorlog*, p. 152.
[76] NA, SG 4974, Field deputies to the SG, on board the barges before Bergen op Zoom, 15 June 1639.
[77] NA, SG 4974, Field deputies to the SG, Philippine, 23 June 1639, in the evening.

and a half without either making a move. On 31 July 1639 Frederik Hendrik sailed back to Bergen op Zoom with the Dutch army. The trek continued from there to Rheinberg, where the troops arrived on 16 August. From this position Frederik Hendrik threatened Venlo and Roermond, but he was not intending to actually besiege these two towns. As soon as the Spanish army had reached the River Meuse as well he wanted to return to Flanders post-haste and at last invest Hulst. On 29 August the commander-in-chief briefed the field deputies on his *'stratègèma'*, which he acknowledged was dependent on a 'favourable wind' for its success. The Spaniards needed six days to return to the environs of Hulst, while the Dutch troops would be able to cover the same distance by barge via the Rhine in four or five days. The Spanish cavalry would probably be able to reach Hulst in four days, but Frederik Hendrik was not concerned by this because 'the army of this State [is] fairly strong and in good health'. He did, however, immediately add the caveat that the siege operation itself would be difficult and protracted, probably lasting well into November: 'That the siege would prove costly, wear out and consume [i.e. cost the lives of] many soldiers.' On 1 September 1639 Frederik Hendrik again broached the question of whether they should lay siege to Hulst during a council of war with the field deputies. This time he asked them to pronounce a decision, but the field deputies had no intention of complying with this. There was, after all, a considerable threat that, due to unforeseeable circumstances, specifically the reliance on the aforementioned 'favourable wind', the Dutch troops would lose their head start on the Spanish army, whereupon it would be impossible to undertake the siege of Hulst, so that 'for the second time in a single summer season one would have landed [to no avail] in Flanders, which would be seriously detrimental to the reputation of this State'. The field deputies therefore passed the responsibility for taking a decision on to The Hague. The States-General endorsed the proposed operation nevertheless. Decisive in this undertaking was that it would be easy and cheap to transport provisions from Zeeland to the siege camp before Hulst and, moreover, that the siege would make a good impression in Paris.[78] The undertaking was not, however, blessed by the gods. Due to an initial 'contrary wind' and subsequent calm it took eight days before the Dutch army reached the environs of Hulst. By this point the Cardinal-Infante had already reached the threatened town with his army's vanguard and had reinforced its garrison with 2,000 men. Frederik Hendrik considered the siege 'unfeasible' under such circumstances.[79] The Dutch army remained in the vicinity of Hulst until the end of the month, but the campaign was over.

The disappointing course of the 1639 campaign meant that Frederik Hendrik found himself in straits even more dire than before. He had repeatedly hammered home that the French alliance was indispensable for the Republic and that in

---

[78] NA, SG 4563, Secret res. SG, 4 September 1639, early morning.
[79] NA, SG 4974, Field deputies to the SG, in the Kruispolder in the Land of Hulst, 10 September 1639, in the evening.

order to safeguard this collaboration the Dutch army could not be reduced. The Hollanders had until then allowed themselves to be persuaded by this argument. However, the 1638 and 1639 campaigns fed the uncertainty of whether their interests were being served by allowing the burden of debt to mount even further. Would it not be wiser to reduce the Dutch army to an effective strength of 60,000 men? This force was more than adequate to guarantee the Republic's security. However, developments that occurred at sea shortly thereafter seemed to increase the likelihood of an aggressive war on land being successful. In August 1639 a fleet of no fewer than seventy-seven galleons had set sail from Spain with 9,000 troops on board, destined for the Spanish army in the Low Countries.[80] In mid-September the 'second Spanish Armada' entered the Straits of Calais, where the Dutch fleet under Lieutenant-Admiral Maerten Harpertsz. Tromp (1598–1653) was lying in wait. The Spaniards sought refuge off the south coast of England in the expectation that the Dutch fleet would not venture to join battle in English coastal waters. However, this did not deter The Hague and on 21 October 1639 Tromp gained a resounding victory over the Spaniards. In the naval battle of the Downs the Spanish fleet was well-nigh obliterated. Approximately 5,000 Spanish troops were put safely ashore in time and were later ferried across to Dunkirk in English and Spanish ships, but it was obvious that the maritime route could no longer be used for the transportation of large numbers of soldiers from Spain.[81] The connection over land had already been severed a year earlier – Breisach had fallen into French hands in December 1638[82] – so from then on the Spanish Netherlands primarily had to rely on their own resources.

Besides the victory at the Downs, Frederik Hendrik had another argument that he could use to overcome the aversion of the Hollanders for a new offensive. In January 1640 he entered into lengthy discussions with Louis Godefroy, comte d'Estrades (1607–1686), who had served as French ambassador at The Hague since 1639. Groningen's deputy to the States-General, Wigbold van Aldringa (1604–1644), informed Stadholder Hendrik Casimir I that 'without doubt something remarkable was to be expected in the spring', because the envoy had given the undertaking that France would pay 1.5 million guilders 'in banco' to Amsterdam. Some 800,000 guilders of this sum was intended for the payment of the unrepartitioned Dutch troops and the remainder to make it possible to enlist 8,000 extra men for the duration of the forthcoming campaign 'without

---

[80] According to Bruijn, *Varend verleden*, p. 24, and Ten Raa, *Het Staatsche leger*, IV, p. 111, there were no fewer than 24,000 troops on board the 'second Spanish Armada'. However, in late August 1639 Philip IV informed the Cardinal-Infante that he could expect reinforcements of 9,000 Spanish infantry. See Parker, *Army of Flanders*, p. 78 n. 1.
[81] Bruijn, *Varend verleden*, p. 34.
[82] Parker, *The Thirty Years' War*, p. 137.

cost to the provinces'.[83] In other words, in 1640 France assumed responsibility for the funding of the *waardgelders*. Moreover, speaking on behalf of Richelieu, Estrades could promise that *maréchals* La Meilleraye and Châtillon would lay siege to Arras, an operation for which they had at their disposal a total of 46,500 men (an effective force of c. 32,000 men).[84] The expectation was that the Cardinal-Infante would advance with the majority of his field troops to relieve Arras, whereupon Frederik Hendrik would be able to lay siege to Bruges or Hulst without much difficulty.

In May 1640 Frederik Hendrik landed near Philippine with between 26,000 and 27,000 Dutch troops and subsequently took up a position by Assenede. On 20 May he dispatched Hendrik Casimir I to Bruges with a vanguard of 5,000 foot and 2,000 horse together with an artillery train of six demi-cannon and six 12-pounders. Hendrik Casmir I had orders to surround Bruges, but as he was approaching this town he encountered a strong Spanish force that blocked his path. For the whole of the following day (21 May) they exchanged fire with musket and cannon, but on the Dutch side 'all those with an understanding of war' were of the opinion that it would be impossible to force the Spaniards from their positions, whereupon Hendrik Casimir I sounded the retreat. During the exchange of fire the Dutch side suffered about one hundred killed and wounded.[85] Now that the besieging of Bruges was out of the question, the Dutch had to await the start of the siege of Arras, at which point an attempt would be made to invest Hulst. On 1 July 1640 the French appeared before Arras. The Dutch troops at Philippine were embarked that same day and landed to the north of Hulst. At eleven o'clock at night on 3 July, Frederik Hendrik ordered the storming of a fort that defended the road to Hulst. In the dark the Dutch and Spanish troops became so thoroughly intermingled that

> the one party could not properly recognise the other, in part because of the night, in part because of the abundant shooting that lasted for an hour and a half, until the great intensity of the fight caused everyone to look for his own party, which is how they were separated from each other, both sides making an honourable retreat.

The fierceness of the fighting is evident from the number of casualties: both sides suffered 300 to 400 dead and hardly any prisoners were taken. During the battle, Willem Frederik, the younger brother of Hendrik Casimir I by just a year, had fought extremely bravely, 'lost two horses from under him and broke his third rapier on the enemy, yet was not injured'. Hendrik Casimir I was less fortunate: he was 'dangerously injured' by a pistol bullet that penetrated his spine, and nine

---

[83] KHA, A24-IV-C-3, Wigbold van Aldringa to Hendrik Casimir I, The Hague, 7 January 1640.
[84] Parrott, *Richelieu's Army*, pp. 209–10.
[85] NA, SG 4975, Field deputies to the SG, Sluis, 23 May 1640.

days later he died from the infected wound (12 July 1640).[86] Frederik Hendrik succeeded him as stadholder of Groningen and Drenthe, but Friesland elected Willem Frederik.

The Dutch troops had fought bravely on 3 July 1640, but it was still impossible for them to invest Hulst. On 9 July the field deputies consulted with Frederik Hendrik about the further 'employ' of the army, 'because the enemy near Hulst ... is so strong that it seems beyond all apparency that it shall be possible to accomplish something fruitful to the service of the Land, either here or in the other quarters of Flanders'. A decision was taken to embark the Dutch army onto barges and transfer it to Bergen op Zoom, 'where its employ shall be deliberated on further'. Frederik Hendrik could then come up with nothing better than a re-run of his campaign plan of 1638, when, following the failed attempt to invest Antwerp, the Dutch army had headed to Gelder. On 30 July 1640 the Dutch troops drew up before Gelder once more, but yet again fortune failed to smile on Frederik Hendrik: because of heavy rain the surrounding fields were inundated, so food supplies could not be brought in and siegeworks could not be dug or raised. Hereupon a decision was taken to go to Rheinberg and to allow the Dutch soldiers to 'refresh' there.[87] On 9 August the French captured Arras, but the French army was by then so riven by hunger and desertion that it was unfit for use in any new operation. By the middle of September the effective strength of the French force was just 22,000 men, some 10,000 fewer than at the start of the campaign.[88] The Dutch army dispersed to the winter quarters that same month.

Frederik Hendrik had by now been vainly endeavouring to invade the Spanish Netherlands for six years. Breda may well have been captured in 1637, but the realisation of the actual war objective was not a single step closer. The Hollanders, Arminians as well as Counter-Remonstrants, were not prepared to postpone the army reduction any longer. Their province's share in the Republic's total war expenditure for the year 1640 had amounted to no less than 10.24 million guilders. The domestic expenses included, Holland had in 1640 been required to defray more than 16.52 million guilders in expenditure. Tax revenues amounted to 10.84 million guilders, leaving a shortfall of 5.68 million guilders.[89] Holland's creditworthiness was threatening to collapse under the swelling burden of debt. However, Frederik Hendrik still wanted to hear nothing of army reduction. Eventually a compromise was reached on the matter. In February 1641 the States of Holland adopted a resolution in which they declared that they would delay the reduction until some means was found to pay the troops promptly from then

---

[86] NA, SG 4976, Field deputies, Sanden, 4 July 1640, in the evening, with a list of the losses as an appendix (quote); Bergsma, *Poppo van Burmania*, entries for 22 June/2 July 1640.
[87] NA, SG 4976, Field deputies to the SG, Rheinberg, 15 July 1640.
[88] Parrott, *Richelieu's Army*, p. 210.
[89] NA, RAZH, AJC 84, 'Voor den jaere 1640'.

on.[90] The only consolation for the monetary malaise was that the Spanish king had financial worries that were much weightier. In May 1640 a revolt had broken out in Catalonia and Portugal seceded from Spain in December. Supported by France the Catalans maintained their resistance for twelve years; the struggle with Portugal was not resolved until 1668.[91]

Frederik Hendrik wanted to open the 1641 campaign by laying siege to Gennep. He then intended to transfer his troops to Philippine and invest Bruges before the Spanish army had arrived in the vicinity, a repeat of his 'stratègèma' of two years earlier. In a treaty concluded on 14 February 1641, France once again promised to furnish a subsidy of 1.2 million guilders to pay for the unrepartitioned Dutch troops, but 'only' 900,000 guilders was paid.[92] Richelieu also promised that the main French army (with an effective strength of 21,000 men[93]), once again under the command of La Meilleraye, would lay siege to Aire.[94] In mid-June 1641 Frederik Hendrik laid siege to Gennep with an effective force of 19,500 men. The garrison of about 2,200 men persevered with the defence for a month and a half, but was forced to capitulate on 29 July.[95] Frederik Hendrik had at last chalked up another success. La Meilleraye had captured Aire three days earlier, whereupon he advanced towards Lille.[96] The new Spanish commander in the Netherlands, Francisco de Melo (1597–1651) – the Cardinal-Infante was seriously ill – managed to protect Lille, Douai and Saint-Omer against the French, but he could not prevent the loss of Lens, La Bassée and Bapaume. As soon as Frederik Hendrik was certain that the Spaniards were interested in only the French, he ordered preparations to be made for conveying the Dutch army to Philippine, which required no fewer than 800 barges. The Dutch troops landed at Philippine on 14 September 1641, but the Spanish positions, along the Sas-Ghent canal as well as along the River Leie, proved to be too strong to breach. Frederik Hendrik was yet again forced to abandon his plans to besiege Bruges or Hulst. On 29 September the Dutch army left for Bergen op Zoom.[97] The war in the south of the Spanish Netherlands continued with great intensity. Melo recaptured Aire from the French on 7 December 1641.[98]

---

[90] NA, RAZH, ASH 74, Res. SH, 2 February 1641.
[91] Lynch, *Spain under the Habsburgs*, II, pp. 113 and 123–4.
[92] Tresoar, FSA 26, Overview of the payment and receipt of the French subsidy in the period 1637–1643.
[93] NA, SG 6766, Tieleman Aquilius to the SG, before Aire, 4 July 1641.
[94] Parrott, *Richelieu's Army*, p. 214.
[95] NA, SG 4978, Frederik Hendrik to the SG, Offelen, 29 July 1641; Field deputies to the SG, before Gennep, 29 July 1641.
[96] Vermeir, *In staat van oorlog*, p. 163; Parrott, *Richelieu's Army*, p. 148.
[97] NA, SG 4978, Field deputies to the SG, near Gennep, 7 August 1641; and Assenede, 17 and 19 September 1641.
[98] Parrott, *Richelieu's Army*, pp. 149–50.

Francisco de Melo goes on the offensive (1642–1643)

The Cardinal-Infante died on 9 November 1641. Madrid appointed Melo as interim governor-general of the Spanish Netherlands. He was determined to continue his offensive against the French. In April 1642 Melo assembled 25,000 men and advanced on Lens. He then recaptured La Bassée as well. On 29 May 1642 he joined battle with the French at Honnecourt.[99] The French army of 10,000 men suffered a heavy defeat: 1,200 Frenchmen lost their lives and the Spaniards took about 2,000 of them as prisoners of war.[100] The Spanish triumph at Honnecourt was a serious setback for France as well as for the Republic. As long as it remained unclear what Melo would then 'want to take in hand', Frederik Hendrik dared not take a decision about the deployment of the Dutch army.[101] The Dutch commander of Maastricht reported on 11 June that Melo was encamped near Namur with 20,000 to 21,000 men, so he possibly had his sights set on Maastricht or on the 'Wimarischen' in French service, of which there were 15,000 to 16,000 men encamped near Uerdingen, a small town just east of Krefeld. At Zons, about fifteen kilometres south of Neuss, lay an Imperial army, so the 'Wimarischen' were in danger of being caught in a pincer movement and annihilated.[102]

The Imperialists had been on the offensive since their crushing defeat of the Swedes at Nördlingen (6 September 1634). To turn the tide, Paris had in 1635 concluded a contract with Bernhard, duke of Saxe-Weimar (1604–1639), a military enterpriser formerly in Swedish service. Saxe-Weimar had pledged to mobilise an army of 18,000 men in exchange for a substantial subsidy. When Saxe-Weimar died in July 1639, his troops threatened to disband because of a lack of money, prompting Louis XIII to take Saxe-Weimar's entire army into French service and place it under direct French command.[103]

On 21 June 1642, the Dutch army, with an effective strength of between 18,500 and 19,500 men, established a position near Rheinberg,[104] from where they could ensure the supply of food and forage to the Saxe-Weimar army camped nearby. The Dutch troops were still encamped near Rheinberg in late August. 'In our army all is calm,' Stadholder Willem Frederik wrote to the States of Friesland from the Dutch headquarters, 'and one must take special care that the Saxe-Weimar troops are provided with vivres and provisions, for otherwise they have

---

[99] Vermeir, *In staat van oorlog*, pp. 244–9.
[100] Israel, *The Dutch Republic and the Hispanic World*, p. 316; Parrott, *Richelieu's Army*, p. 157.
[101] NA, SG 4979, Field deputies to the SG, Fort Sint-Andries, 11 June 1642.
[102] NA, SG 4979, same to same, Fort Sint-Andries 12 June 1642; Tresoar, FSA 30, Willem Frederik to the SvF, in the redoubt at Vooren, 13 June 1642, minute, between Rheinberg and Orsoy in Botbergen, 22 June and 8 August 1642.
[103] Geoffrey Symcox (ed.), *War, Diplomacy, and Imperialism, 1618–1763* (London 1974), source nos. 7 and 8; Parker, *The Thirty Years' War*, p. 133; Parrott, *Richelieu's Army*, pp. 201–2, 143 and 157–8.
[104] NA, SG 4979, Field deputies to the SG, Rheinberg, 22 June 1642.

no supplies and must fetch everything at great expense and with strong convoys from Rheinberg.'[105] The positions of both the Imperialist forces and the Weimar army were too strong to attack, so nothing significant happened despite the presence of four armies. By mid-September there was no more fodder to be found within many miles of the Rhine. The Saxe-Weimar army therefore decided to depart 'and perforce to seek their winter quarters somewhat deeper within the Stift of Cologne'. The Dutch army decamped at the same time and headed via Gennep to the Meijerij of 's-Hertogenbosch in order to recuperate. The 1642 campaign in the Low Countries was effectively over.[106]

During the summer of 1642 the States of Holland had continued making preparations to reduce the Dutch army to an effective strength of 60,000 men in early 1643.[107] A redistribution of the payment of wages among Holland's tax collectors meant it would from then on be possible to guarantee that the repartitioned troops received their pay promptly and for the most part in full. The reduction would come into effect on 1 March 1643.[108] Frederik Hendrik lamented this decision. He warned that France would then refuse to continue paying the subsidy for the unrepartitioned troops. His concern proved to be well founded, because at the end of January 1643, when the Republic's ambassador in Paris, Willem van Lier (1588–1649), lord of Oisterwijk, urged the French secretary of state for foreign affairs, Léon le Bouthillier (1608–1652), comte de Chavigny, to remit as large a subsidy as possible, he responded that The Hague was in no position to make demands, because the States-General were refusing to make ten warships available to France and 'because they [the States-General], due to the intended reduction of her army, would not be bringing the number of soldiers agreed upon in the treaties into the field'. Van Lier parried this critique with the argument that the number of effective troops in Dutch service would not be diminished by the reduction.[109] The Republic's ambassador could also have pointed out that the French king himself had each year brought an effective force of far fewer troops into the field than was agreed, but he refrained from mentioning this. This was because the French threat to discontinue the payment of the subsidy could not be taken terribly seriously. The alliance with the Republic was far too important to France for her to jeopardise it: Richelieu had died on 4 December 1642, Louis XIII's state of health was cause for serious concern, and everything indicated that in 1643 the main Spanish assault would again be directed against France. Chavigny's remark must therefore be seen as a means to place the Republic under pressure to make men-of-war available for the siege of Dunkirk, which Paris had decided to undertake that year. Without the

---

[105] Tresoar, FSA 30, Willem Frederik to the SvF, Rheinberg, 23 August 1642.
[106] Tresoar, FSA 30, same to same, Rheinberg, 13 September (quote), Gennep, 23 September 1642; NA, SG 4979, Field deputies to the SG, Nijmegen, 17 September 1642.
[107] Tresoar, FSA 30, Willem Frederik to the SvF, Rheinberg, 23 August 1642.
[108] See p. 80.
[109] NA, SG 6767, Willem van Lier to the SG, Paris, 31 January 1643.

assistance of the Dutch fleet it would be impossible to prevent Brussels bringing fresh troops and supplies into this coastal town during the siege.

France renewed the subsidy treaty with the Republic on 30 March 1643.[110] The sum that was eventually transferred may well have been considerably lower than the 1.2 million guilders promised – in fact only 852,000 guilders[111] – but the treaty was nevertheless of great value to Frederik Hendrik, because it enabled him to prevail upon the Hollanders to support a new offensive campaign. Once again it was Hulst that was on Frederik Hendrik's agenda. The captain-general of the Union had great expectations for this undertaking, because Melo was at that time advancing on Paris with the bulk of the Spanish field troops (an effective force of approximately 22,000 men). With Louis XIII at death's door, the Spanish commander-in-chief hoped that the uncertain political situation would make the queen of France willing to reach a peace settlement with Madrid before the Spaniards had reached the gates of the French capital. There was, after all, a very real danger that domestic uprisings would break out after the death of Louis XIII. The successor to the throne, the later Sun King, was barely four years old, and his mother, Anne of Austria (1601–1666), was a sister of Philip IV. Louis XIII died on 14 May 1643. However, the volte-face in French foreign policy that Melo was expecting failed to materialise, because the queen-dowager, together with her chief minister, Cardinal Jules Mazarin (1602–1661), continued down the political course plotted out by Richelieu. Only five days after Louis XIII's death Melo suffered a serious defeat to a French military force led by Louis II de Bourbon (1621–1686), duc d'Enghien, the later 'Great Condé', who was only twenty-one. The French triumph at Rocroi (19 May 1643) signalled the end of the Spanish offensive. From then on it was not the Spaniards but the French who could for a time make conquests undisturbed.[112] D'Enghien laid siege to Thionville. The capture of this stronghold would close the gateway to France via the Moselle valley. For the time being the planned attack on Dunkirk was shelved.

Frederik Hendrik had less success against the Spaniards in 1643. 'The contrary westerly winds and the great calm from the south-south-east that ensued, which lasted for two days, have in no small way hindered our intentions in these quarters [of Flanders]', Willem Frederik complained in a letter to the States of Friesland.[113] The sluggishness with which the Dutch assault on Hulst built momentum left the Spaniards with plenty of time to take countermeasures. The Dutch army stood idle before the Spanish lines covering Hulst for two weeks. During a war council adjourned on 30 June 1643 with the field deputies and the

---

[110] NA, SG 6767, Léon le Bouthillier, comte de Chavigny, and Willem van Lier, Paris, 30 March 1643.
[111] Tresoar, FSA 26, Overview of the payment and receipt of the French subsidy in the period 1637–1643.
[112] Bonney, *The King's Debts*, pp. 190–1, 193 and 195; Vermeir, *In staat van oorlog*, pp. 252–3.
[113] Tresoar, FSA 30, Willem Frederik to the SvF, near Hulst, 28 June 1643.

senior army officers, Frederik Hendrik proposed heading to the River Meuse and recapturing Venlo and Roermond. He won the support of Field-Marshal Johan Wolfert van Brederode (1599–1655) and all the colonels for this plan, who shared his opinion 'that it was the most sound, [that it] would make the enemy depart from here and [that it would create] perhaps yet an opportunity to return here to do something [later] this year'. On 1 July the Dutch troops boarded the transport ships, but instead of heading for Bergen op Zoom the barges sailed to Philippine. Holland's three field deputies – Johan van Mathenesse (1596–1653), François Herbert (†1661) and Johan van der Camer (†1669) – had not agreed with the decision to abandon the assault on Hulst and 'after long debates and harsh words' they had their way.[114] Before transferring the army to the River Meuse they wanted Frederik Hendrik to make another attempt to invest Hulst by means of an assault from the west, and otherwise they wanted him to besiege Sas van Gent.[115] A few days later the Dutch troops established a position near Assenede and from there the march could be continued to Sas van Gent or Hulst, but now Frederik Hendrik saw no opportunity to attack either of these places. This was because Melo had amassed all his remaining field troops – 14,000 infantrymen and no fewer than 136 cavalry companies – behind the Sassevaart, a waterway connecting Ghent to the Westerscheldt estuary, 'and had left the upper quarters, including Thionville, exposed to the French under the command of the duc d'Enghien'. There were just 5,500 Spanish troops in Luxembourg.[116] For Brussels retaining control of Bruges and Ghent was of much greater importance than keeping hold of the outlying fortress of Thionville. The duc d'Enghien could therefore beleaguer this town undisturbed.[117]

Neither Sas van Gent nor Hulst could be attacked, but the Dutch army remained in place near Assenede for a month and a half, 'in order to hold up the mass of the enemy's army and thus to give the French better opportunity that they might be able to bring the conquest of Thionville to a good conclusion'.[118] Thionville fell into French hands on 10 August 1643. Thirteen days later the Dutch troops struck camp and left for Bergen op Zoom. It seemed as if the 1643 campaign would turn out to be a great disappointment for the Republic, so in the night of 3/4 September Frederik Hendrik dispatched all his cavalrymen to Antwerp in order that he might have something positive to report. In the early morning of 4 September a small vanguard launched an assault on the Spanish sentry posts, while the main Dutch force waited in ambush. The Spaniards

---

[114] Visser, *Dagboeken van Willem Frederik*, pp. 12–13.
[115] NA, SG 4980, Field deputies to the SG, before Philippine, 2 July 1643.
[116] Tresoar, FSA 30, Willem Frederik to the SvF, Assenede, 5 July (quote) and 9 July 1643; NA, SG 4980, Frederik Hendrik to the SG, Assenede, 3 July 1643.
[117] 'Here one considers Thionville as well-nigh lost,' Willem Frederik wrote from the Dutch army camp at Assenede, 'for all the Spanish are betaking themselves from there and into these quarters.' Tresoar, FSA, to the SvF, Assenede, 9 July 1643.
[118] Tresoar, FSA 30, Willem Frederik to the SvF, Assenede, 24 July 1643.

launched a sally with 1,000 men, on horse as well as on foot. In the ensuing struggle six Spanish infantry companies were surrounded and taken prisoner. Their fate was shared by a lieutenant-general, a major-general of the cavalry, a major-general of the infantry, ten rittmasters and a couple of hundred Spanish cavalrymen. At the cost of a mere fifteen to eighteen lives and a few wounded men the Dutch troops had captured a total of 500 to 600 Spaniards.[119] On 13 September the Dutch troops departed by regiment for the frontier towns.[120] The 1643 campaign was over.

Antwerp for the last time – the Peace of Münster (1644–1648)

In the wake of the 1643 campaign Frederik Hendrik was even more convinced that he would never succeed in breaking the strategic deadlock in the Low Countries unless he managed to seize control of Antwerp. The States of Holland gave its consent for this operation, providing Frederik Hendrik agreed to the Republic simultaneously intervening in favour of Sweden in a war that had broken out between Sweden and Denmark in December 1643. The Amsterdammers considered this to be an ideal opportunity to teach King Christian IV of Denmark for once and for all to refrain from encumbering Holland's trade by imposing high tolls on merchant vessels travelling via the Sound.[121] In 1644 a Dutch fleet of forty-one ships sailed for the Sound.[122] On 7 June the Dutch army (an effective force of c. 20,000 men) landed near Philippine, whereupon Frederik Hendrik sent Brederode on ahead with 6,000 to 7,000 men to clear the way to the Land of Waas.[123] The Spanish resistance proved too strong, however, so the field-marshal had to return mission unaccomplished. The French (with an effective force numbering 21,000 to 22,000 men) had more success in the interim. They laid siege to Gravelines.[124] This placed Frederik Hendrik in a predicament: the French alliance obliged him to remain in Flanders with the Dutch army to prevent Melo advancing to relieve Gravelines, but by doing this he exposed himself to the critique that he was allowing himself to be used as an instrument

---

[119] NA, SG 4980, Field deputies to the SG, Bergen op Zoom, 4 September 1643; Frederik Hendrik to the SG, Bergen op Zoom, 4 September 1643; Tresoar, FSA 30, Willem Frederik to the SvF, Bergen op Zoom, 4 September 1643.
[120] NA, SG 4980, Field deputies to the SG, Bergen op Zoom, 13 September 1643.
[121] Elias, *Het Amsterdamsche regentenpatriciaat*, p. 112; J.J. Poelhekke, *De Vrede van Munster* (The Hague 1948), p. 178; Parker, *The Thirty Years' War*, p. 156.
[122] Ten Raa, *Het Staatsche leger*, IV, p. 137.
[123] NA, SG 4981, Frederik Hendrik to the SG, Assenede, 10 June 1644; Field deputies to the SG, Assenede, 13 June 1644; Tresoar, FSA, Willem Frederik to the SvF, Assenede, 9 June 1644.
[124] NA, SG 4981, Field deputies to the SG, Assenede, 23 June 1644.

of French foreign policy. He therefore proposed to the field deputies that they might study the possibility of laying siege to Bruges.[125]

By mid-July 1644 the Dutch troops were within fifteen kilometres of Bruges. Frederik Hendrik broached the possibility of undertaking the siege during a council of war, but none of the field deputies or senior army officers present considered it feasible: 'All things properly considered, [those] present found that nothing could be accomplished here, because the enemy had such forces here.' An estimated 10,000 to 12,000 Spanish troops covered Bruges, Hulst and Antwerp. Frederik Hendrik then sought The Hague's permission to remain in Flanders until the conclusion of the siege of Gravelines. Frederik Hendrik was initially planning to set off next with the Dutch army for the River Meuse in order to recapture Venlo and Roermond,[126] but shortly thereafter he changed his mind. From the reports of scouts it seemed that the Spaniards were only interested in the security of Antwerp, Ghent and Bruges and were abandoning the fortresses along the Westerscheldt estuary to their fate. On the evening of 25 July, as soon as Frederik Hendrik was informed of this, he set out 'stealthily' for Sas van Gent. Two days later the Dutch troops stormed three forts that guarded the Sassevaart waterway and on 28 July they surrounded Sas van Gent, where a garrison of about 2,350 men was billeted. Sas van Gent would provide the Republic with a second strong base, in addition to Sluis, on the Westerscheldt.[127]

Frederik Hendrik spared neither cost nor effort to bring the siege of Sas van Gent to a successful conclusion. After years of setbacks he owed it to his fame as the 'Tamer of Towns' to at last carry a victory that did justice to this epithet. On 30 July, Willem Frederik, who was first assigned a military command of any importance in 1644, when Frederik Hendrik put him in charge of one of the three *attaques*, wrote to the States of Friesland: 'The entrenchments of our camp are now complete and one is starting to furnish this camp with outworks, thus hoping with God's help to be in [a state of] complete protection [against attack] from the outside within a few days.'[128] The soldiers worked under great time constraints, because Gravelines had fallen into French hands on 28 July 1644. In the Dutch headquarters they initially cherished the hope that this loss would 'without doubt keep the Spanish from our throats'[129] – since the fall of Gravelines the French posed a threat to Fort Mardyck and Dunkirk – but the French army was too severely weakened to undertake another siege during this campaign. This presented Melo with the opportunity to advance with approximately 20,000 men to relieve Sas van Gent. He arrived in the vicinity of the Dutch army on 5 August, but he did not dare launch an assault on the robust line of circumvallation; he limited himself to cannonades. When the Spaniards

[125] NA, SG 4981, same to same, Assenede, 26 June 1644.
[126] Visser, *Dagboeken van Willem Frederik*, p. 56.
[127] Tresoar, FSA 30, Willem Frederik to the SvF, Zelzate, 29 July 1644.
[128] Tresoar, FSA 30, same to same, Zelzate, 30 July 1644.
[129] Tresoar, FSA 30, same to same, Zelzate, 29 and 30 (quote) July 1644.

received news that the French *maréchal* Jean de Gassion (1609–1648) was leading a marauding expedition of 6,000 cavaliers in Flanders, Melo broke camp and left for Ghent to take countermeasures.[130] The siege of Sas van Gent proceeded without any other noteworthy incidents. On 5 September 1644, the defenders, still about 2,000 strong, made it known that they wished to capitulate, and Frederik Hendrik agreed to their free withdrawal to Ghent. The field deputies informed the States-General about this important success: 'It is highly surprising that they did not defend the place better. We cannot as yet actually know what they were lacking, because they were still so amply furnished with soldiers, vivres and ammunition that in the first eight days they would have had little shortage, but it is probable that the soldiers were unwilling [to fight on].'[131] In early October 1644, after the trenches had been levelled and the fortifications restored, the Dutch army left for Bergen op Zoom. A strong garrison of sixty infantry companies was left behind to guard Sas van Gent.[132]

The reduction of Sas van Gent had saved Frederik Hendrik's reputation as a general in the nick of time, but he was not in the least satisfied with the outcome of the 1644 campaign: for him all that counted was Antwerp. The capture of this still very important mercantile city would at last allow him to emerge from the shadow of the French successes and justify the high war expenditure that he demanded from the provinces and most particularly Holland. In 1645 Frederik Hendrik therefore wanted to undertake a new attempt to invest Antwerp. He set forth his ideas during a conclave with the *secrete besogne* on 21 December 1644. The captain-general of the Union began by stating his view that the siege of Antwerp would tax the Dutch army to its limits. A report drawn up by siege experts computed that an army of at least 30,000 men was required for this undertaking: 8,000 to 10,000 men were needed to blockade Antwerp on the Flanders side and 20,000 to 22,000 men to box it in on the Brabant side. Two substantial forts would have to be built on either bank of the River Scheldt,

> in order to lay the bridge between them. Connecting these forts to each other above and below the bridge, straight across the current, with floating structures made of beams, masts and barrels, topped with a parapet, from which it will be possible to effect its [i.e. the bridge's] competent defence. And in some places realised with projecting flanks, to be able to use small pieces of cannon on it.[133]

Frederik Hendrik pointed out that this safeguarded communications between the two siege-corps, whereby a repeat of the defeat at Kallo (1638) could be avoided. The execution of this ambitious plan required a temporary augmentation of the

---

[130] Tresoar, FSA 30, same to same, before Sas van Gent, 7 and 13 August 1644.
[131] NA, SG 4981, Field deputies, before Sas van Gent, 12 September 1644.
[132] NA, SG 4981, Frederik Hendrik, Assenede, 5 October 1644.
[133] NA, RvS 2490, 'Rapport aen sijn princel. Ex.tie duer Cornelis de Bruyne en Jan van Brussel', 1644. Cornelis de Bruyne was a fortifications contractor.

Dutch army with an extra 13,000 men: 5,000 infantry, 2,000 cavalrymen and 6,000 *waardgelders*, at a cost of 1 million guilders.[134]

Frederik Hendrik declared that if the provinces did not wish to consent to this then he would forgo the siege of Antwerp and the States-General would then have to be satisfied with an assault on Ghent, Bruges or Hulst, in which case a force of approximately 20,000 men would be sufficient. On the face of it these operations seemed like attractive alternatives, but they presented two incidental yet major disadvantages. The first was that wholly investing Bruges or Ghent was feasible only if the French provided assistance, when the majority of the regents had no desire to see the French penetrate into the heart of Flanders. The Republic could, however, lay siege to Hulst independently and the reduction of this town was certainly important from a strategic viewpoint – the Republic could thereby tighten her grip on the Westerscheldt – but the drawback here was that it did not break through the military impasse.[135] The members of the *secrete besogne* therefore agreed to the siege of Antwerp, but this decision was more easily taken than it was implemented, because then the consent of the principals (i.e. the provincial States) had to be obtained.[136] A complicating factor was that, since the rift with Amsterdam in 1633, Frederik Hendrik no longer admitted representatives of this major town to the *secrete besogne*.[137] Amsterdam's regents were not ill-disposed towards the capture of Antwerp, but they wanted the assurance that the operation would not be at the expense of the Republic's intervention in the Danish-Swedish war. As a prerequisite for their support for this 'grand design' they therefore insisted that the other provinces put their money where their mouths were, in order that they could once again dispatch warships to the Sound in 1645. This fleet would, moreover, have to be stronger than that of the previous year and would have to take along 5,000 landing troops.[138]

In March 1645, more than two months after Frederik Hendrik had submitted his petition for 13,000 extra men, the Amsterdam regents were still holding to their demand for an expedition to the Sound, and until this was agreed they refused to approve the States-General's secret resolution of 21 December 1644 to undertake the siege of Antwerp. Johan van Veltdriel, Friesland's deputy to the States-General, complained vociferously to his principal:

---

[134] The States-General's secret resolution of 21 December 1644 mentions only 11,000 men (5,000 infantry and 6,000 *waardgelders*), but based on Willem Frederik's journal (*Dagboeken*, p. 160) and the memoirs of Alexander van der Capellen (*Gedenkschriften*, II, p. 107) it seems that the decision to recruit 2,000 cavalrymen as well must have been taken a short time later.
[135] Visser, *Dagboeken van Willem Frederik*, p. 90.
[136] NA, SG 4563, Secret res. of the SG, 21 December 1644, 'In His Highness' chamber'.
[137] KHA, A14-XI-D1, 'Namen van de heeren zoo wt de Generaliteit als wt Hollant die met mij [Frederik Hendrik] besoigneeren over de zaeke van orlooch voor anno 1640'; 'Ut de regering van Hollandt heb ick bi mij geasumeert om te delibereeren en resolveeren op de zaeke van orloch de heeren.'; Israel, *Empires and Entrepots*, p. 98.
[138] Ten Raa, *Het Staatsche leger*, IV, p. 143.

> It appears that ... Holland is more prepared for [and] also more devoted to the project of Sweden and Denmark than the forthcoming campaign.... Many sensible people [in the States-General] are astonished at Holland's sluggish and slow resolve [i.e. decision-making]. It seems as if it is the doing of a mischief-maker: one wants it this way and the other wants it that way. Many cautious people also fear that the grand design [to take Antwerp] has already been ruined by the protracted tarrying.

The French envoy, Estrades, tried to influence the decision-making in Holland in favour of Frederik Hendrik's plan by offering, over and above the standard subsidy of 1.2 million guilders, 'to do his utmost to procure more money',[139] but he does not seem to have had much success in this. The Hollanders cuttingly pointed out that the level of the French subsidy actually turned out to be much lower: since 1641 no more than 850,000 to 900,000 guilders per annum had been transferred.[140] However, Estrades had kept a sweetener in reserve: over and above the normal subsidy he pledged an additional 300,000 guilders 'for the recruitment of some soldiers', namely 3,000 men. This sum of money would make it possible to comply with Holland's requirement that 5,000 troops be sent to the Sound with the fleet, but without this weakening the field army and endangering the execution of the 'grand design'.[141] This more or less coincided with the States-General granting Holland permission to impose an extraordinary tax, the receipts earmarked to equip the fleet for the Baltic Sea. All the merchant vessels that passed through the Sound under the protection of the Dutch fleet – that is without paying toll – would have to pay a 'safe passage', a levy on the value of the goods carried. The two obstacles to launching an assault on Antwerp were thus eliminated.[142]

In early June 1645 a fleet of forty-seven warships under Vice-Admiral Witte de With (1599–1658) set sail for the Sound. There were 4,300 sailors on board, but no landing forces. The 5,000 troops had been enlisted, but the States-General had decided that they would only leave if the king of Denmark declared war on the Republic. In the middle of June the Dutch fleet dropped anchor in the Sound, allowing some 300 merchant vessels to continue their journeys to the Baltic without paying the toll. There was no need for the Dutch warships to take action; flying the flag proved to be enough to force Christian IV into submission. A short time later Denmark and Sweden concluded the Peace of Brömsebro (23 August 1645), which weakened the Danish position in the Baltic region appreciably: Christian IV was forced to cede territories including Halland and the island of Gotland to Sweden.[143]

---

[139] KHA, A25-VII-C-256, Johan van Veltdriel to Willem Frederik, The Hague, 5 March 1645.
[140] KHA, A25-VII-C-256, same to same, The Hague, 19 April [1644].
[141] KHA, A25-VII-C-256, same to same, The Hague, 22 March 1645.
[142] Ten Raa, *Het Staatsche leger*, IV, p. 144.
[143] Gerhard Wilhelm Kernkamp, *De sleutels van de Sont. Het aandeel van de Republiek in den*

While the Dutch fleet sailed for the Sound, Frederik Hendrik massed the Dutch army close by Dordrecht, but the Dutch commander-in-chief's enthusiasm for laying siege to Antwerp had flagged considerably; from spy reports he was aware that the Spaniards had a numerical superiority of cavalry.[144] The field deputies, on the other hand, drew hope from the advance of a French army with an effective strength of 23,000 to 24,000 men 'with the intention to march straight into Flanders and assail the enemy',[145] and they therefore insisted that Frederik Hendrik should proceed with the 'grand design'. Field-Marshal Brederode subsequently departed for Sas van Gent with the vanguard, and from there he continued the march towards Antwerp. On 8 June 1645 he captured Fort Miseria, the gateway to the Land of Waas. It was at last possible to invest Antwerp, but Frederik Hendrik no longer dared to proceed. On 10 June he convened a council of war with the field deputies and the senior army officers in Bergen op Zoom. According to the Dutch commander-in-chief, in view of the strength of the Spanish mounted arms it was too 'periculous' to divide the Dutch army between the two banks of the River Scheldt, as this would place Brederode in danger of being surprised and annihilated by the Spaniards. Would it not be preferable, Frederik Hendrik suggested to those present, for him to head for Sas van Gent, 'to land, to conjoin ourselves with … Brederode, to head into the midst of their [i.e. the enemy's] territory, whence he could lay siege to Hulst, Antwerp, Ghent, Rupelmonde [and] Dendermonde'?[146] The proposal of the captain-general of the Union was approved, but at the end of July 1645 the Dutch army was still encamped in the vicinity of Sas van Gent; it had in the meantime swollen to 322 infantry companies and seventy-one cavalry companies, more than 30,000 men.[147] The States-General had never before assembled a field army of such proportions, yet Frederik Hendrik did nothing. Brederode told Willem Frederik that the commander-in-chief 'did not yet know what he would do, spoke no longer of Damme, [said] also that he would not dare to attack Bruges, because he feared the enemy's cavalry'.[148]

The French, under the command of *maréchals* Gassion and Josias, comte de Rantzau (1609–1650), had in the meantime been working away vigorously. On 9 July 1645 they had captured Fort Mardyck and the following day the 700 Spanish defenders were permitted to withdraw to Dunkirk.[149] Estrades subsequently urged Frederik Hendrik to undertake something as well. It seemed as if

---

Deensch-Zweedschen oorlog van 1644–1645 (The Hague 1890), pp. 193–4, 196 and 201; Bruijn, *Varend verleden*, p. 37.
[144] Visser, *Dagboeken van Willem Frederik*, p. 134.
[145] NA, SG 4982, Field deputies to the SG, Breda, 31 May and 1 June (quote) 1645.
[146] Visser, *Dagboeken van Willem Frederik*, p. 142.
[147] NA, SG 4982, Field deputies to the SG, Sas van Gent, 4 July, Oosteeklo, 7 and 27 July 1645.
[148] Visser, *Dagboeken van Willem Frederik*, p. 152.
[149] NA, SG 6769, Tieleman Aquilius to the SG, Gravelines, 21 June, and Fort Mardyck, 10 July 1645.

he was intending to invest Antwerp after all, but on 5 August, when the Dutch troops were ready to leave for IJzendijke, from where they would sail up the River Scheldt by barge, the wind turned to the east 'and wholly contrary to His Highness's design'. Hereafter, Frederik Hendrik once again sank into inaction for weeks. Estrades was furious that the captain-general of the Union 'accomplished nothing of note'. Why did he not lay siege to Bruges, the French envoy wondered aloud. Frederik Hendrik placed the blame for this on the Hollanders, because if they had not insisted that 5,000 infantrymen be earmarked for the expedition to Denmark, then he would have been able to assemble two field armies 'to move into Flanders from two sides'.[150] This argument is hardly convincing, because Frederik Hendrik had previously put forward the Spanish cavalry's superior strength as the reason he considered it impossible to lay siege to Antwerp and, furthermore, at that time he had more than 30,000 men at his disposal, so he was strong enough to divide his force without risk. The most probable reason for Frederik Hendrik's disinclination to participate in an offensive in Flanders is that he did not wish to lay himself open to the critique that he was using the Dutch army to promote French interests. It is likely that Frederik Hendrik's deteriorating health played a part – he had to contend with all manner of ailments, such as gout, dropsy and stomach cramps[151] – because his lethargic attitude was far from sensible.

Towards the end of August 1645 the French resumed their offensive, with Gassion and Rantzau laying siege to Béthune on 27 August. Its Spanish defenders surrendered just two days later. The two *maréchals* then invested Lillers and Saint-Venant. The former fell on 1 September and the latter surrendered the following day. The capture of these three towns was strategically significant for the French because it enabled them 'to weigh down heavily' on Aire and Saint-Omer. The unprecedented speed of the French advance was purely thanks to the weakness of the Spanish garrisons. There had been only 200 Spaniards garrisoned in Béthune, some 350 in Lillers and 400 in Saint-Venant. Manuel de Moura y Cortereal (†1661), marquis of Castel Rodrigo, who had succeeded Melo as interim governor-general of the Spanish Netherlands in late 1644, employed all his field troops for the protection of Dunkirk, Bruges, Ghent and Antwerp; he abandoned the county of Artois to its fate.[152]

In the Republic the series of French successes was followed with suspicion. There was growing ill-ease among the regents about Frederik Hendrik's lack of derring-do. On his insistence they had assented to taking 30,000 men into the field, but then he did nothing of significance with such a sizeable force while, to quote Alexander van der Capellen's characterisation of the situation, 'the French,

---

[150] Visser, *Dagboeken van Willem Frederik*, pp. 157 and 160.
[151] Poelhekke, *Frederik Hendrik*, pp. 548–51.
[152] NA, SG 6769, Tieleman Aquilius to the SG, Béthune, 30 August and 2 September; and Arras, 4 September 1645.

favoured by our army, on account of our keeping so great a force [i.e. the enemy's troops] from their throats, were resoundingly victorious'.[153] Shortly thereafter the French caused Frederik Hendrik even greater embarrassment. On 26 September 1645, Gassion and Rantzau informed him that they had marched on Sint-Joris, a post along the Ghent–Bruges canal, with 16,000 men. There was huge consternation about this in the Dutch headquarters. Frederik Hendrik made haste to write to the States-General to assure them that prior to this he had heard nothing at all of this French exploit.[154] The French push fuelled suspicion among the regents that Paris had her sights trained on Bruges, while on the basis of the 1635 alliance this town appertained to the Republic. Frederik Hendrik immediately dispatched Major-General Lodewijk of Nassau-La Leck (1604–1665), lord of Beverweert, and Estrades to the two *maréchals* 'to be informed verbally of their good intentions in more detail'.[155] Frederik Hendrik wanted above all to know whether they were willing 'to do him a service and go with [him] to Antwerp, that His Highness [Frederik Hendrik] wanted to advance with them and attack everything that they encounter'. Gassion and Rantzau assured Nassau-La Leck that the only purpose of their advance had been to make it possible for Frederik Hendrik to act offensively. They agreed that the two armies would meet each other at Mariakerke, a village just northwest of Ghent, whereupon they would discuss the operational objectives further.[156]

On 28 September 1645 Frederik Hendrik convened a council of war with Gassion and Rantzau. They agreed that the French forces would remain close to Ghent to 'give a diversion', while the Dutch army would approach Hulst – Frederik Hendrik no longer breathed a word about Antwerp – by means of an outflanking manoeuvre from the south.[157] This decision drove the field deputies, most of whom felt 'that one ought to have gone straight for Antwerp, but the prince raised many difficulties against this',[158] to their wits' end. It would stir up an uproar in The Hague. They therefore decided to keep it secret from the States-General until Hulst was surrounded. The Dutch army arrived in the vicinity of this town on 5 October. The following day the field deputies informed The Hague about the change to the campaign plan. This caused great astonishment, as they had anticipated. As recently as 5 October, Karel van Roorda (1609–1670), a Friesland deputy to the States-General, had been convinced

---

[153] Van der Capellen, *Gedenkschriften*, II, p. 107.
[154] NA, SG 4982, Frederik Hendrik to the SG, Oosteeklo, 27 September 1645; Field deputies to the SG, Oosteeklo, 26 September 1645.
[155] NA, SG 4982, Frederik Hendrik to the SG, Oosteeklo, 27 September 1645. Lodewijk of Nassau-La Leck was an illegitimate son of Maurits and Margaretha van Mechelen (c. 1580–1662).
[156] Visser, *Dagboeken van Willem Frederik*, pp. 164–5.
[157] NA, SG 4982, Field deputies to the SG, before Hulst, 6 October 1645.
[158] Van der Capellen, *Gedenkschriften*, II, p. 110.

that the Dutch army would march into the Land of Waas, 'the proper road to resuming the grand and original design'.[159] Frederik Hendrik's reversal came as no surprise to Willem Frederik: he believed that the captain-general of the Union had suggested laying siege to Antwerp only to lure the French away from Bruges.[160]

The siege of Hulst proceeded without major problems. The Spaniards had been completely surprised and there was a garrison of just 1,600 men in the town, so an active defence was impossible and the defenders capitulated on 3 November.[161] This was followed by the departure of the Dutch army for the winter quarters on 19 November. In December the Spaniards managed to wreak some revenge by recapturing Fort Mardyck from the French,[162] but this success would not halt the French advance. Developments in the political arena did, however, give Madrid hope of better prospects.

The Holy Roman Emperor had from 1641 been working on a diplomatic solution for the wars that had torn Europe asunder since 1618. The efforts of Ferdinand III (1608–1657), Holy Roman Emperor from 1637, were formally limited to the lands involved in the Thirty Years' War, but because the Republic was allied to France she was also approached to participate in the negotiations. The original plan was to bring together all the warring factions in Münster and Osnabrück in July 1643,[163] but the time was not yet ripe and by the following year 'the Münster business ... [had] fallen totally dormant'.[164] In 1645 it came to the fore once again.[165] However, Frederik Hendrik insisted that before a Dutch delegation departed for Münster the provinces had to agree among themselves about their collaboration after the war. Three issues were pivotal in this: union, religion and the militia, the three pillars on which the mutual cooperation, internal stability and joint security of the Dutch Republic was founded. The *union* was the Union of Utrecht (1579). By *religion* they meant the true Christian Reformed religion as specified by the Synod of Dordrecht (1618–1619) and proclaimed from the pulpit in the public church. Lastly, the *militia* was understood as the peacetime strength of the Dutch army. Frederik Hendrik considered consensus on these three 'preliminary points' to be necessary to preclude the risk of a repeat of the internal strife that had ravaged the Republic in 1617–1618.[166] Over the course of

---

[159] KHA, A25-VII-C-237, Karel van Roorda to Willem Frederik, The Hague, 5 October 1645.
[160] Visser, *Dagboeken van Willem Frederik*, pp. 164–6.
[161] NA, SG 4982, Field deputies to the SG, before Hulst, 2 November 1645; Visser, *Dagboeken van Willem Frederik*, pp. 177–8.
[162] Van der Capellen, *Gedenkschriften*, II, p. 117.
[163] Simon Groenveld, 'Unie, Religie en Militie. Binnenlandse verhoudingen in de Nederlandse Republiek voor en na de Munsterse vrede', in 1648. *De Vrede van Munster*, special issue of *De Zeventiende Eeuw*, XIII, 1 (1997), 67–87, esp. p. 68.
[164] KHA, A25-VII-C-256, Johan van Veltdriel to Willem Frederik, The Hague, 9 July 1644.
[165] KHA, A25-VII-C-256, same to same, The Hague, 22 March 1645.
[166] Groenveld, 'Unie, Religie en Militie', pp. 68–70; Wiebe Bergsma, 'De godsdienstige

1645 the provinces reached agreement about the interpretation of the notions of union and religion, but Holland, Zeeland and Friesland still considered it too early to take a decision about the size of the Dutch army during peacetime. They took the position that the strength of the army had to be the subject of further discussion.[167] Frederik Hendrik reconciled himself to this. In exchange for this concession Holland's deputies agreed that in 1646 a final attempt would be made to capture Antwerp. On 5 January 1646 the States-General sent a legation to Münster, so that the negotiations with Spain, initially only about a truce, could officially begin.

Now that Holland had endorsed the siege of Antwerp everything seemed to be cut and dried, but then events in France threatened disruption. First Mazarin raised objections to the payment of the usual subsidy of 1.2 million guilders,[168] and then to cap it all in February 1646 it became common knowledge in The Hague that the seven-year-old Louis XIV had purportedly married the eldest daughter of Philip IV, Maria Theresia (1638–1683), also aged just seven, 'and that the King of Spain would … be giving his daughter as a wedding gift the Netherlandish provinces that he still has under his authority, to be annexed to the crown of France for all eternity'. This caused great alarm in the Republic. Some, according to Alexander van der Capellen, were convinced that all the Netherlandish provinces, including those united in the Dutch Republic, 'were also promised in marriage in secret articles'. Other regents believed that France had concluded a separate peace with Spain.'[169] The rumour of the French-Spanish betrothal threatened to paralyse the preparations for the 1646 campaign. The French plenipotentiaries in Münster denied the story's veracity most emphatically, but distrust was more easily sown than dispelled. In Holland 'people began to be more apprehensive about the proximity of France, through [her] occupation of Flanders together with the other Spanish Netherlands, than they were fearful of the Spaniards'.[170] On 28 February 1646 the States of Holland promulgated a resolution in which they declared: 'That France, having been enlarged with the Spanish Netherlands, shall represent a formidable body for this State. That having over-powerful neighbours has always been deemed highly dangerous for all states. That the nature of the French nation is touchy and restless.'[171] In an attempt to calm the mood and limit the damage, with the aid of Holland's deputy

---

verhoudingen tijdens de Vrede van Munster', in Jacques Dane (ed.), *1648 Vrede van Munster. Feit en verbeelding* (Zwolle [1998]), pp. 83–105.

[167] Groenveld, 'Unie, Religie en Militie', pp. 70–1.
[168] NA, SG 6769, Willem van Lier to the SG, Paris, 3 February 1646.
[169] Van der Capellen, *Gedenkschriften*, II, p. 141. See also Poelhekke, *Vrede van Munster*, pp. 241–2.
[170] Van der Capellen, *Gedenkschriften*, II, p. 143.
[171] Quoted in Poelhekke, *Vrede van Munster*, p. 256. See also Werner Hahlweg, 'Barriere – Gleichgewicht – Sicherheit. Eine Studie über die Gleichgewichtspolitik und die Strukturwandlung des Staatensystems in Europa 1646–1715', *Historische Zeitschrift*, CLXXXVII (1959), 54–89, esp. p. 59.

to the States-General, Amelis van den Bouchorst (†1669), lord of Wimmenum, a member of Holland's Knighthood, Frederik Hendrik engineered the approval by 'Holland' of a resolution in which the States-General instructed their ambassador in Paris to ask for clarification from Mazarin while also giving him orders to press for renewal of the subsidy treaty. Van Lier was at the same time to request an additional sum of 400,000 guilders as a mark of France's good faith, over and above the usual subsidy of 1.2 million guilders, 'to herewith extraordinarily … levy' 4,000 infantrymen for the Dutch army.[172] Frederik Hendrik hereby hoped to rebut the rumour and simultaneously safeguard the execution of the 'grand design'. As soon as Wimmenum's high-handed actions came to the attention of The Hague, the States of Holland distanced themselves in the most vigorous terms,[173] but the resolution could no longer be withdrawn because Van Lier had in the meantime delivered it to Mazarin.

Mazarin swore to the Dutch ambassador that there was no question of a marriage with the Spanish Infanta. According to the cardinal, Madrid had disseminated this rumour in the hope of 'tempting [the Republic] into separate negotiations through jealousy'.[174] He was, however, forced to acknowledge that there had been talks with the king of Spain about the possibility of an engagement and that it was correct that the Spanish Netherlands had been mentioned as dowry.[175] The rumour of a marriage might not have been correct, but the plans for an engagement, the start of the peace negotiations in Münster and the actions of the French during the 1645 campaign – their unexpected advance on Bruges – were, according to the leading regents in Holland, more than enough reason to question the desirability of a new campaign. When, during an assembly of the States of Holland on 23 March 1646, Wimmenum disclosed that 'serious efforts' were being undertaken in the States-General to persuade Holland to consent to the recruitment of 6,000 *waardgelders*, the release of 1 million guilders for the costs of the forthcoming campaign – 'the half of this to be promptly furnished before the middle of April' – and the renewal of the subsidy treaty with France, Holland's deputies decided to postpone a decision on all these matters indefinitely.[176] The Hollanders were, however, forced to admit that the position of the Dutch negotiators in Münster would be bolstered greatly if the Republic had a large army in the field. To sound out the mood, in mid-April 1646 the stadholder of Friesland, Willem Frederik, held an informal meeting

---

[172] NA, SG 6769, Willem van Lier to the SG, Paris, 17 March 1646.
[173] In a resolution of 16 March 1646 the States of Holland declared 'that which has been done by the lord of Wimmenum at [the assembly] of the Generality shall be disavowed and will be disavowed herewith by their Noble Great Mightinesses as having taken place without the knowledge of the State [and] contrary to the order of the government, likewise contrary to the instruction of the deputies of their Noble Great Mightinesses at the assembly of the Lords States-General'. NA, SG 6769, Extract res. SH, 16 March 1646.
[174] NA, SG 6769, Willem van Lier to the SG, Paris, 17 March 1646.
[175] Poelhekke, *Vrede van Munster*, p. 242.
[176] NA, RAZH, ASH 79, Res. SH, 23 March 1646.

in Amsterdam with the bailiff, Pieter Pietersz. Hasselaer (1583–1651), and the two burgomasters, Gerard Simonsz. Schaep (1598–1666) and Cornelis Bicker (1592–1654), a younger brother of Andries, the leader of the 'Bickers League', the dominant political faction in Amsterdam. During the meal they talked about all manner of business, but then alcohol started to loosen tongues, as Willem Frederik recorded in his journal.

> Towards the end it went to our heads somewhat, then Bicker began to open up [to me] and said they no longer had any appetite for the war and must first pay their debts before they consented to new consents for the costs of a campaign.... Ultimately, being very inebriated, he did [however] tell me that I could assure His Highness [Frederik Hendrik] that they [Amsterdam's regents] would table a fine resolution. For His Highness's sake they would still be prepared to do it [i.e. fight another campaign] should it come to that.[177]

The subsidy treaty between France and the Republic had in the meantime, on 17 April 1646, been renewed in Paris. On 3 May the States of Holland affixed its stamp of approval, but not whole-heartedly. Now their critique was that ambassador Van Lier, pressurised by Mazarin, had given the undertaking that the Republic would besiege a major town in the Spanish Netherlands and would in addition provide a fleet to support the French in the besieging of Dunkirk.[178] According to the Hollanders he had exceeded his mandate, 'as howbeit ... [his] power ... was to strive after no other end than [to broker] a treaty of subsidy'.[179] Despite this objection the renewed treaty was ratified on 11 May,[180] but only after Holland had received the assurance from Frederik Hendrik that negotiations in Münster would be pursued with gusto.[181] The following day Estrades promised an additional subsidy of 300,000 guilders, sufficient to employ 3,000 infantrymen for the duration of the campaign, and shortly thereafter Amsterdam consented to the raising of 6,000 *waardgelders*. Frederik Hendrik could begin with the preparations for the 'grand design'.[182]

At the end of June 1646 approximately 25,000 Dutch troops were ready to sail for Sas van Gent, from where the expedition to Antwerp would be continued over land. Frederik Hendrik had received the commitment from Paris that the French army would dispatch an auxiliary corps of 6,000 men, so he would have more than 30,000 men at his disposal to invest Antwerp. The main French army would in the meantime threaten Dunkirk and thereby tie the majority of the Spanish field troops to the coast. The prospects of a successful siege of

---

[177] Visser, *Dagboeken van Willem Frederik*, pp. 228–9.
[178] NA, SG 6769, Willem van Lier to the SG, Paris, 7 and 28 April 1646.
[179] NA, RAZH, ASH 79, Res. SH, 17 April 1646 (quote); Visser, *Dagboeken van Willem Frederik*, pp. 228–9.
[180] NA, RAZH, ASH 79, Res. SH, 17 April and 3 May 1646; SG 6769, Extract res. SG, 11 May 1646.
[181] Poelhekke, *Vrede van Munster*, pp. 263 and 270.
[182] Visser, *Dagboeken van Willem Frederik*, pp. 232, 237, 246 and 248.

Antwerp were therefore more favourable than ever before, but an unexpected demand from the French side threw everything into the air again. As a precondition for providing troops the French stipulated 'that in this place [Antwerp] which we [the Dutch] are taking with their assistance, one would allow the Catholic religion'. This stipulation was in accordance with the alliance of 1635, but over the previous decade the French had not even mentioned it. The French demand meant the deathblow for the 'grand design'. The Amsterdammers were not adamantly against the allocation of a few churches to the Catholics, but then their city had to be allowed 'to build two papist churches in Amsterdam in order to keep the [Catholic] merchants in Amsterdam who would otherwise move to Antwerp'.[183] For the Counter-Remonstrant faction this solution was, however, unacceptable. In order to achieve something of significance with the Dutch army in 1646, Frederik Hendrik turned his attention to Bruges. The French ambassador promised him that France would likewise make 6,000 men available for this siege operation.

In Münster the negotiations between the Republic and Spain had by now reached a decisive phase. The growing distrust between The Hague and Paris gave the Spanish plenipotentiaries a wonderful opportunity to elaborate a separate peace settlement with the Republic. On 17 May they had already hinted that Philip IV was prepared to recognise the independence of the Republic and would assent to the permanent 'closure' of the River Scheldt (the relevance of this was that all shipping to and from Antwerp would be regulated by Dutch tariffs and trade stipulations), would permit the levying of import duties in the Flemish seaports as high as those on the River Scheldt, and would agree to cede the Meijerij of 's-Hertogenbosch. The provision concerning the seaports offered the Hollanders and Zeelanders guarantees against Antwerp's possible plans to transform Ostend into an outport by digging canals, thus re-establishing her former trading status.[184] The king of Spain and his new chief minister, Don Luis Mendez de Haro (1598–1661), were prepared to grant these concessions because they thought they offered the only means of retaining the Spanish Netherlands. Because of the uprisings in Catalonia and Portugal, Madrid could no longer contend with France and the Republic simultaneously.[185] After the conclusion of the previous year's campaign, Castel Rodrigo had warned Madrid that he considered the loss of the Spanish Netherlands but a question of time.[186] In the summer of 1646 it seemed his prediction would become reality. On 29 June the French captured Courtrai, so that Lille and Ghent were threatened with a siege. The negotiations in Münster gained momentum. The Dutch and Spanish

---

[183] Ibid., pp. 250–1.
[184] Israel, *The Dutch Republic and the Hispanic World*, p. 360; Victor Enthoven, 'Zeeland en de opkomst van de Republiek. Handel en strijd in de Scheldedelta c. 1550–1621', Ph.D. diss., Leiden University (1996), pp. 109–10.
[185] Lynch, *Spain under the Habsburgs*, II, pp. 125–9.
[186] Vermeir, *In staat van oorlog*, p. 287.

negotiators reached agreement on almost all the important points within the week, so the signing of a truce or perhaps even a separate peace agreement was imminent.[187]

In mid-July 1646 the Dutch army landed near Sas van Gent. Maréchal Antoine III, duc de Grammont (1604–1678), arrived at the Dutch army camp on 22 July with 4,500 French troops, which was 1,500 fewer than promised. Frederik Hendrik then established a position near Lokeren, midway between Ghent and Antwerp, but nothing else happened.[188] A stroke temporarily robbed him of his power of speech and forced him to rest for several weeks.[189] The main French army had in the meantime laid siege to Bergues. This fortress fell on 1 August. The French wanted to push on to Dunkirk, but Frederik Hendrik, who had by now recovered somewhat, had no intention of assisting them by diverting Spanish troops to Bruges, Ghent or Antwerp.[190] The prospect of the notorious privateers' nest falling into French hands filled the people of Holland and Zeeland with horror. Frederik Hendrik's personal motives also played a part in his passive stance. After all, was it not the attitude of the French that was to blame for his being denied his most coveted prize? Capturing Antwerp would have silenced the critics of his generalship once and for all. When Grammont kept on insisting that the Dutch should create a 'diversion' to clear the way to Dunkirk for the French, Frederik Hendrik responded in no uncertain terms on 21 August 1646: 'The times are now very different to before, for since you visited me the States have made peace, so my doing this is out of the question.'[191] Formally speaking this was incorrect, but in point of fact this was the case. Three days earlier the States of Holland had adopted a resolution which stated that the States-General had to impress upon the French ambassador that the Republic's depleted finances justified the signing of a separate agreement with Spain.[192]

The French continued their triumphal march in Flanders. They captured Fort Mardyck on 25 August 1646 and Veurne (Furnes) on 5 September. There was no longer anything preventing the investment of Dunkirk.[193] The Hague urged Frederik Hendrik 'to act ... with the army of our State', because otherwise France

---

[187] Poelhekke, *Vrede van Munster*, p. 271.
[188] NA, SG 4984, Field deputies to the SG, Sas van Gent, 21 and 24 July; Locheren, 30 July 1646.
[189] Poelhekke, *Frederik Hendrik*, p. 549. On 4 July 1646 Willem Frederik noted in his journal (p. 251) that Frederik Hendrik was terribly 'weak' and that he 'is now very childlike towards Her Highness [Amalia van Solms]'. According to Schöffer ('De Republiek', p. 241), Frederik Hendrik had 'grown old early and [was] mentally enfeebled [when he] died in 1647'; L.J. Rogier, *Grote Winkler Prins* (7th edn, Amsterdam and Brussels 1968), VII, p. 718, points out that from 1641 Frederik Hendrik's 'physical and mental powers ... diminished rapidly'.
[190] NA, SG 4984, Field deputies to the SG, Sint-Gilles, 22 and 28 August 1646.
[191] Visser, *Dagboeken van Willem Frederik*, p. 265.
[192] Poelhekke, *Vrede van Munster*, pp. 306–7.
[193] NA, SG 6769, Tieleman Aquilius to the SG, before Fort Mardyck, 16 and 25 August; Veurne, 6 September 1646.

alone would pluck the fruits of this last coordinated attack on the Spanish Netherlands. Frederik Hendrik briefly toyed with the idea of laying siege to Antwerp, Ghent, Bruges or Damme, but his senior officers were unanimous that 'under these circumstances and in this expiring season … [it is] impossible'.[194] Frederik Hendrik then proposed sending the army to the garrisons, but the States of Holland would hear nothing of it.[195] The Dutch commander-in-chief subsequently ordered the troops to be transferred to Bergen op Zoom in the hope of being able to launch a surprise attack on Lier, but the Spaniards took up a position near Duffel, a village midway between Mechelen (Malines) and Lier, and from there covered both towns.[196] Next Frederik Hendrik resurrected an old plan: he proposed heading to the River Meuse and clearing the lines of communication with Maastricht. The Hague granted its consent, as this was better than doing nothing. On 2 October 1646 the French cavalry left the Dutch army; the infantry had already left to join the main French army before Dunkirk some three weeks earlier. The following day the Dutch troops set out for Venlo, arriving there a week later (10 October 1646).[197] The French captured Dunkirk that same day.[198]

In Venlo lay a garrison of only 400 to 500 men. To save time and money Frederik Hendrik decided neither to realise a line of circumvallation nor to await the arrival of all the siege artillery. A couple of days later he had to pay a heavy price for this. On 16 October, at about nine in the morning, an estimated 600 to 700 Spanish soldiers managed to enter the town. That same afternoon the defenders launched a succession of three 'furious' sorties, 'drove our men far away and if it were not for Colonel Wijnbergen who came to relieve Colonel Erentreiter in the approaches, the enemy could have gained a great advantage over us, but were repulsed'.[199] Five days later, on 21 October, the Spaniards succeeded in bringing fresh troops into Venlo once again, this time a 'whole' regiment of no fewer than 900 men. The field deputies then asked Frederik Hendrik whether he still saw a chance of capturing Venlo under such circumstances, to which he curtly responded in the negative.[200] The siege of Venlo was raised on 29 October and

---

[194] NA, SG 4984, Field deputies to the SG, Sint-Gilles, 28 August (first quote) and 16 September 1646 (second quote); Visser, *Dagboeken van Willem Frederik*, p. 267.
[195] The Waller Manuscript Collection, Uppsala University Library (http://waller.ub.uu.se/images/Waller_Ms_benl/00151/f_001a.jpg, accessed 24 September 2009), Jacob Cats to Frederik Hendrik, n.p., 10 September 1646, copy. My thanks to M. van Groesen for this reference.
[196] NA, SG 4984, Frederik Hendrik to the SG, Bergen op Zoom, 22 September 1646; field deputies to the SG, same place and date.
[197] NA, SG 4984, Field deputies to the SG, Sint-Gilles, 11 September, before Venlo, 11 October 1646.
[198] NA, SG 6769, Tieleman Aquilius to the SG, Dunkirk, 11 October 1646.
[199] NA, SG 4984, Field deputies to the SG, before Venlo, 19 October 1646.
[200] NA, SG 4984, same to same, before Venlo, 21 October 1646.

the Dutch troops departed for the garrisons. This marked the conclusion of the final campaign of the Eighty Years' War.

The States of Holland had in September 1646 already proposed to the other provinces that the Republic should no longer negotiate with Spain about a truce but about an enduring peace. Three months later the last obstacles to a Dutch-Spanish peace had been removed. Philip IV had declared he was prepared to recognise as Dutch possessions all the conquests won by the Dutch East and West India Companies in America and Asia since 1641. The king of Spain had opted for this remarkable step because the loss of these territories did not affect Spain but hit the rebellious Portuguese, and in exchange the Republic promised to suspend trade with the Spanish colonies forthwith.[201] Alexander van der Capellen thought that peace could now be concluded as soon as the provinces had reached agreement about the Dutch army's peacetime strength. He warned his brother that France and Sweden, 'being intent on continuing the war, shall undoubtedly enlard and promote all the impediments that are raised by one or other of our provinces and would prefer nothing less than to see that ... we continue to bear the burden of the war [on our shoulders] if they might part company with advantage'.[202] According to Van der Capellen, the French stance justified a breach of the French-Dutch alliance, in which it was agreed that only a collective peace would be concluded with Spain. Holland nevertheless maintained its standpoint that the determination of the Dutch army's peacetime strength was not yet under discussion. The Hollanders were moreover of the opinion that the size of the armed forces should not be fixed for a long period of time but should be the subject of further discussion each year.[203] The preliminary points were signed by the Dutch and Spanish negotiators in Münster on 8 January 1647.[204]

Frederik Hendrik did not witness the conclusion of the peace between the Republic and Spain: he died on 14 March 1647, aged sixty-three. His health had long been cause for concern, as noted, but he had reacted furiously to any insinuation of devolving his offices of stadholder and captain-general of the Union to his twenty-year-old son.[205] Concern about whether Willem II actually had the abilities to take the helm of the Republic at this critical juncture was the main reason why he had not been willing to relinquish these positions until his

---

[201] Poelhekke, *Vrede van Munster*, pp. 308–10; Israel, *The Dutch Republic and the Hispanic World*, pp. 366–7 and 369.
[202] GA, FAvdC 70, Alexander van der Capellen to his brother Henrik, Boedelhof, 25 February 1647.
[203] Groenveld, 'Unie, Religie en Militie', pp. 70–1.
[204] Israel, *The Dutch Republic and the Hispanic World*, p. 370.
[205] In August 1646, frustrated by Frederik Hendrik's passivity, *maréchal* Grammont had wanted to tell the captain-general of the Union 'that His Highness could no longer lead an army, must entrust it to [his son] Prince Willem'. However, the field deputies had dissuaded him from speaking to Frederik Hendrik in such a manner. Visser, *Dagboeken van Willem Frederik*, p. 265.

death. It was, after all, to be expected that Holland's opinion about the peacetime strength of the Dutch army would lead to considerable tension between the provinces, and many regents questioned whether Willem II possessed sufficient political acuity and tact to prevent the differences of opinion being carried to an extreme. On 17 March 1647, three days after the death of Frederik Hendrik, Alexander van der Capellen wrote to his brother:

> The discords between and within the provinces require a leader who holds the members together, restraining the extravagant within the limits [of the Union] with authority and offering a firm hand at the helm of the ship [of state] that [will face] all manner of winds created to drive it hither and thither. It would have been desirable that this lord [i.e. Frederik Hendrik] would have been allowed [to live] to witness the conclusion of the negotiations with Spain.

Van der Capellen had no confidence that Willem II could assume this role: 'The respect for the young ... prince is too weak.'[206]

In 1650 the disagreements about the size of the Dutch army would lead to a profound political crisis in the Republic, but for the moment the concerted struggle against Spain held the provinces together. The formal signing of the peace between the Republic and Spain took place on 30 January 1648. The ratification followed on 4 April, carried by five votes against two (Zeeland and Utrecht). The Thirty Years' War drew to an end in October 1648, with the emperor, France, Sweden and the German princes abandoning their struggle in the Holy Roman Empire. Yet the war between France and Spain continued unabated; Paris and Madrid did not conclude the Peace of the Pyrenees until 1659.

Conclusion

The Republic's campaigns from 1635 to 1646 were dominated by Antwerp. Without this major town on the River Scheldt an invasion of the Spanish Netherlands from the north was a well-nigh impossible undertaking. Bruges and Ghent could also have served as operational bases for the Dutch army, but the problem with this route of attack was that the Spaniards could defend the canal from Ghent to Bruges very effectively. There was no other route by which the Dutch troops could penetrate into the Spanish Netherlands, as demonstrated by the fiasco of the 1635 campaign. On the face of it the possession of Maastricht, Venlo and Roermond offered the Republic an ideal opportunity to approach Brussels from the east, but it was impossible to exploit this strategic advantage due to the lack of the appropriate logistical facilities. A large field army gave the aggressor no advantage when the steady flow of food supplies was uncertain; all it created was difficulties. A force of 20,000 to 25,000 men could live for a

---

[206] GA, FAvdC 70, Alexander van der Capellen to his brother Henrik, Boedelhof, 17 March 1647.

while on the stocks of food that were available in nearby towns and villages, but an army of 50,000 men faced starvation almost immediately. Frederik Hendrik's 1635 plan to press on to Brussels via Tienen and Louvain was sound from a purely military perspective, but from a logistical viewpoint it was extremely risky. It was at least ill-considered to allow the food supply for 50,000 soldiers to be almost wholly dependent on provisions that would have to be seized in hostile towns. Frederik Hendrik should have known better. He had, after all, participated in the 1602 campaign himself.

There were also risks associated with the siege of Antwerp. After all, this undertaking required that the attacking army split itself into two parts, because wholly investing Antwerp was possible only when army camps were established on both the Brabant and Flanders sides of the River Scheldt. This resulted in an extremely long circumvallation, extending over a distance of approximately forty kilometres, no less than an eight-hour march.[207] To guard this line effectively required an army of at least 30,000 men, of which 8,000 to 10,000 were needed to man the positions on the Flanders side of the Scheldt and 20,000 to 22,000 to man the positions on the Brabant side. For the attackers the greatest danger during the siege resided in the security of the lines of communication between the two encampments, which would have to be ensured via bridges. High water or storm conditions would, however, endanger the bridges' integrity and the Spaniards would then have an opportunity to crush the smaller Dutch force.

It is likely that Frederik Hendrik's repeated attempts to capture Antwerp, Ghent or Bruges would have been crowned with success if 35,000 to 40,000 men had been available to him instead of 25,000 to 30,000. It would, however, be incorrect to ascribe the lack of these extra 10,000 troops to misplaced frugality on the part of Holland. The statement of financial incapacity that the States of Holland presented to the States-General in August 1646 was not an opportunistic argument to justify the breach of the French alliance. In April 1647 the Hollanders were justified in pointing out that 'the great work of the war has now for many years in succession been built on a simple negotiation, floating only on a sniff of credit ... such that ... Holland in particular cannot be considered anything but a hollow tree, the fruits of which are sufficiently consumed by the payment of the annual interests'.[208] The seriousness of this problem had for quite a while remained hidden due to the system of military solicitors, but from the mid-1630s it was evident that war expenditure had to be reduced. Responsibility for the annual shortfalls could no longer be shifted onto the shoulders of the solicitors and the company commanders. It was due to this rather than Holland's disinclination to support Frederik Hendrik's war policy that the Dutch army had an effective strength of 60,000 men instead of the 80,000 men on paper.

[207] Visser, *Dagboeken van Willem Frederik*, p. 248.
[208] Zeeland's deputy to the SG, Jacob Veth, 19 April 1647. Quoted by Kluiver, *De souvereine en independente staat Zeeland*, p. 208.

Frederik Hendrik was fully aware that conquering the Spanish Netherlands was beyond the powers of the Republic, which was the very reason he considered the French alliance necessary. He was, however, insufficiently aware that the interests of the Republic and France did not always run parallel with one another and from the 1640s were even diametrically opposed. Louis XIII and Richelieu were focused on destroying the might of the Spanish Habsburgs, while for the Dutch regents the struggle against Spain was about safeguarding the Republic's sovereignty. The Dutch were therefore proponents of the reduction of Antwerp, but their distrust of the functionality of the French alliance grew once it became evident that the military operations in the Spanish Netherlands were almost exclusively to France's advantage. Breda, Gennep, Sas van Gent and Hulst were no more than consolation prizes compared with the conquest of Antwerp, Ghent, Bruges and Dunkirk. The French were much more successful in combating Spain: in 1637 they captured Landrecies, in 1640 Arras, in 1643 Thionville, in 1644 Gravelines, in 1645 Béthune, Lillers and Saint-Venant, and in 1646 Courtrai, Bergues, Fort Mardyck, Veurne and lastly even Dunkirk. The Spanish readiness to comply with all the Republic's demands in exchange for peace contrasted starkly with the 'egoistic' behaviour of the French ally. Frederik Hendrik's opposition to concluding a peace with Spain without France evaporated in 1646 due to the French demand of permitting open observance of the Catholic faith in Antwerp. Though Paris was formally acting in accordance with the treaty of 1635, until then the French had not even mentioned it. The French government bringing forward its standpoint 'on principle' and making French military support for the siege of Antwerp conditional on compliance with it can only be described as a political stroke, intended to deny the Republic the most important reward that might have resulted from the French-Dutch alliance. For Frederik Hendrik himself the French position represented a slap in the face: the 'Tamer of Towns' was being humiliated, and not by the Spanish fiend but by his French friend.

Concluding Remarks to Part I

Could the Republic of the United Netherlands have decided the Eighty Years' War by military means? This question can only be answered in the negative, by reason of weapons technology, fortifications engineering and logistical factors, but the root cause of this military incapacity was the nature of relations between the state and the armed forces. This complex of issues has been central to the preceding chapters. To conclude Part I they will be revisited and viewed as a cohesive whole.

The tacticks of Aelian and *The art of embattailing an army, or The second part of Aelian's tacticks*, translated and annotated by Captain John Bingham, a veteran of the Dutch army, were published in England in 1616 and 1629, respectively.[1] In both works Bingham stressed the importance of studying the tactics from classical antiquity for combat in his own era. Willem Lodewijk also attached great import to the *Tactica*, written circa AD 100 by the Greek military author Aelian. In his famous letter to Maurits of 18 December 1594 he translated the commands used by Aelian into Dutch and provided a commentary to Aelian's treatise on the drill and tactics of the infantry.[2] Willem Lodewijk did not indiscriminately adopt Aelian's views. Although there were important similarities between sixteenth-century combat and classical warfare – the armies were predominantly infantry and the taking of towns was pivotal – there was also a fundamental difference: the Greeks and Romans did not have firearms. During the winter of 1594/5 and the following summer Willem Lodewijk devised a new firing method known as the 'conversion', an adaptation of the 'choreian' or 'Cretan' countermarch. After firing a salvo the soldiers first cleared the unit's front by marching to its flank and then filed to the rear instead of immediately making an about-turn and retiring individually. This solution meant that each battalion presented a more serried front and, as the soldiers were not allowed to shoot until given the command, made it possible to maintain strict firing discipline.

The development of a method that made orderly volley fire possible is widely considered to be one of the most important military innovations of the early modern era. The admiration for volley fire did, however, have a tendency to wane among contemporaries, witness Bingham feeling it necessary to passion-

---

[1] Captain John Bingham, *The tacticks of Aelian* (London 1616; facsimile edn, Amsterdam and New York 1968) and *The art of embattailing an army* (London 1629; facsimile edn, Amsterdam and New York 1968).
[2] Hahlweg, *Die Heeresreform der Oranier*, pp. 607–10; Parker, 'From the House of Orange to the House of Bush', p. 180.

ately advocate battle in the open field in his preamble to *The art of embattailing an army*:

> And whereas many hold opinion that it sorteth not with the use of our times, they must give me leave to be of another mind. Indeed our actions in warre are onely now a dayes and sieges oppugnations of cities. Battailes wee heare not of, save onely of a few in France and that of Newport in the Low-Countries. But this manner will not last always, nor is there any conquest to be made without battailes.[3]

The major pitched battles during the Thirty Years' War – Breitenfeld (1631), Lützen (1632) and Nördlingen (1634) – as well as the battle of Rocroi (1643) seemed to prove Bingham right. However, none of these victories achieved a decisive outcome: the struggle in the Holy Roman Empire continued through to 1648 and the Franco-Spanish War did not end until 1659. During the second phase (1621–1648) of the Eighty Years' War, the Dutch and Spanish troops skirmished frequently, but Frederik Hendrik never once gave battle.

Writing in the early eighteenth century, the French quartermaster-general and theorist, Puységur, retrospectively formulated the view that

> the greatest change in the ancient battle orders has occurred since the employment of firearms. For since then it has not been possible for the men to bear defensive arms, to protect themselves from strikes, as they did previously. The long range and power of firearms have obliged the armies to maintain an even greater distance from one another.[4]

In other words, the introduction of firearms and the development of orderly volley fire in particular had fundamentally altered tactics, but the likelihood of achieving a decisive victory was at the same time reduced. Owing to the fact that joining battle at a distance had become prevalent, from then on hand-to-hand fighting rarely arose in the open field. Infantry armed with pikes, halberds and swords had an offensive capability and could carry the battle by knocking out the enemy in the hand-to-hand struggle. The introduction of the matchlock musket in the mid-sixteenth century had reinforced the defensive, because battle could then be joined at a distance.[5]

Volley fire transformed the troops equipped with firearms into the most important category of foot soldiers by potential, but the matchlock's sensitivity to weather conditions, the complicated loading process, the impossibility of ranging the musketeers shoulder to shoulder – 'for the musquettiers cannot be so close in files, because they must have their arms at liberty'[6] – and the lack of a weapon which the marksmen could use when unable to shoot meant that the musketeers were a vulnerable group. A functional bayonet which did not hamper the

---

[3] Bingham, *The art of embattailing an army*, 'The epistle dedicatory'.
[4] Puységur, *Art de la guerre*, I, p. 105.
[5] Hall, *Weapons and Warfare in Renaissance Europe*, pp. 170 and 175.
[6] Bingham, *The tacticks of Aelian*, p. 154.

loading and firing of the musket would only be developed towards the end of the seventeenth century. Without such a weapon the musketeers could not expose themselves to the perils of hand-to-hand combat, and this was exacerbated by their vulnerability to the fast-moving cavalry. This was why Willem Lodewijk and Maurits continued to attach great importance to pikemen. Pikemen were the only infantrymen who could withstand a cavalry attack, as demonstrated in September 1643 when the Dutch cavalry lured part of the garrison of Antwerp into an ambush. Six companies of Spanish infantry formed a square and put up 'great resistance'; they did not allow themselves to be taken prisoner until they were completely surrounded by the Dutch infantry.[7] By the late sixteenth and early seventeenth century the offensive might of pikes was exploited but rarely. Assaults against fortifications and field positions formed an exception, as in 1640, when Dutch troops stormed a fort near Hulst, which was described by a Dutch colonel who witnessed the assault:

> They [the Spaniards] then fled to a large, square, stone redoubt ... [which was furnished] all around with embrasures and was flat on top, whence they fired bravely.... Because it was very rainy weather ... we could do them no harm with muskets. But they could amongst us. So we brought our pikemen in front of the embrasures from which they were shooting down, through which [our pikemen] thrust with pikes from all sides, so that the enemy had to retreat up above onto the flat section.[8]

The inability of the Dutch and Spanish army commanders to decide the Eighty Years' War by means of victories on the battlefield was not simply a result of shortcomings in weaponry; the widespread adoption of the bastion system in the Low Countries was another contributory factor. The besieging of towns and forts protected by thick, earthen ramparts with bastions required an enormous investment of time. With the exception of stratagems and surprise attacks – such as the peat barge of Breda (1590) and the surprise attacks on Wesel in 1629 and on Fort Schenkenschans in 1635 – a fortified town could, as a rule, be reduced only after a formal siege of several weeks or months. In an area with a dense network of strongholds it was difficult to achieve a strategic breakthrough, and even more so when the belligerents were numerically and qualitatively well matched, which resulted in wars of attrition. However, the more deep-seated reason for the Republic failing to achieve final victory in the Eighty Years' War was inherent in the relationship between the state and the armed forces, in conjunction with the absence of the need to modify this. After 1590 it was no longer a question of the Republic being involved in a 'struggle for existence'.[9] Spain's intervention in the French civil war, which had flared up again in 1589, allowed the Dutch rebels to consolidate and reinforce their territorial basis. In

---

7   Tresoar, FSA 30, Willem Frederik to the SvF, Bergen op Zoom, 4 September 1643.
8   Bergsma, *Poppo van Burmania*, Entries for 22 June/2 July 1640.
9   Hahlweg, *Heeresreform der Oranier*, p. 9.

1597 the 'garden of the Republic' had been ring-fenced. This transformed the Revolt into a war between states, the struggle being played out along the frontiers. The Republic was no longer embroiled in a struggle for survival, but was increasingly pursuing an offensive war with the object of eliminating Spanish power in the Low Countries.

When one surveys the organisation of the Dutch army in the period 1588–1648 one is immediately struck by the mutual distrust between government and troops. There was no basis for trust whatsoever: the provincial States and the Council of State suspected the officers of perpetrating fraud in every way imaginable; the officers, in turn, were convinced that the paymasters were trying to shift as much as possible of the responsibility for the costs of waging war onto their shoulders. Both accusations were justified, but it would be incorrect to conclude from this that the company commanders were keen to engage in fraudulent practices or that the regents intentionally left the troops in the lurch financially. The latter was indeed the case in France,[10] but the Republic could hardly afford to pursue such a policy. The French government, ruling a population more than ten times greater than the Republic (approximately 18 million people compared to between 1.5 and 2 million), could, after all, draw from a much greater reservoir of captains of foot and of horse than the seven provinces.

To a large extent foreign troops made up for the limited recruitment potential within the Republic, but the financial footing of foreign officers was often less secure than that of indigenous company commanders. In the Republic there was therefore a more acute awareness of the exigency to be sparing with the officer corps than in France. With the exception of the unrepartitioned troops, who were largely left to their own devices, the States-General and the provincial States strove to care for the Dutch army as well as possible, at least as far as the payment of wages was concerned. However, the regents did not properly appreciate that this would not suffice: because the company commanders were saddled with footing the bill for the replacement of soldiers killed in action or seriously wounded – on top of the costs incurred as a result of desertion – they were 'forced, against their will, to steal'.[11] Instead of the government providing the captains and rittmasters with the requisite financial elbow-room, thus making it possible for them to replace those lost in action swiftly, the company commanders were actually penalised by the reduction in pay ordinances. The captains and rittmasters could expect an increase in the company's pay only after a subsequent muster, and until then they had to maintain the recruits from their own pockets. This resulted in a vicious circle: the government ascribed more or less the entire discrepancy between the army's paper and effective strengths to fraud and was therefore hardly inclined to defray part of the company commanders' expenses or to lend them financial support; to hedge against this the officers made wide-

---

[10] Parrott, *Richelieu's Army*, pp. 350–3.
[11] NA, Tweede Afdeling, CG 305, no. 36.

spread use of *passe-volants* during muster to make it seem their companies were at full strength.

The deep-seated distrust between the paymasters and the army had grave consequences for the war effort. While the government still regarded the company commanders as suppliers of mercenaries instead of as leaders of professional soldiers recruited by order of the state there would continue to be a gaping chasm between the actual and paper strengths of army units. During the campaign, losses were rarely replaced, if at all, which resulted in the fighting strength of the armies dwindling rapidly. Commensurate with this, the ability of the military and political leaders to force a decisive breakthrough in the conflict was reduced. The transfer of the costs of the company's upkeep to the officers had the added effect of curbing army expansion. The choice of company commanders was thereby limited to those who possessed sufficient financial reserves or could access enough credit to be able to bank-roll a company independently. With the *solliciteurs-militair* the Republic held an important trump card, but the events of the 1630s and 1640s demonstrated that there were also limitations to this form of army finance. Holland's financial problems led to unacceptable pay arrears that could no longer be absorbed by the officers and their private financiers.

This naturally broaches the question of how on earth it was possible that the States of Holland were unable to raise sufficient revenue from taxation and loans to alleviate the army's financial problems while the volume and scope of Holland's mercantile economy saw an enormous spurt in the seventeenth century. The explanation for this must be sought in a combination of three factors: 1. the way in which warfare was generally regarded until the 1660s; 2. the military situation in which the Republic found itself after 1590; and 3. the peculiar character of its model of governance. In short, the early modern state wanted its involvement with the armed forces to remain as indirect as possible, with all the adverse consequences that have been mentioned. That said, with a difference of about one-quarter between paper and actual strengths the Dutch army still compared very favourably with the French and Spanish forces. In the 1630s and 1640s the French army boasted 120,000 men on paper but was in reality no more than 80,000 strong; the Spanish army surpassed this with a strength on paper in 1625 of no fewer than 300,000 men but an effective strength of 'only' 150,000.[12] In Spain's case this spectacular discrepancy was the result of empty government coffers, while in France an extremely inefficient system of tax collection and deliberate neglect of the army were to blame.[13]

For the Republic, the circumstance that new taxes could not be imposed from above but had to be introduced by the States of the individual provinces was the reason why the riches of her inhabitants could not be tapped without restraint. The regents were mindful not to incur the wrath of the populace by imposing

---

[12] Parker, *The Military Revolution*, p. 45.
[13] Parrott, *Richelieu's Army*, pp. 237 and 348–53.

too high a tax burden. The unfettered floating of loans was equally impossible, because then an ever-greater proportion of each year's tax revenues would be absorbed by the payment of interest and repayment of the principal. Otherwise the government's creditworthiness would be undermined. Between 1600 and 1632 the Dutch Republic's war effort was indeed escalated further, but this was far from whole-hearted. The regents were prepared to consent to army reinforcements only when specific circumstances made this unavoidable, as in 1629, when the Republic had to wage war on two fronts. They lacked the will to foreshorten the struggle by means of a war effort temporarily intensified to the maximum possible level. As a result the officers could not count on government support, and the raising of extra troops was permitted only under exceptional circumstances. The size of the Dutch army in the 1630s and 1640s therefore remained at a ceiling of 80,000 men on paper and 60,000 men in reality. The exigency of leaving behind garrisons in approximately one hundred strongholds, forts and sconces meant, moreover, that there were on average no more than 20,000 to 25,000 troops available for field service each year.

Logistical factors exacerbated the strategic deadlock in the Low Countries. Difficulties with provisioning not only imposed a ceiling on the size of the field armies but also hampered their deployment. The lack of a specialised logistical apparatus meant that military operations within enemy territory were a highly risky enterprise and was also the reason why troop concentrations were subject to a maximum of 25,000 to 30,000 men even within one's own borders.[14] Larger field armies evaporated into thin air because of hunger. While the armies were operating close to their bases, for their proviant the soldiers could turn to the sutlers, the independent vendors who accompanied the troops on campaign and purchased their supplies *in situ* from local bakers, farmers, brewers, butchers and suchlike. Deep inside enemy territory this method of provisioning was feasible only when the army managed to capture a large town or city, or when the inhabitants of several smaller towns and villages in the army's vicinity could be persuaded to trade with the sutlers; provisioning then proceeded in the same manner as within one's own borders. One strict precondition for this form of provisioning was that discipline among the troops and the army-followers had to be rigorously enforced and plundering had to be refrained from, for otherwise the villagers and farmers took flight *en masse*, giving rise to a guerrilla war which meant that provisioning the army camp was wholly impossible. One can find innumerable examples of this during the Thirty Years' War, and the Low Countries were certainly not spared such excesses.

The sacking of Tienen in 1635 provides the most telling example of this, though it is true that it was primarily the French who were guilty of wholesale

---

[14] Parrott underscores this in his article 'Strategy and Tactics in the Thirty Years' War', p. 239: 'Even in the more prosperous 1630's, battles involving substantially more than 20,000 troops were rare. Breitenfeld [1631], with 41,000 Swedes and Saxons set against Tilly's 31,000 troops, was unique down to the 1660's.'

37. Looting of a village in the Netherlands. Oil painting by Pieter Snayers (c. 1592–1669). (Royal Netherlands Army Museum, Delft, 050702)

plunder and pillage. In September 1641, for example, they torched more than thirty villages in Flanders and destroyed a further 500 houses on the outskirts of Lille.[15] In July 1646 the French did not baulk at plundering churches, country manors and villages, even though their owners and inhabitants had paid their contributions. 'Which causes even greater scarcity of vivres here,' the field deputies reported from the Dutch headquarters, 'the people of the countryside fearing to use the roads.'[16] It is therefore hardly surprising that the Southern Netherlanders hated the French the most vehemently and that the French troops suffered more greatly from hunger than the Republic's men. The rural population and the Dutch company commanders benefited from Frederik Hendrik's efforts to limit war damage, but it yielded the Union's captain-general no military-strategic advantage so long as he did not simultaneously have special logistical facilities available to him that would enable him to assemble an army of 30,000 or more men. Maurits and Willem Lodewijk had ensured there were mobile field-ovens in 1602, but this was no more than a one-off experiment. Frederik Hendrik occasionally ordered the milling of a quantity of flour and in 1635 he also ordered the baking of long-lasting rusk, but these supplies were sufficient for only a limited time; even the Dutch depended on local supplies for their

---

[15] NA, SG 4978, Field deputies to the SG, Assenede, 17 September 1641.
[16] NA, SG 4984, same to same, Locheren, 30 July 1646.

vivres. In addition they lacked the requisite number of waggons to be able to transport the bread from magazines to the army camp over greater distances.

Field armies of 20,000 to 25,000 men were advantageous from a logistical viewpoint, because the victualling did not present any insurmountable problems, but this was too small a force to penetrate into the Spanish Netherlands from the north. An army of this size was sufficient for an attack from the east using Maastricht as a base, but this route of invasion was hardly attractive for logistical reasons; the supply lines would have soon become far too long. This could have been resolved by establishing a depot in Louvain, but Brabant's geography meant that the Spaniards were able to establish strong positions in this particular region. This left just one viable path of invasion: Antwerp. Possession of this city would afford the Republic access to four rivers: the Scheldt, Leie, Dijle and Demer. Control of these major waterways was indispensable for a successful push into Brabant and Flanders; otherwise the transport of foodstuffs, siege artillery and munitions was well-nigh impossible. Besieging Antwerp called for a military force of at least 30,000 men: 20,000 to 22,000 men were needed to hem in the city on the Brabant side; the remaining 8,000 to 10,000 men were needed on the Flanders side. Because of the proximity of Bergen op Zoom, the Republic enjoyed the fortunate advantage that provisions for 30,000 men could be conveyed with ease during such an operation, but with the exception of 1645 and 1646 Frederik Hendrik had never been in command of so many troops. The Spaniards, moreover, enjoyed the advantage of the inner lines, so they could swiftly shift troops between the Flanders and Brabant sides of the Scheldt.

The need to commit tens of thousands of Dutch soldiers to garrison duties and the disparity of approximately 20,000 men between the Dutch army's paper and effective strengths were the two main reasons why Frederik Hendrik failed to break the strategic deadlock in the Low Countries. He had himself to blame for a third factor: because of his rift with the Arminian faction in 1633 he had estranged the wealthiest regents, who had the greatest vested interest in persecuting the war in Europe. The alliance with France (1635) ought to have obviated the harmful consequences, but an undesirable side-effect of the close cooperation with Catholic France was that the Counter-Remonstrant faction grew distrustful of continuation of the war as well. The Counter-Remonstrants were deeply unhappy about Article V of this treaty, 'as it speaks of the Romish religion and the promise to leave it and the clergy in the state one finds them in towns apportioned to us [by treaty]'.[17] By devoting due consideration to the trading interests of the Arminian faction when determining the operational goals it seemed that Frederik Hendrik's plan for an invasion of the Spanish Netherlands could depend on broad support from the regents. The capture of Dunkirk, Bruges, Ghent and Antwerp would, after all, be advantageous to the Republic's

---

[17] NA, Aanwinsten Eerste Afdeling 105, Notes from the memoirs of Alexander van der Capellen, 9 April 1635.

security as well as to its trading interests. The mood started to shift when it became clear that only France was reaping the benefits of the Franco-Dutch alliance. Frederik Hendrik did too little to effect a change in this situation; in the years after 1632 there is little evidence of the Republic's commander-in-chief's pluck and resourcefulness. Either the 'contrary winds' prevented him launching a surprise attack or he deemed the Spanish positions to be too strong to force and too 'periculous' to outflank. At long last, in 1645, Frederik Hendrik had 30,000 men at his disposal, but instead of exploiting this opportunity to lay siege to Antwerp he did nothing. The following year, when it came to light that Madrid and Paris were negotiating the betrothal of the king of France with one of Philip IV's daughters and when, as a precondition for providing assistance to the Dutch for an assault on Antwerp, the French stipulated that observance of the Catholic faith would have to be permitted there, any lingering support within the Republic for continuing the war evaporated.

Given the Republic's inability to decide the Eighty Years' War militarily, what import should be attached to the military reforms of the Nassaus? Is the British historian David Parrott right to assert that their significance was largely propagandistic in nature?[18] It is true that the army reforms of the Nassaus had barely any impact on the structure of the Dutch army and nor did they effect a change in relations between government and troops. In fact there is no evidence of army reforms whatsoever. It would, instead, be better to speak of the *tactical* reforms of the Nassaus, which immediately indicates their significance. Because they ensured the constant drilling of the Dutch troops and the development of a method for effective volley fire, Maurits and Willem Lodewijk must be given credit for the Republic having at its disposal an army that could hold its own against the best troops in Europe, namely the Spaniards. The renowned nineteenth-century Dutch army officer and historian W.J. Knoop took the view that Maurits and Frederik Hendrik were each other's equals as commanders-in-chief, but that 'there is one aspect which elevates Maurits above his brother: when Frederik Hendrik served as general he found a fine, pre-established army; Maurits created his army himself'.[19] However, Maurits must share this honour with Willem Lodewijk, the driving force behind the development of effective volley fire. The high level of proficiency among the Dutch troops became the benchmark by which all European armies set the bar from then on. With the States of Holland's resolution of 6 October 1627, which obliged the captains to

---

[18] See Parrott, *Richelieu's Army*, p. 26: 'Military success in the decade of the 1590s, when the reputation of the reformed army was established, owed more to the absence or reduced scale of the Spanish army than to any demonstrable superiority of Dutch fighting methods. However, encouraging the notion that the Dutch army had undergone a decisive improvement in organization and fighting techniques was obviously in the interests of the Republic and its princely generals, as a means to convince both wavering citizens and undecided foreign powers that the United Provinces could sustain their independence into the future.'
[19] Knoop, *Willem den Derde*, I, p. 12.

collect new firearms from the arsenal in Delft from then on, the tactical revolution was accomplished. Volley fire would dominate the battlefield within Europe and beyond until the mid-nineteenth century.

Developments in France during the 1660s were to lead to a revolution in military organisation that resulted in a massive expansion of army establishments. As a result the Dutch army would also undergo structural reforms. A decade earlier the Dutch navy had undergone a similar development in response to the lessons learnt during the first Anglo-Dutch War. In the years 1657–1666 all manner of deficiencies and abuses in the Dutch army came to light during military operations against the bishop of Münster, but domestic political matters specific to the Republic had precluded the land-based forces being reformed by that time. No reforms were initiated until 1667, when the Republic was faced with the threat of war with the France of the Sun King. From 1672 these reforms gained momentum and a structural shift came about in the relationship between state and army. In the years 1667–1688 the Dutch army would be transformed into a standing army of professionals, which is the development addressed in Part II of this book.

PART II

1648–1688

✦ 7 ✦

The Dutch Army under Johan de Witt and William III (1648–1688)

During the first half of the seventeenth century the Dutch army was reputed to be the 'school of Mars',[1] but just a few years after the Peace of Münster there was little evidence of the renowned discipline and high level of proficiency of the Republic's troops. During the war with Münster (1665–1666) the Republic was barely able to withstand Prince-Bishop Christoph Bernhard, *Freiherr* von Galen (1606–1678), and the first great trial of strength against the Sun King – the 'Guerre de Hollande' or Dutch War (1672–1678) – almost spelled the demise of the United Provinces.

This chapter addresses three pivotally important issues: first, how the decline of the Dutch army might be explained; this is followed by an analysis of why the attempts to restore the army undertaken in the 1650s and 1660s were such an uphill struggle and remained incomplete in their elaboration, when during those same years the Republic managed to establish a new war fleet; and lastly, an examination of how it was possible to structurally reform the Dutch army in short order after 1672. The development of the new Dutch army meant that, following the conclusion of the Peace of Nijmegen in 1678, the Republic had a well organised, highly disciplined and superbly drilled standing army at its disposal, an army which a decade later, at the start of the Nine Years' War (1688–1697), could be brought up to fighting strength easily without sacrificing quality.

The long shadow of the assault on Amsterdam (1650)

The desired peacetime strength of the Dutch army had been a point of controversy since 1643, the year in which the reduction demanded by the States of Holland was implemented. Frederik Hendrik and the Council of State had insisted on specifying its strength immediately, but Holland, Zeeland and Fries-

---

[1] Petrus Valkenier, *'t Verwerd Europa* (reprint; Amsterdam 1688), p. 20.

land had preferred not to commit themselves at that time. In 1647 the Council of State proposed retaining 39,000 men in service,[2] but Holland thought this was excessive. Three years later there was still no agreement on this point, though by then the discord was no longer about the desired size of the army but about its composition. In July 1650 a States-General committee chaired by Alexander van der Capellen had recommended reducing the Dutch army to 3,000 cavalrymen (52 companies) and 26,415 infantrymen (410 companies).[3] With a military force of this magnitude it would be possible to ensure the 'security and reputation of the State' during peacetime, but with fewer troops it would be impossible 'in times of hasty need to be able to bring into the field a corps sufficient for the preservation of the countryside and the rivers'.[4] Tens of thousands of soldiers had already been disbanded from Dutch service in 1648 and 1649, so only a further 5,095 men had to be dismissed to reduce the army to the intended size. The Van der Capellen committee proposed disbanding 1,340 cavalrymen and fifty-five infantry companies of fifty men each as well as reducing 201 infantry companies by five men apiece. The States of Holland were prepared to consent to this provided that two supplementary conditions were met: a further 300 cavalrymen had to be dismissed and the fifty-five infantry companies to be disbanded would have to be selected exclusively from the regiments of foreign troops. This would reduce the number of French, English and Scottish companies in Dutch service from 175 to 120. For Willem II this was unacceptable. The young captain-general of the Union had since 1641 been betrothed to Mary Stuart (1631–1661), eldest daughter of Charles I of England, who was beheaded in 1649. Willem II was keen to intervene in the English civil war which had broken out in 1642 in support of his brother-in-law, the later Charles II (1630–1685). He then intended to resume the struggle against Spain in conjunction with France.[5] However, the only chance of his ambitious plans succeeding was if he maintained his hold over the Dutch army so that he could ultimately compel the unwilling regents to comply.

Maurits, Willem Lodewijk and Frederik Hendrik had, as we have seen, exploited the ousting of Van Oldenbarnevelt in 1618 to curtail the power of the provincial States in commissioning officers. From then on, as provincial captains-general, they had the final word in the appointment of officers of Dutch and German companies and of field officers. Their influence in the conferment of the captaincies and lower-ranking offices of 'foreign' companies (French, English and Scottish) was even greater, because new officers for these units were commissioned without first consulting the provincial States. The States of Holland's 1650 proposal to dismiss only French, English and Scottish troops was therefore

---

[2] Ten Raa, *Het Staatsche leger*, IV, pp. 138 and 158.
[3] GA, FAvdC 119, 'Staet van[de] militie met de voorslagh van reductie ende verminderinge gedaen 25 jul[i] 1650'.
[4] GA, FAvdC 119, Alexander van der Capellen, 'Voorslagen en[de] consideratiën op den nieuwen Staet van Oorlogh [1650]'.
[5] P. Geyl, *Oranje en Stuart 1641–1672* (2nd edn, Zeist 1963), pp. 41 and 57.

clearly intended to reduce Willem II's hold over the Dutch army and to reassert the authority of the provinces over the troops. That this was the main concern of the regents of Holland is unequivocally demonstrated by the provincial resolution already voted on in April 1650 to proceed with further army reduction, if necessary on their own authority. On 4 June 1650 they acted accordingly: Holland notified Willem II and the Council of State that thirty-one French, English and Scottish companies – precisely the province's share in the fifty-five infantry companies mentioned – would be disbanded within a fortnight.[6]

Willem II responded to Holland's coup with the infamous assault on Amsterdam. Through his domination of the *secrete besogne* he managed to garner an authorisation from the States-General to restore 'order' in Holland. Six prominent Holland regents were rounded up and imprisoned in Loevestein Castle. Willem II's cousin Willem Frederik had in the meantime been furtively preparing a military operation against Amsterdam. However, the surprise attack planned for the night of 29/30 July 1650 had to be aborted: when Willem Frederik's troops arrived before Amsterdam the gates were closed and the cannon had been positioned on the city walls. The Frisian stadholder still hoped to be able to change the minds of the Amsterdammers by presenting a justification for the military action authored by Willem II,[7] but the gates remained closed. However, after a blockade of four days, the great city had no choice but to acquiesce: Amsterdam was forced to accept the army size as proposed by the States-General, as well as agree to the six prisoners at Loevestein Castle being dismissed from their governmental posts and to the Bicker brothers, Andries and Cornelis, who had long held sway over Amsterdam's politics, being required to relinquish their offices.[8] Nevertheless, Willem II's triumph was a hollow victory. Even in Gelderland, which as a frontier province stood to benefit greatly from a powerful commander-in-chief, news of the assault on Amsterdam was received without jubilation. Gerlach van der Capellen (1627–1685) warned his father, Alexander, that in Zutphen there was

---

[6] J.A. Wijnne, *De geschillen over de afdanking van 't krijgsvolk in de Vereenigde Nederlanden in de jaren 1649 en 1650 en de handelingen van prins Willem II* (Utrecht 1885), pp. 36, 46–7; GA, FAvdC 119, Alexander van der Capellen. In the margin of the 'Voorslagen' (Proposals) it states: 'On June 4th 1650 this was delivered in duplicate to His Highness, who agreed to consider it.'

[7] Willem II (The Hague, 29 July 1650) wrote: 'Lately, when officially in your city on behalf of the Land, I was received so strangely by you that, in order not to be subjected to such again, I wanted to billet Count Willem [Frederik] of Nassau with accompanying troops in your city, with orders to maintain everything there in peace and quiet, in order that what I have yet to propose to you regarding the service of the Land should not be denied me by anyone who is of ill intent.' An explanatory address was added to this letter at a later date: 'Missive from Prince William of Orange intended to be delivered by Count Willem [Frederik] ... into the hands of the burgomasters if he should have come into the city by surprise, in which, God be praised, he has failed.' See GAA, Missives to burgomasters 86 (microfilm 8040).

[8] Elias, *Het Amsterdamsche regentenpatriciaat*, pp. 128–9 and 132.

great alteration [i.e. displeasure] among the commoners about this Amsterdam affair. That His Highness, as stadholder, has committed an infraction against the right of the States of the province of Holland, and for this they shall relieve him of his stadholderate and appoint another. Most of the *jonkers* [i.e. landed gentry] here also judge His Highness to have acted highly irresponsibly.[9]

The seriousness of the unrest sparked in the provinces by Willem II's actions is demonstrated by the States-General's resolution of 18 August 1650. Though the members consented unanimously to the strength of the Dutch army as desired by Willem II, a majority demanded that the fifty-five infantry companies to be dismissed should belong exclusively to the 'foreign nation'. Remarkably the States of Friesland justified this decision by pointing out that if the domestic soldiers' market were no longer to be tapped then the Republic would become overly vulnerable: 'That ... the soldiery recruited [at home] in the [time] of need is unskilled and could not be had at the appropriate time, all the more because the inhabitants of these lands are more competent on water than on land and cannot be compared with the Swiss, [who] exercise with their weapons daily.'[10] Nothing came of Willem II's plan to intervene in the English civil war either. Holland and Zeeland continued to oppose this with might and main. Parliament had the powerful English fleet at its disposal, and Holland's and Zeeland's trading interests would therefore be damaged if the Republic sided with Charles II.[11] A couple of months later, on 6 November 1650, Willem II died of smallpox at the age of twenty-four. The First Stadholderless Era (1650–1672) had dawned.

Prince William III of Orange was born eight days after the death of Willem II, but the States of Holland, Gelderland, Zeeland, Utrecht and Overijssel decided to leave the office of stadholder vacant. To preclude the possibility that Dutch troops would ever again be deployed to bring towns with voting rights to their knees, Holland's deputies in the States-General swiftly pushed through the convening of a Great Assembly in The Hague.[12] The aim of this extraordinary gathering of delegates from all seven provincial States, which lasted from 18 January to 21 August 1651, was to take all kinds of decisions meant to wholly submit the Dutch army to the authority of the provincial States. The Hollanders pronounced that they regarded the following to be provincial concerns: 1. the appointment of stadholders 'or to refrain from doing so'; 2. 'the bestowal of the colonelcies, captaincies and lesser charges [in the companies] repartitioned to them'; 3. the appointment of commanders of towns and forts within the provinces with voting rights; and 4. troop movements within these provinces. The authority to appoint generals, colonels of foreign regiments and governors and commanders of towns and forts outside the voting provinces would reside

---

[9] GA, FAvdC 89, Gerlach van der Capellen to his father, Alexander, Budelhof, 5 August 1650.
[10] Wijnne, *Geschillen over de afdanking van 't krijgsvolk*, p. 163 and Appendix 17 (quote).
[11] Geyl, *Oranje en Stuart*, p. 53.
[12] Schöffer, 'De Republiek', p. 243.

with the States-General, while the issuing of marching orders or patents for the assembly of a field army remained the preserve of the Council of State. However, before withdrawing troops from voting towns – or indeed marching into them – prior permission had to be obtained from the town councils, and for marching across the territory of a province with voting rights a separate patent was required from the respective provincial States.[13]

The other provinces adopted Holland's proposals, which was understandable in the light of recent experiences with Willem II, but it led to all kinds of abuses and procedural rigmarole which had grave consequences for the cohesion, fighting strength and employability of the Dutch troops. These measures caused a fragmentation of the Republic's land-based forces, when for the quality of the Dutch army reduced to a minimal peacetime establishment it was vitally important that regimental cohesion should be preserved and the competence of the officers kept up to standard. The troops formally still fell under the Generality, but the Dutch army had effectively been broken up into seven small provincial armies. At the start of the eighteenth century the Dutch statesman Simon van Slingelandt commented in retrospect that it was as if 'the militia repartitioned among the respective provinces in the State of War is actually ... the militia of the province by which they are paid, in such a manner, however, that this province is obliged to use it and to allow it to be used for the Common Defence'.[14] Officer commissions were no longer decided by the candidate's experience and qualities, but rather by their relationships with provincial and urban factions. Petrus Valkenier (1638–1712), the author of 't Verwerd Europa – 'Europe in confusion' – a political-military history that was published during the Dutch War, complained that in Holland commissions to lieutenant and ensign were 'given away in turns by the Delegated Councillors and subsequently assigned to cousins and nephews'.[15] Though he was exaggerating, Valkenier's complaint was not unfounded, because the 'Ordre' of December 1618 had been rendered obsolete by the decisions of the Great Assembly. The appointment of captains and rittmasters was from then on the preserve of the States assembly of the province to which the company was repartitioned. In a resolution of 16 March 1651 the States of Holland had set out the procedure to be followed, which included the clause that 'in the appointment of the officers the procedure to be followed henceforth is by nomination of three persons and immediately thereafter to election, during the same session [of the States of Holland]'.[16] The lieutenant and the ensign or cornet were no longer automatically contenders for a captaincy or

---

[13] Lieuwe van Aitzema, *Saken van Staet en Oorlogh* (The Hague 1669), III, pp. 537–8 (quote); Ten Raa, *Het Staatsche leger*, V, p. 27.
[14] NA, RAZH, FAvS 246, Simon van Slingelandt, 'Memorie concerneerende de betrekking van de militie staande op den Staat van Oorlog tot de Generaliteit en tot de provinciën respectivelijk'.
[15] Valkenier, *'t Verwerd Europa*, pp. 253–4.
[16] NA, RAZH, FAH 5, Extract res. SH, 16 March 1651.

rittmastership that had fallen vacant and the stipulation that candidates should have at least four years of military experience lapsed.

The roundabout regulation of the patent right had a devastating effect on the Dutch army's employability: the Council of State was unable to maintain oversight of the location of all the Dutch troops, because the provincial States were empowered to move the troops within the province on their own authority. This lack of clarity was muddied even further by companies that, according to an official of the Council of State, 'are being sent to sea [with the fleet], but one does not know which, nor in which towns they have been garrisoned on their return'. He complained that there were also instances of patents being issued 'without name, date or place of destination' and that the provincial States issued marching orders to another captain without informing the Council of State, 'with the outcome that there are companies which have arrived in Generality garrisons from the provinces without knowledge of how and in what manner they have come to be there'.[17] The consequence of this confusion was that the Republic was unable to act decisively. In 1657, for example, the States of Overijssel high-handedly detained several companies from Utrecht and Gelderland in Zwolle 'until further orders', while the Council of State had ordered the captains and rittmasters to proceed to the army camp near Groenlo to prevent the bishop of Münster seizing the town of Münster by force.[18] This town was embroiled in a dispute with its bishop and had called on the Republic to help mediate in the conflict.

The Dutch army under Johan de Witt (1653–1672)

Johan de Witt (1625–1672), Grand Pensionary of Holland from 1653 to 1672, has entered history as the founder of Holland's new war fleet. He paid less attention to the Dutch army. According to the historian S.B. Baxter, De Witt deliberately ignored the abuses in the land-based forces because the only means of improving the army would have been to appoint William III as captain-general of the Union and De Witt feared that this would lead to the restoration of the stadholderate in Holland.[19] This serious allegation is baseless, though it is true that De Witt underestimated the problems in the Dutch army. In his voluminous biography of the Grand Pensionary, H.H. Rowen contends that what De Witt 'failed to see was the importance of a specific army esprit developed over

---

[17] NA, RAZH, FAvS 50, Petition to the SG from Pieter van Peene, transcript, with 'Remarques op de lijste van besetting' as an appendix. There is another copy of this petition in AJdW 2724-a. Van Peene was engaged in 1658 'for the despatch of the patents'.
[18] NA, SG 5016, Frederik Magnus von Salm-Neufville, Wald- and Rhinegrave, to the SG, Groenlo, 17 October 1657; SG 12548.353, Extract res. SG, 21 December 1657, with a letter from the RvS, The Hague, 21 December 1657, as an appendix.
[19] Stephen B. Baxter, *William III* (London 1966), pp. 57 and 59.

time; for him an army was a relatively simple apparatus, something to be bought, used, and dismissed, as the occasion required'.[20] For the Dutch army the lack of a commander-in-chief was not necessarily disadvantageous, as demonstrated by the military successes during the War of the Spanish Succession (1701–1713). This was, however, conditional on there being no fresh developments requiring a swift military response, when a captain-general of the Union would be indispensable, as he alone possessed sufficient authority to push through reforms effectively. The States-General was not the appropriate body for taking swift decisions and the Dutch generals were wary of shouldering responsibility for drastic military innovations, in the battle array, for example, 'because in case of defeat the blame would be attributed to that'. The generals were of the opinion that only a captain-general of the Union had a mandate to make such decisions.[21] Only a blood descendant of Prince William I of Orange was eligible for this most senior military office; in 1653 William III was only three years old. Moreover, for the anti-stadholderian faction his being appointed captain-general was out of the question under any circumstances.

Having an admiral-general of the Union was not a prerequisite for the Dutch navy's modernisation, because its organisation, financing, maintenance and deployment were assigned to five admiralty colleges. Fleet-related business was wholly dominated by Holland, where three of the five admiralties were based. The First Anglo-Dutch War, which broke out in 1652, caused the Republic considerable difficulties. The Dutch fleet was traditionally augmented with armed merchantmen during wartime, but such vessels were no match for the specialised English warships, which were armed with many more cannon. This prompted the States-General to order the construction of sixty new warships in 1653, and in January 1654 they decreed that none of the new ships could be sold without the unanimous consent of the seven provinces, marking the establishment of the Dutch standing navy. In the 1660s the Dutch battle fleet was expanded substantially. Between 1664 and 1667 a further sixty warships were laid down on the stocks, including twelve very large ships of the line. During the Second Anglo-Dutch War (1665–1667) the Dutch fleet won spectacular victories.[22]

The verve demonstrated in the transformation of the Dutch navy into a standing war fleet in the 1650s and 1660s contrasts starkly with the lethargy that took possession of the army during the same period. The explanation for this is that at sea the Republic was confronted with a superior opponent, while a comparable situation on land would not arise until 1667. The task of reforming the fleet was of a different order, both in magnitude and nature, than the task of reforming the Dutch army. The maritime historian J.R. Bruijn estimates the extent of the fleet personnel during the three Anglo-Dutch Wars of 1652–1654,

---

[20] Herbert H. Rowen, *John de Witt, Grand Pensionary of Holland, 1625–1672* (Princeton, NJ 1978), pp. 599 and 601 (quote).
[21] NA, CvdH 124, Memorandum by Lieutenant-General Daniël de Savornin (1669–1739).
[22] Bruijn, *Varend verleden*, pp. 90–103 and 112–15.

1665–1667 and 1672–1674 at between 20,000 and 25,000 sailors and soldiers, more than twice its size in 1642. 'These huge numbers', writes Bruijn, 'gain even more gravity if one takes into account that during these years the VOC [Dutch East India Company] needed at least four thousand men as well.'[23] In other words, in *wartime* the crew of the fleet was more or less equal in number to that of the Dutch army in *peacetime*. It is true that the navy had to compete with the merchant navy, but the Dutch army was just as reliant on an open labour market for recruits and the soldiers who were deployed on the warships were drawn from the Republic's army. The success of the fleet reform was therefore less a question of personnel than of material, involving the investment of millions in new warships. The 1664 decision to build twelve capital warships involved an outlay of 3 million guilders. A total of 12 million guilders was needed for the various fleet-building programmes during the 1650s and 1660s.[24] The costs of 'equipping', crewing and preparing the battle fleet for action came over and above this. It cost more than 7 million guilders to keep a fleet of eighty-four large warships, six 'robust frigates' and twenty-four fire-ships at sea for half a year.[25]

The appointment and quality of Dutch officers

Following the death of Willem II, Field-Marshal Johan Wolfert van Brederode, aged fifty-one, stood at the head of the Dutch army, though his authority could hardly be compared with that of Maurits, Frederik Hendrik or Willem II. Because of the combination of their functions of stadholder/provincial captain-general and of supreme commander they had the decisive say in the commissioning of officers, whether of 'indigenous' or foreign troops. Brederode's command extended over the Dutch field troops, and 'for the rest the field-marshal is without function when there is no army in the field'.[26] He had no influence over the appointment or promotion of officers and nor was he empowered to dismiss company or regiment commanders. The abolition of the post of captain-general of the Union had a noticeably adverse effect on discipline in the Dutch army almost immediately. Field-Marshal Brederode cautioned De Witt in December 1653:

> Your Honour is to please take into account *that the English troops ought to be regulated on a different footing*, for it is shameful and scandalous how licentiously the officers in all the frontier towns talk about the Republic and, furthermore, their companies are not very special and rob the State to such an extent that it is insufferable.[27]

---

[23] Ibid., p. 165.
[24] Ibid., p. 101.
[25] NA, SG 3932, Secret res. SG, 25 December 1673, minute.
[26] Van Slingelandt, *Staatkundige geschriften*, IV, p. 133.
[27] NA, RAZH, AJdW, Johan Wolfert van Brederode, 's-Hertogenbosch, 14 December 1653.

Brederode had few positive things to say about the Dutch officers either, for when the States-General decided to combine twenty-nine Dutch cavalry companies into a field corps in the winter of 1653/4, at the review it came to light that only six rittmasters were actually present: 'There are companies among them that do not have a single officer with them, but are led only by a corporal.' Brederode urged De Witt to reprimand the absent rittmasters.[28]

Brederode died in 1655. Stadholder Willem Frederik of Friesland and Lieutenant-General Johan Maurits of Nassau-Siegen were both contenders for the vacant position of field-marshal, but looking to the future the States of Holland did not deem it prudent to place a cousin of the prince of Orange at the head of the Dutch army. In 1657, when the three northern provinces and Zeeland persisted in pressing for the appointment of a field-marshal, the regents of Holland declared 'that the army was provincial and that no military chief could be imposed upon any province by the Generality.'[29] There was no urgency to appoint a new field-marshal, according to the States of Holland, until it was made necessary by a threat of war. With this standpoint the Hollanders made it abundantly clear that, in their view, the highest authority over the troops resided with the individual provinces to which the companies were repartitioned. In effect the provincial States were now appropriating the supreme command for themselves. De Witt, who already effectively fulfilled the tasks of an admiral-general, now assumed responsibility for more than half the Dutch army as well. An arduous task awaited him, as insubordination had increased hand over fist since the death of Brederode. In order to gain a clearer picture of the gravity of the situation, in early November 1657 the States-General asked Major-General Frederik Magnus von Salm-Neufville (1607–1673), Wald- and Rhinegrave, to report on the condition of the army, 'now it had been resting and rusting for nine to ten years.'[30] The Rhinegrave, as this officer was usually referred to, had just returned from the camp by Groenlo, where he had been in command of fifty-three infantry companies and fourteen cavalry companies. He presented his findings on 20 November 1657, whereupon the Council of State instigated an investigation into the state of the Dutch army. On 27 December the findings were presented to the States-General, prompting a committee from the States of Holland to subject the report to further scrutiny. This ultimately resulted in a voluminous report which was published on 5 April 1658 under the title 'Redres ende reglement op 't stuck van de militie' (Redress and regulations on the matter of the army).

Its authors began by pointing out that 'the respect which the lesser officers owe their commanding officers has degenerated appreciably'. As a cause for this they pointed out the procedure followed since 1651, by which lieutenants

---

[28] NA, RAZH, AJdW, Johan Wolfert van Brederode, 's-Hertogenbosch, 5 December 1653.
[29] NA, FAF 1023, Notes by Hendrik Fagel regarding the appointment of field-marshals. See also Ten Raa, *Het Staatsche leger*, V, p. 55.
[30] Van Aitzema, *Saken van staet en oorlogh*, IV, p. 91.

38. Frederik Magnus von Salm-Neufville (1607–1673), Wald- and Rhinegrave, Dutch major-general and governor of Maastricht. (Collection NIMH)

and ensigns were appointed directly by the province's Delegated Councillors. Maurits and Frederik Hendrik, by contrast, had always consulted with the colonels first. The report's authors recommended the revival of this practice 'in order to be well informed of the capability, length of service and comportments of the candidates'. The authority of the colonels would have to be bolstered further by requiring new lieutenants and ensigns to present their letters of appointment to the regiment's commander within a specified, short timeframe 'in order thereby to become known to them'. The critique of the rapporteurs was not, however, limited to the lieutenants and ensigns; the quality of captains and rittmasters also left a lot to be desired. Many of the company commanders were young and inexperienced. They therefore recommended the strict enforcement of the stipulations of the 'Ordre' of 1618 insofar as these had any bearing on the criteria that someone had to meet in order to be eligible for an officer's rank.[31] The States of Holland concurred with the committee's conclusions and decided that in the appointment of new company commanders they would once again 'seriously and primarily pay heed to those who have made themselves recommendable through their services and courageous deeds'. Furthermore, if someone had not 'effectively served the Land under arms' for at least four years he was ineligible for the rank of rittmaster or captain, and in addition the candidates had to be of a certain age, set at nineteen and seventeen years, respectively. A minimum age of seventeen and at least three years of military experience was established for the ranks of ensign, cornet and lieutenant. It is remarkable that attention was also devoted to the sergeant who, 'although belonging to the lowest officers, [is] of no small consideration in respect of exercises, order and otherwise'. Research had revealed that this office was often entrusted to 'domestic' servants of the captains and lieutenants. To banish this abuse, from then on nobody 'who is not completely expert and singularly proficient' could be promoted to sergeant. To ensure that this was the case, only someone who had served for at least four years as a soldier was considered a candidate for the rank of sergeant, and as proof of his ability he had to undergo a practical exam.

When strictly adhered to, the 'Redres en reglement' of 1658 was advantageous to veterans as well as to promising young officers who lacked the right connections. James Balfour, for example, had already served in the Dutch army for thirty-two years, twenty of them as a lieutenant, when the captain of his company died in November 1657. The colonel of the regiment, John Kirkpatrik, petitioned Holland's Delegated Councillors to 'beneficе' Balfour with this vacant captaincy.[32] Fifteen years later this same colonel advised assigning a company to Lieutenant Alexander Hay. Holland's Delegated Councillors paid heed to this

---

[31] NA, RAZH, ASH 91, Res. SH, 5 April 1658; HUA, HAA 2970, Extract res. SH, 5 April 1658 (quotes).
[32] NA, RAZH, AJdW, John Kirkpatrik to the Delegated Councillors of Holland's South Quarter, Poederoijen, 24 November 1657.

advice, despite 'this same Hay having absolutely no kinfolk here in this land'.[33] In 1659 Johan Maurits of Nassau-Siegen recommended the appointment of Johan Adolfsen Groothuysen as cornet in his company. Groothuysen was 'not only ... of a fine and eminent house, but since his youth ... [has] also practised all the noble exercises and has served in my company of horse for more than eight years now, so [I] have no doubt at all about his capacity'.[34] Promotion on the basis of merit and military experience was a prerequisite for professionalisation of the Republic's officer corps, but once abuses had become the norm they were difficult to eradicate. In early July 1658, Hieronymus van Beverningk (1614–1690), a highly influential Holland regent and treasurer-general of the Union since 1657, sent word to De Witt from Maastricht that the whole garrison was in uproar,

> on the assumption that the Lords States of Holland currently in session, were intending to dispose of vacant [i.e. captainless] companies.... And I am therefore importuned by various people [to write] some letters of recommendation to my friends, but have thus far declined to do so, because I am not in the least of the opinion that there is the semblance of such a disposition, and in any case I am not pleased to meddle with such solicitations. Yet this fine old officer, Rittmaster Hay, who in his long-lasting and considerable services still deserved to be taken into consideration ... has not desisted from pressing me for this.[35]

English and French officers even endeavoured to use diplomatic channels to exact a promotion from The Hague. In 1661, some three years after the introduction of the new regulations, there were still companies to be found 'where none of the three high officers [the captain, the lieutenant and the ensign] understood the evolution [i.e. the manual of arms] or the ... drill'.[36] It was obvious that the 1658 regulations required further sharpening to be properly effective. Holland's Delegated Councillors were commissioned to formulate improved regulations concerning 'the conferment of the companies ... that fall vacant'.

On 9 April 1661 De Witt advised upon the plan of the Delegated Councillors, whereupon the States of Holland promulgated a new 'Ordre en[de] forme op 't begeven van[de] compagni[e]ën' (Order and procedure for the conferment of companies). At the next meeting of the States of Holland the companies of the 'indigenous nation' with a vacant captain's position would first be allocated to 'reformed' (i.e. unemployed) captains and rittmasters, as well as to lieutenants who commanded the companies of colonels, lieutenant-colonels or majors 'in so far as these lieutenants have in time of war served as lieutenants or as ensigns'. If additional captaincies were vacant, then these posts were to be filled from among the lieutenants who served in the company of the deceased commander. On the face of it this measure seemed to ensure that from then on it would be experience alone that counted in the appointment of new captains and rittmasters, but

---

[33] NA, RAZH, AJdW, same to same, 's-Hertogenbosch, 27 May 1672.
[34] NA, RAZH, AJdW, Johan Maurits of Nassau-Siegen, Cleves, 14 May 1659.
[35] NA, RAZH, AJdW, Hieronymus van Beverningk, Maastricht, 7 July 1658.
[36] NA, RAZH, AJdW, Amory van Hallart, The Hague, 23 July 1661.

appearances are deceptive. The number of men from the first two categories who would be eligible for the captaincy of a vacant company would be decided in the States assembly 'by separate rounds with the most votes ... and subsequently which persons among them shall be employed to that same defined number'. For this round of promotions the members would therefore have to present sound arguments for wanting to pass over an experienced 'reformed' captain or lieutenant for a younger lieutenant with no war experience, but the influence of connections was certainly not eradicated by this supplementary rule. Quite the contrary, because all the captaincies that fell vacant thereafter would be assigned as of old in the next meeting of the States of Holland 'by prior nomination ... and will then be bestowed by election from among the nominees during that same session'.[37] Abuses therefore continued. In September 1661, for example, the States of Holland assigned a company to Cornelis de Groot, *landdrost* or country sheriff of the Meijerij of 's-Hertogenbosch, 'in order therewith to partly extinguish the pretensions owing to Hugo de Groot's heirs by power of the ... sentence to their advantage pronounced by the Court of Holland against the town of Rotterdam'. Based on this same judicial pronouncement, Jean Barton de Bret (1623–1696), vicomte de Montbas, who was married to one of Hugo de Groot's daughters, was 'given to expect the first French regiment that shall come to fall vacant.'[38] His appointment as colonel followed on 9 December of that year.

*

While the abuses in the Dutch army were certainly not unique, the consequences were more serious than for other European armies, given that the Republic had relied on a small army for her security since the Peace of Münster and part of that force had to be deployed on the fleet because of the wars with England. In 1667, for example, more than 2,600 Dutch troops served on warships.[39] Most alarming, however, was that in those same years all kinds of measures were taken in France to improve the quality, employability and fighting strength of her land-based forces. This meant that in relative terms the Dutch army fell even further behind. That Holland failed to make haste with redressing 'the list of Holland's regiments', which had been specified in the 'Redres en reglement' of 1658, was therefore a missed opportunity. Preserving regimental structures had not been taken into consideration at all when the army's peacetime establishment

---

[37] NA, RAZH, AJdW 2720-2, Extract res. SH, 9 April 1661. 'The States of Holland have today bestowed their charges: Dolleman colonel, Cromwel lieutenant-colonel and the oldest captain of that regiment once again major. The Lord of Ghent's son and the youngest Dorp have each obtained a company of foot with unanimous votes, according to reports by those who were present', wrote Egbert van Baerdt, Friesland's deputy at the SG, to Willem Frederik, The Hague, 14 September 1663 (KHA, A25-VII-C84).
[38] KHA, A25-VII-C156, Willem van Haren (1626–1708), Friesland's deputy at the SG, to Willem Frederik, The Hague, 20 September 1661.
[39] NA, RAZH, AJdW 2724-a, 'Volck op zee gesonden den 28.en april en[de] 13.en mey 1667'.

was determined in 1650, and as a result there were cavalry regiments that were comprised of just two companies and captains 'who do not know whether they are ranged under a regiment and under which regiment, which could then cause disorder during combat with the colours, drumbeat and otherwise'. Until there was some improvement in this there was no means of restoring the Republic's army to its former 'glory and discipline'.[40]

In 1659, when the Peace of the Pyrenees was signed, the French army was in a sorry state and the companies fell far short of their establishment strengths. By disbanding half the infantry regiments and the majority of cavalry companies and incorporating these men into the units that remained in service, Louis XIV had a force with an effective strength of approximately 55,000 men at his disposal, which could serve as the basis for a 'new' French army.[41] Close collaboration between the Sun King and his two secretaries of state for war, Michel Le Tellier (1603–1685) and his son, François Michel (1641–1691), marquis de Louvois, led to a radical reorganisation of the French army between 1667 and 1671. The French land-based forces were for a while unrivalled. Le Tellier had held the post of secretary of state for war since 1643. In 1662 Louvois was appointed as the second secretary of state for war. During the War of Devolution (1667–1668) against Spain, the French army captured one stronghold after another in the Spanish Netherlands, but the Sun King understood that these successes were due to the weakness of the Spaniards rather than the superiority of the French army. A diversity of shortcomings that were detrimental to the French army's deployability had come to light during the campaign. Louvois was ordered to remedy these shortcomings so that in a subsequent war France would truly be the strongest military power. He could, in part, fall back on improvements already introduced by his father. Le Tellier's acumen lay primarily in logistics. He had been a driving force behind a permanent magazine system, but intervened in the army's organisation only when an acute problem brooked no further delay.[42]

Louvois' efforts were aimed at increasing the government's control over the army; only then could the discrepancy between paper and effective strengths be reduced to acceptable levels and the companies to a large extent rendered uniform in size and quality. Commissions for colonel and captain were still venal, but the functional ranks of lieutenant-colonel and major were from then on bestowed by the French crown. This made it possible to ensure that career officers retained oversight of a regiment's day-to-day management, and there were other advantages too. In 1667 and 1668 Louis XIV introduced a

---

[40] HUA, HAA 2970, Extract res. SH, 5 April 1658.
[41] Kroener, 'Die Entwicklung der Truppenstärken in den französischen Armeen', pp. 185 and 190–1; François Bluche, *Louis XIV* (New York 1990), p. 222.
[42] Douglas C. Baxter, *Servants of the Sword. French Intendants of the Army 1630–70* (Urbana, IL 1976), pp. 142–3, 164 and 169–70; Ronald Martin, 'The Army of Louis XIV', in Paul Sonnino (ed.), *The Reign of Louis XIV* (Atlantic Highlands, NJ 1991), pp. 111–26, esp. 112 and 115; John A. Lynn, *Giant of the Grand Siècle. The French Army, 1610–1715* (Cambridge 1997), p. 111.

new senior rank for the French infantry and cavalry, that of brigadier-general. It was customary for several regiments to be combined into brigades during the campaign. The question of who was allowed to command such brigades often sparked heated quarrels among the colonels, and the rank of brigadier-general was introduced in order to bring an end to this. Lieutenant-colonels and even majors could be promoted to this office, opening up other generalships to them in the future. More or less simultaneously Louis XIV decreed that the deciding factor among officers of equal rank was seniority of service, namely the date on which their commission was granted, and that the social status of the officers should no longer pertain. The Sun King and Louvois considered insubordination unacceptable, irrespective of a soldier's social background. In October 1668, Jean Martinet (killed in action in 1672), lieutenant-colonel in the 'Régiment du Roi', was appointed as inspector general of the infantry. It was his responsibility to introduce and enforce the drill and strict discipline of the French regiment of Guards across the whole infantry. A separate inspector general was appointed over the French cavalry.[43]

*

The war with Münster (1665–1666) and the War of Devolution (1667–1668) brought about a growing awareness in the Republic that measures needed to be taken to improve the organisation of the Dutch army, but vigorous measures were still not forthcoming. Thanks to hiring in Brunswick-Lüneburg's troops and the arrival of a French auxiliary corps – the Republic still being allied with France at the time – the bishop of Münster, being short of money, was forced to abandon his assault on the Republic after just one campaign and conclude the Peace of Cleves (18 April 1666), while the establishment of the Triple Alliance between the Republic, England and Sweden seemed to be sufficient to dissuade Louis XIV from attempting further conquests in the Spanish Netherlands, compelling him to conclude the Peace of Aix-la-Chapelle (2 May 1668). As a consequence, implementing swift and forceful reforms in the Dutch army was deemed unnecessary. 'There is peace, it is not so very urgent now', to quote a Dutch general's characterisation of the regents' prevailing attitude during peacetime.[44] This was a grave miscalculation. The majority of the Dutch troops had for almost two decades, since 1648, done nothing but sentry duty. Experience of fighting in formations above company level (battalions and brigades) was long forgotten and there were only a few Dutch officers who were still prepared to follow orders from superiors. In March 1666, when serving as commander of

---

[43] Guy Rowlands, *The Dynastic State and the Army under Louis XIV. Royal Service and Private Interest, 1661–1701* (Cambridge 2002), pp. 192–3; André Corvisier, 'Louis XIV, la guerre et la naissance de l'armée moderne', in Philippe Contamine (ed.), *Histoire militaire de la France*, i: *Des origines à 1715* (Paris 1992), pp. 383–413, esp. 402.

[44] Lieutenant-General Johan Dibbetz (1685–1745), foreword to *Het groot militair woordenboek* (The Hague 1740).

Groenlo, Colonel Otto, count of Limburg-Stirum (†1679), exacted a fire-tax in the bishopric of Münster, even though the Council of State had already issued safeguards. 'We hereby want to denounce to you our profoundly felt displeasure and indignation, with command and precise order to punctually respect our aforementioned safeguards and ensure they are respected', the Council of State fulminated.[45] Sometimes a fraudulent company commander was dismissed,[46] but absence without leave essentially remained unpunished. Captains, rittmasters, lieutenants and ensigns or cornets were often absent from their companies for weeks – if not months – on end. The Council of State could call upon officers to return to their units, but had no means at its disposal of punishing recalcitrants.[47] In June 1669, Major Joseph Bampfield, an officer who regularly advised Johan de Witt on military affairs, complained to the Grand Pensionary: 'I wish that all those who command in your army were Caesars, Hannibals and Gustavus Adolphuses, but in their present state an encampment lasting three months would be very much required to teach them the most necessary things before facing an enemy.'[48] The regulation of the ranks was the only improvement to have been implemented prior to the French attack of 1672.

Within the Dutch army a hierarchy of ranks had evolved over time. Until the mid-seventeenth century the hierarchy had been straightforward: Maurits, Frederik Hendrik and Willem II stood at the head of the Dutch army, and if a dispute arose about precedence then they themselves resolved it. In the infantry the ascending hierarchy of ensign, lieutenant, captain, major, lieutenant-colonel and colonel was widely accepted. In the cavalry this was more complicated. In 1635 the cavalry companies were also assigned to regiments, but the rittmasters contended that they 'must all be considered as colonels', and therefore considered themselves to outrank the infantry captains.[49] In 1665 this led to a problem in Zutphen: when the town's commander convened a council of war, the captains who held a commission longer than the rittmasters insisted 'that they also ought to sit and vote above these rittmasters, and the rittmasters argue the contrary ... consequently neither wanted to take their seats and therefore separated without [attending to] any business'.[50] In a wartime situation any quarrels about precedence could have serious consequences. In January 1668 the States-General therefore asked the Council of State to formulate an opinion 'on the subject of rank'. The outcome was presented on 21 April of that year. The Council of State

---

[45] NA, Tweede Afdeling, CvLS LN 38, RvS to Count Otto of Limburg-Stirum, The Hague, 3 March 1666.
[46] NA, RvS 488, Res. RvS, 2 November 1667.
[47] NA, RAZH, FAvS 50, RvS to the officer in command of the troops at Schoonhoven, The Hague, 17 February 1668.
[48] NA, RAZH, AJdW, Joseph Bampfield, n.p., 16 June 1669. See also Rowen, *John de Witt*, p. 809.
[49] NA, CvdH 124, Missive from the SG to the States of Friesland, 23 March 1671.
[50] KHA, A4-1466g, Major Alexander Schimmelpenninck van der Oye to Johan Maurits of Nassau-Siegen, Zutphen, 23 September 1665.

was of the opinion, first, 'that on the point of rank, with regard to the military functions, there ought to be no reflection on the quality [i.e. the social status] of persons invested with that [function], but only on the dignity of the function itself'. Secondly, that for officers of equal rank 'the prerogative of rank must be regulated according to the seniority of the commissions'. And lastly, no distinction was to be made between officers of the infantry and of the cavalry 'and that with no semblance of reason can it be asserted that any prerogative of rank appertains to the cavalry'. The Council of State recommended that the order of rank should be established as follows: 1. general or chief of the army; 2. field-marshal; 3. generals of the cavalry and infantry; 4. general of the artillery; 5. lieutenant-generals of the cavalry and infantry; 6. sergeant-majors of the army; 7. commissaries-general of horse; 8. colonels of foot and of horse; 9. lieutenant-colonels of foot and of horse; 10. majors of foot and of horse; 11. rittmasters and captains; 12. captain-lieutenants (i.e. a lieutenant who takes charge of a company in the absence of the commander); 13 lieutenants; and 14. cornets and ensigns. The Council of State concluded with the suggestion of modifying the function of the army's sergeant-major in such manner 'that it only came to extend over the infantry … and consequently that the said function is made parallel and equal to that of commissary-general of the cavalry'.[51]

The States-General failed to heed the advice of the Council of State until almost three years later, when on 23 March 1671 the recommendations were adopted almost unamended. A transitional arrangement was struck to lessen the pain somewhat for the majors, rittmasters, lieutenants and cornets of the cavalry. The cavalry officers who had received their commissions prior to 23 March 1671 would have 'precedence' over majors, captains, lieutenants and ensigns in the open field, but within strongholds and fortified positions the 'anciency' of an officer's commission would be the deciding factor. The rank of sergeant-major of the army and that of commissioner-general of the cavalry were put on the same footing – these general officers were subsequently designated as 'major-generals' – and the distinction between captain-lieutenants and normal lieutenants also lapsed.[52]

'Redress of the militia': attempts to restore the Dutch army's fighting strength

For the first twenty-five years after the Peace of Münster the company administration did not deviate from the practices in the era of Maurits and Willem Lodewijk. When assigned a company, the new captain or rittmaster had to pay the departing company commander or his widow an indemnity for the weapons

---

[51] NA, CvdH 124, Extract res. SG, 9 May 1668, with a missive from the RvS, The Hague, 21 April 1668, as an appendix.
[52] NA, CvdH 124, Extract res. SG, 23 March 1671.

and equipment, which often gave rise to disagreement. In 1649, Steffen Henrich van der Capellen, a nephew of Alexander van der Capellen, received a commission as captain of an infantry company repartitioned to Zeeland. His elation about this was short-lived: 'The company is not much to boast about, for the soldiers are for the greater part poorly clothed and so badly armed as I have never seen heretofore in the service of these Lands.'[53] The provincial paymaster's office continued to calculate the amount of pay that was remitted to the company commander based on the muster-rolls. However, the costs of maintaining a company proved to be higher in peacetime than in wartime, because in peacetime the commanders were unable to report some of the deserted soldiers as killed in action and were therefore forced to keep their units closer to their full complement. They could, of course, try to mislead the muster commissaries by hiring *passe-volants*. The repartition system worked to their advantage in this regard, for although Article VI of the 'Placaat op het stuk van de monsteringe' (Placard on the matter of the musters) dating from 1599 gave each province the right to muster all the troops in a particular garrison – including the troops paid by other provinces – until 1662 not a single province had made use of this right. However, in June of that year two of Holland's deputies appeared in Maastricht together with a muster commissary. They told the Rhinegrave, governor of Maastricht, that they wanted to muster the entire garrison, but he refused to cooperate, on the grounds that 'such a muster on the orders of one particular province was not in force and that on the basis of rumours the militia was apprehensive about Their Noble Great Mightinesses [the States of Holland] introducing some new measures, to which the companies standing on other repartitions could not defer'.[54] The Rhinegrave proposed the compromise of having the whole garrison 'pass in review' before mustering Holland's troops. This would prevent Holland's captains borrowing soldiers from colleagues to make their companies seem complete. This would achieve the States of Holland's objectives, but without causing unrest among the troops repartitioned to other provinces. On 30 June 1662 the whole garrison marched across the St Servatius Bridge to the suburb of Wijk, on the eastern bank of the River Meuse, in the presence of Holland's deputies, after which the troops from the other provinces returned to their lodgings and those paid by Holland were formally mustered.[55]

In early 1665 the impending war with Münster and England necessitated the reinforcement of the Dutch army. According to the Council of State the frontiers could only be secured if all the Dutch infantry companies were reinforced with twenty-five or thirty-six men and if 4,000 marines were recruited. The recruitment of marines meant that fewer ordinary soldiers had to be deployed on the

---

[53] GA, FAvdC 89, Steffen Henrich van der Capellen to Alexander van der Capellen, Fort Moerspui in States Flanders, 9 March 1649.
[54] NA, CvdH 107, Boll and Aemilius Cool, deputies of the States of Holland, to the Rhinegrave, Maastricht, 29 June 1662.
[55] NA, CvdH 107, The Rhinegrave to the RvS, Maastricht, 30 June 1662, copy.

fleet. This brought two advantages: more troops became available for the field army – in 1652 no fewer than 5,000 to 6,000 musketeers had been required to serve on the fleet[56] – and it facilitated the raising of recruits in the Holy Roman Empire, because among the Germans 'the apprehension about going to sea was so tremendously great that no persuasions, oaths, yea even written assurances that they would be let go as soon as there was the least apparency of going to sea, can be of any help'.[57] On Holland's insistence the States-General agreed to the captains receiving a recruitment fee of ten guilders for each new soldier levied on the frontiers of the Republic. In September 1665, when the war with Münster was a fact, this had to be raised to fifteen guilders, 'providing ... the aforesaid soldiers shall effectively ... be levied on the borders'.[58] The States-General concluded contracts for the raising of two new cavalry regiments of 500 horse each that same month. The rittmasters received 'riding money' of no less than 100 guilders per trooper.[59] Compared with the travel allowance that was remunerated prior to 1648 – three to five guilders for a Dutch or German recruit and ten to fourteen guilders for a cuirassier – in 1665 the government granted company commanders a much higher fee. The War of Münster compelled the Republic to reinforce her army quickly and this naturally worked to the advantage of the officers, whose negotiating position was strengthened. In 1668 the captains contracted to raise a new infantry regiment of 1,555 men stipulated a recruitment fee of fifteen guilders plus five guilders for marching money.[60] In 1671 the Council of State fixed the recruitment fee at twenty guilders for a footsoldier and 100 guilders for a trooper.[61]

The captains were not required to arm and equip new units themselves; the Council of State took care of this. For a company of 100 men, the depots of the Generality or the provinces provided sixty-two muskets, musket rests and bandeliers for the musketeers, thirty-four pikes, body armour, helmets and collars for the pikemen, two halberds for the sergeants, and two drums.[62] The monetary value of the weapons supplied – about 1,100 guilders – was as usual deducted from the men's pay, 'for the one half on the first ordinance of their pay and for the other half in the three subsequent ordinances'.[63] For the mounted arm the

---

[56] KHA, A25-VII-C-158, Cornelis Haubois (†1670), burgomaster of Sneek and deputy at the SG, to Willem Frederik, The Hague, 22 June 1652.
[57] NA, RAZH, AJdW, Major Christian van Wartensleben, Minden, 28 May 1672.
[58] NA, Tweede Afdeling, CvLS LN 38, RvS to Count Otto of Limburg-Stirum, The Hague, 29 September 1665 (quote); NA, RvS 86 and 488, Res. RvS, 22 and 30 January, 21 March and 30 September 1665.
[59] NA, Res. RvS, 29 September 1665, Contracts for two cavalry regiments.
[60] NA, RvS 89, Res. RvS, 4 April 1668.
[61] NA, RvS 548, Missive from the RvS to the SG, 17 November 1671.
[62] NA, RvS 86, Res. RvS, 1 and 7 October 1665.
[63] NA, RvS 548, Missive from the RvS to the SG, 17 November 1671. A musket with its rest cost three rix-dollars, a bandelier cost one rix-dollar and a complete pikeman's equipment cost five rix-dollars. NA, RvS 1902, 'Rekeninge van de wapenen van captein Lintelo van 't jaer 1672'.

39. A Dutch cavalry officer painted by Hendrick Berckmans, c. 1656. (Royal Netherlands Army Museum, Delft, 059183)

rittmasters were required to provide their cavalrymen with a fine steed, a sword, a carbine, a pair of pistols, a thick leather jerkin, a cloak, a cuirass protecting front and back, and a visored helmet.[64]

The proficiency of the Dutch troops had declined steeply after 1648. In 1657 the Rhinegrave was complaining that the fighting strength of the cavalry was

[64] NA, RvS 86, Res. RvS, 29 September 1665.

paltry. Most of the troopers were green and inexperienced, 'folk who had virtually bought their places [from the rittmasters] by offering to serve for a few months without pay, were concerned only with farming and civilian trades, [and] knew of war only by hearsay'. The horses were young and poorly trained. The Rhinegrave was equally unimpressed by the infantry: many soldiers did not recognise their officers and their weapons were for the most part worn out.[65] The Rhinegrave's report prompted the formulation of the 'Redres ende reglement op 't stuck van de militie' of 5 April 1658. The governors and fort commanders were from then on responsible for their garrisons being drilled in the 'most necessary exercises'. From 1 April to mid- or late September the soldiers on guard duty had to exercise every two or three days, the companies at least 'every month as a whole', and the regiments every two or three months.[66] Cavalry corporals were instructed to ensure that the troopers cared well for their geldings and that each of them 'knows how to bridle and saddle his horse adroitly and swiftly'. They had to have the cavalrymen ride their horses at least twice a week. The corporals were required to become more intensively involved with the training of raw recruits as well and had to instruct them individually: 'Teach him to handle the weapons competently: to load and fire his pistols and carbine, to grasp his rapier properly, to present it well and to re-sheath it with dexterity.' After the recruits had mastered the handling of their weapons they had to be 'drilled in squadrons, in the presence of the lieutenant or cornet', at least twice a week. When the rittmaster was present he had to exercise his company in person at least once a month.[67]

The reform of the cavalry bore fruit. Willem Frederik, who led a military operation in East Friesland in 1664, wrote to the States-General in May of that year that the cavalry in his corps 'was a delight to see, consisting of very fine men and advantageously mounted and equipped with such weapons that there is nothing to be improved or to be wished for therein'.[68] By contrast, no headway had yet been made with the reorganisation of the infantry. The infantry's much greater numbers – 25,790 men compared with 2,600 troopers – were certainly a factor, but more important was the lack of a central authority to maintain oversight of all military affairs. In November 1665 the States-General petitioned the Council of State to report on the expansion of the Dutch army which had been decreed earlier that year. The Council of State apologised for being unable to provide any precise information, as such figures were not forthcoming from

---

[65] Van Aitzema, *Saken van staet en oorlogh*, IV, p. 91, Report by the Rhinegrave.
[66] HUA, HAA 2970, Extract res. SH, 5 April 1658. Repeated in the 'Ordonnantie van den Raad van State ... op de exercitie van 's Lands militie', The Hague, 3 February 1671 (HCO, ASO 1458).
[67] NA, SG 12548.353, 'Loopende stucken raeckende het redres van 's Lants militie 1657 en[de] 1658' (quote); NA, Tweede Afdeling, CvLS LN 38, Delegated Councillors of Holland to Count Otto of Limburg-Stirum, The Hague, 14 April 1665.
[68] NA, SG 5034, Willem Frederik to the SG, Ulsen, 12 May 1664.

the provinces. In addition it came to light that the States of Gelderland, Zeeland, Utrecht, Friesland, Overijssel and Groningen had been remiss in a reinforcement of the companies of horse and of foot with thirty-one troopers and thirty-six infantrymen to which they had consented in June 1665. Only eight of the twenty-five cavalry companies and just fifty-five of the 165 infantry companies had been strengthened and even then incompletely.[69] The regiments deployed in the field in 1665 were therefore highly uneven in number and often composed of companies which had been randomly cobbled together. For the cavalry this had not been an issue – the might of the mounted arm resided in the courage and skill of small groups of troopers – but the infantry, which relied on firing discipline at battalion level, was at a serious disadvantage.

In January 1666 Johan Maurits of Nassau-Siegen, commander of the expedition against Münster, tabled a raft of proposals to improve the infantry's fighting strength. He insisted that the regiments earmarked for field service should as far as possible be composed of companies which belonged to that unit, and that 'the colonels, lieutenant-colonels and majors have their own companies included thereunder, in order to be better able to act, with greater obedience and affection, with their own men'.[70] Each regiment had to be provided with flags in a specific colour, so that soldiers on the march or in battle could easily relocate their unit, 'it having been learnt during the last campaign that the soldiers were unable to find their respective companies for three or more days, because they had forgotten the name of their captain and could not distinguish between the colours'.[71]

The great conquests achieved by the French in the Spanish Netherlands in 1667 prompted Johan Maurits and the Council of State to propose further improvements to the Dutch army. They recommended bringing all the regiments up to the same strength: the infantry regiments to 1,400 men (fourteen companies of 100 men) and the cavalry regiments to 480 horse (six companies of eighty horse). But this was not yet sufficient. Regimental structures would have to be kept intact in times of war as well as of peace to maintain cohesion by billeting the companies that belonged to the same regiment in a single garrison and 'dividing the same regiment across the neighbouring garrisons when fewer companies are required there'. The regiments were to be exercised *en corps* 'by the field officers themselves' at least once a week and the drill would have to be performed by all the troops in the same manner 'without regard to nation'.[72]

---

[69] NA, SG 5039, RvS to the SG, The Hague, 16 November 1665.
[70] NA, SG 5040, Exhibitum, 27 January 1666, 'Poincten van remarcques door de heeren hare Ho. Mo. gedep[uteer]den ende den heere prince [Johan] Maurits van Nassauw sedert de laetste expeditie te velde op papier gebracht achtervolgens hare Ho. Mo. resolutie van[de] 21 january 1666'.
[71] NA, RAZH, AJdW 2725-4, Anonymous and without date, but very probably drafted by Johan Maurits in 1667. The content is wholly in keeping with the document of January 1666.
[72] NA, RAZH, AJdW, 2724-b, 'Poincten van consideratie raackende het redres van 't volck

Lastly, Johan Maurits and the Council of State underscored the importance of holding manoeuvres with an army corps at least once a year, to give the generals the opportunity to try out different battle arrays. The States-General followed this last piece of advice by immediately ordering exercises with 9,000 men to be held near Bergen op Zoom from April to June 1668.[73]

The Peace of Aix-la-Chapelle (2 May 1668) quickly drained the enthusiasm of the regents to ready the army for war. The plan to regroup the infantry and cavalry into regiments of fourteen and six companies 'of one and the same repartition', namely in the pay of the same province, was indeed adopted,[74] and Holland proposed that in peacetime 'the majority of the army of the State should be assembled once a year in one or more suitable, flat places to be exercised there for several days in succession'.[75] The advantageous effects of this were largely negated by it at the same time being decided to slash the strength of the army by more than half, from 69,000 to 33,000 men, when the Council of State deemed a peacetime strength of 39,000 men to be essential.[76] In view of France's threatening stance this was a false economy. It was, after all, foreseeable that the army would soon have to be brought back up to wartime strength, thus incurring high recruitment costs. Besides, the massive reduction could only be detrimental to the quality of the troops. In early 1668 the Dutch army was in fine condition. The officers and men had gained plenty of practical experience during the war with Münster and for the most part the companies were at full strength. Cornelis de Witt, who had attended the manoeuvres of the corps assembled near Bergen op Zoom as a field deputy, reported with satisfaction to his brother, the Grand Pensionary, in April 1668: 'The militia of the State [is] in general very complete and so well constituted as it has not been for many years heretofore.'[77] The review which took place shortly thereafter corroborated this assertion. The companies counted an average of 82.8 per cent of the prescribed strength in rank and file.[78] The only aspect in which they fell short was the size of the tactical

---

te voet sijnde ten dienste der Vereenigde Nederlanden' (quotes); FAH 5, Extract of a missive from the RvS to the SG, The Hague, 15 June and 14 September 1667.

[73] NA, RAZH, AJdW, Cornelis de Witt, Bergen op Zoom, 29 April, 4 and 26 May, 5 and 9 June 1668.

[74] NA, RAZH, FAH 5, Extract res. SH, 1 December 1667, Missive of the States-General, The Hague, 24 May 1668; NA, RvS 488, Res. RvS, 15 June 1667.

[75] NA, RAZH, FAH 5, Extract res. SH, 3 August 1668. This proposal was adopted by the States-General on 29 August 1670.

[76] NA, RAZH, FAH 5, Advice from the RvS, 27 July 1668.

[77] NA, RAZH, AJdW, Cornelis de Witt, Bergen op Zoom, 23 April 1668.

[78] NA, RAZH, AJdW 2725, 'Lijste van de troupes tot het employ omtrent Bergen op den Zoom gedestineert soo als deselve gevonden sijn op de reveue door de heeren haer Ho. Mo. gedeputeerden en[de] gevolmachtichden, gedaen den 3.e may 1668'. In early 1668 the paper strength of a standard infantry company was set at nine officers, eighty-two men in rank and file (three corporals, one clerk and seventy-eight soldiers) and three boys, a total of ninety-four men. Ten Raa, *Het Staatsche leger*, V, p. 453.

formations: the troops were divided among twenty battalions of an average of 400 men, when 700 to 800 men was considered desirable for field service.

The States of Holland failed to hasten the bringing of all infantry regiments to similar strengths until late 1671, when there could no longer have been any doubt that France, in conjunction with Münster and Cologne, was preparing an attack on the Republic on an unprecedented scale. Johan Maurits ordered ninety-six standards in eight different colours for the infantry: orange, *bleu mourant* (pale blue), grass-green, yellow, red, white, sea-green and Isabella (a brownish yellow). Each regimental colour was seven feet square and 'old pikes' were used as poles.[79] The threat of war made military expansion imperative. Besides reinforcement of all the infantry and cavalry companies to 100 foot and eighty horse, respectively, the States-General ordered the recruitment of 14,000 infantry to form ten regiments and 2,880 cavalrymen to form six regiments,[80] bringing the Dutch army's strength on paper up to 64,715 men. But this was not sufficient; the French war preparations continued unabated. In February, March and April 1672 the provinces consented to three further augmentations of 19,760, 22,560 and 25,200 men, respectively. Had all the enlistments been completed the Dutch army would have numbered no fewer than 132,000 men. But time ran out to complete the last two augmentations before the French assault was launched in June 1672, when the Dutch army numbered only 95,000 men.[81] The augmentations of 1671 and February 1672 had essentially been completed by that point, so the army's strength was more than 80,000 effectives,[82] but apart from the fact that the majority of the Dutch army was scattered across garrisons, the Dutch troops could not match the French in quality. 'It would have been better if one had taken on some ready-made troops [i.e. pre-existing regiments],' Colonel Godard van Reede-Ginkel (1644–1703) complained in February 1672, 'for I fear these recruitments shall be very sluggish and of poor men.'[83] His critique was aimed at the officers rather than the rank and file.[84] 'These troops are all brave

---

[79] KHA, A4-1477, Jean van Weert, Amsterdam, 22 March and 1 April 1672.

[80] NA, SG 12548.454, 'Extraordinaris Staet van Oorlogh te water ende te lande met eene absolute esgaliteyt geformeert in voldoeninge van haer Ho. Mog. resolutie van den 22 en 30 december 1670'.

[81] NA, RAZH, FAvS 44, Overviews of the strength of the Dutch army in June 1672; NA, CvdH 123, Notes by Adriaan van der Hoop about the 'Militia'.

[82] This estimate is based on the strengths of the Maastricht garrison as mustered on 22 April 1672. The muster-rolls of seventy ordinary infantry companies and eight cavalry companies show that in rank and file these companies numbered an average of 86.34 per cent and 88.52 per cent of their strength on paper, respectively. NA, SG 12579.97, 'Lijste van[de] reveue over de compagni[e]ën infanterie door den heere van Crommon, haer Ho. Mog. Gedep[uteer]de ende Gevolm[achtig]de te velde ten overstaen van den heere Rhijngraeff binnen Maestricht gedaen op den 22 april 1672'.

[83] HUA, HAA 2731, Godard van Reede-Ginkel to his father, Godard Adriaan van Reede-Amerongen (1621–1691), Utrecht, 10 February 1672.

[84] 'At The Hague and in Utrecht one has appointed the officers for the new recruitments, it is said there are some fine folk among them, but mostly such poor and drunken blood that

men, but God grant that our military discipline might regain its former state and glory', wrote another Dutch colonel, Diderik Stecke (†1689), to the stadholder of Friesland. 'Your Serene Highness would scarce believe what disorder and disobedience I am finding in my regiment among all the inexperienced young officers.'[85]

The development of the new Dutch army under William III (1672–1688)

The impending war with France led to the appointment of William III as captain-general of the Union in February 1672, initially for just one campaign. With at most 22,000 field troops at his disposal it was impossible for the commander-in-chief, just twenty-one years of age, to hold back the French invasion force of an estimated 80,000 to 100,000 men at the River IJssel. A rapid retreat to Holland was the only means of escaping annihilation. The defence could be continued from behind the Holland Water Line, and at the same time it would be possible to prepare a counter-offensive to recapture the occupied provinces of Gelderland, Overijssel and Utrecht. William III began the withdrawal to Holland in mid-June, with the French following close on his heels. French troops occupied Naarden on 20 June 1672 and Utrecht fell three days later. For William III the retreat to Holland was merely a temporary measure; he wanted to launch a counterattack as soon as possible. However, before the Dutch troops could emerge from behind the inundations with any hope of success, the fighting strength of the seriously weakened and utterly disheartened army had to be restored. Three complementary and mutually reinforcing conditions had to be met in order to turn the French onslaught: the restoration of discipline, regular payment of wages and financial support for the officers to replace their losses. This third condition was a novelty in the Dutch army, because the captains and rittmasters had previously been required to replace even men lost in battle at their own expense, but the critical position of the Republic in 1672 forced the government to support the officers financially in restoring their companies to full strength and maintaining them at that level. Moreover, the company commanders could henceforth be called to account for any deficiencies ascertained.

William III collaborated closely with Gaspar Fagel and the two generals, Johan Maurits and Georg Friedrich, count of Waldeck and Culemborg, to achieve the rebuilding of the Dutch army. Fagel (1634–1688) was an experienced administrator at provincial and federal tiers of government. From 1663 to 1670 he served as Pensionary of Haarlem, was then appointed *griffier* or principal clerk of the States-General, and on 20 August 1672, on William III's insistence, he

---

it is saddening.' HUA, HAA 2722, Margaretha Turnor (1613–1700) to her husband, Godard Adriaan van Reede-Amerongen, Amerongen, 15 February 1672. She had doubtless garnered this information from her son, Godard van Reede-Ginkel.
[85] Tresoar, FSA 48a, Diderik Stecke to Hendrik Casimir II, with the army at Nieuwbeek, 16 May 1672.

40. William III (1650–1702), prince of Orange, captain-general of the Union from 1672. Engraving c. 1700. (Royal Netherlands Army Museum, Delft, 00101308)

was appointed Grand Pensionary of Holland.[86] Johan Maurits, aged sixty-eight, knew the Dutch army from bottom to top – he had first 'carried the pike' under the guards of Willem Lodewijk in 1618 as a fourteen-year-old.[87] His great knowl-

---

[86] A. de Fouw, *Onbekende raadpensionarissen* (The Hague 1946), pp. 94–8 and 101.
[87] NA, RAZH, AJdW 2718, 'Memorie' with Johan Maurits of Nassau-Siegen's record of service.

41. Gaspar Fagel (1634–1688), Grand Pensionary of Holland, 1672–1688. Jan Wagenaar, *Vaderlandsche historie* (Amsterdam 1749–1759). (Royal Netherlands Army Museum, Delft, 00100656)

edge of military affairs and his tenacity were of considerable value in the critical years of 1672 and 1673, but his advanced years and *'fréquentes indispositions'* made it terribly taxing for him to participate in the campaigning. In 1674 he headed into the theatre and fought in the battle of Seneffe, but from 1675 he was granted permission to stay behind in Utrecht or Cleves.[88]

William III was energetic and possessed an attacking spirit bordering on recklessness, but his understanding of how to plan a military operation was sorely inadequate. Moreover, he had no experience whatsoever of leading troops

---

[88] CWB, II, ii, no. 82, Johan Maurits of Nassau-Siegen to William III, 12 February 1676; no. 83, William III to Johan Maurits, 22 February 1676 (quote).

42. Georg Friedrich, count of Waldeck and Culemborg (1620–1692), Dutch field-marshal. (Collection NIMH)

in combat, never mind a siege or pitched battle. It was therefore of the utmost importance that a capable second-in-command stood at his side in the theatre of operations. Waldeck (1620–1692), aged fifty-two at the time, was the best choice to serve as the Dutch army's second-in-command. Waldeck was related to Count Floris II of Culemborg via his mother's side of the family. He had begun his military career under Frederik Hendrik, who promoted him to rittmaster in 1642. After the Peace of Münster he continued his career in the army of Brandenburg, which he left in 1658 as a lieutenant-general. He subsequently served in the armies of Sweden, the Holy Roman Empire and Brunswick. He fought in the Second Northern War (1655–1660), he participated in the battle at St Gotthard Abbey against the Ottomans in 1664, and as commander of the Brunswick-Lüneburg troops he was closely involved in the planning of the campaign to defeat the bishop of Münster in 1665.[89] Waldeck's great expertise in military affairs and his diplomatic acuity – an indispensable quality in a coalition war – made him ideally suited to assist William III and rein him in if necessary. Their relationship was generally good, but in 1676 it would come to a great 'quarrel' between them, when William III laid siege to Maastricht against Waldeck's advice. The operation was a failure. Waldeck did not mince any words in his critique of the commander-in-chief, witness an account of a confidential discussion with Johan Pesters (1620–1703), an influential Utrecht regent. 'His lordship the count of Waldeck did me the honour at the camp of communicating his sentiments on what had come to pass during and after the beleaguering of Maastricht, but they discrepate to a large extent with those of His Highness, even to some discontent', Pesters confided to a correspondent.[90]

William III was in a unique position to mould the Dutch army as he saw fit. Having been overrun by the French, the payment of troops repartitioned to the provinces of Gelderland, Utrecht and Overijssel ground to a halt. As early as 20 June 1672, Count Heinrich Trajectinus of Solms-Braunfels (1637–1693), colonel of a Gelderland regiment, tendered his resignation to the Council of State because he could no longer pay his troops. The field deputy Hendrik van Gockinga (1624–1674) feared the worst, because 'others will have to follow that example, and the fear is that with the departure of the senior officers the soldiers will disband'. He warned Gaspar Fagel, at that time still *griffier* of the States-General, that an emergency solution needed to be found, and quickly.[91] In The

---

[89] P.L. Müller, *Wilhelm III. von Oranien und Georg Friedrich von Waldeck. Ein Beitrag zur Geschichte des Kampfes um das europäische Gleichgewicht* (The Hague 1873), I, pp. 13–16, 23–4 and 27–8; Ten Raa, *Het Staatsche leger*, V, pp. 59 and 93; Baxter, *William III*, p. 93; Peter H. Wilson, *German Armies: War and German Politics, 1648–1806* (London 1998), p. 63; Abraham de Wicquefort, *Histoire des Provinces Unies des Pais Bas*, III (Amsterdam 1866), p. 221.
[90] HUA, HAA 2813, Johan Pesters to Godard Adriaan van Reede-Amerongen, Utrecht, 18 September 1676, PS.
[91] NA, SG 12579.98-I, Hendrik van Gockinga to Gaspar Fagel, *griffier* of the SG, Bodegraven, 20 June 1672. On 2 June the States of Overijssel had already warned the States-General that because of the invasion by Münster's troops and the inundation of land they

Hague they had already reached the same conclusion, because Holland decided that very same day to assume temporary responsibility for the payment of the troops from the three 'conquested' provinces.[92] A new repartition among the four remaining provinces was to be computed, following an audit of all the troops the Republic still effectively had at its disposal.[93] In late September 1672 a provisional State of War that would remain in force until 31 December was approved. Holland paid some 517 of the Dutch army's 781 infantry companies and no fewer than 124 of its 166 cavalry companies.[94] The Dutch army had in effect become the army of Holland for the time being. For 1673, the 'quotas' or percentages that were decisive for the repartition were established as follows: instead of the usual quota of a good 58 per cent, Holland now shouldered responsibility for almost 69 per cent of the army costs, while Zeeland, Friesland and Groningen shared the remaining 31 per cent between them.

The new Dutch army: revision of the system of *solliciteurs-militair* and government support for recruiting and maintaining companies

The reorganisation of the Dutch army was embarked upon with impressive vigour. To prevent its total collapse, on 16 July 1672 the States of Holland promulgated various emergency measures. Besides the decision to transfer the troops employed by Gelderland, Overijssel and Utrecht onto Holland's payroll, the commissaries of the muster were ordered to pay out a month's salary to all companies which had retired 'within the territory of the province of Holland' immediately after the muster was completed. In addition, the States of Holland decided that companies which numbered forty or more men in rank and file had to be made complete as quickly as possible. For this the company commanders could draw on a considerable reservoir of soldiers 'who have become dispersed by the enemy, and are staying at various places'. The Council of State designated assembly points for these troops, whereupon they would be 'enrolled anew and subsequently ranged under companies'. Captains who failed to bring their companies to full strength were threatened with dismissal. An exception was made for commanders whose companies had shrunk to less than forty men in rank and file. These were required to reinforce their companies to at least forty men, 'with sufficient recognizance to restitute the monies received [i.e. pay] in the event that these persons [i.e. captains] do not bring the companies to at

---

were facing serious financial difficulties, as a consequence of which 'we find ourselves utterly impeded with the payment of the militia repartitioned to this province'. SG 12579.98-I, States of Overijssel to the SG, Kampen, 2 June 1672.

[92] NA, RAZH, FAH 6, Extract res. SH, 20 June 1672.

[93] NA, RAZH, FAH 6, 'Voorslagen tot redres van[de] militie'. See also KHA, A4-1476aI, William III to Johan Maurits of Nassau-Siegen, The Hague, 2 August 1672.

[94] NA, RAZH, FAH 7, Extract res. SH, 27 September 1672; Ten Raa, *Het Staatsche leger*, V, pp. 272–82.

least the aforementioned tally of forty heads within a certain short, peremptory time'. Should they fail to achieve this then their companies would be disbanded and the men assigned to other companies. In conjunction with this strict stance, the States of Holland lent the captains a helping hand, shouldering the costs for ransoming prisoners of war. The company commanders received a remuneration of three rix-dollars for each soldier whose freedom they procured from France, Münster or Cologne.[95] This made it possible for an estimated 20,000 or more Dutch prisoners of war to be reunited with their units.[96]

The measures introduced in July 1672 saved the Dutch army from disintegration, but they were still insufficient. Despite Holland assuming payment of the troops from the 'conquested' provinces, the military solicitors were wary of serving these companies because their commanders were unable to stand any surety. By November 1672 the Utrecht colonel, Godard van Reede-Ginkel, already owed his cavalrymen two months' pay,[97] while Count Heinrich Trajectinus of Solms-Braunfels informed Gaspar Fagel in December that it was impossible for him to restore his Gelderland regiment to full strength. In October his unit had participated in a bloody encounter near Woerden, leaving him with only 150 men. Restoring this corps to its full complement would have required the recruitment of more than 800 men for sky-high bounties of eight to ten *patagons* (i.e. twenty to twenty-five guilders). Gelderland's officers could acquire credit nowhere, 'having lost all theirs', so there was not a single solicitor who wanted to do business with them, Solms-Braunfels explained.[98] The threat of mutiny reared its head. In mid-December 1672 all the soldiers from Captain Purcel's company left the redoubt near the Woerdens Verlaat, a lock on a strategic waterway, and headed for Bodegraven to convey their grievances to Lieutenant-General Konrad Christoph, count of Königsmarck (1634–1673). The commander of the post at the Woerdens Verlaat, Captain Jan de Roode van Heeckeren, could sympathise with these soldiers, because 'for 6 or 7 weeks they have not had a stiver in money and the captain has not yet returned, and these soldiers are suffering from great hunger and poverty, such that a person who sees it would have to lament'.[99] Königsmarck, however, was less sympathetic and had the mutinous troops

---

95 NA, RAZH, FAH 6, 'Voorslagen tot redres van de militie' and Extract res. SH, 16 July 1672.
96 André Corvisier, *Louvois* (n.p. 1983), p. 260; John A. Lynn, *The Wars of Louis XIV 1667–1714* (London 1999), p. 117.
97 HUA, HAA 2731, Godard van Reede-Ginkel to Godard Adriaan van Reede-Amerongen, with the army at Vlijtingen, between Tongeren and Maastricht, 29 November 1672.
98 NA, RAZH, AGF 117, Count Heinrich Trajectinus of Solms-Braunfels, Breda, 14 December 1672.
99 NA, RAZH, AGF 116, Lieutenant-General Konrad Christoph, count of Königsmarck, [Bodegraven], n.d., with a letter from Captain Jan de Roode van Heeckeren as an appendix, Woerdens Verlaat, 12 December 1672.

'immediately ... lodged with the military provost'.[100] Colonel Johan van Stockheim (†1674), commander of Weesp, a village near Amsterdam, had that same month received reports that the men from the Van Dam-d'Audignies infantry regiment were 'resolved to set their weapons before my house tomorrow and go their separate ways'. In order to gain some time, Stockheim sent ten *dukatons* (thirty guilders) in cash, so that they could at least buy food, 'for already two men on watch at the Hinderdam ... have died of hunger'.[101] However, such a sum of cash was insignificant. Jacob van Paffenrode, lieutenant-colonel of the Van Dam regiment, informed the burgomasters of Amsterdam that he needed 1,400 guilders: 'Today the whole regiment is to receive its pay advance and it is to be feared that if we do not give them something then great calamities shall come about', he wrote. 'I have given everything that I had and last week I advanced eleven hundred guilders to the regiment, and I have therefore divested myself in one go. We have officers [who] have not eaten for two days.'[102] The Amsterdam regents were swift to provide the money, but the need for a permanent solution was glaringly obvious.

In 1643 the total collapse of the army finances had been averted by a sharp reduction in the number of Dutch troops. In the winter of 1672/3 a repetition of this was inconceivable, as all the soldiers and cavalrymen were needed to withstand the French assault. In early 1673 Gaspar Fagel presented a plan intended to guarantee the payment of wages to the 'Hollandish' troops. He divided all the companies of foot and of horse, numbering 505 and 123 at the time, into eight groups, respecting the regimental structures. Each group, comprised of an average of sixty-three companies of foot and fifteen of horse, was assigned to an army pay director. Holland's commissary for finance was ordered to distribute the pay ordinances only to these eight military solicitors. These 'directors' were obliged to pay the units assigned to them promptly 'not by companies but by whole regiments simultaneously, without favouring anyone therein in the least or making any furnishment to one company before the other'. This meant they were not allowed to refuse less creditworthy captains and rittmasters. Holland deposited no less than 1 million guilders into a special fund, so that the directors could immediately issue a full month's pay. The money for this was obtained by a levying of extraordinary taxes to the substantial tune of more than 5.5 million guilders 'for the payment of the army and the military affairs affected'.[103] If necessary, however, the directors would also have to use their personal credit or that of their associates to appropriate funds for the army. Over this advance they would receive interest at a rate of 0.8 per cent per pay-month of forty-two days (6.95

---

[100] NA, RAZH, AGF 116, Lieutenant-General Konrad Christoph, count of Königsmarck, [Bodegraven], n.d.
[101] GAA, Missives to burgomasters 66 (microfilm 8006), Johan van Stockheim to Major-General Otto, count of Limburg-Stirum, Weesp, 2 December 1672, translation.
[102] GAA, Missives to burgomasters 67 (microfilm 8007), Jacob van Paffenrode, n.p., n.d.
[103] See p. 356.

per cent per annum) and in addition they received a fixed monthly fee for each company they served: twenty-eight guilders for a company of horse, twenty-five guilders for a company of dragoons and twelve guilders for a company of foot.[104]

How long the 1673 regulations remained in force is unclear, but it is clearly documented that thirty-three solicitors were appointed to serve Holland's troops in March 1676. It had evidently proven impossible to limit the number of solicitors to just eight, because from a resolution promulgated by Holland's Delegated Councillors dated 13 March 1676 it is evident that in the meantime there had been a proliferation in the number of solicitors and that several unscrupulous moneylenders were trying to defraud the troops.[105] In order to put a stop to this wholly unsatisfactory situation and prevent the culprits volunteering their services as solicitors again, their number was limited to thirty-eight at most, and these could not be 'persons of very limited means and credit, and their having no understanding whatsoever, or very little, of the business of the soliciting of companies nor of the negotiation of money'. Nobody was allowed to 'solicit' a company without prior permission from the States of Holland and each solicitor was also required to possess a financial reserve from which he could advance at least six months' pay per company. As an extra precaution each solicitor had to deposit a sum of 5,000 guilders as surety. Each of the thirty-three solicitors eventually appointed in March 1676 had to assume responsibility for a proportional share of all the troops on Holland's payroll, and those who served the smallest number of companies were obliged to accept 'the rittmasters and captains who shall not be able to find any solicitors'.[106]

The States of Holland also provided direct assistance to the officers. In December 1672 Holland's field deputies at the army headquarters in Alphen aan de Rijn – Cornelis Geelvinck (1621–1689), Adriaan van Bosvelt and Pieter Burgersdijck (c. 1623–1691) – had advised Gaspar Fagel to reduce all the infantry companies to seventy-five men in rank and file, 'because the hundred soldiers on paper cannot usually amount to 70 effective combatants in rank and file'. This measure would be advantageous for both the company commanders and the government, as the captains would be able to put the pay of five men into their own pockets while Holland 'would be able to save a whole quarter of the ordinary pay without licensing [i.e. dismissing] a single man'.[107] The States of Holland decided to go a step further: all the companies, with the exception of the Foot Guards, having been reduced to eighty-nine men in January 1673, in July

---

[104] NA, RAZH, AGF 126. The division of the regiments into eight classes is to be found in RAZH, FAH 7, Extract res. of the Delegated Councillors of Holland's South Quarter, 28 February 1673.

[105] In November 1675 the troops repartitioned to Holland had 'not yet ... received more than three pay-months of wages'. HUA, ASU 637-12, Secret res. SG, 25 November 1675.

[106] NA, RAZH, AGRH 3026, Res. Delegated Councillors of Holland's South Quarter, 13 March 1676.

[107] NA, RAZH, AGF 121, Field deputies, Alphen aan de Rijn, 23 December 1672.

1673 they decreed that a company which numbered seventy men in rank and file at muster 'and including the officers [and their servants] stood at 81 effectives ... shall be treated ... as complete' and would therefore receive the month's pay in full. The sick and wounded could be counted among this tally of seventy men. This arrangement yielded the captains a financial advantage of eight men's pay, seeing as a company of eighty-nine men was composed of eight officers – the captain, the lieutenant, the ensign, two sergeants, two drummers and the surgeon – plus seventy-eight rank-and-file soldiers and three boys. The three corporals and the clerk were considered 'common officers' and as such were counted among the rank and file. There was a similar arrangement for the cavalry: for every fifty-seven troopers the rittmasters received pay for sixty-one men. This bonus arrangement was intended to compensate company commanders for the losses they suffered during the campaign, namely to replace broken-down or lost baggage waggons, weapons and equipment the men had lost or discarded during a fight, and tents. In part it also served as compensation for the recruitment costs incurred by the captains to replace men and horses who fell victim to disease or accidents and, of course, deserters.

The States of Holland introduced a special financial arrangement for replacing troops killed in action. The captains and rittmasters could from then on depend on full compensation for men lost in battle or siege. 'Such that the recruitment money for men who are enlisted to replace those who have died in attacks against the enemy shall be reimbursed to the captains by the Land.'[108] Thus a new custom was born that would be applied until the demise of the Republic. From then on the provinces bore the risk that was inherent to the military enterprise. Holland's Delegated Councillors set the compensation for a soldier killed in action at thirty-three guilders, for a trooper with horse at 150 guilders, for a horse alone at 120 guilders, and for a trooper 'whose steed had been recovered' at thirty guilders. After the bloody battle of Mont-Cassel (11 April 1677), William III increased the allowance for each soldier 'left behind' in this battle to fifty guilders 'with the proviso that a precise sixth part of the number of the aforesaid men and horses would be deducted from the rittmasters and captains and charged at their expense.'[109] This meant that the net compensation for a soldier killed in action amounted to more than forty-one guilders. It remains unclear why the company commanders had to make up for one-sixth of the losses from their own pockets, but the probable reason for this was that the captains and rittmasters inflated the tally of fatalities with men who had deserted. The government paid out fifty guilders for each soldier killed in action during the Nine Years' War (1688–1697) as well. For a deceased trooper the compensation

---

[108] *Recueil van verscheide placaaten, ordonnantiën, resolutiën, instructiën, ordres en lijsten &c. betreffende de saaken van den oorlog te water en te lande*, I (The Hague, n.d.), no. 9, 'Placaat en ordre op het stuk van de monsteringe', promulgated by the States of Holland on 19 July 1673.
[109] HUA, HAA 2732, Godard van Reede-Ginkel to his father, near Ghent, 26 April 1677; RAZH, AGRH 3027, Res. of the Delegated Councillors of Holland, 8 May 1677 (quote).

43. Dutch recruiting scene, early eighteenth century. E.W. van Bilderbeek, *Ordre und Wörter von Commando auff die Handgriffe [vom Schnap]haan*, manuscript. (Royal Netherlands Army Museum, Delft, P 451)

was thirty guilders, for a horse and equipment 130 guilders, and for a trooper together with his gelding 160 guilders.[110] From 1702 to 1781 the compensation for the loss of a soldier amounted to sixty-two guilders and ten stivers (twenty-five rix-dollars), that for a trooper with steed some 225 guilders (ninety rix-dollars).[111]

The payment of compensation for men killed in action had a significant impact on the employability of the Dutch army. Shortly after the battle of Mont-Cassel, Johan Pesters wrote to the Utrecht regent, Godard Adriaan van Reede-Amerongen: 'I do not doubt that, due to the arrival of 17 fresh regiments and through the recruitment of ... the battalions [which have seen action], our army shall once again be in a complete state within six weeks.'[112] After a bloody battle or siege operation the Dutch army had previously been forced to retire to the garrisons – as after the battle of Nieuwpoort in 1600 – but it could now remain in the field and venture a new confrontation after a short recovery period of six to eight weeks. Almost immediately after the battle of Mont-Cassel the Council of State had submitted a petition for 600,000 guilders 'for the recruitment and restoration of the militia of the State, it having been severely weakened in the recent battle with the enemy near St Omer'. All the provincial States promptly granted their consent.[113]

---

[110] NA, Collectie De Jonge van Ellemeet 115, Extract res. SG, 27 July 1690.
[111] NA, CvdH 102, 'Recruts- of aanritsgelden'.
[112] HUA, HAA 2817, Johan Pesters to Godard Adriaan van Reede-Amerongen, Utrecht, 24 April 1677.
[113] NA, Collectie De Jonge van Ellemeet 115, Extract res. SG, 23 April 1677.

Deserters 'and those who died in other ways' remained the responsibility of the captains and rittmasters,[114] though the government did not leave them to fend for themselves. Besides introducing the bonus system, the decree of July 1673 stipulated that if the company commander had refilled a vacancy as a result of desertion or illness within ten days of the muster then payment of this recruit's salary would commence immediately. There was thus no delay until the following muster, as had been the norm until then. In addition the government turned a blind eye to the captains and rittmasters amassing a special reserve fund from which 'the accidents of desertion' could be paid. From the pay of each soldier or trooper in their company they held back six and ten stivers a week, respectively. This money was officially intended for the repair and replacement of weapons, 'but a captain does not need six stivers [for this], this exceeds that'. The company commander put the difference 'in his pocket'. The rittmasters were also permitted to deduct half a rix-dollar from each trooper in their company as a contribution towards the cost of replacing a horse that died or fell lame.[115] These financial compensations provided the captains and rittmasters with sufficient money to be able to replace three deserted soldiers or two troopers with their steeds every pay-month.[116]

In addition William III did everything possible to push back desertion and to limit its damaging consequences. In September 1673 he asked the burgomasters of Amsterdam to take measures 'against … certain persons within your city named "soul-sellers", who … are constantly apprehending the deserters from the Land's militia and are seducing others to that end'.[117] Three years later he urged the States of Overijssel to ensure that in the towns and in the countryside all the soldiers who could not show a passport were rounded up, 'and not to act laxly and to see it is carried out'. The deserters then had to be assembled in a major town 'where the said soldiers shall be kept at the expense of their respective captains, who on our orders, after settlement of the aforesaid costs, shall have them collected and bring them back to the army'.[118] Sometimes a deserter

---

[114] NA, Collectie Bisdom 162, Extract res. RvS, 15 April 1746, question XXI: 'If and what is to be compensated for a man shot dead or injured by the enemy in battle, as well as for a deserter or deceased?'
[115] NA, CvdH 102 and 107, Notes by Adriaan van der Hoop about the pay of the Dutch troops; *Recueil … betreffende de saaken van den oorlog*, I, no. 74, 'Ordre en reglement op het stuk van de monteeringe en kleedinge der cavallerie', The Hague, 26 January 1687, Art. II.
[116] Based on an infantry company of sixty men in rank and file and a cavalry company of fifty troopers in rank and file.
[117] GAA, Missives to burgomasters 86 (microfilm 8040), William III, The Hague, 28 September 1673.
[118] HCO, ASO 5156, William III to the States of Overijssel, before Maastricht, 31 July 1676. See also Tresoar, FSA 48b, Hendrik Casimir II to the States of Friesland and the States of Groningen, Louvain, 11 July 1675.

was sentenced to death,[119] but this was only to set an example. The high demand for experienced soldiers disallowed the execution of all the deserters, and such an approach would also have landed the company commanders in dire financial straits. For example, between 17 April and 13 August 1676 some eighty-three men deserted from Colonel Utenhove's regiment, while between 19 April and 24 June of that same year the regiment of the Prince-Count Palatine of Birkenfeld saw its strength diminish by at least 157 deserters.[120] Instead of receiving the death penalty, the sentences handed down for deserters usually involved corporal punishment, though this could be very severe. In December 1672, for example, the General Court Martial sentenced the infantryman Jan Swol 'to be thrice hauled up on the strappado and, moreover, to be branded with a gallows on the cheek'.[121]

Severe measures were also taken against *rouleurs*, soldiers who enlisted and then made off with the bounty, thereby pocketing plenty of cash. A certain Jacob Bourgogne, for example, received a bounty of six *dukatons* (eighteen guilders) from Captain Van der Dussen when he had already enlisted with Captain Panin. Bourgogne was sentenced 'thrice to pass and run the gauntlet of one hundred men and furthermore ordered that he ... will then have to report back to the company of Captain Panin'.[122] Running the gauntlet involved the convict having to walk or run bare-backed between two rows of soldiers, each of whom struck him with a long, thin birch-rod.

*

The States of Holland did not resort to introducing the above-mentioned measures merely to oblige the officers; it was also in their own interests. The pay bonus for companies numbering at least seventy men in rank and file was a great incentive for the captains to maintain their companies at this strength. Commanders who had sixty to sixty-nine soldiers or fifty to fifty-six troopers on the muster-roll received the pay 'according to the precise count of the heads', while captains and rittmasters whose companies numbered fewer than sixty soldiers or fifty troopers could expect stiff fines; their pay was reduced by the wages of the missing men 'in proportion to a complete company'. Moreover, if the following muster revealed that they had failed to make up the shortfall, then they faced a punishment 'deemed fitting to the exigency of the matter, either by cassation, suspension or disbanding of the company'.[123] In other words, the

---

[119] NA, AHK 353-I, no. 40, Sentence of 3 March 1673; HUA, ASU 278-5, William III to the States of Utrecht, Aarschot, 8 July 1675.
[120] GA, AHGC 1240, Muster-rolls of the Utenhove regiment, 13 August 1676, and 'Liste van de deserteurs van 't regiment van Birkenfeld', 19 April–24 June 1676.
[121] NA, AHK 353-I, no. 19, Sentence of 6 December 1672.
[122] NA, AHK 353-I, no. 18, Sentence of 6 December 1672. For similar cases see sentence nos. 20 and 22.
[123] *Recueil ... betreffende de saaken van den oorlog te water en te lande*, I, no. 9.

government offered the company commanders a helping hand in maintaining their companies and in exchange for this they demanded that the captains and rittmasters did not allow their companies to fall below the minimum strength of sixty soldiers or fifty troopers, and if this happened then they had to answer for it before the General Court Martial.

In November 1673 Holland temporarily expanded its financial support for the captains even further. On William III's advice, the Delegated Councillors declared that from 21 October 1673 to 25 March 1674 they would exceptionally issue pay ordinances for complete companies, no matter whether a company numbered seventy men in rank and file, 'thereby amply to enable the captains to [enlist] the prescribed recruits'. Officers whose companies were not complete in April 1674 would be dismissed on the spot with 'infamy'.[124] It was, however, difficult to impose this threat, because the distribution of the pay did not always proceed flawlessly. As an excuse for the weakness of his company, on 4 April 1674 Captain Godefroy Mom de Swartzstein argued 'that I to date am still owed 1,608 guilders, and God knows when it shall please the lords at Hoorn to order this, and without this money, God be my witness and knowing of my lack of wherewithal, such recruitment is beyond my power'.[125] Thus the earlier decree of July 1673 remained in force and also applied for the troops repartitioned to Zeeland, Friesland and Groningen. The bonus of the pay of four cavalrymen was, however, withdrawn in 1674. The mounted arm was less prone to desertion and the officers could often supplement their income with the proceeds from booty. On the other hand, the outbreak of an infectious horse disease could easily ruin a rittmaster. In 1676 such an outbreak in conjunction with a shortage of fodder led to high mortality rates among the cavalry's horses. 'My loss [is] at least so great as if I should have to raise a whole new company', Godard van Reede-Ginkel complained to his father.[126]

The regulation of July 1673 was highly effective. From then on roughly half the infantry companies (53 to 54 per cent) numbered seventy men in rank and file, and 44 to 45 per cent were at least sixty strong. These percentages are based on the muster-rolls of fifty-seven infantry regiments (650 companies) mustered in January 1676 and partly also at later dates (see Appendices III and IV). In January 1676 there were ten regiments (127 companies) with an average strength per company of sixty or more men in rank and file; the average company strength of twenty regiments (234 companies) was fifty or more men at that time. Of a similar number of regiments (221 companies) the companies were between forty and fifty men strong, and of five regiments (fifty-six companies) they numbered between thirty and forty men. One regiment (Widdrington) was exceptionally weak: its twelve companies counted an average of just 23.42 men in rank and

---

[124] NA, RAZH, FAH 7, Extract res. SH, 17 November 1673.
[125] GA, AHGC 1224, Captain Godefroy Mom de Swartzstein to Georg Friedrich von Waldeck, Gorinchem, 4 April 1674.
[126] HUA, HAA 2732, Godard van Reede-Ginkel to his father, The Hague, 12 October 1676.

file. After this muster the captains were granted more than two months, namely until 1 April 1676, to bring their companies to strength. It is likely that companies which already counted fifty or more effectives in January were strengthened to seventy men before the start of the campaign. The regiments of Birkenfeld, Utenhove, Slangenburg and Torsaye provide evidence of this: in January the average effective strengths (i.e. without the sick and soldiers on furlough) of the companies in these four regiments were 46.75, 44.75, 49.40 and 51.85 men in rank and file, respectively. At the start of the 1676 campaign these strengths had risen to an average of 62.33, 66.33, 63.67 and 63.69 men, respectively. The six or seven men who were missing at the time must have been sick, wounded or absent with furlough, as well as deserters and fatalities who had not yet been replaced. The majority of companies numbering forty to fifty men would have been strengthened to sixty men or more before the start of the campaign. If a company was weaker then the captain was subject to financial and disciplinary sanctions. As a result of all of these measures, from 1674 the Republic could bring a substantial force of 30,000 men into the field each year and could maintain this strength *throughout* the campaign season.

There was still a difference between paper and effective strengths, but this was now considerably smaller than in the era of Maurits and Frederik Hendrik. Back then the effective strength in the field had been a quarter to a third lower than on paper,[127] while the Dutch infantry companies which were deployed in the field between 1674 and 1678 had an average effective strength of sixty men in rank and file and sixty-nine to seventy men including the officers (see Appendices III, IV and V), only 14 to 15 per cent below the prescribed paper strength of eighty-one men (eight officers, three boys and seventy rank and file). The most complete regiments were obviously detailed for field service, while the weaker units performed garrison duties.

In the cavalry the difference between the strength on paper and the effective field strength was as great as for the most highly complete of the infantry companies. The paper strength of a cavalry company was sixty-nine men and eighty horses: eight officers with nineteen horses and sixty-one troopers with one horse each. The muster-rolls reveal an average field strength of fifty-two troopers, which is a difference of 15 per cent. A company of dragoons was meant to be comprised of ninety-four men and 100 horses: fourteen officers, three boys and seventy-seven men in rank and file (including three corporals). The average field strength was seventy-one men in rank and file, no less than 92 per cent of the paper strength.

Based on the data above, the total strength of the Dutch army between 1675 and 1678 can be estimated at 10,000 horse and dragoons and 60,000 infantry, a total of 70,000. According to the army establishments presented in the States of War, from 1675 to 1678 the paper strength should have amounted to 88,588

---

[127] See pp. 45–6.

men, but calculated on the basis of the prescribed paper strengths it was approximately 80,000 men – 148 cavalry companies of eighty horse, twenty companies of dragoons of 100 horse and 823 infantry companies of eighty-one foot. This means that the army fell short of the establishment strength by between 14 and 15 per cent. The permanent presence of a commissary of the musters at the field headquarters meant that the company commanders had to be prepared for a muster-call at all times.[128]

In conjunction with the enforcement of strict discipline, the financial measures introduced by the States of Holland ensured that within a period of two years (1673–1674) the demoralised and weakened Dutch army could be sufficiently restored to contend with the French in the open field. William III was, however, aware that the permanent restoration of the Dutch troops 'in splendour and discipline' required constant care and attention and that it would have all been for nothing if the government itself remained in default. The return of Gelderland's, Utrecht's and Overijssel's troops to their former repartition was therefore an important test. In early 1674 the troops of France, Münster and Cologne had essentially left the Republic's territory. Gelderland and Utrecht had suffered a great deal from the invasion – damage in Overijssel had remained limited[129] – but Holland, Zeeland, Friesland and Groningen had no desire to take this into account and demanded that from 1 January 1675 the defence expenditure would be borne by the seven provinces based on the old distribution formula. This meant that Gelderland, Utrecht and Overijssel had to pay 166 infantry companies and nine cavalry companies. The three former 'conquested' provinces attempted to shirk reassuming this burden. William III had to intervene in person on a regular basis in order to save the stricken captains and rittmasters from financial ruin. In March 1675 he urged the States of Utrecht to pay the Prince of Brunswick-Osnabrück's regiment 'without putting forward the excuse of incapacity or otherwise to delay, the said militia being apportioned to your charge ... and the Province of Your Noble Mightinesses thereby being taxed according to its quota, the settlement of which cannot be avoided in this present necessity of the State'.[130] In November 1675 he instructed the States of Utrecht that they also had to ensure that the captains, 'on returning from the field to the garrisons with their companies, may be promptly furnished with at

---

[128] NA, RvS 1501 and RvS 1905, 'Staat van de militie na de Vreede van Munster'; Ten Raa, *Het Staatsche leger*, VI, pp. 185 and 210–11; NA, CvdH 150, Extract res. RvS, 23 February 1677, concerning a commissary of the musters in the field army. On 27 July 1675, William III promulgated an order whereby anyone reporting a fraudulent captain or rittmaster could expect a reward of no less than 100 rix-dollars, and if the informant was a soldier or trooper he was also offered the prospect of promotion or an honourable discharge, 'according to his preference and request'. See NA, RvS 2096.

[129] W. Fritschy, *Gewestelijke financiën ten tijde van de Republiek der Verenigde Nederlanden*, vol. I, 'Overijssel (1604–1795)', RGP kleine serie 86 (The Hague 1996), p. 65.

[130] HUA, ASU 278-5, William III to the States of Utrecht, The Hague, 9 (quote) and 14 March 1675.

least two months' pay in order to enable them to carry out their recruitments'.[131] Colonel Frederik Eybergen complained in that same month that the captains of his regiment whose companies were repartitioned to Overijssel had received no pay since June 1675. William III's intervention resulted in the States of Overijssel issuing two pay ordinances, but this did not fully resolve Van Eybergen's troubles, because 'there is no way ... to negotiate the payments on them', namely convert them into cash. Eybergen warned William III that under such circumstances the captains were in no position to restore their companies.[132]

As stadholder and provincial captain-general of Holland, Zeeland, Gelderland, Utrecht and Overijssel, William III could keep watch on the quality and payment of the companies repartitioned to these five provinces, but over the troops from Friesland, Groningen and Drenthe he had little say, as the three northern provinces had their own stadholder. However, Hendrik Casimir II (1657–1697) was still too young and inexperienced to keep his officers in check. In July 1675 William III petitioned the States of Groningen 'to authorise [him] during the current campaign to be able to cashier such officers ... that we shall judge to be incompetent and neglectful [of their duties] and appoint others in their places'.[133] The regents of Groningen raised no objection to William III dismissing incompetent officers, but they pointed out that the appointment of new officers was the preserve of their own stadholder and the province's States assembly.[134] But William III would not be defeated so easily. In January 1677 he instructed the legal expert Henric Piccardt (1636–1712) to contend that he was entitled to confer vacant officers' posts in the field, because 'His Highness must not be considered in the quality of stadholder or captain-general of the one province or the other, but as captain-general of the Union, for in the army [in the field] the quality of stadholder does not enter into the matter'. Piccardt warned that if William III were to be denied the right to appoint Friesland's and Groningen's officers during the campaign then he would not be able to assert his authority, seeing as it was 'incontrovertible that he who cannot make any rewards to the militia during the military operations can neither hold nor gain adequate respect, obedience and gravitas among the militia'.[135] The States of Groningen

---

[131] HUA, ASU 278-5, William III to the States of Utrecht, Soestdijk, 4 November 1675.
[132] KHA, A16-XIe-23, Frederik Eybergen to William III, Coevorden, November and 19 December (quote) 1675.
[133] GrA, ASSO 1399, William III to the Delegated States of the province of Groningen, Louvain, 13 July 1675, transcript.
[134] GrA, ASSO 1399, Response of the Delegated States of the province of Groningen to William III, 30 July 1675, transcript.
[135] GrA, ASSO 1399, 'A proposition delivered by the syndic [Henric] Piccardt in the name of His Highness, the lord prince of Orange in the assembly of the lords the Delegated States of Groningen, on account of His Highness's assertion and sentiment concerning the bestowal of all the military charges that fall vacant in the field, even of the provinces of Friesland and Groningen, notwithstanding that they have their own stadholder'. This proposition was submitted verbally on 26 January 1677.

and Friesland stood their ground all the same, so the abuses in Groningen's and Friesland's regiments persisted undiminished. In December 1676, for example, the Frisian infantry regiment of Colonel Stecke numbered no more than 269 men when it should have counted at least 720 (twelve companies of sixty men in rank and file). Stecke complained to the Frisian stadholder that it was not his fault that his regiment was so weak:

> [I] left it here [in Sas van Gent] 454 men strong, including the officers and a few sick. Now [on my return I] find there are 269 present, with 3 captains, some lieutenants and ensigns, sergeants and drummers, all the rest have left with and without furlough for Friesland. The lieutenant-colonel and sergeant-major are also in Friesland.

By 20 January 1677 the regiment's strength had shrunk to just 242 men. The following week some fifty men returned from Friesland, but 266 soldiers as well as about half the officers were still absent, with or without leave.[136]

Johan de Vassy, the commander of Fort Philippine, had difficulties with the Frisian officers, too. In March 1677 he informed the States-General that just one of the four Frisian companies of his garrison was in good condition, namely that of Taco van Burmania. All the officers in Burmania's company were present and it boasted sixty men in rank and file. The other three companies, by contrast, counted just thirty-eight, forty-two and forty men. Captain Elias Lycklama had not been seen by his company for a year and a half, 'and according to the officers does not impose any order in the least on his company'. Captain Joachim van Amama was also absent, 'being about 14 years old'. Captain Alexander Papelay was present and proffered as an excuse for the poor state of his company that over the last three pay-months of forty-two days he had received no more than 400 *dukatons* (1,200 guilders) and was 'therefore not in a position to make any recruitments.'[137]

The disciplining of Dutch officers

The government measures introduced in July 1673 meant that the company commanders were no longer forced to commit fraud in order to be able to maintain their units, as had been the case at the time of Maurits and Frederik Hendrik. The captains and rittmasters were transformed from suppliers and leaders of mercenaries into professional officers employed by the state. The officers did, however, have to pay a price for the government support. From now on they had to respect the rules. Whereas previously only the rank and file were subject to strict discipline, William III now tightened the reins for the

---

[136] Tresoar, FSA 48b, Diderik Stecke to Hendrik Casimir II, Sas van Gent, 8 December 1675 (quote) and 17 January 1676.
[137] NA, SG 5075, Johan de Vassy to the SG, Philippine, 29 March 1677, with appendix.

officers as well. Financial support was reserved for captains and rittmasters who had acquitted themselves properly; those who were found guilty of 'laxness and cowardice', insubordination or fraud by the General Court Martial could not count on any clemency from William III whatsoever.[138]

In autumn 1672 all the officers who had surrendered strongholds or forts to the French were called to account by the General Court Martial. Lieutenant-Colonel Ditmaer van Wijnbergen, commander of Rees, was acquitted of treason and cowardice, but the judges thought that he could have negotiated a better capitulation and therefore ordered him 'to recruit three hundred men at his own expense and to present these to His Highness for the service of the Land'.[139] Colonel Stecke, commander of Deventer at the time, received a similar sentence: he was suspended for four months and was ordered 'to recruit [his company] at his own expense'.[140] A harsher fate awaited Lieutenant-Colonel Daniël d'Ossory, commander of Rheinberg, and Alexander d'Hinyossa, captain of the garrison at Wesel: both were found guilty of cowardice and treason and were subsequently beheaded.[141] The most notorious case was that of Moise Pain et Vin (c. 1620–1673), the army's quartermaster-general, who in December 1672 had abandoned his post at the Nieuwerbrug sconce without putting up the least resistance. The General Court Martial sentenced him to life imprisonment and ordered the confiscation of all his property. As captain-general of the Union William III had to approve all the sentences, but he refused to be satisfied with this. He wanted an example to be set and therefore demanded the death penalty. The General Court Martial revised its sentence and ordered that Pain et Vin be taken to the scaffold 'and that there the sword shall be struck over the prisoner's head by the executioner', whereupon he would be transferred to the gaol. William III rejected this sentence for being too light for a second time. Pain et Vin was ultimately sentenced to death by the sword on 23 January 1673 and was beheaded that same day, 'the head being severed only with the third blow'.[142]

After these death sentences the Dutch officers took good care not to behave in a cowardly manner, but insubordination and fraud proved more difficult to eradicate. 'The negligence of all the captains, lieutenants and ensigns, as well as the abuse of their charges, is so great that it is unbelievable and insupportable', Johan Maurits fulminated in February 1673. 'They are so impertinent that they quit their posts at night and go to the lodgings to bed down between two sheets.'[143] During the winter months 'many officers [went] as they themselves saw

---

[138] NA, RAZH, FAH 6, 'Voorslagen tot redres van de militie'.
[139] NA, AHK 353-I, no. 14, Sentence of 24 December 1672.
[140] NA, AHK 353-II, no. 90, Sentence of 12 February 1674, transcript.
[141] HUA, HAA 2731, Godard van Reede-Ginkel to his father, Nieuwpoort, 14 September 1672; Ten Raa, *Het Staatsche leger*, V, pp. 575–6.
[142] NA, AHK 353-I, no. 35, Sentence of 23 January 1673; *Vervolg van 't Verwerd Europa*, p. 173.
[143] KHA, A4-1476aI, Johan Maurits of Nassau-Siegen to William III, Muiden, 16 February 1673.

fit', without asking the colonel's permission, in order to conduct their affairs at The Hague.[144] William III did not take kindly to disobedience towards superiors and ordered the General Court Martial to impose stiff sentences. Three captains and three lieutenants from the garrison of Blokzijl who in May 1673 had refused to follow the orders of the commander to dispatch some troops to a position, were not merely cashiered but also sentenced 'to carry the pike for the period of one year in His Highness's guards regiment', so that they should better learn their 'duty' under the direct supervision of William III. The captains also had to pay a fine of 100 silver *dukatons* and the lieutenants a fine of fifty.[145] These sums were equivalent to twice the monthly salary of a captain (150 guilders) and three times the salary of a lieutenant (forty-five guilders).

When mustered on 16 December 1672 the strength of the company of Captain Snaerts was 140 men; two days later they numbered just forty. The lieutenant contended that 100 men had deserted in a single night. 'Your High Honour can judge for yourself that a deception underlies this', Lieutenant-General Königsmarck wrote to Gaspar Fagel.[146] What became of Snaerts is unknown, but the General Court Martial dismissed Captain Willem Padburch, on the charge that he had tried to entice two civilians from Haarlem to pretend to be soldiers in his company during the muster.[147] Johan Maurits hoped to deter such *passe-volants* by threatening, following the example of the French army, to brand them with a 'P' on their foreheads and, if they were caught for a second time, to hang them 'without mercy'.[148] Padburch's transgression was minimal compared with that of Captain Daniël Kriex, who had signed a contract to raise a new company during the winter of 1673/4. An investigation had revealed that Kriex, 'seeing that he could not make his company complete ... has engaged various soldiers, some on condition that these men would be free when it pleased them, some when the city of Utrecht had been retaken [from the French], and others ... when the first ships would sail to the West Indies'. Engaging soldiers on temporary or provisional contracts was forbidden and not the only punishable offence that Kriex had committed. The contract required him to levy recruits outside the Republic, but the muster commissaries discovered that 'almost all the ... soldiers [were] recruited here in the land', and it came to light that Kriex had embezzled a large part of the pay. Kriex was sentenced to pay the soldiers 'their proper unpaid salaries' and the General Court Martial also imposed a fine of 1,000 guilders.[149]

---

[144] KHA, A16-Xie-15, Frederik Eybergen to William III, Coevorden, 22 October 1675.
[145] NA, AHK 353-I, no. 56, Sentence of 6 June 1673.
[146] NA, RAZH, AGF 116, Konrad Christoph, count of Königsmarck, Bodegraven, 18 December 1672.
[147] NA, AHK 353-II, no. 108, Sentence of 18 April 1674.
[148] GAA, Missives to burgomasters 66 (microfilm 8006), Johan Maurits, Muiden, 26 November 1672. In France the punishment of branding was in 1676 replaced by cutting off the culprit's nose. See Corvisier, 'Louis XIV', p. 394; Lynn, *Giant of the Grand Siècle*, pp. 405–6.
[149] NA, AHK 353-II, no. 108, Sentence of 19 April 1674.

William III and Waldeck were severe in their actions against company commanders, but they deemed malfeasance by colonels to be even more serious. In November 1673 Waldeck ordered the disbanding of four of the six companies in Colonel Melchior van Brodden's regiment and 'to have the captains arrested ... and if according to my orders one would send me the colonel Brodden I will have him judged as he deserves'.[150] The General Court Martial deemed the defendants responsible for the poor state of their companies and dismissed them from their posts. Van Brodden was also ordered to pay a fine of no less than 10,000 guilders.[151] Colonels Jan Albert Jorman and Hannibal van Degenfelt received a similar punishment. Their incomplete regiments were disbanded in April 1673 and 'the one amalgamated into the other ... and this completed regiment assigned to the Count-Palatine of Birkenfeld'. These three colonels got away fairly lightly, considering that Colonel Louis François de Grisperre had been executed for his fraudulent practices.[152]

William III and the restoration of the Dutch army's morale

In the winter of 1672 the morale of the Dutch troops was at an all-time low. On 23 December Holland's Delegated Councillors wrote to Gaspar Fagel from the army headquarters at Alphen aan de Rijn: 'It is incomprehensible with what a scrupulous circumspection our militia seeks to preserve itself and how greatly preoccupied one is with the belief that the enemy is planning and ready to take some post or other by surprise, and how little weight our arguments against it carry'.[153] In the Dutch as well as other European armies the sergeants and corporals had traditionally been charged with maintaining discipline among the rank and file. They punished disobedience during drill or sentry-go by administering 'arbitrary correction' on the spot, giving the culprit a thrashing, which was not discussed with superiors. An eye-witness report reads as follows:

> Thus it came to pass that yesterday, when the parade was to be held, there was a soldier in the regiment of the young Prince Maurits who with filthy invectives refused his corporal's orders to stand watch, so that the corporal was compelled to strike the soldier over the head with [the flat side of] the rapier.[154]

The regiment in question was that of Colonel Willem Maurits of Nassau-Siegen (1649–1691).

---

[150] NA, FAF 1950, Georg Friedrich von Waldeck to Gaspar Fagel, Geertruidenberg, 24 November 1673.
[151] Ten Raa, *Het Staatsche leger*, VI, p. 337.
[152] *Vervolg van 't Verwerd Europa*, pp. 145, 180 and 441–2.
[153] NA, RAZH, AGF 121, Delegated Councillors at the headquarters in Alphen aan de Rijn, 23 December 1672.
[154] GA, AHGC 1200, Johan Belgicus, count of Hornes, to Georg Friedrich von Waldeck, Namur, 31 January 1678.

In 1672 such methods were inadequate, because it was not about reprimanding or correcting the reprehensible behaviour of a few, but exorcising the general sense of defeatism which had gripped the Dutch army since the launch of the French attack. William III saw just one means of combating this perilous situation: the foot-soldiers and cavalrymen had to fear the General Court Martial more than the enemy. Field-Marshal Waldeck, who was entrusted with the difficult task of readying the Dutch troops to meet the French in the open field, informed Grand Pensionary Fagel in November 1672 that there were many fine soldiers serving in the Dutch army, but there were also many 'whose nonchalance and weakness is inexcusable'.[155] The combative spirit demonstrated by several Dutch regiments in a fierce fight with the French near Woerden on 12 October 1672, when Colonel Palm's marines in particular had distinguished themselves for their great bravery, offered hope of a speedy recovery:

> The marines ... having put to the sword everything that they encountered with their cutlasses, with the exception of about 200 Frenchmen and among them a good 60 officers, who they spared on account of their pitiful pleas, which gives new heart and courage to our men, who now, as in former times, find that the French are also but human and like our men are subject to the sword and death.[156]

There had already been incidental attempts to restore discipline in the Dutch army in the 1660s, 'whereby the militia of Your High Mightinesses [the States-General] has at all times excelled above all others', but these measures had been intended only to protect the rural population and not in order to elevate the fighting strength of the troops. In 1664, for example, Willem Frederik had ordered the hanging of a waggon-driver travelling with the Dutch intervention force in East Friesland 'who, with an inhumanity unheard of in former times, has dared to tie down a farmer in a large basket and set it before the fire, to burn him gradually and just like a ham *à petit feu* and thereby to extort ham and other goods from him'.[157] William III was less concerned about this, the main object of his disciplinary measures being to achieve the absolute obedience of subordinates to their superiors, so that they would perform better when under fire. On 13 December 1672 the General Court Martial sentenced a Scottish sergeant who had publicly beaten his lieutenant with a stick 'to appear before the whole regiment ... and there to beg the aforesaid lieutenant for forgiveness on his bare knees'. He was then to be brought to the scaffold 'and being blindfolded with a handkerchief, have three soldiers shoot above his head'. And this was not the end of his suffering, because the executioner then administered twelve strokes with

---

[155] NA, FAF 1946, Georg Friedrich von Waldeck to Gaspar Fagel, Dichem, 28 November 1672 (quote); HUA, HAA 2802, Georg Friedrich von Waldeck to Godard Adriaan van Reede-Amerongen, Zwammerdam, 22 and 24 Ocober 1672.
[156] HUA, HAA 2801, G.v.K., Pensionary of Delft, to Van Reede-Amerongen, Delft, 14 October 1672.
[157] NA, RAZH, AJdW, Willem Frederik to the SG, Velthuysen, June 1664, transcript.

a stick to the sergeant's bare back and broke his sword, 'banishing the aforementioned prisoner from the United Provinces for all eternity'.[158]

In March 1673 a corporal and a few soldiers had to answer to the General Court Martial for mutiny. The corporal had demanded payment of his wages from his company's lieutenant and when he had wanted to have him placed under arrest for this the thronged soldiers had prevented it. The soldiers were sentenced 'to sit on the donkey or wooden horse in front of the parade for three days in succession, each time for two hours'. The corporal had to run the gauntlet of 150 men four times over and was also sentenced to permanent guard duty.[159] The wooden horse was a construction in the form of a horse with a sharply ridged back. The condemned man had to mount it, sometimes with weights attached to his legs as extra punishment.[160] These defaulters got away lightly all the same, seeing as the death penalty could be imposed for cowardice in the face of the enemy. The General Court Martial condemned ten soldiers and fourteen troopers who on 2 June 1673 had taken flight during a skirmish near Lopik, 'to draw straws for four of their twenty-four to be arquebusiered', namely executed by firing squad. The others had to 'run the gauntlet thrice in succession' for three days in a row.[161]

In the summer of 1673 the Dutch army was sufficiently restored to launch a counter-offensive. After the unexpectedly swift recapture of Naarden in September 1673, William III decided to lay siege to Bonn. At the end of October he invaded the Electorate of Cologne with about 12,000 men (including 3,000 Spaniards).[162] The Dutch troops missed no opportunity to wreak revenge on Cologne's civilian population. 'They spare nothing and many atrocities have already been committed', Colonel Van Reede-Ginkel wrote to his father. 'My only fear is that our army will become so wild that in the end one shall no longer have any command over the soldiers. Monasteries and churches, all were plundered.'[163] Van Reede-Ginkel's fear became reality a few days later, when things got totally out of hand at the small town of Rheinbach. William III had Rheinbach stormed, after repeatedly enjoining the inhabitants to open the gates to no avail. According to the historian S.B. Baxter what happened next provided the evidence that the Dutch troops, unlike the French, committed no atrocities. 'When it was taken ... the Prince would allow the soldiers only to plunder the town. ... and strict orders were given for the protection of women. They were

---

[158] NA, AHK 353-I, no. 25, Sentence of 13 December 1672.
[159] NA, AHK 353-I, no. 40, Sentence of 3 March 1673. For a similar case see no. 54, Sentence of 12 February 1673.
[160] Dibbetz, *Groot militair woordenboek*, s.v. 'Houte paard'.
[161] NA, AHK 353-I, no. 57, Sentence of 19 June 1673.
[162] *CWB*, II, i, nos. 414 and 416, William III to the *secrete besogne* of the States-General, Santhoven, 15 October, and Mol, 18 October 1673.
[163] HUA, HAA 2731, Godard van Reede-Ginkel to his father, Vleysen (three hours from Cologne), 29 October 1673.

obeyed.'[164] Alas the reality was different. The Dutch troops put a great many of the inhabitants and farmers who had fled to the town to the sword and hanged the burgomaster in the town's gateway. Field deputy Adriaan van Bosvelt sent a report to the States-General about this operation. 'In general one senses a very great esprit and courage among our troops, which has also been demonstrated [in the assault on] Rheinbach', he proudly boasted.[165] Bonn fell into the hands of the allies on 12 November 1673 after a short siege.

During the winter of 1673/4, Waldeck pushed on with the reorganisation of the Dutch army. William III had empowered him 'on his Highness's provision and approbation, to appoint in his absence capable persons as captains over the companies which shall fall vacant'.[166] Waldeck's most important task involved the revision of the 'State of War' army establishment and making preparations to facilitate the dispatch of a substantial field army to the Spanish Netherlands in 1674. In 1673 the establishment of the Dutch army was 147 companies of horse, twenty companies of dragoons and 948 infantry companies. The revised State of War was established at 149 cavalry companies, twenty companies of dragoons and 900 infantry companies. Waldeck was ordered to disband the fifty weakest infantry companies and divide their troops among the remaining companies as he 'shall judge best'.[167] One of the captains dismissed by Waldeck was Bredemus. At the muster in March 1674 it had come to light that his company was just thirty-seven strong. 'The weapons are worthless and many [of the men] have none whatsoever. The men are so poorly clothed that one would take them for beggars rather than soldiers.' Nevertheless, the recently appointed captain did his utmost to restore the company so that it would not have to be disbanded.[168] Waldeck's efforts bore fruit: in June 1674 the Dutch army was in a 'very good state'.[169]

Owing to his severity, William III was not well-liked among his soldiers – in an instruction dated 19 February 1673 he had instructed the Dutch army's provost-general to hang troops who were caught *in flagrante delicto* 'without any delay or form of trial', and after the battle at Mont-Cassel (11 April 1677) he had one soldier from each company in the Van Weede-Walenburg regiment, which had taken to its heels, executed by drawing lots; the rest were rehabilitated.[170] He was, however, respected by the men, because he did not spare himself either.

---

[164] Baxter, *William III*, p. 107.
[165] NA, SG 12579.99, Adriaan van Bosvelt, before Bonn, 4 November 1673.
[166] NA, FAF 1950, Georg Friedrich von Waldeck to Gaspar Fagel, The Hague, 30 October 1673, with William III's authorisation as an addendum, The Hague, 28 September 1673.
[167] CWB, II, i, no. 412a, 'Memorie voor den heer grave van Waldec wegens de te doene reductie van het voetvolck', 12 October 1673.
[168] GA, AHGC 1216, Colonel Nicolaus Friedrich von Zobel to Georg Friedrich von Waldeck, Breda, 25 March 1674.
[169] NA, FAF 1952, Georg Friedrich von Waldeck to Gaspar Fagel, Blasfelt, 26 June 1674.
[170] HUA, HAA 2732, Godard van Reede-Ginkel to his father, Zedigem, 11 May 1677; *Hollantse Mercurius* (Haarlem 1677), p. 46. The provost-general and his staff rode 'piebald

During the battles of Seneffe (11 August 1674), Mont-Cassel and Saint-Denis (14 August 1678) he was always to be found where the danger was greatest. He led the troops in battle in person, but was 'miraculously preserved by God Almighty in and amongst his enemies', wrote an eye-witness after the battle at Seneffe.[171] Three years later, during the battle of Mont-Cassel, William III took two shots in his breastplate, and Hendrik van Nassau-Ouwerkerk (1640–1708) saved his life during the battle at Saint-Denis by shooting down, in the nick of time, a French officer who had already placed 'the pistol to his body'.[172]

William III also took great risks in siege operations. During the siege of Maastricht in 1676 he was constantly present in the foremost trenches, which resulted in him being hit by a musket-ball two fingers above the elbow on 24 July. The wound was not life-threatening but 'considering the subtle [i.e. sensitive] temperament of His Highness's body' it had to be watched carefully, according to Johan Bruynstein, William III's personal physician. William III was not blessed with a strong physical constitution. Nonetheless, he was already to be found in the saddle or in the trenches the following day, 'and that in this hot weather', a concerned Bruynstein wrote to Gaspar Fagel.[173]

*

William III made strenuous demands on the Dutch troops, but he also endeavoured to care well for them. He devoted plenty of attention to the provisioning (see the following chapter) and medical care. In December 1673 the States-General decided to establish a field hospital staffed by an intendant, two *medicinae doctores* (physicians in the true sense), two surgeons-general, a hospital master and an unspecified number of servants and washerwomen. In addition each regiment was from then on required to have a surgeon-major present and at least one barber-surgeon for every two companies. The barber-surgeons had to treat uncomplicated wounds and provide first aid to the seriously injured, so that casualties could then be transferred to the field hospital. Each regiment had its own field-chest containing medications, linen and 'plaster'. The level of skill of the barber-surgeons was not consistent and in 1677 it was therefore decreed that each brigade should appoint a master-surgeon in order to supervise. The intendant was charged with the management of the field hospital. The doctors, the surgeons 'and, in addition, those who shall attend to the sick and wounded in the army' were to keep him informed of the number of patients, specifying their sickness or 'discomforts'. The intendant then reported this to William III or Waldeck. The 'hospital master' was responsible for purchasing and distrib-

---

horses in order to be recognised by the soldiers from afar'. NA, CvdH 150, Notes by Adriaan van der Hoop about the 'provost-general of the army'.
[171] NA, RAZH, AGF 54, A. Nyenborch van Naeltwijk, Mons, 24 August 1674.
[172] NA, RAZH, AGF 121, Revixit van Naerssen to the Delegated Councillors of Holland, Saint-Denis, 15 August 1678.
[173] NA, RAZH, AGF 43, Johan Bruynstein, Smeermaas, 24 and 27 July 1676.

44. Field hospital, c. 1670–1690. Oil painting by Hendrick Verschuring. (Royal Netherlands Army Museum, Delft, 105901)

uting food and drink to the sick and wounded. In addition he had to 'visit the sick and wounded ... from bed to bed ... with the doctors; receive the orders concerning the patients from them ... and execute these, with regard to the ordained medicaments as well as to the distribution of food and drink'. The sick and wounded whose recovery 'shall require a considerable time' had to be transferred by waggon or barge to a town or city hospital, and the sooner the better. The capacity of the field hospital was, after all, limited and intended to care for the soldiers only until they were stable enough to be moved. As a rule, two out of three wounded men would recover. The deceased were as swiftly as possible to be 'buried [in] deep pits at remote places ... for the prevention of all the infection and contagion'. A fee of six stivers was charged for every day that a soldier was nursed in the field hospital or hospice: four stivers was deducted from the pay and the paymasters made up the difference of two stivers.[174]

The government's interests were directly affected by the treatment and recovery of a wounded soldier, because a soldier's dying constituted a double blow for the state: the loss of an experienced soldier and the company commander's costs for

---

[174] *Groot Placaet-boeck*, III (The Hague 1683), pp. 182–4, 'Reglement ende ordre van de Hoogh Mog. Heeren Staten-Generael der Vereenighde Nederlanden tot voorkominge ende redres van sieckten onder des Landts militie in 't leger en elders', 11 December 1673 (quotes); Antoon Hubert Marie Kerkhoff, *Over de geneeskundige verzorging in het Staatse leger* (Nijmegen 1976), pp. 56 and 68–76; Ten Raa, *Het Staatsche leger*, VI, pp. 305–7.

the recruitment of a replacement which had to be reimbursed. Companies were traditionally accompanied by 'field-shearers' (*veldscheerders*), but these were effectively barbers. These men were able to deal with uncomplicated wounds, but for the seriously wounded they were unable to do anything. As a result, during the journey from the battlefield to the town hospice an unnecessarily high number of soldiers had died from their wounds. The establishment of a field hospital was therefore a significant improvement, but a permanent military hospital where the troops could be cared for until they were fully recovered was still lacking. The civilian hospices of the Spanish Netherlands were as ill-equipped as those in the Republic to cope with a great influx of wounded men. After the battle of Seneffe some 2,000 wounded soldiers 'and many officers from our army' had to be cared for in the nearby stronghold of Mons.[175] The Republic did not proceed with the establishment of a main army hospital based in Brussels until 1690.[176]

In early January 1676, Everard van Weede (1626–1702), lord of Dijkveld, the States-General's extraordinary envoy in Brussels, impressed upon the duke of Villa Hermosa, governor-general of the Spanish Netherlands from 1675 to 1680, that 'good care ought to be provided for the [Republic's] soldiers who might end up being hurt or sick, because the orders about this given by his Excellency [Villa Hermosa] in the campaign before last were not properly followed or obeyed, causing serious inconvenience and complaints among the men, and many soldiers deserted'. To prevent a repeat of these abuses in 1676, Villa Hermosa designated hospitals in Brussels, Mons, Louvain, Mechelen and Ghent for the Dutch sick and wounded, where they would be 'cured and attended to' for six stivers a day. The troops had to pay the usual four stivers themselves and the remaining two stivers would be covered by the government in Brussels.[177] In early August 1676, however, it came to the attention of the Dutch field deputy, Nicolaas Witsen (1641–1717), that in Ghent 'a papist has assisted our patients and our chaplains have acted very badly in not having proffered their services'. Rittmaster Diederik Hoeufft (1648–1719), the Republic's liaison officer at the Spanish headquarters, was instructed to lodge a protest and point out that in 1672 'at the hospital in Amsterdam one permitted Catholic clergy for the Spanish sick and thus far one is not raising any great objections to it'.[178]

The improved medical care resulted in fewer Dutch soldiers succumbing to their injuries, but when an epidemic broke out the doctors often stood powerless. Armies and garrisons were extremely susceptible to infectious diseases. In 1672,

---

[175] NA, RAZH, AGF 54, A. Nyenborch van Naeltwijk, Mons, 24 August 1674.
[176] Kerkhoff, *Geneeskundige verzorging*, p. 85.
[177] NA, SG 12588.106, Everard van Weede-Dijkveld to the SG, Brussels, 1 (quote) and 5 January 1676. See also SG 5075, Exhibitum, 24 May 1677, Convention agreed by Alexander de Baillencourt Courcol and Van Weede-Dijkveld as plenipotentiaries of Villa Hermosa and William III, respectively, Brussels, 22 February 1677, Article XIV.
[178] NA, RAZH, Familiearchief Hoeufft van Velsen 123, Nicolaas Witsen to Diederik Hoeufft, Coppegem, 8 August 1676.

when the Dutch army was gathered at the River IJssel, the surrounding towns ended up 'so packed full of troops ... that if they do not swiftly march out then they shall stink themselves out'.[179] In November 1673 there broke out in Naarden an epidemic 'of dysentery as well as other infectious fevers, from which a multitude of people are being consumed and dying, to which the churchyards bear the ample and surest witness'. Of the 3,400-strong garrison by 10 November 1673 some 183 had already died and 933 others were infected.[180] Towards the end of the campaign season in particular, when the nights were cold and it often rained, many soldiers fell sick. In early October 1674, William III had the troops billeted in farmhouses 'to prevent sickness', but by then many were already ill. 'The Imperialists are also starting to long for their winter quarters and the Spanish are shrinking [in number] from day to day. So the end of this campaign is beginning to approach', according to A. Nyenborch van Naeltwijk, the representative in the army of the Delegated Councillors of Holland.[181]

The birth of the Republic's standing army

The Republic concluded a peace with France on 10 August 1678. A month later the States-General voted to reduce the Dutch army to its peacetime establishment. In contrast to the troop reductions that were implemented after the Peaces of Münster (1648) and of Aix-la-Chapelle (1668), they now paid careful attention to keeping army organisation intact. Thousands of soldiers were dismissed, but the regimental structures were in large part retained in order to prevent loss of the expertise and experience gained over the previous seven years of war. The Republic could not allow itself to become involved in a war with France wholly unprepared ever again. By holding manoeuvres on a regular basis during peacetime, the discipline and proficiency of the troops would be kept up to the mark. The soldiers and officers could be taught the drill in the garrisons, but training camps were needed for fighting in brigade and army formations. On New Year's Eve 1678 the peacetime strength of the Dutch army was set at 40,000 men, in line with William III's advice.[182] Of the infantry, besides the Foot Guards (2,522 men), two companies of guards from Friesland and Groningen (354 men) and four companies in Emden (440 men), some forty-eight infantry regiments were retained. Each regiment was composed of ten or twelve companies of fifty-five men. The cavalry was composed of twenty-two regular regiments, each with an

[179] HUA, HAA 2731, Godard van Reede-Ginkel to his father, Middachten, 10 May 1672.
[180] GA, AHGC 1221, The joint officers of the garrison of Naarden to Georg Friedrich von Waldeck, Naarden, 10 November 1673.
[181] NA, RAZH, AGF 54, A. Nyenborch van Naeltwijk, Affligem Abbey, east of Aalst, 10 October 1674.
[182] NA, Res. RvS, 2 January 1679; Tresoar, Familiearchief Thoe Schwartzenberg en Hohenlansberg 3242, 'Provisionele staet van militie bij sijn Hooch.t en Hollandt voorgeslagen', 1679; Ten Raa, *Het Staatsche leger*, VI, p. 150.

average of three companies of fifty horse, the Horse Guards (480 horse) and the Life Guards of William III (160 horse), plus ten companies of eighty-six mounted dragoons and eight companies of fifty-five dragoons on foot.[183]

The care and attention that William III devoted to the Dutch army is evident from the muster-rolls of eighty-nine infantry companies (4,348 men) and eleven cavalry companies (398 men and 410 horses) which were mustered in September 1681, for the most part in the encampment near Breda.[184] A regular infantry company of fifty-five men was composed of eight officers, forty-four men in rank and file (including three corporals) and three boys. The captains were required to maintain their companies at the strength on paper. The eighty-nine companies mustered counted an average of 47.99 effectives, which is 87.25 per cent of the paper strength. If only the rank and file are considered, then the percentage is more than 3.5 per cent higher (an average of forty men per company). This discrepancy arises from the fact that in peacetime there were always several officers absent on furlough. A regular company of horse consisted of eight officers with thirteen horses and thirty-seven troopers with one horse each, a total of fifty horses. The eleven companies mustered counted an average of thirty-six effective men and thirty-seven horses, namely 80.4 per cent and 74.5 per cent of the paper strength. If one considers only the rank and file then both percentages amount to 87 per cent. In 1683 almost 11,000 infantry (202 companies) were gathered at an encampment in Gelderland. On average each company present mustered 90 per cent of its prescribed strength.[185]

That is why the Dutch army could be brought up to wartime strength without sacrificing quality in 1689. The ordinary infantry companies were at this time reinforced with sixteen men in rank and file, so the proportion of veteran soldiers to recruits was approximately 3:1. According to contemporaries this ratio was acceptable.[186] During the Nine Years' War the Dutch captains were once again allowed to have eight men less on the muster-roll than was prescribed as the paper strength,[187] but from the War of the Spanish Succession the company commanders were obliged to keep their companies at full strength. An order promulgated by William III on 25 April 1701 specified that 'the captains … [shall] be obliged to keep their companies complete and a soldier who comes to die or desert, the captain shall be obliged immediately to enlist another competent soldier in his place'.[188] It can therefore be stated without exaggeration that the Republic's standing army was born under the captain-generalship of William III.

[183] Ten Raa, *Het Staatsche leger*, VI, pp. 162–5, 190–201 and 228–65.
[184] NA, SG 12548.488.4, Muster-rolls.
[185] HUA, HAA 3610, 'Camp 1683 op [de] Velue'.
[186] Van Nimwegen, *De Republiek als grote mogendheid*, p. 110.
[187] John M. Stapleton, 'Forging a Coalition Army: William III, the Grand Alliance, and the Confederate Army in the Spanish Netherlands, 1688–1697', Ph.D. diss., Ohio State University (2003), p. 117.
[188] Dibbetz, *Groot militair woordenboek*, s.v. 'Compleethouding der compagni[e]ën'.

The transformation of the Dutch army into a standing army of professional soldiers was also evident from the men's clothing. It is unclear when the decision to dress the troops 'uniformly' per regiment was taken, though this was certainly the case during the Dutch War.[189] The custom would be formally established in the 1680s. A 'Naadere ordre en reglement op het stuk van de kleedinge der infanterie' (Further orders and regulations on the matter of the clothing of the infantry) appeared on 17 October 1686,[190] providing the basis for all the later rules and regulations concerning the uniform of the Dutch troops. The soldiers had to be provided with 'fine and sufficient *surtouts* or overcoats', as well as a waistcoat and a pair of breeches every two years, and a new hat, a pair of stockings and a pair of shoes each year. There was a similar regulation for the cavalry: a trooper received a 'tight-fitting coat or *juste au corps*, a hat, a scarf ... and gloves' every two years and, in addition, a cloak, a sash, a shabrack, and holster-caps for his two pistols every four years.[191] The new clothing had to be distributed in May, at the start of the campaign. The colonels were free to determine the colour and cut of the coats, but they were expressly forbidden to charge the men a higher amount for this than they could afford from the weekly deductions. 'And in order that the common soldiers might be [financially] burdened as little as possible by the clothing, all unnecessary costs and decorations shall be eschewed.'[192] The troops had to pay for their clothing themselves, the company commanders deducting a set amount from their weekly pay: six stivers per soldier and six and two-thirds stivers (two guilders per pay-month of forty-two days) per trooper.[193] To keep the costs as low as possible, most of the regiments wore coats of rough, undyed cloth known as 'kersey', which was usually light grey in colour. By contrast the elite Foot Guards were dressed in blue, thus underscoring their special place in the Dutch army. The ordinary infantry units were distinguishable by their regimental colours, their different facings and the lacing of the buttonholes.

---

[189] KHA, A26-343, Contract signed at Leeuwarden in March 1678, between Major Menno van Coehoorn, an authorised representative of Hendrik Casimir II, and the cloth merchants Hessel Hessels and Pieter Cornelis Backer, for the supply of worsted to clothe the Frisian stadholder's regiment. The uniform consisted of a blue coat with red facings and red trousers.
[190] *Recueil ... betreffende de saaken van den oorlog te water en te lande*, I, no. 73; Van Nimwegen, *Subsistentie van het leger*, p. 356 n. 73 (Res. RvS, 2 March 1706); Ten Raa, *Het Staatsche leger*, VI, pp. 219–20; F.G. de Wilde, 'De ontwikkeling van de infanterie-uniformen in het Staatse leger gedurende de 18e eeuw', in *Armamentaria*, XVII (Leiden 1982), pp. 90–105, esp. 90 and 92.
[191] *Recueil ... betreffende de saaken van den oorlog te water en te lande*, I, no. 74.
[192] Ibid., I, no. 73.
[193] NA, CvdH 102 and CvdH 107, Notes by Adriaan van der Hoop about the payment and clothing of the troops.

Holland's financing of the Republic's war effort during the 'Guerre de Hollande' (1672–1678)

The First and Second Anglo-Dutch Wars (1652–1654 and 1665–1667) and the associated fleet-building programmes swallowed up millions of guilders during the 1650s and 1660s. The army costs during these years stand out for being so slight. From 1650 to 1665 the Dutch army had a modest peacetime establishment of slightly less than 30,000 men, their maintenance costing about 6.57 million guilders per annum.[194] During the war against Münster, army expenditure increased to approximately 8.5 million guilders.[195] After the Peace of Aix-la-Chapelle (May 1668) the Dutch army was once again reduced to about 30,000 men, but 'the storm looming in the year 1671' made necessary a huge military build-up of land-based forces. The reinforcement of the Dutch army in November 1671 with 30,000 men cost 5.5 million guilders (including 576,120 guilders in recruitment costs). Yet this was insufficient, given that France's military build-up continued unabated. The augmentation of 4 February 1672 with 14,000 foot and 5,760 horse amounted to an expenditure of more than 4.35 million guilders (including 866,640 guilders for recruitment expenses). The decree of 28 March 1672 to establish two cavalry regiments (960 men), two regiments of dragoons (2,000 men) and fourteen infantry regiments (19,600 men) cost more than 3.87 million guilders (recruitment costs included). The third and last augmentation in April 1672 provided for the raising of eighteen infantry regiments (25,200 men), with Holland shouldering the costs for ten of them. The total cost, recruitment outlay included, was 3.7 million guilders.[196] At the same time millions of guilders had to be found for the equipping of the battle fleet. The financing of this enormous defence expenditure made it necessary to introduce several special measures, in which Holland took the lead as usual. In December 1670 the States of Holland had already decided to double the tax on the milling of grain for two years in succession. In anticipation of these revenues the towns had to advance 1 million guilders; based on the new repartition approved in 1668, Holland's South Quarter had to provide 81.75 per cent and Holland's North Quarter the remaining 18.25 per cent. Interest would be paid at a rate of 4 per cent per annum over this advance.[197] The States of Holland also attempted to float a loan of 3 million guilders on life annuities issued at a rate of 7.14 per cent.[198] Approximately half this offering was subscribed, making

---

[194] NA, CvdH 24, 'Staedt van 't innecomen en[de] lasten van Holl.t', 7 December 1651.
[195] Ten Raa, *Het Staatsche Leger*, V, pp. 382–3.
[196] NA, SG 12548.454, 'Extraordinaris Staet van Oorlogh', 1671; RvS 548, RvS to the SG, 17 November 1671; Ten Raa, *Het Staatsche leger*, V, pp. 255–64.
[197] NA, CvdH 24, Extract res. SH, 6 December 1670; HCO, ASO, Deputies at the SG to the States of Overijssel, n.p., n.d., received 10 July 1668.
[198] NA, CvdH 24, 'Ordinaris en extraordinaris inkomen en lasten van Hollandt 1671–1676'.

it necessary to issue redeemable annuities and bonds at an interest rate of 4 per cent for the remainder.[199]

In 1671 Holland's ordinary receipts amounted to 11.25 million guilders, while the year's expenditure amounted to 17.41 million guilders, which, including the extra 4 million guilders in revenue, left a shortfall of 2.16 million guilders. The following year expenditure increased to 31.08 million guilders, but by levying extra taxes – including a wealth tax of 0.5 per cent (raising 2 million guilders) and a surcharge of 50 per cent on the existing land tax (receipts of 1.32 million guilders) – and by issuing forced loans (8 million guilders in receipts) as well as normal loans to the total value of 13.12 million guilders (against which 11.4 million guilders in cash was eventually netted), at the start of 1672 there was a surplus on Holland's budget of about 3 million guilders.[200] The unexpectedly swift advance of the French armies in June 1672 immediately eliminated this relatively favourable financial situation.

The lynching of the De Witt brothers in August 1672 and the subsequent purge of Holland's town councils (*wetsverzettingen*), which involved the replacement of anti-Orangist regents and burgomasters with members of the Orangist faction,[201] allowed William III, who had been appointed stadholder of Holland and Zeeland in early July, to seize firm political control, though from a financial viewpoint the ousting of many experienced regents proved to be less advantageous. 'Everywhere and in all matters [there is] an irremediable confusion', a correspondent of the Republic's ambassador in Berlin reported from The Hague in November 1672. 'To sum up, everything here is in confusion, the majority of the regents being new and inexperienced steersmen who do not know how to steer the ship straight.'[202] The fact that Holland had to shoulder almost 69 per cent of the army costs compounded the situation. Holland's budget for 1673 amounted to 33.5 million guilders, an increase of more than 2.4 million guilders on 1672. In order to raise the money required, Grand Pensionary Gaspar Fagel felt there was no alternative but to impose a raft of extraordinary taxes, to the tune of 14 million guilders – of which 6.2 million was earmarked for army pay – supplemented by forced loans to a sum of almost 6.5 million guilders.[203] In 1673 the payment of the troops was ensured by levying of a hundredth-penny *gevens-gelt*, which was a '*don gratuit*' or compulsory interest-free 'gift' of 1 per cent on all bonds, redeemable annuities and life annuities, on shares in the East India Company and on real estate.[204] This raised more than 5.5 million guilders, which was 711,000 guilders less than estimated but a great success all the same. The

---

[199] Dormans, *Het tekort*, p. 67.
[200] NA, CvdH 24, 'Ordinaris en extraordinaris inkomen en lasten van Hollandt 1671–1676'.
[201] Franken, *Coenraad van Beuningen*, p. 111.
[202] HUA, HAA 2802, Jacob le Maire to Godard Adriaan van Reede-Amerongen, The Hague, 22 November 1672.
[203] NA, RAZH, AGF 88, Extract res. SH, 8, 9 and 16 March and 22 December 1673.
[204] NA, RAZH, AGF 88, Extract res. SH, 15 June 1673.

double imposition of a two-hundredth penny tax *gevens-gelt* on property (both moveable and fixed) yielded a similar sum of more than 5.5 million guilders in receipts, albeit 718,000 guilders less than estimated. The forced loans, however, failed to yield more than 4 million guilders. Total extraordinary revenues in 1673 amounted to more than 19.6 million guilders, including a loan of almost 1.6 million guilders provided by the East India Company.[205] The extraordinary receipts made it possible for the Republic (Holland) to persevere with the war, but the financial situation remained precarious, because the paymaster's offices of Holland's South Quarter and of the Receiver-General were by then already 'weighed down' by debts of no less than 67.68 and 39.67 million guilders, respectively.[206] The substantial impost of additional taxes was intended to afford some breathing space.

In December 1673 the States of Holland voted to levy a tax on property and income of each household, called a *familiegeld*.[207] This proposal came up against strong resistance from Amsterdam's inhabitants and as a consequence the requisite registers were 'never completed or introduced, because of the difficulty one anticipated in its execution and because one was concerned about bringing the mob into the street'.[208] Three months earlier, in September 1673, the Amsterdammers had impressed upon the Delegated Councillors of the South Quarter that they had already paid an excess of more than 800,000 guilders into Holland's coffers and in forthright terms they had added that if these 'advanced monies' were not swiftly repaid then they would be forced 'to our hearts' sorrow ... to have to set aside everything that is of concern to Your Noble Mightinesses'.[209] In the wake of such threats of filibuster, the Amsterdam regents eventually consented to the floating of a substantial forced loan (four times the two-hundredth penny on property) against bonds at 4 per cent interest, but the proceeds were disappointing: 6.9 million guilders instead of the estimated 8.1 million guilders. This was followed by a new forced loan in July 1674, which raised more than 3.4 million guilders. In that same month it was decided to levy a surcharge of 50 per cent on the existing land tax (raising 1 million guilders), and in December

---

[205] NA, CvdH 24, 'Ordinaris en extraordinaris inkomen en lasten van Hollandt', 1673, 'Staet van hetgene bij Hugo Mouthaen als ghecommitteert tot ontfangh van de extraordinaris consenten van den jare [1673] ontfanghen is op de eerste capitale leeningh ende den hondertsten penningh in denselven jare geconsenteert ende tot betalinge van de militie ende militaire saecken geaffecteert' and 'Staat van 'tgeene is ontfanghen uyt den tweehondertsten penningh'; NA, RAZH, FAH 10, no. 75, 'Staet van de eerste capitaele leeninge in gevolge van het consent van den 10 january 1673'.
[206] NA, RAZH, FAH 10, no. 76, 'Staet van de lasten en schulden waermede de volgende comptoiren sijn beswaert', 1673.
[207] NA, RAZH, AGF 88, Extract res. SH, 22 December 1673.
[208] J.F. Gebhard, *Het leven van Mr. Nicolaas Cornelisz. Witsen (1641–1717)*, vol. I, 'Levensbeschrijving' (Utrecht 1881), p. 118.
[209] NA, RAZH, AGF 30, Burgomasters of Amsterdam to the Delegated Councillors of Holland's South Quarter, Amsterdam, 4 September 1673, transcript.

1674 the two-hundredth penny was levied twice (yielding almost 3.9 million guilders). The extraordinary income in 1674 amounted to 21 million guilders, a few hundred thousand guilders more than a year earlier. Nevertheless, after subtracting a surplus of 1 million guilders on the ordinary income there was still a budget shortfall of 1.5 million guilders.[210]

In 1675 the three former 'conquested' provinces were once again assessed on the basis of their usual quotas in the State of War military overviews.[211] Holland's share in the defence expenditure amounted once again to a good 58 per cent, as of old. This reduction of about 10 per cent represented a substantial reduction in costs for the province – expenditure decreased by 6 million guilders to about 26 million guilders per annum – but it was still Holland's finances on which the Dutch war effort depended. Land-based warfare required millions of guilders in hard cash. The soldiers had to be paid in specie for digging activities and storm assaults during siege operations, establishing the bread magazines required large sums of money, and lastly hundreds of waggons and horses had to be hired for the conveyance of artillery and provisions. The Council of State computed the outlay for the 1676 campaign at 1.6 million guilders. On 24 November 1676 Holland had transferred 884,727 guilders towards this amount (almost 95 per cent of its quota in the army costs), while the six other provinces still owed 214,808 guilders (more than 32 per cent of their combined share of 667,049 guilders).[212] Between 1672 and 1677 Holland paid a total of 7.9 million guilders in army expenses, 1.3 million guilders more than the province was obliged to contribute based on its quota.[213] In addition, Holland paid more than 6.9 million guilders in subsidies between 1673 and 1678, mostly in cash, to Austria, Denmark, Brandenburg, Trier, Brunswick-Lüneburg, Lorraine, Osnabrück and Münster.[214]

In 1675 Holland's budget deficit amounted to more than 1.76 million guilders. The following year the war expenditure rose by approximately 1.22 million guilders, which increased the deficit on the budget in 1676 to 2.61 million guilders. In 1675 two 'capital' loans were floated (yielding 3.28 million guilders) and the two-hundredth penny was levied twice (raising almost 3.2 million guilders). The two-hundredth penny was imposed on another two occasions, in July 1676

---

[210] NA, CvdH 24, 'Staet van den ontfangh ende uytgeef ten Comptoire-Generael van Hollandt ... gehadt ende gedaen op de extraordinaris consenten bij haer Edele Groot Mog. geconsenteert voor den jare 1674, 1675 ende 1676 tot ultimo july 1677 incluys, ende noch voor den jare 1677 tot den 15 augusti desselven jaers mede incluys'.
[211] Ten Raa, *Het Staatsche leger*, VI, pp. 142–4.
[212] HUA, HAA 2815, 'Staet van 'tgeene de navolgende provinciën hebben betaelt in minderinge van[de] legerlasten voor den jare 1676 geconsenteert tot den 24e novemb. 1676 incluys'. The most serious defaulters were Zeeland (submitting barely 16 per cent of its share), Groningen (almost 20.4 per cent) and Friesland (23.3 per cent). Gelderland had paid 33.8 per cent, Overijssel 53.6 per cent, and Utrecht 72.6 per cent.
[213] NA, CvdH 93, Holland's share in the army expenses, 1672–1677.
[214] NA, CvdH 93, 'Subsidiën. Geduurende den oorlog met Vrankrijck van den jaare 1672 tot 1678 is bij Holland betaalt aan subsidiën'.

and March 1677, this time yielding 3.1 and 2.5 million guilders, respectively. In Holland, especially in Amsterdam, there was a groundswell of opposition to continuing the war. The defence of the Spanish Netherlands had been shifted almost entirely onto the Republic's shoulders. There was practically no assistance to be expected from Spain and support from the Austrian Habsburgs failed to materialise. In December 1676 the Republic's resident in Brussels, Thomas van Sasburch (1611/12–1687), sent word to the *griffier* of the States-General, Hendrik Fagel: 'It is nought but certain that the affairs here are in a very sober state. And I believe I am able to state truthfully that one is scraping together everything in order to be able to pay one month's wages to the [Spanish] army (which is nevertheless not very considerable).'[215]

The bloody battle at Mont-Cassel was fought in April 1677. The faction which backed William III's foreign policy feared that this French victory would cause the collapse of trade on the Amsterdam stock exchange. The Republic would therefore be forced to conclude a separate peace with France. Johan Pesters, a confidant of William III, was therefore relieved to learn that:

> One generally, and in Amsterdam in particular, is more contented with the battle than I had feared, the price of neither shares nor bonds having depreciated in the least, stemming from the fact that our people, truthfully said, have fought very well, a very small number of battalions excepted, and that the French losses were greater than ours.[216]

The Amsterdammers expressed their satisfaction by consenting to the levying of a two-hundredth penny tax in July 1677, and the following month they endorsed a loan of 250,000 guilders to allow William III to undertake a 'considerable' siege operation.[217] However, in 1678 the French would once again demonstrate their superiority in military organisation. In March the French laid siege to Ghent, while the Dutch and Spanish troops were still billeted in their winter quarters, and this major Flemish town capitulated on 12 March 1678. A deputy of Groningen to the States-General, Lucas Alting, informed his principals about the impact of this grave loss on public opinion in Holland: 'On my arrival here [at The Hague I] found a general consternation about the loss of ... Ghent, whereby the shares in the East India Company ... have also fallen considerably lower than ever they were in the year 1672.'[218] The French advance seemed unstoppable. Ypres was lost on 26 March 1678 and in July the stronghold of Mons was also in danger of falling into French hands. This uncomfortable military situation sparked panic on the Amsterdam stock exchange. On 12 July 1678, Revixit van

---

[215] NA, SG 12588.106, Thomas van Sasburch to the *griffier* of the SG, Hendrik Fagel, Brussels, 20 December 1676, late evening.
[216] HUA, HAA 2818, Johan Pesters to Godard Adriaan van Reede-Amerongen, Utrecht, 24 April 1677.
[217] NA, RAZH, AGF 30, Extract res. of Amsterdam's city council, 5 August 1677.
[218] GrA, ASSO 1376, Lucas Alting to the City of Groningen, The Hague, 19 March 1678.

Naerssen, one of Holland's Delegated Councillors, warned Gaspar Fagel 'that late yesterday evening here [in Amsterdam] there was such concern and consternation among the people that the shares had by that time already tumbled by 15 per cent'. Van Naerssen had travelled to Amsterdam to negotiate a loan of 100,000 guilders for the States of Holland, but nobody was ready or willing to subscribe to it unless Amsterdam's receiver of taxes, De Willem, offered 130,000 guilders in bonds as collateral, personally stood surety, offered an interest rate of 5 per cent and in addition promised to repay the principal after six months. It was clear that in Amsterdam the will to persist with the war had evaporated, and without the support of this major city a new campaign in 1679 was inconceivable. Of the loans issued by the States of Holland, Amsterdam shouldered responsibility for approximately a third of the South Quarter's quota of 79.5 per cent.[219] Immediately after the fall of Ypres, Holland's military solicitors had to go to great pains 'to make credit on the pay ordinances'.[220] On 10 August 1678, France and the Republic concluded the Peace of Nijmegen.

Holland's burden of debt had increased by 38 to 39 million guilders between 1672 and 1678. The war expenditure for 1675 and 1676, after the reinstatement of the old quota, came to an average of 17.39 million guilders per annum. At that time the province's ordinary income and expenditure ran to approximately 11.5 and 9.3 million guilders, respectively, so after subtracting a surplus on the ordinary expenditure of about 2.1 million guilders there was still an annual shortfall of 15.3 million guilders, which had to be produced by extra taxation and loans. During the Dutch War it was almost impossible to float a voluntary loan, so the money required was primarily obtained by levying a two-hundredth penny tax (a 'compulsory gift') or 'in the form of a capital loan', by which a total of 23.24 million guilders was raised in the period 1674–1676.[221]

---

[219] NA, CvdH 24, Notes by Adriaan van der Hoop concerning the 'negotiation of funds'.
[220] NA, RAZH, AGF 92, Extract res. SH, 29 March 1678.
[221] NA, CvdH 24, 'Staet van den ontfangh ende uytgeef ten Comptoire-Generael van Hollandt ... gehadt ende gedaen op de extraordinaris consenten bij haer Edele Groot Mog. geconsenteert voor den jare 1674, 1675 ende 1676'.

♦ 8 ♦

The Conduct of War (1650–1688)

The revolution in military organisation that was achieved in the Republic between 1667 and 1688 extended to logistics and siege warfare. In 1675, for the first time in its history, the States-General promulgated orders for the establishment of several sizeable rye magazines for the Dutch army, so that bread supplies for the troops were assured throughout the campaign. Provisioning had repeatedly caused Maurits, Willem Lodewijk and Frederik Hendrik problems when they were operating beyond the immediate vicinity of their bases, but thanks to the magazine system William III enjoyed a greater degree of freedom of action. Food supplies were assured up to a distance of between forty and sixty kilometres from the magazine, thus removing the obstacle which had thwarted the growth of field armies; the old ceiling of 25,000 to 30,000 men no longer applied. During the campaigns in the Spanish Netherlands from 1674 to 1678, William III would still encounter serious hindrance due to the lack of forage magazines. The French had such magazines at their disposal and the armies of Louis XIV could therefore already begin their operations before forage for the horses was to be found in the theatre.

Developments in siege warfare influenced the methods of besieging a fortress, the structure and design of fortifications, and the use of strongholds in national defence. The greater scale of the military operations and the employment of innovative siege tactics devised by the French siege expert Vauban meant that an inchoate collection of fortified towns was no longer sufficient to halt an enemy advance; a cohesive system of extremely robust strongholds that formed an impenetrable chain was required. A military zone made up of two or more lines of fortifications should bring the enemy army's push to a halt and allow breathing space to launch a counter-offensive. Within the buffer zone a number of towns served as so-called *places des armes*, very large strongholds which functioned as depots from which the field armies could collect their food, forage, munitions and heavy artillery. In the event of a defeat the men could also seek refuge there. Because of their strategic position, Maastricht and Bergen op Zoom were two of the Dutch strongholds ideally suited to serve as *places des armes*.

There was no breakthrough in tactics in the years 1667 to 1688, though the tactical revolution ushered in by Maurits and Willem Lodewijk was properly embedded in the organisational revolution during this period. It would, however, be incorrect to conclude from this that nothing changed in the sphere of combat. The gradual replacement of the matchlock musket with flintlock firearms, the phasing out of the musket rest and the development of the socket bayonet facilitated the optimisation of volley fire. Such developments in weapons technology and tactics are addressed in the conclusion at the end of this chapter.

The magazine system

The War of Devolution (1667–1668) confronted the European powers with a military strategic problem that was completely new. On 24 May 1667 Louis XIV invaded the Spanish Netherlands at the head of 50,000 men. Frederik Hendrik had preceded him with a force of similar size some thirty-two years earlier, but while the Dutch commander-in-chief had soon been forced to make an about-turn because of logistical difficulties, the young Sun King could continue his campaign of conquest unhindered. He captured Valenciennes, Binche, Charleroi, Ath, Bergues, Veurne (Furnes), Tournai, Douai, Courtrai, Cambrai, Oudenaarde and Aalst in quick succession. On 28 August, without pausing to rest, the French laid siege to Lille. Vauban, aged thirty-four, was placed in charge of digging the trenches and raising the batteries. Lille fell on 27 September 1667 and was annexed by France.[1] Though the French triumphal march must in part be attributed to the imbalance in military strength – the Spanish army in the Netherlands numbered a total of 35,000 men[2] – the primary cause of the French being so successful was that they allowed the Spaniards no time to take countermeasures. For more than four months, from 24 May to 27 September, the use of the magazine system made it possible for the French to press their attack without relent.

Establishing food depots for the troops in the field was not unknown, but the scale on which it was implemented after 1667 was wholly unprecedented. In 1629 Frederik Hendrik had ordered the stockpiling of an emergency reserve of rye to prevent hunger forcing the Dutch army to raise the siege of 's-Hertogenbosch. He did the same during the sieges of Maastricht and Breda in 1632 and 1637.[3] As soon as these operations were concluded the supplies were sold, so there was no question of a permanent magazine system. During the Thirty Years' War the French crown ordered the stockpiling of victuals along the lines of march, so that the French soldiers could be supplied with food and drink *en route* to

---

[1] Christopher Duffy, *The Fortress in the Age of Vauban and Frederick the Great 1660–1789* (London 1985), p. 7; Lynn, *The Wars of Louis XIV*, p. 108; Bluche, *Louis XIV*, pp. 241–2.
[2] Etienne Rooms, 'De materiële organisatie van de troepen van de Spaans-Habsburgse monarchie in de Zuidelijke Nederlanden (1659–1700)', Ph.D. diss., Vrije Universiteit Brussels (1998), p. 20.
[3] See p. 131.

the Holy Roman Empire and the Spanish Netherlands. The *étapes* or staples, as these food depots were known, were meant to preserve France's rural population from being plundered by their own soldiers. For operations in enemy territory Paris drew up contracts with purveyors who were required to supply the French troops with bread no matter where they were. In practice the French soldiers often went hungry, because their wages were distributed erratically and without payment the *munitionnaires* refused to continue the bread deliveries. During the Fronde – the internal uprisings that tore France asunder between 1648 and 1653 – the system of *étapes* was placed under serious strain.[4] Consequently the small armies of the various factions essentially lived from the land: the soldiers harvested the ripe grain themselves or simply stole it from the barns, had it milled into flour in the proximity of the camp and baked into bread in the ovens of the surrounding villages. 'The cavalry has greater facility for this manner of living than the infantry', wrote Puységur, seeing that the mounted arm's radius of action was much greater than that of foot-soldiers. As a result the war degenerated into a series of predatory raids. After the Fronde had waned, Paris could once again better organise the food supply, though troop concentrations of more than 15,000 to 20,000 men were rare between 1653 and 1659 due to the depletion of the French crown's financial reserves.[5] The Franco-Spanish War (1635–1659) made it clear that as long as the payment of wages and the logistics were not properly organised then France could not exploit her military might effectively. After the Treaty of the Pyrenees, the two secretaries of state for war – the aforementioned Le Tellier and his son Louvois – reformed the logistical organisation of the French army. The role of the government remained limited to the issuing of instructions and making money available, but thanks to improved oversight and greater financial certainty for the *munitionnaires* the supply of bread to the French troops could from then on be guaranteed for the duration of the campaign. The introduction of a permanent magazine system at last made it possible to break through the ceiling of 25,000 to 30,000 men in the scale of field armies. Troop concentrations of many tens of thousands of men, even as many as 120,000, became feasible.

'Le principal des armées': the provisioning of the Dutch troops

The magazine system was based on what Field-Marshal Waldeck termed the *'principal des armées'*, the notion that the provisioning could not be left to uncertain factors. 'We have to take care that we do not suffer a shortage of proviant, considering that it is the mainstay [*le principal*] of armies', he wrote to Grand

---

[4] Kroener, *Les routes et les étapes*, pp. 121–3 and 137; Parrott, *Richelieu's Army*, pp. 507–17; Lynn, *Giant of the Grand Siècle*, pp. 110–12 and 132–9.
[5] Puységur, *Art de la guerre*, II, pp. 150 (quote) and 152.

Pensionary Gaspar Fagel in September 1673.[6] Even in densely populated regions such as the Low Countries it was impossible to be certain that sufficient grain would be available locally to feed 30,000 or more men. Fields of grain and barns could, after all, be reaped, stripped bare or, if necessary, razed to the ground by the adversary, and even if this did not occur then an unforeseen delay could result in local grain supplies being exhausted. The army command then had no other option but to leave for other parts with the troops, but this was not the only difficulty the generals had to contend with. The enemy often rendered the existing wind- and watermills in the theatre of war unusable, so that there was insufficient milling capacity. During the war with Münster (1665–1666) the Dutch defenders successfully delayed the advance of Bishop von Galen's troops by wrecking the mills in Gelderland, Overijssel and Groningen. In November 1665 the field deputies ordered the burning of the windmill in the village of Beerta in East Groningen, and a few days later, when it came to their attention that there were also two horse-mills there, they once again dispatched troops to this village, who 'smashed [the horse-mills] and their stones to pieces and ruined them completely'.[7] Instead of wrecking the windmills, the belligerents sometimes made do with removing the spindles and the sails,[8] a solution which was often just as effective in rendering a mill unusable but without the attendant damage.

Milling the grain presented problems enough, but baking the bread required even greater organisation. Some of the grain could be milled into flour before the start of the campaign – rye flour could be kept for three to four months under favourable conditions – but this expedient did not apply to the baking of bread. During the summer months rye-bread remained edible for six to eight days at most, so it made no sense to bake a large supply before the start of the campaign. Nor could the soldiers be expected to carry bread for more than six days, this weight being in addition to their arms and marching kit,[9] as underscored by a Dutch officer in the late eighteenth century:

> And if one considers that the poor soldier on campaign, without bread, must carry 52 lb 17 loths [almost 26kg; 1 loth was 1/32 of a local pound], one ought to strive as far as possible to spare him. Should someone doubt this truth, then let him take the trouble to walk just 2 hours with a soldier's complete armament and kit, as I have done. I have no doubt that he shall come round to my sentiment.[10]

The ovens in the villages and farms were not designed to bake a bread supply for thousands of soldiers within a few days. The baking capacity in towns was,

---

[6] NA, FAF 1950, Georg Friedrich von Waldeck to Gaspar Fagel, Naarden, 18 September 1673.
[7] NA, SG 5039, Field deputies to the SG, Scheemda, 13 November 1665.
[8] NA, SG 12579.98-I, Hieronymus van Beverningk to the *griffier* of the SG, Zutphen, 4 June 1672.
[9] Van Nimwegen, *Subsistentie van het leger*, pp. 10–11.
[10] NA, RvS 1902-II, 'Gedagten tot soulaes en beeter bestaan der trouppes van den Staat', 1789. Probably written by a captain in the Orange-Nassau regiment.

of course, much greater – in 1665 the bakers in the towns along the River IJssel produced bread for about 25,000 Dutch and French troops[11] – but they too fell short when the military force numbered 30,000 men or more. The populations were simply too small. In 1672 Zutphen counted 5,000 inhabitants and Zwolle 10,000. In 1665 's-Hertogenbosch had a population of an estimated 9,000, while in 1650 Maastricht counted 18,000 inhabitants, Arnhem some 6,000 and Nijmegen almost 8,200. Counting 30,000 inhabitants in 1670, Utrecht was among the most populous cities in the Republic, while Amsterdam with its population of 200,000 was exceptional.[12]

The provisioning of field armies of 30,000 or more men therefore required the employment of specialists. The French government entered into contracts with the *munitionnaires*. In exchange for reimbursement of his outlay, exemption from tax and compensation for goods that were seized or destroyed by the enemy, the *munitionnaire* promised to acquire a quantity of grain, store it in various places as instructed, and have a portion of the stockpile milled into flour immediately. He then had to have the flour baked into bread using ovens he had rented or had built himself and he was required to transport the loaves by waggon to the army camp, where the loaves were sold to the soldiers at a fixed price. French troops were traditionally entitled to a daily bread portion of one and a half pounds, as were Spanish and Dutch armies. The *munitionnaires* usually baked loaves weighing three or six pounds and a new bread convoy left the magazine every four days. At a distance of up to about forty kilometres (a two-day march) the bread waggons could travel back and forth between the magazine and the encampment within four days. By deploying twice the number of waggons this distance could be increased to sixty kilometres. Such a shuttle service made it possible to deliver a new four-day bread supply every fourth day. Sometimes the troops received bread for five or six days in one go, usually when the army was about to besiege a town or had to travel a great distance. The bread supplier needed time to move his supplies and get his ovens ready. If the army managed to capture an enemy town then the *munitionnaire* established a new magazine there to serve as a base for the onward push into enemy territory. The *intendant d'armée*, a high-ranking government official who stayed at or close by the headquarters during the campaign, was responsible for supervising the *munitionnaire*.[13]

The War of Devolution demonstrated that, thanks to the magazine system, many more troops could be concentrated into a single theatre than was ever thought possible, but the implications of this were not immediately evident to everyone. The Spanish had put up hardly any resistance and military opera-

---

[11] NA, SG 5039, Field deputies to the SG, Zutphen, 4 December 1665.
[12] Piet Lourens and Jan Lucassen, *Inwoneraantallen van Nederlandse steden ca. 1300–1800* (Amsterdam 1997).
[13] Lynn, *Giant of the Grand Siècle*, pp. 107–27; Van Nimwegen, *Subsistentie van het leger*, p. 41.

45. Tombstone of Moses *alias* Antonio Alvares Machado (†1706) and his wife, Rachel Ximenes Cardoso, in the Portuguese-Israelite cemetery at Ouderkerk aan de Amstel, just south of Amsterdam. Besides a reference to Machado's surname in the form of an axe, this large and handsomely decorated tombstone features a cornstalk. The inscription below reads: 'em sua vida provedor general das armadas de Ingalatera e Holande' – 'during his life *provediteur-generaal* of the armies of England and Holland'. (Photo: author)

tions had been limited to a single campaign. It was therefore the 'Guerre de Hollande' (Dutch War) which incontrovertibly demonstrated the importance of the magazine system. The Republic adopted the French logistical system in 1675, with the three previous years serving as a transitional period. The names of Moses *alias* Antonio Alvares Machado (†16 December 1706) and Jacob Pereira (†1707) are inextricably linked with the provisioning of the Dutch troops during the 'Forty Years' War' (1672–1712) between Louis XIV's France and the Dutch Republic. The first contract with the firm of Machado and Pereira dates from October 1672. On 19 October William III informed Johan Maurits of Nassau-Siegen that he had concluded an agreement with 'Antoine Alvarez Machado, a Portuguese merchant from Amsterdam, concerning the supplying of bread for our army'.[14] Why William III specifically contracted out the provisioning of the Dutch troops to Sephardic Jews remains uncertain. Jonathan Israel points out that they could quickly borrow large sums of money because of their close ties with fellow Jews in Amsterdam and Antwerp.[15] In the critical months of 1672 this was of vital importance for the Republic. The payment of wages had, after all, been in utter disarray for some time, so the troops could not pay for the delivered food promptly. Machado and Pereira could fall back on sufficient financial reserves to be able to advance the costs of the bread supplies for a while.

[14] KHA, A4-1476aI, William III to Johan Maurits van Nassau-Siegen, Bodegraven, 19 October (quote), Roosendaal, 7 November 1672.
[15] Jonathan I. Israel, *European Jewry in the Age of Mercantilism 1550–1750* (2nd edn, Oxford 1991), p. 128.

In 1673 Machado was closely involved with the planning of the first major Dutch counter-offensive, the recapture of Naarden. William III entrusted the provisioning of 25,000 men to Machado. Each soldier was to receive one and a half pounds of bread and half a pound of Edam cheese a day, as well as a cask of beer to be shared among 100 soldiers.[16] Machado had to ensure that the bakers 'shall make the bread ... not round but in a rectangular form of six pounds [Brabant weight, c. 2.8kg], so that it can be carried by the soldiers with the least hindrance'.[17] The rectangular loaves were also a better fit for the bread chests used to transport the bread from the bakeries to the army camp. A bread chest held 133 six-pound loaves and had a wooden lid to protect the bread from rain. A farmer's waggon could transport a single bread chest or three casks of beer.[18] Machado insisted that the bread contract stipulated that he would be exempt from the 'excise on grain-milling'. Amsterdam's tax-farmers demanded payment of this tax all the same. On 3 September 1673 William III wrote a letter to the city's burgomasters from his headquarters near Loosdrecht:

> By reason of the great urgency for the army here to be supplied with bread, of which it suffers great want, we cannot be remiss in requesting that Your Honours arrange at the speediest that the *provediteur* Machado is afforded sufficient freedom and the means to be able to bake without hindrance and in accordance with the conditions agreed with him.[19]

Once the problems caused by the tax-farmers had been resolved, Machado resumed regular deliveries of fresh bread to the Dutch army.

Naarden fell into Dutch hands on 12 September 1673 after a short siege. William III then marched for Bonn, the linchpin of French operations in the Republic. The reduction of Bonn on 12 November severed the lines of communication between the French occupying army and its bases. The French left Utrecht and evacuated all the captured Dutch strongholds with the exception of Grave and Maastricht. Louis XIV continued the Dutch War in the Spanish Netherlands. The States-General were prepared to deploy the majority of their field troops, more than 30,000 men, for the defence of the Spanish Netherlands, provided that Brussels shouldered most of the costs of provisioning. Machado employed bakers and millers and supplied the grain and the means of transport – 100 Brabant waggons, each with a loading capacity of 1,200 pounds and furnished with watertight tarpaulins[20] – but Brussels would have to arrange

---

[16] NA, RAZH, ASH 6120, 'Memorie wat vivres dat duysent man dagelijcx van noden hebben', 1673; *Vervolg van 't Verwerd Europa*, p. 484.
[17] GAA, Missives to burgomasters 68 (microfilm 8007), Pieter Burgersdijck and Cornelis Hop, The Hague, 23 January 1673.
[18] NA, RAZH, ASH 6120, 'Memorie wat vivres dat duysent man dagelijcx van noden hebben', 1673.
[19] GAA, Missives to burgomasters 86 (microfilm 8040), William III, Loosdrecht, 3 September 1673.
[20] NA, RvS 95, Res. RvS, 26 February 1674.

storage space and provide the milling and baking facilities. Juan Domingo de Zuñiga y Fonseca (1649–1716), count of Monterrey and Fuentes, who had served as governor-general of the Spanish Netherlands since 1670, promised William III that he would do everything in his power to assist Machado. He kept his word. On 17 June 1674 he wrote to William III: 'I have seen to it that your purveyor of vivres has been given some mills in order to provide himself with flour. Nothing shall be forgotten in providing him the means to produce his provisions.'[21] Such sharing of responsibilities was not, however, satisfactory. There was no reason to doubt Monterrey's good intentions, but it was understood that his favourable attitude towards the Republic was not shared by everyone in Brussels and Madrid. It would therefore be better to maintain central control of the whole process of supplying bread. This prompted William III to decide that from 1675 the supply of bread would be assigned exclusively and in its entirety to the firm of Machado and Pereira. The captain-general of the Union was so pleased with the way they had performed their duties since 1672 that they were henceforth permitted to style themselves *provediteurs-generaal van den Staat*. Contenders for the bread contract could register their interest with the Council of State in advance of each new campaign, but in Machado's lifetime this was no more than a formality, because William III had ordered the Council of State 'in all undertaking of contracts … to prefer [Machado] before all other entrepreneurs'. This integrated Machado into the stadholder's small circle of 'specially close friends'.[22]

On 23 January 1675 Machado and Pereira signed an undertaking to establish five or six bread magazines in the Spanish Netherlands before 1 May: 'In order to establish these magazines, the quantity of 500 lasts of [Prussian] rye shall be delivered to the contractors at Amsterdam or in some other places in Holland, [the sum of] one hundred and fifty gold florins per last to be paid in cash by the contractant on receipt of the same.' Since the sixteenth century, Amsterdam had functioned as an entrepôt for rye and wheat from Poland-Lithuania and Prussia, the greatest grain-producing regions in Europe. A gold florin (*goudgulden*) was the equivalent of twenty-eight stivers, so Machado and Pereira paid a total of 105,000 guilders for the rye supplied. This was exceptionally expensive. Since the outbreak of the Dutch War the price of rye had risen sharply, which naturally had consequences for the price of army bread. An army of 30,000 men could be supplied with bread for sixty days with 500 last of rye, and the campaign season usually lasted from late May to early November. During the course of the campaign the *provediteurs* would therefore have to replenish their magazines on a regular basis and thus incur further high outlays. Machado and Pereira refused to accept less than one and three-quarter stivers for a bread portion of one and a half pounds.[23]

---

[21] NA, FAF 430, Monterrey to William III, Brussels, 17 June 1674, at three o'clock in the morning.
[22] Van Nimwegen, *Subsistentie van het leger*, pp. 27 and 353 n. 29.
[23] NA, SG 5076, William III to the SG, Sombref, 17 August 1677.

Table 4. Average price of a last of Prussian rye on the Amsterdam corn exchange (1670–1679)

Year	Price in g.fl.	in fl.
1670	60-8 1/5	84-8 1/5
1671	68-5 4/5	95-11 4/5
1672	93-7	130-11
1673	95-18	133-18
1674	112-23 2/5	157-19 2/5
1675	154-21 3/5	216-13 3/5
1676	134-2 2/5	187-14 2/5
1677	109-21	153-13
1678	87-17	122-13
1679	68-7 3/5	95-11 3/5

Key: g.fl. = gold florin of 28 stivers; fl. = guilder of 20 stivers. A last was the largest grain measure. One last of rye yielded on average 5,400 pounds of bread (900 six-pound loaves).

Source: N.W. Posthumus, *Nederlandsche prijsgeschiedenis*, I, 'Goederenprijzen op de beurs van Amsterdam 1585–1914' (Leiden 1943), p. 574.

Machado and Pereira had to bake more than 45,000 pounds of bread every day,[24] for which they needed six large ovens, each with a baking capacity of 7,200 pounds of bread per twenty-four hours.[25] The bread contract of 23 January 1675 stipulated that the purveyors had to bake loaves weighing three pounds, but in practice this did not happen; they continued distributing the oblong 'ammunition bread' of six pounds, the loaf of three pounds being intended only as a unit of account.[26] The soldiers had to pay for the bread themselves. Based on the bread price in 1675 this amounted to twelve and a quarter stivers per week (seven portions of one and a half pounds at one and three-quarter stivers). The troops were meant to settle this bill every six weeks, but Machado and Pereira were not confident that this would proceed without difficulties. It was, after all, highly uncertain whether the companies which had once again been repartitioned to Gelderland, Utrecht and Overijssel would receive their pay on time. The solution was to call on Holland's credit. The above-mentioned bread contract stipulated that the deliveries would be paid for from Holland's quota in 'the campaign expenses to be petitioned for the year 1675'. The settling up with the troops would take place afterwards. All that the soldiers and troopers

---

[24] GA, AHGC 1240, 'Lijste van 't broot dat den 30 juny 1675 aen de regimenten is gedistrib[uee]rt op dry tagen'.
[25] Van Nimwegen, *Subsistentie van het leger*, p. 11.
[26] In the bread contracts from the War of the Spanish Succession the *provediteur* is also instructed to bake loaves of three pounds, but at the end of each contract it states: 'In accordance with all the preceding conditions, [name of the *provediteur*] has agreed to the aforementioned delivery, each loaf of six Brabant pounds in weight, for [price].' See, for example, NA, RvS 1548, Bread contract of 9 December 1707.

were required to pay to the purveyors immediately was a 'victualling fee'. For an infantry company this amounted to seventy guilders per annum and for a cavalry company sixty guilders per annum. The paymasters had to deduct these amounts from the pay of each company 'being employed on campaign' in three instalments and transfer these funds to the *provediteurs-generaal*. Machado and Pereira received this payment 'for the delivery, preparation and keeping in readiness of the … supplies and provision of the grain and of the bread [in compensation] for interest, damage and leakage'.[27]

In December 1675 the Council of State entered into a new agreement with Machado and Pereira. The bread contract for 1676 diverged from the previous year's contract on two important points. The purveyors had complained that it was unreasonable that they had to advance the purchase price of the grain themselves, in view of the high price of rye and the large quantity they were required to purchase in one go; they should instead be granted an interest-free loan by the government. The purveyors impressed upon the Council of State that this was also in the troops' interests, because if they were not required to pay interest then they would be able to supply the bread at a lower price. The States-General appreciated the rationale behind Machado and Pereira's request and lent their stamp of approval. The States of Holland furnished the *provediteurs* with a loan of 100,000 guilders at the Generality's expense and in exchange for this Machado and Pereira reduced the price of a three-pound loaf by half a stiver, from three and a half to three stivers. The second important revision in 1676 was that the payment for the bread deliveries would no longer be advanced from the petitioned 'campaign expenses', because Holland deducted the loan of 100,000 guilders from its quota in this petition. If payment for the bread deliveries also had to be advanced from the campaign expenses then there would be insufficient funds remaining for the army expenditure required during the course of the campaign. From then on, at the end of each pay-month of forty-two days the *provediteurs-generaal* presented the bill for the bread directly to the provincial States to which the companies were repartitioned. The Council of State made an urgent request to the provinces to withhold 150 guilders from the pay ordinances of each infantry company and 100 guilders from each cavalry company, 'in order that the payments might be made more promptly … and to continue with this from month to month during the campaign'.[28] These amounts covered about two-thirds of the value of the monthly bread supplies. The agreement of December 1675 served as a model for all later bread contracts.

Despite all the assurances, Machado and Pereira soon had reason to complain. 'Seeing that in four months of petitioning by my son at The Hague he has not obtained any payment in the least,' Machado wrote to Gaspar Fagel on 26 July 1676, 'Your Honour must be aware that the accord reached with the State

---

[27] NA, RvS 96, Res. RvS, 23 January 1675, which includes the bread contract for 1675.
[28] NA, RvS 96, Res. RvS, 21 December 1675, which includes the bread contract for 1676.

was to be paid all our arrears, and in consideration of this we have undertaken [to supply] the bread at half a stiver less than the previous year.' He reminded the Grand Pensionary that William III had personally guaranteed to Pereira and himself that all arrears would be settled before the commencement of the campaign, and in conclusion Machado cuttingly commented 'that not one day passes when it is not necessary to supply more than four thousand guilders of bread'. The Republic was thus deeply indebted to Machado and Pereira's enterprise and it would therefore be a '*grande disgrace*' for the Republic if they were forced to halt their bread deliveries to the troops because of the government being in default.[29] No solution was found until months later, in October 1676, when the Amsterdam regent Nicolaas Witsen informed Gaspar Fagel that, following consultations with Machado and Pereira,

> a proposal has been made, not displeasing to His Highness, which I propose to you in His ... Highness's name, in order to make it appealing to the members of our college [Holland's Delegated Councillors], namely that one has given the Jews one's word and assured [them] in writing that Holland ... would pay them a major portion of their arrears.

The total sum in question was 85,350 guilders.[30]

In the second half of 1676 the price of rye began to fall. In December, a last of rye cost 110½ gold florins, which was forty gold florins less than at the start of that year. Machado lowered the price of a three-pound loaf by half a stiver once again. In 1677 the soldiers paid one and a quarter stivers for a portion of one and a half pounds, and this price was maintained in 1678.[31] The reduction in the bread price was highly significant for the troops. They received an advance on their pay of twenty-eight stivers per week from their captain, so a soldier had to manage on four stivers per day. Besides the bread he had to purchase all the other victuals from this, such as cheese, butter, salt fish, bacon, baked or stewed apples, gin and beer. Expressed in percentages, in 1677 and 1678 a soldier spent 31.25 per cent of his weekly advance on bread. In 1675 and 1676 this had been 43.75 and 37.5 per cent, respectively. During the War of the Spanish Succession it would be officially stipulated that a soldier should spend no more than ten stivers per week (35 per cent of his advance) on bread. If the bread was more expensive then the paymasters were to make up the difference.[32]

The task of the *provediteurs* was far from simple. Machado and Pereira travelled along behind the army to keep a watchful eye on everything *in situ*. The

---

[29] NA, RAZH, AGF 53, Antonio Alvares Machado and Jacob Pereira, Brussels, 26 July 1676.
[30] NA, RAZH, AGF 121, Nicolaas Witsen, Bergen op Zoom, 16 October 1676. Reproduced in Gebhard, *Witsen*, pp. 141–3.
[31] NA, RvS 98 and RvS 1544, Res. RvS, 14 January and 26 December 1677, bread contracts for 1677 and 1678.
[32] Van Nimwegen, *Subsistentie van het leger*, p. 37.

order book kept by Waldeck during the 1676 campaign provides useful insights into their activities. For example, on 19 July he wrote:

> An order to the *provediteur* Pereira (1) to report how many days of bread he has in stock at Brussels; (2) to ensure that in Brussels bread for four days is always ready until further notice; (3) and at Louvain for six days; (4) at Ghent and Dendermonde to arrange that flour is kept ready so that the army arriving thereabouts can be supplied with bread.

Eight days later Pereira was ordered to suspend the baking of bread in Louvain and Brussels, 'and in Ghent without fail to have ready six days of bread through until this coming Friday for the army, also in Ypres and Ghent to arrange and organise that the army arriving in the quarters can be provided with the necessary bread'. In Ypres Pereira had to stockpile sufficient grain to be able to supply the Dutch army with bread for a fortnight.[33]

For the smooth operation of their enterprise, Machado and Pereira depended on the cooperation of the Spanish governor-general. Holland's cargo ships were too large for the rivers of the Spanish Netherlands and it was sometimes necessary to transport grain over land. Carlos de Gurrea, Aragón y Borja, duke of Villa Hermosa (†1692), who had succeeded Monterrey as interim governor-general in January 1675, tried to shift responsibility for the transportation costs onto the Republic, because the stockpiles of the *provediteurs* were already exempt from import duties and they could also make use of the warehouses for free. The Hague, however, was of the opinion that seeing as the Dutch troops were being deployed for the defence of the Spanish Netherlands, Brussels also had to pay the skippers and provide the requisite number of bread waggons.[34] In accordance with their contract, in 1675 Machado and Pereira had provided 150 waggons, but this number had proven to be insufficient when the army was more than a two-day march from the magazine. For the 1676 campaign they would therefore use 400 bread waggons, each one harnessed with three horses. In 1676 greater mobility was required, because William III hoped to recapture Maastricht that year. Waldeck would in the meantime cover Flanders and Brabant with approximately 20,000 Dutch troops and 6,000 Spaniards, but when the main French army advanced to relieve Maastricht he would have to be able to head there swiftly. Villa Hermosa initially asserted that it would be impossible for him to bear the expense of the freightage and the extra waggons, but after Van Weede-Dijkveld, the Republic's extraordinary envoy in Brussels from 1676 to 1678, had threatened that the Republic would therefore be forced to limit herself to defensive action he declared that the requisite transport ships would be made available to the *provediteurs* for free. He also promised to transfer 42,000 Holland guilders a month to Machado and Pereira for the hire of the 400 bread

---

[33] GA, AHGC 1237, Orders issued by Georg Friedrich von Waldeck during the 1676 campaign.
[34] NA, SG 12588.106, Everard van Weede-Dijkveld to the SG, Brussels, 1 January 1676.

waggons. Though this amount fell 8,000 guilders short, the States-General were satisfied.[35] In 1677 and 1678 Machado and Pereira hired 250 bread waggons, each drawn by four horses, with which a six-day bread supply for 30,000 men could be transported.[36] Once again it was Brussels which shouldered these costs.[37]

Sutlers

The sutlers were certainly not rendered obsolete by the introduction of the magazine system, seeing as the *provediteurs* supplied only bread. As before, the troops were dependent on the sutlers for all other victuals. In December 1674 William III stipulated that each infantry company had to have at least one sutler who would follow the troops everywhere for the duration of the campaign.[38] The transfer of hostilities to the Spanish Netherlands had major consequences for these small-scale vendors and their clientele, the troops. Spanish officials taxed the products the sutlers imported from the Republic with all manner of tolls and duties. It was the soldiers who suffered, because the sutlers passed on the extra costs in the price of their wares. Coenraad van Heemskerck (1646–1702), the States-General's envoy extraordinary in Brussels in 1675, therefore petitioned Villa Hermosa to grant the sutlers exemption from these levies like the *provediteurs*. He pointed out that this would also be in the interests of the population of the Spanish Netherlands, because the reduced purchasing power of the Dutch troops might otherwise give rise to plundering. Van Heemskerck assured the Spanish governor-general that he was not aiming to flood the Spanish Netherlands with merchandise from Holland: 'The intention not being anything other than to allow the army to subsist much more easily, to deny the soldiers any pretext for living dissolutely.' Villa Hermosa appreciated the reasonableness of this argument and promised to exempt the Dutch sutlers from import duties from then on. Van Heemskerck then impressed upon the Spaniard that the Dutch troops would have even more reason to be satisfied if they and the sutlers were to be allowed to pay with Holland's coinage throughout the Spanish Netherlands at the same rate as in Holland, 'that is to say, one *dubbeltjen* for two sols, a *schellingh* for six sols, and so on for the rest'.[39] Van Heemskerck argued that this

---

[35] NA, SG 12588.106, same to the *griffier* of the SG, Brussels, 5 January (Art. IX of the appendix), 15 and 22 January, 2 February 1676; NA, RAZH, FAHvV 123, Nicolaas Witsen to Diederik Hoeufft, Haelen, 27 July 1676, PS, and Diegem, 12 August [1676], 'in haste'.
[36] NA, RvS 1544, Bread contracts of 14 January and 26 December 1677.
[37] NA, SG 5075, Exhibitum, 24 May 1677, Agreement with regard to the subsistence concluded between Alexander de Baillencourt Courcol and Everard van Weede-Dijkveld, Brussels, 22 February 1677.
[38] GA, AHGC 1246, William III to Georg Friedrich von Waldeck and the officers of his regiment, The Hague, 22 December 1674, transcript.
[39] NA, SG 12579.102, Coenraad van Heemskerck to the *griffier* of the SG, Brussels, 26 May (quote), Duffel, 3 June 1675.

was necessary because the difference in silver content meant there was a great difference of exchange between the coins of Holland and those of the Spanish Netherlands.[40] Were this not taken into account then the Dutch soldiers would have even more reason to complain, because as soon as the army pitched its tents for any length of time then local sutlers, innkeepers and pedlars descended in large numbers to offer their goods and services to the soldiers. The troops naturally had to pay for such goods and services with hard cash and were therefore paying over the odds. The Dutch sutlers also suffered greatly from this, because for fresh meat and other perishable foodstuffs they were dependent on the markets in the vicinity of the army camp.[41]

Villa Hermosa was not prepared to accept payment in Holland's coinage without constraints, because he feared, not unjustifiably, that the difference in exchange would lead to a shortage of cash in the Spanish Netherlands. He was therefore not prepared to go beyond granting the concession that traders from the Southern Netherlands could accept the money from Holland against the higher exchange rate, but on the strict condition that there would be no settlement with Spanish currency and nor would Holland's coinage be allowed to enter into circulation in the Spanish Netherlands. However, Spain's military weakness forced Villa Hermosa to renege on this standpoint shortly thereafter. Van Weede-Dijkveld, the Republic's envoy extraordinary in Brussels, conveyed this to the *griffier* of the States-General in January 1676:

> His Excellency [Villa Hermosa] has ordained that in all the towns where the army of monsieur, the Prince of Orange, approaches there shall be sufficient of the small coinage of his Majesty [the King of Spain] with which to cater for the officers and soldiers, because for the coinage of Holland the loss would be from twenty to twenty-five per cent compared against that of his Majesty.[42]

The impact of the magazine system on the conduct of war

It would be difficult to overestimate the impact of the magazine system on the conduct of war. In April 1672, Colonel Godard van Reede-Ginkel informed his father that in Borken, a small town in Münster, '700 small copper field ovens were brought [there] six to seven days ago, so it is certain that we shall be attacked as soon as they can to some extent subsist [i.e. gather forage] in the field'.[43] Sparsely populated regions such as the eastern parts of Gelderland and Overijssel no longer represented an obstacle for the advance of enemy armies. From 1676,

---

[40] H. Enno van Gelder, *De Nederlandse munten* (2nd edn, Utrecht 1966), pp. 134 and 137.
[41] Van Nimwegen, *Subsistentie van het leger*, pp. 44–5, and *De Republiek als grote mogendheid*, pp. 130–1.
[42] NA, SG 12588.106, Everard van Weede-Dijkveld to the *griffier* of the SG, Brussels, 5 January 1676, Article X of the appendix.
[43] HUA, HAA 2731, Godard van Reede-Ginkel to his father, Middachten, 12 April 1672.

merely the news that Louvois had been spotted somewhere was cause for great alarm in The Hague and Brussels. In April of that year there were fears that the French had designs on Ypres, 'but the reports received today state that, on the arrival of an express courier from the court, Louvois had furtively returned to Paris', so this threat seemed to have abated.[44] However, the French laid siege to Condé soon thereafter (21 to 26 April) and then proceeded to invest Bouchain (6 to 11 May). The allies were subsequently on tenterhooks. In December 1676 Louvois arrived in Arras. According to Thomas van Sasburch, the Republic's resident in the Spanish Netherlands, 'considering that this gentleman rarely undertakes such journeys to no avail, here one fears with good reason that his sights might be set on Valenciennes'.[45] Three months later the Spaniards were proved correct, when on 9 March 1677 the French opened the trenches in front of Valenciennes, which fell on 17 March.

The French successes in 1676 and 1677 were so spectacular because they were achieved in a season when major military operations were normally out of the question. Looking back in 1702, the Council of State commented:

> Experience has demonstrated that the great progress which the enemy made in the Spanish Netherlands during the war that was ended by the Peace of Nijmegen, in the winter and early in the spring or before one could subsist in the field, was not only attributable to the enemy's great strength, but most especially that in seasons otherwise unsuitable for military operations their troops could find their subsistence from magazines established on the frontiers and could subsequently act, while those of the State lay dispersed in the garrisons and could not be assembled because of a lack of forage.[46]

Without special facilities it was impossible to open the campaign before the grass and the grain had grown sufficiently to provide sustenance for the horses, which was usually not until middle or late May. The turning point came in 1676: in February and March Louvois ordered the stockpiling of substantial quantities of dry forage at Ath, Tournai and Oudenaarde, so that the fodder for the horses of the cavalry, the artillery train, and the bread and baggage waggons could be collected there 'until the grass time has arrived'.[47] This enabled the French army to leave its winter quarters as early as April 1676 and lay siege to Condé unopposed. There was great frustration about this in the allied camp. William III marched to the stronghold's aid with a courage born out of desperation:

> My concern is not that we shall now be forced to give battle, but that because of a shortage of fodder [our horses] shall surely die if we do not end up involved in battle presently.... For if we must stand facing the enemy for any length of time

---

[44] NA, SG 12588.106, Everard van Weede-Dijkveld to the SG, Brussels, 8 April 1676.
[45] NA, SG 12588.106, Thomas van Sasburch to the *griffier* of the SG, Brussels, 8 December 1676.
[46] Ten Raa, *Het Staatsche leger*, VII, p. 41.
[47] NA, SG 12588.106, Thomas van Sasburch to the *griffier* of the SG, Brussels, 1 March 1676.

then our horses shall certainly perish from hunger, because in these quarters there is no forage in the world.[48]

By then most of the farmers' hay supplies had been consumed by their own livestock or carried off by the French.

Military operations in the spring certainly took a heavy toll on the horses. The animals suffered a great deal from the cold and rain, and it was therefore of essential importance that there was a break in operations in May to let the animals loose in the meadows. Grazing the 'fat', young grass was essential for the horses to regain their strength. Without this protein-rich nourishment the weakened horses were highly susceptible to infectious diseases. Grazing in the meadows was even more important because the horses were fed unripe grain (green forage) in June and July, which was not good for the animals. In June 1667, for example, there was massive mortality among the horses in the French army, 'from eating green corn'.[49] For practical reasons it was impossible to allow the horses to graze in the field when the armies were in each other's vicinity, as the thousands of beasts would end up being scattered over too large an area and it would be impossible to assemble them in time to withstand an enemy assault.

Though there were also disadvantages to beginning the campaign early, these were more than outweighed by the strategic advantages, as was demonstrated once again in 1677, when the French laid siege to Valenciennes in March. Never before had a major military operation been launched so early in the year, as Van Reede-Ginkel complained to his father: 'God grant that they do not succeed, though I am seriously afraid of this in the event of us remaining in the vicinity of Antwerp any longer, as [I] think we must, because we cannot travel anywhere far away, having no magazines and the forage having been consumed everywhere.'[50] After Valenciennes it was the turn of Cambrai (28 March to 17 April) and St Omer (4 to 22 April), and in December the French rubbed even more salt into the wound by investing Saint-Ghislain. Waldeck had no option but to look on powerlessly, 'because of a lack of everything which is required for subsistence'.[51] Saint-Ghislain fell on 10 December 1677.

This does not imply that the feeding of army horses during the campaign was unheard of in the Dutch army. Maurits and Frederik Hendrik had distributed oats to the cavalry in the autumn, and each year from 1676 to 1678 the Council of State ordered the stockpiling of 260,000 oat rations in Mechelen (Malines), Diest and Louvain.[52] From a strategic viewpoint it was an important advantage

[48] CWB, II, ii, no. 98, William III to Gaspar Fagel, n.p., 21 April 1676.
[49] NA, SG 7061, Thomas van Sasburch to the SG, Brussels, 12 June 1667.
[50] HUA, HAA 2732, Godard van Reede-Ginkel to his father, Amerongen, 14 March 1677.
[51] NA, SG 12579.106, Georg Friedrich von Waldeck to the SG, n.p., n.d., received 8 December 1677.
[52] NA, SG 12588.106, Everard van Weede-Dijkveld to the SG, Brussels, 15 January 1676; RvS 1544, Contracts for the supply of oats, 14 January 1677 (fols 361v–363) and 1 February 1678 (fols 379–81).

if the units intended for the campaign were already gathered in the villages and towns along the front line in the spring. The campaign could then be opened as soon as the grass had grown sufficiently. Until then the horses were fed hay that had been stored in farmers' barns. The proximity of the enemy entailed the risk that they would attempt to surprise the Dutch troops in their cantonments and it was therefore of the utmost importance that a corps could be assembled in the event of an emergency, for which these oats were intended. After the threat had abated the troopers returned their steeds to the stables, because oats provided insufficient nutrition to keep the horses strong, for which hay, supplemented with straw if necessary, was essential. Louvois therefore ordered the stockpiling of 'complete' forage rations composed of oats, hay and sometimes also straw. The usual proportions were fifteen pounds of hay and eight pounds of oats or six pounds of hay, twelve pounds of straw and ten pounds of oats. The complete forage rations provided all the nourishment a horse needed. The dry forage was ferried as close to the army camp as possible by barge. Hay was too bulky to be transported by waggon, so the troops had to collect it from the unloading point in person.

The dearth of forage magazines on the allied side was primarily a question of money. In the latter half of the seventeenth century, field armies were composed of approximately one-third cavalry and two-thirds infantry. In May 1674 the Dutch army in the Spanish Netherlands numbered 16,000 infantry and 8,000 cavalry; in July 1677 it counted some 17,800 infantry and more than 9,000 cavalry.[53] However, the total number of horses in an army was one and a half to two times higher than the number of cavalrymen. Thousands of draught horses were needed for the conveyance of artillery, munitions, baggage and victuals. Feeding a total of 13,500 to 18,000 horses from mid-March to mid-May required the purchase and storage of between 800,000 and 1 million complete forage rations. As far as Mechelen the transportation costs were small because it was possible to use large ships from Holland and there was little fear of a French attack, but for the onward transportation along the River Demer these vessels were unsuitable, having too deep a draught. The freight therefore had to be transhipped into several smaller barges and in addition the skippers charged danger money. Van Weede-Dijkveld forewarned The Hague of the extra costs on 15 January 1676:

> The transportation costs for the conveyance of the provender and the munition from the places where these must be transhipped will also be of great consequence, because for a ship with a cargo capacity of just six or seven lasts a sum of 180 guilders must be paid for transportation from Mechelen to Diest and 120 guilders from Mechelen to Louvain.[54]

---

[53] *Vervolg van 't Verwerd Europa*, p. 915; HUA, HAA 3209, 'Lijste de la force de l'armée le 9.me juillet 1677'.
[54] NA, SG 12588.106, Everard van Weede-Dijkveld to the SG, Brussels, 15 January 1676.

A trooper received a weekly advance of seventy-six stivers (twenty-three guilders per pay-month of forty-two days), which was considerably more than a foot-soldier's advance of twenty-eight stivers, but they also had to care for their horse from this amount.[55] The Council of State calculated that a trooper could afford a maximum of six stivers per day for dry forage. After deducting the price of the ammunition-bread he was left with about three stivers per day for all his other expenditure. However, the forage suppliers charged an average of eight stivers for a complete ration.[56] It did not become standard practice for the Dutch paymasters to make up the difference between the six stivers and the contracted price until the Nine Years' War; during the Dutch War the Republic was not prepared to do this. At that time The Hague, not wholly incomprehensibly, was still of the opinion that the Spanish Netherlands had to supply the hay and straw. The realisation that this could not be asked of Spain's depleted coffers dawned only gradually. During the Nine Years' War, the Council of State submitted a petition for an average of 2 million guilders each year that was specifically for the forage magazines,[57] so that the Dutch army could be assembled as early as March or April, whereby the French undertakings in this war would be 'rendered fruitless and thwarted'.[58]

Field operations

Increased government involvement with the army had a considerable impact on the conduct of war. The financial support for the captains and rittmasters ensured that the companies remained in large measure at strength during the campaign, and the magazine system made it possible to deploy the troops in sizeable field armies. From 1674 to 1678 the armies in the Spanish Netherlands numbered between 30,000 and 60,000 men (see Appendix VI), the strength varying over the course of the campaign depending on whether the belligerents were operating defensively or offensively. The French usually launched their offensive in the spring and thereafter, during the campaign season proper (May–October), assumed a defensive stance. In July 1675, for example, the Republic's envoy extraordinary in Brussels estimated that the main French army was no more than 25,000 to 30,000 strong, 'but positioned in such a manner that from the garrisons lying to the rear [it] can always be reinforced in case of need'.[59]

---

[55] NA, CvdH 102, Notes by Adriaan van der Hoop about the payment of the Dutch troops.
[56] NA, RvS 1544, Contract for the delivery of 650 lasts of oats, 1 February 1678. The contractor charged seventy-eight guilders for a last of oats, sufficient for 400 oat rations.
[57] NA, CvdH 122, Notes by Adriaan van der Hoop concerning the 'Petitions regarding the forage magazines'.
[58] Van Nimwegen, *Subsistentie van het leger*, p. 15.
[59] NA, SG 12579.102, Coenraad van Heemskerck to the *griffier* of the SG, Lembeek, 27 July 1675.

At least 50,000 men were needed to persecute an offensive war in the Spanish Netherlands,

> because the situation of the ... Spanish Netherlands is such that it is impossible to undertake something [i.e. an operation] to any advantage there if one does not have two armies, the one to observe the army that the enemy shall surely bring there and continually stand up to that army; and a [second] army that attaches itself to the towns and strongholds while the other army faces the enemy.[60]

The problem William III had to contend with was that the Republic had brought 30,000 or more men into the field, but the Spanish contribution lagged far behind. In 1674 Brussels mobilised 10,000 to 15,000 Spanish troops for field service, and because the emperor had for that year's campaign sent an additional 25,000 men to the Spanish Netherlands the allied army attained an impressive scale of 70,000 men. There was, however, no further direct assistance from the emperor after 1674, while the strength of the Spanish military contingent in the Low Countries was highly uncertain. In 1675 only 4,000 to 5,000 Spanish cavalry participated in the campaign. In April 1676 the Spanish court swore to the Republic's envoys in Madrid that Villa Hermosa would lead between 20,000 and 22,000 men into the field, 'but the way things are looking that is hardly likely, the Duke of Villa Hermosa having recently urged their High Mightinesses [the States-General] to send him eight [Dutch] infantry regiments in order to man the forts there [in the Spanish Netherlands]'.[61] Otherwise it was impossible for Villa Hermosa to release troops for field service.

In the summer of 1676 the allies eventually managed to gather 56,000 men, 36,000 of them Dutch troops, from which they assembled two armies: William III lay siege to Maastricht with 30,000 men (more than half of them Dutch and the remainder German), while Waldeck and Villa Hermosa had to cover Flanders, Brabant and the siege operation with the remaining 26,000 men (20,000 Dutch infantry and cavalry and 6,000 Spanish troopers). This latter task proved to be impossible, because the French field army was between 40,000 and 45,000 strong. In the latter half of 1677, the strengths became more evenly balanced, when 24,000 troops from Brunswick and Münster joined the Spanish army in the Netherlands, putting a total of 60,000 men at the disposal of the allies. However, their assault on Charleroi ended in failure and the state of the Spanish finances precluded hiring a similar number of German troops in 1678, so the numerical superiority was once again on the French side.

William III hoped to ameliorate the adverse strategic situation of the allies in the Spanish Netherlands by winning pitched battles. A French defeat would have freed up thousands of Spanish garrison troops for field service. Maurits,

---

[60] HUA, ASU 637-12, Secret res. SG, 25 November 1675.
[61] NA, RAZH, AGF 387, Coenraad van Heemskerck and Sébastien de Chièze (1625–1679), the Republic's envoy extraordinary to the Spanish court from 1675 to 1679, Madrid, 8 April 1676, appendix A.

Willem Lodewijk and Frederik Hendrik had been forced to be terribly sparing with their troops, because the captains would have been unable to bear heavy financial losses. This was less of a consideration for William III. He could not sacrifice troops lightly, of course, but it was no longer necessary to steer clear of battles. The greater fire-power of the infantry (see below) and the more mobile field artillery seemed to be to the assailant's advantage. In 1668 the Council of State had ordered the casting of sixty-four regimental 3-pounder field pieces, namely twenty-four muzzle-loaders and forty breech-loaders, as well as twelve howitzers. The barrel of the 3-pounders weighed on average just 400 pounds, making these pieces light enough to accompany the infantry on the attack. Loaded with canister shot they could inflict serious damage among the enemy's battalions. Canister shot consisted of a tin box filled with musket balls. When fired the box ripped open, ejecting the balls from the barrel as a hail of shot. The ammunition for the howitzers consisted of a grenade, a hollow iron sphere filled with powder that weighed twenty pounds. Since this type of artillery lobbed the projectile in a high-arced trajectory, a very short barrel was sufficient, which allowed for considerable weight savings. Howitzers were ideally suited for use against cavalry: the loud explosions caused the horses to start and could therefore scupper a charge.[62]

Compared with the battle of Nieuwpoort, those at Seneffe (1674), Mont-Cassel (1677) and Saint-Denis (1678) were bloodbaths. The French losses in the battle of Seneffe were estimated at 8,000 to 10,000 dead and wounded, while the losses of the allies stood at 10,000 to 12,000, perhaps even 15,000 men, including those taken prisoner.[63] At Mont-Cassel some 3,000 Dutch troops lost their lives and between 4,000 and 5,000 were wounded; the French suffered 1,200 dead and 2,000 wounded.[64] The battle of Saint-Denis was less gory: an estimated 2,500 dead and wounded on the French side and 3,000 on the allied side.[65] None of these three battles was decisive, however. The military organisation lacked the requisite tactical flexibility and the terrain in the Spanish Netherlands also made a vigorous pursuit of the defeated adversary difficult. After the battle of Saint-Denis, an eye-witness reported:

> This is for all that the truth that the French have been beaten back from their advantageous positions to such an extent that they have left that place without drumbeat, marching the whole night (so one says) in disorder higher up towards Mons, leaving their dead unburied and leaving many of their injured lying there, leaving to us the *camp de bataille*. This [result] is first and foremost the work of

---

[62] Kuypers, *Geschiedenis der Nederlandsche artillerie*, III, p. 8; Ten Raa, *Het Staatsche leger*, V, pp. 509–10; Van Nimwegen, 'Kanonnen en houwitsers', p. 57.
[63] Bluche, *Louis XIV*, p. 252; Knoop, *Willem den Derde*, II, p. 81; Lynn, *Wars of Louis XIV*, pp. 125–6; Rooms, *Materiële organisatie*, p. 35.
[64] Knoop, *Willem den Derde*, II, p. 257.
[65] Rooms, *Materiële organisatie*, p. 52.

the Dutch infantry, the cavalry having been unable to pass through the forests and the broken terrain there.[66]

Warfare in the late seventeenth and eighteenth centuries was wholly focused on realising as great a fire-power as possible and outflanking the opponent. The battle arrays were therefore elongated. By dividing the formation into a centre and two wings, each two lines deep, the army commanders attempted to gear the movements of the brigades of foot and of horse to one another, but in practice they had little success. Usually all the infantry stood arrayed in the middle, with the cavalry to the left and right. William III divided his field army into infantry brigades of 6,000 to 7,000 men, cavalry brigades of an average of 1,900 troopers and a separate brigade of dragoons of 1,400 men.[67] This meant that brigades were no longer composed of two types of arms, as in the age of Maurits and Frederik Hendrik. Before battle was joined, the battle arrays of the belligerents formed an impressive spectacle. 'It is the most beautiful sight in the world to see two mighty armies like this so close to each other on such a level plain', William III wrote to Gaspar Fagel on 11 May 1676.[68] But as soon as battle was joined such orderliness quickly degenerated into separate combats without cohesion. William III, Waldeck and the French *maréchals* led the troops in person, thus demonstrating great courage, but as a result they could not retain any oversight of the general course of the battle. A lack of experience with leading large armies was a serious drawback for the Dutch and Spanish generals, too. After the battle of Mont-Cassel (1677), William III asked a few young colonels 'what the cause of the confusion had been', in confidence. The thirty-one-year-old Frederik Johan van Baer (1646–1713), lord of Slangenburg, responded that the Dutch generals 'were not worth a fig'.[69] Slangenburg was hardly renowned for his tact, but Johan Pesters was wholly in agreement with his critique: 'I do not [see] us being a match for France with battles.'[70] The only consolation was that the French could not draw any advantage from the inexperience on the allied side. The French may well have achieved victory at Mont-Cassel, but they failed to follow through with a vigorous pursuit of the Dutch-Spanish army; they limited themselves to the continuation of the siege of Saint-Omer. It is not difficult to find a plausible explanation for the pursuit not being followed through: without the baggage and

---

[66] NA, RAZH, AGF 121, Revixit van Naerssen to the Delegated Councillors of Holland, Saint-Denis, 15 August 1678.
[67] GA, AHGC 1240, 'Lijste van 't broot dat den 30 juny 1675 aen de regimenten is gedistrib[uee]rt op dry tagen'; HUA, HAA 3209, 'Lijste de la force de chacque regim[en]t de cavallerie et infanterie selon la revue faite par S.A. [William III] au camp de Drongene et Marikercke', 9 July 1677.
[68] CWB, II, no. 106, William III to Gaspar Fagel, near Valenciennes, 11 May 1676, at five o'clock in the afternoon.
[69] HUA, HAA 2819, Johan Pesters to Godard Adriaan van Reede-Amerongen, Utrecht, 30 April 1677.
[70] HUA, HAA 2818, same to same, Utrecht, 19 April 1677.

bread waggons the victorious army would soon have been seriously weakened by disease and desertion.

*

From 1676 a Dutch infantry regiment of twelve companies was followed by eighteen baggage waggons and about ten sutlers' carts. During the Eighty Years' War, the war with Münster and the first three years of the Dutch War the baggage waggons were not organised until after the commencement of the campaign. This had presented few problems, because at that time the Dutch army operated almost exclusively within the territory of the Republic or just outside it. The situation changed in 1674 when the Dutch troops set out for the Spanish Netherlands. The horses and waggons suffered a great deal from the long marches and other privations, and the waggoners objected to serving so far from home. During the winter of 1674/5 the Council of State therefore ordered the colonels and captains 'by the forthcoming campaign … to furnish themselves with their own army waggons and horses'. The colonel had to procure two waggons for himself and his company, the lieutenant-colonel, the major and the captains one each, and the regimental staff 'together' (chaplain, adjutant, surgeon, provost and quartermaster) shared two waggons between them.[71] The Council of State reimbursed the officers for the rental costs of their draught horses. For this they received a daily stipend of three guilders (one guilder per horse). In 1676 the three field officers were granted permission to hire one extra waggon each, thus increasing the number of baggage waggons per regiment from fifteen to eighteen.[72]

During the campaign the field officers, captains, lieutenants and ensigns slept on camp-beds in tents. They transported their linen and clothing, 'and especially their best uniform, which is not suitable to wear every day', in trunks or valises. The sergeants and the rank and file also slept in tents, but instead of a camp-bed they had to content themselves with a straw-filled mattress known as a palliasse and in addition the soldiers had to share their quarters with several comrades, usually seven or eight men. The structure of soldiers' tents was simple: two tent-posts were interconnected by a horizontal ridge-pole. The tent-canvas was stretched across this and secured in the ground using pickets (tent-pegs). During the march the canvas was carried on a sturdily built baggage horse, but the soldiers had to carry the tent-posts, pickets, palliasses and cooking equip-

---

[71] GA, AHGC 1246, William III to the officers of the infantry regiment of Georg Friedrich von Waldeck, The Hague, 22 December 1674, transcript; NA, Archief Bogaers 81, Extract res. SH, 5 April 1675, Statement of the number of baggage waggons of the campaign-bound regiments repartitioned to Holland.
[72] NA, Archief Bogaers 81, Extract of a missive from the Council of State to the SG, 8 June 1689; NA, CvdH 109, Notes by Adriaan van der Hoop about the baggage waggons.

ment themselves.[73] Besides carrying the baggage of the officers the waggons were also intended for the conveyance of the hand-mills or querns – in an emergency the troops could then mill the grain themselves – and for carrying the weapons and equipment of wounded or exhausted soldiers, 'and the soldier himself when he is so hurt or enfeebled that he cannot follow the company'.[74] Besides the baggage waggon, experienced captains provided themselves at their own expense with 'a servant's horse in order to carry thereon a blanket and some linen for his person, [for] when the main baggage [i.e. the baggage waggons] is sent off ... a captain misses his tent, must make do in a sergeant's tent on straw and then uses the blanket to cover himself'. The cavalry did not use any baggage waggons. The troopers carried the tent-posts and the canvas on the back of their horses, 'which the cavaliers who constitute a chambre [i.e. tent-fellows] do by turns'. Special baggage horses hauled the larger tents of the rittmasters, lieutenants and cornets.[75]

*

The impossibility of deciding the struggle on the battlefield meant that in spite of army expansion, improved logistics and greater fire-power, wars dragged on for years. The 'crisis in strategy' was heightened by improvements in the design and construction of forts and the realisation of lines of fortification along the frontiers.[76] The War of Devolution and the Year of Disaster proved to have been great exceptions. The reform of the Dutch army between 1672 and 1674 and the participation of the emperor and a great many German princes in the struggle against Louis XIV restored the military balance of power in Europe. France was still the strongest national power, but the days when the Sun King could occupy towns and whole regions almost without firing a shot were definitively over. The epoch of the great wars of attrition had dawned. 'The war aim now', writes the Hungarian historian G. Perjés, 'was to avoid decision [i.e. a battle of annihilation] more than before, to protract the war even more, to exhaust the enemy as much as possible, and to put him in a position where he had no choice but to sue for peace'.[77] Johan Pesters had expressed a similar opinion in April 1677, shortly after the battle of Mont-Cassel: 'If while reinforcing our army with new regiments ... and while restoring the scattered or vanquished ones, the Emperor and the other allies take to the field and can be disposed of [i.e. hired] ... and

---

[73] NA, CvdH 108, Isaac Kock, baron of Cronström (1661–1751) to Adriaan van der Hoop, Ypres, 1 August 1742 (quote); Guillaume le Blond, Elémens de tactique (Paris 1758), pp. 333–4.
[74] NA, CvdH 108, Isaac Kock, baron of Cronström to Adriaan van der Hoop, Ypres, 1 August 1742.
[75] NA, CvdH 108, Notes by Adriaan van der Hoop about the baggage.
[76] Perjés, 'Army Provisioning', pp. 36–7.
[77] Ibid., p. 46.

if one manages to avoid joining battle, then I still foresee a fine campaign and a desired peace this year.'[78]

Siege warfare

With the benefit of hindsight, Major General Hobbe, baron van Aylva (1696–1772), had little difficulty explaining the spectacular French advance during the Year of Disaster. In 1741 he remarked:

> When one calls to mind the lamentable and fatal year of 1672 one [shall] very easily ... be able to discern that one of the principal reasons why France at that time progressed with her conquests with such rapidity was that nowhere were the [munitions] magazines stocked and all the garrisons, on account of one [i.e. the Dutch] wanting to preserve and defend everything, were everywhere so weak that nowhere was one in a position to effect any defence.[79]

So long as the field armies numbered 20,000 to 25,000 men, every bastioned town with a garrison of 2,000 to 2,500 men could persevere with its defence for two months or more: the besiegers were too small in number to approach the fortifications across a broad front – a portion of the troops were needed for guarding the line of circumvallation – and this presented the defenders with excellent opportunities to launch sorties, in which the cavalry could also be deployed to great effect. The garrison could therefore time and again create a local military predominance. The numerical growth of armies after 1650 at last gave the besiegers the chance of confining the defenders within the stronghold. With an army of 50,000 to 60,000 men the besieger was strong enough to deal with the garrison and simultaneously hold off a relief army.

The significance of the siege of Maastricht in 1673

The altered balance of power between attack and defence was made dramatically manifest during the siege of Maastricht in 1673. Louis XIV arrived before this town with 35,000 to 40,000 men on 6 June. The garrison numbered 5,000 to 6,000 men, some 3,000 fewer than the military command had requested,[80] but compared with the number of troops which had defended Maastricht in 1632 – about half that number – it could still be considered strong. This notwith-

---

[78] HUA, HAA 2818, Johan Pesters to Godard Adriaan van Reede-Amerongen, Utrecht, 19 April 1677.
[79] NA, CvdH 124, Hobbe, baron of Aylva, 'Memorie vervattende eenige consideratiën waarom een potentaat sijne vestingen behoorde te voorsien van goede magasijnen en[de] in cas van atacque van een guarnisoen bekwaam tot een lange deffensie', Maastricht, 1741.
[80] NA, RAZH, FAvS 21, Jacob Pieck and Hendrik van Raesfelt to Govert van Slingelandt, Maastricht, 1 November 1670.

standing the Dutch governor was forced to capitulate on 30 June, just thirteen days after the besiegers had opened the trenches in the night of 17/18 June 1673. In 1632 the Spaniards had maintained the defence for no fewer than seventy-four days. The arrival of a Spanish-Imperial relief army had certainly played a major part in prolonging the siege back then, but the swift capitulation of Maastricht in 1673 was primarily to Vauban's credit. That year he employed a new siege technique which made it possible for the attacker to approach the stronghold 'as good as in battle order'.[81] At a distance of some 300 *toises* (585m) from the covered way he ordered the digging of a broad trench that extended across the full breadth of the fortified front that was to be attacked. From this first parallel the French began to approach the stronghold. These trenches (*approches*) were dug in a zigzag in order to avoid enfilading cannon-fire. Vauban secured the territorial gain using a second parallel at some 150 *toises* (292.5m) from the covered way; well beyond the maximum range of the muskets. Once the foot of the glacis had been reached he ordered the digging of a third parallel, from which the assault on the covered way could begin, the besiegers approaching the crown of the glacis at several points simultaneously via saps. A sap was a trench that was immediately dug to the full depth, so that the soldiers were hidden from the view of the defenders. This was necessary to keep losses within reason, because the glacis not only offered a wholly unobstructed field of fire but also had a depth of 40 to 50 metres, precisely the range at which musket-fire from the covered way became truly effective. The three parallels made the construction of redoubts unnecessary. When the garrison launched a sortie, then the workers in the forward trenches fled to the closest parallel, from which the counterattack was launched.[82]

The siege of Maastricht in 1673 had major consequences both for the attack and the defence of strongholds. A protracted defence was from then on possible only if the governor had a substantial garrison with which he could await the attackers outside the main ditch in pre-established, strong emplacements. Only then would the defenders always have the advantage in the struggle for the covered way. During the Eighty Years' War the key objective had been to capture the main rampart. The outworks were intended 'only' to delay the assault on the bastions for as long as possible. After 1672 these roles were reversed. Henceforth the artillery on the bastions had the task of supporting the troops in the outworks, so that the struggle there could be pursued to the bitter end, because after the loss of the covered way the stronghold was as good as lost. The altered division of tasks called for the construction of bastions with plenty of space to deploy artillery. The parallels and batteries of the besieger could be fired upon

---

[81] Knoop, *Willem den Derde*, I, p. 272.
[82] Le Blond, *Elémens des fortifications*, pp. 13 and 29; and by the same author, *Traité de l'attaque des places* (3rd revised edn, Paris 1780), p. 39; Duffy, *The Fortress in the Age of Vauban*, p. 10. A *toise* measured six feet or 1.95 metres.

from the faces (the two outward-facing sides of the bastion), while the covered way and the ditches could be swept by fire from the flanks.

A properly defensible covered way made hornworks obsolete. On the face of it the disappearance of such outworks would seem to weaken the defence, but this was not the case. On the contrary, their abolition actually worked to the advantage of the garrison. Hornworks required large numbers of defenders and therefore led to taxing sentry duties, and once the hornwork was captured it gave the besieger an excellent position for the attack on the main defences. There was an abundance of earth available, so the attacker could easily entrench himself and raise batteries. By constructing only a covered way he was denied this advantage.

The recapture of Grave in 1674 and the unsuccessful siege of Maastricht in 1676

The changes in siegecraft ushered in by the siege of Maastricht in 1673 initially escaped the attention of the Dutch army commanders entirely, but they would suffer the consequences. The recapture of Grave in 1674 cost the lives of thousands of Dutch soldiers and William III's siege of Maastricht in 1676 ended in failure.

The siege of Grave began on 29 July 1674. The Dutch besiegers, about 16,000 men under the command of Lieutenant-General Karl Rabenhaupt (1602–1675), baron von Sucha, who had led Groningen's defence in 1672, approached the fortifications in the traditional manner, across a narrow front. The French governor, Noël de Bouton (1636–1715), marquis de Chamilly, made the most of this opportunity to inflict heavy losses on the enemy. Grave was amply stocked with ordnance and munitions and the garrison was 4,000 to 5,000 strong. Chamilly could therefore order one sortie after the other and the fortress cannon played incessantly, so in mid-September the besiegers had made little progress. The seventy-one-year-old Poppo van Burmania, lieutenant-colonel of the stadholder of Friesland's regiment since 1657, lay with his troops within musket range of the covered way at that point, 'so that the heads, arms and legs of many were blown off by the constant cannonade'. A couple of days earlier the French had launched a sortie 'on horse and on foot'. The three Dutch companies that were standing watch were completely surprised, 'so that of Tiddinga's company, excepting the dead and injured as well as those taken prisoner, which included lieutenant Muller and sergeants, only 25 men came fleeing unscathed to us in the quarter, and of captain Rademaecker's company 27 men and he himself with his officers were taken prisoner. [They] have lost all their weapons.'[83] Heavy rain-

---

[83] Tresoar, FSA 48a, Poppo van Burmania to Hendrik Casimir II, before Grave, 15 September 1674. Several weeks earlier Rabenhaupt had written to Gaspar Fagel: 'The enemy is putting up a great resistance here with cannon-shot, musket-fire and canister-shot, at night throws fireworks into the field to illuminate it and makes many sorties, such that on our side as well

fall exacerbated the misery in the Dutch camp. Chamilly refused to capitulate until 27 October 1674, after a siege of ninety days, William III having reached Grave with reinforcements on 9 October and Chamilly having realised that there was no hope whatsoever of relief. The garrison had lost more than 2,000 men, but the losses on the Dutch side were much greater: 7,000 to 8,000 dead and wounded.[84]

*

In July 1676 William III appeared before Maastricht with approximately 30,000 men.[85] The siege would not be simple. The French garrison numbered 7,000 men and the French had also reinforced the weakest part of the fortified town, its northwest side, where the high ground precluded the construction of water-filled moats, with seven detached bastions. These outworks lay just forty to fifty paces in front of the covered way, thus within the effective range of the muskets. On the advice of Maximiliaan van Hangest Genlis, called d'Yvoy (1621–1686), who was quartermaster-general of the Dutch army as well as an engineer and inspector of the Republic's fortifications, William III initially decided to focus the main assault against the detached Dauphin bastion and then against the High France (*Hoog Frankrijk*) hornwork. Capturing the main rampart itself would present few problems, because Maastricht had retained its medieval walls.[86] The struggle for the outworks would be decisive and everything therefore depended on confining the defender to the covered way, so that the troops in the Dauphin bastion could neither be refreshed nor assisted by sorties. However, the Dutch troops approached Maastricht in precisely the same way as their predecessors in 1632, across a narrow front, thus giving the French governor excellent opportunities to launch major sallies.

By late July 1676 the Dauphin bastion had been severely damaged by intense bombardments, but the French were still holding firm. William III then ordered the storming of this bastion. The French repulsed the Dutch assault and a second storming on 31 July also failed. The Dutch therefore had to turn to the miners, but the French twice managed to lob a bomb precisely 'into the entrance of the mine', causing the collapse of most of the mine gallery. The captain of the miners hoped to at last be able to spring the mine on 4 August, but William III felt he could not wait any longer, having received reports that the French army had captured the Spanish stronghold of Aire. There was a very real danger that 'the enemy on account of such a swift conquest could easily formulate ideas to

---

as on the enemy's side rather a lot of officers and common soldiers are being killed as well as injured'. NA, RAZH, AGF 117, Balgoij, 22 August 1674.

[84] Knoop, *Willem den Derde*, II, p. 144.

[85] NA, FAF 555, 'Liste des troupes à piedt et à cheval que S.A. [William III] a destiné pour le chiège de Mastricht'. This document is mistakenly included in a sheaf of papers concerning the 1674 campaign.

[86] *Vervolg van 't Verwerd Europa*, p. 318.

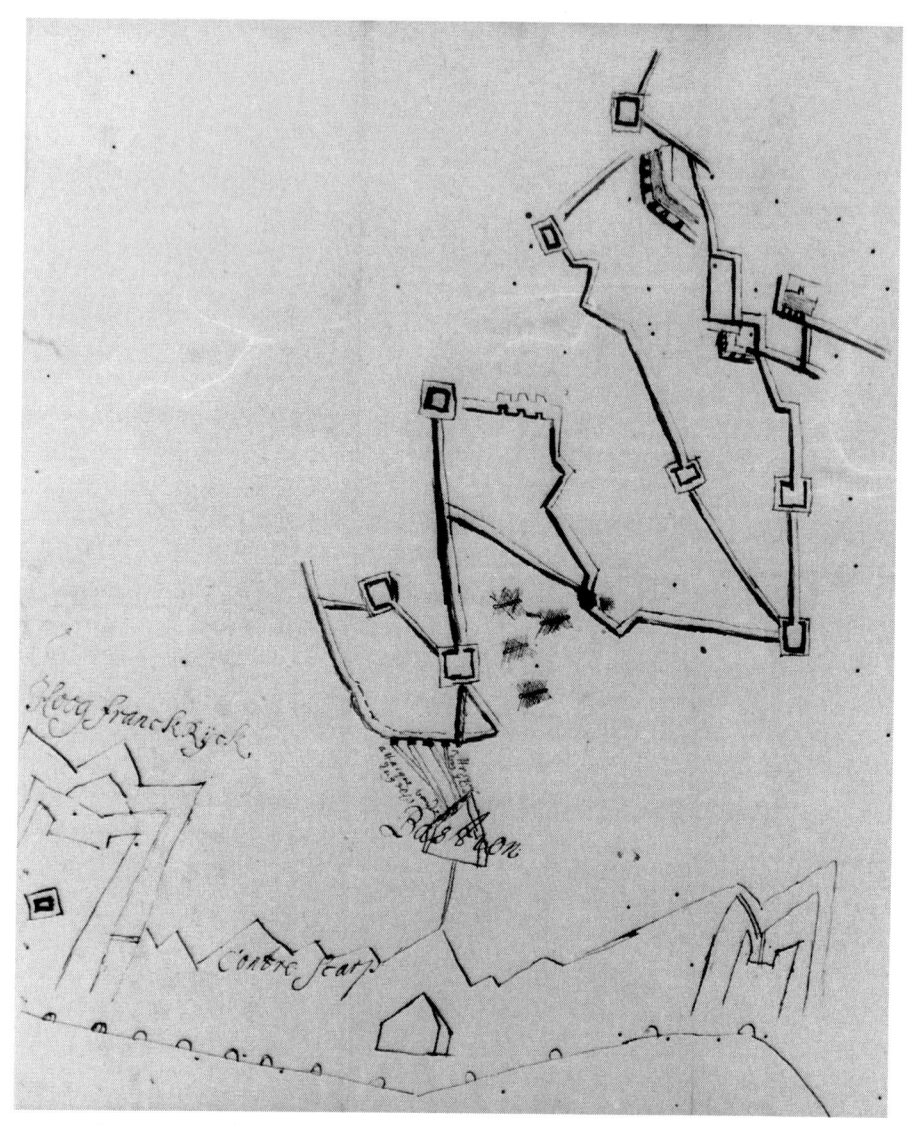

46. A plan sketched by field deputy Everard van Weede-Dijkveld during the siege of Maastricht in 1676. It depicts the Dutch approaches and the outworks constructed by the French – the *Dauphin* detached bastion, the *Hoog Franckrijck* hornwork and the *contrescarp* (covered way) – which were so significant in this failed siege. (NA, SG 12588.106, Smeermaas, 5 August 1676)

besiege yet another place or to come and incommode His Highness in the execution of his plan'.[87] Maastricht therefore had to be taken as quickly as possible. Six hundred Dutch troops stormed the Dauphin bastion for the third time at seven o'clock in the evening on 4 August, with three cavalry regiments providing cover to the rear. Their task was 'to prevent any of the French cavalry, who might come out from the town, from attacking the infantry'. The attackers quickly reached the breach, but it proved difficult to scale. The French hurled down hand grenades and fired incessantly, with muskets from the covered way and with cannon from the main rampart. The Dutch grenadiers gave the French a taste of their own medicine, 'lobbing multitudes of hand grenades into the bastion, even picking up those that the enemy rolled down'. After a struggle of almost half an hour the Dutch troops had seized control of the bastion. However, the French regrouped and after they had sprung three mines they launched the counterattack. This was again followed by heavy fighting, but the French failed to recapture the bastion. Field-deputy Van Weede-Dijkveld reported to the States-General's military committee in The Hague:

> It is unbelievable Your Noble Mightinesses and difficult to describe with what courage, intrepidity and tenacity our men have performed this task. It hailed grenades, cannon- and musket-balls ... the mines, filled with grenades, stink-pots and all manner of foulnesses exploded, and everything shone in fire and flame, and the soldiers remained on the bastion without wavering.[88]

The grenadiers who played such an important part in the struggle for the Dauphin bastion were elite troops. Following the example of the French army, the first company of Dutch grenadiers was established in 1670. Two more grenadier companies were formed three years later and in December 1674 William III ordered the colonels 'to ensure that among each company of the regiment under his command there are twenty grenadiers, to be able to serve when needed during the coming campaign'.[89] This decree was prompted by lessons learnt during the siege of Grave. 'And because the enemy also uses a great many grenadiers for all the sorties, against them [I] must also by necessity provisionally order and recruit some grenadiers for when the occasion requires it', Rabenhaupt had explained on 22 August 1674.[90] Grenadiers carried out all kinds of dangerous missions: they kept watch in the forwardmost trenches, lobbed hand grenades, from which they derive their name, and in storm assaults they formed the vanguard. Armed with axes and flintlock weapons equipped with bayonets they had to clear the way for

---

[87] NA, SG 12588.106, Everard van Weede-Dijkveld to the SG, Smeermaas, 3 August 1676, late in the evening.
[88] NA, SG 12588.106, same to the SG, Smeermaas, 5 August 1676, between eleven o'clock at night and midnight.
[89] *Groot Placaetboeck*, III, p. 187, 'Ordre van sijne Hoogheydt ... waernae ... dat al de collonels en officieren der Vereenighde Nederlanden haer sullen hebben te reguleren', 22 December 1674.
[90] NA, RAZH, AGF 117, Rabenhaupt, Balgoij, 22 August 1674.

47. Dutch grenadier's cap, c. 1700, regiment of Johan Werner, baron of Pallandt (†1741). (Royal Netherlands Army Museum, Delft, 112626)

the other troops. In connection with their special tasks, only highly courageous officers and soldiers were suitable as grenadiers.[91]

The French made every effort to recapture the Dauphin bastion. On 6 August 1676 they carried out two sorties. The first took place at about ten o'clock in the morning and was initially successful. Between 300 and 400 Frenchmen managed to penetrate into the bastion 'because our [men] were not properly on their guard',

---

[91] NA, RAZH, AJdW, Commander Lewis Erskine, Maastricht, 30 January 1670; H.L. Zwitzer, 'In Staatse dienst', in C.M. Schulten and F.J.H.Th. Smits (eds), *Grenadiers en Jagers in Nederland 1599 1829 1979* (The Hague 1980), pp. 11–22, esp. 15–16.

but when the Dutch resistance became more intense the French abandoned their assault. They tried again in the evening. 'The captain of the miners had positively guaranteed that all the mines under the bastion had been sprung or discovered,' field-deputy Van Weede-Dijkveld informed the States-General, 'and all the same the enemy ignited another one ... at between ten and eleven in the evening.' A great many Dutch soldiers were thrown into the air, whereupon the French attack was launched. Nevertheless, Dutch troop reinforcements which had rushed to the scene managed to turn the tide. Two days later, at six o'clock in the morning, the French made a third 'furious sortie', this time with 400 to 500 men, 'but because the Guards of His Highness who had the watch in the bastion and at the head of the approaches received [them] in such manner that after a small but keen fight they were forced back head over heels'.[92] The Dutch troops showed great bravery once again, but this could not disguise the fact that the Dutch army's leadership had failed. If, following Vauban's example, they had dug a parallel at the foot of the glacis, the French would probably not have dared to launch the three counterattacks. Vauban had brought Maastricht to its knees in just two weeks, while after three weeks of heavy fighting William III could boast of capturing only a lone detached bastion.

After the seizure of the Dauphin bastion the besiegers turned their attention to the High France hornwork and the section of the covered way directly behind the detached bastion. Once more it was storm assaults that were used to drive the French from their emplacements. Six Dutch infantry regiments stormed the hornwork in the night of 11/12 August 1676. The assault was a partial success, with the Dutch troops managing to lodge themselves in a few places in the covered way, but the losses were huge, the French springing several mines. 'At the moment we do not have a single regiment which has 400 men,' William III wrote to Waldeck afterwards, 'which is why, after this siege, it would be better not to rely on this infantry.' At the start of the siege the Dutch infantry regiments had numbered 600 men in rank and file.

In the night of 12/13 August the besiegers resumed their attack. The French stood their ground, so the besiegers suffered heavy losses once again. At last William III began to realise that he would have no army left if he persisted with the siege operations in this manner. Almost all the Dutch engineers had by then been killed or wounded – d'Yvoy, for example, was hit by a hurtling stone.[93] Over the following days the besiegers therefore took things slightly more calmly. 'As far as I might surmise, one wants to spare the men for a few days, who one sees spilt too liberally because of a lack of experience or misplaced zeal', Johan Pesters reported to Van Reede-Amerongen from Liège. 'One is not yet sufficiently experienced in war to employ the necessary precautions against countless accidents.'[94]

---

[92] NA, SG 12588.106, Everard van Weede-Dijkveld to the SG, Smeermaas, 8 August 1676.
[93] Müller, *Wilhelm III und Waldeck*, II, pp. 305–6.
[94] HUA, HAA 2813, Johan Pesters to Godard Adriaan van Reede-Amerongen, Liège, 21 August 1676.

In the night of 26/27 August 1676, following the arrival of a French relief army in the vicinity of Maastricht, William III ordered the raising of the siege. The captain-general of the Union blamed the Dutch artillerists and miners for the failure. According to Pesters this was only partly correct, because 'the shortage of miners, inexperience of some officers, jealousy between the generals ... and suchlike have also played their parts in this tragedy'.[95] Louis XIV had assigned the overall leadership of siege operations to Vauban, in order that one single person coordinated all the siege activities, such as choosing the point of attack, the digging of the trenches and the raising of batteries. In the Dutch army everyone to a large extent went their own way. William III was to be found 'twice or thrice a day on the batteries, in the approaches – even the forwardmost ones – making comments, investigating and pointing out all the defects, including the most minor, in order to have them improved'.[96] The valour of the soldiers and William III's inexhaustible energy could not, however, make up for the lack of leadership and professionalism on the Dutch side.[97]

The New Netherlandish fortification system

Curiously enough, the need to adapt the design of fortifications to the altered siege technique was appreciated immediately in the Republic. In 1673 the States of Holland had already decided to have Naarden reconstructed as a modern fort and the work began three years later. The small, earthen bastions were replaced with large bastions with concave high and low flanks, so that the artillery could be positioned on two levels. Ravelins were constructed in the moat between the bastions. An envelope, a continuous wall with a covered way, surrounded the whole fortress. The bastions, the rampart and the ravelins were demi-revetted, only the lower half of the works being clad with brick and the rest consisting of earth. The crown of the glacis hid the masonry from the besieger's direct lines of fire, so the siege artillery could only breach the revetment with cannonades after the covered way had been captured. A demi-revetment provided just as much protection against a rampart subsiding as a retaining wall that encased the rampart to its full height, but the construction of the former was markedly cheaper.[98] The construction of Naarden's new fortifications took ten years in all, reaching completion in 1685. In 1676 a start was also made on the modernisation of the defences of Sas van Gent and Grave, and from 1679 this work was also carried out in Breda and 's-Hertogenbosch, though none of these four projects

---

[95] HUA, HAA 2813, same to same, Utrecht, 18 September 1676.
[96] NA, RAZH, AGF 239, Everard van Weede-Dijkveld, Smeermaas, 25 July 1676.
[97] Knoop, *Willem den Derde*, II, p. 210.
[98] Le Blond, *Elémens des fortifications*, pp. 166–7.

48. Menno, baron van Coehoorn (1641–1704), fortifications engineer, artillerist and siege expert. (Author's collection)

was completed when the Nine Years' War broke out in 1688.[99] The construction programme was only resumed after the Peace of Rijswijk in 1697.

The name of Menno van Coehoorn (1641–1704) is inextricably linked with the development of the New Netherlandish (*Nieuw-Nederlands*) fortifications system. In 1673 he took part in the defence of Maastricht as a captain and the following year he was involved with the siege of Grave. In the 1680s, on the basis of his experiences during the Dutch War, he developed a 'new method of fortification', in fact an improvement of the French method that was already being

---

[99] J.S. van Wieringen, 'Menno van Coehoorn in de praktijk van de vestingbouw', in *Jaarboek Stichting Menno van Coehoorn*, 1990/1 (The Hague 1991), pp. 56–66, esp. 57–8.

implemented at Naarden. Coehoorn adhered to bastions with double concave flanks, but besides making these works even bigger he also provided them, after the Italian example, with oreillons, a round extension at the tips of the faces. The oreillons protected the artillery on the flanks from the besieger's enfilading fire. Coehoorn's most important innovation concerned the expansion of the covered way. He reinforced the re-entrant places of arms with lunettes, thus transforming these works into small, autonomous forts. A lunette is a V-shaped work consisting of two demi-revetted faces which extend as far as the ditch. The faces are often 'broken', which means that the rampart is recessed slightly at the midway point or thereabouts. The opening that this creates made it possible for the troops in the lunette to launch sorties. A heavy, pivoted fence known as a barrier closes off the opening. The gorge of the lunette is open, so if this work fell into enemy hands then it was covered from the ravelins and the main rampart. Coehoorn also held the view that the besieger should be allowed the least possible opportunity to dig himself in, and he therefore wanted the covered ways and dry ditches to be dug down to just above the water-table.[100]

During and after the Nine Years' War, Coehoorn had the opportunity to put his ideas about fortress-building and siege warfare into practice. In 1691 William III commissioned him to build a fort intended to cover the approach to the citadel of Namur. The following year the French laid siege to Namur. Coehoorn led the defence of this fort, which fell only after an extended struggle, in person. In 1695 it was the allies who laid siege to Namur. Initially the siege progressed with difficulty, but once Coehoorn was assigned overall command the end was soon in sight. Coehoorn's method of attack consisted of a combination of heavy artillery bombardments followed by storm assaults. He attached a great deal of importance to the use of mortars. A continuous hail of bombs and grenades was intended to break the morale of the defenders. The recapture of Namur established Coehoorn's reputation as a besieger. In September 1695 the States-General promoted him to lieutenant-general of the infantry and a month later they also appointed him as director-general of the fortifications.[101] After the Peace of Rijswijk (1697), Coehoorn was commissioned to inspect the Republic's frontier forts along with three towns in the Spanish Netherlands (Ostend, Nieuwpoort and Courtrai) and to draw up plans for the improvement of the fortifications. Coehoorn devoted most attention to Bergen op Zoom and its three satellite forts: 'And because the sandy ground around Bergen op Zoom does not allow the construction of any works from earth without revetting them, it shall be necessary that all the ravelins and further outworks, as well as the ramparts of the town itself, are consistently raised with a [masonry] wall.' He estimated

---

[100] Duffy, *The Fortress in the Age of Vauban*, pp. 67–70; J.P.C.M van Hoof, 'Nieuwe manieren, sterke frontieren. Het bouwconcept van Menno van Coehoorn en zijn aandeel in de verbetering van het verdedigingsstelsel', in *BMGN*, CXVIII (2003), no. 4, 545–66, esp. pp. 551–3.
[101] Van Hoof, 'Nieuwe manieren, sterke frontieren', pp. 555–6.

the cost, including the improvement of the three forts and putting the adjacent town of Steenbergen in a state of defence, at 2.6 million guilders. Ostend, by contrast, could be modernised for just 200,000 guilders – lines of inundation covered the perimeter of the town almost completely, so the construction of 'some brick-clad and solid outworks' on the side facing Nieuwpoort would suffice. Coehoorn estimated the cost of modernising Courtrai's fortifications at no less than 3 million guilders: 'I have found [this town's defences] to be of little or no defensive value, but the terrain and the situation there are nevertheless highly favourable and suitable for turning it into a strong fortress, and it would be possible to completely enclose it with eight large stone bastions.'[102]

William III and the States-General adopted Coehoorn's proposal for the modernisation of Bergen op Zoom, and the fortifications of Zutphen, Zwolle, Coevorden and Groningen were to be improved at the same time. Grave, 's-Hertogenbosch and Breda were added to this list later on. For the time being the provinces made 4 million guilders available for these modernisation projects. Brussels would have to shoulder the costs for Ostend and Courtrai.[103]

After the Peace of Nijmegen (1678), the 'rampart' of the Republic was formed by Maastricht, Bergen op Zoom and States Flanders, while the Spanish Netherlands had to be regarded as the 'glacis with the covered way'. This was the only means of establishing sufficient strategic depth to prevent a repeat of 1672. The *frontière de fer* designed by Vauban along France's northern border served as a model for this fortified buffer zone.[104] At the Peace of Aix-la-Chapelle (1668), Louis XIV had retained several strongholds in the Spanish Netherlands. A number of these – Lille, Tournai and Douai – were of great military-strategic value, but Courtrai, Oudenaarde, Ath and Charleroi lay deep within the Spanish Netherlands and were therefore difficult to provision and maintain. In January 1673 Vauban wrote to Louvois: 'Seriously, Sir, the King ought to take a little care in looking after his *pré carré* [i.e. the fortified zone covering France's northern frontier]. This confusion of pell-melled friendly and enemy places does not

---

[102] NA, RAZH, Archief Bicker 39, 'Schriftelijk rapport van den generael Coehoorn wegens de gedaene visitatie van de frontieren van den Staet in de maenden van february en maert 1698', transcript by engineer Adriaan van Helden (†1787/8).

[103] J.W. van Sypesteyn (ed.), *Het leven van Menno baron van Coehoorn beschreven door zijnen zoon Gosewijn Theodoor baron van Coehoorn* (Leeuwarden 1860), notes by Van Sypesteyn, pp. 113–17.

[104] The concept of the Spanish Netherlands as a buffer against France would eventually result in the realisation of the Dutch Barrier during the War of the Spanish Succession. From 1715 some 12,000 Dutch troops permanently manned seven barrier towns: Veurne (Furnes), Fort Knokke, Ypres, Waasten (Warneton), Menen (Menin), Tournai and Namur. The Austrian emperor, who gained sovereignty over the Spanish Netherlands as part of the Utrecht peace settlement, had to guard the remaining strongholds. If France attacked what was by now known as the Austrian Netherlands, then Great Britain was obliged to assist the Republic and Austria with the defence. See Van Nimwegen, *De Republiek als grote mogendheid*, pp. 13–35.

please me at all. You are obliged to maintain three for one.'[105] In September 1675 he advised the king that he should capture Condé, Bouchain, Valenciennes and Cambrai, so that he could realise his plan for a line of fortifications from the North Sea to the River Meuse. In line with Vauban's strategic concept the French reduced Condé, Bouchain and Aire in 1676, took Valenciennes, Cambrai and Saint-Omer in 1677, and ultimately captured Ypres in 1678. Louis XIV ceded Courtrai, Oudenaarde, Ath and Charleroi to Spain in the negotiation of the Peace of Nijmegen, but he retained the conquests of 1676–1678.

Vauban elaborated his ideas about the *frontière de fer* in a memorandum dated November 1678. He proposed rendering France's northern border unapproachable by establishing a double line of defences. These strongholds would dominate the approach roads to France and would at the same time serve as storage depots for food and fodder to enable the French army to tackle the enemy in the Spanish Netherlands. Should the enemy prove too strong or if Louis XIV wanted to engage in offensive operations elsewhere, then the struggle would be continued along and within the lines of fortification. Vauban assumed that this war of attrition would be beyond the powers of the opponent. The *frontière de fer* was completed before the outbreak of the Nine Years' War.[106]

The weaponry and tactics of the Dutch troops

Soon after the conclusion of the Peace of Münster the Dutch troops were no longer fighting in battalions with a depth of ten ranks. Following the example of the Swedes, from the 1650s they were arrayed in formations six ranks deep.[107] When giving fire the depth of the formations was reduced even further. The musketeers in ranks four to six walked forward and took up position between the files of the front three ranks. This doubled the number of musketeers in the front of the battalion. A drum signal told the musketeers to prepare to fire, 'the front rank on the knee, the second on the musket rest, the third standing upright', whereupon 'the salvo is begun from the right-hand side'.[108] Instead of all the ranks firing a salvo simultaneously, they also fired alternately by rank. The two foremost ranks kneeled, whereupon the third rank gave fire. The second

---

[105] Anne Blanchard, 'Vers la centure de fer', in Contamine, *Histoire militaire de la France*, I, pp. 449–83, esp. 476.
[106] Henry Guerlac, 'Vauban: The Impact of Science on War', in Peter Paret (ed.), *Makers of Modern Strategy: From Machiavelli to the Nuclear Age* (Princeton, NJ 1986), pp. 64–90, esp. 86–87; Werner Gembruch, 'Vauban', in Werner Hahlweg (ed.), *Klassiker der Kriegskunst* (Darmstadt 1960), pp. 150–65, esp. 152; Duffy, *The Fortress in the Age of Vauban*, pp. 9 and 12.
[107] HUA, Verzameling van Buchel Booth 83, 'Ordre der bataille van 4 compaignie infanterije gesteld door den ingenieur Melder ter presentie van de wel Ed. Heeren Borgem.rs, Schepenen ende Vroetschap der stadt Utrecht op de exercitieplaets boven 't Accademie den 25 augus. an.o 1658'.
[108] Boxel, *Vertoogh van de krijgsoeffeninge*, vol. III, p. 25.

rank then stood up and fired a volley, after which it was the turn of the first rank. Only after everyone had reloaded his weapon in a standing position could this shooting procedure be repeated. It was impossible to reload while kneeling 'due to the length of the fusil and the pressure [i.e. closeness] of the files. It is therefore necessary that they remain standing in order to reload, and that they interrupt the continuity of the firing action', according to the French mathematician and military theorist Guillaume le Blond (1704–1781).[109] The 'conversion' devised by Willem Lodewijk was also still in use, as demonstrated by the accounts of a skirmish that took place on 2 June 1673 near Lopik, a hamlet located sixteen kilometres to the southwest of Utrecht. The Dutch troops approached to within 'about sixty or seventy paces' (45 to 52.5 metres) of the French, whereupon 'the first rank fired on the enemy, which then took up a position again in the rear [to reload]; after that the second rank also fired'. It was then the third rank's turn to give fire.[110] The officers, however, preferred the firing method by which the troops loaded and fired their weapons 'on the spot', because this reduced the risk of disarray. During the skirmish near Lopik, the third rank fell into 'confusion'.

From 1660 the composition of the battalions also changed. Until the end of the Eighty Years' War approximately half a company was armed with pikes, but in the 1660s and 1670s it was just a third.[111] The reduction in the number of ranks and the shift in the ratio of firearms to polearms are often attributed to technical improvements that the king of Sweden, Gustavus II Adolphus, is said to have applied to the musket circa 1626. The resulting reduction in the musket's weight is reputed to have made the musket rest redundant. Freed from this impediment, the musketeers would be able to reload their weapons more quickly. There is, however, no evidence whatsoever for this hypothesis.[112] Until the 1660s the musket rest continued to be part of the standard equipment of every European musketeer. The explanation for the decrease in the number of pikemen must therefore be sought in tactical changes in the mounted arm rather than in an improvement of the musket. After the Peace of Münster the heavily armoured cuirassiers were transformed into ordinary cavalrymen in almost all European armies. In the Dutch army this change was effected in 1656.[113] The 'arquebusiers' were in the first place intended to harass the opponent with carabine fire. After

---

[109] Le Blond, Elémens de tactique, p. 405.
[110] NA, AHK 353-I, no. 57, Sentence of 19 June 1673.
[111] NA, RAZH, ASH 1354B** contains the muster-rolls of seven companies reviewed on 7 June 1658; NA, RvS 86, Res. RvS, 7 October 1665; KHA, A4-1466f, 'Lijste van de [12] compagnie[ën] gemonstert binnen Weesel', 29 July 1665; NA, RAZH, AJdW 2725, 'Lijste van de troupes [113 compagnieën] tot het employ omtrent Bergen op den Zoom gedestineert', 3 May 1666; NA, SG 12579.97, 'Lijste van[de] reveue over de [71] compagniën infanterie door den heere van Crommon, haer Ho. Mog. gedep[uteer]de ende gevolm[achtig]de te velde, ten overstaen van den heere Rhijngraeff binnen Maestricht gedaan', 22 April 1672.
[112] Michael Roberts, 'Gustav Adolf and the Art of War', in Essays in Swedish History (London 1967), pp. 56–81, esp. 69.
[113] Ten Raa, Het Staatsche leger, V, p. 409.

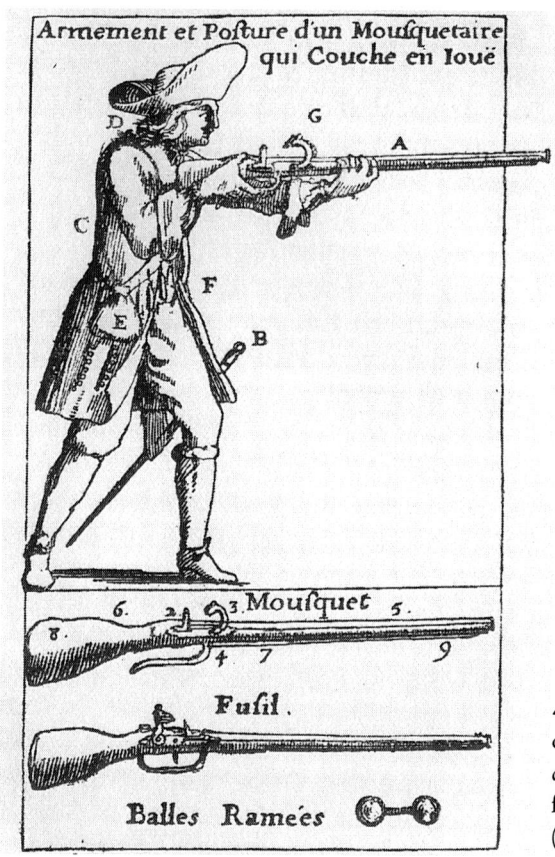

49. French musketeer, c. 1670. Gaya, *Traité des armes* (1678; facsimile 1911). (Author's collection)

firing, the cavalrymen rode away quickly in order to reload at a safe distance. The *caracole*, as this manoeuvre was called, continued until the opponent had been thrown into disarray and only then did the cavalry charge with swords drawn. It called for a deep block of pikemen to absorb the shock of charging cuirassiers. According to contemporaries, the more lightly armoured cavalrymen could, by contrast, be kept at a distance by fewer pikemen and firearms of a smaller calibre.[114] The use of smaller balls made it possible to lighten the musket, as the diameter of the barrel could be reduced. Together with a lighter butt and stock (the wooden support below the barrel) this resulted in weight savings of one to two kilograms. From the 1660s muskets no longer weighed an average of seven kilograms but between five and six kilograms.[115] A rest was unnecessary for aiming and firing the lighter muskets.

According to F.J.G. ten Raa, author of *Het Staatsche leger*, a multi-volume history of the Dutch army, 'the musket without rest [was] already being used by

---

[114] Puységur, *Art de la guerre*, I, p. 252.
[115] Boxel writes that in 1670 a musket had an average weight of 12.5 Amsterdam pounds (6.175kg). See *Vertoogh van de krijghsoeffeninge*, vol. III, pp. 4–5.

THE CONDUCT OF WAR (1650–1688)　　　　399

the majority of [Dutch] units in 1672. In accordance with previous regulations the musket was bored to 10 balls to the pound, but the calibre was now reduced to 12 balls to the pound, so the musket rest could be dropped.'[116] Ten Raa's assertion is only partly correct. As late as December 1674 William III decreed that the musket barrels had to be bored to a calibre of ten 'tight-fitting' balls to the pound (a diameter of 20mm), 'as prescribed of old in the regulations of the Land',[117] though in practice the majority of captains did not adhere to this. In November 1673 the officers of the garrison of Naarden had jointly petitioned Waldeck to send '30 iron bullet moulds [of fourteen balls to the pound] ... because the balls of the Land's calibre are too big'.[118] Usually the barrel had a bore of no more than twelve 'tight-fitting' balls to the pound, a calibre of 18 millimetres. The munition for these muskets consisted of balls with an average diameter of 17 millimetres (fourteen 'rolling' balls to the pound).[119]

Even though William III wanted to retain the musket calibre as prescribed by Maurits and Willem Lodewijk, he was certainly not ill-disposed towards new weapons. In December 1674 he also ordered the colonels to ensure that in each company there were 'twenty snaphance locks to be found, suitable for application on muskets when the occasion [requires it]',[120] thus turning the matchlock musket into a snaphance. The use of the term 'snaphance' is confusing in this context, because the firing mechanism referred to here was the flintlock, a simplified version of the snaphance.[121] In the 1650s and 1660s the flintlock had wholly superseded the much more costly wheel-lock and snaphance lock.[122] A higher rate of fire could be achieved with the flintlock than with the musket, but not one European army immediately dared to replace the trusted musket wholesale. Because of the quality of the flints and springs in the mechanism, which was

[116] Ten Raa, *Het Staatsche leger*, VI, p. 217.
[117] *Groot Placaetboeck*, III, no. 50 (p. 187), 'Ordre van sijne Hoogheydt ... waarnae ... dat al de collonels en officieren der Vereenighde Nederlanden haer sullen hebben te reguleren', 22 December 1674, Art. II.
[118] GA, AHGC 1221, The officers of the garrison of Naarden to Georg Friedrich von Waldeck, Naarden, 10 November 1673. See also NA, RvS 1544, fol. 316, 'Lijste van ammunitiën van oorloghe door ordre van sijn Hooch.t [William III] bij den commis Martiny ingestelt om op het spoedichste gebracht te werden in 't leger omtrent Bodegrave', 5 July 1672. This list mentions: 'Lead [balls] of 12, 14 and 18 to the pound, together 12,000 lb.'
[119] J.P. Puype and M. van der Hoeven (eds), *The Arsenal of the World. The Dutch Arms Trade in the Seventeenth Century* (Amsterdam 1996), p. 110; Jerzy Gawronski, *De equipagie van de Hollandia en de Amsterdam. VOC-bedrijvigheid in 18de-eeuws Amsterdam* (Amsterdam 1996), p. 187.
[120] *Groot Placaetboeck*, III, p. 187, 'Ordre van sijne Hoogheydt ... waarnae ... dat al de collonels en officieren der Vereenighde Nederlanden haer sullen hebben te reguleren', 22 December 1674.
[121] See p. 95.
[122] Jan Piet Puype describes many examples of flintlock guns and pistols in his 'Dutch Firearms from the Seventeenth Century' and 'The Arms Catalogue', in Puype (ed.), *The Arsenal of the World*, pp. 71–5 and 77–143.

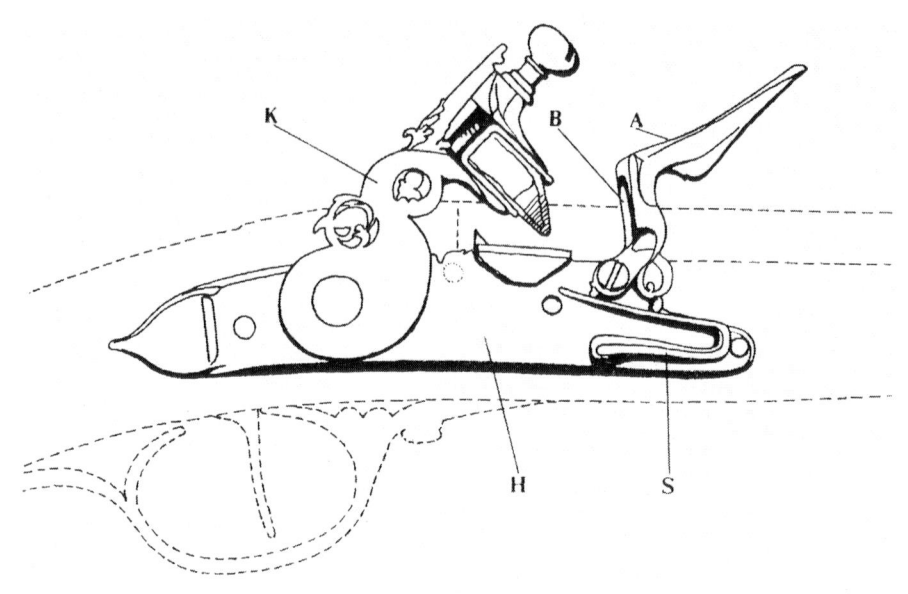

50. Flintlock (line drawing by Jan Piet Puype).
Key: A. steel; B. pan-cover (A and B together form the 'battery'); H. lockplate; K. cock; S. steel spring.

often mediocre in the flintlock's infancy, many veterans were mistrustful of the blanket introduction of the new weapon.[123] They deemed the risk of this weapon misfiring to be too great. Money was also a factor, with a flintlock weapon costing one and a half guilders more than a musket: six guilders and eighteen stivers compared with five guilders and eight stivers.[124] Nevertheless, the advantages of the flintlock weapon amply outweighed these two drawbacks. For the French officer Puységur there was no question about the superiority of the new firearm. Before the matchlock musket could be fired the match had to be positioned and the pan opened, so

> if the wind was blowing the powder would not stay there; if it was raining it was wet in an instant.... It is true that it [a musket] fires more durably than a fusil [a flintlock], but seeing as all engagements in the field demand a rapid and promptly redoubled fire, instead of slow and longer-lasting firing; ... that one fires four shots with a fusil against two with a musket; that the grenadiers ... have all been armed with fusils, and see more action than the other soldiers, there is no good reason not to arm them with the same.[125]

[123] In his *Traité des armes*, p. 26, Gaya writes: 'Flintlocks are more prone to misfirings than muskets, because of the failure of the flints and the springs.' In 1695, when 150,000 flints purchased for the Dutch army were tested it turned out that 'barely ten or eleven thousand are good to use and that all the rest are of the worst and most defective sort'. See Ten Raa, *Het Staatsche leger*, VII, p. 287.
[124] Ten Raa, *Het Staatsche leger*, VI, p. 218.
[125] Puységur, *Art de la guerre*, I, p. 147.

The rearming of the Dutch troops with flintlocks was achieved gradually between 1665 and 1698. The Dutch marines were armed with them from the start – smouldering slow-match was hardly practical at sea. In the ordinary infantry regiments a few soldiers in each company were equipped with flintlocks in 1672. The calibre was usually the same as for the lighter muskets, at fourteen balls to the pound, but there were also guns in use with a calibre of just eighteen balls to the pound. The maximum range of the flintlock weapon was the same as that of a musket, about 300 paces (225m). In January 1673 Holland's Delegated Councillors entered into a contract with the Liège-based arms manufacturer Dieudonné de Bael for the supply of 12,000 muskets and 6,000 flintlock weapons with a calibre of twelve rolling balls to the pound, which was the traditional bore. The States of Holland probably hoped that this would prevent all the soldiers being equipped with firearms of a smaller calibre, but to little effect. As noted, in December 1674 William III ordered the colonels to ensure that from then on each company included twenty flintlocks – the grenadiers were required to be armed with them – and in April 1675 he also introduced the flintlock for the entire regiment of Guards, which was more than 2,000 strong.[126] After the Peace of Nijmegen (1678) William III no longer objected to a calibre of fourteen balls to the pound. By this time body armour had disappeared almost completely in both the infantry and the cavalry – only the pikemen continued to wear a cuirass and a helmet – so the principal reason for heavier balls, namely their greater 'stopping power', was no longer relevant. At the start of the Nine Years' War the commissaries of the Republic's magazines were granted permission 'to have all the musket-balls that were not of 14 pieces to the lb recast into 14 to the lb.'[127] By 1701, on the eve of the War of the Spanish Succession, almost all the muskets had been replaced by flintlock firearms,[128] which weighed as much as the lighter muskets, namely five to six kilograms.[129]

---

[126] Ten Raa, *Het Staatsche leger*, V, p. 458; VI, p. 218.

[127] NA, RvS 490, Res. RvS, 1 October 1688. From a list of the weaponry of thirteen Dutch infantry regiments drawn up after the battle of Fleurus (1 July 1690) it appears that eight regiments were armed with firearms with a calibre of fourteen rolling balls to the pound, one with a calibre of sixteen rolling balls to the pound, and just four with a calibre of twelve rolling balls to the pound. From this overview it is unfortunately impossible to ascertain whether the calibres referred to muskets or to flintlock weapons. NA, SG 12579.122, Report by Anthonie Heinsius and Everard van Weede-Dijkveld, exhibitum, 15 July 1690, Appendix V. My grateful thanks to Dr John Stapleton for directing me to this source. See also the same author's 'Forging a Coalition Army', pp. 322–5.

[128] On 18 October 1698 the Council of State wrote (NA, RvS 490): 'And while since the recent wars [the Dutch War and the Nine Years War] almost all the muskets have been converted into snaphances shooting 14 and 16 balls in a pound, the commissary of the Land's magazines in 's-Hertogenbosch has been given orders to recast this lead into balls of 14 and 16 to the pound.' See also KHA, A16-X-19, Anonymous memorandum dated 1701.

[129] David Chandler, *The Art of Warfare in the Age of Marlborough* (2nd edn, Tunbridge Wells 1990), p. 137, lists the weight and calibre of several representative flintlocks. A *'fusil ordinaire'* used by the French army dating from 1703 had a calibre of 17.272 millimetres and

51. Plug bayonet, Dutch, first half of the eighteenth century. (Royal Netherlands Army Museum, Delft, 011572)

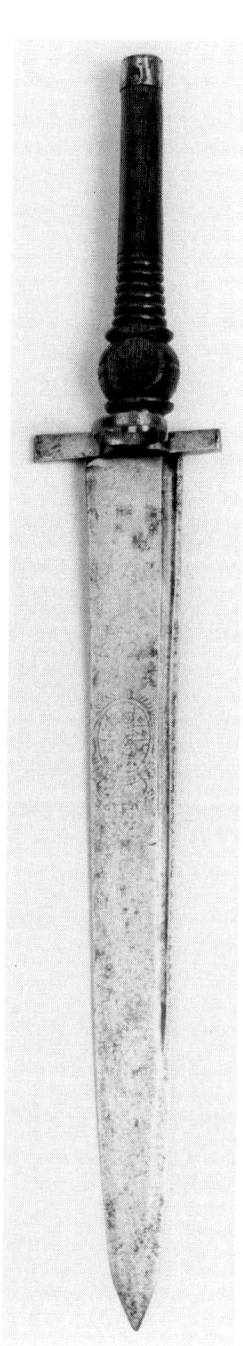

52. Ring bayonet derived from the plug bayonet, probably German or Swedish, 1703. (Royal Netherlands Army Museum, Delft, 011571)

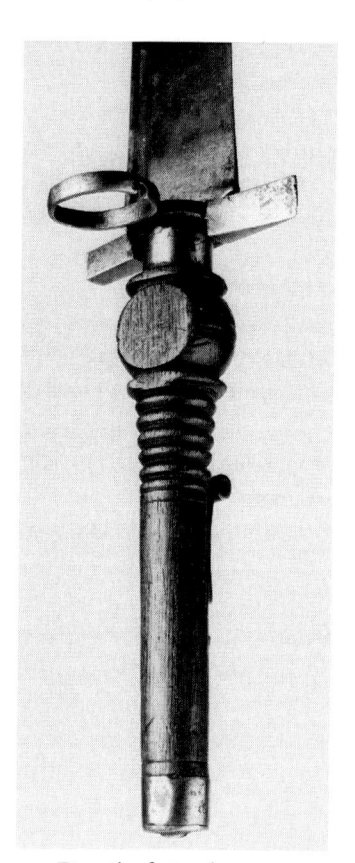

53. Detail of ring bayonet. This example is noteworthy for its crossguard fashioned as tools (a 'small hammer' and a 'screwdriver'). (Royal Netherlands Army Museum, Delft, 011571)

The reduction of the calibre and the introduction of flintlock firearms presented the possibility of using more mobile and aggressive tactics. However, until the musketeers possessed a weapon they could use if they were unable to shoot, the battalions had to be manoeuvred very cautiously. The number of pikemen had since the 1660s been too negligible to be able to play a significant part in hand-to-hand combat. The musketeers could, of course, beat each other with the butts of their firearms or could draw their swords, but then the chaos was complete. The battalions fell into disarray and the officers lost all control over their troops. It was therefore better to conduct the fight at a distance. However, the only way of optimising fire-power was by reducing the number of pike even further or by dispensing with them altogether. Experienced officers did not dare to take this step, because without the protection of 'the queen of arms' the enemy cavalry would make short work of the defenceless musketeers. The bayonet was the answer needed. The mere sight of a serried wall of glistening steel would usually be enough to deter the cavalry from making contact.

Hunters had long been familiar with plug bayonets, which they used to kill wounded game. This type of bayonet was less suitable for military purposes, because it was impossible to load and fire the weapon once it had been plugged into the barrel.[130] Some French regiments experimented with a ring bayonet during the Dutch War. 'Before the Peace of Nijmegen [1678], I saw a regiment that was carrying épées which had nothing but the point, and instead of the hilt there was a ring of brass and another next to the pommel, into which one fitted the end of the barrel of the fusil, which held it securely', Puységur informs us.[131] However, the loading of a musket equipped with a ring bayonet was no simple matter. Because the ring was affixed directly onto the hilt, when ramming down the charge the soldier had to be careful not to cut himself on the blade. Another problem was that the heat generated by firing made the barrel expand, so a snugly fitting ring could no longer be slipped over the muzzle. The rings could not be too generous in size either, because then the bayonet could easily fall off the barrel. The invention of the socket bayonet provided the eventual solution. Developed around 1700, this weapon consisted of a blade attached to a sleeve with a recessed slot shaped like a carpenter's square down one side. A pin that fitted into the slot was attached to the muzzle of the barrel. By then giving the

---

weighed five kilograms including the bayonet; during the War of the Spanish Succession the English infantry was armed with a flintlock with a calibre of 19.304 millimetres (0.76 inches) which weighed 5.362 kilograms (11 pounds 13 ounces). The balls were 18.034 millimetres (0.71 inches) in diameter. During the Nine Years' War (1668–1697) the English troops were using flintlock weapons with a calibre of 19 millimetres and a weight of 5.9 kilograms. For this see F. Myatt, *Geïllustreerde encyclopedie van de 19de-eeuwse vuurwapens. Een geïllustreerde geschiedenis van de ontwikkeling van de militaire vuurwapens in de 19de-eeuw* (Deurne 1982), pp. 14–15.

[130] Beaufort-Spontin, *Harnisch und waffe Europas*, p. 134; Jan Piet Puype, *Blanke wapens. Nederlandse slag- en steekwapens sinds 1600. Zwaarden, degens, sables en ponjaards. Historisch overzicht en typologie* (Lochem 1981), p. 55.

[131] Puységur, *Art de la guerre*, I, p. 220.

sleeve a half turn it sat firmly affixed to the barrel. In addition the blade was attached to the sleeve by an offset neck, so that the musketeer could reload his weapon quickly and safely with the 'fixed' bayonet. The pike could at last be dispensed with: in the French army it was abolished in the winter of 1703, the English followed a year later, the Austrians in 1705, and in 1708 the pike also disappeared from the Dutch army's armoury.[132]

The general introduction of flintlocks fitted with a socket bayonet led to a further refinement of volley fire. During the Nine Years' War the Dutch troops experimented with an improved firing tactic: platoon fire.[133] Platoon fire was based on the principle that the battalion did not give fire by rank, but alternately by platoon. The battalions were therefore usually subdivided into eighteen platoons of an average of thirty men. Usually the first platoon on the right flank began firing first, after which it was the turn of the first platoon on the left flank. This alternation continued until all the platoons had by turn given fire with all three ranks simultaneously. The great advantage of platoon fire compared with the complicated conversion and firing by ranks was that it was easier to maintain firing discipline and the salvoes followed each other incessantly. Officers now had to keep an eye on only a small group of soldiers, there was no need for the men to march back to the rear of the unit, and all the weapons were ready to fire again at the same time, because all three ranks of a platoon fired simultaneously. Platoon fire could also be used in attack: two platoons stepped three paces forward, gave fire alternately and began to reload. In the meantime the battalion's other platoons joined them, whereupon two other platoons stepped forward and gave fire, and so on.[134]

---

[132] Olaf van Nimwegen, 'Van vuurkracht naar stootkracht en vice versa. Veranderingen in de bewapening van het Staatse leger tijdens de Spaanse Successieoorlog (1701–1712)', in *Armamentaria*, XXX (Delft 1995), pp. 47–60, esp. 54–7.
[133] Stapleton, 'Forging a Coalition Army', pp. 334–5.
[134] Van Nimwegen, *De Republiek als grote mogendheid*, pp. 118–19.

✦ 9 ✦

War on Two Fronts against England and Münster: The Dutch Army Falls Short (1650–1667)

The Dutch army's fragmentation – mounting tensions with the bishop of Münster (1652–1657)

The Peace of Münster brought the Eighty Years' War with Spain to an end, but the Republic soon became embroiled in new conflicts, at sea and on land. The First Anglo-Dutch War (1652–1654) worked out highly unfavourably for the Republic, as already noted.[1] The antiquated Dutch fleet reinforced with merchantmen proved to be no match for the large English warships. In the Treaty of Westminster (15 April 1654) the States-General were forced to accept the Act of Navigation promulgated by the Parliament of the English Commonwealth in October 1651, which decreed that goods could only be transported to England by English vessels or by vessels from the land of origin, curtailing the Republic's carrying trade. The Hollanders also had to tolerate interference in their internal affairs. On 7 May 1654, the day on which the ratification of the treaty with England was announced in the States-General, an anonymous correspondent wrote to Count Georg Friedrich von Waldeck:

> [M]any faithful patriots would with reason be most highly gladdened [by this], were it not for their righteous joy having been reduced, even negated, by the resolution taken and adopted the day before yesterday here [in The Hague] by the States of Holland, which is that this still-young prince [the three-year-old William III] and his descendants now and forever shall not be admitted to any political or military charges here in this land.

Oliver Cromwell (1599–1658), Lord Protector of the Commonwealth of England, Scotland and Ireland from 1653 to 1658, had stipulated this secret annex, the 'Act of Seclusion', to prevent Charles II, the exiled son of King Charles I of England

---

[1] See p. 307.

(who had been executed in 1649), acceding to the English throne with the military backing of the Dutch Republic. This was a very real threat if William III were to be appointed stadholder as well as captain- and admiral-general of the Union, seeing as Charles II was his uncle and that William III's deceased father, Willem II, had made no secret of his intention to intervene in the English civil war. The States of Holland had consented to the Act of Seclusion by a majority of votes. The Knighthood was divided, while the towns of Haarlem, Leiden, Alkmaar, Enkhuizen and Edam voted against.[2] The thirteen remaining towns with voting rights and the new Grand Pensionary of Holland, the twenty-eight-year-old Johan de Witt, who was elected to that office in July 1653, felt that the adverse situation at sea made continuation of the war irresponsible, so the English stipulation had to be accepted.[3] Most of the Hollanders had no regrets about the definitive abolition of the stadholderate. After all, in 1651, during the first Great Assembly, they had decided that every province was at liberty to appoint a stadholder 'or desist from doing so', and Holland had opted for the latter.[4]

The First Anglo-Dutch War certainly had consequences for the Republic as a maritime power, but the impact was wider-ranging in scope. The deployment of thousands of musketeers on the warships – they fired on the enemy's sailors and on boarding a ship they fought with their cutlasses – brought to light 'how damaging the great reduction [of 1650] has been'. Just 29,000 strong, the Dutch army was far too small to properly perform the three-pronged task required of it: guarding the coastline against an English landing, protecting the Republic's frontiers, and detailing musketeers to the fleet. As early as June 1652, Cornelis Haubois (†1670), Friesland's deputy to the States-General, had commented:

> If the gentleman Pauw [re-elected as Grand Pensionary in 1651 and serving until his death in February 1653] does not set the [political] compass differently, I fear that we shall end up in an open war with the English, and because one will be needing many of the Land's musketeers on the ships I am confident one shall once again be forced to recruit five- to six-thousand men for the reinforcement of the companies.[5]

This indispensable troop augmentation had, however, failed to materialise, leaving the Republic militarily powerless on land when the fleet was at sea. Because an average of twenty or so musketeers from each infantry company served on the warships the fighting strength of the troops left behind in the garrisons was paltry: it was therefore impossible to achieve the desired ratio of one-third pikemen to two-thirds musketeers. The weakness of the Dutch cavalry,

---

[2] GA, AHGC 1135, Anonymous correspondent of Georg Friedrich von Waldeck, The Hague, 7 May 1654.
[3] Herbert H. Rowen, *The Princes of Orange. The Stadholders in the Dutch Republic* (Cambridge 1988), pp. 104–5.
[4] See p. 304.
[5] KHA, A25-VII-C-158, Cornelis Haubois to Willem Frederik, The Hague, 22 June 1652.

'wherein the might of the war on land resides', caused Field-Marshal Brederode even greater concern. Part of the cavalry was needed to patrol along Holland's North Sea coast, but this left insufficient troopers to protect both the area around Maastricht and States Brabant. The war between Spain and France was still in full swing, so marauding gangs had to be taken into account. In October 1653 Brederode impressed upon De Witt that the weakness of the Dutch field troops made it necessary to make a choice: 'Prince [Frederik] Hendrik, [who we keep in] eternal remembrance, who was such an old and experienced soldier, at least a hundred times warned us and taught us that one ... must not divide one's force, for one sometimes believes it is possible to preserve all things, and one loses one thing with the other.'[6]

The Treaty of Westminster (1654) delivered De Witt from this dilemma, but developments in the Baltic region soon demanded the utmost from the Dutch military apparatus once again. The Second Northern War broke out in 1655. Charles X Gustav (1622–1660), king of Sweden since 1654, invaded Poland and in early 1656 ordered the investment of Danzig (present-day Gdansk). For the Republic this was a highly dangerous development, for if the Swedes were to gain control of the mouth of the River Vistula (Weichsel) then they would be able to exclude the Dutch merchants from the large Polish grain market.[7] The Hague therefore decided to send forty-two warships and 1,400 Dutch troops to Danzig to break through the Swedish blockade. The soldiers who were assigned to this expeditionary corps were over and above the musketeers detailed to serve on the ships as marines. The Dutch fleet appeared before the blockaded town in late July 1656, whereupon the Dutch auxiliary corps joined Danzig's garrison.[8]

The weakening of the Dutch army did not pass unnoticed in the Republic's neighbouring states. After the Peace of Münster, Dutch garrisons had remained behind in Emden, Leerort, Emmerich, Rees, Wesel, Büderich, Rheinberg, Orsoy and Meurs. The Republic considered East Friesland, the county of Bentheim, the bishopric of Münster and the area between the rivers Meuse and Rhine to be within her sphere of influence. Maximilian Heinrich of Bavaria (1621–1688), elector of Cologne and prince-bishop of Liège, and above all Christoph Bernhard, *Freiherr* von Galen, prince-bishop of Münster from 1650, refused to resign themselves to this situation. The Court of Gelderland's allocation in 1615 of the seigniory and town of Borculo – claimed by Von Galen as a fief of Münster – to a count of Limburg-Stirum, the heirs of the last lord of Borculo, and the

---

[6] NA, RAZH, AJdW, Johan Wolfert van Brederode, Wageningen, 29 October 1653.
[7] Joan Römelingh, *De diplomatieke betrekkingen van de Republiek met Denemarken en Zweden 1660–1675* (Amsterdam 1969), pp. 16–17.
[8] Johannes Kunisch, 'Der Nordische Krieg von 1655–1660 als Parabel frühneuzeitlicher Staatenkonflikte', in Kunisch, *Fürst – Gesellschaft – Krieg. Studien zur bellizistischen Disposition des absoluten Fürstenstaates* (Cologne 1992), pp. 43–82, esp. 76–7; Robert I. Frost, *The Northern Wars. War, State and Society in Northeastern Europe, 1558–1721* (n.p. 2000), pp. 171 and 175–6; Ten Raa, *Het Staatsche leger*, V, pp. 63–5 and 68.

Republic's interference in the conflict between the city of Münster and its bishop, were a thorn in Von Galen's side. His desire to subject the city to his authority did not square with the Republic's interests, in view of the fact that Münster and the other Free Imperial Cities 'have always obstructed the plans of the princes ... to wage war ... and, beside God, were the only reason' that throughout the Eighty Years' War the Republic, the authority of the emperor notwithstanding, had remained 'without formal rupture' with the Holy Roman Empire.[9]

Tensions between the Republic and the two German potentates mounted rapidly over the course of 1656. In March of that year, even before the Dutch fleet with 1,400 troops set sail for Danzig, Johan Maurits of Nassau-Siegen, the Brandenburgian stadholder of the duchy of Cleves and the Dutch governor of Wesel, had warned De Witt that a 'good friend and patriot' had in confidence informed him that the elector of Cologne was preparing an assault on the Dutch garrison in Rheinberg. Johan Maurits had made no secret of his incredulity about this: 'I replied to the aforesaid person that I could not believe that the elector of Cologne would offend the State ... to which I received the response that one had little regard for the might of the ... State, but considered it very minor.' A month later Johan Maurits reported to De Witt that the attack 'had for certain been in the offing'. With the assistance of the electors of Mainz and Trier, Maximilian Heinrich of Bavaria and Von Galen had assembled troops for this purpose, but on learning that Rheinberg had been brought into a state of defence they had called off the operation at the last moment. The situation remained tense. In May 1656 Von Galen arrived in Cleves with two noblemen, all three 'disguised in shabby, old burghers' clothes'. After this was brought to Johan Maurits's attention he set off in pursuit and followed the bishop to Emmerich,

> and with the carriage in which they were riding coming into view, and their noticing this, they jumped off and tried to hide, but I managed to find them. I greeted them with every civility and then spoke with the bishop apart ... on the assumption that he would have made himself known, but he maintained his cover, whereupon I took my leave of them.[10]

The cold war between Münster and the Republic threatened to finally break loose the following year.

Von Galen laid siege to Münster in August 1657. The city appealed to the Republic for assistance and Amsterdam's regents thought that this could not be ignored. Amsterdam merchants had commodities warehoused in Münster worth more than 1 million guilders and in addition the city's government had borrowed 150,000 guilders from Amsterdam.[11] To place the bishop under pres-

---

[9] Floris der Kinderen, *De Nederlandsche Republiek en Munster gedurende de jaren 1650–1666*, vol. I (Leiden 1871), pp. 2, 5, 10–11, 47–9 and 432–7 (quote).
[10] NA, RAZH, AJdW, Johan Maurits of Nassau-Siegen, Cleves, 6 March, 5 April and 17 May (quote) 1656.
[11] Der Kinderen, *De Republiek en Munster*, I, p. 68.

sure the States-General decided to assemble 3,200 men near Groenlo, but this decision was more easily reached than implemented. The States-General suggested bringing the companies earmarked for this corps to their full complement by borrowing troops from garrisons which would not be participating in the expedition to Münster. The Council of State rejected this plan, pointing out that it would wholly upset the company administration, because

> such reinforced companies [shall] be a commingling of two and three sorts of soldier from diverse companies and garrisons, to whom the payment of the pay advances cannot be organised as well as for whole companies, besides it having to be kept in mind that the ... companies ... are so weakened, first by the sending of troops to Danzig and by the musketeers who are detailed to the fleet and are fighting at sea, that no soldiers can be missed from them.[12]

The States-General eventually managed to assemble part of the intended corps, but as already noted the discipline and skill of the troops was in a sorry state,[13] and their equipment also suffered from several shortcomings. 'Many weapons [were] so neglected and have become so dilapidated ... that in times of urgency they would barely be serviceable.'[14] The Hague could count itself lucky that the bishop did not yet dare enter into an open confrontation with the Republic and therefore concluded an agreement with the magistrates of Münster before the Dutch troops set out on their march to the beleaguered city.[15]

In December 1657 the Dutch auxiliary corps that was billeted in Danzig returned to the Republic, but the following year the Dutch troops were heading back to the north of Europe again. In early 1658 the king of Sweden had closed the Sound to foreign warships and in the autumn he laid siege to Copenhagen. The Republic decided to intervene militarily in support of her ally Denmark. Besides warships the States-General dispatched an auxiliary corps of 2,000 infantry. On 8 November 1658 the Dutch fleet gained victory over the Swedes in the naval battle in the Sound, and the Dutch troops then joined Copenhagen's garrison.[16] In 1659 the States-General increased their military presence in Denmark with a further 3,000 men, so in all some 5,000 Dutch musketeers were stationed there. In June 1660, after the Swedes had been driven from the island of Fyn and the passage to the Baltic Sea was freely navigable again, the warring factions concluded a peace. For the Republic the most important outcome was

---

[12] NA, SG 5016, RvS to the SG, The Hague, 14 October 1657.
[13] See pp. 309 and 320–1.
[14] Aitzema, *Saken van staet en oorlogh*, IV, p. 91, Report by the Rhinegrave, commander of the corps at Groenlo.
[15] Der Kinderen, *De Republiek en Munster*, I, pp. 99–100; Ten Raa, *Het Staatsche leger*, V, pp. 71–3.
[16] Bruijn, *Varend verleden*, p. 109.

that Sweden's attempt to close the Sound to Holland's merchant vessels had been scuppered.[17]

Expedition to the Dijlerschans (1664)

Though the First Anglo-Dutch War, the tensions with Münster and the interventions in the Baltic had clearly exposed how overstretched the Dutch army had become, the regents chose to ignore the signs. The Peace of the Pyrenees (1659) between France and Spain, the end of the Second Northern War and the vacillations of the bishop of Münster seemed to assuage the urgency to expand and reform the Dutch army. On Holland's insistence, the States-General decided in February 1661 to reduce the Dutch army even further. No fewer than 5,000 men were dismissed, shrinking the army to just 24,000 men, a decision that was bound to have consequences. In March 1661 Von Galen ordered his troops to occupy the city of Münster and in May he ordered the construction of a citadel. De Witt harboured no illusions about Von Galen being satisfied with this success; what the Republic needed was a strong ally. In April 1662 De Witt restored the ties with France which had been broken since 1648. The French alliance was meant to provide cover to the Republic's rear against Münster, so that if the struggle with England were to flare up again then it would be possible to focus all attention on the naval war.[18] The Treaty of Westminster failed to dispel the tensions between the two maritime powers; in Asia as well as the Americas the interests of the English and Dutch trading companies still clashed. Nor did the restoration of the English monarchy in 1660 improve the situation; Charles II upheld the Act of Navigation, supported the war in the colonies and had personal reasons to undermine the position of De Witt's faction: if Charles II's nephew William III were to be elected stadholder through his agency, then William III would probably allow his uncle to control the Republic's foreign policy. The danger of war with England breaking out again was therefore still present and if the estuary of the River Ems were to fall into Münster's hands then an alliance with Von Galen would enable the English to attack the Republic from the rear as well.[19]

Restoration of the Franco-Dutch alliance was attractive for Louis XIV as well as for the Republic, so he readily promised to assist the Republic with 6,000 French troops in the event of an enemy attack. The king of France hoped to put the Republic under an obligation to him in view of the imminent partition of the Spanish inheritance. In 1660 he had married the Spanish Infanta, Maria

---

[17] Kunisch, 'Der Nordische Krieg', pp. 67–8 and 78–9; Ten Raa, *Het Staatsche leger*, V, pp. 89, 91 and 97–8.
[18] M.A.M. Franken, *Coenraad van Beuningen's politieke en diplomatieke aktiviteiten in de jaren 1667–1684* (Groningen 1966), p. 48; Rowen, *John de Witt*, p. 469.
[19] Geyl, *Oranje en Stuart*, pp. 160–1.

Theresia. Don Carlos (1661–1700) was born a year later, but nobody expected her 'sickly wretch' of a half-brother to survive for long,[20] never mind produce any progeny. On the death of Philip IV, his father-in-law, Louis XIV was intent on securing the Spanish Netherlands for France. The procurement of such a strategically important region was inconceivable without the Republic's cooperation. Despite De Witt's strong distaste for France's intentions he solicited a rapprochement, for he regarded an alliance with France as a suitable means of curbing the ambitions of Louis XIV, barely twenty-three years old. The historian P. Geyl judiciously points out that until 1667, the year in which the French invaded the Spanish Netherlands, cooperation with France was in the Republic's interests; in 1662 'Louis was yet to emerge as the tyrant of Europe, the insatiable conqueror'.[21]

It was not long before Von Galen and the Republic came into sharp conflict. In December 1663 between 800 and 900 of the bishop's troops marched into the county of East Friesland, an agitation that Von Galen could formally justify. The emperor had authorised him to collect an old debt of 300,000 rix-dollars from the prince of East Friesland, Georg Christian (1634–1665), if necessary using military means,[22] but it was obvious to everyone that this operation was primarily aimed against the Republic, because the bishop's troops laid siege to the Dijlerschans. The reduction of this fort overlooking the River Ems posed a direct threat to the Generality land of Westerwolde on the eastern border of Groningen and Drenthe, and to the Dutch garrisons in Leerort and Emden. The handful of East Frisian defenders surrendered after just a few cannon-shots on 18 December 1663.[23] The capture of the Dijlerschans caused an outcry in the Republic, particularly in Friesland and Groningen. On 26 December the States-General were 'unanimously resolved that with this exigency … a field army shall be formed from the militia of this State, strong enough to effect the dislodgement of Münster's troops from East Frisia without having to fear suffering any affront'.[24] As a justification for this military operation the Republic would first lend a sum of 135,000 rix-dollars to Prince Georg Christian, so that he could repay the first instalment of his debt. 'If on the presentation of this first instalment the bishop's troops should not want to leave, then the matter has already been set in motion', according to Friesland's deputy to the States-General, Epeus van Glinstra (1605–1677). Glinstra considered it unlikely that Von Galen would receive assistance from the emperor and the German princes, 'because they currently have enough to do with the common enemy, the Turk'.[25] In 1663

---

[20] Ibid., p. 175.
[21] Ibid., p. 176.
[22] KHA, A25-VII-C-144, Epeus van Glinstra to Willem Frederik, The Hague, 10 August 1663; Der Kinderen, *De Republiek en Munster*, I, pp. 210–11.
[23] NA, SG 12568.61, R. de Sijghers to Willem Frederik, Leerort, 8 [December] 1663.
[24] KHA, A25-VII-C-144, Epeus van Glinstra to Willem Frederik, The Hague, 26 December 1663 (quote); Tresoar, FSA 25, Extract res. SG, 26 December 1663.
[25] KHA, A25-VII-C-144, Epeus van Glinstra to Willem Frederik, The Hague, 25 January (quote), 6 February 1664.

the Ottomans had invaded Hungary. In short the situation was auspicious for the Republic to undertake a medium-sized expedition with the limited military means available to her. The Frisians and Groningers were eager to launch the assault on the Dijlerschans as soon as the season permitted and wanted their stadholder, Willem Frederik, to assume overall command of the operation. The Hollanders gave their consent immediately, this being a superb opportunity to oblige the Frisians and Groningers to them and in addition the capture of the Dijlerschans directly served Holland's interests.

On 30 December 1663 the Council of State submitted a list of troops who could be deployed for the expedition to East Friesland: twenty cavalry companies and seventy-six infantry companies grouped into three regiments of horse and seven regiments of foot. When selecting the companies the Council of State had taken into account the garrisons from which these men could most easily be missed, choosing moreover 'as far as possible the officers and companies which had been in Denmark', approximately 5,000 men with recent battle experience. The complete corps would have to be assembled at the rendezvous near Deventer in early May 1664.[26] The assault on Fort Dijlerschans was the first important land-based operation that the Republic had undertaken since the Peace of Münster. On paper the force available for this had a strength of 1,125 cavalry (including 100 horse-guards from Friesland) and 4,496 infantry (including 200 foot-guards from Friesland and eighty men from Willem Frederik's colonel's company), but the effective strength was much lower: 750 horse and approximately 2,100 foot. Willem Frederik's whole army numbered in reality only half its strength on paper, the infantry regiments being on average just 300 strong.[27] The siege artillery of three demi-cannon and three 12-pounders was the only thing properly in order.[28]

The expedition to the Dijlerschans set out on 6 May 1664. Marching via the county of Bentheim, Willem Frederik had by the middle of May reached the River Ems, along which his small army continued its advance into the county of East Friesland. Willem Frederik hoped to prove himself as an army commander – he had long had his eyes on the vacant office of field-marshal, which had remained unfilled since the death of Brederode in 1655 – and he therefore maintained strict discipline, but the German countryfolk remained apprehensive. Willem Frederik reported to the States-General: 'At every place to which we come we find no people in the houses, although I have by public drumbeat had the soldiers forbidden, on [the threat of] corporal punishment, besides cursing and swearing, that they shall not plunder, burn or do anyone any harm.'[29] This

---

[26] Tresoar, FSA 25, RvS to the SG, 30 December 1663.
[27] Tresoar, FSA 25, 'Sijn Furstelijcke Doorluchticheit prins Wilhelm [Frederik] van Nassauw generael van de geheele armée'.
[28] Tresoar, FSA 25, 'Lijste van drie halve canons schietende 24 lb ijser ende drie lange veltstucken van 12 lb om te lande te marcheren, tot ieder stuck 200 schoten'.
[29] NA, SG 5034, Willem Frederik to the SG, Dalmen, 14 May 1664.

54. Willem Frederik (1613–1664), count of Nassau-Dietz, stadholder and captain-general of Friesland. (Royal Netherlands Army Museum, Delft, 00102275/03)

unexpected setback was an embarrassment for Willem Frederik, because the Dutch troops had brought along bread rations for only a few days. He therefore ordered Thomas Kien, the commissioner of the victualling, to have a bread supply baked in Deventer immediately. He hoped to tide over the time it would take for the first bread convoy to arrive by living from the land: 'In the end I therefore decided, in consultation with his lordship, the prince of Tarente,[30] [commander of the cavalry] to send a party of three companies of horse and 300 infantrymen ... across the Ems in order to see whether there was something to be found there whereby the said shortage could be overcome.'[31] It turned out that the farmers east of the Ems had likewise hidden all their food supplies, 'and refuse, even for money, to contribute something for the alimentation of Your High Mightinesses' troops'.[32] In order to deal with this emergency Kien decided on his own initiative to have bread baked in Neuenhaus and Lingen. He wrote to Willem Frederik and his second-in-command, Colonel Ernst van Ittersum van de Oosterhof (†1681), explaining that the terms demanded by the German bakers were disadvantageous – they were only prepared to bake bread for a cash payment of between 3,000 and 4,000 guilders – but that this still far outweighed the difficulties of having bread baked in Deventer. The great distance between the army and Deventer aside, there was the problem of the 'changing of the tracks' – the bread waggons had been prepared for the roads in the Holy Roman Empire, where the gauge of the tracks was different from that in the Republic. Kien was able to dispatch an initial consignment of 8,000 pounds of bread to the army on 18 May 1664.[33] Two days later the Dutch troops arrived before Fort Dijlerschans.

Willem Frederik divided the small Dutch army into two parts, one under his personal command and the other under Colonel Van Ittersum. There was a garrison of some 400 men within the fort. On 25 May 1664 the Dutch batteries were ready, whereupon the artillery let loose with great ferocity from both sides. A Dutch colonel wrote to his father: 'From last Monday until Tuesday evening [26–27 May] I had watch duty in the approaches, where God Almighty miraculously preserved me several times, principally on entering the trench, when they [the defenders in the fort] cannonaded furiously, and with double arquebuses they fired whole salvoes at me, no different than if it were with muskets.'[34]

On 28 May a couple of the prince-bishop's deputies arrived at the Dutch encampment, claiming they had been sent by Von Galen to work out an amicable

---

[30] Henri Charles de la Tremouille (†14 September 1672), prince de Tarente et Talmont, a great-grandson of William I of Orange.
[31] NA, SG 5034, Willem Frederik to the SG, Wesuwe, 16 May 1664.
[32] NA, SG 5034, same to same, Wesuwe, 17 May 1664.
[33] Tresoar, FSA 25, Thomas Kien, commissioner of the victualling, to Willem Frederik, Neuenhaus, 17 May 1664; same to Colonel Ernst van Ittersum van de Oosterhof, Neuenhaus, 17 May (quote), and Lingen, 18 May 1664.
[34] Tresoar, Familiearchief Thoe Schwartzenberg en Hohenlansberg 276, Colonel Georg Wolfgang (1638–1674) to his father, Georg Frederik I, Dreval, 29 May 1664.

settlement. Willem Frederik agreed to a three-day truce (28–31 May), but the negotiations led to nothing, for when Willem Frederik asked them to show their 'letters of credence' it came to light that they had none. He then lifted the ceasefire and the Dutch cannon reopened fire on 1 June. After a bombardment of three days the fort had been transformed into a mole-hill. At half past seven in the morning on 4 June the defenders started 'to sound the drum in order to parley'. Willem Frederik granted the garrison a free withdrawal to Meppen and the exodus took place two days later. First to depart the fort were 160 ablebodied men, followed by '80, both sick and injured, who lay on waggons, the majority of whom had been damaged by the splinters and chips of [shattered] palisades'. Including about sixty men who were guarding the baggage, the garrison still numbered more than 300 men. The number of Münster soldiers who lost their lives is unknown, as are the losses on the Dutch side. On 20 June, after the damage to the fort had been repaired, Willem Frederik struck the Dutch army camp and headed for Deventer, leaving behind a garrison of 160 men in the Dijlerschans.[35] Willem Frederik's hope of promotion to field-marshal failed to transpire; in October 1664 he was killed in a mishap while cleaning a pistol.

War with Münster and the Second Anglo-Dutch War (1664–1667)

In the same month that the Dutch troops headed for the Dijlerschans, the tensions between England and the Republic were mounting. In early May 1664 the English Parliament called on Charles II to take measures to counteract the growth in Dutch trade. This provoked a sharp reaction in Holland, as Friesland's deputy to the States-General, Van Glinstra, reported to Stadholder Willem Frederik on 11 June 1664:

> The lords of Holland are altogether highly agitated by the English war preparations, reminding us often that they were the first to have backed the expedition to reduce the Dijlerschans in order to free the neighbouring provinces of the fear of Münster's troops, and that under these circumstances [they] therefore expect no less from the same [provinces against England].[36]

In other words the Hollanders expected the States of Friesland and of Groningen to agree to a petition to ready the Dutch fleet for battle. In the latter half of 1664, there were more and more reports reaching The Hague about English actions against the West India Company's trading posts. The news of the capture of Nieuw Amsterdam (the later New York) by the English on 7 September reached

---

[35] NA, SG 5034, Willem Frederik to the SG, before the Dijlerschans, 21 May, and Stapelmoer, 23 May 1664; NA, RAZH, AJdW, Willem Frederik to the States of Holland, Stapelmoer, 1, 2, 4 (quote), 7 (quote) and 20 June 1664; Tresoar, Familiearchief Thoe Schwartzenberg en Hohenlansberg 276, Colonel Georg Wolfgang to his mother, Agatha Tjaerda van Starckenborg, Dreval, 5 June 1664.

[36] KHA, A25-VII-C-144, Epeus van Glinstra to Willem Frederik, The Hague, 11 June 1664.

the Republic in October.[37] An open war between the two maritime powers was now just a question of time. The recruitment of Dutch troops was tackled in great haste. In December 1664 the States-General ordered the temporary levying of 4,000 marines, though this was too small a number to be able to man all the warships properly, so musketeers would still have to be seconded from the army. In March 1665 the provinces consented to a reinforcement of the Dutch infantry with 11,000 men. The marines included, this strengthened the Dutch army to 39,500 men on paper.[38]

Charles II officially declared war on the Republic that same month. Thanks to De Witt's efforts the Republic could mobilise a fleet of no fewer than eighty-one ships of the line, eleven heavily armed East Indiamen, nine frigates and six other vessels, with an armament totalling 4,864 cannon. The crewing amounted to 21,500 men, including marines and musketeers. The first trial of strength between the Dutch and English fleets was on 13 June 1665, the battle of Lowestoft, which ended in a defeat for the Republic, primarily due to a lack of leadership and tactical insight on the part of Lieutenant-Admiral Jacob van Wasseraar-Obdam (1610–1665). Seventeen Dutch ships were lost and approximately 5,000 men died (including Obdam), were wounded or were taken prisoner. The English lost just one frigate and 720 men.[39]

In the wake of the English naval victory, the bishop of Münster felt the time was ripe to launch his own assault on the Republic.[40] On the same day as the battle of Lowestoft an offensive alliance had been forged between Münster and England. In exchange for the pledge of subsidies to the sum of half a million rix-dollars from England, Von Galen promised to expand his army to 30,000 men. The payment would take place as soon as the bishop had captured a harbour in the estuary of the River Ems.[41] Münster's war preparations did not go unnoticed in the Republic. An anonymous correspondent sent a warning to De Witt:

> There [in Münster], in towns and villages throughout the land, hard work is being carried out on all manner of things useful to war.... In conclusion, wherever I have been, from Coesfeld to Münster and from there to Telgte and Warendorf, and thus back to Dülmen again, in whatever villages and towns that I passed through I found that people were busily smithying, making wheels, attaching iron reinforcements [bands and strips] to waggons and gun carriages, etc.

One of Von Galen's major-generals had boasted to the correspondent that the bishop would soon have 25,000 men assembled.[42] The summer of 1665 also

---

[37] Geyl, *Oranje en Stuart*, p. 161.
[38] NA, RAZH, FAH 5, Advice of the Council of State, 27 July 1668; Ten Raa, *Het Staatsche leger*, V, pp. 139–42.
[39] Bruijn, *Varend verleden*, p. 112.
[40] Rowen, *John de Witt*, p. 598.
[41] Der Kinderen, *De Republiek en Munster*, I, p. 281.
[42] NA, RAZH, AJdW 2722-3, Anonymous to the gentleman Croock, Schermbeeck, 17 July 1665.

brought greater clarity about the bishop's operational plans. Johan Maurits was informed that 'the bishop's secret intention is reputedly to seize control of Greetsiel in [the county of] East Friesland and to conjugate with the English there'.[43]

Nevertheless, De Witt was not hugely concerned. The number of Dutch troops available for field service was not great – approximately 1,700 cavalry (twenty-eight companies) and 9,500 infantry (121 companies)[44] – but this would be only temporary, because Gelderland, Zeeland, Utrecht, Friesland, Overijssel and Groningen had in June 1665 consented to a further reinforcement of the companies repartitioned to these six provinces: a total of 165 companies of foot and twenty-five of horse were each to be strengthened by thirty-six soldiers and thirty-one troopers, respectively; by way of compensation, Holland footed the bill for the equipping of the warships. The raising of these troops would naturally take time, but given the poor reputation of Münster's army the Dutch officers did not expect there would be any negative consequences.[45] Moreover, during the siege of Fort Dijlerschans, Willem Frederik had sent assurances to The Hague: '[I]t is by no means the case that some Electors and Princes (namely Brunswick, Württemberg, Hessen and others) would disapprove of Your High Mightinesses' actions against the bishop, but that they are on the contrary secretly gladdened by this and desire that ... his wings would be clipped.'[46] In other words the States-General would always be able to hire immediately deployable regiments from the friendly German princes.

Duke Georg Wilhelm (1624–1705) of Brunswick-Celle and his brother Ernst August (1629–1698), the Evangelical bishop of Osnabrück, did indeed demonstrate their readiness to support the Republic in her struggle against Münster. At the end of July 1665, The Hague hereupon sent Colonel Arent Jurrien van Haersolte (†1672) to Calenberg, one of Georg Wilhelm's residences, to negotiate the terms for the hiring of Brunswick's auxiliary troops. The two dukes offered to make ready 4,000 cavalrymen and 8,000 infantrymen and to immediately make half of these available to the States-General, followed by the remainder a month later, 'provided that ... the States[-General] form with them a league of mutual defence and promptly furnish the money for the levying of half of these troops'.[47] As an additional token of goodwill, the two brothers advertised that

---

43 KHA, A4-1466f, 'Bericht den 28 aug.ti 1665 ingecomen'.
44 KHA, A4-1466f, 'Comp[agnie]ën tot het leger gedestineert bij haer Ho. Mo. den 28.en july 1665'. The effective strength of the companies is calculated on the basis of the muster-rolls that were closed between 19 and 21 September 1665.
45 On 27 August 1665, Willem Copes, acting commander of Wesel, wrote to Johan Maurits of Nassau-Siegen: 'His Princely Grace of Münster takes great pleasure in ... having the new cavalry exercised, but they amuse themselves the most when sometimes man and horse fall. They shoot at the targets there [so violently] that the farmers quack [i.e. are as frightened as ducks].' KHA, A4-1466f.
46 NA, RAZH, AJdW, Willem Frederik to the SG, Stapelmoer, 3 June 1664.
47 KHA, A4-1466f, Colonel Arent Jurrien van Haersolte to Johan Maurits of Nassau-Siegen, Calenberg, 18 August 1665.

55. Johan Maurits (1604–1679), count of Nassau-Siegen, commander of the Dutch army in the war with Münster (1665/6). (Royal Netherlands Army Museum, Delft, 00102168)

they wanted to assign the command over their troops to Georg Friedrich von Waldeck, who as noted had close ties with the Republic. Van Haersolte was highly satisfied with the offer from the two dukes. He wrote to Johan Maurits, to whom the States-General had assigned command over the Dutch troops in the imminent 'field expedition against the bishop of Münster', that if they also succeeded in bringing the third brother – Duke Johann Friedrich (1625–1679) of Brunswick-Hanover – into the alliance, then an additional 6,500 men would become available. This would mean the bishop of Münster having to reckon with a substantial army of at least 12,000 men to his rear. Van Haersolte impressed upon the Dutch commander that

> this being the case and if one were to march from the other side with the army of … the States, which might well be equally strong, if one could not [thereby] expedite the end of the war, during this autumn [one] can still at least reduce the bishop of Münster to such a condition that there would be nothing to fear from him.[48]

The long-term prospects for the Republic were not unpropitious, but Van Haersolte warned Johan Maurits that this did not imply no haste was called for in commencing the recruitment of the dukes of Brunswick's troops, seeing as Münster's assault could be launched at any moment. As far as Van Haersolte had been able to ascertain, Von Galen's 'grand design' entailed invading Overijssel with his main corps and then attempting to cross the River IJssel, 'in order to establish his winter quarters there [on the Veluwe], hoping to take some fortified town for his safety'.[49]

Von Galen's 'grand design' being made public was cause for plenty of commotion in the Republic. In The Hague they had not envisaged that the bishop might be planning to lay siege to one of the towns along the River IJssel. They had always assumed that he would vent his rage on the Republic by launching predatory raids into the Achterhoek and Twente (the eastern quarters of Gelderland and Overijssel), Drenthe and Groningen. De Witt had wanted to wait out Münster's incursions until the enlistments for the Dutch army were complete, the 6,000 French auxiliary troops had arrived and the Dutch fleet had returned to port – more than 2,000 musketeers could then disembark and rejoin their companies. The rationale was that, after the arrival of all these reinforcements, it would require little effort alongside the allies from Brunswick to drive out the bishop of Münster's troops and recapture the lost territory. Until that time Johan Maurits would have to thwart Von Galen's marauding expeditions as best he could. Münster's imminent advance towards the River IJssel made a patient stand-off undesirable, but the Dutch commander could do little else. Johan Maurits was faced with a strategic dilemma: he could either man the endangered IJssel towns with adequate garrisons or he could assemble a field army. With the

---

[48] KHA, A4-1466f, same to same, Calenberg, 18 August 1665.
[49] KHA, A4-1466f, same to same, Calenberg, 20 August 1665.

Dutch troops available doing both was impossible. On 19 September 1665 the Republic entered into a league with two of the Brunswick dukes, Georg Wilhelm and Ernst August[50] – the third brother remained aloof – but a herald sent by Von Galen arrived in The Hague the following day. The bishop demanded the immediate restitution of Borculo.[51] He did not await a response to his ultimatum, and on 21 September 1665 the bishop's troops – about 20,000 men under the command of Major-General Johann Georg Gorgas – marched into Twente.[52]

Johan Maurits established his headquarters in Zwolle, Overijssel's main city. From 19 to 21 September he mustered the garrisons along the eastern frontier.[53] There were 15,000 infantry (191 companies) and 1,470 cavalry (twenty-four companies) spread across thirty-one strongholds and forts. Two more cavalry companies arrived in Deventer a few days later, swelling the mounted arm to almost 1,600 men, but then, after discounting the sick men, the strength of the infantry stood a good 3,700 men lower. When Johan Maurits informed the field deputies that he was in command of 12,800 effectives at best, there was therefore widespread bewilderment. They sent the overview specifying unit strengths to The Hague immediately:

> From these Your High Mightinesses shall be able to see the true constitution and endowment of the said garrisons, which ... ought to be treated with the utmost care and without keeping any minutes thereof, much less making copies, [but should only] be imparted by word of mouth in secret, and as an extra precaution and certainty torn up at once.

The field deputies were in no doubt that the States-General would concur with their assessment of

> how extremely difficult it shall be to form an army corps from this, without denuding many towns of garrisons and putting them in evident danger. And we shall therefore request once again that ... as quickly as possible, whether by new recruitments or otherwise, extra soldiers might be sent to us, in order to obstruct the enemy's designs all the better and with greater force.[54]

---

[50] Ten Raa, *Het Staatsche leger*, V, pp. 499–500.
[51] Rowen, *John de Witt*, p. 604.
[52] Theodor Verspohl, *Das Heerwesen des Münsterschen Fürstbischofs Cristoph Bernard von Galen 1650–1678* (Hildesheim 1909), p. 125.
[53] KHA, A4-1466f, Muster-rolls of the Dutch garrisons in the towns of Meurs, Orsoy, Rheinberg, Büderich, Wesel, Rees (including the fort), Emmerich, 's Gravenweert, Nijmegen, Arnhem, Zutphen, Doesburg, Groenlo, Borculo, Bredevoort, Deventer, Kampen, Zwolle, Hasselt, Gennep, Grave, Ravenstein and Coevorden, as well as the forts of Ommerschans, Bourtange, Langakkerschans, Bellingwolderschans, Leeroort, Dijlerschans and Delfzijl, 19–21 September 1665.
[54] NA, SG 12579.83, Field deputies to the SG, Zwolle, 23 September 1665. According to the lists that the field deputies sent to The Hague, which despite their urgent requests were not destroyed and are therefore still extant, the effective strength of the available Dutch force amounted to just 12,780 men (1,560 cavalry and 11,220 infantry). This calculation is based on sixty troopers and sixty soldiers per company, while the muster-rolls in the archives of Johan

On 27 September 1665 Münster's troops appeared before Borculo. The Dutch garrison surrendered after just one day. Count Otto of Limburg-Stirum, governor of Groenlo and lord of Borculo, informed Johan Maurits about this loss: 'It would take too long to particularise everything, [I] shall only say that in 24 hours under siege about 100 [men] were killed and injured. Four bombs fell in the castle but did not hurt any people.' He was furious about the lax defence and the unfavourable terms on which the castle was surrendered to the bishop's army, namely 'on condition that they [the Dutch troops] leave everything behind up above [in the castle] and would march out with only their side-arms, which so transpired, having to [their] eternal disgrace so dishonourably surrendered the colours along with the artillery to the enemy'.[55]

Besides Borculo, the Achterhoek towns of Lochem, Lichtenvoorde, Doetinchem, Keppel and Ulft were lost, and in Twente the towns of Oldenzaal, Almelo, Ootmarsum and Diepenheim. Johan Maurits stood helpless. He could assemble only 1,500 cavalry and 1,250 infantry. With this small corps he posted himself near Dieren.[56] He did, nonetheless, achieve his most important objective: the protection of the towns along the River IJssel. Gorgas had wanted to take Doesburg or Arnhem by surprise, but Johan Maurits's position prevented this. A formal siege was equally impossible, because persistent rain had left the roads in such a parlous state that Münster's troops had been forced to leave behind their very considerable siege artillery in Coesfeld.[57] The bishop's troops therefore continued their assault in a northerly direction. On 12 October 1665 some 8,000 of them attacked the Dutch post by Rouveen. The 280 defenders took to their heels almost immediately. Hasselt and Zwartsluis could now be invested, but Johan Maurits also had to take into account that Münster's advance on Rouveen was only intended as a feint to draw the Dutch field troops away from Dieren – Gorgas had left 3,800 men behind in the Achterhoek, so that he would be able 'in all haste' to assemble 2,000 to 3,000 men along the IJssel. After the departure of the Dutch corps by Dieren it would be impossible to prevent the bishop's troops establishing a bridgehead on the IJssel between Doesburg and Zutphen.[58]

The capture of Rouveen was in retrospect the turning point in the war with Münster. Instead of laying siege to Hasselt or launching an attack on the IJssel line, part of the bishop's army marched onward into the province of Groningen. The reason for this must be sought in financial problems and the aforemen-

---

Maurits of Nassau-Siegen (KHA, A4-1466f) reveal an average effective strength of seventy-eight men per infantry company and sixty men per cavalry company.
[55] KHA, A4-1466g, Count Otto of Limburg-Stirum to Johan Maurits of Nassau-Siegen, Groenlo, 4 October 1665.
[56] KHA, A4-1466g, 'Dieren en daer ontrent lancx den IJssel', early October 1665.
[57] Bosscha, *Neerlands heldendaden te land*, II, p. 18; De Wicquefort, *Histoire des Provinces Unies*, III, p. 218.
[58] NA, SG 5038, Johan Maurits of Nassau-Siegen to the SG, Deventer, 10 October, and Hasselt, 13 October 1665; Field deputies to the SG, Zwolle, 14 October 1665; SG 12579.83, Field deputies to the SG, Zwolle, 16 October 1665.

tioned absence of the requisite siege artillery. In August 1665 the acting Dutch commander in Wesel, Willem Copes, had already noted the financial difficulties in a letter to Johan Maurits:

> The difficult time [for the bishop of Münster] is starting to approach: the soldiers want to be paid and still no wages have been distributed ... so the men are already starting to desert. If Their High Mightinesses were to start recruiting now then I have no doubt that we shall be riding horses that someone else has saddled.[59]

There was no means for Von Galen to take receipt of the subsidy promised by Charles II until he had established contact with the English fleet, so the bishop ordered his army commanders to capture the port of Delfzijl.[60]

The departure of Münster's army for East Groningen gave the Republic some breathing space to prepare a counter-offensive. The Council of State drew up contracts for the raising of six new regiments: two cavalry regiments of 500 troopers each, and four infantry regiments of 1,000 men each. By mid-November 1665 some 760 cavalry and almost 2,900 foot-soldiers had been recruited.[61] However, in general things did not proceed smoothly with the reinforcement of the companies of foot and of horse which had been voted in June. The Council of State informed the States-General that by November only fifty-five of the 165 infantry companies and only eight of the twenty-five cavalry companies had been reinforced, and even these augmentations were deficient.[62] The arrival of the French auxiliary corps near Maastricht on 10 November therefore came as a boost. As soon as the 6,000 Frenchmen had joined the Dutch troops along the IJssel, Johan Maurits hoped to launch a large-scale counter-offensive with the aim of dislodging the bishop of Münster's troops from Twente and the Achterhoek. Then, in conjunction with the dukes of Brunswick, he wanted to transfer the theatre of war to the bishopric of Münster itself. Until then he endeavoured to inflict as much damage as possible on the bishop's troops with small-scale operations. On his advice the field deputies set a bonus of three rix-dollars on the head of each Münster soldier taken prisoner.[63]

The French reached the River IJssel in mid-November 1665 and were billeted between Doesburg and Zutphen. Preparations for the Dutch-French counter-offensive were, however, beset by problems. The Rhinegrave, second-in-command of the Dutch field army, complained about the situation:

> [S]ince the companies everywhere in the vicinity and in particular those of foot are very weak, because but few of the soldiers who were seconded to the fleet have

---

[59] KHA, A4-1466f, Willem Copes to Johan Maurits of Nassau-Siegen, Wesel, 27 August 1665.
[60] Rowen, *John de Witt*, p. 604.
[61] NA, SG 5039, RvS to the SG, The Hague, 16 November 1665, with the appendix 'Lijste van de sterckte der nieu geworvene regimenten te peert & te voet'.
[62] NA, SG 5039, RvS to the SG, The Hague, 16 November 1665.
[63] NA, SG 5039, same to same, The Hague, 9 November 1665.

returned to their companies yet, and in the other [companies] there are many sick starting to emerge, the number [of Dutch troops] shall not be able to equal that of the French.[64]

Various captains and rittmasters informed the field deputies that in addition they 'were six, seven, others even nine months in [pay] arrears and ... therefore wanted to know from us whether, [when they] were in the field [with their companies], we would be prepared to step in with a loan of two to three [weeks' pay]'.[65] On top of this there were problems of a logistical nature. At the end of November the commissioner of the victualling had still not arrived in the headquarters at Zutphen, making it impossible to organise the supply of bread, and the readying of the siege artillery was also beset by problems. Two mortars had arrived, but without munitions, 'so the aforementioned mortars are useless here', the field deputies complained.[66] These setbacks caused Johan Maurits's enthusiasm for a counter-offensive to flag. He was primarily concerned about the discontent among the Frenchmen. The French intendant, Etienne Carlier, complained incessantly about the shortage of beer, food and oats. According to him, 'the soldiers of the king [were] not accustomed ... to carrying loads other than their weapons, and that the vivres must be delivered to them from day to day in the respective quarters'. General François de Vilanders et Pradel, commander of the French corps, went so far as to advise the field deputies to abandon the whole expedition and 'to send all the troops to the respective garrisons as swiftly as possible'.[67] On hearing the utterances of this Frenchman, Johan Maurits gave up any hope of succeeding. On 1 December 1665 he informed the States-General that he no longer considered an incursion into the bishopric of Münster to be realistic:

> Your High Mightinesses are requested to take into consideration the already late season ... and the very poor roads that must be used, over which one can barely make any progress with the baggage and provisions, without my even mentioning the artillery.... Furthermore, it is to be feared and is highly probable that, because of the cold and discomfort, many soldiers shall fall sick and both armies [the Dutch as well the French corps] shall therefore melt away greatly.[68]

De Witt refused to endorse their suspending the struggle against Münster.[69] The Dutch fleet had by then returned to port and the commissioner of the victualling had arrived in Zutphen at the start of December, where he had ordered the baking of bread for more than 20,000 men. The Grand Pensionary therefore insisted that the counter-offensive should be executed.

---

[64] NA, SG 5039, Field deputies to the SG, Arnhem, 18 November 1665.
[65] NA, SG 5039, same to same, Arnhem, 27 November 1665.
[66] NA, SG 5039, same to same, Arnhem, 29 November 1665.
[67] NA, SG 5039, same to same, Zutphen, 1 December 1665.
[68] NA, SG 5039, Johan Maurits to the SG, Zutphen, 1 December 1665.
[69] Rowen, *John de Witt*, p. 606.

On 7 December 1665 the Dutch-French army crossed the IJssel. The Republic's force was composed of eighty-eight companies of foot and thirty-eight of horse,[70] more than 9,000 effectives.[71] The plan was to recapture Lochem and then seize Bocholt. '[F]or otherwise it would be well-nigh unfeasible to advance further into the See of Münster, because it would not be possible to convey the necessary vivres to us in security', according to the field deputies.[72] Lochem fell into Dutch hands after a four-day siege, but the assault on Bocholt had to be abandoned, because 'the [artillery] train was reduced to speed the march and no more than six 6-pounder field-pieces, four 3-pounders, together with a 24-pounder chamber-piece ... [were] brought along'. This artillery was suitable for reducing some castle or other that happened to be 'lying in the way', but inadequate to besiege a town. Bocholt would therefore have to be taken by surprise, but the plan was discovered and the 800-strong garrison was in readiness. Johan Maurits then decided to beat a retreat to the Republic.[73]

After the close of the 1665 campaign Johan Maurits travelled directly to The Hague. He presented a report to the States-General in which he made a whole raft of proposals aimed at improving the employability and fighting strength of the Dutch army,[74] so that in 1666 the Republic would be able to decide the war with Münster to her advantage. Shortly thereafter Waldeck sent a plan to De Witt in which he proposed launching an attack against a Münster town on the River Ems using 9,000 Brunswick troops and 6,000 Dutch troops. In contrast to 1665, the Republic would thus be able to profit directly from the availability of Brunswick's auxiliary troops.[75] De Witt was sympathetic to this, but he wanted the elector of Brandenburg to be involved in this operation as well. Because the Grand Pensionary was keen to have his hands free for the next round with England, the struggle with Münster had to be decided before the Dutch fleet returned to sea. On 16 February 1666 the States-General entered into an alliance with Friedrich Wilhelm (1620–1688) of Brandenburg. The Great Elector would first try to persuade Von Galen to agree to a diplomatic solution, but if he declined then 7,000 of Brandenburg's troops would be made available to the Republic immediately.[76] In early March 1666 a delegation from the States-General travelled to Cleves for further consultation with Friedrich

---

[70] NA, SG 5040, Johan Maurits to the SG, The Hague, 3 January 1666.
[71] Calculated on the basis of eighty men in rank and file per infantry company (including twenty men who had served on the warships) and sixty rank-and-file troopers per cavalry company.
[72] NA, SG 5039, Field deputies to the SG, near Rhede, a village to the east of Bocholt, 22 December 1665.
[73] Aitzema, *Saken van staet en oorlogh*, V, p. 771, Report by Johan Maurits of Nassau-Siegen regarding the 1665 campaign (quote); NA, SG 5039, Field deputies to the SG, Wesel, 18 December, Rhede, 22 December 1665.
[74] See p. 322.
[75] NA, RAZH, AJdW 2723-2, Plan by Georg Friedrich von Waldeck, February 1666.
[76] Der Kinderen, *De Republiek en Munster*, I, pp. 296 and 371.

Wilhelm. Cornelis de Witt informed his brother that the Great Elector 'assures us emphatically that from this hour forward more than 7,000 men are absolutely ready and waiting to be employed in accordance with the intention of Their High Mightinesses'. This was no overstatement, the muster having revealed that the effective strength of the Brandenburg corps amounted to 7,700 men.[77] Von Galen's acceptance of the Great Elector's mediation meant that there was no need for the Brandenburg troops to take action. On 18 April 1666 the Republic and Münster concluded the Peace of Cleves. The bishop renounced the 'territorial right' to Borculo – formally the seigniory remained a fief of Münster – and in addition he committed himself to reducing his army to a peacetime strength of just 3,000 men.[78] The end of the War of Münster made the presence of the French auxiliary corps redundant, so on 13 June 1666 the French returned home.

For the Republic the resumed war with England initially proceeded highly favourably. In the Four Days' Battle (11–14 June 1666), Lieutenant-Admiral Michiel Adriaansz. de Ruyter (1607–1676) inflicted a painful defeat on the English navy. The Dutch fleet lost four ships and suffered 2,850 dead and wounded, but the English losses were considerably greater: four ships were sunk and six were captured by the Dutch; 2,450 Englishmen were killed or wounded and 1,800 were taken as prisoners of war. The English did, however, manage to revenge themselves in the Two Days' Battle, also known as the St James's Day Battle (4–5 August), and later that month they captured 140 Dutch merchant vessels and subsequently plundered the island of Terschelling. The struggle was carried forward in 1667, when in June the renowned Raid on the Medway was organised by De Witt. The burning or sinking of the core of the English fleet and the severe plague epidemic which had ravaged England the previous year forced Charles II to make peace with the Republic: the Peace of Breda was signed on 26 July 1667.[79] De Witt was satisfied with measured peace terms, the critical situation in the Spanish Netherlands making a swift end to hostilities with England highly desirable. In May 1667 Louis XIV had invaded the Spanish Netherlands at the head of 50,000 men and there was the threat that France would become the Republic's immediate neighbour.

Conclusion

The Second Anglo-Dutch War was a triumph for the Republic in general and for De Witt in particular. Within ten years of the poorly executed First Anglo-Dutch War, the organisation and composition of the Dutch fleet had been so

---

[77] NA, RAZH, AJdW, Cornelis de Witt to the States of Holland, Cleves, 24 March 1666, with the 'Lijste der troupen welcke sijne Cheurfurstel[ijke] doorlu[chtighei]t van Brandenburch etc. gereet heeft om te konnen gemonstert werden ten dienste van haer Ho. Mo.' as an appendix.
[78] Der Kinderen, *De Republiek en Munster*, I, pp. 399–401; Rowen, *John de Witt*, p. 609.
[79] Bruijn, *Varend verleden*, pp. 112–14.

radically improved that England could be subjected to heavy defeats and forced to sue for peace. The exploits of the Dutch navy stood in stark contrast to the poor performance of the Dutch army over those same years. In 1657 the bishop of Münster had still been intimidated into abandoning his attack on the city of Münster by the Republic scraping together a mere 3,000 Dutch troops near Groenlo, but four years later Von Galen had at last managed to occupy the rebellious city and had ordered the construction of a citadel. The minimal strength of the Dutch army and its limited employability were the reason why he was no longer to be deterred. With the exception of the 5,000 or so men who had taken part in the operations in the Sound in 1658 and 1659, the Dutch troops had gained no combat experience since the end of the Eighty Years' War. It would have been possible to obviate much of this lack of proficiency by holding training camps on a regular basis and drilling the garrisons in regimental formations every week, but this would not be introduced until the War of Devolution had begun.[80] In 1658 a Dutch ensign had complained to De Witt that he would have liked to temporarily enter into the service of the city government of Münster, and thus 'by gaining rather more battle experience to become more skilled in the practice of my profession in the service of Their High Mightinesses ... but it seems that I have once again been unable to achieve this goal, because the current differences between the bishop and the city of Münster shall apparently be reconciled'.[81]

The expedition to the Dijlerschans in 1664 may well have been successful for the Republic, but it simultaneously exposed how severely the organisation of the Dutch army had deteriorated. Instead of the force of 1,125 cavalry and 4,496 infantry as specified by the Council of State, Willem Frederik had in effect just 751 troopers and 2,137 foot-soldiers available to him. Only fifty-nine of the seventy-eight infantry companies he was allocated had appeared at the rendezvous.[82] The war with Münster (1665–1666) made the weakness of the Dutch army painfully evident. On the face of it the sizeable recruitment drives to which the provinces had consented in March and June 1665 seemed as if they would provide the Republic with a force that was amply up to the task – including two supplementary augmentations in August and September this amounted to a reinforcement of 18,600 infantry and 1,540 cavalry in all – but because there was no oversight of the implementation of the decrees by the provinces, in practice the effect of this fell far short of expectations. The Republic was now paying the price for the lack of a captain-general of the Union. The States-General tried to overcome the shortage of troops by establishing four new infantry regiments (4,000 foot-soldiers) and two cavalry regiments (1,000 troopers) in

---

[80] NA, RAZH, AJdW, Joseph Bampfield, n.p., 16 June 1669.
[81] NA, RAZH, AJdW, J. van der Muelen, Nijmegen, 16 October 1658.
[82] Tresoar, FSA 25, 'Sijn Furstelijcke Doorluchticheit prins Wilhelm [Frederik] van Nassauw generael van de geheele armee'.

September 1665, but by mid-November only 60 per cent of these 5,000 men had been enlisted. As long as the bishop's troops continued to threaten the IJssel towns, Johan Maurits could assemble only 1,500 cavalry and 2,760 infantry. The Republic was saved from this awkward predicament by the arrival of the French auxiliary corps, the stance of the dukes of Brunswick and above all Von Galen's lack of finance.

In December 1665 Johan Maurits could at last mount a counter-offensive, but the 9,000 or so Dutch troops available for field service was still small. Moreover, the weakness of the Republic's mounted arm – twenty-four cavalry companies in all – made it impossible to impose contributions on the bishopric of Münster during the winter of 1665/6. At the end of March 1666, Georg Groenewaldt, the receiver of the contributions, had 'received in all no more than 1,420 rix-dollars of it'. When the field deputies asked for clarification, Groenewaldt proffered the excuse that he lacked the means to coerce the people of Münster: 'In earlier times, if one wanted to impose contributions on the Hessians then one first went there with one thousand men, [or] two or three, one instilled fear in the inhabitants, and thus they were brought to obedience.' It was impossible to imitate this tried and tested method with the handful of cavalrymen that Groenewaldt had at his disposal. According to the Dutch receiver, the inhabitants of the bishopric brazenly wondered out loud: 'Why should we contribute when we have seen no Dutch soldiers?' The field deputies therefore advised The Hague to revoke the contribution treaty with Münster and grant the Dutch and French troops permission to undertake marauding expeditions on their own initiative, 'so that the inhabitants of [the land of] the said bishop are continually incommoded and damaged by raiders and forays, and he [Von Galen] may by such means be spurred on and compelled with greater pressure to make peace'.[83] The countryfolk were spared this destructive measure, because on 11 April 1666, before the States-General had voted on it, the Peace of Cleves was a fact.

The end of the war with Münster made it possible for De Witt to focus all his attention on the struggle with England. This favourable circumstance was, however, of short duration, because of the 50,000 Frenchmen who invaded the Spanish Netherlands in May 1667; and five years later Louis XIV would attack the Republic at the head of twice as strong an army and almost annihilate her. During the Third Anglo-Dutch War (1672–1674), the sizeable and modern Dutch navy would once again prove itself to be a formidable adversary, but in 1672 the Dutch army would only escape destruction by means of a huge effort on the part of the States of Holland and the indomitability of William III. The large-scale land-based warfare that France first put into practice in 1667 left no

---

[83] RAZH, AJdW, Cornelis de Witt to the States of Holland, Wesel, 2 April 1666, with Georg Groenewaldt to the deputies in Wesel as an appendix, Wesel, 30 March 1666, transcript (quote).

leeway for stopgap solutions; the substantial and superbly provisioned French armies could only be stopped by a radical reorganisation and considerable expansion of the Dutch army. The Year of Disaster would embroil the Republic in a 'struggle for survival' (*Existenzkampf*) with the France of the Sun King.[84]

[84] Hahlweg, 'Die Oranische Heeresreform', p. 150.

✦ 10 ✦

The Dawn of Large-Scale Land-Based Warfare: The War of Devolution and the 'Guerre de Hollande' (1667–1674)

The War of Devolution:
France threatens to overrun the Spanish Netherlands (1667–1668)

Philip IV died in September 1665. The power struggle this sparked off at the Spanish court, between the queen dowager, Maria Anna of Austria (1635–1696), and her favourites on the one hand, and Don Juan of Austria (1629–1679), a bastard son of Philip IV, and the leading Spanish aristocracy on the other, soon led to serious tensions with France. During the minority of the four-year-old Charles II – Spanish kings reached their majority at fourteen years of age – his mother was to govern over the Spanish empire, advised by a council (*Junta de Gobierno*). However, the *grandes* hoped to exploit the weakening of monarchical authority to regain their former position and status, while Don Juan strove to establish himself as a powerful figure. As a foreigner Maria Anna had to rule without the benefit of a personal network of clients and therefore sought the support of her brother, Leopold I (1640–1705), Holy Roman Emperor from 1658. In 1666 Leopold married his niece, Margaretha Theresia (1651–1673), sister of the Spanish king. This was unacceptable to Louis XIV, because in Philip IV's last will and testament he had stipulated that Margaretha Theresia would inherit the Spanish possessions if her sickly brother were to die childless.[1] This presented the real threat that Charles V's empire would be restored. To avert this danger, Louis XIV decided to annex the Spanish Netherlands. As a pretext he cited the right of devolution which obtained in parts of the Southern Netherlands, whereby daughters from an earlier marriage succeeded before sons from

---

[1] F.J.L. Krämer, *De Nederlandsch-Spaansche diplomatie vóór de Vrede van Nijmegen* (Utrecht 1892), pp. 31–2; Lynch, *Spain under the Habsburgs*, II, pp. 249–50, 253 and 258–60; Derek McKay and H.M. Scott, *The Rise of the Great Powers 1648–1815* (3rd edn, London 1986), p. 20.

any subsequent union.[2] Louis XIV may well have relinquished all rights to the Spanish inheritance as a condition for his betrothal to Maria Theresia, but he did not consider himself bound by this pledge because her dowry had not been paid.[3]

The French assault on the Spanish Netherlands in May 1667 caused a shockwave in the Republic. A political adviser to Grand Pensionary Johan de Witt sounded a warning:

> I consider that one can assume, without being mistaken, 1. that having France as a neighbour is the worst thing that could happen to this State, and 2. that this is inevitable if one does not oppose it now.... If one wants to make a comparison of the incommodities of the English [i.e. Anglo-Dutch] War and of those that France presently wages against the Spanish and will one day apparently visit upon this State, one would readily judge that one must not make any less of an effort in this instance than that which one has made in the other. The former [i.e. defeat against England] could inconvenience the State and commerce; the latter [i.e. French victory over the Spanish] would absolutely ruin the one and the other.

The anonymous author of this *Raisonnement op[de] oorloch in[de] Spaensche Nederlanden* (Reasoning on the war in the Spanish Netherlands) also advised De Witt to forge a grand coalition composed of the Republic, Brandenburg, the dukes of Brunswick-Celle and Brunswick-Osnabrück, Sweden, and possibly also England. Yet all the effort would be in vain, he impressed upon the Grand Pensionary, 'if the State does not organise its militia promptly, so that it can enhance its [i.e. the Republic's] reputation, by rendering the companies complete and placing fine officers at their head'.[4] This reasoning closely mirrored De Witt's personal ideas. The Grand Pensionary agreed with Paris that it would be highly undesirable for the Austrian and Spanish territories to be united under a single ruler, but De Witt wanted to go no further than detaching the Spanish Netherlands from the House of Habsburg. Transforming the Southern Netherlands into a 'cantonment', a republic of independent cantons after the Swiss model, would serve the interests of France as well as those of the Republic: it would deprive the Habsburgs of their most important line of march for an assault on Paris and would spare the Republic having to contemplate France as an immediate neighbour.[5]

The War of Devolution made it patently clear to De Witt that Louis XIV had no interest in a cantonment; he was intent on France's full-blown annexation of the Spanish Netherlands. The Republic started to bring its army to wartime strength and to make overtures towards potential allies in order to dissuade the king of France from implementing his plan, if necessary by means of a military

---

[2] Van Nimwegen, *De Republiek als grote mogendheid*, p. 14.
[3] Bluche, *Louis XIV*, p. 87.
[4] NA, RAZH, AJdW 2725-7, 'Raisonnement op[de] oorloch in[de] Spaensche Nederlanden'.
[5] Rowen, *John de Witt*, pp. 474–6; Israel, *The Dutch Republic*, p. 778.

intervention. At the start of 1668 the States-General voted for an army expansion of 11,900 men, including 1,200 marines. The Hague entered into an agreement with the dukes of Brunswick-Celle and Brunswick-Osnabrück for the hire of 3,000 infantry and 1,600 cavalry; Paulus Wirtz (1612–1676), baron of Orneholm, who had previously served as a Swedish general and a Danish field-marshal, was contracted to raise a regiment of 1,500 men; the remaining 4,600 foot-soldiers were levied in individual companies, 'but once these have been established [they are] to be assigned to such regiments as can be effected most properly'.[6] This would render all the regiments sufficiently strong for deployment in the field. De Witt was, however, aware that expansion of the Dutch army would not on its own be sufficient to dampen Louis XIV's desire to press ahead with his campaign of conquest in the Spanish Netherlands. It would also have to be possible to deploy the Dutch troops offensively in order to achieve this, which called for field-marshals. Since the death of Brederode in 1655 the States of Holland had doggedly resisted the appointment of a new field-marshal, but the French assault in 1667 prompted the Hollanders to change their minds. On 17 January 1668 the States-General appointed Johan Maurits of Nassau-Siegen as first field-marshal and Wirtz as second field-marshal.[7] In that same month the Republic entered into an alliance of necessity with her two rivals, England and Sweden.

In this so-called Triple Alliance of 23 January 1668 the contractants agreed that they would first offer the belligerents their services as arbitrators. Madrid would have to singe her feathers to achieve the restoration of the peace, because 'it is true that the imprudence of the Spaniards merits punishment', to quote the anonymous author of the *Raisonnement*. The marriage between Leopold I and Margaretha Theresia had, after all, been extremely rash,[8] and the Spanish court could therefore be blamed for having provoked the French attack itself. De Witt was therefore prepared to leave Louis XIV in possession of the eleven towns in the Spanish Netherlands which his troops had captured in 1667, namely Armentières, Charleroi, Ath, Bergues, Veurne (Furnes), Tournai, Douai, Courtrai, Oudenaarde, Lille and Aalst. However, if he refused to be satisfied with this and persisted in his campaign of conquest in 1668, then a military response was the only option. In a secret article of the Triple Alliance, De Witt made sure it was stipulated that in this event the Republic, England and Sweden would cooperate to compel Louis XIV to acquiesce and would reinstate the *status quo ante* as set out in 1659 by the Peace of the Pyrenees.[9] To show their teeth the States-General ordered the equipping of forty-eight men-of-war and the assembly of two army corps, one of almost 11,000 men at Bergen op Zoom and a second of 6,800

---

6   NA, RvS 89 and RvS 488, Res. RvS 14, 17 March, 1 (quote) and 4 April 1668.
7   Ten Raa, *Het Staatsche leger*, V, p. 201.
8   NA, RAZH, AJdW 2725-7, 'Raisonnement op[de] oorloch in[de] Spaensche Nederlanden'.
9   Franken, *Coenraad van Beuningen*, pp. 54–5.

men at Zutphen.[10] The task of the force on the River IJssel was to facilitate the arrival of Brunswick's auxiliary corps. Its line of march traversed the bishopric of Münster and The Hague was not confident that Von Galen would allow this,[11] in the knowledge that France had provided him with money in order to expand his army to 10,000 men.[12] However, the bishop of Münster did not feel the time was ripe for a new confrontation with the Republic, and Brunswick's troops therefore reached the IJssel without encountering any difficulties.

There was no need for the Dutch troops to rise in action against the French, as noted above. At the Peace of Aix-la-Chapelle (2 May 1668) the Sun King for the meantime contented himself with France's annexation of the eleven towns. The end of the War of Devolution seemed like a triumph for De Witt: the Spanish Netherlands were indeed left battered, but the damage had been limited to the loss of strongholds that were but partly to France's advantage: Courtrai, Oudenaarde and Ath were surrounded by Spanish towns and were therefore difficult to defend.[13] This disappointing conclusion to the War of Devolution for France meant that there was scant prospect of an enduring peace. Moreover, there was a high risk that the struggle would soon flare up again, because the collaboration among the Republic, England and Sweden was far from unqualified; Charles II of England had joined the Triple Alliance only to enable him to deal the deathblow to the Franco-Dutch alliance of 1662 – he had immediately informed Louis XIV about the secret article[14] – while the Swedes had signed to boost their value as a future ally for France.[15] The reduction of the Dutch army in the latter half of 1668 to 33,000 men was therefore a highly injudicious decision.[16] In July 1669 Johan Maurits had already warned De Witt that he thought it certain that the French king was planning

> to break [the alliance] with the Republic of the United Netherlands, but would delay a declaration of war until he had first taken a few fortified towns on the Rhine, IJssel and Meuse by surprise, to which purpose the bishop of Münster is in every way diligently helpful [to Louis XIV], so various armies shall act…. The Triple Alliance is nought but scoffed at, my having been told with certainty that during the past month a very large sum of money has been transferred by the Crown of France to England.[17]

---

[10] NA, RAZH, AJdW 2725-7, 'Lijste van de troupes tot het employ omtrent Bergen op den Zoom gedestineert sooals deselve gevonden sijn op de reveue door de heeren haer Ho. Mo. gedeputeerden en[de] gevolmachtichden, gedaen den 3e may 1668'; Ten Raa, *Het Staatsche leger*, V, p. 207.
[11] Der Kinderen, *De Republiek en Munster*, II, pp. 9, 13–14 and 36.
[12] NA, RAZH, AJdW 2725-7, 'Lijste van 't voetvolck in het Stifft Munster tegenwoordig in dienst sijnde'.
[13] Duffy, *The Fortress in the Age of Vauban*, p. 12.
[14] Herbert H. Rowen, 'The Peace of Nijmegen: De Witt's Revenge', in *The Peace of Nijmegen*, pp. 275–83, esp. 278–9.
[15] McKay, *Rise of the Great Powers*, p. 21.
[16] See p. 323.
[17] NA, RAZH, AJdW, Johan Maurits of Nassau-Siegen, Siegen, 3 July 1669.

It would be another three years before Johan Maurits's prescient warning became reality.

The build-up to the 'Guerre de Hollande' (1669 to May 1672)

In 1667 Europe had become acquainted with a new manner of warfare. In the first half of the seventeenth century the Spaniards had still been able to deride the lack of discipline in the French army – the French soldiers being 'more adept at winning a place than retaining it'[18] – but the War of Devolution silenced such mutterings altogether. However, in the context of the 'Forty Years' War' (1672–1712), 1667 was nothing more than a foretaste of the large-scale warfare that France would put into practice from 1672, the Republic barely escaping becoming her first victim. Between 1669 and 1672 more than 100,000 French troops were put in readiness to ensure Louis XIV's triumph over the Republic. A military operation on this scale had never before been planned in European history. The aim of the 'Guerre de Hollande' was to make it possible for Louis XIV to complete the annexation of the Spanish Netherlands by eliminating the Republic as a great power.[19] For his plan to render the Republic powerless the king of France could depend on the support of the bishop of Münster, the elector of Cologne and King Charles II of England. A new war with England's most important trade rival could count on broad support in England, but for Charles II himself there was a motive that carried even more weight: French subsidies would release him from dependence on Parliament and provide him with the means to achieve his 'grand design', namely the restoration of the Catholic Church in England.

The pact between Louis XIV and Charles II was made official in June 1670 in the Secret Treaty of Dover, by which the two kings agreed that they would jointly declare war on the Republic. Charles II left the decision about the appropriate moment to do this to Louis XIV,[20] who opted for postponement. All manner of deficiencies in the French army's organisation had come to light during the War of Devolution, and Le Tellier and Louvois therefore wanted to be certain that the payment of wages and the provisioning would run like clockwork before launching an attack, especially one involving more than twice as many troops as in 1667.[21] The invasion of the duchy of Lorraine in the latter half of 1670 served

---

[18] Van der Capellen, *Gedenkschriften*, II, p. 117.
[19] Carl J. Ekberg, *The Failure of Louis XIV's Dutch War* (Chapel Hill, NC 1979), p. 112; Paul Sonnino, *Louis XIV and the Origins of the Dutch War* (Cambridge 1988), p. 89; Klaus Malettke, 'Ludwigs XIV. Außenpolitik zwischen Staatsräson, ökonomischen Zwängen und Sozialkonflikten', in Heinz Duchhardt, *Rahmenbedingungen und Handlungsspielräume europäischer Außenpolitik im Zeitalter Ludwigs XIV* (Berlin 1991), pp. 43–72, esp. 50.
[20] Geyl, *Oranje en Stuart*, pp. 258–9; Franken, *Coenraad van Beuningen*, p. 82–3.
[21] Sonnino, *Louis XIV and the Origins of the Dutch War*, p. 121; Baxter, *Servants of the Sword*, pp. 169–70.

as a 'dress rehearsal'.[22] This campaign also presented the possibility of experimenting with new tactics, such as the cavalry charge with swords drawn instead of the *caracole* with the pistol,[23] without taking major risks. The occupation of the duchy of Lorraine was also strategically important for France. The close ties between Spain and Charles IV (1604–1675), duke of Lorraine, had long been a thorn in the side for Paris. Charles IV not only made his troops available to Spain, but Lorraine also formed an important bridge in the line of communication between the Spanish Netherlands, Franche-Comté and Lombardy.

The occupation of Lorraine caused a great deal of consternation in the Republic. The regents realised they had taken the decision to reduce the Dutch army too hastily and that there was no time to be lost in readying the Dutch troops for action, because a well-drilled company 'would, on joining battle, have greater effect than two untrained ones. The exercising [i.e. drill] is also very necessary for the soldiers: if they have nothing to occupy them then they are prone to laziness and bad behaviour.'[24] The provinces had already consented to the advice of the Council of State to strengthen all the infantry companies to 100 men and the cavalry companies to eighty troopers in December 1670. Three months later, on 7 March 1671, the States-General voted for a further army augmentation of thirty-six cavalry companies and 141 infantry companies and also instructed the Council of State to make preparations for the staging of manoeuvres, 'so that the said troops learn not only the manual [i.e. the handling of the musket and the pike] and the exercise with the weapons, but also and especially the performance of all kinds of evolutions – marching, wheeling, merging, retreating – and everything else on which this task depends'. The Council of State did not, however, deem it necessary to organise the training camps that year, because until the French food magazines had been stocked and the enlistments for the French army were complete the Council of State thought it impossible that Louis XIV would launch hostilities in 1671.[25] This proved to be a judicious appraisal, but there was no question of the French abandoning their assault on the Republic. Quite the contrary, on 27 July 1671 the king of France, his two secretaries of state for war and the *maréchals*, Henri de La Tour d'Auvergne (1611–1675), vicomte de Turenne, and Louis II de Bourbon, prince de Condé, the victor at Rocroi in 1643, met at the castle of Saint-Germain-en-Laye near Paris to decide the operational plan for the invasion. Like Condé, Turenne was a veteran of the Thirty Years' War and the Franco-Spanish War with an impressive service record. The plan of attack that was decided upon involved the following: 1. the majority of the French field troops (80,000 to 90,000 men) are to operate in two main armies with Charleroi and Sédan as bases; 2. the campaign will be opened with

---

[22] Lynn, *Giant of the Grand Siècle*, p. 112; Ten Raa, *Het Staatsche leger*, V, p. 225.
[23] Puységur, *Art de la guerre*, I, p. 252.
[24] NA, RAZH, AJdW, J. Neidecker, a correspondent of De Witt, Bergen [op Zoom], 8 March 1668.
[25] NA, RvS 548, Advice of the RvS to the SG, 22 May 1671.

56. Henri de La Tour d'Auvergne (1611–1675), vicomte de Turenne, French *maréchal*. (Royal Netherlands Army Museum, Delft, 00101168)

an advance towards Maastricht, but this would be merely a feint, as the attack proper will be directed against the Dutch strongholds along the rivers Rhine and IJssel; 3. the invasion of the Republic is to be continued until there is a pretext for Louis XIV to direct his forces upon the Spanish Netherlands; 4. the French troops will begin their push into the Republic in May 1672.[26]

By late 1671 the States-General were receiving more and more intelligence which pointed to a French assault being at hand and indicated that the bishop of

---

[26] Sonnino, *Louis XIV and the Origins of the Dutch War*, p. 158; Sonnino, 'Louis XIV and the Dutch War', in Ragnhild Hatton (ed.), *Louis XIV and Europe* (London 1976), pp. 153–78, esp. 155–6.

Münster and the elector of Cologne would be lending their support.[27] Captain Hendrik Mulert wrote on 3 November 1671 from Orsoy: 'Within Uerdingen, Neuss, Düsseldorf, Kaiserswerth [and] Dorsten it is crammed full with troops, and more and more arrive daily.'[28] On the basis of these and other reports, the Council of State advised the States-General to recruit an additional 20,000 men.[29] On 4 February 1672 the provinces consented to this second augmentation, but it quickly became clear that even this was insufficient. According to estimates, Louis XIV had 148,000 men under arms and the bishop of Münster had already strengthened his army to between 17,000 and 18,000 men,[30] so the Dutch army – approximately 84,000 men – would be facing a numerically superior force. On 28 March 1672 the States-General ordered a third augmentation of 22,500 men and a month later, on 29 April, this was followed by a fourth augmentation of 25,000 men. Nothing came of this last army reinforcement and about a third of the third augmentation was still lacking when the Dutch War broke out.

Uncertainty about where the main French attack would be directed presented the Republic's political and military leaders with a strategic dilemma. Were the French really planning to bypass Maastricht or were the French preparations for a campaign along the Rhine intended solely to lure Dutch troops away from Maastricht? For Brussels, on the other hand, there was no shadow of a doubt that a French advance between the Meuse and the Rhine served no other purpose than to distract attention from France's true operational goal, namely the conquest of the Spanish Netherlands.[31] In accordance with a defensive alliance formed in December 1671 by the Republic and Spain, the governor-general of the Spanish Netherlands, Monterrey, therefore requested that the States-General send between 10,000 and 12,000 Dutch troops to Spanish Brabant. Monterrey, in turn, kept a cavalry corps with an effective strength of 3,000 men on standby, 'to be employed as assistance for the State in case this should be requested'. He could as yet spare no infantry, but as soon as the Spanish army in the Low Countries had been reinforced he would make infantry available, too.[32]

The Hague paid heed to Monterrey's request. Six infantry regiments left for Mechelen (Malines) and seven others were assembled by Bergen op Zoom. Maastricht was not forgotten either: in April 1672 an effective force of 6,000

---

[27] NA, SG 12579.96, Members of the States of Gelderland to the SG, Arnhem, 11 December 1671, and RvS to the SG, The Hague, 29 December 1671.
[28] NA, SG 12579.96, Captain Hendrik Mulert to the SG, Orsoy, 3 November 1671.
[29] NA, RvS 548, RvS to the SG, 13 and 17 November 1671.
[30] NA, RAZH, FAH 6, 'L'estat des troupes infanterie et cavallerie sur pied pour le service du roy [Louis XIV] ... 1672'; CWB, II, i, no. 29, Godard Adriaan van Reede-Amerongen to William III, Münster, 27 March 1671.
[31] NA, SG 12588.100, Cornelis de Witt and Cornelis van Vrijbergen to the *griffier* of the SG, Brussels, 26 February 1672, at two o'clock in the afternoon.
[32] NA, SG 12588.100, Cornelis de Witt to his brother, [Brussels, n.d.], received 12 February (quote) and 7 February 1672; Coenraad van Beuningen and Cornelis van Vrijbergen to the *griffier* of the SG, Brussels, 15 May 1672.

was garrisoned there.[33] Nevertheless, the governor of Maastricht, the Rhinegrave, pressed for reinforcements of no less than 2,000 to 3,000 men,[34] but Hieronymus van Beverningk, who was serving as a field deputy in 1672, felt that this request could not be honoured. He and a fellow field deputy sneered that for the Rhinegrave it 'would not be disagreeable if all the Republic's force were to come and encamp before his gates, but we are of the opinion that 5,597 effective soldiers ... not counting the officers, is a sufficient body of soldiers to defend a town.'[35] What everything hinged upon, according to Van Beverningk, was the integrity of the IJssel line. The Rhine strongholds were in a neglected state, so an attack on the Republic's eastern frontier could only be repelled by gathering as many soldiers as possible along the IJssel. In Büderich, for example, of the eighteen cannon there 'barely two were employable for defence.... The moats [were] completely dry, the walls without palisades.'[36] Colonel Godard van Reede-Ginkel took a grave view of things. 'I hear that Prince [Johan] Maurits is very busy along the IJssel', he wrote to his father, the Republic's envoy in Berlin, in early 1672. 'We may all of us hope that something good shall be made of the defences there, because the whole land depends on that post.'[37] He personally believed the chance was slight that the Dutch troops would manage to thwart the French at the River IJssel, because 'one is confident that the king of France shall march on the first of May with all his armies, estimated at 200,000 men.'[38] Van Reede-Ginkel may well have overestimated France's superior numbers – a few weeks later he would revise his estimate to 80,000 men, in addition to 20,000 troops from Münster and Cologne – but this did nothing to detract from the fact that the prospects for the Republic were grim.

The only ray of hope during this dark period was the restoration of the captaincy- and admiralcy-generalcy of the Union which had been voted in February 1672. Within Holland several regents had long been pressing for the appointment of a supreme commander. The experience gained during the war with Münster (1665–1666) had convinced the influential Haarlem regent, Gaspar Fagel, and the Amsterdam burgomaster, Gilles Valckenier (1624–1680), that the restoration of the Dutch army was feasible only if the troops stood under the permanent supervision of a captain-general of the Union. But the appointment of a commander-in-chief required the amendment of the Act of Seclusion,

---

[33] NA, SG 12579.97, 'Lijste van[de] reveue over de compagni[e]ën infanterie ... binnen Maestricht gedaen op den 22 april 1672' and 'Lijste van de cavallerie'.
[34] According to the Rhinegrave the garrison of Maastricht needed to be 8,000 to 9,000 strong during wartime. See NA, RAZH, FAvS 21, Jacob Pieck and Hendrik van Raesfelt (†1678), Maastricht, 1 November 1670.
[35] NA, SG 11670, Hieronymus van Beverningk to the *griffier*, Doesburg, 1 May 1672, transcript.
[36] NA, SG 12579.97, Otto de Roode van Heeckeren, commander in Büderich to the SG, 9 February 1672.
[37] HUA, HAA 2731, Godard van Reede-Ginkel to his father, Amerongen, 28 March 1672.
[38] HUA, HAA 2731, same to same, Amerongen, 7 April 1672.

because only descendants of William the Silent were eligible for the rank of captain- and admiral-general of the Union. To make this far-reaching step palatable to the other regents, Fagel and Valckenier had in 1667 proposed declaring that the functions of stadholder and commander-in-chief were irreconcilable. They thus hoped to allay the concern among the regents about a repetition of the events of 1618 and 1650. A majority of the Hollanders were able to come to terms with their proposal. In a resolution of 5 August 1667 they had informed the other provinces that they would no longer obstruct the appointment of a captain-general of the Union, provided that the States-General established in a resolution that he to whom 'the supreme command over the militia at sea and on land shall ever be deferred [i.e. tendered] may not be nor remain stadholder of any province or provinces'. The 'Perpetual Edict', as this resolution has entered the annals of history, also specified that William III would be appointed as commander-in-chief as soon as he had reached the age of majority of twenty-three years, in November 1673. Until then he would be allowed to take a seat in the Council of State.[39] It took until 1670 before Holland's decision was adopted by the States-General, as the 'Act of Harmony'. The threat of war with France actually led to William III being appointed as captain-general of the Union on 24 February 1672, a good year and a half earlier than planned, though initially his appointment was for just a single campaign. France and England's long-expected declarations of war against the Republic followed six weeks later, on 6 April 1672. 'In the opinion of everyone we are to expect a very heavy summer', the English-born Margaretha Turnor (1613–1700) wrote to her husband, Godard Adriaan van Reede-Amerongen, a few days later.[40]

The attack on the Republic (May–June 1672)

The position in which twenty-one-year-old William III found himself on the eve of the French assault was far from enviable: he had been burdened with an impossible task. With at most 22,000 men he had to defend a line extending no less than a march of twenty hours and to make matters worse the water level in the IJssel also started to drop. The troops who had been assigned to the Dutch field army were indeed 'altogether splendid, excellent men',[41] but they would not be able to hold their own against a predominance of four to one. Van Reede-Ginkel warned his father that unless reinforcements were sent to

---

[39] NA, RAZH, FAH 6, Extract res. SH, 5 August 1667 (quote); N. Japikse, *Prins Willem III de stadhouder-koning*, 2 vols (Amsterdam 1930–1933), I, pp. 137–8; Groenveld, *Evidente factiën*, p. 50; Elias, *Het Amsterdamsche regentenpatriciaat*, p. 160.
[40] HUA, HAA 2722, Margaretha Turnor to her husband, Godard Adriaan van Reede-Amerongen, Amerongen, 11 April 1672.
[41] Tresoar, Familierachief Thoe Schwartzenberg en Hohenlandsberg 276, Georg Wolfgang to Prof. Michael Buschig at Franeker, Zwolle, 5 May 1672.

the IJssel immediately it would be 'impossible for us to obstruct the crossing. The French are marching directly hither with 80,000 men and shall without any doubt be here within eight days.'[42] De Witt was livid when he heard that the Dutch generals had contemplated 'abandoning' the IJssel line without putting up a fight. He wrote to Van Beverningk, who was staying in the Dutch headquarters:

> I would like to hope that if among the ... senior officers there should ever again be such narrow-minded thoughts and opinions, or that they should be uttered, that Your Honour shall resolutely dismiss them with remonstrations of an exceptional seriousness, and shall not tolerate such proposals or views becoming known within the army among the lower officers and common soldiers.

The Grand Pensionary reiterated that reinforcements of 8,000 men were *en route* to the IJssel, in addition to a few thousand armed peasants, and that the French first had to capture Maastricht and the Rhine strongholds, thus 'giving us the opportunity to strengthen the army there [along the IJssel] considerably'.[43] Van Beverningk soon opened De Witt's eyes, preparing him and the other regents in The Hague for the worst, because he did not expect the Rhine strongholds would hold back the French for long, 'because ... the burghers [there] are not only fearful and miscontented, but some of them are fleeing, others remain and yet others threaten to cause harm, so those poor garrisons are in an awful situation, expecting an attack from without and obstruction from within'.[44]

At the end of May 1672 the French crossed to the eastern bank of the Meuse by Visé and speeded onward to the Rhine. Major Everwyne Kirkpatrik (killed in action on 11 April 1677) wrote from Maastricht to his father, Major-General John Kirkpatrik, that the French army numbered 71,000 men in all and that a further 25,000 were ready to follow.[45] On 1 June the French laid siege to four Dutch strongholds simultaneously – Wesel, Büderich, Orsoy and Rheinberg – while the troops of the bishop of Münster and the elector of Cologne marched into the Achterhoek and Twente (the eastern quarters of Gelderland and Overijssel). Van Beverningk's gloomy prediction proved to be more than prescient. Orsoy capitulated on 3 June, Büderich on 4 June, Wesel on 5 June and Rheinberg on 6 June. Rees and Emmerich were next in line, both towns falling into French hands on 9 June. These garrisons numbered on average just a couple of hundred men, so putting up a serious struggle had been out of the question.

---

[42] HUA, HAA 2798, Godard van Reede-Ginkel to his father, in the cavalry encampment between Zutphen and Deventer, 25 May, and Middachten, 2 June 1672 (quote); KB HS 70 C 9, fol. 16, William III to Hieronymus van Beverningk, Dieren, 28 May 1672, transcript.
[43] R. Fruin and N. Japikse (eds), *Brieven van Johan de Witt*, IV (Amsterdam 1913), pp. 345–7, to Hieronymus van Beverningk, 4 June 1672.
[44] NA, SG 12579.98, Hieronymus van Beverningk and S. van Huls to the *griffier* of the SG, Zutphen, 2 June 1672.
[45] NA, RAZH, AJdW, Everwyne Kirkpatrik to his father, John Kirkpatrik, [Maastricht], 25 May 1672.

Wesel and Rheinberg – the two strongest fortified towns – were the exceptions, each manned by fairly substantial garrisons of between 1,500 and 2,000 men. Initially the citizens of Wesel were prepared to defend the town alongside the Republic's troops, but the mood changed after the French had captured a sconce and put the soldiers standing guard there to the sword. Utrecht's field deputy, Gaspar Schadé (1623–1692), sent word to the *griffier* of the States-General: 'The burghers had at first taken up arms as well, but on seeing the said redoubt lost had thrown them down and, with the women of the town walking alongside them, forced the governor to open the gate.'[46] This stood in sharp contrast to the turn of events in Rheinberg, where the burghers 'displayed a great zeal and readiness to defend that town to the utmost'. This notwithstanding, the Dutch governor, Colonel Daniël d'Ossory, opened the gates of Rheinberg for the French without a single shot being fired. As the Dutch troops left the town the populace yelled after them: 'You scoundrels, neither before God nor the world shall you be able to defend your deeds. You all deserve to be punished with the gallows.'[47] Colonel d'Ossory did not escape scot-free either: a few months later he died on the scaffold.

The swift capture of the towns along the Rhine led to great agitation in The Hague. Now a quick choice had to be made between the two evils: relinquish Gelderland, Overijssel and Utrecht to the enemy or run the risk that the French would cut off the field army's retreat to Holland by means of an outflanking movement via the Betuwe. There was no third alternative, the morale of the Dutch troops being at such a low ebb that, the numerical imbalance notwithstanding, there was no question of being able to march to meet the French and bring them to a standstill by means of forcing a battle. Since the start of the French assault the Dutch soldiers had been terrified, while the 'enemy [is] by contrast powerful [and] courageous'.[48] The States-General's committee for 'secret military affairs' travelled to Arnhem for crisis talks with William III, Van Beverningk and Schadé. During a fraught council of war held on 5 June 1672, William III and the field deputies declared that they deemed the IJssel indefensible, but that there might be the devil to pay militarily and politically for the voluntary evacuation of this line and that they would therefore rather go down fighting.[49] A week later, on 12 June, the French penetrated into the Betuwe and laid siege to the Schenkenschans. The twenty-year-old Hendrik ten Hove, this fort's commander, warned The Hague that he would be able to maintain the defence for but a short time: 'Officially we have eighteen companies quartered here, but what is to be

---

[46] NA, SG 12579.98, Gaspar Schadé, Utrecht's field deputy, to the *griffier* of the SG, Zutphen, 7 June 1672.
[47] NA, SG 12579.98, Marinus van Crommon, Zeeland's field deputy, and Johan van Egmond van der Nijenburch (1618–1712), member of the Council of State, to the *griffier* of the SG, Maastricht, 12 and 15 (quote) June 1672.
[48] NA, RAZH, FAvS 22, Notes by Govert van Slingelandt.
[49] NA, RAZH, FAvS 22, Notes taken during the council of war on 5 June 1672.

lamented is that the majority are very weak and four of them combined could not constitute a single complete company.'[50] This predicament left no room for bravura. The threat of communications with Holland being lost was now acute and without the Dutch field troops this province would be undefendable. Van Beverningk and Schadé therefore gave orders on their own authority 'to break up the army [along the IJssel] because one now has the enemy to the back and to the front'.[51] William III was in Arnhem at this dramatic juncture, so the decision was taken without consulting him, but there was no alternative on hand. 'It is high time that in Holland one did everything one can with water, because [the French] are whole-heartedly professing to march on Amsterdam', Van Beverningk wrote to the city's burgomasters.[52]

After dispatching two infantry regiments to Friesland and Groningen, and reinforcing the garrisons of Doesburg, Zutphen, Deventer and Zwolle with a total of seven to eight infantry regiments, William III marched on Utrecht with the entire cavalry (5,000 men) and the remaining infantry (4,000 men). Some 2,000 Spanish cavalry joined this small Dutch army *en route*. On 16 June 1672 the States-General ordered William III and the field deputies to evacuate Utrecht and withdraw to Holland with all the troops.[53] The French captured Arnhem that very same day and four days later, on 20 June, a vanguard of the French army seized Naarden by surprise. On 22 June troops from Münster and Cologne penetrated as far as Harderwijk and the following day the main French army occupied Utrecht. Hastily implemented inundations prevented the French being able to press onward to Amsterdam or any other town in Holland.

The French advance had been brought to an abrupt halt, but this did not lessen the dismay about the events of the past three weeks. Godard van Reede-Ginkel wrote to his father on 23 June, the day the city of Utrecht fell into French hands: 'Our whole country, for which our forefathers fought for 80 years, is on the brink of being lost, and that in the space of three weeks ... and the most appalling thing is that we are losing our country without even having strongly resisted the enemy.'[54] The implications of the revolution in military organisation achieved in France between 1667 and 1671 had been made brutally evident. The age when wars could be conducted and sustained on the basis of temporary solutions was consigned to the past once and for all. From now on the security of states could only be guaranteed by ensuring that the proficiency and cohesion of the armed forces were kept up to standard in peacetime as well. This was

---

[50] NA, SG 12579.98, Hendrik ten Hove to the committee for military affairs, Schenkenschans, 13 June 1672.
[51] NA, RAZH, FAvS 22, Hieronymus van Beverningk and Gaspar Schadé, Zutphen, 12 June 1672, transcript.
[52] GAA, Missives to burgomasters 65 (microfilm 8006), Hieronymus van Beverningk to the SG, Rhenen, 14 June 1672, transcript.
[53] NA, RAZH, FAvS 22, Res. SG, 16 June 1672.
[54] HUA, HAA, Godard van Reede-Ginkel to his father, Amsterdam, 23 June 1672.

the harsh lesson that Europe in general and the inhabitants of the Republic in particular were taught in June 1672.

Behind the Holland Water Line (June–September 1672)

The Holland Water Line extended from the Zuiderzee to the River Meuse. This improvised line of redoubts linked by defensively inundated tracts of land was not consistently wide. The sector near Bodegraven was the weak point, so William III established his headquarters there. The remaining field troops established positions at Muiden, Goejanverwellesluis, Schoonhoven and Gorinchem. Every French attempt to cross the water line had to be repulsed from these and a great many smaller positions, but it was uncertain whether that would be effective. Hundreds of Dutch soldiers managed to escape from French captivity and join the troops in Holland, but with just as many men deserting, on balance this was of little help. Johan Maurits, who was in command of the sector near Muiden and was therefore responsible for the protection of Amsterdam, wrote to William III in late June 1672:

> Many of our soldiers pass through here every day, their having been captured in the surrendered towns and having escaped. They have in many days seen no bread, never mind having a stiver to their name. Give to each of them a guilder.... Our soldiery, which is already weak enough, is deserting every day by reason of the taxing sentry duties, the great deal of digging, and primarily those who have their wife and children in those towns that have been captured by the enemy.[55]

Johan Maurits elaborated on this in another letter: 'I have a [great] quantity of young officers without experience and many companies of fifteen, twenty and thirty men who have been prisoners but are without arms, and because of [a lack of] money they are deserting.'

From the middle of July the situation started to improve gradually. As we have seen, on 16 July the States of Holland proclaimed a raft of emergency measures intended to preserve the Dutch army from total collapse,[56] and a start could be made with the restoration of the discipline and fighting strength of the Dutch troops. The circumstances under which this had to be achieved were very difficult. The summer and autumn of 1672 allowed a few months of respite, but the French would probably resume their offensive as soon as the freeze set in; frozen inundations would no longer form an obstacle. In 1672 everything depended on bringing the ubiquitous defeatism to an end. The Dutch troops had to regain their self-confidence as quickly as possible. Only then was there a chance of their being able to persevere with the war through the winter. The

---

[55] KB, HS 70 C 9, Johan Maurits of Nassau-Siegen to William III, [June 1672], and same to the burgomasters of Amsterdam, Muiden, 30 June 1672.
[56] See p. 330.

spring of 1673 would then have to be used to tackle the reform of the Dutch army more thoroughly, after which the struggle could be resumed with more evenly balanced odds. Four factors converted this scenario into reality: 1. the indomitability of William III and of the Hollanders, Groningers, Frisians and Zeelanders; 2. Louis XIV's actions; 3. the successful deployment of the Dutch fleet; and 4. the international reaction to the French invasion.

Three days after the fall of Utrecht a majority in the States of Holland had voted to send a delegation headed by Pieter de Groot (1615–1678), the Republic's former envoy in Paris, to the French headquarters in Zeist. De Groot was authorised to cede the Generality Lands to Louis XIV in exchange for peace. The Sun King refused to settle for this, demanding Nijmegen, Grave and Bommel, as well as the forts of Schenkenschans, Voorne, Sint-Andries, Crevecoeur and Loevestein. Possession of these strongholds and forts would give the king of France total control of the land between the rivers Meuse and Waal.[57] On top of this there were still the English demands. Charles II was only prepared to abandon the assault if English garrisons were permitted in Sluis, Vlissingen and Den Briel, and if in addition the Republic paid an indemnity of 10 million guilders. Compliance with these demands would have been tantamount to sacrificing the Republic's independence, because French and English troops would henceforth be able to march into Holland, Zeeland, Utrecht and Gelderland at a moment's notice. For the Amsterdam regents, who had after all wanted nothing to do with granting a mandate to De Groot, this prospect brooked just one possible response to Louis XIV: negotiations had to be broken off immediately. William III, stadholder of Holland and Zeeland since 4 July 1672, was of exactly the same opinion, and in conjunction with Amsterdam's stance his position was decisive. De Witt was also against a peace at any price, but since being seriously injured in an attempted assassination on 21 June he no longer pulled any political weight.[58] The Dutch navy's successful actions buoyed up William III in his determination to maintain the resistance to the bitter end. On 7 June De Ruyter had surprised the combined Anglo-French fleet at its anchorage off Solebay, to the south of Lowestoft. The battle may have been undecided, but the threat of an English landing on Holland's coast was scuppered for that year.[59] This released a great many Dutch soldiers, who would otherwise have been needed to guard the beaches, for duties along the Holland Water Line.

The decision 'to prefer to await the ultimate fate of the war with the remaining allies [i.e. the provinces of Groningen, Friesland and Zeeland], and to take a gamble instead of settling for such scandalous and highly disadvantageous conditions' soon began to bear fruit.[60] Monterrey made an additional 6,000 to

---

[57] Valkenier, 't Verwerd Europa, Appendix no. 59.
[58] Franken, Coenraad van Beuningen, pp. 100–2 and 107.
[59] Bruijn, Varend verleden, pp. 116–17.
[60] GrA, ASSO 1399, Egbert Horenken (†1679), Johan Eeck (†1713), L.T. van Starckenborg and G. Aldringa, The Hague, 4 July 1672.

7,000 men available to the Republic, the Spanish auxiliary force thus swelling to between 9,000 and 10,000 men. The Spaniards replaced the Dutch garrisons in 's-Hertogenbosch, Breda and Bergen op Zoom, releasing the units billeted there for the defence of Holland.[61] In July 1672, thanks to Louis XIV's actions, thousands more troops became available for this. After negotiations with De Groot were broken off, the Sun King returned to France with part of his army (15,000 men). He felt that more than enough had been achieved that year and he therefore raised no objections to all the Dutch prisoners of war, an estimated 20,000 men, being freed after payment of the ransom. The French historian André Corvisier denounces this decision,[62] and with the benefit of hindsight it was indeed highly injudicious. While it is true that releasing prisoners of war was an age-old military tradition, this does not detract from the fact that the king of France and his right-hand man, Louvois, made a grave error, because they had not taken advantage of the opportunity to make political capital from the military victory over the Republic. 'There are strategic assaults which have immediately led to peace,' writes Clausewitz, 'but few are of this nature.'[63] The 'Guerre de Hollande' was no exception to this, but Louis XIV largely had himself to blame. By demanding too high a price for peace he forced the Republic to continue the struggle, and by setting free the prisoners of war he provided the Republic with the means to do this.[64] This hardly served France's best interests, because so long as the 'Guerre de Hollande' dragged on, tens of thousands of French soldiers were needed to guard the captured towns in the Northern Netherlands and these men were therefore not available for an assault on the Spanish Netherlands. The Sun King was thus playing into the hands of his arch-enemies – the Spanish and Austrian Habsburgs. Looking back from the mid-eighteenth century, the assessment of the French military theorist Guillaume le Blond was that:

> This prince [Louis XIV] has taken all the precautions that prudence might suggest in order not to be distracted from the pursuit of his objective in the least, and if the happy events of this war had not excited him to continue beyond the bounds necessary to humiliate this Republic ... he would have achieved his goal [of procuring the Spanish Netherlands] without obstacles on the part of neighbouring powers.[65]

The Republic was already receiving military support from Spain and in July this was fleshed out by assistance from the emperor and the elector of Brandenburg.

---

[61] GrA, ASSO 1399, Egbert Horenken and G. Aldringa, The Hague, 1 July 1672.
[62] Corvisier, *Louvois*, p. 260. See also Knoop, *Willem den Derde*, I, pp. 134–5.
[63] Clausewitz, *Vom Kriege*, p. 777.
[64] Three-quarters of a century later, during the War of the Austrian Succession, the French would not make this mistake anew. In 1746 and 1747 more than 18,000 Dutch troops were taken prisoner by France. They were marched off to France and the majority (almost 14,000 men) were allowed to return to the Republic only after the war had been concluded. See Van Nimwegen, *De Republiek als grote mogendheid*, p. 137.
[65] Le Blond, *Elémens de tactique*, p. 452.

On 25 July 1672 the Republic and the emperor entered into a pact with the object of ensuring 'observance of the Peace of Cleves [1666] and preventing that someone ... should do something to the detriment of the Peace of Westphalia [1648]'. Leopold I promised to raise 16,000 men in exchange for a subsidy of 30,000 rix-dollars a month, and as soon as these troops were ready to march they would be deployed against the enemies of the Republic in conjunction with a Brandenburgian army of 20,000 men. In May 1672, prior to the launch of the French assault, the States-General and the Great Elector had entered into a defensive alliance, but the speed with which the French had trampled over the Republic's strongholds had thus far prevented Friedrich Wilhelm from meeting his obligations.[66]

William III incorporated the ransomed Dutch prisoners of war into the regiments quartered in Holland and Zeeland. Groningen's deputies to the States-General pressed the prince of Orange and Gaspar Fagel to send some men to the north as well, in order to lend a hand in their province's defence against the troops from Münster and Cologne – on 11 July 1672 they had captured Coevorden, whereupon they advanced on the city of Groningen – but this fell on deaf ears. From The Hague Groningen's deputies reported back to their principals about the attitude in the States of Holland:

> There is nobody who of his own volition concerns himself with the defence and protection of the other remaining [free] provinces. And the urgent requests from those which it concerns, no matter with what assiduity and effort these are made, are disposed of so weakly and so tardily that we must verily declare not to know what we should make of it.[67]

William III and Holland's regents were justifiably of the opinion that the preservation of the city of Groningen could by no means outweigh the integrity of the province of Holland. So long as the enemy was kept outside this province there was still a chance of recapturing the lost territories. It was, moreover, still doubtful whether troops from Münster and Cologne would be able to besiege Groningen successfully. A substantial garrison of 4,000 to 5,000 men under the command of the experienced General Rabenhaupt was quartered in Groningen. On paper the bishop of Münster and Elector Maximilian Henry of Bavaria could deploy 24,000 men for this operation, but their army was evaporating because of a lack of money and food supplies. One of Georg Friedrich von Waldeck's correspondents reported that the bishop of Münster's infantry 'was half dead and very miserable before Groningen.... [I] can assure you that, if they receive any substantial shock, all the German troops [of the bishop] shall disband by whole

---

[66] Valkenier, 't Verwerd Europa, Appendix nos. 12 and 78 (quote); Der Kinderen, De Republiek en Munster, II, p. 187.
[67] GrA, ASSO 1399, Egbert Horenken and G. Aldringa, The Hague, 30 June (quote) and 1 July 1672.

companies or regiments.'[68] The 'siege' of Groningen (19 July to 27 August 1672) therefore went no further than a protracted bombardment that, incidentally, caused few casualties on the side of the defenders: when the siege was lifted the Dutch fatalities amounted to about 100, while the losses suffered by the besiegers amounted to no fewer than 11,000 men, including 5,600 deserters.[69]

The war preparations of the Imperialist and Brandenburgian forces and the successful defence of Groningen were an important boost for the Republic. Johan Maurits thought there was no longer any danger that the French would launch a surprise attack on Amsterdam that summer. 'The enemy continues to sniff at us on all sides,' he wrote from Muiden on 24 August 1672, 'but rest assured that by letting in the water [in the meadows] with this fine wind [he] shall change his mind.' The following day was the feast-day of Saint Louis, the French monarch's name day, and in the French army it was customary during wartime to celebrate this with a daring military operation, but the French exercised restraint.[70] Louis XIV's attention was wholly focused on the German troop concentration. He sent Condé with 18,000 men to Alsace and Turenne with 20,000 men to the Rhine. An occupying force of approximately 50,000 men remained behind in the Republic: between 18,000 and 19,000 men in the province of Utrecht and on the Veluwe, more than 25,000 men in the county of Zutphen and the Nijmegen quarter, and a mounted corps of about 7,000 men in the vicinity of Maastricht. Condé had been ordered to guard France's eastern borders, while Turenne was to prevent the Imperial and Brandenburgian army compelling Münster and Cologne to acquiesce. The Sun King assigned the task of keeping an eye on William III to Lieutenant-General François Henri de Montmorency-Bouteville (1628–1695), duke of Luxembourg, who was commander in the province of Utrecht and the Veluwe. Luxembourg was a pupil of Condé and renowned as a highly enterprising military leader.[71]

For William III the enfeeblement of the French army in the Republic was the signal to start preparing for a counter-offensive. This was intended to restore the Dutch troops' self-confidence and to demonstrate to Europe that the Republic was not beaten yet. William III was aware that he lacked the experience to embark

---

[68] GA, AHGC 1218, 'Staett von Monsterse armé' in 1672. Three days after the raising of the siege, the field deputies wrote to Albertina Agnes (1634–1696), widow of the Frisian stadholder Willem Frederik: 'One can well imagine how he [the enemy] with this exceptionally rainy weather shall be perplexed in his retreat and, because of shortages, many of his [men] must have deserted and starved.' Tresoar, FSA 48a, Tietjerk, 30 August 1672.
[69] Valkenier, 't Verwerd Europa, p. 796; Knoop, Willem den Derde, I, pp. 165–72.
[70] GAA, Missives to burgomasters 66 (microfilm 8006), Johan Maurits of Nassau-Siegen, Muiden, 24 August 1672.
[71] GA, AHGC 1200, Count Willem Adriaan de Hornes to Georg Friedrich von Waldeck, Gorinchem, 7 August 1673, with a 'Lijste van de [Franse] regimenten soo te voet als te peerde in de naervolgende steeden en forten' as an addendum; Vervolg van 't Verwerd Europa, p. 660; Knoop, Willem den Derde, I, pp. 302–4 and 311; J. den Tex, Onder vreemde heren. De Republiek der Nederlanden 1672–1674 (Zutphen 1982), p. 29.

on this alone, and he therefore agreed to Waldeck accompanying him as his second-in-command.[72] As soon as the 'allied soldiers', namely the Imperial forces and the Brandenburgers, had arrived on the banks of the Rhine, the Republic's troops were to emerge from behind the Holland Water Line. Waldeck took advantage of the interim to restructure the Dutch army. 'One has carried out a major reformation among the troops here by disbanding companies and redistributing the men', according to a correspondent of Van Reede-Amerongen.[73] However, from Brussels, the States-General's two envoys extraordinary, Coenraad van Beuningen (1622–1693) and Cornelis van Vrijbergen, warned that all the effort would be to no avail if there was not an immediate end to the 'domestic commotions in sundry towns of the Republic … because these make such a perilous impression on many people [abroad], as if the State were on the point of descending into total anarchy and thus in no position to be of any use either to itself or to its friends.'[74] The appointment of William III as stadholder of Holland and Zeeland had failed to dispel the populace's fury with the De Witt faction. De Witt resigned as Grand Pensionary on 4 August 1672, but he and his brother were lynched on 20 August all the same. The States of Holland appointed Gaspar Fagel as Grand Pensionary that very same day. Fagel and many others were of the opinion that the struggle against France could be brought to a successful conclusion only if William III was able to pursue a vigorous military strategy. The States of Holland therefore empowered their stadholder 'on this occasion' to 'change the law', namely to reconstitute the councils of the voting towns as he saw fit. Eventually some 130 of the 460 Holland regents were purged and replaced by persons who were prepared to support William III's policy, at least for the time being. William III reorganised the magistrature in Amsterdam in accordance with the wishes of Gilles Valckenier, who thereby managed to assure himself of the highest authority in this major city, the 'magnificat'. William III would be able to count on the solid backing of Amsterdam until 1675.[75] On 16 September 1672 a correspondent of the Republic's envoy in Berlin wrote to Godard Adriaan van Reede-Amerongen:

> We would like to hope that now we have domestic calm we shall be capable of bringing our army into the field on the arrival of the auxiliary troops [the Imperialists and Brandenburgers]. Today it was resolved at the meeting of Their High Mightinesses [the States-General] to have the land's fleet return to port, seeing

---

[72] See p. 329.
[73] HUA, HAA 2800, Rudolf van Ommeren (1619–1689), burgomaster of Wageningen and a deputy of Gelderland at the States-General, to Godard Adriaan van Reede-Amerongen, The Hague, 16 September 1672.
[74] NA, SG 12588.100, Coenraad van Beuningen and Cornelis van Vrijbergen to the *griffier* of the SG, Brussels, 11 September 1672.
[75] Elias, *Het Amsterdamsche regentenpatriciaat*, pp. 171 and 175; Groenveld, *Evidente factiën*, p. 61.

that the season is so advanced ... whereby it shall then be possible to reinforce our army with a sizeable contingent of soldiers or marines [who had been detached to the fleet].[76]

The failed assault on Naarden and the battle of Woerden (September–October 1672)

The Imperial and Brandenburg armies were at last conjoined on 26 September near Hildesheim. The expectations in The Hague were that this force, with a combined strength of 36,000 men, would then thrust ahead into the bishopric of Münster and the electorate of Cologne, thus ridding the Republic of two of her four opponents in one fell swoop and leaving the French with no option but to withdraw from the conquered provinces. This, however, failed to transpire.[77] The Holy Roman Emperor was not yet prepared to allow things to degenerate into open hostilities with France and in addition he wanted to prevent Brandenburg taking advantage of the enfeeblement of Münster and Cologne. He had therefore secretly instructed his commander, the renowned General Raimondo, count of Montecuccoli (1609–1680), who had famously won victory over the Turks in the battle of St Gotthard Abbey (August 1664), to limit the campaign to a 'demonstration' along the Lower Rhine.[78] But even this came to nothing, because Turenne was one step ahead of Montecuccoli. The French *maréchal* had ordered the land on both sides of the Rhine from Wesel to Koblenz to be stripped bare, in order that the Imperial and Brandenburgian troops would find no more forage or proviant there. Rather than stand idle, Montecuccoli decided to head for Frankfurt am Main. The French would then at least have to be on the alert for an enemy advance along the Moselle or an incursion into Alsace.[79]

The march of the emperor's and Brandenburg's troops to Frankfurt meant that the Republic would have to manage without direct help from her allies, but William III, Waldeck and Johan Maurits thought that this could no longer serve as a reason to keep the Dutch troops within the water line. After all, the only way to restore their dented morale was by achieving successes against the French. Johan Maurits devised a plan for a surprise attack on Naarden. He pointed out to William III that the way would then be clear to thrust ahead to Amersfoort and Harderwijk.[80] The capture of Amersfoort would make the conveyance of

---

[76] HUA, HAA 2800, Rudolf van Ommeren to Godard Adriaan van Reede-Amerongen, The Hague, 16 September 1672.
[77] CWB, II, i, no. 119, Godard Adriaan van Reede-Amerongen to William III, Halberstadt, 12 September 1672.
[78] Wilson, *German Armies*, p. 46; Gunther E. Rothenberg, 'Maurice of Nassau, Gustavus Adolphus, Raimondo Montecuccoli, and the "Military Revolution" of the Seventeenth Century', in Paret, *Makers of Modern Strategy*, pp. 32–63, esp. 55–8.
[79] Valkenier, *'t Verwerd Europa*, pp. 857–8; H.M. Hozier, *Turenne* (1885; reprint Tonbridge 1992), p. 167.
[80] Bosscha, *Neerlands Heldendaden te land*, II, p. 90.

supplies to the city of Utrecht very difficult and would probably force Luxembourg to retreat back to the IJssel. The recapture of Harderwijk would make it possible to launch an assault on the IJssel towns in conjunction with the troops in Friesland and Groningen. William III sanctioned Johan Maurits's plan. The early morning of 28 September 1672 was the moment chosen for the surprise attack on Naarden. Johan Maurits expected little resistance: the French garrison was not strong – estimates ranged from 1,000 to 1,400 men – the moats were wadeable, no ravelins had been constructed and it also lacked a covered way, so the Dutch troops would be able to storm the main rampart and gates without further ado.[81] Yet this operation turned out to be a débâcle. Four infantry regiments from different garrisons were meant to take part in the storm assault and were supposed to arrive before Naarden simultaneously. The Guards under the command of Colonel Karel Florentijn, Wald- and Rhinegrave von Salm (†1676), son of the governor of Maastricht, had to be transported from Amsterdam by ship while the three other regiments travelled over land. William III and Johan Maurits appeared before Naarden at the agreed time with the troops from Muiden, 'tensely awaiting the lord Rhinegrave, who, having come via the water and having landed, would carry out the first attack'. Having waited in vain for the Guards for two whole hours, William III summoned Johan Maurits. He told him that he had just received news that a lack of wind had prevented the Guards sailing any further than Muiden and that the position of the other two regiments was a mystery – they had probably lost their way in the dark. After consulting with Johan Maurits, William III decided to call off the operation.[82] The failure of the assault on Naarden sparked a furore in Holland. To mollify the popular outrage, Johan Maurits insisted that the burgomasters of Amsterdam should publish the written report of the operation which he had submitted to them. He was prepared to pay for the printing of several hundred copies himself.[83]

After the failed assault on Naarden, William III did not throw in the towel; he immediately hatched the plan to recapture Woerden. He was aware that the reduction of this small town might result in substantial losses – the French garrison numbered 2,000 men and in the wake of the assault on Naarden the French sentry posts were on high alert – but this was a risk he was prepared to take, because the recapture of Woerden would yield two major advantages. In the first place Luxembourg would then have to be constantly on the alert

---

[81] KHA, A4-1468, Description of Naarden's defences; Valkenier, *'t Verwerd Europa*, p. 825.
[82] GAA, Missives to burgomasters 66 (microfilm 8006), Johan Maurits of Nassau-Siegen, Muiden, 29 September 1672.
[83] 'Given that in these present times not even the benefactors of the populace are spared reproach, and that there is already much ado about the Naarden venture, I humbly request Your Honours, that, since public opinion shall probably place the blame at my door rather than that of God, who governs everything, you will permit me to make known in print the short report that I presented about this to the lord burgomasters ... of the city of Amsterdam, to avoid such calumny somewhat.' See GAA, Missives to burgomasters 66 (microfilm 8006), Johan Maurits of Nassau-Siegen, Muiden, 29 September 1672.

for an assault on Utrecht and thus be forced to keep a strong garrison there permanently – this would leave him with fewer troops to launch an invasion into Holland across the ice during the winter – and in the second place the possession of this outlying post would at last make it possible to take advantage of the Dutch cavalry – Holland's marshy ground was unsuitable for the mounted arm. 'If we could get to terra firma, one would act with greater freedom and employ the cavalry', according to the Utrecht regent Johan van Reede-Renswoude (1593–1682), who had fled to The Hague.[84] These strategic considerations aside, something that for William III weighed no less heavily was his above-mentioned view that the Dutch troops could only regain their self-confidence by attacking the French wherever possible. Seventy years later, during the War of the Austrian Succession, the States-General formulated this standpoint as follows: 'It has often ... been observed ... that when troops who previously did not perform well in every respect are brought before the enemy for a second time ... they have accomplished their task with double the courage.'[85]

William III assembled 6,500 to 7,000 men for the assault on Woerden, including some of the best Dutch troops, such as the marines of Lieutenant-Colonel François Palm (died of wounds on 18 August 1674). The plan of attack was as follows: Woerden was to be enclosed on the western side by William III and Waldeck with four infantry regiments (3,500 to 4,000 men) and hemmed in on its eastern side by the general of the artillery, Count Willem Adriaan van Hornes (†1694), with 1,600 infantrymen, including the marines. After a cannonade lasting a day or two the small town was to be stormed from both sides simultaneously. It was self-evident that the French defenders would call on Luxembourg for assistance using signal fires. Given the short distance between Woerden and Utrecht he would be able to march to the town's relief in short order. William III had taken this eventuality into account. He entrusted the extremely important task of blocking the road from Utrecht to Woerden to the general of the infantry, Frederik of Nassau-Zuylensteyn (1624–1672), with about 1,500 men (including the Solms regiment).[86] Nassau-Zuylensteyn, a natural son of Frederik Hendrik, had received this command position primarily owing to his personal ties with William III. He had been charged with the prince of Orange's upbringing from 1659 to 1666 and William III had become deeply attached to him.[87] The choice of Nassau-Zuylensteyn would prove to be rather unfortunate: though he did have military experience – he had been promoted to lieutenant-colonel in 1645 – he had seen no action after 1648 and had not been promoted to general until April 1672.

---

[84] HUA, HAA 2801, Johan van Reede-Renswoude to Godard Adriaan van Reede-Amerongen, The Hague, 15 October 1672.
[85] NA, CvdH 143, Secret resolution of the SG, 8 June 1745.
[86] Knoop, *Willem den Derde*, I, p. 181.
[87] Geyl, *Oranje en Stuart*, pp. 207–8.

The attack on Woerden began in the night of 10/11 October 1672. Nassau-Zuylensteyn marched past this small town and dug in by Grovenbrugge, on the road to Utrecht. However, he did this only on the side facing Utrecht, because local farmers had assured him there 'was no passable route whereby it would be possible to be attacked from behind' and Nassau-Zuylensteyn did not think it necessary to check the veracity of this.[88] In the meantime Hornes had twelve cannon brought to bear and William III and Waldeck arrived before Woerden. At four o'clock in the morning the French discovered the presence of the Dutch troops and warned Luxembourg using fires and cannon-shots. The French commander assembled a corps of between 8,000 and 9,000 men and marched to the town's relief. At between two and three o'clock in the morning on 12 October he launched a 'furious' assault on Nassau-Zuylensteyn's position, but the Dutch troops repulsed the attack. Luxembourg then investigated whether it was possible to reach the rear of the Dutch position and it turned out that this was indeed a possibility, despite the assertions of the farmers. The French did, however, have to march 'through water above the knees' for part of the way. Like the king of Sparta, Leonidas, at the battle of Thermopylae in 480 BC, Nassau-Zuylensteyn died a hero's death in the midst of his troops – his corpse bore no fewer than thirty-six wounds.[89]

For the people of the sixteenth, seventeenth and eighteenth centuries, Greek and Roman warfare was the benchmark for war in their own era and to them the similarity of the situation facing the Republic in 1672 and that faced by Greece and Rome during the Persian Wars (490–479 BC) and the Second Punic War (218–201 BC), respectively, went without saying. Besides the death of Nassau-Zuylensteyn there was, however, another much more important parallel with the battle of Thermopylae: at Woerden the Dutch troops fought with a valour that was in no way inferior to that of the Spartans. The Solms regiment lost more than three-quarters of its strength – after the battle it counted just 150 soldiers – and the fierceness with which the troops under Hornes beat back the advancing French came as a complete surprise not only to Luxembourg but to everyone in the Republic.

> In this encounter our men – senior and lesser officers as well as the rank and file – have in general acquitted themselves admirably and courageously. The lord count of Waldeck declares that … [he] cannot understand how it is possible, given that our troops have [on this occasion] held their ground so courageously and determinedly, that we have so scandalously lost so many fortified towns in so short a time.

The marines particularly distinguished themselves during this battle. After the first musket salvo, Lieutenant-Colonel Palm ordered his men 'to set their muskets

---

[88] Valkenier, 't Verwerd Europa, p. 827.
[89] HUA, HAA 2801, Godard Willem van Tuyl van Serooskerken (1647–1708) to Godard Adriaan van Reede-Amerongen, The Hague, 15 October 1672.

down on the ground and ... storm through the enemy with cutlass in fist, with such success that they took flight'.[90] Yet Luxembourg exploited the fighting to smuggle 1,500 men into Woerden as reinforcements via another route. The opportunity to take this town by storm had been frittered away and William III ordered the beating of the retreat.[91]

Despite calling off the operation, William III was very satisfied with the outcome of the battle at Woerden. The aura of French invincibility had at last been fractured. It turned out that the French soldiers were also mere mortals, 'as subject to the sword and death as ours'.[92] The French losses amounted to between 1,500 and 2,000 men, three times as many as on the Dutch side. Van Beverningk wrote proudly to Van Reede-Amerongen that the French themselves had to acknowledge that the Dutch troops had fought 'admirably'.[93] 'Such that one could say that the enemy achieved their objective and we gained the victory', added another correspondent of the Republic's envoy in Berlin.[94] William III promoted Palm to colonel as a reward for the courage he had shown. Besides words of praise there were, however, more critical voices to be heard. Margaretha Turnor, who had been residing in Amsterdam since the French attack, commented to her husband that the Dutch soldiers had fought 'courageously' but that this could not disguise the fact that the discipline in the Dutch army was not yet fully restored:

> It appears that disorder persists there [in the army], because although the worthy lord of Zuylensteyn has paid with his life, many still say that his nonchalance alone was the cause of that setback before Woerden.... One says that even when the artillery arrived before Woerden there was not a single ball with which one could actually fire, these being either too big or too small and [having] other such shortcomings.

She warned her husband that in Holland all attention was focused on the arrival of the Imperial-Brandenburgian army, 'for here one foresees no relief without them'.[95] Waldeck concurred with her critique. 'The disorder and nonchalance

---

[90] HUA, HAA 2801, G. v. K. to Godard Adriaan van Reede-Amerongen, Delft, 14 October 1672.
[91] HUA, HAA 2801, Johan van Reede-Renswoude to Godard Adriaan van Reede-Amerongen, The Hague, 15 October 1672.
[92] HUA, HAA 2801, G. v. K. to Godard Adriaan van Reede-Amerongen, Delft, 14 October 1672.
[93] HUA, HAA 2802, Hieronymus van Beverningk to Godard Adriaan van Reede-Amerongen, Zwammerdam, 24 October (quote); Rudolf van Ommeren to the same, The Hague, 21 October; and Johan van Reede-Renswoude to the same, The Hague, 3 November 1672; Valkenier, 't Verwerd Europa, p. 830.
[94] HUA, HAA 2801, Rudolf van Ommeren to Godard Adriaan van Reede-Amerongen, The Hague, 21 October 1672.
[95] HUA, HAA 2722, Margaretha Turnor to Godard Adriaan van Van Reede-Amerongen, Amsterdam, 21 October 1672.

[of the Dutch troops] have caused us the failure of two enterprises',[96] he wrote to her husband, referring to the assaults on Naarden and Woerden. Even after the events of 12 October 1672 William III did not subscribe to the view that the Dutch army had re-established its former reputation. There was still much work to be done, but for him, as noted, the most important outcome was that the troops had regained their self-assurance. The next task was to convince the regents and the populace at large that the most critical period for the Republic was over. On 17 October, just five days after the battle of Woerden, William III took the decision, in consultation with Waldeck, Johan Maurits and De Ruyter, to leave the Holland Water Line with an appreciable body of men and launch a daring assault on Charleroi.[97]

The expedition to Charleroi (November–December 1672)

The expedition to Charleroi was a risky undertaking, but if it succeeded then the strategic effect would be commensurately great. The capture of this key stronghold would sever the communications between the French army of occupation in the Republic and France, forcing Louis XIV to give the order to evacuate Utrecht and Gelderland and to lift the blockade of Maastricht. The Republic could not perform this operation alone, so success depended on cooperation with Brussels and Vienna. Waldeck calculated that 37,000 men were needed for a formal siege of Charleroi: a siege corps of 12,000 men and an army of observation of 25,000.[98] The Republic could provide 23,000 to 25,000 men for this undertaking, but no more than that. In the autumn of 1672 there were an estimated 41,000 to 43,000 Dutch troops in Holland and Zeeland, of which at least 18,000 were required for the guarding of the Holland Water Line.[99] William III could depend on the Spanish governor-general placing all the Spanish troops he could spare at his disposal for the attack on Charleroi. Monterrey regarded this as a first step in undoing the Peace of Aix-la-Chapelle. Monterrey was prepared to deal with Louis XIV being able to find an excuse to declare war on Spain in the assistance offered to the Republic; he was not mistaken in regarding an overt 'rupture' with France as a foregone conclusion. The assistance of the Spanish governor-general would, however go no further than bringing an effective force of 10,000 to 11,000 men into the field – the army of Flanders numbered 39,000 men in all[100] – so

---

[96] HUA, HAA 2802, Georg Friedrich von Waldeck to Godard Adriaan van Reede-Amerongen, Zwammerdam, 22 October 1672.
[97] Valkenier, 't Verwerd Europa, p. 832.
[98] GA, AHGC 1240, Notes by Georg Friedrich von Waldeck about the number of troops needed for a siege of Charleroi.
[99] HUA, HAA 2802, Georg Friedrich von Waldeck to Godard Adriaan van Reede-Amerongen, Zwammerdam, 24 October 1672; CWB, II, i, no. 180, William III to the SG, Roosendaal, 7 November 1672.
[100] Rooms, 'Materiële organisatie', p. 20.

the success of the expedition to Charleroi ultimately hinged on the action that Montecuccoli undertook. If the Imperial general were to cross the Rhine with the Imperial-Brandenburg army and join forces with the Dutch-Spanish army, then it would certainly be possible to bring the siege to a successful conclusion.

Preparations for the expedition to Charleroi were begun in early November 1672. 'Here one is whole-heartedly gladdened that the troops are on the march', a correspondent of Van Reede-Amerongen wrote from The Hague on 3 November. 'From here ... about 25,000 men, both on foot and on horse, have sailed from Rotterdam by ship for ... Bergen op Zoom.'[101] From there the Dutch troops proceeded to Roosendaal and Wouw, where 6,000 to 7,000 Spanish cavalry were awaiting their arrival. William III mustered the Dutch-Spanish army on 7 November, which numbered 30,000 men: 18,000 cavalry, 2,000 dragoons and 10,000 infantry.[102] William III and Waldeck left for Maastricht the following day with between 10,000 and 11,000 cavalry,[103] along with 5,000 infantry; the remaining 14,000 to 15,000 men stayed behind near Bergen op Zoom. Depending on the circumstances they would follow William III at a later point in time or would in part quickly return to Holland to enable Johan Maurits to drive the French from Utrecht.

Travelling via Herentals, Peer and Lanaken, the Dutch-Spanish corps arrived in the vicinity of Maastricht on 12 November. Initially everything went precisely as anticipated: Jacques Henri de Durfort (1626–1704), duke of Duras, commander of the French cavalry corps of 7,000 horse that was holding Maastricht invested, hastily raised the blockade of this stronghold, while Luxembourg assembled the bulk of his troops and therefore seemed intent on abandoning the province of Utrecht and the Veluwe. As soon as William III was informed of this he sent the 5,000 infantrymen back to Bergen op Zoom. 'I believed', he wrote to Johan Maurits, 'that perhaps, having this infantry, you would be able to undertake something.'[104] The 'something' that William III was alluding to was the recapture of Kampen, Zwartsluis, Naarden, Utrecht, Amersfoort or Woerden. However, Johan Maurits had to disappoint William III, because Luxembourg had no intention whatsoever of evacuating the province of Utrecht.[105] The Utrecht regent Johan Pesters, pensionary of Maastricht and a confidant of William III, made no secret of his disappointment about this: 'It is good for the reputation of

---

[101] HUA, HAA 2802, H. van Heteren to Godard Adriaan van Reede-Amerongen, The Hague, 3 November 1672.
[102] Valkenier, 't Verwerd Europa, p. 832.
[103] HUA, HAA 2731, Godard van Reede-Ginkel to his father, Navaigne, 20 November 1672; HAA 2802, Johan Pesters to Godard Adriaan van Reede-Amerongen, Maastricht, 15 November 1672.
[104] KHA, A4-1476aI, William III to Johan Maurits of Nassau-Siegen, Kastel, 11 November 1672 (quote); CWB, II, i, no. 180, William III to the SG, Roosendaal, 7 November, and from the headquarters at Kastel (Gastel), 11 November 1672.
[105] CWB, II, i, nos. 184 and 223, Johan Maurits of Nassau-Siegen to William III, Muiden, 16 November (quote) and 19 December 1672.

the State that this army [of the Republic and Spain] is coming into the field ... but it would have been desirable that this diversion had achieved a better result with regard to [the French occupation of] Utrecht and that one had been able to remove that thorn.'[106]

William III had by now placed all his hopes on the effect that the threat to Charleroi and the approach of Montecuccoli would exercise on Louis XIV. He hastily transferred to his army infantry from Bergen op Zoom, and the Spanish governor-general augmented the Spanish contingent with a 'notable reinforcement', comprised of 1,500 cavalry and about 3,000 infantry.[107] Including several regiments that were pulled from Maastricht this swelled the Dutch-Spanish army to 24,000 men.[108] Van Reede-Ginkel hoped that William III would then quickly leave the environs of Maastricht, as he wrote to his father on 29 November 1672: 'It would be desirable for one to begin something quickly, because in the fourteen days that they have stood still [since the 15th] our cavalry has been more badly affected than from the preceding march, [for we] have had quarters where the French had eaten up everything within a radius of about six hours.'[109] Yet William III wanted to postpone the march to Charleroi until he was certain that Montecuccoli would cross the Rhine, and against his better judgement he remained hopeful about this until mid-December.[110] Waldeck had already given up hope at the end of November. In a letter to Grand Pensionary Fagel he stated with candour that he considered the campaign to have been a failure: 'The tardiness of the allies has ruined our measures for the great coup [against Charleroi].' However, it was not an option to call off the operation while the Imperial-Brandenburg army was still in the field, because the emperor would then be able to place the blame for the joint operation's abandonment squarely on William III's shoulders. According to Waldeck there was no other choice but to continue for form's sake, seeing it as an opportune incidental circumstance that 'this raid [i.e. the advance on Charleroi] would at least serve to lick our people into shape and make us aware of the shortcomings.'[111]

---

[106] HUA, HAA 2802, Johan Pesters to Godard Adriaan van Reede-Amerongen, in the headquarters of William III, 18 November 1672.
[107] NA, SG 12588.100, Cornelis van Vrijbergen to the *griffier* of the SG, Brussels, 20 November 1672; SG 12579.98, William III to the SG, Eijsden, 23 November 1672.
[108] *Vervolg van 't Verwerd Europa*, p. 203.
[109] HUA, HAA 2731, Godard van Reede-Ginkel to his father, Vlijtingen, 29 November 1672.
[110] William III wrote to Godard Adriaan van Reede-Amerongen on 18 November: 'I have ... with sorrow seen that one vacillates so much in deciding to cross the Rhine. I must admit that I do not understand these maxims and have suspicious thoughts about them.' HUA, HAA 2802, Eijsden.
[111] NA, FAF 1946, Georg Friedrich von Waldeck to Gaspar Fagel, Dichem, 28 November 1672. On 13 December Johan Pesters fulminated, 'We have had it up to our necks with the German auxiliary troops, hoping that they shall at least serve as a bogeyman [i.e. instil fear into the French] and will come into action towards the spring.' See HUA, HAA 2802, Johan Pesters to Godard Adriaan van Reede-Amerongen, Maastricht.

On 15 December 1672 William III invested Charleroi. Machado and the Spanish *proveedor de víveres* had established bread magazines in Namur, so the provisioning of the Dutch and Spanish soldiers was assured. The horses were also provided for – oat supplies sufficient for 11,000 to 12,000 animals had been stockpiled there – though so late in the season many of the beasts were already so severely weakened that they were dying in droves.[112] William III pressed ahead nevertheless, because Charleroi's garrison numbered just 700 to 800 men and the governor, Montalto, was absent, so the siege seemed to promise a good chance of success.[113] The undertaking ended in an anticlimax despite these favourable circumstances for the attackers. Though the Spaniards were to provide the siege artillery it took three to four days to arrive. The French governor had in the meantime managed to re-join his garrison and to make matters worse the freeze set in, forcing William III to lift the siege.[114] In addition, incidents along the water line demanded his speedy return to Holland.

Luxembourg threatens to cross the Holland Water Line (November–December 1672)

While William III and Waldeck were in the Spanish Netherlands, Johan Maurits was in command of the troops in Holland together with Field-Marshal Wirtz. On paper they had 18,000 men at their disposal for the defence of the Holland Water Line, but the actual strength was about 4,000 lower. In the middle of November the 5,000 men who William III had sent back from the field army arrived, but this made the task of the two field-marshals no easier. Their force attained an effective strength of 19,000 men, just a thousand more than the strength that was called for as an absolute minimum. Johan Maurits wrote to Wirtz on 28 November 1672:

> We are standing together as if positioned in a counterscarp [i.e. a covered way], but the most important fortress and town that we have to defend, namely the whole of Holland, is denuded of soldiers, so it presents no small danger if the enemy should break through, because of the great length of that counterscarp (if I might describe our posts thus).[115]

---

[112] CWB, II, i, nos. 205, 206 and 207, 'Mémoire de ce qu'il est nécessaire pour nostre dessin', 4 December 1672; 'Mémoire des choses nécessaires pour le dessin gognu'; William III to Georg Friedrich von Waldeck, n.p., n.d.; HUA, HAA 2731, Godard van Reede-Ginkel to his father, from the duchy of Jülich, 24 October 1673.

[113] NA, FAF 421, Gaspar Fagel to Holland's Delegated Councillors at Alphen aan de Rijn, The Hague, 21 December 1672, transcript.

[114] CWB, II, i, no. 224, William III to the SG, Gilly, 20 December 1672.

[115] NA, RAZH, AGRH 3881, Johan Maurits of Nassau-Siegen to Paulus Wirtz, Muiden, 28 November 1672, transcript.

This threat was greatest if it began to freeze, as noted, because the French could then carry out surprise attacks anywhere.[116] Johan Maurits and Wirtz calculated that of the 379 infantry companies and ten cavalry companies under their command at least 276 of foot and six of horse were needed for the manning of the posts along the water line. This left just 103 companies of foot and four of horse for the containment of a French assault, and these were 'so incomplete and weakened by diseases, discomforts and other inconveniences ... that these can provide at best no more than 5,000 effective combatants'.[117] Johan Maurits warned William III that Luxembourg could assemble two to three times as many soldiers.[118] The erratic and incomplete payment of wages was also cause for serious disquiet among the Republic's soldiery.[119] How dangerous this made the situation was demonstrated on 27 November 1672, when the French made an attack on the post near Ameide, a village on the River Lek midway between Vianen and Schoonhoven. The Dutch troops stood their ground for half an hour, but then took to their heels.[120] Wirtz sent a report to the States-General: 'If the soldiers of Bampfield's regiment [garrisoned in Ameide] had not been so long without pay, starved and exhausted, and if there had been more means to hand, then with such open and reasonably high water [i.e. the inundations] this misfortune would not have come about.'[121] Colonel Joseph Bampfield had for weeks been complaining to the States of Holland about his regiment's pay arrears, and on 11 November he had confronted Grand Pensionary Fagel: 'The soldiers are performing a very unpleasant task ... without money or anything to eat or clothes on their backs or shoes on their feet.... I do not even have wages for myself and am in serious arrears for my company.'[122] Two weeks later he complained that the company of the lieutenant-colonel counted just eighteen effectives, another company twenty, his own company thirty-five, 'and the strongest not even 40 soldiers'.[123]

The assault on Ameide had no serious consequences – the French withdrew after plundering the village and setting it ablaze – but the writing was on the

[116] NA, RAZH, AGRH 3881, Johan Maurits of Nassau-Siegen, Alphen aan de Rijn, 11 December 1672, 'Consideratiën op den tegenwoordigen toestandt van des vijants macht ende wat bij tijden van vorst tot conservatie en beschermingen de provincie van Hollandt ... het best dient geobserveert ende bij der handt genomen te worden'.
[117] NA, RAZH, AGRH 3881, Minutes of a meeting between the Delegated Councillors of Holland's South Quarter with the Republic's generals on 13 December 1672 and 'Lijste van[de] militie die 't samen getrocken soude konnen werden'.
[118] KHA, A4-1476aI, Johan Maurits of Nassau-Siegen to William III, Muiden, 27 December 1672.
[119] See pp. 331–2.
[120] NA, RAZH, AGF 116, Colonel Caspar de Mauregnault, Schoonhoven, 28 November 1672.
[121] NA, SG 12579.98, Paulus Wirtz to the SG, Gorinchem, 28 November 1672.
[122] NA, RAZH, AGF 116, Joseph Bampfield, Ameide, 11 November 1672.
[123] NA, RAZH, AGF 116, Joseph Bampfield, Ameide, 25 November 1672.

wall. This caused the mood in Holland, already jittery, to deteriorate further, as a correspondent of Van Reede-Amerongen noted in a letter:

> In The Hague one is starting to be apprehensive about the impending danger, which is why some people are already starting to send their belongings to safety and it has prompted those [i.e. the magistrates] of Leiden to decide to chop down all the trees lining the canals [around the city perimeter], and to demolish all the buildings situated roundabout the city [i.e. outside its walls]. Amsterdam is constructing diverse defensive works outside its main ramparts. In conclusion, everyone is taking measures against a [French] surprise attack, all the more now that His Highness [William III] is so far from home with so substantial an army.[124]

In the middle of December 1672, as frost set in, the situation threatened to turn critical. Johan Maurits received reports from every quarter that Luxembourg was assembling 12,000 to 13,000 men for a surprise attack on Gouda or Leiden and would then attempt to press on to The Hague.[125] It was therefore of the utmost importance to render the post near Bodegraven as strong as possible. William III had ordered the commander of this sector, the experienced Lieutenant-General Königsmarck,[126] 'not to abandon [Bodegraven] except in the utmost extremity', but Grand Pensionary Fagel thought that the Dutch officers gave too broad an interpretation to this notion.[127] The Delegated Councillors of Holland therefore wanted all the available field troops in the region, 5,000 men, to be assembled near Bodegraven and Zwammerdam.[128] They sent several of their own deputies to Alphen aan de Rijn to be able to set things in order *in situ*. Their arrival seemed to be sorely necessary, because 'we ascertain that the lord count of Königsmarck is starting to take measures for a retreat to ... Leiden'. Of no less concern to the deputies was the lack of discipline among the Dutch soldiers. 'Furthermore we must state that the farmers hereabouts are being seriously mistreated by our troops ... and it is barely possible to bring the food to the posts without it already being plundered by the soldiers.'[129]

In the final days of December it seemed the most pessimistic predictions would become reality. Luxembourg marched into Holland across the frozen water with 12,000, perhaps even 15,000 men. However, the ice proved to be too

---

[124] HUA, HAA 2802, Jacob le Maire to Godard Adriaan van Reede-Amerongen, The Hague, 22 November 1672.
[125] GAA, Missives to burgomasters 66 (microfilm 8006), Johan Maurits of Nassau-Siegen, Muiden, 23 December 1672; KHA, A4-1476aI, same to William III, Muiden, 27 December 1672.
[126] He was the grandfather of Maurice de Saxe, the renowned French *maréchal général* from the later War of the Austrian Succession. See Jon Manchip White, *Marshal of France. The Life and Times of Maurice, Comte de Saxe (1696–1750)* (London 1962), p. 4.
[127] NA, FAF 421, Gaspar Fagel to Holland's field deputies in Alphen aan de Rijn, The Hague, 18 December 1672.
[128] NA, RAZH, AGRH 3881, Extract of a secret resolution of the SH, 21 December 1672.
[129] NA, RAZH, AGF 121, Cornelis Geelvinck, Adriaan van Bosvelt and Pieter Burgersdijck, Alphen aan de Rijn, 23 December 1672.

thin for a force of such magnitude and he therefore sent the majority back to Woerden. He continued onward to Zwammerdam with approximately 3,000 men, 'aiming to cut off Königsmarck together with the troops who are quartered in Bodegraven and Zwammerdam'. He did not succeed in his scheme, because Königsmarck got wind of it and fell back towards Gouda with his troops in time.[130] The French then seized control of Zwammerdam and Bodegraven, going on a terrible rampage of murder, rape and pillage. Yet it was not so much the nature of the atrocities that shocked public opinion, but the circumstances under which these were committed. Bodegraven and Zwammerdam were hardly strong fortresses which had been taken by storm only after a long and bloody siege. Nothing could extenuate the behaviour of the French, a fact that pamphleteers in Holland seized upon with rapacity.[131] The setting in of the thaw put Luxembourg in an awkward position, because the only way back to Woerden was blocked by a redoubt at Nieuwerbrug which was manned by fifteen Dutch infantry companies. But the commander of these troops, Quartermaster-General Pain et Vin, was stricken with panic and ordered the evacuation of the redoubt, a decision for which he would pay with his life on 23 January 1673; his cowardice gave Luxembourg the opportunity to lead his men to safety.[132]

At the very last moment the Republic managed to close the Year of Disaster with an important military success. In the early morning of 30 December 1672, Lieutenant-Colonel Frederik Eybergen managed to recapture Coevorden by surprise. The Münster garrison had failed to keep the moats clear of ice, so the 1,100 Dutch soldiers could penetrate the 'renowned stronghold' without much difficulty 'and, in addition to the commanding officer De Moy, capture [that part of] the garrison which [was] still alive'. Approximately 250 of the 550 defenders died, while the rest fled into the church and surrendered themselves there. The fatalities on the Dutch side ran to about a hundred.[133]

Louis XIV captures Maastricht – the Dutch counter-offensive (1673)

The failed expedition to Charleroi and Luxembourg's incursion had highlighted how the Dutch army was still too numerically weak to operate far beyond its own borders and that discipline could not be restored while the chaos in the payment of the troops persisted. In the first half of 1673 the States of Holland

---

[130] HUA, HAA 2803, Hendrik Jacob van Tuyl van Serooskerken (1642–1692) to Godard Adriaan van Reede-Amerongen, The Hague, 2 January 1673.
[131] On the atrocities see Valkenier, 't Verwerd Europa, p. 841, as well as the famous series of etchings by Romeyn de Hooghe (1645–1708) which appeared in 1673 under the title *Spiegel der France tirannye* (The Mirror of French Tyranny). See also C.H. Slechte, 'De propaganda-campagnes voor koning-stadhouder Willem III. Een verkenning', in *Jaarboek Oranje-Nassau Museum 2002*, pp. 71–108, esp. 80.
[132] Knoop, *Willem den Derde*, I, pp. 208–11.
[133] NA, SG 5063, Rabenhaupt to the SG, Groningen, 31 December 1672.

introduced a series of measures that offered the officers and soldiers financial and social security.[134] In addition the States-General ordered the levying of seven new infantry regiments and a regiment of dragoons.[135] Speed was of the essence with this expansion of the army, because there was every indication that France was preparing a large-scale military operation in the Low Countries. The Spaniards were gravely concerned that Louis XIV would no longer leave the Spanish Netherlands unmolested. Monterrey received intelligence from all quarters that thousands of French troops were being assembled near Courtrai and that the French had amassed a large stock of shovels, spades and pickaxes at Oudenaarde. 'Information has also been obtained about the state of all the ovens, and a calculation has been made of what quantity of bread it shall be possible to bake each day [for the French troops] both in Oudenaarde and in the vicinity.' The Spaniards used this intelligence to estimate the French troop build-up at between 20,000 and 22,000 men.

Monterrey suspected that the French would open the campaign by laying siege to Brussels.[136] This was incorrect, because Louis XIV had decided to capture Maastricht first. The Sun King wanted to have his hands free for the showdown with Spain and he hoped that the loss of Maastricht would at last compel the Dutch to acquiesce and opt for peace, 'and in the process sell out the Spanish Netherlands', according to the American historian Paul Sonnino.[137] The siege of the renowned stronghold on the Meuse was thus from the start intended to demonstrate France's military might. Besides the aforementioned troops, a further 20,000 would be redirected to Maastricht, so that the whole siege army would be 40,000 strong. Louis XIV would command this army in person. There was no danger of a loss of face, because the French reckoned on stalwart resistance from the garrison of 5,000 to 6,000 men under the command of Major-General Jacques de Fariaux (1627–1695) – the Rhinegrave had died in January 1673 – but the outcome of the siege was a foregone conclusion, because the defenders could not expect any outside help. Under threat of the devastation of all his possessions in Westphalia, the elector of Brandenburg had in April 1673 been forced to make peace with France (the Peace of Vossem) and without the assistance of his German ally it was out of the question that William III could venture a confrontation with the main French army.[138] The Dutch commander-in-chief could for the time being assemble 18,000 men at most.[139] In addition to the defence of the Holland Water Line, now that the season for fleet opera-

---

[134] See pp. 332–5.
[135] HUA, HAA 2731, Godard van Reede-Ginkel to his father, The Hague, 19 January 1673.
[136] NA, RAZH, AGF 221, Cornelis van Vrijbergen, Brussels, 10 May (quote), Dendermonde, 24 May, and Antwerp, 5 June 1673.
[137] Sonnino, 'Louis XIV and the Dutch War', p. 160.
[138] Ekberg, *Failure of Louis XIV's Dutch War*, pp. 14–15.
[139] HUA, HAA 2731, Godard van Reede-Ginkel to his father, The Hague, 5 February 1673; NA, RAZH, ASH 6120, 'Memorie wat vivres dat duysent man dagelijcx van noden hebben'; *Vervolg van 't Verwerd Europa*, p. 392.

tions had come round again he also had to be prepared for any attempt by the English to land on the coast of Zeeland or Holland. The tactical victories gained by De Ruyter on 7 and 14 June 1673 over the superior English-French fleet on the Schoneveld sandbanks before the mouth of the Scheldt estuary might well have earned him plenty of glory, but it did not dispel the threat of a landing.[140]

In the meantime, on 6 June 1673, Louis XIV had ordered the investment of Maastricht. This was followed by the opening of the trenches under Vauban's leadership in the night of 17/18 June, and just thirteen days later Maastricht was in French hands. The number of dead and wounded who fell during this short siege is uncertain. The losses of the defenders were estimated at between 1,200 and 1,700 men, those of the French at least 2,300 or as many as 9,000, even 10,000. Louis XIV granted the garrison a free withdrawal to 's-Hertogenbosch.[141] William III expected the Sun King to continue the campaign by laying siege to Breda,[142] but this failed to transpire. In the French headquarters Louis XIV and his advisers were by now firmly convinced that the emperor was planning to invade France via the Moselle. This fear was not unfounded, because Leopold I had ordered the assembly of an army with an effective strength of 31,000 men near Eger (Cheb), a town on Bohemia's westernmost frontier,[143] and on 1 July 1673 he had also entered into an alliance with the king of Spain and the States-General as well as the exiled duke of Lorraine. Austria, Spain and the Republic promised to provide Charles IV with the means to raise an army of 18,000 men and thus enable him to regain his duchy.[144] These developments prompted Louis XIV to decide to postpone his assault on the Spanish Netherlands once again and to make a pre-emptive foray into the electorate of Trier, the eastern gateway to Lorraine. For France this decision had a counterproductive effect; the German princes asked the emperor for protection against French aggression and Leopold I did not allow this opportunity to profile himself as protector of the Holy Roman Empire, pass him by.[145]

On 21 August 1673 the Dutch fleet clashed with the English and French for the third time that year. Lieutenant-Admiral-General Michiel de Ruyter had under his command more than sixty ships of the line and fifteen frigates, armed with more than 4,200 cannon and manned by 17,300 sailors and 2,100 soldiers.

---

[140] Bruijn, *Varend verleden*, p. 117.
[141] NA, RAZH, AGF 221, Cornelis van Vrijbergen, Brussels, 9 July 1673; *Vervolg van 't Verwerd Europa*, pp. 314 and 317; Knoop, *Willem den Derde*, I, p. 270.
[142] NA, SG 12579.99, William III to the *griffier* of the SG, Gorinchem, 2 July 1673, transcript.
[143] NA, RAZH, AGF 221, Cornelis van Vrijbergen, Brussels, 9 and 12 July 1673. The Imperial army was in fine fettle: 'This being such a wonderful army that it was a joy to behold, all the cavalrymen wearing ... leather jerkins and cuirasses, to wit back- and breastplates, casques on the head, superbly mounted.' See *Vervolg van 't Verwerd Europa*, p. 464.
[144] *Vervolg van 't Verwerd Europa*, p. 163.
[145] Ekberg, *Failure of Louis XIV's Dutch War*, pp. 26–7; Lynn, *The Wars of Louis XIV*, pp. 120–1.

The fleet of the opponent was at least a third stronger, but a lack of coordination between the English and French officers prevented them being able to exert their superiority and De Ruyter seized victory once again.[146] This victory also gained the Republic a major political prize. At last Leopold I elected to openly support the Republic. On 30 August 1673 a triple alliance was concluded by Austria, Spain and the Republic. In exchange for large Spanish and Dutch subsidies – Spain promised to transfer 50,000 rix-dollars per month to Vienna, while the Republic promised 45,000 rix-dollars – Leopold I agreed to send the army assembled near Eger to the Rhine and to continue the war until the States-General had 'recaptured from France all the towns and places they have already lost during this war or might lose in the future, likewise all the towns and places that the Spanish Crown has lost since the Treaty of the Pyrenees was concluded [in 1659]'.[147] Some 11,000 Dutch troops arrived near 's-Hertogenbosch that same day. Brigadier-General Van Reede-Ginkel wrote to his father about William III and his field-marshals:

> They give the impression of heading for Grave [on the Meuse], but I am certain they have designs on a totally different stronghold and that the soldiers which one is loudly proclaiming have gone to Friesland are not so far away, but have landed at a Zuiderzee port somewhere in the province of Utrecht or Gelderland, where they shall have to invest some stronghold or other, and we shall then follow up immediately with the main army.[148]

Van Reede-Ginkel had read the situation correctly. On 6 September 1673 William III appeared before Naarden with 25,000 men. Despite the French governor, Philippe de Pracé du Pas, being in command of a considerable garrison of 3,000 men and the French engineers having extended the defensive works with a covered way, he timidly kept his troops within the fortifications and even the French artillery fire was but 'feeblish'. Because of this the digging of the trenches progressed so swiftly that the besiegers were soon able to prepare for the storming of the covered way. The morale of the Dutch troops was excellent and not even the news that Luxembourg had assembled 18,000 men – the actual strength was 10,000 men – and was marching to the relief of Naarden, caused their fighting spirit to flag. Field deputy Adriaan van Bosvelt wrote with satisfaction to Gaspar Fagel that Luxembourg's approach 'has not ended up causing the least agitation here; on the contrary, one observes a great courage among the officers as well as the soldiers, who are full of self-assurance about combating the approaching enemy'. It would be hard to imagine a contrast more stark than that between this self-confidence and the 'great terror' which had seized all the Dutch troops in 1672. The disregard for death which William III demonstrated by appearing

---

[146] Bruijn, *Varend verleden*, p. 117.
[147] *Vervolg van 't Verwerd Europa*, pp. 167–8; Japikse, *Willem III*, I, pp. 305–6.
[148] HUA, HAA 2731, Godard van Reede-Ginkel to his father, near Oisterwijk, 30 August 1673.

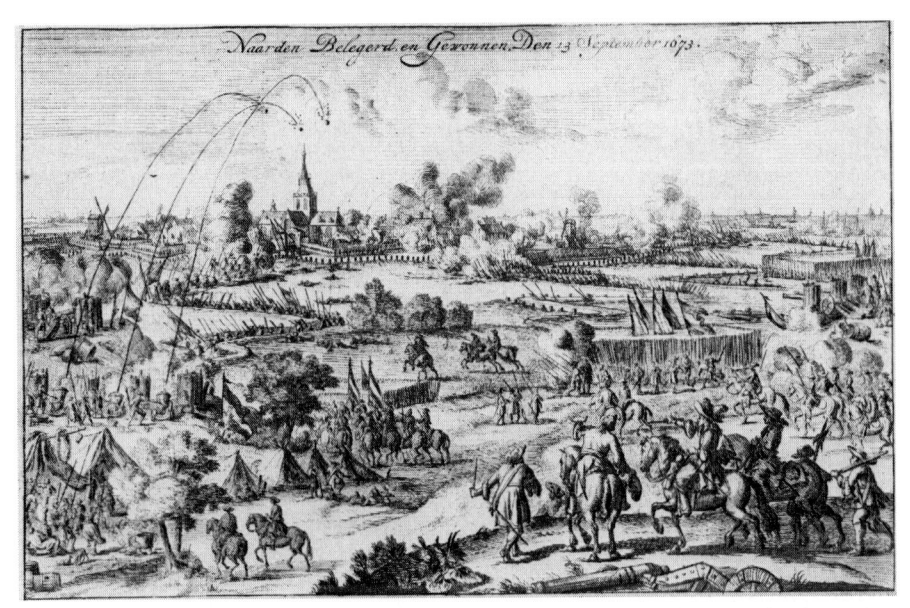

57. Siege and recapture of Naarden by the Dutch army on 13 September 1673. Engraving by Caspar Luyken (1672–1708). Illustration in L. van den Bos, *Het leven en bedrijf van Willem de Darde*, vol. I (Amsterdam 1694). (Royal Netherlands Army Museum, Delft, 00112038/008)

'twice to thrice a day in person' in the forwardmost trenches stirred the fighting spirit of the soldiers even further.[149] The storming of the covered way took place at about eleven o'clock at night on 11 September 1673. Colonel Palm's marines more than lived up to the reputation they had gained at Woerden of being hardened combatants. 'Palm's regiment has fought uncommonly well and effectively captured it [i.e. the covered way] on his own', according to Van Reede-Ginkel.[150] The following day the French governor raised the white flag and the evacuation took place on 13 September. During the three-day siege approximately 300 dead and wounded had fallen on each side.[151] The faint-hearted defence of Naarden was a disgrace for the French army, and Van Reede-Ginkel was jubilant: 'The French have hereby squandered much of their reputation, having defended this place much more poorly than any of ours [i.e. the Dutch garrisons] last year.... They undertook no sortie nor anything else, but surrendered as soon as our troops were on the counterscarp.'[152]

[149] NA, RAZH, AGF 121, Adriaan van Bosvelt, Bussum, 10 September 1673.
[150] HUA, HAA 2731, Godard van Reede-Ginkel to his father, Amsterdam, 16 September 1673.
[151] *Vervolg van 't Verwerd Europa*, pp. 487 and 490.
[152] HUA, HAA 2731, Godard van Reede-Ginkel to his father, Amsterdam, 16 September 1673.

58. The recapture of Naarden by the Dutch army on 13 September 1673. Published by Marcus Doornik (Amsterdam 1673). (Royal Netherlands Army Museum, Delft, 053918)

The war worked out equally unfavourably for Louis XIV within the Holy Roman Empire. In September 1673 his troops had indeed captured Trier, but the Imperial forces set out on their march to the Rhine that same month. Turenne tried to hold back Montecuccoli, but the Imperial general was more adept than anyone else in constantly staying one step ahead of his opponent.[153] There was at last a real chance of a conjunction of the Dutch-Spanish army and the Imperial army. William III, Monterrey and Montecuccoli agreed that they would jointly lay siege to Bonn, residence of the elector of Cologne. The reduction of this fortified town would force Maximilian Heinrich of Bavaria to switch allegiances, laying the bishopric of Münster open to invasion, and to crown it all it would sever the lifeline between the French army of occupation in the Republic and Charleroi and from there to its home bases. In mid-October William III set out for Bonn with 5,000 to 6,000 cavalry, 1,500 dragoons and 2,000 infantry. Monterrey added 800 cavalrymen, 200 dragoons and 2,000 foot-soldiers to this, so the whole Dutch-Spanish army numbered between 11,500 and 12,500 men.[154] On 23 October the Dutch and Spanish troops crossed the Meuse into the duchy of Jülich. Initially Van Reede-Ginkel had cherished no high expectations for this expedition:

> What further plans there are I cannot write with certainty, because they are being kept highly secret, but the majority are of the opinion that we shall go and visit something upon the [inhabitants] of the territory of Jülich and Cologne, eat them up [i.e. go plundering] and otherwise not accomplish much. I hope that it shall not be a repeat of the [failed] expedition to Charleroi.[155]

It quickly became evident to Van Reede-Ginkel that he had been mistaken. More or less simultaneously Louis XIV and Louvois came to the realisation that William III had set his sights on Bonn. Luxembourg received orders to evacuate Utrecht and the Veluwe and head for Maastricht with all the troops under his command – 18,000 to 19,000 men.[156] If possible he and Turenne were to hamper the investment of Bonn.[157]

Since the retaking of Naarden the clearance of the French conquests to the north of the major rivers in the Republic had been but a question of time, but the expedition to Bonn made the immediate implementation of this decision ineluctable. The 10,000 to 12,000 Dutch field troops who had been left behind near Naarden under the command of Waldeck posed a constant threat to Woerden, Utrecht, Amersfoort, Harderwijk, Elburg and Kampen. If the French were to delay the evacuation of these towns until Bonn had been captured and

---

[153] Ekberg, *Failure of Louis XIV's Dutch War*, pp. 69, 71 and 74.
[154] CWB, II, i, nos. 414 and 416, William III to the SG, Santhoven, 15 October, and Mol, 18 October 1673.
[155] HUA, HAA 2731, Godard van Reede-Ginkel to his father, from the duchy of Jülich, 24 October 1673.
[156] *Vervolg van 't Verwerd Europa*, p. 660.
[157] Ekberg, *Failure of Louis XIV's Dutch War*, pp. 134–5.

William III had returned to the Republic with his army, then the withdrawal of their garrisons would be cut off and Waldeck would then have been able to take them prisoner one by one. *Maréchal* Bernardin Gigault (1630–1694), marquis de Bellefonds, commander in the Gelderland quarters of Zutphen and Nijmegen, had in the meantime concentrated all his troops, 26,000 men in all, in Zutphen, Arnhem, Nijmegen and Grave for this very reason. If Luxembourg and Turenne managed to prevent the investment of Bonn then these four bridgeheads on the IJssel, Rhine, Waal and Meuse would make it possible to penetrate into the heart of the Republic anew; if they failed in their plan, then the French could quickly retreat to France along the Meuse.[158] In this latter instance, the three towns to the north of the Meuse would be abandoned, but a substantial garrison of 4,000 to 5,000 men would be left behind in Grave. Besides the possession of this fortified town denying the Republic the use of the Meuse, it also served as a collection point for artillery and munitions from the evacuated towns in the provinces of Utrecht and Gelderland, as well as for the Dutch hostages who served as collateral for payment of the contributions imposed. The city of Utrecht, for example, was taxed at 616,000 guilders, of which 250,000 guilders had to be paid in cash when the French departed and the rest at a specified later date. In order to be assured of payment, Luxembourg had 'twenty-four of the most eminent burghers and gentlemen and clergymen ... taken away'.[159] Besides retaining a garrison in Grave, Maastricht would be left with a strong French garrison.

Luxembourg's attempt to catch up with the Dutch-Spanish army failed, their having too great a head start. 'While we are here in the land of Cologne the plundering has been horrendous and this territory is being no less ruined than are our own poor provinces', Van Reede-Ginkel wrote to his father on 29 October 1673. 'Your High Honour is invited to imagine what astonishment this has caused in these parts, where very few [inhabitants] had taken flight, and the people could not have imagined that our army would come so far [from the Republic's borders].'[160] A low point was the massacre of the armed burghers carried out by the Dutch troops after their storming of the small town of Rheinbach.[161]

On 6 November the Dutch-Spanish army was approaching Bonn. Montecuccoli was already there with the Imperial troops, so the siege could start immediately. The Dutch commander-in-chief opened the trenches on the northwest side of Bonn (facing towards Cologne) and the Imperial general on the south

---

[158] Knoop, *Willem den Derde*, I, pp. 302–4 and 311.
[159] NA, RAZH, AGF 43, Bosschaert, Woerden, 22 November 1673 (quote); NA, SG 12579.100, Marinus van Crommon, J. van Gemmenich and Scato Gockinga (1624–1683) to the *griffier* of the SG, Utrecht, 30 January 1674, with a letter from the French intendant Louis Robert as an appendix, Nijmegen, 28 January 1674.
[160] HUA, HAA 2731, Godard van Reede-Ginkel to his father, 'Vleysen', three hours from Cologne, 29 October 1673.
[161] See pp. 347–8.

side.¹⁶² The siege proceeded propitiously. The garrison of troops from France and Cologne had a strength of about 2,000 men but put up little resistance. On 11 November the besiegers began the undermining of the main rampart, 'thus necessitating the enemy to turn his thoughts to a reasonable capitulation'. The parley about the fort's surrender began the following day, agreement being reached at eleven o'clock at night.¹⁶³ The 1,200 defenders remaining were granted a free withdrawal to Neuss, but only a small portion actually arrived there, because 'a great many of them have entered into service with the Imperial forces and our troops', William III informed the States-General.¹⁶⁴ After the damage to Bonn's fortifications had been repaired, Montecuccoli and William III cleared away the remaining garrisons of troops from Cologne and France within the electorate. In Linnich and Kerpen there were garrisons of a mere 200 men, who surrendered after putting up a 'very feeble resistance'.¹⁶⁵ William III then headed for Herentals with the Dutch-Spanish troops, arriving there in early December 1673. Waldeck had in the meantime marched to meet him with the troops under his command and Monterrey had sent 6,000 Spanish troops, so the allied forces grew to between 27,000 and 28,000 men.¹⁶⁶ William III hoped to defeat Luxembourg's army with these amassed forces, but the French commander managed to evade a battle and reached Charleroi in safety.

The end of the 'Guerre de Hollande': the peace treaties of Westminster and Cologne (February–April 1674)

The military successes the Republic and her allies had achieved in 1673 continued to reverberate on the diplomatic battlefield. With an English victory at sea not forthcoming and the second marriage in September 1673 of James, duke of York (1633–1701), brother of the childless king of England, to the Catholic Maria d'Este, princess of Modena – James's first wife, Anna Hyde, had died in 1671 – the appetite of the English to continue the struggle had been seriously dampened. The rumour that Charles II was cooperating with Louis XIV in order to establish absolutism and popery in England and to bring about the establishment of a French 'universal monarchy' in Europe became widespread in the arena of public opinion. Parliament consequently refused to continue providing money for the struggle against the Republic, compelling Charles II to discontinue the war. In the second Peace of Westminster (19 February 1674)

---

[162] NA, SG 12579.99, Adriaan van Bosvelt to the SG, before Bonn, 4 November 1673; William III to the SG, before Bonn, 6 November 1673.
[163] NA, SG 12579.99, Adriaan van Bosvelt to the SG, before Bonn, 12 November 1673, at eleven o'clock at night.
[164] *CWB*, II, i, no. 424, William III to the SG, near Bonn, 15 November 1673.
[165] NA, SG 12579.99, same to same, Blatzheim, 25 November 1673.
[166] Ten Raa, *Het Staatsche leger*, VI, pp. 20–1.

he waived the demand of garrisoning Sluis, Vlissingen and Den Briel, and the Republic was to pay him an indemnification of just 2 million guilders instead of 10 million.[167] On 22 April 1674 the bishop of Münster also left the French camp. Without the protection of the French army he could not safeguard his bishopric against Imperial incursions. Von Galen had initially hoped that the States-General would be prepared to conclude a peace for the cession of all the towns in Gelderland and Overijssel, excepting Borculo and Lingen, which had been captured by his troops. The Hague, however, would have nothing of it, so the bishop eventually had to be satisfied that he was not required to pay any damages to the Republic and that his land was spared the devastations which had befallen Cologne. Soon thereafter the elector of Cologne also made peace (11 May 1674). In exchange for the retrocession of all the places captured by his troops in the Republic, the States-General waived its right to a garrison in Rheinberg.[168] In that same month of May the French evacuated the Gelderland towns of Zutphen, Arnhem and Nijmegen. According to plan, strong French garrisons of between 4,000 and 5,000 men and more than 7,000 men remained behind in Grave and Maastricht, respectively, but the loss of three allies by no means deterred Louis XIV from continuing the war. Quite the contrary, the end of the 'Guerre de Hollande' meant his armies were at last available for the war aim that he was really pursuing, namely the subjugation of the Spanish Netherlands, a region ideally suited to bringing France's military might to full maturity. The French troops would be operating at a short distance from their bases and there was no line of inundation that could halt the advance of a superior army. Louis XIV was convinced that there could never be any question of a 'peaceful coexistence' between France and Spain, mirrored in his credo: 'One cannot elevate the one without humbling the other.'[169]

Conclusion

The War of Devolution and the Year of Disaster had ushered in a new phase in the conduct of war. By establishing large food magazines Louis XIV was able to wage war with armies of unprecedented size. In 1667 he had invaded the Spanish Netherlands with 50,000 men and in 1672 he attacked the Republic at the head of twice as many soldiers. The unprecedented scope of the 'Guerre de Hollande' made a big impression on contemporaries as well as later generations, though this admiration remained limited to the military operation itself; there was wide condemnation of the way in which Louis XIV and his right-hand man, Louvois,

---

[167] Troost, *Willem III*, p. 131; K.H.D. Haley, 'English Policy at the Peace Congress of Nijmegen', in *The Peace of Nijmegen*, pp. 145–55, esp. 146.
[168] *Vervolg van 't Verwerd Europa*, pp. 798 and 801–4.
[169] Malettke, 'Ludwigs XIV. Außenpolitik', pp. 49–50. According to Valkenier, 'Christendom is comprised of two mighty kingdoms, namely France and Spain, which together hold the balance of war and peace for all other states.' See *'t Verwerd Europa*, p. 64.

allowed the opportunity to end the war in 1672 resplendently to slip through their fingers. The French peace terms were indeed inordinate, but in the flush of victory not wholly incomprehensible. Originally the sole aim of the 'Guerre de Hollande' had been to render the Republic powerless, but with the speed of the French advance in June 1672 exceeding the boldest expectations, annihilation of the opponent seemed to be within reach. The implications of the organisational revolution in the art of war surprised not only the Republic's political and military leaders, but also Louis XIV himself. Nor could the Sun King have suspected that William III would prove to be an adversary to be reckoned with; in 1672 the twenty-one-year-old prince of Orange was still an unknown factor. There was, lastly, the Holland Water Line, which gave William's policy of resistance to the bitter end a chance of success. Louis XIV unintentionally involved the Republic 'in the second great struggle for survival in her history', the German historian Werner Hahlweg noted.[170] The spectre of utter annihilation was the driving force behind the Dutch army reforms. Grand Pensionary Fagel and field-marshals Waldeck and Johan Maurits of Nassau-Siegen were the lead players in the financial and organisational aspects of this. The contribution of William III was primarily focused on restoring the morale of the Dutch troops. He astutely realised that the Dutch soldiers would only overcome their 'great fear of the French' by being deployed offensively. Johan Maurits concurred wholeheartedly and encouraged the young captain-general of the Union to miss no opportunity to launch a counter-offensive. The sixty-eight-year-old field-marshal understood that a life-and-death struggle left no leeway for circumspection or being humane. On 30 November 1672 he wrote to Gaspar Fagel:

> Now that the enemy has begun this unchristian and merciless manner of warfare, which involves burning to the ground, and persists with it daily, whereby poor, innocent people, children and livestock are ravaged and destroyed, it is in my judgement necessary to combat it rigorously. We dare not burn down everything in return, because the Republic's own subjects would be ruined by it, so we must find a different means.

As an alternative he proposed offering all the troops and farmers who 'went on a raid' into territory occupied by the French the prospect of a bounty for each enemy soldier they took prisoner or killed, ranging from ten guilders 'for every French soldier alive or dead' to sixty guilders for a captain.[171] William III's decision to attack Woerden demonstrates that he did not eschew heavy losses and nor was he in the least concerned about the fate of the inhabitants of enemy territory: there is no substantial difference between the French massacres in

---

[170] Hahlweg, 'Die Oranische Heeresreform', p. 150.
[171] NA, RAZH, AGF 117, Johan Maurits of Nassau-Siegen, Willes, 30 November 1672. See also his 'Consideratiën' to the Delegated Councillors of Holland (AGRH 3881, Alphen aan de Rijn, 11 December 1672).

Bodegraven and Zwammerdam and the bloodbath perpetrated by the Dutch troops in Rheinbach.

Once the French offensive in the Republic had ground to a halt on 23 June 1672, it seemed as if the era of large-scale warfare was precipitously over. The size of field armies dwindled to between 15,000 and 20,000 men, at times increasing to 25,000 to 30,000 men, and circumstances determined the course of operations. The following year, however, it became evident that warfare had in fact changed definitively, when Louis XIV laid siege to Maastricht at the head of 40,000 men. Such a military force was large enough to be divided into a siege army and an army of observation. The capture of Naarden and Bonn in September and November 1673, respectively, led to the evacuation of Utrecht, Gelderland and Overijssel by the occupying forces from France, Münster and Cologne, but the security of the Republic was still at issue, because the French were still occupying Grave and Maastricht and Louis XIV was still intent on conquering the Spanish Netherlands. It would be impossible to prevent him doing this unless the Republic, Spain and Austria could match the French troop build-up. The Republic's *Existenzkampf* might have been over by early 1674, but the struggle to preserve the European balance of power had only just begun.

♦ 11 ♦

War in the Spanish Netherlands: The Republic is Still Ill-Equipped for the New, Large-Scale Manner of Warfare (1674–1678)

The Republic, Spain and the emperor wage war in the Spanish Netherlands together, but success remains elusive (1674)

On 31 March 1674 the German princes declared 'Imperial War' against Louis XIV,[1] so the Holy Roman Empire was now formally supporting the Republic in her struggle against France. The importance of this decision lay primarily in the domain of the provision of troops: the declaration of war legitimised making battle-ready units available (for payment) to the emperor, the States-General and the king of Spain. William III hoped that it would hereby be possible to counterbalance the numerical superiority of France's military. On the basis of reports about French troop concentrations and movements, he and the Dutch generals assumed that France would in 1674 bring 65,000 men into the field, divided across four theatres of war: the Low Countries, Alsace, Franche-Comté and Roussillon. On paper the allies could muster twice as many troops, and diplomatic deliberations involving The Hague, Madrid, Brussels and Vienna led to the determination of the main thrust of an operational plan that covered all fronts. France's war preparations left no shadow of a doubt that Louis XIV would no longer pull his punches with regard to the Spanish Netherlands. Condé would in all probability invade this territory at the head of 30,000 men, but Monterrey could for the time being assemble no more than 10,000 men for the defence of the Spanish Netherlands – the majority of the Spanish troops (c. 30,000 men) had to remain behind in the garrisons until there was greater clarity about France's plan of attack. This meant that at least 20,000 extra men were needed to stand up to the French in the Spanish Netherlands. The States-

---

[1] Malettke, 'Ludwigs XIV. Außenpolitik', p. 52.

General promised Monterrey that William III would set out with an army of 24,000 men.

The emperor and the German princes promised to mobilise two armies, one along the Upper Rhine and the other on the Moselle. The Imperial army's field-marshal-general Alexandre Hippolyte Balthasar de Hennin (1620–1690), prince de Bournonville, commander of 40,000 men, was given the task of preventing Louis XIV from dispatching his army from Franche-Comté to the Spanish Netherlands – in February 1674 the king of France had invaded this Spanish possession at the head of 15,000 men. The allied objective could best be achieved by laying siege to Philippsburg, a stronghold on the Rhine which had been in French hands since 1648. The capture of Philippsburg would provide the Imperial forces with a bridgehead for operations in Alsace. Though Turenne wielded the command in this region, his army was estimated to be 13,000 strong at most – its actual strength was 4,000 lower.[2] The expectation was that an Imperial push into Alsace would compel Louis XIV to deploy his army in Franche-Comté for the defence of France's eastern border. The second German army was 31,000 strong – 20,000 Imperial troops, 9,000 from Münster and 2,000 from Cologne – and was commanded by the sixty-six-year-old Imperial field-marshal Louis Raduit, comte de Souches (1608–1683), son of a French nobleman from La Rochelle, and was to operate along the Moselle, 'and ensure that it always remains ahead and is able to join with Bournonville's army or that of the Low Countries, as need requires'. Lastly, 16,000 Spanish troops in Catalonia were to threaten Roussillon, where an estimated 6,000 Frenchmen were dispersed across garrisons.[3]

In early May 1674, Waldeck travelled to Brussels for further deliberations with Monterrey and the most senior Spanish officers. The Spanish governor-general informed him that if Condé should receive reinforcements then he would ask the emperor to send Souches to the Low Countries, but not before. The poor pay and deficient logistical organisation of the Imperial forces meant they were highly undesirable guests.

> As the greatest interest of the allies [the Spanish and Dutch] is the preservation of their country and that the Imperial army should [therefore] act offensively outside it, one is in agreement that so long as there is not an extreme and ultimate necessity ... one shall not call on the said Imperial army to come to the aid of these countries on this side of the Meuse.[4]

---

[2] According to A. Cousine, in April 1674 Turenne had barely 9,000 effectives at his disposal. See 'La campagne de 1674–1675 du maréchal de Turenne', in *Troisième centenaire de la mort de Turenne. Actes du colloque international sur Turenne et l'art militaire*, held in Paris, 2–3 October 1975 (1978), pp. 221–34, esp. 224.

[3] NA, FAF 555, 'Forces de l'ennemy en ca[m]pagne' and operational plans.

[4] NA, FAF 554, 'Relation succincte de ce qui s'est passé de plus considérable sous le commandement de son Altesse monseigneur le prince d'Orange dans la campagne de 1674', Appendix A.

However, only a week after this was settled it came to light that the military prospects for the allies were less favourable than assumed. Louis XIV captured Besançon in the middle of May 1674. The reduction of the capital of Franche-Comté meant the campaign there was effectively at an end, and the bulk of the 15,000-strong invading army was therefore available for operations elsewhere. Louis XIV sent reinforcements to Turenne's army, but directed the majority of his troops, estimated by the allies at between 8,000 and 10,000 men, to the Spanish Netherlands. In anticipation of the arrival of these reinforcements, Condé captured two castles on the Meuse between Liège and Maastricht: Argenteau on 17 May and Navagne five days later. In response to the question from Brussels as to why William III had failed to march with the Dutch army to the relief of the castles, Waldeck countered that the Dutch company commanders had not been required to have their companies complete before 1 May 1674: 'If one had made them march sooner they would have had this pretext for not acquitting themselves of their duty.' After this the Dutch troops were immediately sent to the rendezvous at Roosendaal and headed for Mechelen (Malines) on 15 May. But even if the companies had been up to strength sooner, Waldeck continued, then William III would still have been unable to assemble the Dutch troops any sooner, because the Spaniards had failed to establish any forage magazines, so the Dutch cavalry, which had already suffered greatly from the expedition to Bonn the previous winter, would have been utterly ruined. And lastly, Waldeck perceptively remarked that the Spanish troops had been equally unfit to march.[5]

The capture of Argenteau and Navagne was of great strategic importance for the French, making them master of the Meuse corridor to the north and south of Maastricht. They therefore no longer had to be wary of an unexpected investment of this stronghold. The Dutch as well as the Spanish siege artillery would now have to be transported over land. Condé could then begin preparations for a large-scale offensive operation. Namur and Mons were the most likely candidates for a siege; the capture of Namur was important with a view to the safety of Charleroi and would at the same time block an important route of access into France (the River Meuse) for the allies, while the capture of Mons would drive a wedge between Flanders and Spanish Brabant.

With the campaign beginning so inauspiciously for the allies, Monterrey pressed Waldeck to immediately seize back the initiative from Condé by giving battle, but the Dutch field-marshal resolutely rejected that proposal: 'I am obliged to convey to Your Excellency that it would be temerity to go and seek a battle with Monsieur the prince of Condé and imprudence to place the well-being of all Europe on the decision of a single battle.'[6] The reason for this was that the latest intelligence indicated that Condé's army was 10,000 men stronger

---

[5] Ibid., under the header 'Reasons why the Dutch troops could not head into the field early' (quote); *Vervolg van 't Verwerd Europa*, p. 915.
[6] NA, FAF 1952, Georg Friedrich von Waldeck to Monterrey, Rumpst, 24 May 1674, minute.

than estimated – 40,000 men instead of 30,000 – and, moreover, it was soon to be joined by 8,000 to 10,000 troops from Franche-Comté. William III, who arrived at the Spanish headquarters in Vilvorde on 31 May 1674, was, unlike Waldeck, not averse to a battle, though he agreed with his field-marshal that the French numerical superiority was too great and there was therefore no other option but to ask Souches to join them in the Spanish Netherlands. William III was intent on seeking out the French and giving battle as soon as the Imperial troops had crossed the Meuse at Namur and conjoined with the Dutch-Spanish army. Monterrey resigned himself to the inevitable, whereupon a courier was dispatched to the Imperial army.[7] Souches replied that he would head to the River Meuse but not with the promised 31,000 men, because the emperor was afraid that Louis XIV would further reinforce Turenne's army and that this corps would subsequently launch an invasion into Breisgau or the Swabian Circle. Bournonville's army was still far from complete – it would be the end of July 1674 before it numbered 30,000 men, swelling to 36,000 in October. Souches was thus compelled to send part of the Münster contingent to the Upper Rhine, his own force shrinking to just 25,000 men. 'God willing, I shall not in the future be obliged to send more forces from this side ... because the troops of Münster, who must number 9,000 men, have rebelled', Souches opined to William III.[8]

The weakening of Souches' force and the flurry of activity that was simultaneously to be seen in Condé's army – in Le Quesnoy and Ath he was amassing a large bread supply – gave Monterrey cause for graver concern about the safety of Mons, but he also had to bear in mind the peril of the French *maréchal* preparing a surprise attack on Ghent. He therefore urged Souches to come to the Spanish Netherlands as quickly as possible and lay siege to Charleroi.[9] Souches had to disappoint him, however, as he also had no forage magazines at his disposal and the grain was not yet ripe enough for the horses to be able to live from the land. It was therefore the end of June 1674 before the Imperial troops arrived near Namur. Souches then travelled onward to Landen, a small town eleven kilometres southeast of Tienen (Tirlemont), in person. On 2 July he had a meeting there with William III, Waldeck and Monterrey. To their great displeasure they noted that Souches displayed 'a very great repugnance to crossing the Meuse'. This notwithstanding they tried to persuade him to do so 'and to conjoin himself with us, in order jointly to go and defeat the prince of Condé, who lies close by Ath'. However, Souches stood by his standpoint that the Dutch-Spanish army,

---

[7] NA, FAF 554, 'Relation succincte de ... la campagne de 1674', Appendix F, 'Résolution prise le 31e de may 1674 à Vilvorden aux Trois Fontaines'.
[8] Ibid., Appendix G, Souches to William III, Niedecken, 2 June 1674 (quote); NA, FAF 430, Monterrey to William III, Brussels, 8 June 1674, at midnight; CWB, II, i, no. 506, Jacob van Borssele van der Hooghe, lord of Geldermalsen, to William III, Eschweiler, 16 June 1674.
[9] NA, FAF 430, Monterrey to William III, Brussels, 3 and 8 June 1674; FAF 554, 'Relation succincte de ... la campagne de 1674', Appendix K1, the council of war 'aux Trois Fontaines le 18 juin'.

which had by then swelled to 45,000 men, was strong enough to attack the French successfully even without Imperial assistance.[10] Waldeck rebutted this argument by pointing out that Condé was expecting substantial reinforcements from Franche-Comté and that his army would therefore be 50,000 strong. The allies would then be unable to risk giving battle or laying siege to Charleroi, unless Souches conflated his troops with those of the Republic and Spain. However, the Imperial field-marshal categorically refused to cross the Meuse, and when Waldeck asked him the reason for this he replied, 'Because Bournonville does not have a force sufficient to oppose Turenne.'[11] Turenne had crossed to the right bank of the Rhine at Philippsburg in the middle of June 1674 and had defeated a corps from Bournonville's army by Sinzheim.[12] After this defeat the emperor had 'definitely ordered' Souches to remain on the east bank of the Meuse.[13]

Souches at last volunteered an alternative: he proposed heading for Dinant, a small stronghold within the prince-bishopric of Liège, with the Imperial army and part of the Dutch-Spanish force. William III and Monterrey were not in the least enthusiastic about this plan. The occupation of Dinant would have no effect on the strategic situation in the Spanish Netherlands whatsoever. They therefore resorted to a ruse in order to persuade Souches to cross the Meuse after all. William III informed the Imperial field-marshal that he would in person join the Imperial army with 17,000 to 18,000 Dutch troops and would lend assistance to the siege of Rocroi. This stronghold's reduction would clear the way to attack Charleville-Mezières, a fortress on either side of the Meuse on which Souches had set his sights. In exchange for this offer, William III expected that Souches would 'have his cavalry [cross the Meuse] in order to ensure the conjunction'. The French army stood near Charleroi at that time and William III therefore had no doubt that Condé would attempt to block the passage of the Dutch corps, 'being able to be there [at Namur] in three marches, as easily as us'. This was what he was actually hoping for, because if Condé abandoned his positions by Charleroi then Souches would be forced to come to the aid of the Dutch corps with his main army.[14]

---

[10] NA, FAF 554, 'Relation succincte de ... la campagne de 1674', Report of the war council of 2 July 1674 (first quote), and Appendix L3, Borssele van der Hooghe to William III, Namur, 6 July 1674; *Vervolg van 't Verwerd Europa*, p. 920; CWB, II, i, no. 530, William III to Coenraad van Heemskerck in Vienna, at the headquarters in Savants, 6 July 1674 (second quote).
[11] NA, FAF 1952, Notes by Georg Friedrich von Waldeck, 2 July 1674.
[12] Childs, *Warfare in the Seventeenth Century*, pp. 172–3.
[13] CWB, II, i, no. 530, William III to Coenraad van Heemskerck in Vienna, from the headquarters in Savants, 6 July 1674.
[14] NA, FAF 1952, Georg Friedrich von Waldeck to Gaspar Fagel, Blasfelt, 11 July 1674 (quote); FAF 554, 'Relation succincte de ... la campagne de 1674', Appendix R1, Souches to William III, Namur, 9 July 1674, Notes and Appendix S, Souches to William III, near Rochefort, 12 July 1674; KHA, A16-Xic-1369, William III to Jacob van Borssele van der Hooghe, lord of Geldermalsen, near Louvain, 12 July 1674, minute (quote).

Souches informed William III that as soon as he had taken Dinant he would proceed with his entire cavalry – 8,000 horse – to the allied encampment near Perwez, a village eighteen kilometres north of Namur, to collect the Dutch corps. Some 1,800 Imperial troops marched into Dinant on 18 July 1674, and ten days later Souches arrived at Perwez. William III, Waldeck and Monterrey then tried to persuade him to take advantage of the superior numbers of cavalry the allies currently had at their disposal and either launch an attack on Condé or at least block his lines of communication with France. They pointed out that a victory in the Spanish Netherlands would also alleviate the pressure on Bournonville. Souches yielded to these arguments, resulting in the decision 'to march to meet the enemy with all these forces combined'.[15] Souches now ordered the Imperial infantry to cross to the left bank of the Meuse as well, so no fewer than 70,000 allied troops were assembled there: 30,000 Dutch, 15,000 Spanish and 25,000 Imperial. This meant the allies were 20,000 stronger than the French, but this failed to yield the advantage that William III had hoped for: Condé refused to give battle and his positions near Charleroi were too strong to attack frontally. Namur and Mons were indeed no longer in danger of being besieged by the French, but this was a terribly meagre result considering the huge number of soldiers then available to the allies in the Spanish Netherlands. They had to find a means to compel Condé to forsake his advantageous positions.

Monterrey tabled the proposal of laying siege to Ath during a council of war convened on 10 August 1674. He stressed that the reduction of Ath would be advantageous to the safety of Brussels and that victuals, artillery and munitions could easily be conveyed from Brussels and Mons during the operation. William III, Souches and the Dutch and Imperial generals were, however, unimpressed by Monterrey's proposal. They pointed out 'the disadvantageousness of the terrain, where the cavalry would scarcely be able to act, the minimal harm that France would suffer from this loss and, lastly, the devastation that an army without discipline [i.e. the Imperial troops] would cause in the lands of the king of Spain'. With this last argument William III and Souches were nimbly exploiting an excuse that Monterrey had himself put forward earlier that year to defer the arrival of the Imperial army. Rather than laying siege to Ath, the Dutch commander-in-chief and Souches advised heading to Hainaut 'in order to attack, if possible, a place on the frontier of France', such as Le Quesnoy, Douai or Saint-Quentin.[16] With one of these towns as an operational base the allies would be able to exact contributions from large tracts of France. Monterrey hereupon withdrew his proposal and preparations were then made to head straight to the French border the following day (11 August). There was a serious risk attached to this decision, because the allied army would pass within a short distance of the front of the French army. The hilly terrain, criss-crossed by morasses and ditches

---

[15] NA, FAF 554, 'Relation succincte de ... la campagne de 1674', Notes.
[16] Ibid., War council of 10 August 1674.

provided some protection against a flank attack, but Condé would still be able to attack the rearguard of the allied army with superior numbers and would then be in a position to defeat the main body piecemeal. William III, Souches and Monterrey were well aware of this danger, but they underestimated its gravity. Near Seneffe, a small town fifteen kilometres northeast of Charleroi, they positioned a corps of 3,000 cavalry, 500 dragoons and five Dutch infantry battalions under the command of Charles Henri of Lorraine (1649–1723), prince de Vaudemont,[17] one of the most capable Spanish commanders, but these covering troops would be unable to stand their ground against 50,000 Frenchmen for long.

The battle of Seneffe (11 August 1674) began at about ten o'clock in the morning with a French storm assault on the village itself. After a brief exchange of fire the Dutch infantry sought cover amidst the cavalry. Brigadier-General Godard van Reede-Ginkel commanded the Dutch cavalry in two successive charges, leading Obdam's squadron in person:

> [I]t came about that, for me personally, I penetrated a little too far into the enemy force, when the said squadron [Obdam's] loosed a salvo, in which I was shot through and through by a pistol ball just under my left shoulder, which because of the unusually profuse bleeding made me slightly faint and forced me to retreat.[18]

Under the persistent French assaults the allied cavalry began to lose ground and eventually fled. The five Dutch battalions were abandoned to their fate and just about annihilated. Condé had scored an important success, but he was by no means satisfied with this. His ultimate goal was to crush the entire allied army, and in order that this major prize should not elude him he gave chase without first regrouping his troops. This presented the allies with the opportunity 'to arrange themselves in battle array, adjusting themselves as best they may to the circumstances of the battlefield. The battle only really began thereafter, and lasted from three o'clock to eleven o'clock at night.' The battle proceeded with varying success and was extremely bloody. There was no question of coordinated attacks. The French and allied generals led one unit after the other into combat. The hand-to-hand fighting continued until the closing in of darkness made further fighting impossible. Condé then ordered the retreat to Charleroi. Losses on both sides were huge, as reported by the field deputy of Holland's Delegated Councillors, A. Nyenborch van Naeltwijk: 'People proclaim that there has never been such a bloody battle and thus far the prince of Condé refuses to allow us to ransom our officers taken prisoner … giving as a reason that neither our troops nor the Imperial troops lent any quarter to his, but shot them all dead.'[19] The number of casualties is proof enough that this was no exaggeration. In the French army no fewer than 36 field officers, 163 captains, and 260

---

[17] HUA, HAA 2731, Godard van Reede-Ginkel to his father, Mons, 12 August 1674.
[18] Ibid.
[19] NA, RAZH, AGF 54, A. Nyenborch van Naeltwijk, Mons, 24 August 1674.

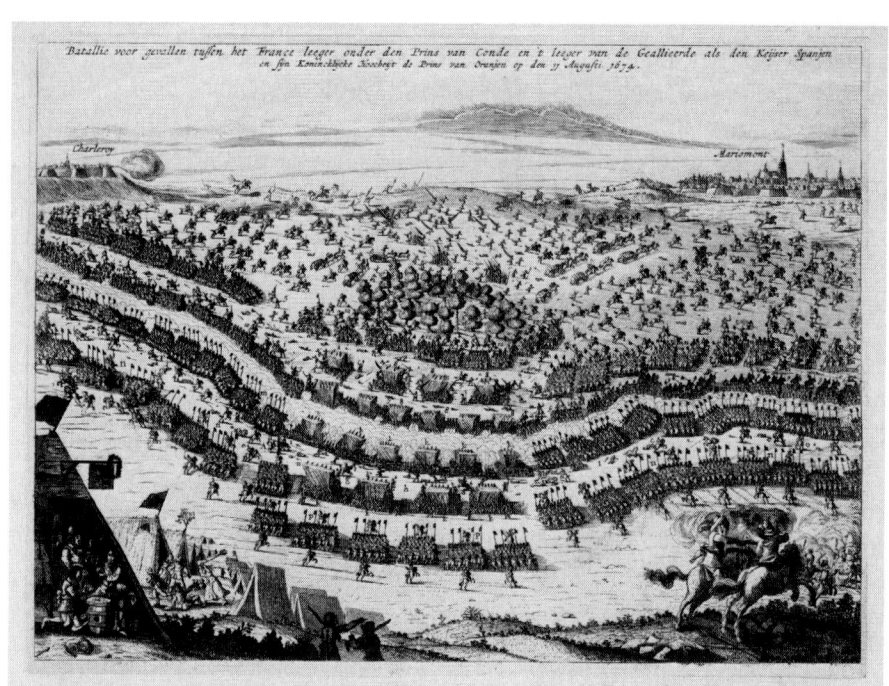

59. Battle of Seneffe, 11 August 1674 (Royal Netherlands Army Museum, Delft, 00121753). Fictional depiction of the battle. The Dutch-Spanish-Imperial army and the French army are standing in a battle array that is wholly in keeping with the rules of warfare, in neat lines with the infantry in the middle and the cavalry on either flank.

lieutenants and lower-ranking officers lost their lives.[20] The allies lost hundreds of officers as well. 'One sees hardly any officers among the infantry,' the wounded Van Reede-Ginkel wrote to his father the day after the battle, 'either [they] are dead or injured.'[21] The total losses on the allied side amounted to between 10,000 and 12,000 men, perhaps even 15,000, of whom 6,000 were Dutch troops. The French had suffered 8,000 to 10,000 dead and wounded.[22] Condé could show off a great many colours and standards captured from the allies and his troops had also seized most of the Dutch army's baggage waggons, but this could not conceal that his intention of inflicting a crushing defeat on the allies had failed.

The allied army reached Mons on 13 August 1674. Before any further operations could be contemplated they needed to find shelter for more than 2,000 wounded and allow the Dutch troops the opportunity to procure new tents, field-beds and clothing. Brigadier-General Godard van Reede-Ginkel, for example, informed his father that he had

> not retained one single shirt, not even my slippers.... Of my spare horses I have, thank God, lost no more than one. My chaplain, maid, valet, baker and kitchen boy have been taken prisoner or are dead. My waggonmaster and two grooms aside, one does not know their whereabouts. All in all I have lost everything.[23]

Van Reede-Ginkel was a wealthy man, so he could recover from this setback, but for less well-heeled officers the loss of baggage, saddle horses and personnel was a heavy financial blow, because the government did not compensate such losses. On 31 August a convoy of 'several hundred waggons' with provisions and new equipment (weapons and accoutrements) for the Dutch troops arrived in Mons, as well as the clerk of the States of Holland, Simon van Beaumont (1641–1726), with a large sum of money, 'for the advancement of one month's pay for a large part of the army'. Five fresh Dutch infantry regiments arrived in the allied camp at the same time, bringing the Dutch corps to the same strength as before the battle of Seneffe. William III then proposed resuming the march to the French border,[24] but by then Souches wanted to hear nothing of it. Monterrey

---

[20] NA, RAZH, AGF 131, 'Les tués de l'armée de France à la dernière bataille'.
[21] HUA, HAA 2731, Godard van Reede-Ginkel to his father, Mons, 12 August 1674.
[22] Bluche, *Louis XIV*, p. 252; Knoop, *Willem den Derde*, II, p. 81; Lynn, *Wars of Louis XIV*, pp. 125–6; Ten Raa, *Het Staatsche leger*, VI, p. 32.
[23] HUA, HAA 2731, Godard van Reede-Ginkel to his father, Mons, 12 August 1674. Dutch preachers actively participated in battle, witness the experience of Agidius van Couendael during the battle of Seneffe. As minister to the Dutch Guards, Van Couendael provided the 'thirsty' guardsmen with water and helped carry their wounded to safety, besides supplying the soldiers with muskets, powder, lead and matches. Van Couendael's bravery knew no bounds: he lay under the dead for half an hour and thus saved one of the regimental colours from capture by the French, 'which he will be able to prove with the testimony of several officers should it be required'. NA, SG 7498, 'Requeste van Agidius van Couendael, predicant', 1676.
[24] NA, SG 12579.100, William III to the SG's committee for secret affairs, Kevering, 1 September 1674 (quote). See also *Vervolg van 't Verwerd Europa*, p. 979.

60. Godard van Reede-Ginkel (1644–1703), Dutch general of horse, earl of Athlone from 1692 (Author's collection)

broached the possibility of laying siege to Ath again, which in his view had a good chance of success now, Condé having reduced the garrison to between 3,100 and 3,300 men. Souches agreed to this proposal, but a couple of days later he suddenly changed his mind; he was only prepared to lend assistance for the besieging of Oudenaarde.

On 16 September 1674 the allies arrived before Oudenaarde and the opening of the trenches followed a day later (17/18 September).[25] Oudenaarde had a garrison of approximately 2,500 men under Rochepère, a seventy-year-old 'soldier of fortune [i.e. risen through the ranks] and of low social status, reputed to be a fine soldier'.[26] He was assisted by Vauban, who had betaken himself to this stronghold when it became apparent that the allies no longer had designs on Ath. The Dutch and Spanish troops approached the covered way energetically, but the Imperial troops did nothing. On 19 September there was news that Condé had crossed to the left bank of the River Scheldt at Tournai and was advancing to the relief of the beleaguered town. For William III and the Spanish general Villa Hermosa this was an extra incentive to capture Oudenaarde as quickly as possible, and the Dutch and Spanish trenches reached the covered way that same night. Souches, however, drew a different conclusion. 'Of his own volition and without communicating this to any of us, that same evening [he had ordered] his artillery ... be carried off from the trenches', William III snorted. And the following night Souches dispatched his entire field artillery and all the munitions to Ghent. This not only scuppered the possibility of besieging Oudenaarde but also forced the allies to make a hasty retreat, because without their field artillery and munitions the Imperial troops could not take part in a battle and with only the Dutch and Spanish troops William III and Villa Hermosa could not hazard a battle against Condé.[27]

The actions of Souches caused a storm of indignation in the Republic. Grand Pensionary Gaspar Fagel ordered the States-General's envoy in Vienna to lodge an official protest with the emperor. He was instructed to underscore that the Republic's war effort had amounted to more than 30 million guilders for the year, 'and that this sum was raised by extraordinary taxes from the [Republic's] inhabitants.... That the said inhabitants ... would become reluctant to contribute if they were to learn that the outlays were poorly spent due to such poor conduct.'[28] William III no longer wanted to serve in the same army as Souches. On 8 October 1674 he headed for Grave, which Lieutenant-General Rabenhaupt had

---

[25] NA, FAF 554, 'Relation succincte de ... la campagne de 1674', Entries for August and September 1674, and appendix AA3.
[26] NA, RAZH, AGF 54, A. Nyenborch van Naeltwijk, before Oudenaarde, 18 September 1674.
[27] NA, SG 12579.100, William III to the SG's committee for secret affairs, Zevergem, 25 September 1674.
[28] NA, SG 12579.100, Gaspar Fagel to the SG's committee for secret affairs, Balgoij, 30 September 1674.

been besieging since late July, with 3,000 foot-soldiers and eight cavalry regiments. The French had in the meantime headed for their winter quarters, so for this year the campaign in the Spanish Netherlands was over.[29]

The siege of Grave – Turenne's winter campaign (July–December 1674)

In Grave there was a garrison of 4,000 to 5,000 men under the command of the thirty-eight-year-old Chamilly, a highly capable and bellicose officer. Chamilly used this town as a base for his marauding forays into the Nijmegen quarter. In order to bring an end to this and to liberate the hostages whom Luxembourg had carried off from Utrecht and gaoled in Grave in late 1673,[30] in mid-July 1674 Rabenhaupt advanced on Grave with 155 companies of foot and fourteen of horse. This army was insufficient to wholly invest this town, allowing Chamilly to have the hostages transferred to Maastricht. Rabenhaupt's force was not strong enough to begin the siege proper until August. The Brandenburg troops arrived at the Dutch siege camp on 11 August, swelling Rabenhaupt's siege army to approximately 16,000 men.[31] After the Holy Roman Empire had declared war on France, with the emperor mobilising two sizeable armies and the Republic fighting together with Spain against France in the Spanish Netherlands, the Great Elector felt the time was ripe to participate in the struggle again. He thought the renewal of the pact with the Republic was desirable primarily in view of the ominous threat of war with Sweden. Charles XI (1655–1697), king of Sweden from 1660, was an ally of Louis XIV. In accordance with an alliance concluded with France in 1672, the Swedish king was obliged to help discourage the German princes from assisting the Republic by assembling an intervention force of 16,000 men, but he was for a long time hesitant to meet this commitment. In 1674 he was nevertheless forced to keep his word, because otherwise Louis XIV threatened to make overtures to Denmark, Sweden's arch-enemy. Charles XI therefore augmented his army in Swedish Pomerania from 15,000 to 22,000 men and ordered preparations to be made for a campaign in the north of the Holy Roman Empire.[32]

The progress of the siege of Grave was ponderous. The strong garrison and the huge supply of artillery and munitions in the stronghold – a good 450 pieces

---

[29] NA, RAZH, AGF 54, A. Nyenborch van Naeltwijk, Abbey of Affligem, one and a half hours from Aalst, 10 October 1674; *Vervolg van 't Verwerd Europa*, p. 983.
[30] See p. 466.
[31] NA, RAZH, AGF 117, Lieutenant-General Rabenhaupt, Nijmegen, 10 and 15 July, with a 'Lijste van de militie soo hier tot Nimmegen alsmede tot Ravenstein bij het vliegende leger vergadert' as an addendum, and Balgoij, 11 August 1674; Knoop, *Willem den Derde*, II, pp. 125 and 129.
[32] Frost, *Northern Wars*, p. 210; Göran Rystad, 'Sweden and the Nijmegen Peace Congress', in *The Peace of Nijmegen 1676–1678/79* (Amsterdam 1980), pp. 131–43, esp. 133–4.

and a million pounds of gunpowder[33] – made it possible for Chamilly to conduct a highly active defence.[34] William III arrived in the camp of the besiegers on 9 October 1674. The troops that he brought with him were a welcome reinforcement. Colonel Gaspar Richard Hundebeck wrote to Waldeck on 22 October:

> This siege ... is currently not proceeding as desired. We are losing many soldiers. The enemy is very well equipped in his positions, with all the advantages [i.e. strong fortifications] and mines, which do us great damage. Yet I believe the enemy shall run into a shortage of flour and other necessities, and will therefore have to surrender in eight to ten days, otherwise they are pretty much immune to the siege assault as it is now being carried out. Our regiments have become very weak. I have no more healthy captains, never mind a senior officer. They are all injured and have fallen sick, thus I shall once again have to think about raising recruits.[35]

Chamilly beat the chamade on 27 October, three days earlier than Hundebeck had expected. The French garrison was granted a free withdrawal. Both sides had suffered heavy losses: the defenders had suffered more than 2,000 dead and wounded, while the besiegers had lost between 7,000 and 8,000 men. After the recapture of Grave William III dispersed the Dutch troops across the garrisons, but in the Holy Roman Empire there was no question of a military hibernation. Quite the reverse – Turenne exploited the winter months to begin an offensive along the Rhine.

In October 1674 Bournonville had established his winter quarters along the left bank of the Upper Rhine with 30,000 to 40,000 Imperial troops and 20,000 Brandenburg troops. Turenne had just 20,000 to 30,000 men at his disposal, but he managed to turn his numerical inferiority to his advantage. In December he drove the Imperial and Brandenburg troops from Alsace. Guillaume le Blond explains that Turenne brought about this remarkable achievement 'by capturing all the quarters of the enemies, one after the other. He foresaw that the Imperials, because of their great number, would be able neither to march together nor remain united in an army corps because of the difficulties with subsistence.'[36] Turenne's offensive demonstrated once again that logistics was the Achilles' heel of the Imperial forces. While the Republic and Spain had adopted the French magazine system, at least with respect to the bread supplies, the emperor was still trying to provision his troops as he had during the Thirty Years' War, namely by requisitioning supplies. This method was effective with small armies, but it forced large armies to spread themselves out. Souches' troops were faced with the same problem, but because Brussels had taken care of the bread supplies during

---

[33] *Vervolg van 't Verwerd Europa*, pp. 984–5; Knoop, *Willem den Derde*, II, pp. 115–16.
[34] On the siege of Grave see pp. 386–7.
[35] GA, AHGC 1202, Caspar Richard Hundebeck to Georg Friedrich von Waldeck, by Velp before Grave, 22 October 1674.
[36] Le Blond, *Elémens de tactique*, p. 211. See also Childs, *Warfare*, pp. 173–6.

their sojourn in the Spanish Netherlands the Imperial troops had not suffered any hunger there.[37]

Another disappointing year for the allies (1675)

After the experiences with Souches, William III was convinced that the French could be successfully combated in the Spanish Netherlands only 'if the ... allies could decide to conjoin the armies that are to be found in the Spanish Netherlands or thereabouts, to be commanded by a single general or chief'. In a discussion about this with Grand Pensionary Fagel, William III expressed the view that this commander-in-chief should preferably be authorised, having heard the counsel of the commanders of the 'separate armies', to 'decide [upon the course of action] as he judges will best serve' the common cause, but William III realised it was unlikely that Vienna and Madrid would consent to this. As an alternative he therefore proposed 'with authority to concert the military operations with those who will be in command of the separate armies [and] to come to a decision by plurality [i.e. a majority] of votes'. William III assumed that this would obviate the objection that the Imperial and Spanish generals might harbour against his appointment as allied commander-in-chief in the Netherlands. For William III it was a foregone conclusion that the rank of supreme commander would fall to him. In 1635 the French *maréchals* had, after all, raised no objections to serving under Frederik Hendrik, he reminded Gaspar Fagel.[38] William III could count on the unreserved support of the States-General's committee for secret affairs for his plan – the behaviour of Souches during the siege of Oudenaarde had, after all, caused 'great commotion and annoyance', among the regents as well.[39] William III entrusted Waldeck and the Amsterdam regent Coenraad van Heemskerck with the difficult task of raising this delicate matter in Vienna and Brussels, respectively. Waldeck was partly successful in his diplomacy: Leopold I suspended Souches and assigned the command over a 'powerful army corps on the banks of the Rhine' to Montecuccoli, but at the same time the emperor explained that he was in no position to dispatch an army to the Low Countries again. The remaining Imperial troops were needed to help the Great Elector against the Swedes – in the winter of 1674/5 a Swedish force of 13,000 men had invaded the Uckermark, a province of Brandenburg-Prussia, and then marched on Berlin.[40]

---

[37] CWB, II, i, no. 532, Jacob van Borssele van der Hooghe, lord of Geldermalsen, to William III, Namur, 7 July 1674.
[38] NA, SG 12579.100, Gaspar Fagel to the SG's committee for secret affairs, Balgoij, 27 October 1674.
[39] NA, RAZH, AGF 4, Johan Mauregnault, deputy of Zeeland to the SG, The Hague, 28 September 1674.
[40] Frost, *Northern Wars*, p. 210.

Nor were there auxiliary troops available from Brunswick and Lorraine, because they were destined for a campaign along the Moselle.[41]

The emperor's response came as an extremely unpleasant surprise for the Republic. In early 1675 the Dutch army was in fine condition, but the same could not be said of the Spanish army. In December 1674 William III had ordered the Dutch captains to have their companies complete by 1 April 1675 at the latest.[42] He had learned the lesson of May 1674, when Condé had besieged Argenteau and Navagne without the least opposition from the allied side. William III could therefore have over 30,000 men – 'all of them fine and well-disposed soldiers' – in readiness by early April 1675,[43] but Villa Hermosa, who had replaced Monterrey as governor-general in January 1675, was in no position to follow this example; the Spanish contingent consisted 'for the present of nought but about 5,000 horse'.[44] On paper the Spanish army in the Southern Netherlands numbered 49,000 men,[45] but the companies fell far short of their establishment strengths and Villa Hermosa had distributed all the infantry among the threatened forts. Mutual distrust between Brussels and The Hague was an important factor in this decision. Not without reason, the Spaniards suspected that, if the worst came to the worst, the regents would be satisfied with the creation of an effective barrier between the Republic and France, and would no longer mention the restoration of the 1659 situation. After all, since the end of the 'Guerre de Hollande' and the recapture of Grave the Republic was no longer embroiled in a struggle for survival with France, so for the majority of regents a compromise peace with Louis XIV was no longer unthinkable. A precondition for this was that the king of France consented to the Spanish Netherlands serving as a rampart between the Republic and France. Otherwise the Republic would have to be prepared for the possibility of a French invasion at all times, even in peacetime, and thus be forced to keep her army at wartime strength and permanently maintain the forts in a state of defence. Establishing the Spanish Netherlands as a buffer zone required France's retrocession of Veurne (Furnes), Courtrai, Oudenaarde, Ath and Charleroi. Louis XIV would have to be indemnified for this and the Spanish therefore harboured suspicions that the Dutch would accept France pursuing conquests in Artois and Cambrai and not make any troops available for the defence of these provinces.[46]

---

[41] CWB, II, ii, no. 8, Georg Friedrich von Waldeck to William III, Vienna, 14 February 1675.
[42] *Groot Placaetboeck*, III, p. 187, no. 50, 'Ordre van sijne Hoogheydt', 22 December 1674.
[43] GA, AHGC 1240, 'Lijste van 't broot dan den 30 juny 1675 aen de regimenten is gedistrib[uee]rt'.
[44] NA, SG 12579.102, Coenraad van Heemskerck to the *griffier* of the SG, more than a quarter of an hour from Louvain, 11 June, and Lembeek, 27 July 1675 (quotes); Krämer, *Nederlandsch-Spaansche diplomatie*, p. 221.
[45] Rooms, 'Materiële organisatie', p. 54.
[46] Baxter, *William III*, p. 134; Hahlweg, 'Barriere – Gleichgewicht – Sicherheit', p. 69; Troost, *William III*, p. 139.

The French operational plans for 1675 were almost identical to those for the previous year. Turenne would continue his offensive against the Imperial forces and Condé would lay siege to Namur. The 1674 campaign had, however, demonstrated that the Republic, Spain and the emperor could jointly assemble an army that was superior to the French army in the Spanish Netherlands. Internal discord had prevented the allies being able to take advantage of this, but there was no assurance that this would also be the case in 1675. Louis XIV therefore ordered Condé to seize control of Dinant, Huy and Limbourg before laying siege to Namur. After capturing these three towns, all the fortified crossing places upstream of Maastricht on the River Meuse would be in French hands – Liège had been occupied by French troops since 31 March 1675 – and it was highly unlikely that the emperor would once again dispatch troops to the Spanish Netherlands when his lines of communication would have to run via Roermond. In an emergency it would then be impossible to quickly pull back the Imperial troops to the Moselle or the Upper Rhine.

Condé was assigned more than 40,000 men for his offensive, augmented later to between 50,000 and 60,000 men in all.[47] In order to be left with as much time as possible for the siege of Namur, Condé would for the most part omit putting the horses to pasture that year and go on the offensive as early as mid-May 1675. The distribution of oats was meant to prevent the horses becoming too seriously weakened. Condé appeared before Dinant on 19 May. The garrison of this small fort, just 250 strong at the time, capitulated on 30 May. Next in line was Huy, where the 550 defenders surrendered on 6 June. Four days later the French invested Limbourg, where the garrison of 1,000 men kept up the defence until 21 June.[48]

The French offensive caused great consternation in Brussels. William III and Villa Hermosa advanced with the Dutch and Spanish troops, 35,000 men in all, on Louvain, but the French superiority was too great to hazard a battle. They therefore agreed to go to Roermond and await the arrival of a corps of cavalry from Brunswick and Lorraine before launching a counter-offensive.[49] However, this plan soon had to be abandoned, because Condé led the French army to Ath, stoking fears about the safety of Brussels, Mons and Ghent. William III and Villa Hermosa struck camp and, travelling via Mechelen (Malines), at the end of July 1675 they reached the environs of Halle, a small town to the southwest of Brussels, with forced marches. From there they could soon reach Ghent. The allied army was just 29,000 strong at this time. Field deputy Coenraad van Heemskerck reported to the *griffier* of the States-General on 27 July: 'Excepting the units left behind (namely one regiment in Brussels, two in Malines, one in Dendermonde, some soldiers in Roermond, Venlo, Louvain, etc.), the State's army ... probably still consists, by estimation, of 25,000 combatants.... The Spaniards

---

[47] Lynn, *Wars of Louis XIV*, pp. 136–7.
[48] Ibid., pp. 136–9; Knoop, *Willem den Derde*, II, pp. 170–3.
[49] NA, FAF 1956, Georg Friedrich von Waldeck to Gaspar Fagel, near Louvain, 12 June 1675.

in the field have 4,000 men in all, both cavalry and dragoons.' He did, however, expect that the allied army would soon be reinforced again, because besides the various regiments which had been ordered to leave their garrisons and join the field army, there were also hundreds of soldiers who had fallen behind *en route* during the long march from Roermond to Halle and would trickle into the allied camp over the coming days.[50]

On the same day that Van Heemskerck penned his letter there was an event on the Rhine that would also have major repercussions in the Netherlandish theatre of war: Turenne was killed by a cannon-ball on 27 July 1675, during a reconnaissance of the Imperial positions near the small town of Sasbach. Without their brilliant leader the French were no match for Montecuccoli and they beat a swift retreat to Alsace. To prevent the Imperial forces crossing the Rhine, Louis XIV ordered Condé to head to Alsace with part of his army immediately and to assume command over the Rhine army. Fifteen days later, on 11 August, another French army under *Maréchal* François, marquis de Créqui (1624–1687), suffered a defeat against Brunswick's and Lorraine's troops at the battle of Consarbruck, after which the duke of Lorraine laid siege to Trier. This city fell on 6 September 1675, due to its French garrison rising in mutiny.[51]

After Condé's departure, Luxembourg assumed command over the French army in the Spanish Netherlands. It still numbered approximately 40,000 men, which was too scant to lay siege to Namur or to seek battle with the Dutch-Spanish army. Luxembourg was therefore ordered to limit himself to the defensive for the rest of the campaign. For William III and Villa Hermosa it was impossible to gain any advantage from Turenne's death, because they had too few troops at their disposal to compel Luxembourg to give battle and nor were they in a position to lay siege to a French-controlled town. The division of the allied army into a siege force and a covering force would, after all, give Luxembourg the opportunity to act aggressively. As a consequence the Dutch, Spanish and French troops remained in the field until early November 1675, but there were no more operations of any import that year.[52]

France's spring offensive (January–June 1676)

The emperor could look back with satisfaction on the war year 1675, and the elector of Brandenburg had reason to be contented, too; on 28 June of that year he had beaten the Swedes in the battle of Fehrbellin. The Swedish losses amounted to just 600 men, but because the Great Elector immediately

---

[50] NA, SG 12579.102, Coenraad van Heemskerck to the *griffier* of the SG, Lembeek, 27 July 1675.
[51] Childs, *Warfare in the Seventeenth Century*, p. 176; Knoop, *Willem den Derde*, II, pp. 176–7; Lynn, *Wars of Louis XIV*, p .141.
[52] Ten Raa, *Het Staatsche leger*, VI, p. 45; Knoop, *Willem den Derde*, II, p. 179.

exploited this triumph the strategic outcome was great. He drove the Swedes from Brandenburg and occupied Swedish Pomerania. Denmark then involved herself in the struggle as well, capturing Wismar and Bremen.[53] In the Republic and Spain, however, there was growing disappointment about military successes failing to materialise. In December 1674 Amsterdam's deputies to the States of Holland had still consented to the States assembly approving the 'State of War' army overview without referring it to the town councils, but hereafter they were no longer prepared to do this.[54] The Amsterdammers had no intention of shouldering Spain's dirty work and were of the opinion that the Spaniards had to make a much greater contribution to the defence of the Spanish Netherlands. In December 1675 Van Heemskerck left for Madrid to elucidate the Republic's standpoint. He was instructed to impress upon the king of Spain that the war in the Spanish Netherlands could be decided to the advantage of Spain and the Republic only if Villa Hermosa likewise 'may be strong and capable of bringing into the field an army of 25,000 or at least 20,000 men, over and above the requisite garrisons of the forts'. Together with 30,000 troops from the Republic it would then be possible to put together a siege corps and an army of observation. An offensive was out of the question if this precondition was not met. Besides this demand for more Spanish troops, Van Heemskerck had to insist that the Republic be relieved of payment 'of all the subsidies' to the emperor and the German princes in 1676.[55]

Van Heemskerck arrived in Madrid in early January 1676. He soon came to discover that there was little to be expected from Spain 'before the arrival of the galleons [from the Americas], which are said already to be delayed by two months more than usual and are awaited with impatience'. However, he warned The Hague not to cherish high expectations, because even if the treasure fleet were to put into port soon, William III still could not count on many Spanish troops being sent to the Low Countries: '[W]e think it will amount to 1,000 men at most, because of the minimal enthusiasm among the [Spanish] people to serve [i.e. take up arms] as well as by reason of the depopulation of Spain in general.' If the Spanish managed to levy recruits then these were sent to Catalonia or to Sicily, where an uprising backed by France had broken out in 1674. Only when Van Heemskerck had threatened that without a substantial military contribution from Spain the Republic would be compelled to broker a separate peace with France, did the Spanish court at last, on 25 February 1676, give the undertaking that Villa Hermosa would be provided with the means to field 20,000 to 22,000 men.[56] However, the regents were soon forced to acknowledge that this

---

[53] Frost, *Northern Wars*, pp. 210–14; Fiedler, *Kriegswesen und Kriegführung im Zeitalter der Kabinettskriege*, p. 97.
[54] Franken, *Coenraad van Beuningen*, p. 36.
[55] HUA, ASU 637-12, Secret resolution of the SG, 25 November 1675.
[56] NA, RAZH, AGF 387, Coenraad van Heemskerck and Sébastien de Chièze, Madrid, 15 January (quote), 29 January, 12 and 26 February, and 11 March 1676.

extorted promise was of no practical significance whatsoever, because in early April 1676 Villa Hermosa made an urgent request to The Hague to loan him eight Dutch infantry regiments (5,000 to 6,000 men) immediately. The Spanish governor-general complained that he would otherwise be unable to man the forts in the Southern Netherlands properly.[57] Thomas van Sasburch, the Republic's envoy to Brussels, endorsed this assertion:

> The greatest difficulty that I ... ascertain is that here one has no troops to provide the towns with adequate garrisons, not even against a sudden attack, so all hope is vested in a speedy dispatch of some [Dutch] regiments ... in order to be able to properly reinforce [the garrisons in] the places and towns that are most in peril and by such means to repel the first strike by the French.[58]

There was every indication that the French were preparing a spring offensive on a massive scale.

The 1675 campaign had not only taken a disappointing course for the Republic and Spain, but for France as well. Though Liège, Huy, Dinant and Limbourg had been captured, none of the strongholds which were of true consequence to Louis XIV – Namur, Ghent and Brussels – had fallen into his hands. Turenne's sudden death had precluded this. From this turn of events Louis XIV and Louvois drew the conclusion that the success of the French operational plans had to be less dependent on chance. By carefully planning the military operations in the various theatres of war and mutually attuning them, France would be able to play her two greatest trump cards, namely unity in command and a superior logistical organisation. The weakness of the allies resided in their deficient cooperation and the lack of a sound financial basis to make it possible to assemble the armies early in the year. The Republic was weighed down by the consequences of the Year of Disaster, the Spaniards had been living from hand to mouth for a century already, and the emperor had neither the financial reserves nor the creditworthiness to be able to borrow substantial sums of money. By establishing huge forage magazines the French armies would be able to launch the attack early in the year, in March or April, enabling them to carry out assaults and make conquests while the allies were still in their winter quarters. In 1674 and 1675 they had already achieved positive results with this manner of warfare, occupying Franche-Comté and capturing towns in the bishopric of Liège and Limbourg, respectively. According to Louvois the time had now come to apply this way of conducting war on a truly grand scale. The death of Turenne and the retirement of Condé, tormented by gout, cleared the way for the implementation of the *'stratégie de cabinet'*. Turenne and Condé had to a large extent executed military operations on the basis of their personal insights. From now on it was Louis XIV and Louvois who decided France's 'grand strategy', drawing on the

---

57 NA, SG 12588.106, same to the *griffier* of the SG, Madrid, 8 April 1676, Appendix A.
58 NA, SG 12588.106, Thomas van Sasburch to the *griffier* of the SG, Brussels, 8 and 22 (quote) March 1676.

61. Louis XIV (1638–1715), king of France (1643–1715), his brother Philippe, duc d'Orléans (1640–1701), Louis 'le Grand Dauphin' (1661–1711), and François Michel Le Tellier (1639–1691), marquis de Louvois. *Hollantse Mercurius* (1678). (Royal Netherlands Army Museum, Delft, 00102431/001)

advice of a few experts. Chief among these were Vauban and Quartermaster-General Jules-Louis Bolé (1650–1719), marquis de Chamlay.[59]

From 1676 the French war effort was focused on establishing buffer zones along France's frontiers. The strongest line of fortifications had to be established along the border with the Spanish Netherlands. Vauban had already aired his views on this to Louvois in January 1673: 'Seriously, Sir, the King ought to take a little care in looking after his *pré carré* [i.e. the fortified zone covering France's northern frontier]. This confusion of pell-mell friendly and enemy places does not please me at all. You are obliged to maintain three for one.'[60] In the latter half of 1675 he had elaborated his ideas into concrete measures. Vauban was of the opinion that in the Peace of Aix-la-Chapelle (1668) Louis XIV had acquired various forts that were positioned too far forward, such as Charleroi, Ath, Oudenaarde and Courtrai. He advised the king to give back these places to Spain, their being difficult to defend anyway, in exchange for strongholds that would enable him to establish a *frontière de fer* from the North Sea all the way to the River Meuse. The Sun King approved this ambitious plan, whereupon he began preparations to seize Condé, Bouchain, Valenciennes and Cambrai in 1676.[61] For this large-scale offensive Louis XIV reserved an army of 60,000 men, over which he and his brother, Philippe, duc d'Orléans (1640–1701), known as *Monsieur*, would assume personal command, assisted by no fewer than five French *maréchals*, of whom Louis de Crevant (1628–1694), duc d'Humières, and Friedrich Hermann, comte de Schomberg (1615–1690), were the most competent.

On 17 April 1676 the French invested Condé and four days later the trenches were opened in the presence of the Sun King. The Spanish garrison numbered just 1,500 men, so the siege was unlikely to last long. William III immediately gathered all the available Dutch troops, about 28,000 men,[62] and Villa Hermosa assembled approximately 13,000 Spanish troops. The allied army reached Mons on 26 April, but Condé fell into French hands that same day. The French then marched to Bouchain and invested this stronghold on 2 May. At Villa Hermosa's insistence, William III agreed, despite the imbalance of manpower, to relieve Bouchain by means of a battle. Waldeck informed Grand Pensionary Fagel about this daring decision:

> The decision has been taken to attempt to cross by force the defile that the Most Christian King of France has before him in order to endeavour to relieve Bouchain or at least to save Valenciennes, and it is a plan that, if it succeeds, has never been equalled, as His Highness [William III] will have without doubt written to you.... We are marching tomorrow, the 7th. *Nous serons au mains*.[63]

---

59 Corvisier, *Louvois*, pp. 359, 361 and 363; Bluche, *Louis XIV*, p. 248.
60 Anne Blanchard, 'Vers la centure de fer', p. 476.
61 Duffy, *The Fortress in the Age of Vauban*, p. 12; Knoop, *Willem den Derde*, II, p. 182.
62 Knoop, *Willem den Derde*, II, p. 186
63 NA, FAF 1956, Georg Friedrich von Waldeck to Gaspar Fagel, Mons, 4 April 1675. The date on this letter is incorrect, its content leaving no shadow of a doubt that Waldeck wrote it on 6 May 1676.

62. William III (1650–1702), captain- and admiral-general of the Union. Copy of a painting by Willem Wissing (c. 1656–1687). (Royal Netherlands Army Museum, Delft, 056862)

Three days later (10 May 1676) the allies had approached to within 'a cannon-shot' of the French position, so a battle seemed inevitable and it seemed Waldeck's prediction that it would 'come to blows' was on the mark. Louis XIV was keen to throw down the gauntlet, but Louvois and a majority of the *maréchals* and generals advised him most strongly against giving battle. They pointed out that the allies could easily find refuge under the guns of Valenciennes, but the actual reason was that they did not want to imperil Louis XIV's life. In the meantime Waldeck was trying to persuade William III not to pursue an aggressive course of action. The Republic's army could not be imperilled, he impressed upon the captain-general of the Union, and the key objective of preventing the loss of Valenciennes had been achieved.

Both the Sun King and William III allowed themselves to be dissuaded, albeit with great reluctance, from joining battle.[64] Bouchain's 750 defenders capitulated the following day (11 May). This was followed by a lull in hostilities which lasted more than a month. On 27 May the French established a position on the River Dender between Geraardsbergen and Ninove. From this position they posed a threat to Brussels, Aalst and Ghent, but even more important was that the French horses could recuperate there at the expense of the Spanish Netherlands. The meadows were filled with lush grass, the fields with grain. The horses of the allies were in a state even more parlous than those of the French, because no forage magazines had been established for the Dutch and Spanish troops, leaving them dependent on stores that farmers had amassed for their livestock. William III and Villa Hermosa took up positions between Aalst and Dendermonde with the allied army. In the latter half of June 1676 the French shifted their position. They set up a new camp between Mons and Valenciennes, but they made no moves to attack either of these towns, because the Imperialist forces had been besieging Philippsburg since 24 June and Louis XIV wanted to be at liberty to direct reinforcements from the Spanish Netherlands to Alsace. On 4 July the Sun King returned to France 'having made several detachments' to the French army in Alsace. As soon as William III became aware of this he began preparations for a counter-offensive.[65]

William III's unsuccessful attempt to recapture Maastricht (July–December 1676)

Having provided the majority of the troops for the defence of the Spanish Netherlands for two and a half years, William III thought it only right that the Spaniards should lend their assistance to the recapture of Maastricht. The

---

[64] CWB, II, ii, nos. 98, 106 and 107, William III to Gaspar Fagel, 21 April, 11 and 13 May 1676; Corvisier, *Louvois*, pp. 198–200; Sonnino, 'Louis XIV and the Dutch War', p. 165.
[65] NA, FAF 1958, Georg Friedrich von Waldeck to Gaspar Fagel, Nivelles, 6 July 1676 (quote); Knoop, *Willem den Derde*, II, pp. 193–4; Lynn, *Wars of Louis XIV*, pp. 147–8.

most zealous advocate of this undertaking was Johan Pesters, the town's former pensionary. He acknowledged that the 'liberation' of Maastricht would be an extremely difficult task, but this would be more than compensated by the 'glory' and 'splendour' this operation would garner for the Republic. Pesters wrote to the Grand Pensionary Gaspar Fagel:

> I need neither to remind nor to mention to Your Honourable Worship how much value was attached to Maastricht at the time of the Spanish War [i.e. the Eighty Years' War] – whence one did not merely extend the contributions across four or five provinces, prevented the enemy occupying the winter quarters outside his own bosom, disrupted and made impossible all the [Spanish] recruitment drives, and made difficult the communications between [the Spanish Netherlands] and the German Empire; but moreover one had at the same time also been able to extend her [i.e. the Republic's] influence over the lands of Liège, Jülich, Cologne, Trier and other adjoining territories – and what damage and mockery the Republic has for some years endured from the said town and still experiences daily, running to millions in cash, and being inestimable in its derision.[66]

William III assigned 16,500 Dutch troops for the siege of Maastricht. Together with 2,200 troops from Brandenburg, 4,000 from Palatine-Neuburg and 7,500 from Brunswick this amounted to an army of 30,000 men.[67] William III allocated 20,000 Dutch troops for the army of observation,[68] to which Villa Hermosa contributed a further 6,000 Spanish cavalry. With these 26,000 men, Waldeck and the Spanish governor-general had to cover the siege of Maastricht and at the same time watch over Spanish Brabant and Flanders. Waldeck doubted whether this two-pronged task was feasible, given that the French field army numbered 40,000 to 45,000 men. He therefore advised William III to make the line of circumvallation extremely robust, because 'if your lines [around Maastricht] are not safe from assaults then things could go badly, for this army would not be able to prevent some corps from reaching the besieged [town] as well as watch over Flanders.'[69]

William III appeared before Maastricht on 8 July 1676, but it was eight days before the siege artillery arrived, because the water level in the River Meuse was extremely low. The opening of the trenches eventually took place on 18 July and four days later the siege artillery began to play from thirty cannon. Two

---

[66] NA, RAZH, AGF 56, Johan Pesters, Nijmegen, 27 May 1676, eleven o'clock at night.
[67] NA, FAF 555, 'Liste des troupes à piedt et à cheval que S.A. a destiné pour le chiège de Mastricht'.
[68] GA, AHGC 1240, Muster-rolls of 13 August 1676 for the thirteen Dutch infantry regiments under command of Waldeck. The strength of the eight Dutch regiments that were loaned to Villa Hermosa is based on these muster-rolls. The cavalry strength is an estimate based on the review of Dutch cavalry on 9 July 1677 and the list of cavalry present at the siege of Maastricht. HUA, HAA 3209, 'Lijste de la force de chacque regim[en]t de cavallerie ... selon la revue faite par S.A. au camp de Drongene en Marikercke, le 9.me juillet 1677'; NA, FAF 555, 'Liste des troupes à piedt et à cheval que S.A. a destiné pour le chiège de Mastricht'.
[69] Müller, *Wilhelm III und Waldeck*, II, p. 274, no. 10, Waldeck, Genappe, 19 July 1676.

weeks had passed before the siege of Maastricht really began, a loss of time that the allies could ill afford. 'According to the reports from Monsieur the Duke of Villa Hermosa,' William III wrote to an unknown correspondent, 'the enemy's main army is heading into Flanders to attack a place there.'[70] Schomberg and d'Humières seized the opportunity to lay siege to Aire. They were of the opinion that the relief of Maastricht could wait a few more weeks. The commander there, Jean-Sauveur de Calvo (1625-1690), had sworn that he would defend the stronghold entrusted to him to the bitter end, 'in a word, he would never render it to his Prince's enemies by capitulation', a pledge that he should certainly have been able to keep with a garrison of 7,000 men.[71] Moreover, Aire's garrison counted just 1,200 men, so it was unlikely that the capitulation of this town would take long. Schomberg and d'Humières were therefore satisfied that there was sufficient time to capture Aire first and only then to relieve Maastricht. D'Humières assumed responsibility for the siege with approximately 15,000 men, while Schomberg kept an eye on the troops under Waldeck and Villa Hermosa with the remaining 25,000 to 30,000 men. On 19 July 1676 the French invested Aire. Three days later, on the same day that the Dutch siege artillery began to play, d'Humières ordered the opening of the trenches.

Villa Hermosa was as circumspect as the French *maréchals* about Aire's garrison being able to hold out for long and he therefore wanted Waldeck to assist with an attempt to relieve the stronghold.[72] The Dutch field-marshal agreed, as he feared that otherwise the siege of Maastricht would never be brought to a successful conclusion. After all, as soon as Aire had fallen into French hands Schomberg was at liberty to head for the Meuse. So long as d'Humières was besieging Aire the allies were almost as strong as Schomberg's army of observation, so giving battle or at least threatening to do so was militarily sound. It did not come to a fight, however, because when Waldeck and Villa Hermosa reached Deinze on 2 August 1676 they received news that Aire had capitulated on 31 July. William III was flabbergasted 'that Aire surrendered so brusquely, see there the enemies in a position ... to come and relieve this place [Maastricht]'. The allies now had to choose between two evils, and according to William III the lesser of these was 'that Monsieur the Duke of Villa Hermosa and yourself [Waldeck] shall garrison as best they can the towns that remain in Artois and Flanders, and that with the rest of the army you shall return [to Spanish Brabant] and take up a position to cover the siege [of Maastricht]'.[73] It is not difficult to understand that Villa Hermosa took a different view. He suspected that the army under

---

[70] CWB, II, ii, no. 146, William III to an unknown correspondent, before Maastricht, 21 July 1676.
[71] Le Blond, *Elémens de tactique*, p. 470. On the course of the siege of Maastricht see pp. 387-92.
[72] NA, FAF 1958, Georg Friedrich von Waldeck to Gaspar Fagel, Genappe, 21 July 1676.
[73] Müller, *Wilhelm III und Waldeck*, II, p. 294, no. 39, William III, before Maastricht, 3 August 1676.

d'Humières would invade Flanders as soon as the allies had left for Brabant and he therefore considered it necessary to furnish the Flemish towns which had most to fear with strong garrisons. There was therefore no other option but to split the allied force: Villa Hermosa posted six battalions in Ypres, three in Diksmuide (Dixmude) and as many in Nieuwpoort, and with the remaining Spanish troops and eight Dutch battalions (5,000 men) he established a position near Ghent. Waldeck departed with the majority of the Dutch troops for Brussels, where he would remain until there was clarity about France's plans. If Schomberg marched on Maastricht then Waldeck would immediately follow him and Villa Hermosa promised that the Spanish cavalry would then join the Dutch corps. If d'Humières attacked a Flemish town then Waldeck would in turn place the Dutch cavalry at Villa Hermosa's behest.[74]

On 18 August 1676 Waldeck received news that Schomberg was heading toward Charleroi, which could mean but one thing: the French had decided to relieve Maastricht. Villa Hermosa and the Spanish cavalry joined up with Waldeck, but they could not prevent the French *maréchal* establishing a position that made it possible for him 'to throw troop reinforcements into the town [of Maastricht] from the Wijk side', namely from the east via the stone bridge. Hereafter the allied generals in the siege army were 'unanimously' of the opinion that the 'safest and most necessary was to remove our troops from that side [the eastern bank of the Meuse] and place them with all the others outside our line [of circumvallation] in the vicinity of Lanaken'.[75] In other words they no longer saw any means of continuing with the siege operation. In the night of 26/27 August the allies lifted the siege of Maastricht. '[This] surprises and disconcerts the whole world', a correspondent of Van Reede-Amerongen wrote from The Hague. 'The people of Amsterdam and Rotterdam are spitting fire and flame, but it cannot thereby be remedied.'[76]

William III had no intention of resigning himself to this fiasco. Over the following weeks he tried to force Schomberg to give battle in every way imaginable, 'but he has always tried to evade this, either by changing his route slightly and moving aside, or by taking up advantageous positions, or by giving the impression that he was about to march [with his army] and then remaining standing still', according to the field deputy Van Weede-Dijkveld.[77] On 9 September 1676 the French established a position near Waremme (Borgworm)

---

[74] GA, AHGC 1225, 'Conseil de guerre tenu à Dains [Deinze] le 2 d'aoust 1676 entre son Exc.e Mr. le Duc de Villa Hermosa et son Exc.e Monsieur le Comte de Waldeck comme aussy de touts les généraux des deux armées'.
[75] NA, SG 12588.106, Everard van Weede-Dijkveld to the States-General's deputies for military affairs, Smeermaas, 22 August, at about eleven o'clock at night; same to same, Diepenbeek, 29 August (quote) 1676.
[76] HUA, HAA 2813, H. Heteren to Godard Adriaan van Reede-Amerongen, The Hague, 1 September 1676.
[77] HUA, HAA 2813, Everard van Weede-Dijkveld to the same, at the headquarters, 12 September 1676.

to the west of Liège, 'from which they shall not depart before ours have withdrawn, for there they can subsist better than us, having the town of Liège in their control once again, so the enemy is not bloodthirsty [for battle] now that they have achieved their objective'.[78] The strain became too much for William III: he suffered bouts of fever and therefore felt he had no choice but to retire to the palace at Honselaarsdijk in order to recuperate.[79] Waldeck assumed command of the Dutch army.

The relief of Maastricht effectively marked the end of the 1676 campaign in the Low Countries. The allied and French troops remained in the field for several weeks, but for the remainder of the campaign season there were no operations of any significance. The Dutch army was too severely weakened by the siege of Maastricht – the infantry regiments numbered an average of just 428 men instead of an establishment strength of 700 to 800 men[80] – and setbacks in the Holy Roman Empire once again played tricks on Louis XIV. On 8 September the Imperial forces captured Philippsburg, so Alsace was threatened with an invasion. This important success gave Johan Pesters hope that the war might still be decided to the advantage of the allies, 'if people here [in the Republic] do not want to precipitate the conclusion of the peace, which is what it all boiled down to for France when he [Louis XIV] wanted to direct most of his might hither [in the Low Countries] and thereto subordinated his interests along the Rhine'.[81] The pros and cons of continuing the war were still equally balanced, 'as long as we are certain that trade will not be diverted [i.e. snatched up by other countries, in particular England] or is in evident danger thereof'.[82] After the failure of the siege of Maastricht the Amsterdam regents were, however, of the opinion that the opening of peace negotiations could be delayed no longer. For two years they had been patient, but now that was at an end. As long as Madrid made no serious contribution to the defence of the Spanish Netherlands and tried to mislead the Republic with empty promises, the great city's regents saw no point in continuing the war. A separate peace was going a step too far for the Amsterdammers, but it could do no harm to try to negotiate a general peace plan with France, since the belligerents had already agreed to join a peace congress in Nijmegen.[83]

---

[78] HUA, HAA 2813, H. Heteren to the same, The Hague, 12 September 1676, ten o'clock in the morning.
[79] William III 'has become very thin and is rather feverish, so he shall sorely need the rest'. HAA 2813, H. Heteren to Godard Adriaan van Reede-Amerongen, The Hague, 15 September 1676.
[80] Müller, *Wilhelm III und Waldeck*, II, p. 321 n. 2.
[81] HUA, HAA 2813, Johan Pesters to Godard Adriaan van Reede-Amerongen, Utrecht, 18 September 1676.
[82] HUA, HAA 2816, same to same, Utrecht, 7 December 1676.
[83] Franken, *Coenraad van Beuningen*, p. 124; Groenveld, *Evidente factiën*, p. 64; Haley, 'English Policy at the Peace Congress of Nijmegen', p. 148.

The French resume their offensive (January–May 1677)

During the winter of 1676/7 Louvois ordered the accumulation of enormous forage magazines along France's border with the Spanish Netherlands. The plan was to bring the French troops into the field as early as March 1677, a month earlier than in the previous year. The expectation was that the French would thus be in a position to lay siege to Valenciennes and Cambrai, the two strongholds that Louis XIV had already wanted to capture in 1676, without having to take the allies into account. Besides these two towns the French would lay siege to Saint-Omer, an operation for which the capture of Aire had provided a solid foundation. The *frontière de fer* would then be largely complete and Louis XIV expected that this would deprive the Republic of her determination to continue the war. In order to fan the will for peace among the regents even further, the Sun King assigned the command over the French troops in the Spanish Netherlands – a good 60,000 men – to Luxembourg. Louis XIV would again participate in the campaign in person and he wanted to be certain that there would be no repeat of the events of 10 May 1676, when Louvois and the *maréchals* had prevented him joining battle with William III. Luxembourg would not allow the opportunity to inflict a searing defeat on the allies pass him by. This year the French would conduct a defensive war along the Rhine.[84]

The preparations for France's springtime offensive were no secret to The Hague and Brussels, but the taking of countermeasures was no simple matter. In December 1676 Waldeck drew up memorandums about the strategic situation and the military resources that the allies in general and the Republic in particular could mobilise for the defence of the Spanish Netherlands. Waldeck pointed out that the fortunes of war would never turn in favour of the allies unless they were in a position 'to counter that which the enemy might undertake … and to enter into France with a considerable corps'. In 1677 no fewer than seven towns in the Southern Netherlands were in serious danger of being besieged by the French: Saint-Ghislain, Valenciennes, Cambrai, Charlemont, Ypres, Diksmuide and Saint-Omer. These towns could not be covered with a single army, being too far apart. The French could, after all, lure the allies away from their true target with feints: 'That is why there is a need for two armies: the one to observe Hainault and the Meuse, the other to act in Flanders.' Waldeck was under no illusions about the allies being able to assemble two armies that would both be equal to the French, 'but it seems to be feasible to assemble one [that is] considerable and strong enough to resist the enemy, and the other that will be capable of taking up a position that covers the forts and sufficiently reinforce [the garrisons thereof] as needs require'. With a view to the provisioning it was preferable to have the main army operate from Flanders, but this advantage was wholly negated because in that region the French could establish very

---

[84] Lynn, *Wars of Louis XIV*, p. 150; Rooms, 'Materiële organisatie', p. 41.

strong defensive positions. An invasion into France would therefore have to be directed via Hainaut, even if finding forage there presented problems. The next question broached by Waldeck concerned where they might find the necessary armies. He computed that more than 70,000 men had to be found: 60,000 men from which to assemble the said armies and 10,000 to 12,000 men 'to cover our provinces against the garrison of Maastricht'. Waldeck proposed laying siege to Charleroi with 35,000 men, the majority of them Dutch troops. Villa Hermosa would in the meantime have to observe the main French army with 26,000 men – 5,000 Spanish troops, 5,000 Dutch, 8,000 from Münster and 8,000 from Brunswick-Osnabrück – and protect Flanders against an enemy counterattack. The Republic could supply 4,000 to 5,000 men for the blockade of Maastricht. The electors of Brandenburg and Cologne and the duke of Palatine-Neuburg would have to provide a further 6,000 men to render the blockade effective.[85]

William III and the States-General's committee for secret military affairs adopted Waldeck's operational plan. It then boiled down to ensuring the cooperation of Madrid and Brussels, because the regents wanted Spain to shoulder the cost of the troops hired from Münster and Brunswick-Osnabrück. In a resolution promulgated on 21 December 1676, William III and the committee for secret military affairs issued a warning to the king of Spain, pointing out to him that in the Spanish Netherlands

> without two armies ... nothing in the world can be accomplished or any harm done to the enemy. That they [the States-General] would be pleased to help with the formation of one of the said armies ... but that his Majesty may rest assured that the army of this State shall not enter into the campaign if his Majesty has not also arranged that another army is assembled there [in the Spanish Netherlands] in due time.

William III had no intention of being forced to stand idly by for the third year in succession while the French captured one town after the other, 'because this enemy was much stronger and more powerful in the field than all the troops, both of this State and that of his Majesty, which could be assembled'.[86] The Republic's unequivocal tone made a forceful impression in Madrid, at the very moment the power struggle at the Spanish court was reaching a climax. In early January 1677 Don Juan marched on Madrid together with eighteen Castilian *grandes*, the majority of Aragon's nobility and an army of 15,000 men. He made his entry on 23 January, whereupon Charles II consigned the charge of government to him and banished the queen dowager to Toledo. Don Juan was a champion of a plucky war policy and promised the Republic that Spain would deploy

---

[85] GA, AHGC 1218, 'La disposition des armées pour la campagne de l'an 1677', Culemborg, 5 December 1676 (quotes); AHGC 1240, Lists of troops for the siege of Charleroi; AHGC 1232, Georg Friedrich von Waldeck, Culemborg, 5 December 1676, with 'La distribution de la milice Hollandoise pour l'anné 1677' as an appendix.
[86] HUA, ASU 637-15, Secret res. SG, 21 December 1676.

25,000 men for the campaign in the Spanish Netherlands in 1677.[87] Waldeck and Van Weede-Dijkveld travelled to Brussels immediately for further discussions with Villa Hermosa. He swore to them that he was doing everything possible to hire the German troops and that he was not only negotiating with the bishops of Münster and of Osnabrück but with the duke of Brunswick-Celle as well, 'but as the whole thing rolls [i.e. depends] on the remittances from Spain, which have not been sent yet, everything remains uncertain'. Villa Hermosa warned Waldeck not to cherish any overly high expectations of the coming campaign, because even if the German auxiliary troops were to arrive in the Spanish Netherlands soon it would not be possible to begin the intended offensive into Hainaut directly, 'because there would be no means of finding the bread nor the forage, and the only thing that one could do would be to have the troops advance from the Brabant side and above all from Flanders, in order to be able to prevent the enemy making further progress'.[88] For his part Waldeck advised Villa Hermosa to make haste with the negotiations with the bishop of Münster, 'because he treaties with the whole world'.[89]

The French offensive began on 1 March 1677, when they appeared before Valenciennes, where there was a garrison numbering just 1,150 men. William III assembled the Dutch troops near Roosendaal in all haste.[90] The levying of new recruits was by then largely complete, so he had 30,000 men at his disposal, including 3,800 Spaniards.[91] However, the delivery of forage constituted a major problem, because no hay or oat magazines had been established, as noted above, which forced William III to remain near Antwerp until early April.[92] In the meantime, on 17 March, the French had taken Valenciennes by storm. Louis XIV then ordered the simultaneous besieging of Cambrai and Saint-Omer. On 22 March the main French army under the personal command of the Sun King invested Cambrai, and the opening of the trenches followed six days later. On 4 April the duc d'Orléans did the same before Saint-Omer. William III reached Bruges that same day. The captain-general of the Union considered Cambrai to be lost, but he was determined not to abandon the garrison of Saint-Omer to its fate. In the rush he neglected to have the battleground thoroughly reconnoitred,

---

[87] Krämer, *Nederlandsch-Spaansche diplomatie*, pp. 265 and 267–8; Lynch, *Spain under the Habsburgs*, II, pp. 265–7.
[88] GA, AHGC 1218, 'Rapport de son Exc. [Waldeck] touschant la conférence avec M.r le Duc de Villa Hermosa', The Hague, 12 February 1677, minute.
[89] GA, AHGC 1125, Georg Friedrich von Waldeck to Everard van Weede-Dijkveld, The Hague, 12 February 1677, minute.
[90] H. Heteren wrote to Godard Adriaan van Reede-Amerongen on 2 March 1677: 'All the regiments, on horse as well as on foot, are on the move and several of them have already arrived at the rendezvous [near Roosendaal].' HUA, HAA 2817.
[91] Knoop, *Willem den Derde*, II, p. 251; Rooms, 'Materiële organisatie', p. 41.
[92] HUA, HAA 2732, Godard van Reede-Ginkel to his father, Amerongen, 14 March 1677; Müller, *Wilhelm III und Waldeck*, II, p. 336, E no. 2, William III, Breda, 28 March 1677.

an omission that Luxembourg and d'Humières, the two *maréchals* who were assisting Monsieur, would exploit to the full.

On receiving news of the approach of the Dutch-Spanish army, the duc d'Orléans had established a forward position by Mont-Cassel, about fifteen kilometres west of Saint-Omer. William III was intending to surprise the French in their positions on 10 April, but 'was hampered by a little brook that ran between us and the enemy'. At the break of day on 11 April 1677, the Dutch and Spanish troops marched across the brook, 'yet found, unexpectedly, that there was another little brook that separated us from the enemy'. This gave Monsieur, Luxembourg and d'Humières the opportunity to range their troops in battle array without having to hurry. Moreover, in the course of the night reinforcements had arrived from the main French army, so the French were 5,000 men stronger than the allies. The battle of Mont-Cassel began at ten o'clock in the morning and raged over the whole length of the battle order. The decisive moment fell when the French cavalry managed 'to assail our left wing in the flank', as Van Weede-Dijkveld described it to the Council of State. Two Dutch battalions took to their heels and dragged along three or four more in their wake. William III therefore saw no alternative but to order the retreat to Ypres.[93] The French did not follow on, but baggage, munitions and artillery had to be abandoned on the battlefield. The field deputy Nicolaas Witsen informed Grand Pensionary Fagel about the defeat the following day:

> The spilling of blood that took place there was terrible on both sides.... I had to leave all my baggage and managed to rescue myself from many perils, and at the same time saved the Land's money, which I threw in all haste into the oat sacks, cut free the horses from the waggons and flung it onto their backs.[94]

According to French estimates the Dutch army had suffered 3,000 dead and 4,000 to 5,000 wounded. They estimated their own losses at 1,200 dead and 2,000 wounded.[95] The garrison of Saint-Omer maintained its defence until 22 April, but then had no choice but to capitulate. Cambrai had fallen five days earlier.

The defeat at Mont-Cassel caused but little controversy in the Republic: there was no hint of panic, rather a mood of resignation. There was criticism of the nonchalant manner in which the Dutch troops had approached the French position and of the five to six battalions taking to their heels, but to counterbalance this the bulk of the Dutch army had fought courageously and the French had gained 'only' a tactical victory. They were content with rounding off the sieges

---

[93] HUA, HAA 2818, Everard van Weede-Dijkveld to the Council of State, Ypres, 12 April 1677 (quotes); Knoop, *Willem III*, II, pp. 254–6.
[94] NA, RAZH, AGF 121, Nicolaas Witsen to the Delegated Councillors of Holland, Ypres, 12 April 1677.
[95] Japikse, *Willem III*, II, pp. 60–1; Knoop, *Willem den Derde*, II, p. 257; Lynn, *Wars of Louis XIV*, p. 150.

of Saint-Omer and Cambrai. The French troops then returned to the garrisons and Louis XIV returned to France. 'The French have also led away their army to refresh, so most of her fire has for this year already been spewed out', a correspondent of Van Reede-Amerongen commented.[96]

The pause in hostilities made it possible for the Republic to redress the losses suffered. William III reaped the benefits of the States of Holland's decision of 19 July 1673 henceforth to reimburse the company commanders for the outlay needed to replace soldiers and cavalrymen lost in action. Johan Pesters expected that, with the levying of recruits and the amassing of seventeen battalions from the garrisons, the Dutch army would already be fully deployable again by the end of May 1677. He therefore felt confident about the rest of the campaign,[97] especially because Villa Hermosa was at last making haste with the hiring of the German troops. On 24 April the Spanish governor-general concluded a subsidy treaty with the bishop of Münster for the provision of 9,000 men and the following day he also reached agreement with the representative of the duke of Brunswick-Osnabrück, 'whereupon this lord shall head here shortly with his troops', a force of 7,000 men. Soon thereafter Brussels concluded a contract with his brother, the duke of Brunswick-Celle, who pledged to furnish 8,000 men.[98] The total number of German subsidy troops ran to 24,000 men 'to which number the Spanish shall add 5,000 to 6,000 men to [be able to] act independently of His Highness, who is set to march with 30,000 men in 14 days to 3 weeks [counting from 8 May]'.[99] At the end of May or by early June at the latest, the allies would at last have 'two considerable armies, both capable of being able to act and to face the enemy', at their disposal in the Spanish Netherlands.[100] The French had begun the first round of the 1677 campaign in spectacular fashion. William III and Villa Hermosa hoped to wreak revenge on Louis XIV in the second round by taking Charleroi, and if the Imperial army under the command of Charles V of Lorraine (1643–1690) – he had succeeded his uncle as duke of Lorraine in 1675 – were to lay siege to Thionville simultaneously, then France would be threatened with invasions from two sides.[101]

[96] HUA, HAA 2819, H. Heteren to Godard Adriaan van Reede-Amerongen, The Hague, 8 May 1677.
[97] HUA, HAA 2818, Johan Pesters to the same, Utrecht, 19 and 24 April 1677. See also HUA, HAA 2818, H. Heteren to the same, The Hague, 24 April 1677.
[98] HUA, HAA 2819, Everard van Weede-Dijkveld to the same, Brussels, 25 April 1677.
[99] HUA, HAA 2819, H. Heteren to the same, The Hague, 8 May 1677.
[100] HUA, HAA 2819, Everard van Weede-Dijkveld to the same, Brussels, 25 April 1677.
[101] CWB, II, ii, nos. 182 and 183, William III to Charles V of Lorraine, The Hague, 11 and 15 March 1677.

The allied counter-offensive founders (June–December 1677)

In June the preparations for the allied counterattack were in full swing. The blockading force of 12,000 men intended for Maastricht was assembled by Maaseik, the 24,000 troops from Münster and Brunswick were on their way to Spanish Brabant to join Villa Hermosa and the Spanish troops, and in mid-July 1677 William III was close by Dendermonde with the Dutch army, which boasted an effective strength of 26,900 men in rank and file.[102] William III and Villa Hermosa were in command of a combined total of 60,000 men. They advanced to meet the French army, 'but it is not in their interest to fight [another] battle this campaign', opined Major-General Godard van Reede-Ginkel. 'What we shall do now, time will tell. It must come to a siege.'[103]

Louis XIV had indeed ordered Luxembourg to restrict himself to the defensive during the summer. Besides a military argument – now that the allies were in the field at full strength it would be much more difficult to achieve new conquests – there was also a political argument that weighed heavily in the French king's decision. France could not wage war *too* successfully, because that would force the king of England to intervene in favour of the Republic and Spain.[104] Louis XIV bore in mind that public opinion in England was ill-disposed towards him and that the French victory at Mont-Cassel had not been received kindly. 'The French reports at first informed us ... that they had won a very complete victory.... But when the French noticed the ill effect that the elevation of the magnitude of our defeat caused to [English] feelings, [they] afterwards attempted to extenuate it', according to Coenraad van Beuningen, the States-General's envoy extraordinary to the English court.[105] The French finances did not permit allowing the war to drag on unnecessarily for years.[106] The Sun King had, after all, already reaped ample reward. Lorraine, Alsace and Franche-Comté were occupied by French troops and the *frontière de fer* was well-nigh complete: Ypres was the only missing link in the double line of defence.

On 6 August 1677 William III appeared with the Dutch army before the ramparts of Charleroi.[107] Meanwhile Villa Hermosa kept an eye on the main French army – approximately 50,000 men – near Ath. 'The enterprise is grandiose,' Johan Pesters wrote from William III's headquarters, 'but I still have my

---

[102] HUA, HAA 2820, H. Heteren to Godard Adriaan van Reede-Amerongen, The Hague, 8 June 1677; HAA, HUA 2821, Johan Pesters to the same, Kalken, 16 July 1677; HUA, HAA 3209, 'Lijste de la force de chacque régim[en]t de cavallerie et infanterie selon la revue faite par S.A. [William III] au camp de Drongene et Marikercke, le 9.me juillet 1677'.
[103] HUA, HAA 2732, Godard van Reede-Ginkel to his father, near Aalst, 21 July 1677.
[104] Sonnino, 'Louis XIV and the Dutch War', pp. 167–8.
[105] CWB, II, ii, no. 194, Coenraad van Beuningen to William III, Westminster, 11/26 April 1677.
[106] Malettke, 'Ludwigs XIV. Außenpolitik', p. 56.
[107] GA, AHGC 1240, 'La liste des régiments de l'infanterie' (11,923 foot) and 'Liste de la cavallerie' (4,577 horse).

concerns.'[108] Van Reede-Ginkel shared his apprehension, because 'their weakest fort is in a better state than the best of the Spanish'.[109] William III prepared The Hague for a protracted and costly siege operation. Charleroi was 'because of [its] situation as well as [its] fortifications of a very considerable strength ... and furnished with everything required for a vigorous defence', he informed the States-General. He estimated the garrison to be 5,000 strong.[110] On 8 August a first convoy arrived in the camp of the besiegers with twenty-four demi-cannon and a second convoy was expected two days later. It was, however, doubtful whether the artillery could be brought to bear, because Luxembourg had left his position by Ath and was approaching Charleroi at speed.[111] In the night of 8/9 August he crossed the River Sambre, placing him about twenty kilometres southwest of the invested town. According to William III, '[I]f he continues his march he could be with us tomorrow. It was thereupon decided that the lord duke of Villa Hermosa would likewise cross the Sambre with the army of the allies [the Spaniards and Germans] this coming night [9/10 August] in order to cover the Republic's army and to observe the enemy.'[112] Villa Hermosa failed to catch up with Luxembourg. As the Dutch resident in Brussels observed, the French *maréchal* then dug himself in

> at an advantageous position ... from where he can seriously inconvenience the convoys [between Brussels and the Dutch army] and, in the opinion of all those who are aware of the state of the terrain in the vicinity of Charleroi, he cannot be engaged in any battle, [the French army] being covered by a forest and a small river.... Added to which the forage is starting to run low, [so] one is convinced that the armies shall not be able to hold out there for more than three days.

On 14 August 1677 William III was for the second time in his military career forced to raise the siege of Charleroi.[113] Soon thereafter he left the army and travelled to The Hague.

The failed siege of Charleroi was a bitter disappointment for William III. He now also understood that the restoration of the 1659 situation was unachievable, but at the same time he realised that the war could not be ended unless the Republic had the guarantee that the Spanish Netherlands could serve as an effective buffer against France. As noted, this required the retrocession of various

---

[108] HAA, HUA 2821, Johan Pesters to Godard Adriaan van Reede-Amerongen, before Charleroi, 7 August 1677.
[109] HAA, HUA 2732, Godard van Reede-Ginkel to the same, near Aalst, 21 July 1677.
[110] NA, SG 12579.106, William III to the SG's committee for secret affairs, before Charleroi, 7 August 1677.
[111] NA, RAZH, AGF 117, Quartermaster-General Maximiliaan van Hangest-Genlis, called d'Yvoy, before Charleroi, 10 August 1677.
[112] NA, SG 12579.106, William III to the SG's committee for secret military affairs, before Charleroi, 9 August 1677.
[113] NA, SG 12588.107, Thomas van Sasburch to the *griffier* of the SG, Brussels, 15 August 1677.

strongholds in the Southern Netherlands which had been captured by France, and English assistance was needed to achieve this. William III knew that he could depend on the support of Parliament in this – within the English 'nation' there was consensus that the Spanish Netherlands 'must be preserved to such an extent that they can serve as a barrier against the French'[114] – but the position of the English king was ambiguous. Charles II was still receiving money from Louis XIV. To gain greater insight into the relations between Parliament and the Crown, William III sent his confidant Hans Willem Bentinck (1649–1709) to London. Bentinck was to sound out the king concerning his readiness to arbitrate a general peace settlement between the allies and France. Seeing in this an opportunity to profile himself as an arbiter, Charles II agreed to this proposal and he also granted his consent to a marriage between his fifteen-year-old niece Mary Stuart (1662–1694) and his nephew William III. James, duke of York was firmly set against this, but the Lord Treasurer, Thomas Osborne (1631–1712), earl of Danby, had convinced Charles II that a union of the champion of the Protestants with James's oldest daughter was a suitable means of assuaging the distrust that James's second marriage to the Catholic Maria d'Este had caused in Parliament.[115]

The marriage of William III and Mary Stuart was solemnised on 4/14 November 1677. Charles II then exerted pressure on Louis XIV to break off his assault on the Spanish Netherlands and reach a peace agreement. The king of France would be allowed to keep Franche-Comté and various strongholds that his troops had captured in the Spanish Netherlands, but in accordance with The Hague's demands he would be obliged to return Tournai, Courtrai, Oudenaarde, Ath, Charleroi and Condé to Spain and to cede Maastricht to the Republic.[116] The position of the king of England was not to Louis XIV's liking. He ordered a limited winter offensive in Hainaut in order to demonstrate beyond all question that he would not allow anyone to lay down the law to him. D'Humières was ordered to capture Saint-Ghislain, the possession of this small fortified town being important with a view to a future siege of Mons.

At the end of October 1677 the allied troops were dispersed across the winter quarters. Waldeck's headquarters were in Mechelen (Malines) and Villa Hermosa's in Brussels. The hibernal pause was but short, because in early November the French began to stir. Waldeck suspected that d'Humières had designs on Saint-Ghislain or Halle and he therefore asked Villa Hermosa to consider billeting more troops in Hainaut and Brabant. The Spanish governor-general

---

[114] CWB, II, i, no. 506, Frederik van Reede-Lier, Coenraad van Beuningen and Willem van Haren, Sr. to Gaspar Fagel, Westminster, 22 May/1 June 1674.
[115] David Onnekink, 'The Anglo-Dutch Favourite. The Career of Hans Willem Bentinck, 1st Earl of Portland 1649–1709', Ph.D. diss., Utrecht University (2004), pp. 35–7.
[116] Franken, *Coenraad van Beuningen*, pp. 153–4 and 156; Troost, *William III*, p. 145, and 'De buitenlandse politiek van William III en het begin van de Britse evenwichtspolitiek', in *Jaarboek Oranje-Nassau Museum 2002* (Rotterdam 2003), pp. 41–57, esp. 48.

would, however, hear nothing of it, 'because the regiments here [near Brussels] and in the environs ... were enough to safeguard Halle if the enemy would want to attack it, and should he have designs on Saint-Ghislain that one would have to bear it, being in any case unable to prevent it due to a lack of forage and the requisite magazines'. But when the French actually invested Saint-Ghislain on 1 December, Villa Hermosa took a different view. He now exhorted Waldeck to head there immediately with a relief force, 'because on this town being lost, Mons ... would also certainly follow'.[117] Waldeck had little choice but to heed Villa Hermosa's request, despite him being able 'to see well in advance ... that it shall be very difficult, yea, I might well say impossible [to assist Saint-Ghislain's garrison] because of a shortage of everything that is required for the subsistence of the militia'.[118] Saint-Ghislain fell on 10 December, whereupon Waldeck called off the relief operation.

The French demonstrate their superiority once again – the Peace of Nijmegen (1678)

The year 1677 was a watershed in the war which had been raging in the Spanish Netherlands since 1674. The failure of the siege of Charleroi in combination with the bloody battle of Mont-Cassel undermined any popular support in the Republic for continuation of the war. '[I] do not see us being equal to France with battles', to quote the assessment of Johan Pesters.[119] Only a minority still believed it was feasible to bring France to her knees militarily. Nobody in the Republic doubted the courage, discipline and proficiency of the Dutch troops, but the struggle against the French was too unevenly balanced. It would only be possible to reverse the fortunes of war in the Spanish Netherlands if Spain were (like the Republic) to supply 30,000 men, year in year out, for the operations there and, moreover, shoulder responsibility for building up substantial forage magazines, but the Spanish finances did not allow this and the Republic was neither willing nor able to bear these extra costs. Van Weede-Dijkveld, who in the winter of 1677/8 held discussions with Villa Hermosa in Brussels about the coming year's campaign, complained in a letter to the *griffier* of the States-General: 'I must admit to Your Honour that the finances here are so depleted and the income so minimal that if the king of Spain does not send significant sums the result shall be utter chaos.' Van Weede-Dijkveld warned that as a consequence not only the

---

[117] NA, RAZH, AGF 239, Everard van Weede-Dijkveld to William III, Brussels, 7 December 1677, transcript.
[118] NA, SG 12579.106, Georg Friedrich von Waldeck to the SG, Mechelen, 3 December 1677 and n.d., received 8 December 1677 (quote); same to the *griffier* of the SG, Malines, 4 December 1677.
[119] HUA, HAA 2818, Johan Pesters to Godard Adriaan van Reede-Amerongen, Utrecht, 19 April 1677.

German subsidy troops but also the Spanish army remained unpaid and 'instead of being augmented with recruits it is every day subject to incredible diminution and desertion'.[120] Villa Hermosa complained that for the field operations in 1678 he would be able to provide 16,000 men at most.[121] Together with the Dutch troops this amounted to an army of approximately 46,000 men. An army of this strength was not only too small for an offensive war but would also be unable to obstruct the French continuing their campaign of conquest in the Spanish Netherlands. Concluding a peace before the new campaign was opened presented a solution to this dilemma, but the disadvantage with this was that the odium of treason would beset the Republic, because Spain and the emperor continued to insist on the restoration of the geopolitical situation as it was in 1659, which had been agreed in the treaties of 1673. The Republic would therefore have to make peace with France independently of her two allies. For William III this was out of the question; he still hoped to be able to broker a general peace settlement. In order to force William III to abandon his opposition to a separate peace, Louis XIV instructed *Maréchal* d'Humières to capture Ghent and then Ypres, which would leave just Brabant and parts of Hainaut under Spanish rule within the Spanish Netherlands.[122]

Maréchal d'Humières invested Ghent with 60,000 men on 3 March 1678. Louis XIV arrived in the French encampment the following day and on 5 March the trenches were opened in his presence. The 500 Spanish defenders surrendered a week later. Immediately after the taking of Ghent, the Sun King left for Ypres with the main French army. There was a garrison of 3,000 men in this town, but no sign of a robust defence. Ypres capitulated on 26 March, after just seven days under siege.[123] In the wake of these two conquests, on 15 April Louis XIV let it be known that he would suspend hostilities until 10 May 1678 in order to give the allied diplomats in Nijmegen the opportunity to agree to the French peace terms, of which the three most important articles read: 1. in exchange for the return to Spain of Ghent, Courtrai, Oudenaarde, Ath and Charleroi, the king of Spain must cede Franche-Comté, Ypres, Saint-Omer, Aire, Cambrai, Bouchain, Valenciennes and Condé to France; 2. Maastricht will be returned to the Republic; 3. all the Swedish territories which Brandenburg and Denmark had conquered since 1675 had to be restored to Sweden.[124] Louis XIV expected that these conditions would be acceptable to the States-General, because the Spanish Netherlands would then be able to fulfil its role as a buffer zone between

---

[120] NA, SG 12588.109, Everard van Weede-Dijkveld to the *griffier* of the SG, Mechelen, 13 March 1678.
[121] Rooms, 'Materiële organisatie', p. 55.
[122] Bluche, *Louis XIV*, p. 258.
[123] Ibid., pp. 259–60; Knoop, *Willem den Derde*, II, pp. 293–6; Lynn, *Wars of Louis XIV*, p. 153.
[124] Bluche, *Louis XIV*, p. 261; G. Livet, 'Colbert de Croissy et la diplomatie française à Nimegue', in *The Peace of Nijmegen*, pp. 181–223, esp. 194; Troost, *William III*, p. 145.

the Republic and France. However, the French ultimatum was not favourably received. After the fall of Ghent and Ypres the States of Holland may well have notified William III that there was no reason for him to expect them to provide him with the means to continue the war in 1679, but their distrust of France was equally deep-rooted. Louis XIV stoked up this mistrust himself by insisting on the restoration of the Swedish possessions as a *sine qua non*. This could, after all, only be explained as a French machination to pit Brandenburg and Denmark against the Republic.[125] There was therefore no other option but to assemble the Dutch army and push on with the campaign until Louis XIV had withdrawn his stipulation with respect to Sweden. There was also another reason why it was opportune to allow the war to last a few months longer: after the capture of Ghent and Ypres the king of England could no longer wriggle out of dispatching troops to the Low Countries. In England there were grave concerns that the French were also planning to take Antwerp, Bruges and the seaports of Ostend and Nieuwpoort. This would not only mean the loss of an important market for English merchants; even more threatening was that France would then have bases at her disposal for naval operations in the North Sea. Charles II immediately sent 1,400 English troops to Flanders and had another 20,000 men put in readiness.[126]

On the face of it the English war preparations seemed to make little impression on Louis XIV, because almost immediately after the passing of the deadline he had set, the French seemed to resume the offensive. Van Weede-Dijkveld sent word to the States-General on 18 May 1678:

> Here [in Brussels] one is at present still uncertain about what the king of France shall undertake with his army.... Some reports imply that Bruges is the target and the lord duke [of Villa Hermosa] is also of that opinion. Others [believe] that the king would attack Brussels with the main army .... There are also those who think that Antwerp shall bear the brunt.[127]

But Louis XIV left Brussels, Antwerp and Bruges unmolested and he gave the Republic until 15 August to assent to the French ultimatum, because he realised that if his troops attacked one of these three towns then he would leave Charles II of England no option but to have the 20,000 men being held in reserve conjoin with the Dutch-Spanish army in the Spanish Netherlands. Blockading Mons, the last remaining Spanish stronghold in Hainaut, was a less risky means of increasing the pressure on The Hague and Brussels and bending the negotiations in Nijmegen to his will.

---

[125] D.J. Roorda, 'The Peace of Nijmegen. The End of a Particular Period in Dutch History', in *The Peace of Nijmegen*, pp. 17–28, esp. 24–5.
[126] Nesca A. Robb, *William of Orange, A Personal Portrait*, ii: *The Later Years, 1674–1702* (London 1966), p. 108; George Satterfield, *Princes, Posts and Partisans. The Army of Louis XIV and Partisan Warfare in the Netherlands (1673–1678)* (Leiden 2003), p. 38.
[127] NA, SG 12588.109, Everard van Weede-Dijkveld to the SG, Brussels, 18 May 1678.

A French cavalry corps of between 6,000 and 7,000 men surrounded Mons at the end of June 1678. Luxembourg took up a position with the main French army of about 50,000 men near the abbey of Saint-Denis, about seven kilometres northeast of Mons. As soon as news of the blockade reached Brussels, Van Weede-Dijkveld travelled to the French headquarters together with Jacob Boreel (1630–1697). Boreel, an Amsterdam regent, had arrived in the capital of the Spanish Netherlands in early May to persuade Villa Hermosa to accept the French peace conditions. The Republic's diplomats asked Luxembourg and the *intendant* Louis Robert whether they ought to interpret the blockade of Mons as a resumption of the campaign in the Spanish Netherlands. The French *maréchal* denied this. Louis XIV had in fact instructed him to negotiate a truce with Villa Hermosa and then 'march out of the territory of the king of Spain' with the French troops. All the king of France expected in exchange for this generous gesture was that no victuals would be conveyed to Mons and no troops would enter or leave until the peace was concluded and the ratifications exchanged, 'and in order to be assured of this, only forty or fifty squadrons of cavalry or dragoons … would be left surrounding the town'. Van Weede-Dijkveld and Boreel pointed out to Luxembourg and Robert that a blockade would have the same effect as a formal siege and that this was acceptable neither to Brussels nor The Hague, 'it not being reasonable that during a truce the king of France, no more than the king of Spain, be allowed to invest any places … [while] Mons would by a lack of provisions be placed in dire circumstances and forced to capitulate'. Luxembourg and Robert eventually agreed to allow food to be delivered to Mons intermittently.[128] According to Villa Hermosa this undertaking was of no value whatsoever, because in Mons 'many necessary things are lacking … and there is no confidence that they [the defenders] shall be able to subsist for more than fourteen days or three weeks at the outside'.[129] From this Van Weede-Dijkveld and Boreel drew the conclusion that Luxembourg and Robert were not 'acting candidly'.

At the peace conference in Nijmegen the French negotiators were by now behaving just as intractably. They categorically refused 'to evacuate the places to be restored before the Swedes have been given effective satisfaction'. For William III this provided sufficient proof that Louis XIV did not truly desire peace.[130] The French stance had repercussions in England, too. On 26 July 1678 the States-General and the king of England entered into an offensive alliance, in which it was specified that England and the Republic would jointly attack France if Louis XIV had not forgone his demand with regard to Sweden by

---

[128] NA, SG 12588.109, Everard van Weede-Dijkveld and Jacob Boreel to the SG, Brussels, 1 July 1677.
[129] NA, SG 12588.109, Thomas van Sasburch to the SG, Brussels, 14 July 1678.
[130] NA, SG 12588.109, Everard van Weede-Dijkveld and Jacob Boreel to the SG, Brussels, 3 July 1678 (quote); NA, Collectie Overige Gezanten en Legatiearchieven 130, same to Coenraad van Beuningen, envoy of the SG in London, Brussels, 15 July 1678.

11 August.[131] That very same evening William III left The Hague for Brussels, where the Dutch army (30,000 men) was assembled. 'Everything here [is] in readiness and the Republic's army ready to march in order to attempt to lift the blockade of Mons', Van Weede-Dijkveld and Boreel wrote to the Republic's envoy in London.[132]

The French negotiators in Nijmegen dropped the Swedish demand at the very last moment. At midnight on 10 August 1678 the Republic and France made peace. However, William III had in the meantime arrived in the vicinity of Mons with the Dutch troops. Including 15,000 troops from Brunswick, Brandenburg and Münster, a couple of hundred Englishmen and some Spanish cavalry, he had an army of approximately 45,000 men at his disposal.[133] On 14 August the allies launched a storm assault against the French positions near Saint-Denis. William III later contended that he was unaware that the peace had by then been concluded.[134] It is impossible to ascertain whether he was speaking the truth. It is, however, certain that the smashing of the French blockade was militarily desirable. Spain was still at war with France, after all, and if Mons were to fall into French hands then it was doubtful whether Louis XIV would willingly give up this stronghold again. William III achieved an important victory at Saint-Denis. Johan Pesters, who witnessed the battle, was jubilant: 'The heavens be thanked for this victory, seeing as one stormed not a town but a whole army and caused it to take flight.'[135] The superior strength of the French army notwithstanding, after more than six hours of intense fighting Luxembourg saw no alternative but to beat a retreat, 'leaving behind the dead, injured, tents and provisions.'[136] The allies had suffered about 3,000 dead and wounded, primarily Dutch infantry. The French losses amounted to an estimated 2,500 men.

The victory at Saint-Denis had the desired effect: Luxembourg raised the blockade of Mons and on 17 September 1678 France and Spain also made peace. Louis XIV pledged to restore to Spain those towns annexed by France in 1668, namely Charleroi, Binche, Ath, Oudenaarde and Courtrai, and to evacuate Limbourg, Saint-Ghislain and Ghent (Articles IV and V) immediately after the treaty's ratification. In exchange France obtained the whole of Franche-Comté and the Southern Netherlandish towns of Maubeuge, Condé, Valenciennes, Bouchain, Cambrai, Aire, Saint-Omer, Menen (Menin), Warneton (Waasten), Ypres and Cassel (Article XI).[137] The French withdrew from Maastricht at the

---

[131] Bluche, *Louis XIV*, p. 261.
[132] NA, Collectie Overige Gezanten en Legatiearchieven 130, Jacob Boreel and Everard van Weede-Dijkveld to Coenraad van Beuningen, Brussels, 22 July 1678, transcript.
[133] *Hollantsche Mercurius* (Haarlem 1678), pp. 165 and 167.
[134] Knoop, *Willem den Derde*, II, p. 318.
[135] NA, RAZH, AGF 56, Johan Pesters, at the abbey of Saint-Denis, an hour and a half from Mons, 15 August 1678.
[136] *CWB*, II, ii, no. 296, William III to the SG, by Saint-Denis, 15 August 1678.
[137] GA, AHGC 1136, 'Traitté de la paix entre les couronnes de France & d'Espagne', Nijmegen, 17 September 1678; Bluche, *Louis XIV*, p. 262; Rooms, 'Materiële organisatie', p. 52.

start of November and the Dutch troops returned. The war between France and the Holy Roman Empire was concluded on 5 February 1679: Louis XIV ceded Philippsburg, but Alsace and Lorraine remained under French military occupation. The Sun King had declared his preparedness to return Lorraine to its ousted duke, but under such humiliating terms that their acceptance would have been tantamount to voluntary annexation by France. Duke Charles V decided not to return to Lorraine, but instead to place all hope on a new war between France and the Habsburgs. In the summer of 1679 Brandenburg and Denmark were forced, under French military pressure, to cease their struggle against Sweden and retrocede practically all the conquered Swedish possessions.[138]

Conclusion

'Victory in war', writes the Roman military theorist Vegetius in his renowned *De Re Militari* from the late fourth century, 'does not depend entirely upon numbers or mere courage; only skill and discipline will insure it.... The Ancients, taught by experience, preferred discipline to numbers.'[139] The view articulated by Vegetius resonated widely in the early modern era, with Maurits and Willem Lodewijk as its principal exponents. The emphasis on drill and exercise in the training of soldiers was, after all, the core of the tactical military revolution of the late sixteenth century that they initiated. However, in the second half of the seventeenth century, the marked augmentation of the French army meant that the numerical component became decisive in military enterprises. In combat between a body of disciplined soldiers and a disorderly rabble, victory usually went to the side which operated as a group, but with armies that were fairly similar in training and armament – and in the course of the seventeenth century the tactical reforms of the Nassaus had become widespread across Europe – the number of soldiers was often the deciding factor, 'because God favours the strongest battalions',[140] to quote a saying that was often heard in military circles. This was the key problem the Republic faced in the years 1674–1678. The 'Guerre de Hollande' had seen the revival of the Dutch army as one of the most disciplined and most highly trained European armies, but this was not enough to stop France making her conquests in the Spanish Netherlands, never mind bring her to her knees militarily. The Holy Roman Empire's declaration of war, the arrival of the Imperial army under Souches, the undecided battle of Seneffe and

---

[138] D.E.L. de Boer, *Het oude Duitsland. Een geschiedenis van de Duitse landen van 1450 tot 1800* (Amsterdam 2002), p. 209; McKay, *Rise of the Great Powers*, pp. 35–6.
[139] Vegetius (Publius Flavius Vegetius Renatus), 'The Military Institutions of the Romans', trans. John Clarke, in Thomas R. Phillips (ed.), *Roots of Strategy. The 5 Greatest Military Classics of All Time* (1940; reprint Harrisburg, Penn. 1985), pp. 65–175, esp. 75 and 126.
[140] Th. Bussemaker (ed.), *Archives ou correspondance inédite de la maison d'Orange-Nassau*, 4th series, III (Leiden 1912), no. 605, Notes by Willem Bentinck, 8 December 1756.

the sudden death of Turenne meant that in 1674 and 1675 the French managed to achieve only marginal successes in the Spanish Netherlands, but from 1676 this changed completely. From that year on, Louis XIV and Louvois brought a new factor into the game to ensure the predominance of the French army over the allies. By establishing substantial forage magazines the French could from then on head into the field while the Dutch and Spanish troops still lay scattered across their winter quarters. 'The French with great prudence attack places in the beginning of the Spring, when there is no army to relieve them; and in the Summer, when the whole confederacy [i.e. the allied army] is in the field, they are usually on the defensive, and cover what they have took', a contemporary ascertained in 1677.[141]

The inability of the Spaniards to bring 30,000 men into the field in the Spanish Netherlands every year, as the Republic managed to do, made it extremely difficult for William III to call a halt to the wave of French successes, but it would be incorrect to blame the allied setbacks on this alone. The deficient cooperation between the Republic, Spain and the emperor precluded the possibility of gaining any advantage from developments in the various theatres of war, while the *stratégie de cabinet* placed Louis XIV in a position to achieve this. In addition the weakness of the Spanish field army in the Netherlands was primarily a result of the majority of the Spanish troops having to remain behind to man the garrisons. So long as the French were consistently the first to set out on campaign and thus enjoy the initiative, no improvement could be expected in a situation that was so unfavourable to the allies. This would only be possible if the allies established forage magazines as well, but neither Spain nor the Republic were prepared to shoulder the cost. William III hoped to reverse the fortunes of war in favour of the allies by giving battle, but with the exception of the battle of Saint-Denis (1678) his attempts to defeat the French failed to lead to the desired result. At Seneffe, William III, Monterrey and Souches had allowed themselves to be taken by surprise by Condé – the allies eluded a crushing defeat only because of the discipline and great courage of the Dutch and Spanish infantry – and the inexperience of the allied generals was likewise to blame for the assault on the French position by Mont-Cassel (1677) ending in a fiasco. The sieges of Maastricht (1676) and Charleroi (1677) seemed to promise greater success for William III, but even these undertakings foundered because of a lack of expertise and experience. The revolution in military organisation in the Republic was far from complete. Between 1672 and 1674 the Dutch army had regained its former might and reputation, but without the requisite logistical support, thousands of extra soldiers and experience in the leadership of large-scale undertakings (battles and sieges) there was no chance of the Republic and Spain ever managing to seize the initiative from the French and reversing their

---

[141] Earl of Orrery, *A Treatise on the Art of Warre* (London 1677), quoted in Chandler, *The Art of Warfare in the Age of Marlborough*, p. 18.

conquests. It was, however, impossible for the Republic to bear the costs of a war effort escalated even further on her own. The depletion of Spain's coffers made close cooperation with England a necessity. In 1682 Coenraad van Beuningen expressed this as follows: 'That without England acting powerfully alongside her the Republic can enter into neither an open nor a cold war with France.'[142] Six years later William III would for this very reason sail for England and lay claim to the English throne.

---

[142] Franken, *Coenraad van Beuningen*, p. 208.

Concluding Remarks to Part II

In the second half of the seventeenth century a revolution in military organisation took place in Europe. The 1650s and 1660s saw the establishment of the first modern battle fleets to be composed entirely of warships; the era of the navy being brought to war strength by commandeering and arming merchant vessels was definitively over. The changes that were achieved in the domains of army organisation and growth during the 1660s and 1670s were even more spectacular than the maritime developments. The basis for this was a fundamental shift in relations between state and army; mercenaries were replaced by professional soldiers in the service of a government. Armies of unprecedented size were mobilised and, thanks to special logistical facilities, troop concentrations on a scale hitherto unseen were from then on among the viable military options. In 1678 the effective strength of the French army was 250,000 men, which was three times greater than during the Thirty Years' War. After the Peace of Nijmegen the French army was expanded even further to reach an effective strength of approximately 340,000 men during the Nine Years' War or War of the League of Augsburg (1688–1697) and the War of the Spanish Succession (1701–1713). The effective strength of the Dutch army in the 1630s and 1640s was 60,000 men, from 1675 to 1678 approximately 70,000 men, and during the last four years of the War of the Spanish Succession more than 100,000 men.[1] Difficulties with provisioning meant that field armies had long been subject to a ceiling of between 25,000 and 30,000 men. From 1667, however, strengths of 50,000 to 60,000 men or more were the norm – during the War of the Spanish Succession even the boundary of 100,000 men would be exceeded. The magnitude of the Sun King's wars led to a new form of warfare, namely *'frontière à frontière'*. The Year of Disaster was unique in that the attacker was able to penetrate into the heart of the enemy country at exceptional speed. The 'Forty Years' War' (1672–1712) was primarily fought within fortified zones, of which the *frontière de fer* and the *barrière* are the most renowned. Every offensive foundered within this dense network of strongholds unless one of the belligerents could surpass the opponent militarily. Louis XIV was successful in this from 1674 to 1678, but from the Nine Years' War onward the French and the allied forces (a coalition of the Republic, England and the Holy Roman Empire) were evenly matched.

---

[1] Lynn, 'Recalculating French Army Growth', p. 125; Van Nimwegen, *Subsistentie van het leger*, p. 79. No estimates are available for the effective strength of the Dutch army during the Nine Years' War. At that time its establishment strength was more than 100,000 men. See Stapleton, 'Forging a Coalition Army', pp. 113–19.

The oft-cited marquis de Puységur considered frontier wars with large armies to be the most difficult form of warfare, 'such as they are conducted nowadays with armies of 80,000 men, against others who are of equal strength and who have also sufficiently stocked their bases [i.e. food depots] and their artillery magazines'.[2] The conclusion to Part II of this study places the problem outlined above, which was discussed in detail in Chapters 7 to 11, in a broader context.

Thanks to the tactical reforms introduced by Maurits and Willem Lodewijk, from circa 1600 the Republic had an army at its disposal that could hold its own against the Spanish troops, who had a reputation for invincibility. Frederik Hendrik cherished the Dutch soldiers almost more than Maurits and Willem Lodewijk – he called them 'in general always ... *my children*'[3] – and devoted a great deal of attention to drill and exercise. At the signing of the Peace of Münster the Dutch army was held up as a paragon of discipline and proficiency. Scarcely a decade later there was scant evidence of this to be found. This is usually attributed to the reduction of the Dutch army in 1650 to a strength of only 29,000 men and the dawn of the First Stadholderless Era (1650–1672). This peacetime strength was indeed paltry, even if all the companies were at their establishment levels, which was not the case in practice. 'Many of the rank-and-file soldiers were boys who could barely handle the musket, and such persons who were inhabitants of the garrisoned places and, because of their trade, contracted out their guard duties and watches', Petrus Valkenier opined in his political-military history, *'t Verwerd Europa* (Europe in confusion), which was published shortly after the Year of Disaster. 'There were many mentioned as soldiers [on the muster-rolls] who had been dead for 20 to 30 years. These troops were exercised so little that many did not know how to perform the commands.'[4] Valkenier's dim view of the state of the Dutch army served a political objective – namely justifying his abhorrence of the republicans – but this made it no less true. It would, however, be overly simplistic to place all the blame for the deterioration of the Dutch army in the lap of the De Witt faction. The engineer and quartermaster Christoffel le Hon, compiler of the *Ordres van batailjen* (Orders of battle) military manual which was published in 1672, asserted that the root cause for the lack of military expertise in the Republic lay in the lengthy peacetime after 1648.

> Our Netherlandish war on land having been dormant for about 25 years now (though in the meantime it was once, for a short time, raised from its slumber by the bishop of Münster [i.e. the war with Münster in 1665/6]) is now being reawakened with clamorous belligerence by the king of France.... These *Ordres van bataille* [sic] might [now therefore] be of service to all the commanders and officers.... To the best of my knowledge they have never been made public in print.[5]

---

[2] Puységur, *Art de la guerre*, II, pp. 153 (quote) and 155.
[3] Christoffel le Hon, *Ordres van batailjen*, p. 33v.
[4] Valkenier, *'t Verwerd Europa*, pp. 255–6.
[5] Le Hon, *Ordres van batailjen*, Dedication by the author to William III.

Le Hon had touched on a sore point. Because of the lack of cohesion and tradition in the Dutch army, the experience and proficiency gained during the Eighty Years' War had soon been lost again after 1648. The company was for a long time the only stable component of an army. At the time of Maurits, Willem Lodewijk and Frederik Hendrik, companies were indeed amalgamated into regiments, but the colonels had no direct authority over the day-to-day management of companies. Their principal task was to maintain oversight, in order that the most complete companies headed into the field and the commander-in-chief would therefore have strong battalions at his disposal. In peacetime the regiments had no function and in the reduction of 1650 these larger-scale groupings were not taken into consideration. In organisational terms the Dutch troops did not constitute a unified whole. In this the Dutch army was not unique, but because of the unusual domestic political circumstances the consequences were far more serious in the Republic than elsewhere.

At the inaugural meeting of the first Great Assembly of the States-General in 1651, the States of Gelderland, Holland, Zeeland, Utrecht and Overijssel dispensed with the office of stadholder, which had fallen vacant on the death of Willem II in November 1650, and adopted a series of resolutions that subjected the troops to the authority of the provincial States alone. By doing this they wanted to prevent the Dutch army ever again being misused to influence decision-making processes within the provinces. This is understandable in the light of the assault on Amsterdam (29–30 July 1650), but it did have serious consequences for the deployability and fighting power of the Dutch troops, for, parallel to the abolition of the stadholderate, the highest military office in the Republic also remained unfilled, leaving the Dutch army without a captain-general of the Union and the fleet without an admiral-general until 1672. The Republic's army was effectively fragmented into seven small provincial armies. There was indeed a field-marshal, namely Johan Wolfert van Brederode, but he only exercised command in the field. He had no influence over the commissioning or promotion of officers and nor was he empowered to dismiss company or regimental commanders. From Brederode's death in 1655 through to 1668 the Dutch army also had to manage without a field-marshal. It would be incorrect to surmise that Johan de Witt deliberately ignored the problems that the land-based forces were facing, but he underestimated their gravity and in any case the naval wars with England demanded all his attention.

One must therefore ask why Holland failed to propose the appointment of a captain-general of the Union in the States-General. This was precluded by two factors. In the first place, the highest military office in the Republic was traditionally reserved for a direct descendant of William I of Orange. For the republican faction this was for many years unthinkable, because its adherents regarded it as a first step towards restoration of the stadholderate, apart from the fact that this solution would for a long time have had no practical effect whatsoever. In the 1650s and 1660s, William III (born in 1650) was barely out of the cradle and had no military experience at all. Holland could, of course, have proposed a high-ranking officer for the rank of captain-general of the Union as an alternative, but a proposal to this effect would have had no chance of being accepted. The commander-in-chief of the Dutch army could be appointed only by unanimous vote and for Willem Frederik, already serving as stadholder and captain-general of Friesland and Groningen, it was unacceptable that he should be passed over for this appointment. It was, moreover, well-nigh out of the question that Gelderland, Zeeland, Utrecht and Overijssel would have consented to a candidate from Holland, so the impasse was not broken. Committees and officers proposed all kinds of solutions to rectify the abuses in the Dutch army, but the voluntary cooperation of the provincial States was required for the implementation of these plans, and the upshot of this was that practically nothing happened: 'There is peace, it is not so very urgent now.'[6]

The severity of the Dutch army's deterioration after 1648 was made evident during the war with Münster (1665–1666), when the Dutch succeeded in halting the assault by the bishop of Münster's troops only with the greatest of difficulty. When Louis XIV threatened to overrun the Spanish Netherlands a year later – the War of Devolution (1667–1668) – the regents eventually realised that tackling the abuses in the Dutch army could wait no longer. Johan Maurits of Nassau-Siegen was promoted to field-marshal in 1668, and the Council of State recommended bringing all the regiments to the same strength, keeping the regimental structures intact as far as possible in peacetime, and improving the command structures by establishing an order of rank for officers. This could hardly be described as a true army reform, because Johan Maurits and the Council of State made no proposals to revise the way in which the recruitment and upkeep of the Dutch army were organised. As a result, on the eve of the Year of Disaster several initiatives to raise the standard of the Dutch army had been set in motion, but the discipline was still poor. This was especially worrisome, because during those same years the French army had indeed been structurally reformed. Thanks to the efforts of father and son Le Tellier, the secretaries of state for war, the difference between the paper and effective strengths of the French companies had been reduced to an acceptable level, the exercise of the French Guards regiment had been introduced for the whole of the infantry, and a magazine system had been developed so that supplies of bread and forage to the troops in the field were guaranteed. This meant that the French army was for a while organisationally far superior to other European armies.

It was not until the 'struggle for survival' (*Existenzkampf*), in which the Republic became entangled because of the French invasion in 1672, that a climate was created which made far-reaching structural reforms in the Dutch army possible. At an astonishing speed the Republic's land forces were then transformed from an army of mercenaries into a standing army of professional soldiers. William III collaborated closely with Holland's newly chosen Grand Pensionary, Gaspar

---

[6] Dibbetz, *Groot militair woordenboek*, Foreword.

Fagel, and the field-marshals Johan Maurits and Georg Friedrich von Waldeck. The key to this reform process, which was largely achieved in 1673 and 1674, was a greatly intensified government involvement with its troops. Mercenaries had no close ties with the state for which they fought; for the soldiers and troopers personal loyalty to their captain or rittmaster was most important. The paymasters shared this view until the latter half of the seventeenth century; for them a captain or rittmaster was a military contractor first and foremost, responsible for a company's upkeep as its owner. As noted in Chapter I, the company commanders received no compensation for the replacement of deserters or soldiers who had succumbed to disease or died by accident, and they even had to replace the losses suffered during battles and sieges from their own pockets. The upshot of this was fraud on the muster-rolls.

The year 1673 saw the dawn of a completely new relationship between government and army, with Holland taking the lead. Alongside the companies repartitioned to Holland, the province was at that time also paying the troops repartitioned to the three 'conquested' provinces (Gelderland, Utrecht and Overijssel), almost 69 per cent of the entire Dutch army. From then on the captains and rittmasters received compensation for the costs of recruiting soldiers 'who shall be taken on to replace others who have died in action against the enemy'. Moreover, a captain was entitled to a bonus of the pay of eight soldiers when his company numbered at least seventy men in rank and file,[7] a system that remained in force until 1697. In conjunction with the paymasters turning a blind eye to the captains setting aside part of the soldiers' pay for the replacement of deserters, the state hereby ensured that the company commanders could build up a cash reserve to mitigate the financial risks of desertion, infectious diseases and accidents, because 'deserters and those who have died otherwise are [traditionally] for the captain's reckoning'.[8] At the same time as the States of Holland introduced the above-mentioned pecuniary compensation, the province also revised the system of *solliciteurs-militair*. From then on these financiers had to offer their services to entire regiments, so they could no longer refuse less creditworthy captains and rittmasters.

Government support for the company commanders was the reason why the difference between the paper and effective strengths shrank from 25–30 per cent to just 14 or 15 per cent. No less important was that the Dutch army was in large part maintained at full strength throughout the campaign. The winter months continued to be the main recruitment season, but after a bloody battle the losses were now immediately replenished with fresh recruits. Between 1674 and 1678 William III always had about 30,000 men at his disposal for field operations. The intensified government involvement was also advantageous for the rank and file. Wages were paid more regularly, the colonels ensured that the troops received

---

[7] *Recueil ... betreffende de saaken van den oorlog*, I, no. 9, 'Placaat en ordre op het stuk van de monsteringe', 19 July 1673.
[8] NA, Collectie Bisdom 162, Extract res. RvS, 15 April 1746, Question 21.

a new uniform every two years, the men were assured of their daily bread at set prices due to the establishment of bread magazines, and the wounded received first aid in a field hospital. The six other provinces adopted Holland's measures, though this was far from whole-hearted because of the much heavier financial burden, and William III had to prod the provincial States repeatedly in order to get them to implement the reforms.

The Republic's officers and soldiers had to pay a price for their greater financial security. William III demanded a high degree of preparedness to endure personal sacrifice and the men had to submit to a draconian disciplinary regime. Maurits, Willem Lodewijk and Frederik Hendrik had been hesitant to tackle fraudulent officers, because the provincial States set a poor example by distributing the wages irregularly and incompletely. During the First Stadholderless Era the action taken against abuses was equally timid. The reason for this was that the ties between the officers and the town governments were too close: the regents shielded their kith and kin in the army. By contrast, William III, Johan Maurits and Waldeck were of the opinion that the Dutch troops would never regain their self-confidence if they did not act rigorously against fraud, insubordination and absence without leave, and without regard to the rank or social status of the culprit. The greater financial security that the paymasters provided for the officers not only justified this policy, according to William III, but actually made it viable. During the Eighty Years' War it had been necessary to spare company and regimental commanders, because suitable candidates were difficult to find. Only captains, rittmasters and colonels who had access to sufficient personal means were in a position to maintain the companies and regiments. From 1673 this was no longer a requirement, because from then on the government largely covered the business risk, so capable officers with more limited financial reserves could also be appointed as company commanders. This increased the supply of captains considerably, which for a country with a small population was highly significant. 'Among the Austrians and French [there are] people ... who are soldiers of distinction and who have money, which is something one does not find with us, because most serve for the bread', a Dutch lieutenant remarked.[9] The cavalry was an exception: the mounted arm continued to be the domain of the elite even in the Republic. Horses were very vulnerable, so maintaining a cavalry company was extremely expensive. Officers who were found guilty of fraud by the General Court Martial lost their companies or had to pay stiff fines. In extreme cases they ended up on the scaffold.

William III demanded absolute obedience from the Dutch troops. Insubordination was subject to corporal punishment and troops who were guilty of cowardice in the face of the enemy had to pay with their lives. Maurits, Willem Lodewijk and Frederik Hendrik had been extremely sparing with their veterans;

---

[9] HUA, Familiearchief Van der Muelen, Lieutenant Elias van der Muelen (1720–1784) to his brother Samuel (1715–1775), Auxerre, 10 March 1748. This observation is as applicable to the late seventeenth century as it is to the middle of the eighteenth century.

for William III soldiers were more like 'expendables'. He obviously did not sacrifice Dutch troops pointlessly, but he accepted heavy losses as par for the course. After all, the company commanders received compensation, while in Maurits's day the captains had been required to foot these costs themselves.

Apart from the altered financial conditions under which the captains and rittmasters exercised their profession, there was another reason for the Dutch army's increased resilience during the second half of the seventeenth century. The simplification of volley fire – firing by rank had wholly superseded the complex 'conversion' – meant that soldiers needed fewer hours of drill and decimated units could quickly be rendered deployable again by adding recruits. This largely explains why William III, in contrast to his predecessors, did not hesitate to engage in battle and ordered one storm assault after the other during siege operations. For Maurits, Willem Lodewijk and Frederik Hendrik the tactical reforms were an object in themselves; it was for them solely about achieving a continuous hail of gunfire and they failed to recognise the opportunities presented by the drill programme devised by Johann VII of Nassau-Siegen to train a constant stream of recruits for the army. After 1672 this was self-evident. '[It is] a constant truth that, in case of war or time of recruitment, one can in six to eight weeks train a churl in the drill for him to become a fine soldier', an anonymous officer remarked in the early eighteenth century.[10] Once a recruit had completed this phase of training he could take his place among the ranks and participate in the exercising of the whole battalion.[11] Generals of the late seventeenth century set no great store by complicated tactical formations in which order and fire discipline could only be maintained if the troops performed a complex choreography punctiliously. In the age of Maurits and Willem Lodewijk this had been viable because they were in command of small armies composed of veterans. They were therefore able to supervise everything in person. According to Lieutenant-General Daniël de Savornin (1669–1739), with the much larger armies of the late seventeenth and eighteenth centuries that was an impossibility:

> One knows it is to be found in manifold writings and drawings how highly a figured corpus of infantry was revered at the time of Prince Maurits and thereafter, yet one has seen that subsequently from all these figures has evolved the current, simple and unsurpassed manner of shooting, in advancing as well as retreating, setting aside all that which the speculative and theoretical reasonings have produced.[12]

The 'unsurpassed manner of shooting' that Savornin was referring to was the platoon fire devised and introduced in the Dutch army shortly after the Peace of Nijmegen (1678). This firing system made it possible to fire volley after volley

---

[10] NA, CvdH 106, 'Memorie en reflectie artillery'.
[11] Van Nimwegen, *De Republiek als grote mogendheid*, p. 110.
[12] NA, CvdH 124, Memorandum by Daniël de Savornin.

with the regularity of a clock, in formations just three ranks deep, provided that strict discipline was maintained.

The reforms introduced in the Dutch army during the 'Guerre de Hollande' and the experience gained by the Dutch troops in the many fights against the French in 1672 and 1673 meant that the Republic once again had one of the best trained and most highly disciplined armies in Europe at her disposal. This assessment raises the question of why it proved impossible to halt the French invasion into the Spanish Netherlands. The mediocrity of many Dutch and Spanish generals and the impetuosity of William III were certainly factors, but what was decisive for the outcome of the campaigns of 1674 to 1678 was the unequal balances of power and the superior logistics of the French. The propensity of William III to constantly pursue the offensive and to smash through the impasse by giving battle was to a large degree amplified by frustration about the asymmetric struggle that he was forced to engage in against Louis XIV. For the French there was unequivocal supreme command, so the Sun King could already have over 40,000, 50,000 or even 60,000 men available to him at the start of each campaign in the Spanish Netherlands, while William III could count on only 30,000 Dutch troops. Most of the Spanish army was scattered across garrisons and the Spanish companies were, moreover, in a sorry state. The Spanish governor-general concentrated his field troops only once it became obvious where the French assault would be directed, but usually he had no more than 10,000 to 15,000 men at his disposal. Furthermore, by establishing enormous forage magazines the king of France was in a position to assemble his troops as early as March or April, while the allied forces were still dispersed across the winter quarters. Even the most trenchant critics of Louis XIV had great admiration for the superior French logistics. According to the compiler of the *Vervolg van 't Verwerd Europa* (Sequel to Europe in confusion), the French were able, because

> of their fervent vigilance and diligent work, to come into the field earlier than their enemies every year, which affords them such an appreciable advantage that they conquer towns and provinces before their enemies take to the field with their armies, of which there are testimonies and examples aplenty, to wit, when they conquered Burgundy [Franche-Comté] in the year 1674, the Land [i.e. the bishopric] of Liège as well as the duchy of Limbourg in the year 1675, and Condé and Bouchain in the year 1676, thanks to their early campaigns.[13]

The French springtime offensives could only be brought to a standstill if the Dutch and Spanish troops marched into the field in the spring, but Brussels had no war chest to bear the costs of establishing forage magazines because of the chaos in the Spanish finances and at that time the Republic was not yet prepared to do this. Moreover, it should not be forgotten that military expenditure had risen sharply since the paymasters had decided to provide financial support for the company commanders. In the 1630s – when on paper the Dutch army was

---

[13] *Vervolg van 't Verwerd Europa*, pp. 8–9.

more or less as strong as during the Dutch War – Holland's annual contribution to the war expenditure amounted to an average of 11 to 12 million guilders. In 1675 and 1676 – when Holland was once again paying the usual quota of a good 58 per cent of the defence expenditure – the province's contribution amounted to an average of 17.39 million guilders per annum.

After the Peace of Nijmegen, William III and the regents took stock. Three matters were as clear as day: first, they had to do everything to preserve the knowledge and experience that the Dutch troops had gained over the previous seven years; secondly, France could only be successfully combated in the Spanish Netherlands if the allies also had large forage magazines available to them; and lastly, Spain was incapable of making a substantial contribution to the struggle against France. The security of the Republic could therefore only be assured by defending the Spanish Netherlands in close collaboration with England. The enduring legacy of the Dutch War was the birth of the Republic's standing army, a force the organisation and command structures of which also remained intact in peacetime. This made it possible to bring the Dutch army to wartime strength in 1688 without this being detrimental to quality and deployability. Moreover, during the Nine Years' War which broke out that year, the Dutch, English and Spanish troops had proper forage magazines at their disposal, so the French could at last be given a taste of their own medicine and their enterprises 'rendered fruitless and foiled', as the Council of State observed.[14] The revolution in military organisation of the second half of the seventeenth century was complete.

---

[14] NA, RvS 2227, Petition of 2 October 1702, quoted in Van Nimwegen, *Subsistentie van het leger*, p. 15.

Appendices

Appendix I

Effective strength of the Republic's field army (1591–1646)

Year	Date	Infantry (in rank and file)	Cavalry (in rank and file)	Total strength (officers and men)	Notes
1591	June	9,000	1,500	10,500	Duyck's estimate
	22 July	5,750	1,400	7,150	Counted while crossing the Rhine at Arnhem
	29 July	6,945	1,535	8,480	General review
	16 October	8,500	1,600	10,100	Counted while crossing the Waal at Nijmegen
1592	18 July	5,875			Exercises with the infantry after the conquest of Steenwijk
	20 August		1,500		General review
1593	June	7,250	700	7,950	Duyck's estimate
1594	3 May	9,550	1,872	11,422	Review
1595	13 July	7,800	1,000	8,800	Muster
	19 October	5,392	1,057	6,449	Review
1597	8 September	6,000	1,420	7,420	Review
1598	23 October	6,649	1,767	8,416	Review
1599	18 June	10,625	2,315	12,940	Muster
1600	2 July	10,000	1,200	11,200	Battle of Nieuwpoort; Duyck's estimate
1602	17 June	18,842	5,422	24,264	Muster; cavalry excluding 1,031 *bidets* (servants)
	4 August	15,074	4,827	19,901	Review
	21 September	12,322	4,625	16,947	Review
1603	28 July	8,000	2,800	10,800	Counted while marching past Breda; excluding 3,000 Spanish mutineers
1604	23 August	15,793	1,899	17,692	Muster, excluding 431 *bidets* and 1,325 sick soldiers
1605	28 May	20,000	3,400	23,400	General muster

	28 June	9,827	2,827	12,654	Muster, excluding *bidets*
	26 August	9,502	2,701	12,203	Muster, excluding 847 *bidets*
1606	August	8,400			Estimate
1614	September	14,000	4,000	18,000	Estimate
1629	May	24,000	4,000 to 5,000	28,000 to 29,000	Estimate by Jacob Wijts, sergeant-major general
1632	May	24,000	4,400	28,400	Estimate
	October			12,000	Estimate
1634	September	12,000	3,000	15,000	Estimate
1635	June			20,000	Estimate by Bernhart van Welderen, correspondent of Count Floris II of Culemborg
1637	July	21,000	3,000	24,000	Henry Hexham's estimate
1640	May	21,000 to 22,500	4,600	25,600 to 27,100	Estimate
1641	May	15,000	4,500	19,500	Estimate
1642	June	13,500 to 14,500	5,000	18,500 to 19,500	Estimate
1644	31 May	14,000 to 15,000	4,500	18,500 to 19,500	Willem Frederik's estimate
1645	July	24,000 to 25,000	5,500	29,500 to 30,500	Estimate
1646	20 June	20,000 to 21,000			Estimate

Sources

1591   Duyck, I, pp. 16, 35, 41 and 59.
1592   Duyck, I, pp. 105 and 124.
1593   Duyck, I, p. 241.
1594   Duyck, I, p. 377.
1595   Duyck, I, pp. 611 and 683–4.
1597   Duyck, II, p. 345.
1598   Bor, *Nederlandsche historiën*, IV, p. 482.
1599   NA, SG 4892, 'Monsteringe gedaen den 18.en juny 1599'.
1600   Duyck, II, p. 665.
1602   NA, RAZH, AJvO 2954, 'Staet sommier van[de] monsteringe gedaen den xvii.en juny 1602'; Duyck, III, pp. 389–90, 431–2 and 482–3.
1603   Vervou, *Enige gedenckweerdige geschiedenissen*, p. 150.
1604   NA, SG 4908 and RAZH, AJvO 2954, 'Staet sommier van[de] comp[ag]ni[e]ën ruyteren [en voetknechten] gemonstert in 't leger voor Sluys op ten xxiii.en augusti 1604'.

APPENDICES

1605 NA, SG 4910, Field deputies to the SG, IJzendijke, 5 June 1605; NA, RAZH, AJvO 2956, Muster of 28 June and 'Monsteringe den xxvi augusti 1605 in 't leger voor Deventer gedaen'. In the neighbouring garrisons (Deventer, Zutphen, Zwolle, Rheinberg, Bredevoort and Groenlo), 8,147 men were mustered on 16 August.

1606 NA, SG 4913, 'Liste van de comp[ag]ni[e]ën die bij sijne Ex.cie te velde gebruyckt sullen worden', a total of 84 infantry companies. Based on the muster-rolls for June and August 1605, each infantry company estimated to be 100 strong.

1614 Ten Raa, *Het Staatsche leger*, III, p. 33.

1622 Van der Capellen, *Gedenkschriften* I, p. 106.

1629 HUA, HAA 4128, Jacob Wijts, 'Mémoires des choses qui se sont passées durant le siège de Bois le Ducq en l'an 1629'.

1632 Ten Raa, *Het Staatsche leger*, IV, 59, states that on 22 May the Dutch army had a strength of 281 infantry companies and 58 cavalry companies. The strength of the army is calculated on the basis of Hexham's figures (see 1637). For the strength in October see *Het Staatsche leger*, IV, p. 64.

1634 Ten Raa, *Het Staatsche leger*, IV, p. 76.

1635 GA, AHGC 749, Bernhart van Welderen to Count Floris II of Culemborg, Nijmegen, 7 June 1635. Duffy gives the same strength, see *Siege Warfare*, p. 102.

1637 According to Henry Hexham (Ten Raa, *Het Staatsche leger*, IV, p. 303), at the start of the 1637 campaign an infantry company was on average 85 strong while a cavalry company was 75 strong.

1640 *Archives*, 2nd series, III, no. 599, Hendrik Casimir I to his mother, The Hague, 7 May 1640. He states that the campaign army was comprised of 280 companies of foot and 62 companies of horse at the time. According to Willem Frederik (*Dagboeken*, p. 44), in 1644 a company of foot had an average strength of 75 to 80 men; a company of horse is consistently calculated at 75 strong.

1641 Ten Raa, *Het Staatsche leger*, IV, p. 123.

1642 Tresoar, FSA 30b, Willem Frederik to the Delegated States of Friesland, Schans Ter Voorn, 13 June 1642, minute; Tresoar, FAEVC 713, 'Ordre de bataille comme il a este ordonné par monseigneur le prince d'Orange dans le fort de Voorn le 2e de juin 1642'. At this point the Dutch field army was composed of 180 infantry companies grouped into 36 battalions and 65 cavalry companies.

1644 Visser, *Dagboeken van Willem Frederik*, p. 44.

1645 NA, SG 4982, Field deputies to the SG, Oost Eecklo, 27 July 1645. At this time the Dutch army consisted of 322 infantry companies and 71 cavalry companies, 'altogether fresh and healthy men'.

1646 Visser, *Dagboeken van Willem Frederik*, p. 245.

Appendix II

Important Dutch siege operations (1591–1646) and Spinola's sieges of Ostend (1601–1604) and Breda (1624–1625)

Year	Town	Start of the siege	End of the siege	Duration of the siege	Strength of the garrison	Garrison losses	Besieger's losses	Strength of the garrison on surrender	Capitulation (treaty)
1591	Zutphen	28 May	30 May	3 days	530 men				FW
	Deventer	4 June	10 June	7 days	1,080 men	250 men	135 men	830 men	FW
	Delfzijl	28 June	2 July	5 days	230 men				FW
	Hulst	20 Sept.	24 Sept.	5 days	260 men				FW
	Nijmegen	17 Oct.	21 Oct.	5 days				300 men	FW
1592	Steenwijk	28 May	4 July	38 days	1,080 men	450 men		830 men	A
	Coevorden	27 July	11 Sept.	47 days			1,500 men	560 men	FW
1593	Geertruidenberg	30 March	25 June	87 days	1,000 men		700 men	660 men	FW
1594	Groningen	23 May	19 July	57 days		300 dead	400 dead	395 men	B
1597	Rheinberg	9 Aug.	20 Aug.	12 days				850 men	FW
	Groenlo	11 Sept.	26 Sept.	16 days	1,250 men	100 dead		985 men	C
	Bredevoort	1 Oct.	9 Oct.	9 days	300 men			203 men	D
	Oldenzaal	19 Oct.	22 Oct.	4 days				400 men	E
	Ootmarsum	20 Oct.	21 Oct.	2 days				120 men	E
	Lingen	29 Oct.	12 Nov.	15 days				550 men	E
1601 to 1604	Ostend	5 July 1601	22 Sept. 1604	3 years and 80 days	4,000 men	c. 40,000 dead and wounded	c. 40,000 dead and wounded	3,500 men	FW
1601	Rheinberg	13 June	30 July	48 days	2,000 men	260 dead		1,740 men	FW
1602	Grave	18 July	18 Sept.	63 days	1,340 to 1,440 men			1,200 men	FW
1604	Sluis	23 May	20 Aug.	89 days				3,000 to 4,000 men and 1,400 galley slaves	FW
1624 to 1625	Breda	28 Aug. 1624	5 June 1625	281 days	4,000 men			3,800 men	FW and F
1626	Oldenzaal	24 July	1 Aug.	9 days	1,000 men				FW

Year	Place	Date start	Date end	Duration	Garrison	Casualties	Conditions	Commander
1627	Groenlo	20 July	19 Aug.	31 days	1,360 men		1,000 men	FW
1629	's-Hertogenbosch	1 May	14 Sept.	137 days	2,500 to 3,500 men			FW
1632	Maastricht	10 June	22 Aug.	74 days			1,550 men	FW
1633	Rheinberg	12 May	2 June	22 days			1,660 men	FW
1637	Breda	21 July	7 Oct.	79 days	2,600 to 2,700 men	700 to 800 dead	1,800 to 2,000 'fighting and healthy men'	FW
1641	Gennep	15 June	29 July	45 days	2,200 men	300 dead	1,900 men, including 500 wounded	FW
1644	Sas van Gent	28 July	5 Sept.	40 days	2,350 men	300 dead	2,000 men	FW
1645	Hulst	5 Oct.	3 Nov.	30 days	1,600 men	300 dead	1,300 men	FW

Key
FW Free withdrawal
A   Ban on serving on the right bank of the Rhine for six months
B   Ban on serving on the right bank of the Rhine for three months
C   Ban on serving on the right bank of the Meuse for three months
D   Stormed
E   Ban on serving on the right bank of the Meuse for three months
F   This siege was in fact a blockade

Sources
1591   Duyck, I, pp. 10–12, 15, 22–3, 28 and 64.
1592   Duyck, I, pp. 74, 101, 138 and 140; Hahlweg, *Heeresreform der Oranier*, pp. 689–91.
1593   Duyck, I, pp. 238 and 241.
1594   Duyck, I, pp. 463–4.
1597   Duyck, II, pp. 326, 363, 366, 382, 396–7, 399–400, 430–1 and 436.
1601 to 1604   On the siege of Ostend see pp. 143–4. 173–80 and 183–9.
1601   Duyck, III, pp. 68 and 114–16.
1602   Duyck, III, pp. 419–20 and 479–80.
1604   Orlers, *Nassauschen laurencrans*, p. 203.
1624 to 1625   NA, SG 4946, Field deputies to the SG, Waalwijk, 6 June 1625.
1626   NA, SG 4949, Ernst Casimir and the field deputies to Frederik Hendrik, before Oldenzaal, 25 July 1626, transcript.
1627   NA, SG 4951, Field deputies to the SG, near Groenlo, 21 July; and near Groenlo, 21 August 1627; Frederik Hendrik to the SG, near Groenlo, 20 August 1627.
1629   NA, SG 4953, Field deputies to the SG, Fort Crevecoeur, 1 May 1629. Besides the garrison there were also between 4,000 and 5,000 armed civilians, 'long experienced with the war, all the more because for a long time they have not wanted to receive [i.e. host] a garrison and have several times defended themselves alone against sieges and assaults that one had wanted to undertake against them'. HUA, HAA 4128, Jacob Wijts, 'Mémoires des choses qui se sont passées durant le siège de Bois le Ducq en l'an 1629.'
1632   NA, SG 4961, Field deputies to the SG, near Maastricht, 24 August 1632.
1633   NA, SG 4962, Frederik Hendrik to the SG, near Rheinberg, 3 June 1633; Albert Sonck to the SG, near Rheinberg, 5 June 1633.
1637   NA, SG 4970, Field deputies to the SG, before Breda, 27 July 1637; SG 4971, Field deputies to the SG, before Breda, 8 October 1637; Frederik Hendrik to the SG, Breda, 11 October 1637; HUA, ASU 314–6, Godard van Reede-Amerongen to the States of Utrecht, before Breda, 11 October 1637.
1641   NA, SG 4978, Frederik Hendrik to the SG, Offelen, 29 July 1641; Field deputies to the SG, before Gennep, 29 July 1641.
1644   Visser, *Dagboeken van Willem Frederik*, p. 68.
1645   Visser, *Dagboeken van Willem Frederik*, pp. 177–8.

Appendix III

Fifty-seven Dutch infantry regiments mustered on 20 January and other dates in 1676

Regiment	Number of companies	Effective strength in rank and file	Average company strength	Total no. of officers	Total no. of sick	Date of muster
Foot Guards (H)	25	1648	65.92			
Johan Maurits of Nassau-Siegen (H)	13	799	61.46			
Waldeck (H)	12	762	63.50			
Ditto	12	832	69.33			12 April
Ditto	12	794	66.17			30 April
Ditto	12	792	66.00			2 June
Ditto	12	776	64.67		5	13 August
Aylva (F)	12	608	50.67		22	13 August
Rhinegrave (H)	12	762	63.50			
W.A. van Hornes (H)	13	783	60.23			
Ditto	13	662	50.92		114	13 August
Kirkpatrik (H)	12	636	53.00			
Limburg-Stirum (Gld)	12	570	47.50			
Erbach (H)	12	674	56.17			
Ditto	12	690	57.50		60	13 August
Asperen-Heeswijk (H)	10	418	41.80			
Ditto	10	483	48.30		18	13 August
Watteville (?)	12	674	56.17			
Weede-Walenburg (H)	20	980	49.00			
Birkenfeld (H)	12	561	46.75			
Ditto	12	748	62.33	114 (boys included)		3 May
Ditto	12	572	47.67		107	13 August
J.B. van Hornes (H)	20	1252	62.60			
Cassiopijn (H)	10	567	56.70			
Beaumont (H)	10	649	64.90			
Zobel (H)	10	673	67.30			
Ditto	10	550	55.00		117	13 August
Utenhove (H)	12	537	44.75			
Ditto	12	796	66.33			17 April
Ditto	12	638	53.17		77	13 August
Colyear (H)	12	643	53.58			
Manmaecker-Hofwegen (H)	10	554	55.40			
De la Grandière (H)	13	671	51.62			
Widdrington (Z)	12	281	23.42			
Fenwick (H)	12	476	39.67			
Lillingston (H)	12	489	40.75			
Ter Bruggen (Dr)	10	488	48.80			
Lavergne (H)	12	567	47.25			
Clooster (F)	11	489	44.45			
Slangenburg (H)	10	494	49.40			
Ditto	9	573	63.67	64 + 27		8 July
Ingen Nulant (Gld)	8	371	46.38			
Hundebeck (U)	8	456	57.00			
Eybergen (Ov)	12	429	35.75			
Ditto	12	622	51.83	78 + 36		18 July
Mario (H)	10	571	57.10			
Willem Maurits of Nassau-Siegen (U)	12	710	59.17		67	13 August

Tamminga (G)	15	890	59.33			
Gockinga (G)	15	876	58.40			
Burmania (F)	12	418	34.83			
Reish (?)	9	385	42.78			
Lehndorf (H)	12	674	56.17			
Ditto	12	643	53.58		36	13 August
Reuss van Plauen (H)	12	400	33.33			
Ditto	12	752	62.67	76		1 June
Ditto	10	358	35.80	58	111	27 September
Osnabrück (U)	10	415	41.50			
Eylenburgh (H)	8	297	37.13			
Brumszen (F)	10	449	44.90			
Baye-Du Theill (U)	8	384	48.00			
Horn (H)	11	515	46.82			
Wijnbergen (Gld)	10	544	54.40			
Frederik Hendrik of Nassau-Siegen (H and U)	10	521	52.10			
Ditto	9	479	53.22		30	13 August
Graham (Gld)	12	443	36.92			
Thouars (H)	12	609	50.75			
Coeverden (H and U)	10	458	45.80			
Albrandsweerd (H)	10	455	45.50			
Torsay (H and Z)	13	674	51.85			
Ditto	13	828	63.69			2 June
Stecke (F)	12	454	37.83			November 1675
Ditto	12	269	22.42			December 1675
Ditto	12	242	20.17			
Ditto	12	292 + 266*	46.50			27 January
Frentz (H)	12	701	58.42			
Sedlnitzky (Z)	12	618	51.50			
Schotte (Z)	12	762	63.50			
Mauregnault (Z)	13	821	63.15			
Vrijbergen (Z)	12	742	61.83			

Notes

* 'absent without and with furlough'

The total number of officers in the whole regiment is given, excluding the corporals and the clerk, who are included among the rank and file. The number of boys is given after the plus sign. The guard companies had a divergent strength of 80 men in rank and file.

The province to which the regiment was repartitioned is given in brackets after the names of the colonels: Drenthe (Dr), Friesland (F), Gelderland (Gld), Groningen (G), Holland (H), Overijssel (Ov), Utrecht (U) and Zeeland (Z).

Source: GA, AHGC 1240, 'Review van de armee geschieden den 20 jan[uari] 1676' and muster-rolls for other dates; GA, AHGC 1225, Daniël de Torsay, Ypres, 2 June 1676.

Appendix IV

Five Dutch infantry regiments mustered on various dates in 1676

Date	Regiment	No. of companies	Strength in rank and file	Sick, wounded and on furlough	Deserters	Dead	Average company size in rank and file
17-04	Utenhove	12	796	38	–	–	69.50
13-08	Ditto	12	638	77	83	2	66.66
03-05	Birkenfeld	12	748	60	26	–	69.50
13-08	Ditto	12	572	107	148	24	70.92
12-08	W.A. van Hornes	12	662	137	–	–	66.58
13-08	Willem Maurits of Nassau-Siegen	12	609	82	64	14	64.08
13-08	Zobel	10	550	121	18	14	70.30

Source: GA, AHGC 1240.

Two infantry companies mustered on 19 March 1677

Captain	Effective strength, subdivided into		Sick, wounded and on furlough	Total in rank and file
	Officers	Rank and file		
Antony de Vasch	7 + 3	68	10	78
Frederik Seger	7 + 2	64	–	64

Source: HUA, Familiearchief De Beaufort 84, 'Monsterrolle van de compa[gn]y van de heer capeteyn Antony de Vasch gedaen op de schans [illegible] op den 19 mertius 1677'; muster-roll of the company of Captain Frederik Seger van Wijenhorst, 19 March 1677.

Appendix V

Dutch infantry regiments in the field army mustered on 9 July 1677

Regiment	No. of companies	Total in rank and file	Average per company
Foot Guards	25	1899	75.96
Waldeck	12	775	64.58
Erbach	12	743	61.92
Watteville	12	674	56.17
J.B. van Hornes	20	1430	71.50
Mac Dowell	12	654	54.50
Bellasyse	12	493	41.08
Westley	12	604	50.33
Colyear	12	786	65.50
Albrandsweerd	10	655	65.50
Birkenfeld	12	785	65.42
Brumszen	10	483	48.30
Van Weede	12	753	62.75
Nassau-Ottweiler	12	764	63.67
Rijngraaf	12	772	64.33

Heemstra	11	699	63.55
Mario	10	616	61.60
La Grandière	13	910	70.00
Clooster	11	661	60.09
Sedlnitzky	12	751	62.58
Cassiopijn	10	673	67.30
Aylva	12	634	52.83
Beaumont	10	600	60.00

N.B. The companies of Foot Guards were supposed to number 80 men in rank and file.

Dutch cavalry regiments and dragoons mustered in the field army on 9 July 1677

Regiment	No. of companies	Total in rank and file	Average per company
Dragoon Guards	10	707	70.70
Count of Nassau dragoons	1	142	
Brandt dragoons	8	579	72.38
Life Guards	1	140	
Horse Guards	6	327	54.50
Nassau	6	230	38.33
's-Gravenmoer	6	340	56.67
Flodrof	6	279	46.50
Brederode	6	301	50.17
Truchses	6	299	49.83
Holtzappel	6	322	53.67
Coerland	6	334	55.67
Prince of Nassau	6	277	46.17
Emmenhuysen tot Eppe	6	339	56.50
Montpouillan	6	336	56.00
Weybnom	6	349	58.17
Kingma	6	304	50.67
Croonenburg	6	333	55.50
Burum	6	293	48.83
Quadt-Soppenbroeck	6	339	56.50
Van der Burgt	9	333	37.00
Van Aerssen van Sommelsdijk	7	371	53.00
Berlo	3	171	57.00
Schellart-Doorwerth	6	339	56.50
Van Wassenaer-Obdam	5	282	56.40
Nassau-La Leck	6	325	54.67
Van Reede-Ginkel	6	326	54.33

N.B. All cavalry companies were required to number 80 horses and 69 men (8 officers and 61 rank and file), except for the Life Guards (160 horses strong). A dragoon company stood at 100 horses and 94 men (14 officers, 3 boy-servants and 77 rank and file), except for the Count of Nassau dragoons (200 horses strong).

Source: HUA, HAA 3209 'Lijste de la force de chacque régim[en]t de cavallerie et infanterie selon la Review faite pas S.A. au camp de Drongene et Marikercke, le 9.me juillet 1677'.

Appendix VI

The strength of the field armies in the Spanish Netherlands (1674–1678)

Year		Dutch troops	Spanish troops	Imperial troops	German troops	Total allied forces	French	Notes
1674	May	24,000 men	10,000 men			34,000 men	40,000 men	
	11 Aug.	30,000 men	15,000 men	25,000 men		70,000 men	50,000 men	A
1675	May	30,000 men					40,000 men	
	June	30,000 men	5,000 men			35,000 men	50,000 to 60,000 men	
	July	25,000 men	4,000 men			29,000 men	25,000 to 30,000 men	
	August						40,000 men	
1676	April	28,000 men	13,000 men			41,000 men	60,000 men	
	July	36,500 men	6,000 men		13,500 men	56,000 men	40,000 to 45,000 men	B
1677	April	26,000 men	4,000 men			30,000 men	60,000 men	C
	11 April	26,000 men	4,000 men			30,000 men	35,000 men	D
	August	30,000 men	6,000 men		24,000 men	60,000 men	50,000 men	
1678	March						60,000 men	
	14 Aug.	30,000 men			15,000 men	45,000 men	50,000 men	E

Key

A   Battle of Seneffe.
B   The Dutch, Spanish and German subsidy troops were divided into two armies: a siege army of 30,000 men under William III and an army of observation of 26,000 men under Waldeck and Villa Hermosa.
C   The French field troops were divided into two armies.
D   Battle of Mont-Cassel.
E   Battle of Saint-Denis.

Sources: See Chapter 11.

Bibliography

Manuscripts and primary sources

Koninklijk Huisarchief, The Hague

Archief Johan Maurits van Nassau-Siegen (A4)
- correspondence
    1466g A. Schimmelpenninck van der Oye (1665); 1476aI From and to William III (1672–1673); 1477 J. van Weert (1672) and Johan Pesters (1675).
- military affairs
    1466f 'Expeditie te velde tegens den bischop van Munster 1665'; 1466g Dutch forces at 'Dieren en daer ontrent lancx den IJssel' (Oct. 1665); 1468 Description of Naarden's fortifications (1672).

Archief Maurits (A13)
- correspondence
    XI-A Willem Lodewijk (1595); 'Graeff Wilhems advys op 't onsett van Oostende' (11 Sept. 1604).
- military affairs
    IX-6 'Beschrijvinge van[de] offiçieren ende offitiën der Groot Moegende Heeren Staeten-General ... bij de artillerie ende munitie van oorloghe te velde gedient hebbende'.

Archief Frederik Hendrik (A14)
IX-2 'Ordres de batailles'; XI-D1 Notes by Frederik Hendrik about political and military affairs (1633–1640).

Archief Willem III (A16)
- correspondence
    XIc-1369 To J. van Borssele van der Hooghe, lord of Geldermalsen (12 July 1674); XIe-14-16, 21, 23 F. van Eybergen (1675).
- military affairs
    X-19 Memorandum (1701) regarding the drill manual and the use of flintlock weapons.

Archief Willem Lodewijk (A22)
- correspondence
    VIII-4 To J. van Oldenbarnevelt (19 March 1602), 'Graeff Willems advys over 't ontsett van Oostende ende den tocht in Brabant 1602'.
    IX-A-1 Maurits (1593–1594, 1599, 1602–1606, 1614–1616).
    IX-A-6 Ernst Casimir (1600–1603).

IX-E to Maurits (1594, 1598, 1601–1602, 1605–1606).
- military affairs
   VIII-5, 'Lijste van de geappoincteerde staende op de compaigni[e]ën van Vrieslandt' (Oct.–Dec. 1606).

Archief Ernst Casimir (A23)
- correspondence
   VII-C-340 and 342 E.J. Clant van Stedum (1630–1631); VII-C-555 and 556 J. van Eysinga and J. van Veltdriel (1630); VII-C-564 J. Foutlau (27 July 1629); VII-C-602, 602a, 608 and 612 O. van Gendt, lord of Dieden (1629); VII-C 1055, 1057–1059 J. van Veltdriel (1631).
   VII-Da5 County of Zutphen to the SG (30 July 1629); VII-Db1 J. van Eysinga, G. Schaffer and R. Jensema (1629).
- military affairs
   VII-Db O 'De woorden van commandement waerdoor de capiteynen hunne soldaten gebieden ende exerceren' (1630).

Archief Hendrik Casimir I (A24)
- correspondence
   2, 28, 75, 77, 79, 81, 92, 98, 101, 105, 114a, 114c, 115c, 131 and 133 Frederik Hendrik (1633–1640); IV-B-66 W. of Nassau-Siegen (1638); IV-C-99 J. van Veltdriel (1638); IV-C-3 W. van Aldringa (1640); IV-C-13 Ed. Broune (1638).
- military affairs
   IV-E-1 Ban promulgated by the States-General on the sale of military offices (16 Feb. 1637); IV-E-2 Letters from the Council of State to Hendrik Casimir I as colonel (1634–1639); IV-H-1 and H-2, Papers regarding the valuation of a company's weapons (1638–1639); IV-H-4 Strength of the garrison of Maastricht (December 1634); IV-H-5 The Republic's war expenditure (1635); IV-H-10 Tactical formation of the Frisian regiment (winter 1594/5).

Archief Willem Frederik (A25)
- correspondence
   VII-AII-7, VII-AII-9 and VII-AII-14, Letters from Frederik Hendrik regarding the drill and exercise of soldiers (1643–1644); VII-C-84 E. van Baerdt (14 Sept. 1663); VII-C-144 E. van Glinstra (1663–1664); VII-C-156 W. van Haren (1661 and 1664); VII-C-158 C. Haubois (22 June 1652); VII-C-174 E. van Ittersum (24 and 25 May 1664); VII-C-256 J. van Veltdriel (1643–1645); VII-C-237 C. Roorda (1645).
- military affairs
   VIII-31V 'Consideratiën van[de] h.r Rhijngraeff' (1657).

Archief Constantijn Huygens sr. (G1)
   3 letters from E. Puchler (1645–1646).

Koninklijke Bibliotheek, The Hague

Manuscripts
- texts by Simon Stevin
   128-A-9I Notes about the tactics of the Dutch infantry; 128-A-18 'Formen van

slachorden … van 't leger'; 128-A-9II 'Eenighe stucken der crijchconst beschreven deur Simon Stevin'.
– letters
   70-C-9 'Correspondance de Guillaume III année 1672 à 1677', transcripts.
– drill manual
   72-F-27 'Oude wapenhandel' (c. 1600).

Nationaal Archief, The Hague, Eerste Afdeling

Staten-Generaal (1.01.03 to 1.01.06)
– resolutions (secret and ordinary)
– letters received from the captain-general of the Union, the field deputies, the Council of State and the provincial States
   4883 (1596); 4887 (1597); 4900–4901 (1601); 4902–4904 (1602); 4906 (1603); 4907–4909 (1604); 4910–4911 (1605); 4912–4914 (1606); 4921–4922 (1610); 4929 (1614); 4941 (1622); 4945 (1624); 4946–4947 (1625); 4948–4949 (1626); 4951 (1627); 4952 (1628), 4953–4955 (1629); 4958–4959 (1631) 4562–4563 (1626–1644); 4960–4961 (1632); 4962–4964 (1633); 4965 (1634); 4966–4967 (1635); 6764 (1635); 4970–4971 (1637); 4972–4973 (1638); 4974 (1639); 4975–4976 (1640); 4977–4978 (1641); 4979 (1642); 4980 (1643); 4981 (1644); 4982 (1645); 4984 (1646); 5016 (1657); 5034 (1664); 5038–5039 (1665); 5040 (1666); 5061 and 5063 (1672); 11670 (1672); 5075–5076 (1677).
– letters from Paris from ambassador Willem van Lier and his secretary Euskercken, and from Tieleman Aquilius, agent of the States-General to the French army
   6766 (1640–1641); 6767 (1643); 6769 (1645–1646).
– subsidy treaties with France
   12587.64, 12587.67, 12587.71, 12587.75, 12587.76, 12587.79, 12587.85, 12587.90 and 12587.91 (1637–1644).
– *lias lopende* (military affairs)
   12548.180 'Brieven, lijsten, papieren ende andere stucken alle overgelevert bij de heeren haer Ho. Mo. gedeput.den te velde' (1626); 12548.196 'Memorie dienende tot instructie voor de heeren Gecommitteerden van haer Ho. Mo. gaende naer de provinciën' regarding the 1632 campaign; 12548.211 Exchange and treatment of prisoners of war (1599–1602); 12548.251 Reduction of the Dutch army (1643); 12548.268 'Loopende. Besoinge van den heer Wimmenom wegen hare Ho. Mo. bij sijne Hoocheyt ende de heeren hare Ho. Mo. gedep.en in 't leger tot St.-Gilles A.o 1646'; 12548.353 'Loopende stucken raeckende het redres van 's Lants militie 1657 en[de] 1658'; 12548.454 Assembly of the army corps (1671); 12548.488.4 Muster-rolls (Sept. 1681); 12568.61 R. de Sijghers to Willem Frederik regarding the occupation of the Dijlerschans by the bishop of Münster (8 Dec. 1663).
– secret affairs, letters received from the field deputies, William III and Georg Friedrich von Waldeck
   12579.83 (1665); 12579.96 (1671); 12579.97-I and 12579.98 (1672); 12579.99 (1673); 12579.100 (1674); 12579.102 (1675); 12579.106 (1677); 12579.122 Report by A. Heinsius and E. van Weede-Dijkveld regarding the battle at Fleurus and the state of the Dutch army (1690).

- secret letters about military matters concerning Spain and the Spanish Netherlands

    12588.37-I, Advice of the Council of State regarding the required peacetime strength of the Dutch army (28 October 1643); 12588.100 C. de Witt, C. van Vrijbergen and C. van Beuningen (1672); 12588.103 C. van Vrijbergen (1673); 12588.106 C. van Heemskerck, S. de Chièze, T. van Sasburch and E. van Weede-Dijkveld (1676); 12588.107 T. van Sasburch, E. van Weede-Dijkveld (1677); 12588.109 E. van Weede-Dijkveld (1678).
- ordinary letters concerning Spain and the Spanish Netherlands

    7061 (1667).
- petitions to the States-General

    7498 'Requeste van Agidius van Couendael, predicant' (1676).

Raad van State (1.01.19)
- resolutions
- general indices to the resolutions

    488 (1648–1674); 489–490 (1675–1699).
- strength of the Dutch army

    1251 States of War (1643); 1896I Overview of the number of Dutch troops who served in Ostend during the siege (1601–1604); 1501 and 1905 'Staat van de militie na de Vreede van Munster' (1649–1748); 2061-II Companies in the field and in garrisons (1622); 2090-II Peacetime strengths of the Dutch army (1671, 1681 and 1700); 2486-I State of the Dutch army (1671).
- military affairs

    548 'Advysen aan haar Ho. Mo. van 1670 tot 1671 incluis'; 1907-I *Waardgelders*; 1544 'Actenboek' (1677–1678) with bread contracts and munitions deliveries; 2287 Notes about the artillery and the armament of the Dutch troops (c. 1600); 2490 'Rapport aen sijn princel[ijke] Ex[cellen]tie duer Cornelis de Bruyne en Jan van Brussel' regarding the siege of Antwerp (1644).

Hoge Krijgsraad (1.01.45)

   352–353 Sentences (1672–1674).

Stadhouderlijke Secretarie (1.01.50)

   1449 'Ordre' of Maurits, Willem Lodewijk, Frederik Hendrik and the Council of State 'om deser landen crijchsvolck ... tot derselver landen dienst bequamer te maecken ende te houden' (5 December 1618) and 'Ordre ende reglement op 't begeven van comp[agnie]ën &c. van den 19.en sept. 1668 voor d'heer raedtpensionnaris De Witt' (Res. SH, 19 September 1668); 1454 Tests with artillery (1618–1621).

Collectie Bisdom (1.10.06)

   162 Extract res. RvS, 15 April 1746: '21 vraag. Off en wat voor een in het veld doodgeschooten off van de vijand gekwetste man, als ook voor een deserteur off afgestorven goedgedaan word?'

Archief Adriaan Bogaers (1.10.09)

   46 Composition of Dutch companies (1587, 1599 and 1623); 47 States of War

(1595–1649); 64 Strength of the Dutch army (1647); 81 Baggage waggons of Holland's infantry companies (5 April 1675).

Familiearchief Fagel (1.10.29)
- correspondence of Gaspar Fagel
    1945 J. Deutz (10 April 1672); 1946, 1950, 1952, 1956 and 1958 G.F. von Waldeck (1672–1676).
- correspondence of William III
    430 Monterrey (1674).
- military affairs
    554 'Rélation succincte de ce qui s'est passé de plus considérable sous le commandement de son Altesse monseigneur le prince d'Orange dans la campagne de 1674'; 555 Overview of allied and French field troops (1674), 'Liste des troupes à piedt et à cheval que S.A. a destiné pour le chiège de Mastricht' (1676).

Collectie Van der Hoop (1.10.42)
- notes and papers of Adriaan van der Hoop
    87 and 93 Procedure for submitting the State of War; 102 and 107 Payment, muster procedures and clothing of the Dutch troops; 109 Baggage waggons (1676–1677); 108 Regulations for baggage (1742); 123 Various military matters; 124 Regularisation of the ranks (1668–1671).
- financial affairs of Holland
    24 Income, expenditure, loans and debts (1626, 1651, 1653, 1670–1677); 25 Tax on houses and land (1632, 1665–1666), 1000th penny tax (1621 and 1654) and 200th penny tax (1674); 28 Holland's debts (1671–1678); 93 'Legerlasten', i.e. outlay for the campaign (1672–1677) and subsidies paid by Holland to allied princes (1672–1678).
- provisioning of the Dutch army
    93 Van Werve to Adriaan van der Hoop (30 July 1741); 124 Rules and regulations concerning the sutlers (15 March 1706).
- military affairs
    124 Memorandum by Lieutenant-General D. de Savornin concerning the tactics and deployment of the Dutch troops (first half of the eighteenth century); notes by Hobbe baron van Aylva regarding 1672 (1741).

Collectie De Jonge van Ellemeet (1.10.50)
    'Resolutiën raeckende de recruiteringe, aenrits- en werfgelt militie over de iaeren 1675 tot 1692 beyde incl[uis].'

Collectie Overige Gezanten en Legatiearchieven (1.10.110)
    130 J. Boreel and E. van Weede-Dijkveld to C. van Beuningen (1678); 131 William III to E. van Weede-Dijkveld (4 July 1678).

Aanwinsten (1.11.01.01)
    105 'Uyt de eigenhandige schriften van den h.r Alex[ander] van der Capellen ... gecopieert en aan mij gecommuniceert door desselfs agterkleinsoon de h.r Robb[ert] Jasper van der Capellen'.

Nationaal Archief, Tweede Afdeling

Collectie Goldberg (2.21.006.51)
>305 Documents concerning the strength, financing and payment of the Dutch army (first half of the seventeenth century).

Collectie van Limburg Stirum (2.21.106)
– papers of Joost, count of Limburg Stirum
>LN 25 Contract for the recruitment of 2,000 infantrymen (22 June 1604).
– papers of Otto, count of Limburg-Stirum
>LN 38 Letters from the Council of State and Delegated Councillors (1665–1666).
– papers of Herman Otto, count of Limburg Stirum
>LM 23 Muster-roll of his company of cuirassiers (16 December 1641); LM 24 Muster-roll of his infantry company (15 April 1633).

Nationaal Archief, Derde Afdeling, Rijksarchief in Zuid-Holland

Staten van Holland (3.01.04.01)
– resolutions
– financial affairs pertaining to the army and the campaign
>1293-II 'Staet van 'tgeene aen de naevolgende compagni[e]ën tot in dese lopende maent van january 1643 noch te betaelen staet', 'Voorslach tot beter egaliteyt van betalinge aen de militie te doen' (c. 1643), overview of the outlay for the campaign (1640–1644), Holland's revenues; 1354B* 'Regueste van wegen de gemeene solliciteurs van[de] Zuyt-Hollandtsche comp[agnie]ën ruyteren ende knechten' (1639); 1354f 'Consideratiën over de hooftelijcke betal[ing]e anno 1651'.
– muster-rolls
>1354B** Garrison at Heusden (7 June 1658).
– military affairs
>6120 Provisioning during the siege of Naarden (1673).

Gecommitteerde Raden van Holland (3.01.05)
>3022 Res. GR, 14 and 17 Jan. 1673, regarding the delivery of muskets and flintlocks; 3026 Res. GR, 13 March 1676 regarding the *solliciteurs-militair*; 3027 Res. GR, 8 May 1677 regarding recruitment money to replace men lost in action; 3881 Correspondence from J.M. of Nassau-Siegen and K.C. von Königsmarck regarding the military situation (Dec. 1672).

Financie van Holland (3.01.29)
>797 and 806 'Memorie ofte verhandeling van hetgeene omtrent het stuk van de finantie van ... Holland ... van tijd tot tijd is voorgevallen' (1755); 799 Revenues from Holland's South Quarter (1626).

Archief Johan van Oldenbarnevelt (3.01.14)
– strength of the Dutch army
>2813 and 2954 Effective strength (summer 1602); 2831A Unrepartitioned troops (5 April 1599); 2942A Effective strength (31 Dec. 1587).

- strength of the Spanish army
    3053 Strength in 1598 and 1602.
- military affairs
    460 'Lijste van[de] besettinge voor den somer 1606'; 2875 Composition of the Solms regiment; 2876 Raising of a regiment of a thousand horse (17 January 1599); 2953 Memorandum concerning bread deliveries to the Dutch troops; 2954 'Sommiere gestaltenis der comp[agnie]ën gemonstert den xvii.n en[de] xviii.n nov.bris 1598 tot Bergen op ten Zoom en[de] in den lande van Tholen'; 3000 Res. SG regarding the payment of the unrepartitioned troops (12 July 1603).
- siege of Ostend
    2985 Operational plan for the campaign of 1602; 2997 'Raminge van provisiën van Oostende voor 3 & maenden [voor] 4000 mannen'; 3001 'Staet in 't corte van de oncosten van Osteyn[de]' (July 1601–July 1603); 3008 Strength of the garrison (1599–1604).

Archief Jacob Cats (3.01.15)
- financial affairs
    15, 22, 23, 27 and 84 Holland's income and expenditure (1634–1635 and 1640); 18 'Penningen op intrest tot laste van Holland genegotieert in de naevolgende jaeren' (1621–1634); 25 'Repartitie van 100 pond over d'ontfangers van[de] steden'.
- financial retrenchment and army reduction
    31 'Advys G.R. ontrent de finantie' (19 December 1634); 32 'Rapport ... op 't stuck van de mesnage', 'Pointen van mesnage' and 'Pointen van consideratiën tot redres van de confusiën der finantiën van Hollant' (November 1638); 34 'Besogne op het stuck van 't mesnage' (12 October 1635); 48 Advice of the Council of State concerning army reduction (16 Dec. 1636); 82 'Memorie ofte consideratie van menage' drafted by clerk Van de Broucke (1640).
- military affairs
    27 'Repartitie van betaellinge over de naevolgende [elf] comptoiren'; 45 'Compagni[e]ën buyten de Staeten van[de] Oorloch'; 49 'Staet van 14 compangi[e]ën te voet en[de] één compang[i]e paerden van[de] baron van Charnacé'; 52 'Staet van[de] soldije van ruyteren en[de] knechten in de naevolgen[de] jaeren tot laste van[de] provincie van Holland gestelt' (1621, 1626, 1627, 1628 and 1632); 86 Strength of the Dutch army (1635); 87 'Besettinge van de garnisoenen soo deselve wesen sullen het leger te velde sijnde'.

Archief Johan de Witt (3.01.17)
- correspondence (no inventory numbers available)
    L. Arskyne (30 Jan. 1670); J. Bampfield (16 June 1669); H. van Beverningk (1658); J.W. van Brederode (1653); A. van Hallart (23 July 1661); J. Kirkpatrik (1657 and 1672); J. van der Muelen (16 Oct. 1658); Willem Frederik of Nassau (1664); J.M. of Nassau-Siegen (1656–1669); J. Neidecker (20 Jan. 1665 and 8 March 1668); the Rhinegrave (1669 and 1672); Chr. van Wartensleben (28 May 1672); C. de Witt (1666 and 1668).
- military affairs
    2718-2 Memorandum with Johan Maurits of Nassau-Siegen's service record; 2720-2 Extract res. SH, 9 April 1661, regarding the 'Ordre en[de] forme op 't

begeven van[de] compagnie[ë]n'; 2722-3 Münster's preparations for war (17 July 1665); 2723-2 Georg Friedrich von Waldeck's ideas regarding the war with Münster (1666); 2724-a 'Volck op zee gesonden' (28 April and 13 May 1667), Pieter van Peene 'Remarque op de lijste van besettinge'; 2724-b 'Poincten van consideratie raackende het redres van 't volck te voet sijnde ten dienste der Vereenigde Nederlanden' (1667); 2725-4 'Project van esgualisatie der regementen' (1668); 2725-7 Review of the army corps at Bergen op Zoom (3 May 1668), anonymous, 'Raisonnement op[de] oorloch in[de] Spaensche Nederlanden' (early 1668), recommendations of J.M. of Nassau-Siegen for the Dutch army's restoration (1666).

Archief Gaspar Fagel (3.01.18)
– correspondence
  4 J. de Mauregnault (28 Sept. 1674); 30 Burgomasters of Amsterdam (1673–1674 and 1677); 43 Bosschaert (22 Nov. 1672), J. Bruynstein (1676); 46 Von Eppen (16 Dec. 1674); 53 A.A. Machado and J. Pereira (26 July 1676); 54 A. Nyenborch van Naeltwijk (1674), R. van Naerssen (12 July 1678); 56 J. Pesters (1672–1673, 1676 and 1678); 116 J. Bampfield (1672–1673), G.R. Hundebeck (31 Aug. 1674), K.C. Königsmarck (Dec. 1672–Jan. 1673), J. de Mauregnault (28 Nov. 1672); 117 H.T. von Solms-Braunfels (14 Dec. 1672), J.M. of Nassau-Siegen (30 Nov. 1672), K. Rabenhaupt (1674), G.F. von Waldeck (1673), Yvoy (18 July 1676 and 10 Aug. 1677); 121 Holland's field deputies (23 Dec. 1672, 1673), N. Witsen (1676–1677) and R. van Naerssen (15 Aug. 1678); 221 C. van Vrijbergen (1673); 239 E. van Weede-Dijkveld (1676–1677); 387 C. van Heemskerck and S. de Chièze (1676); 421 Gaspar Fagel to the Delegated Councillors of Holland (1672).
– financial affairs
  88, 89 and 92 Levying of extra taxes and loans (1673–1678); 126 'Instructie en reglement waernaer dat de directeurs van de betalinge der militie te lande ... haer sullen hebben te reguleren' (17 March 1673).
– muster-rolls
  127 Muster-roll of the company of Captain Johan de Vassy (6 Nov. 1673).
– military affairs
  131 French and Dutch losses at the battle of Seneffe (1674).

Archief Bicker (3.20.04.01)
  39 'Schriftelijk rapport van den generael Coehoorn wegens de gedaene visitatie van de frontieren van den Staet in de maenden van february en maert 1698', transcript by engineer Adriaan van Helden (d. 1787 or 1788).

Familiearchief Hoeufft van Velsen (3.20.26)
– correspondence of Diederik Hoeufft
  123 G.F. von Waldeck, N. Witsen, P. van Hattem (1676).

Familiearchief Hop (3.20.28)
– military affairs
  5 Composition of the Dutch army, commissioning of officers (1628, 1651–1670); 6 Strength of the French and Dutch armies, 'Voorslagen tot redres van[de] militie' (1672); 7 Revised State of War (27 Sept. 1672); 8 Pay lists (1673–1678).

– financial affairs
> 7 Arrangement of the troops repartitioned to Holland into eight classes (28 Feb. 1673); 9 Finances of Holland (first half of the seventeenth century); 10 Loans, expenditure and debts (1673).

Familiearchief Van Slingenlandt De Vrij Temminck (3.20.52)
– strength of the Dutch army
> 3 'Nieuwe Staet van Oorloge geformeert & aen de provinciën gesonden in den jaere 1643'; 44 Papers regarding the army's composition in 1672; 237 Instructions for the commissaries of musters in connection with the army reduction (1 February 1643).

– military affairs
> 21 Letters about bringing Maastricht, Wesel and the IJssel towns into a state of defence (1670–1671); 22 'Histoire de l'an 1672', resolutions, lists of company strengths and other matters pertaining to the war with France; 46 Exchange and treatment of prisoners of war (26 May 1673); 50 Garrisons and patents (1668); 239 Res. SG with regard to the field deputies in the seventeenth century; 246 Simon van Slingelandt, 'Memorie concerneerende de betrekking van de militie staande op den Staat van Oorlog tot de Generaliteit en tot de provinciën respectivelijk'.

Familiearchief Van Wassenaer van Duvenvoorde (3.20.87)
> 2050 Treaty with France (1637); 2055 Frederik Hendrik to Cornelis Musch (17 July 1638).

Gelders Archief, Arnhem

Archief heren en graven van Culemborg
– correspondence and papers of Count Floris II of Culemborg
> 581 Ernst Casimir (1622–1625); 671 A. van der Capellen (1635), H. Nobel (1638); 744 A. Pauw (1635); 749 Various correspondents (1635); 770 Lieutenant J. van Welderen (1635).

– papers regarding the political decision-making in The Hague and operations in the field
> 692 Extract res. SG (1631 and 1636); 737 Letters from T. van Eyck (1630–1635); 754 General Petition (17 Nov. 1629).

– papers regarding the infantry company of Count Floris II of Culemborg
> 667 Letters from J. Wagenaer (1632); 763 Account of recruitment costs by ensign J. Catz (1635); 763A Instruction for the company clerk S. van de Waeter (1625); 768 'Missiven van[de] lieute[n]andt Padtborch' (1631–1633); 767 Letter from Floris II to Lieutenant A. Drost (20 Oct. 1632); 769 Contracts with the *solliciteurs-militair* and muster-rolls (1624–1636); 770 Letter from the Council of State concerning the length of the pikes (15 Feb. 1639).

– papers regarding the company of cuirassiers of Count Floris II of Culemborg
> 759 Letters from *solliciteur* D. van Noordinghen (1628–1632); 760 Letters from Lieutenant A. Schimmelpenninck van der Oye (1636), contracts with the *solliciteurs* (1624, 1626 and 1635); 761 Pay ordinances (1625) and contract with the

solliciteur (1636); 770 Correspondence about the company flying its own guidon (1635–1636).
- papers regarding the infantry company of Count Filips Theodoor von Waldeck (d. 1645)
  861 Strength of his company (March 1639).
- correspondence of Georg Friedrich von Waldeck
  1125 To E. van Weede-Dijkveld (12 Feb. 1677); 1135 Anonymous regarding the 'Act of Seclusion' (7 May 1654); 1200 J.B. van Hornes (7 Aug. 1673 and 31 Jan. 1678); 1202 G.R. Hundebeck (22 Oct. 1674); 1216 N.F. von Zobel (25 March 1674); 1221 Papers regarding the siege of Naarden and its garrison (1673); 1224 G. Mom de Swartzstein (4 April 1674), G. Sparre (8 June 1674); 1225 D. de Torsay (1676).
- papers about the provisioning of the Dutch army originating from G.F. von Waldeck
  1237 Orders for the 1676 campaign; 1240 Bread deliveries (1675), strength of the Dutch army (1674, 1676); 1246 Rules and regulations by William III regarding the baggage waggons (1674).
- papers regarding the campaigns of 1672, 1676–1678
  1136 'Traitté de la Paix entre les couronnes de France & d'Espagne' (17 Sept. 1678); 1218 Conferences about the 1677 campaign, strength of Münster's field army (1672); 1225 'Conseill de guerre' (2 Aug. 1676); 1232 Strength of the Dutch army in 1677; 1240 Muster-rolls (1676), dispositions for the siege of Charleroi (Dec. 1676), strength of Dutch forces in the field (Aug. 1677).

Familiearchief Van der Capellen
- correspondence of Henrik van der Capellen, heer van Rijsselt
  70 A. van Capellen (1637 and 1647).
- correspondence and papers of Alexander van der Capellen
  89 S.H. van der Capellen (9 March 1649); To 'monsieur & frère' (11 May 1650); G. van der Capellen (26 July 1650); 119 Papers regarding the State of War (1650).

Groninger Archieven, Groningen

Archief of the Staten van de Ommelanden
- correspondence
  1376 L. Alting (19 March 1678); 1399 Deputies to the SG (1672).
- military affairs
  1250 Strength of the Dutch army (1609, 1621, 1643 and 1648); 1396 Augmentation with 14,000 infantry and 5,967 cavalry (19 Jan. 1672); 1399 Commission of officers (1675 and 1677).

Het Utrechts Archief, Utrecht

Archief of the States of Utrecht
- correspondence
  278-4 Frederik Hendrik (1634–1642); 278-5 William III (1675–1676); 314-6 G. van Reede-Amerongen (1637–1638).
- military and financial affairs
  654-8 Military affairs (1634–1635); 660 'Compaigni[e]ën in dienst van den

Landen zijnde' (11 July 1637); 657 Overview of the petitions submitted by the Council of State (1586–1637).

Huisarchief Amerongen
> 5075 'Instructie voor … Pieter de Sedlintsky … treckende naer Oostende' and other papers concerning the defence of Ostend (1601).

– papers of G. van Reede-Amerongen
> 2689 Companies in the field (1640).

– correspondence of G.A. van Reede-Amerongen
> 2722 M. Turnor (1672); 2731–2732 G. van Reede-Ginkel (1672–1674, 1676–1677); 2798 G. van Reede-Ginkel (1672); 2799–2802 (G.F. von Waldeck, H. van Beverningk, J. Pesters, William III, H. van Heteren, R. van Ommeren, G.W. van Tuyl-Serooskerken, J. van Reede-Renswoude, J. le Maire (1672); 2803, 2805 and 2808 H.J. van Tuyl-Serooskerken, J. van Rhenen and G.F. von Waldeck (1673); 2813, 2815 and 2816 H. Heteren, J. Pesters, E. van Weede-Dijkveld (1676); 2817–2821 H. Heteren, J. Pesters, E. van Weede-Dijkveld (1677).

– military affairs
> 2970 'Resolutie militie. Redres ende reglement op 't stuck van de militie van den 5.en april 1658. Voor de heere raedtpensionnaris &c.'; 3087 Contract with a *solliciteur-militair* (16 Nov. 1673); 3209 'Lijste de la force de l'armée le 9me juillet 1677'; 3610 'Camp 1683 op [de] Velue'.

– papers of Jacob Wijts (d. 1643)
> 4120 Letter from the Council of State concerning the abolition of calivers (22 May 1609); 4121 Letter from the Council of State about bringing the company to its prescribed strength (18 Feb. 1626) and from Holland's Delegated Councillors regarding the collection of weapons from the arsenal at Delft (3 Dec. 1627); 4128 'Mémoires des choses qui se sont passées durant le siège de Bois le Ducq en l'an 1629'.

Familiearchief De Beaufort
> 84 Muster-rolls of the companies of captain Antony de Vasch (19 March 1677) and Frederik Seger van Wijenhorst (19 March 1677).

Collectie Buchel Booth
> 83 'Ordre der bataille van 4 compaignie infanterije gestelt door den ingenieur Melder ter presentie van de wel Ed. Heeren Borgem.rs, Schepenen ende Vroetschap der stadt Utrecht op de exercitieplaets boven 't Accademie den 25 augus. an.o 1658'; 355 Billet-money (1636).

Historisch Centrum Overijssel, Zwolle

Archief Staten van Overijssel
> 992 Letters from Overijssel's deputies to the SG (1631–1635); 994 Quotas of Holland's North and South Quarters (10 July 1668); 1457 Letter from the Council of State regarding the armament of the infantry (19 Aug. 1588); 1458 Drill for Dutch troops (1670–1671); 5156 Letter from William III about desertion (31 July 1676) and from H. Bentinck about conducting musters (17 June 1678).

Tresoar, Leeuwarden

Archief Staten van Friesland
> 1352 Required garrisons and strength of the field army (23 Jan. 1588); 2985 Orders and regulations for muster commissaries (30 April 1587); 3025 Required strength of the garrisons (9 May 1586).

Fries Stadhouderlijk Archief
– correspondence from the stadholders
> 3 Willem Lodewijk to the States-General (1606); 17 Letters from the Council of State and the States-General to Ernst Casimir as colonel of a regiment of German infantry (1599 and 1605) and as stadholder of Friesland regarding Mansfeld's troops in East Friesland; 30 Willem Frederik to the Delegated States of Friesland (1642–1644); 48 D. Stecke, P. van Burmania to Hendrik Casimir II (1672, 1674–1676).

– correspondence from the deputies to the States-General
> 1356 C. Kann and E. van Bootsma (1673).

– military affairs
> 5 'Verscheide slag- en togtordres 1592, 1595, 1601'; 25 Expedition to the Dijlerschans (1663–1664); 321 Request from the joint captains of the Frisian regiment in connection with the heavy losses suffered in 1592.

– financial affairs
> 26 'Staet van den ontfanck ... over het gelt secours bij sijne Ma.t van Vranckrijck ... aen desen Staet belooft' (1637–1643); 29 Letter from the Council of State to the provinces concerning the poor financial circumstances of the unrepartitioned troops (9 Feb. 1644).

Familiearchief Van Eysinga-Vegelin van Claerbergen
> 547 Complaint from the Council of State regarding Friesland's non-payment of its quota (14 Jan. 1637); 713 'Ordre de bataille comme il a este ordonné par monseigneur le prince d'Orange dans le fort de Voorn le 2e de juin 1642'.

Familiearchief van Haren
– correspondence of Willem van Haren (1626–1708)
> 50 To the SG (29 May 1664).

Familiearchief Thoe Schwartzenberg en Hohenlansberg
– correspondence of Georg Wolfgang
> 276 To his father (29 May 1664), his mother (26 May 1664), and Prof. Michael Buschig (5 May 1672).

– military affairs
> 3242 'Provisioneele staet van militie bij Sijn Hooch.t en Hollandt voorgeslagen' (1679).

Zeeuws Archief, Middelburg

Archief Rekenkamer
> C 312–314, 322–324 and 332–335 1st grossa 1st summa I, Muster-rolls of Zeeland's infantry companies (1604–1606).

Gemeentearchief van Amsterdam

Missives to burgomasters (5026)
: 65 (microfilm 8006) H. van Beverningk (1672); 66 (microfilm 8006) J.M. of Nassau-Siegen (1672); 67–68 (microfilm 8007–8008) H. van Beverningk, J.M. of Nassau-Siegen, J. van Paffenrode, William III, P. Burgersdijck, C. Hop (1672–1673) and 'Beverningh raport' (1672); 86 (microfilm 8040) Willem II (1650), William III (1673).

Missives from Amsterdam's deputies to the States of Holland (5029)
: 71 (microfilm 7548) Letters (1633–1636).

Printed sources

AITZEMA, Lieuwe van, *Saken van staet en oorlogh*, vols III–VI (The Hague 1669).

BIJL, M. van der and H. Quarles van Ufford (eds), *Briefwisseling van Godard Adriaan van Reede van Amerongen en Everard van Weede van Dijkveld (27 maart 1671 – 28 juli 1672)* (The Hague 1991).

BINGHAM, John, *The tacticks of Aelian* (London 1616; facsimile edn, Amsterdam and New York 1968) and *The art of embattailing an army; or, The second part of Aelian's Tacticks* (London 1629; facsimile edn, Amsterdam and New York 1968).

BOR Christiaensz., Pieter, *De Nederlandsche historiën*, 4 vols (Amsterdam 1679–1684).

BOXEL, Johan, *Vertoogh van de krijghsoeffeninge soo in 't particulier van musquet en spies, als in 't generael van een corpus of gros der compagniën te voet van de guardes* (The Hague 1670).

BURMANIA, Poppo, *Enege gedenckwerdege geschiedenissen tot naerichtinge der naekomelingen*, KB HS 132-B-10. Transcription and intro. by W. Bergsma.

CAPELLEN, Robert Jasper van, *Gedenkschriften van jonkheer Alexander van der Capellen, heere van Aartsbergen, Boedelhoff en Mervelt*, 2 vols (Utrecht 1777–1778).

CLAUSEWITZ, Carl von, *Vom Kriege*, 'Vollständige Ausgabe im Urtext mit historisch-kritischer Würdigung von Dr. Werner Hahlweg' (1832; 16th edn, Bonn 1952).

DIBBETZ, Johan, *Het groot militair woordenboek* (The Hague 1740).

ENNO VAN GELDER, H., *De Nederlandse munten* (2nd edn, Utrecht and Antwerp 1966).

FLEMING, Philippe, *Oostende vermaerde, gheweldighe, lanckdurighe ende bloedighe belegheringhe ende stoute aenvallen … in de jaren 1601, 1602, 1603 ende 1604* (The Hague 1621).

FRITSCHY, Wantje, *Gewestelijke financiën ten tijde van de Republiek der Verenigde Nederlanden*, vol. I, *Overijssel (1604–1795)* (The Hague 1996).

FRUIN, R., *Brieven aan Johan de Witt*, vol. II (Amsterdam 1922).

FRUIN, R., 'Gedenkschrift van Joris de Bye, betreffende het bewind van Oldenbarnevelt', in *Bijdragen en Mededeelingen van het Historisch genootschap*, XI (Utrecht 1888), 400–59.

FRUIN, R. and N. Japikse, *Brieven van Johan de Witt*, vols II and IV (Amsterdam 1913–1922).

GAYA, Louis de, *Traité des armes* (Paris 1678; facsimile edn with an introduction by Charles Ffoulkes, n.p. 1911).

GEBHARD, J.F., *Het leven van Mr. Nicolaas Cornelisz. Witsen (1641–1717)* (Utrecht 1881).

GROEN VAN PRINSTERER, G., *Archives ou correspondance inédite de la Maison d'Orange-Nassau*, 2nd series, vols II–V (Utrecht 1858–1861).

GROOT PLACAETBOECK, vols II–III (The Hague 1664–1683).

HAHLWEG, Werner, *Die Heeresreform der Oranier. Das Kriegsbuch des Grafen Johann von Nassau-Siegen* (Wiesbaden 1973).

HEXHAM, Henry, *Principii ofte de eerste gronden van de oorloghskonste gelijck se in dese Vereenichde Nederlanden ghepractiseert wort onder het gouvernement van sijn hoogheyt mijnheer den prince van Orangien* (The Hague 1642). Dutch trans. of *The Principles of the Art Militarie: Practised in the Warres of the United Netherlands* (London 1637).

HOLLANTSE MERCURIUS (Haarlem 1677–1678).

HONDIUS, Henricus, *Korte beschrijvinge ende afbeeldinge van de generale regelen der fortificatie* (The Hague 1624).

JAPIKSE, N., *Notulen gehouden ter statenvergadering van Holland (1671–1675) door Cornelis Hop pensionaris van Amsterdam en Nicolaas Vivien pensionaris van Dordrecht* (Amsterdam 1903).

JAPIKSE, N., *Resolutiën der Staten-Generaal van 1576 tot 1609*, Rijksgeschiedkundige Publicatiën, vols 55, 57, 62, 71, 85, 92 and 101 (The Hague 1923–1957).

JAPIKSE, N., *Correspondentie van Willem III en van Hans Willem Bentinck, eersten graaf van Portland*, 2 vols (The Hague 1932–1935).

LE BLOND, Guillaume, *Elémens de tactique* (Paris 1758).

LE BLOND, Guillaume, *Elémens des fortifications* (5th rev. edn, Paris 1764).

LE BLOND, Guillaume, *Traité de l'attaque des places* (3rd rev. edn, Paris 1780).

LE HON, Johan and Christoffel, *Ordres van bataiIjen gepractiseert in de legers der Vereenighde Nederlanden onder het beleydt van sijn excellentie Mauritius en sijn hoogheydt Frederick Hendrick* (Amsterdam 1672).

LOURENS, Piet and Jan Lucassen, *Inwonertallen van Nederlandse steden ca. 1300–1800* (Amsterdam 1997).

MULDER, Lodewijk, *Journaal van Anthonis Duyck, advokaat-fiscaal bij den Raad van State (1591–1597, 1600–1602)*, 3 vols (The Hague and Arnhem 1862–1866).

MÜLLER, P.L., *Wilhelm III von Oranien und Georg Friedrich von Waldeck. Ein Beitrag zur Geschichte des Kampfes um das europäische Gleichgewicht*, 2 vols (The Hague 1873–1880).

MYATT, F., *Geïllustreerde encyclopedie van de 19de-eeuwse vuurwapens. Een geïllustreerde geschiedenis van de ontwikkeling van de militaire vuurwapens in de 19de-eeuw* (Deurne 1982); originally published in English as *The Illustrated Encyclopedia of 19th Century Firearms* (London, 1979).

ORLERS, Jan Jansz. and Henrick van Haestens, *Den Nassauschen laurencrans* (Leiden 1610; facsimile edn, Amsterdam 1979).

PAEN, Louis, *Den korten weg tot de Nederlandsche militaire exercitie. Inhoudende eenige consideratiën tot het manuael, soo van musquet, picq als andere noodige evolutiën, &c.* (Leeuwarden 1679).

POSTHUMUS, N.W., *Nederlandsche prijsgeschiedenis*, I, 'Goederenprijzen op de beurs van Amsterdam 1585–1914' (Leiden 1943).

PUYPE, Jan Piet, *Blanke wapens. Nederlandse slag- en steekwapens sinds 1600. Zwaarden, degens, sables en ponjaards. Historisch overzicht en typologie* (Lochem 1981).

PUYSÉGUR, Jacques François de Chastenet, marquis de, *Art de la guerre, par principes et par règles*, 2 vols (Paris 1748, reprint 1749).

RECUEIL *van verscheide placaaten, ordonnantiën, resolutiën, instructiën, ordres en lijsten, &c. betreffende de saaken van den oorlog, te water en te lande*, vol. I.

RINGOIR, H., *Hoofdofficieren der infanterie van 1568 tot 1813* (The Hague 1981).

SLINGELANDT, Simon van, *Staatkundige geschriften*, 4 vols (Amsterdam 1784–1785).

STEVIN, Simon, *Castrametatio dat is legermeting* (Rotterdam 1617), facsimile edn and trans. as *Castrametatio, that is the Marking out of Army Camps*, in W.H. Schukking (ed.), *The Principal Works of Simon Stevin*, 5 vols (Amsterdam, 1955–1968), iv: *The Art of War* (Amsterdam 1964), 261–397.

SYMCOX, Geoffrey, *War, Diplomacy, and Imperialism, 1618–1763* (London 1974).

SYPESTEYN, J.W. van, *Het leven van Menno baron van Coehoorn beschreven door zijnen zoon Gosewijn Theodoor baron van Coehoorn* (Leeuwarden 1860).

VALKENIER, Petrus, *'t Verwerd Europa*, and anon., *Vervolg van 't Verwerd Europa* (Amsterdam 1688).

VEENENDAAL, A.J. sr., *Johan van Oldenbarnevelt. Bescheiden betreffende zijn staatkundig beleid en zijn familie*, vol. II (The Hague 1962).

VEGETIUS Renatus, Publius Flavius, *De Re Militari*; trans. John Clarke as 'The Military Institutions of the Romans', in Thomas R. Phillips (ed.), *Roots of Strategy. The 5 Greatest Military Classics of All Time* (1940; reprint Harrisburg, Penn. 1985).

VERVOU, Fredrich van, *Enige gedenckweerdige geschiedenissen tot narichtinge der nakomelingen, sommarischer wijze beschreven*, published by Het Friesch Genootschap (Leeuwarden 1841).

VISSER, J. (transcription) and G.N. van der Plaats (ed.), *Gloria Parendi. Dagboeken van Willem Frederik stadhouder van Friesland, Groningen en Drenthe 1643–1649, 1651–1654* (The Hague 1995).

WICQUEFORT, Abraham de, *Histoire des Provinces Unies*, ed. C.A. Chais van Buren, vol. III (Amsterdam 1866).

WIJN, J.W., *Krijgskundige aanteekeningen van Johan den middelste van Nassau* (Utrecht 1947).

WIJNNE, J.A., *De geschillen over de afdanking van 't krijgsvolk in de Vereenigde Nederlanden in de jaren 1649 en 1650 en de handelingen van prins Willem II, toegelicht met behulp van ongedrukte stukken uit het huisarchief van Z.M. den koning* (Utrecht 1885).

Secondary literature

ASCH, Ronald G., '"Wo der soldat hinkömbt, da ist alles sein": Military Violence and Atrocities in the Thirty Years War Re-examined', *German History. The Journal of the German History Society*, 18, III (2000), 291–309.

BAXTER, Douglas C., *Servants of the Sword: French Intendants of the Army, 1630–70* (Urbana, Ill. 1976).

BAXTER, Stephen B., *William III* (London 1966).

BEAUFORT-SPONTIN, Christian, *Harnisch und Waffe Europas. Die militärische Ausrüstung im 17. Jahrhundert* (Munich 1982).

BERGSMA, Wiebe, 'De godsdienstige verhoudingen tijdens de Vrede van Munster', in Jacques Dane (ed.), *1648 Vrede van Munster. Feit en verbeelding* (Zwolle n.d.), 83–105.

BLACK, Jeremy, *European Warfare 1660–1815* (New Haven and London 1994).

BLANCHARD, Anne, 'Vers la centure de fer', in Philippe Contamine (ed.), *Histoire militaire de la France*, vol. I, *Des origines à 1715* (Paris 1992), 449–83.

BLUCHE, François, *Louis XIV*, trans. Mark Greengrass (New York 1990).

BOER, D.E.L. de, *Het oude Duitsland. Een geschiedenis van de Duitse landen van 1450 tot 1800* (Amsterdam 2002).

BONNEY, Richard, *The King's Debts. Finance and Politics in France 1589–1661* (Oxford 1981).

BORDES, J.P. de, *De verdediging van Nederland in 1629* (Utrecht 1856).

BOSSCHA, J., *Neerlands heldendaden te land van de vroegste tijden af tot op onze dagen*, 4 vols (rev. edn, Leeuwarden 1872).

BRUIJN, Jaap R., *Varend verleden. De Nederlandse oorlogsvloot in de zeventiende en achttiende eeuw* (n.p. 1998). This is an expanded and revised version of his *The Dutch Navy of the Seventeenth and Eighteenth Centuries* (Columbia, SC 1993).

BRUIN, Guido de, *Geheimhouding en verraad. De geheimhouding van staatszaken ten tijde van de Republiek (1600–1750)* (The Hague 1991).

CHANDLER, David, *The Art of Warfare in the Age of Marlborough* (2nd edn, Tunbridge Wells 1990).

CHILDS, John, *Warfare in the Seventeenth Century* (London 2001).

CORVISIER, André, *Louvois* (n.p. 1983).

CORVISIER, A., 'Louis XIV, la guerre et la naissance de l'armée moderne', in Philippe Contamine (ed.), *Histoire militaire de la France*, vol. I, *Des origines à 1715* (Paris 1992), 383–413.

COUSINE, A., 'La campagne de 1674–1675 du maréchal de Turenne', in *Turenne et l'art militaire. Troisième centenaire de la mort de Turenne. Actes du colloque international tenu à Paris ... les 2 et 3 octobre 1975* (1978), 221–234.

DAM VAN ISSELT, W.E. van, 'Onze Duitsche bondgenooten tijdens prins Maurits' veldtocht van 1599', in *Bijdragen voor Vaderlandsche Geschiedenis en Oudheidkunde*, 5th series, V (The Hague 1918), 23–77.

DELBRÜCK, Hans, *Geschichte der Kriegskunst im Rahmen der politischen Geschichte*, vol. IV, 'Neuzeit' (Berlin 1920).

DEURSEN, A. Th. van, 'De Raad van State onder de Republiek 1588–1795', in *Raad van State 450 jaar* (The Hague 1981), 47–91.

DEURSEN, A. Th. van, *Maurits van Nassau 1567–1625. De winnaar die faalde* (Amsterdam 2000).

DOORN, J.A.A. van, *Sociologie van de organisatie. Beschouwingen over organiseren in het bijzonder gebaseerd op een onderzoek van het militaire systeem* (Leiden 1956).

DORMANS, Eduard H.M., *Het tekort. Staatsschuld in de tijd der Republiek* (Amsterdam 1991).

DORREBOOM, M.L., '"Gelijk hij gecondemneert word mits deezen". Militaire strafrechtpleging bij het krijgsvolk te lande, 1700–1795', Ph.D. diss., University of Amsterdam (2000).

DUFFY, Christopher, *Siege Warfare: The Fortress in the Early Modern World 1494–1660* (London 1979).

DUFFY, C., *The Fortress in the Age of Vauban and Frederick the Great, 1660–1789* (London 1985)

EKBERG, Carl J., *The Failure of Louis XIV's Dutch War* (Chapel Hill, NC 1979).

ELIAS, Johan E., *Geschiedenis van het Amsterdamsche regentenpatriciaat* (2nd rev. edn, The Hague 1923).

ENTHOVEN, Victor, 'Zeeland en de opkomst van de Republiek. Handel en strijd in de Scheldedelta c. 1550–1621', Ph.D. diss., Leiden University (1996).

FIEDLER, Siegfried, *Kriegswesen und Kriegführung im Zeitalter der Landsknechte* (Koblenz 1985).

FIEDLER, S., *Kriegswesen und Kriegführung im Zeitalter der Kabinettskriege* (Koblenz 1986).

FOUW, A. de, *Onbekende raadpensionarissen* (The Hague 1946).

FRANKEN, M.A.M., *Coenraad van Beuningen's politieke en diplomatieke aktiviteiten in de jaren 1667–1684* (Groningen 1966).

FRITSCHY, Wantje (J.M.F.), *De patriotten en de financiën van de Bataafse Republiek. Hollands krediet en de smalle marges voor een nieuw beleid (1795–1801)* (The Hague 1988).

FROST, Robert I., *The Northern Wars. War, State and Society in Northeastern Europe, 1558–1721* (Harlow 2000).

FRUIN, R., *De oorlog van 1672* (Groningen 1972).

GAWRONSKI, Jerzy, *De equipagie van de Hollandia en de Amsterdam. VOC-bedrijvigheid in 18de-eeuws Amsterdam* (Amsterdam 1996).

GEMBRUCH, Werner, 'Vauban', in Werner Hahlweg (ed.), *Klassiker der Kriegskunst* (Darmstadt 1960), 150–65.

GEYL, P., *Oranje en Stuart 1641–1672* (2nd edn, Zeist, Arnhem and Antwerp 1963); trans. Arnold Pomerans as *Orange and Stuart 1641–1672* (London 1969).

GROENVELD, Simon, *Verlopend getij. De Nederlandse Republiek en de Engelse Burgeroorlog 1640–1646* (Dieren 1984).

GROENVELD, S., *Evidente factiën in den Staet: sociaal-politieke verhoudingen in de 17e-eeuwse Republiek der Verenigde Nederlanden* (Hilversum 1990).

GROENVELD, S., 'Unie, Religie en Militie. Binnenlandse verhoudingen in de Nederlandse Republiek voor en na de Munsterse vrede', in *1648. De Vrede van Munster*, special issue of *De Zeventiende eeuw*, 13, I (1997), 67–87.

GUERLAC, Henry, 'Vauban: The Impact of Science on War', in Peter Paret (ed.), *Makers of Modern Strategy from Machiavelli to the Nuclear Age* (Princeton, NJ 1986), 64–90.

HAHLWEG, Werner, *Die Heeresreform der Oranier und die Antike. Studien zur Geschichte des Kriegswesens der Niederlande, Deutschlands, Frankreichs, Englands, Italiens, Spaniens und der Schweiz vom Jahre 1589 bis zum Dreissigjährigen Kriege* (Berlin 1941).

HAHLWEG, W., 'Barriere – Gleichgewicht – Sicherheit. Eine Studie über die

Gleichgewichtspolitik und die Strukturwandlung des Staatensystems in Europa 1646–1715', *Historische Zeitschrift*, CLXXXVII (Munich 1959), 54–89.

HAHLWEG, W., 'Wilhelm Ludwig von Nassau und das Cannae-Problem', *Nassauische Annalen*, LXXI (Wiesbaden 1960), 237–42.

HAHLWEG, W., 'Die Oranische Heeresreform, ihr Weiterwirken und die Befreiung und Etablierung der Niederlande. Studien und Betrachtungen', *Nassauische Annalen*, LXXX (Wiesbaden 1969), 137–57.

HAHLWEG, W., 'Aspekte und Probleme der Reform des niederländischen Kriegswesens unter Prinz Moritz von Oranien', *Bijdragen en Mededelingen betreffende de Geschiedenis der Nederlanden*, LXXXVI (1971), 161–77.

HAHLWEG, W. (ed.), *Die Heeresreform der Oranier. Das Kriegsbuch des Grafen Johann von Nassau-Siegen* (Wiesbaden 1973), introduction, 1–54.

HALEY, K.H.D., 'English Policy at the Peace Congress of Nijmegen', in *The Peace of Nijmegen 1676–1678/79* (Amsterdam 1980), 145–55.

HALL, Bert S., *Weapons and Warfare in Renaissance Europe. Gunpowder, Technology, and Tactics* (Baltimore and London 1997).

HART, Marjolein C. 't, *The Making of a Bourgeois State. War, Politics and Finance during the Dutch Revolt* (Manchester and New York 1993).

HATTON, Ragnhild, 'Nijmegen and the European Powers', in *The Peace of Nijmegen 1676–1678/79* (Amsterdam 1980), 1–16.

HAUG, C.F., *De Dertigjarige Oorlog. Eene bijdrage tot de krijgskundige geschiedenis. Met de karakterschetsen der beroemdste veldheren*, vol. I (Delft 1826).

HOEK, Jan Johannes van den, *De veldtocht van prins Maurits in 1597* (The Hague 1914).

HOOF, J.P.C.M. van, 'Nieuwe manieren, sterke frontieren. Het bouwconcept van Menno van Coehoorn en zijn aandeel in de verbetering van het verdedigingsstelsel', *Bijdragen en Mededelingen betreffende de Geschiedenis der Nederlanden*, CXVIII (2003), IV, 545–66.

HOUTZAGER, D., *Hollands lijf- en losrenteleningen vóór 1672* (Schiedam 1950).

ISRAEL, Jonathan, *The Dutch Republic and the Hispanic World 1606–1661* (Oxford 1982).

ISRAEL, J., *European Jewry in the Age of Mercantilism 1550–1750* (Oxford 1985).

ISRAEL, J., *Empires and Entrepots. The Dutch, the Spanish Monarchy and the Jews, 1585–1713* (London and Ronceverte, WV 1990).

ISRAEL, J., *The Dutch Republic. Its Rise, Greatness, and Fall 1477–1806* (Oxford 1995).

JAPIKSE, N., *Prins Willem III de stadhouder-koning*, 2 vols (Amsterdam 1930–1933).

JONG, Michiel A.G. de, '"Staet van oorlog". Wapenbedrijf en militaire hervormingen in de Republiek der Verenigde Nederlanden (1585–1621)', Ph.D. diss., Leiden University (2002).

KERKHOFF, Antoon H.M., *Over de geneeskundige verzorging in het Staatse leger* (Nijmegen 1976).

KERNKAMP, Gerhard W., *De sleutels van de Sont. Het aandeel van de Republiek in den Deensch-Zweedschen oorlog van 1644–1645* (The Hague 1890).

KINDEREN, Floris der, *De Nederlandsche Republiek en Munster gedurende de jaren 1650–1679*, 2 vols (Leiden 1871–1874).

KIST, J.B., *Jacob de Gheyn, 'The exercise of armes', a Commentary by J.B. Kist* (Lochem 1971).

KLUIVER, Jan Hendrik, *De souvereine en independente staat Zeeland. De politiek van de provincie Zeeland inzake vredesonderhandelingen met Spanje tijdens de Tachtigjarige Oorlog tegen de achtergrond van de positie van Zeeland in de Republiek* (Middelburg 1998).
KNEVEL, Paul, *Het Haagse bureau. Zeventiende-eeuwse ambtenaren tussen staatsbelang en eigenbelang* (Amsterdam 2001).
KNOOP, W.J., *Krijgs- en geschiedkundige beschouwingen over Willem den Derde*, 3 parts in a single vol. (Schiedam 1895).
KOOPERBERG, L.M.G., 'Een muiterij in den Spaanschen tijd. De muiters van Hoogstraten (1602–1604)', *Bijdragen voor Vaderlandsche Geschiedenis en Oudheidkunde*, 5th series, V (The Hague 1918), 113–72.
KRÄMER, F.J.L., *De Nederlandsch-Spaansche diplomatie vóór den Vrede van Nijmegen* (Utrecht 1892).
KROENER, Bernhard, *Les routes et les étapes. Die Versorgung der französischen Armeen in Nordostfrankreich (1635–1661). Ein Beitrag zur Verwaltungsgeschichte des Ancien Régime* (Münster 1980).
KROENER, B., 'Die Entwicklung der Truppenstärken in den französischen Armeen zwischen 1635 und 1661', in *Forschungen und Quellen zur Geschichte des Dreißigjährigen Krieges* (Aschendorff and Münster 1981), 163–220.
KUNISCH, Johannes, 'Der Nordische Krieg von 1655 bis 1660 als Parabel frühneuzeitlicher Staatenkonflikte', in *Fürst – Gesellschaft – Krieg. Studien zur bellizistischen Disposition des absoluten Fürstenstaates* (Cologne 1992), 43–82.
KUYPERS, F.H.W., *Geschiedenis der Nederlandsche artillerie*, vols II–III (Nijmegen 1871–1872).
LIVET, G., 'Colbert de Croissy et la diplomatie française à Nimeque', in *The Peace of Nijmegen 1676–1678/79* (Amsterdam 1980), 181–223.
LYNCH, John, *Spain under the Habsburgs*, 2 vols (2nd edn, Oxford 1981).
LYNN, John A., 'Recalculating French Army Growth during the Grand Siècle, 1610–1715', in Clifford J. Rogers (ed.), *The Military Revolution Debate. Readings on the Military Transformation of Early Modern Europe* (Boulder, San Francisco and Oxford 1995), 117–47.
LYNN, J.A., *Giant of the Grand Siècle. The French Army, 1610–1715* (Cambridge 1997).
LYNN, J.A., *The Wars of Louis XIV 1667–1714* (London and New York 1999).
MALETTKE, Klaus, 'Ludwigs XIV. Außenpolitik zwischen Staatsräson, ökonomischen Zwängen und Sozialkonflikten', in Heinz Duchhardt, *Rahmenbedingungen und Handlungsspielräume europäischer Außenpolitik im Zeitalter Ludwigs XIV. Zeitschrift für Historische Forschung*, XI (Berlin 1991), 43–72.
MARTIN, Ronald, 'The Army of Louis XIV', in Paul Sonnino (ed.), *The Reign of Louis XIV* (Atlantic Highlands, NJ and London 1991), 111–26.
NICKLE, Barry H., 'The Military Reforms of Prince Maurice of Orange', Ph.D. diss., University of Delaware (1975).
NIEROP, Henk van, *Het verraad van het Noorderkwartier. Oorlog, terreur en recht in de Nederlandse Opstand* (Amsterdam 1999).
NIMWEGEN, Olaf van, *De subsistentie van het leger. Logistiek en strategie van het Geallieerde en met name het Staatse leger tijdens de Spaanse Successieoorlog in de Nederlanden en het Heilige Roomse Rijk (1701–1712)* (Amsterdam 1995).
NIMWEGEN, O. van, 'Van vuurkracht naar stootkracht en vice versa. Verander-

ingen in de bewapening van het Staatse leger tijdens de Spaanse Successieoorlog (1702–1712)', *Armamentaria*, XXX (1995), 47–60.

NIMWEGEN, O. van, 'Maurits van Nassau and Siege Warfare (1590–1597)', in Marco Van der Hoeven (ed.), *Exercise of Arms. Warfare in the Netherlands, 1568–1648* (Leiden, New York and Cologne 1997), 113–31.

NIMWEGEN, O. van, 'Kanonnen en houwitsers. De Staatse veldartillerie in de eerste helft van de achttiende eeuw', *Armamentaria*, XXXII (1997), 50–66.

NIMWEGEN, O. van, *De Republiek der Verenigde Nederlanden als grote mogendheid. Buitenlandse politiek en oorlogvoering in de eerste helft van de achttiende eeuw en in het bijzonder tijdens de Oostenrijkse Successieoorlog (1740–1748)* (Amsterdam 2002).

NIMWEGEN, O. van, 'Het Staatse leger en de militaire revolutie van de vroegmoderne tijd', *Bijdragen en Mededelingen betreffende de Geschiedenis der Nederlanden*, CXVIII (2003), IV, 494–518.

NIMWEGEN, O. van, 'De betekenis van Willem III voor de wederopbouw en vorming van het Staatse leger (1672–1678)', in *Jaarboek Oranje-Nassau Museum 2002* (Rotterdam 2003), 25–39.

NIMWEGEN, O. van, 'De Republiek der Verenigde Nederlanden in oorlog met Frankrijk (1650–1750)', in Jaap R. Bruijn and Cees B. Wels (eds), *Met man en macht. De militaire geschiedenis van Nederland 1550–2000* (Amsterdam 2003), 65–104.

OESTREICH, Gerhard, 'Der römische Stoizismus und die oranische Heeresreform', *Historische Zeitschrift*, CLXXVI (1953), 17–43.

ONNEKINK, David, 'The Anglo-Dutch Favourite. The Career of Hans Willem Bentinck, 1st Earl of Portland 1649–1709', Ph.D. diss., Utrecht University (2004).

ORTENBURG, Georg, *Waffe und waffengebrauch im Zeitalter der Landsknechte* (Koblenz 1984).

OSTWALD, Jamel, 'The "decisive" Battle of Ramillies, 1706: Prerequisites for Decisiveness in Early Modern Warfare', *Journal of Military History*, LXIV (July 2000), 649–77.

OVERDIEP, G., *De Groninger schansenkrijg. De strategie van graaf Willem Lodewijk. Drente als strijdtoneel. 1589–1594* (Groningen 1970).

PARKER, Geoffrey, *The Dutch Revolt* (London 1977).

PARKER, G., *Spain and the Netherlands, 1559–1659. Ten Studies* (London 1979).

PARKER, G., *The Army of Flanders and the Spanish Road 1567–1659. The Logistics of Spanish Victory and Defeat In the Low Countries' Wars* (rev. edn, Cambridge, New York and Melbourne 1990).

PARKER, G., *The Military Revolution. Military Innovation and the Rise of the West, 1500–1800* (2nd rev. edn, Cambridge 1996).

PARKER, G. (ed.), *The Thirty Years' War* (2nd edn, London and New York 1997).

PARKER, G., 'From the House of Orange to the House of Bush: 400 Years of "Revolutions in Military Affairs"', *Militaire Spectator*, 172, IV (2003), 177–93.

PARROTT, David, 'Strategy and Tactics in the Thirty Years' War: The "Military Revolution"', in Clifford J. Rogers (ed.), *The Military Revolution Debate. Readings on the Military Transformation of Early Modern Europe* (Boulder, San Francisco and Oxford 1995), 227–51.

PARROTT, D., *Richelieu's Army. War, Government and Society in France, 1624–1642* (Cambridge 2001).

PERJÉS, G., 'Army Provisioning, Logistics and Strategy in the Second Half of the 17th Century', *Acta Historica Academiae Scientiarum Hungaricae*, XVI (Budapest 1970), 1–51.
POELHEKKE, J.J., *De Vrede van Munster* (The Hague 1948).
POELHEKKE, J.J., *Frederik Hendrik prins van Oranje. Een biografisch drieluik* (Zutphen 1978).
PRAK, Maarten, *Gouden Eeuw. Het raadsel van de Republiek* (Nijmegen 2002). *The Dutch Republic in the Seventeenth Century*, trans. Diane Webb (Cambridge and New York 2005).
PUYPE, Jan Piet, 'Victory at Nieuwpoort, 2 July 1600', in Marco Van der Hoeven (ed.), *Exercise of Arms. Warfare in the Netherlands, 1568–1648* (Leiden, New York and Cologne 1997), 69–112.
PUYPE, J.P., 'Hervorming en uitstraling. Tactiek en wapens van het Staatse leger tot de Vrede van Munster en hun invloed in andere Europese landen', in Jacques Dane (ed.), *1648 Vrede van Munster. Feit en verbeelding* (Zwolle [1998]), 47–81.
PUYPE, J.P. and M. van der Hoeven (eds), *The Arsenal of the World. The Dutch Arms Trade in the Seventeenth Century* (Amsterdam 1996).
PUYPE, J.P. and A.A. Wiekart, *Van Maurits naar Munster. Tactiek en triomf van het Staatse leger/From Prince Maurice to the Peace of Westphalia. Tactics and Triumphs of the Dutch Army*, catalogue of the presentations at the Royal Netherlands Army Museum in Delft (1998).
RAA, F.J.G. ten, *Het Staatsche leger 1568–1795*, vols VI and VII (The Hague 1940–1950).
RAA, F.J.G. ten and F. de Bas, *Het Staatsche leger 1568–1795*, vols I–V (Breda 1911–1921).
REDLICH, Fritz, *The German Military Enterpriser and His Workforce. A Study in European Economic and Social History*, 2 vols (Wiesbaden 1964–1965).
ROBB, Nesca A., *William of Orange. A Personal Portrait*, vol. II, *The Later Years 1674–1702* (London, Melbourne and Toronto 1966).
ROBERTS, Michael, 'Gustav Adolf and the Art of War', in *Essays in Swedish History* (London 1967), 56–81.
ROBERTS, M., 'The Military Revolution, 1560–1660', in Clifford J. Rogers (ed.), *The Military Revolution Debate. Readings on the Military Transformation of Early Modern Europe* (Boulder, San Francisco and Oxford 1995), 13–35.
ROGERS, Clifford J., 'The Military Revolution of the Hundred Years War', in Clifford J. Rogers (ed.), *The Military Revolution Debate. Readings on the Military Transformation of Early Modern Europe* (Boulder, San Francisco and Oxford 1995), 55–93.
RÖMERLINGH, Joan, *De diplomatieke betrekkingen van de Republiek met Denemarken en Zweden 1660–1675* (Amsterdam 1969).
ROOMS, Etienne, 'De materiële organisatie van de troepen van de Spaans-Habsburgse monarchie in de Zuidelijke Nederlanden (1659–1700)', Ph.D. diss., Free University of Brussels (1998).
ROORDA, D.J., 'The Peace of Nijmegen. The End of a Particular Period in Dutch History', in *The Peace of Nijmegen 1676–1678/79* (Amsterdam 1980), 17–28.
ROTHENBERG, Gunther E., 'Maurice of Nassau, Gustavus Adolphus, Raimondo Montecuccoli, and the "Military Revolution" of the Seventeenth Century', in Peter

Paret (ed.), *Makers of Modern Strategy from Machiavelli to the Nuclear Age* (Princeton, NJ 1986), 32–63.
ROWEN, Herbert H., *John de Witt, Grand Pensionary of Holland, 1625–1672* (Princeton, NJ 1978).
ROWEN, H.H., 'The Peace of Nijmegen: De Witt's Revenge', in *The Peace of Nijmegen 1676–1678/79* (Amsterdam 1980), 275–83.
ROWEN, H.H., *The Princes of Orange. The Stadholders in the Dutch Republic* (Cambridge, New York and Melbourne 1988).
ROWLANDS, Guy, *The Dynastic State and the Army under Louis XIV. Royal Service and Private Interest, 1661–1701* (Cambridge 2002).
RYSTADT, Göran, 'Sweden and the Nijmegen Peace Congress', in *The Peace of Nijmegen 1676–1678/79* (Amsterdam 1980), 131–43.
SATTERFIELD, G., *Princes, Posts and Partisans. The Army of Louis XIV and Partisan Warfare in the Netherlands (1673–1678)* (Leiden and Boston 2003).
SCHÖFFER, I., 'De Republiek der Verenigde Nederlanden 1609–1702', in I. Schöffer, H. van der Wee and J.A. Bornewasser (eds), *De Lage Landen van 1500 tot 1780* (3rd edn, Amsterdam and Brussels 1985), 167–267.
SCHULTEN, C.M., 'Prins Maurits (1567–1625), legerhervormer en vernieuwer van de krijgskunde, of trendvolger?', *Armamentaria*, XXXV (2000), 7–22.
SCHULTEN, C.M. and J.W.M. Schulten, *Het leger in de zeventiende eeuw* (Bussum 1969).
SIMONI, Anna E.C., *The Ostend Story. Early Tales of the Great Siege and the Mediating Role of Henrick van Haestens* ('t Goy-Houten 2003).
SLECHTE, C.H., 'De propagandacampagnes voor koning-stadhouder Willem III. Een verkenning', in *Jaarboek Oranje-Nassau Museum 2002* (2003), 71–108.
SONNINO, Paul, 'Louis XIV and the Dutch War', in Ragnhild Hatton (ed.), *Louis XIV and Europe* (London 1976), 153–78.
SONNINO, P., *Louis XIV and the Origins of the Dutch War* (Cambridge 1988).
STAPLETON, John M., 'Forging a Coalition Army: William III, the Grand Alliance, and the Confederate Army in the Spanish Netherlands, 1688–1697', Ph.D. diss., Ohio State University (2003).
SYPESTEYN, C.A. van, *Het merkwaardig beleg van Ostende 5 juli 1601–22 september 1604* (The Hague 1887).
SYPESTEYN, J.W. and J.P. de Bordes, *De verdediging van Nederland in 1672 en 1673*, 2 vols. (The Hague 1850).
TEX, J. den, *Oldenbarnevelt*, 4 vols with a separate index (Haarlem and Groningen 1960–1972).
TEX, J. den, *Onder vreemde heren. De Republiek der Nederlanden 1672–1674* (Zutphen 1982).
TROOST, Wout, *Stadhouder-koning Willem III. Een politieke biografie* (Hilversum 2001).
TROOST, W., 'De buitenlandse politiek van Willem III en het begin van de Britse evenwichtspolitiek', in *Jaarboek Oranje-Nassau Museum 2002* (2003), 41–57.
VERMEIR, René, *In staat van oorlog. Filips IV en de Zuidelijke Nederlanden 1629–1648* (Maastricht 2001).
VERSPOHL, Theodor, *Das Heerwesen des Münsterschen Fürstbischofs Cristoph Bernard von Galen 1650–1678* (Hildesheim 1909).

VLIET, Adri P. van, 'De Staatse vloot in de Tachtigjarige Oorlog', in Jaap R. Bruijn and Cees B. Wels (eds), *Met man en macht. De militaire geschiedenis van Nederland 1550–2000* (Amsterdam 2003), 44–62.

WATERBOLK, E.H., 'Met Willem Lodewijk aan tafel 17-3-1560 – 13-7-1620', in *Verspreide opstellen aangeboden aan de schijver bij zijn aftreden als hoogleraar aan de Rijksuniversiteit te Groningen* (Amsterdam 1981), 296–315.

WATERBOLK, E.H., 'Willem Lodewijk als opvoeder', in *Omtrekkende bewegingen. Opstellen aangeboden aan de schrijver bij zijn tachtigste verjaardag* (Hilversum 1995), 160–78.

WESTRA, F., *Nederlandse ingenieurs en de fortificatiewerken in het eerste tijdperk van de Tachtigjarige Oorlog, 1573–1604* (Alphen aan de Rijn 1992).

WIERINGEN, J.S. van, 'Menno van Coehoorn in de praktijk van de vestingbouw', in *Jaarboek Stichting Menno van Coehoorn 1990/91* (The Hague 1991), 56–66.

WIJN, J.W., *Het krijgswezen in den tijd van prins Maurits* (Utrecht 1934).

WIJN, J.W., 'Onder het vaandel', in *De Tachtigjarige Oorlog* (Amsterdam 1941), 111–31.

WIJN, J.W., *Het Staatsche leger*, VIII, 'Het tijdperk van de Spaanse Successieoorlog 1702–1715', 3 vols (The Hague 1956–1964).

WIJN, J.W., 'Military Forces and Warfare 1610–48', in J.P. Cooper (ed.), *The New Cambridge Modern History*, IV (Cambridge 1970), 202–25.

WILDE, F.G. de, 'De ontwikkeling van de infanterie-uniformen in het Staatse leger gedurende de 18e eeuw', *Armamentaria*, XVII (1982), 90–105.

WILSON, Peter H., *German Armies. War and German Politics, 1648–1806* (London and Bristol, Penn. 1998).

WILSON, P.H., 'Warfare in the Old Regime 1648–1789', in Jeremy Black (ed.), *European Warfare 1453–1815* (Basingstoke and London 1999), 69–95.

ZWITZER, H.L., 'In Staatse dienst', in C.M. Schulten and F.J.H.Th. Smits (eds), *Grenadiers en Jagers in Nederland 1599 1829 1979* (The Hague 1980), 11–22.

ZWITZER, H.L., *'De militie van den Staat'. Het leger van de Republiek der Verenigde Nederlanden* (Amsterdam 1991).

Index of Personal Names and Institutions

ADMIRALTY, boards of the 70, 307
AELIAN, author of *Tactica* (c. AD 100) 289
AERSSEN, François van (1572–1641), lord of Sommelsdijk, regent of Holland, diplomat and confidant of Frederik Hendrik 120, 243, 253
ALBERT (1559–1621), archduke, governor-general (1596–1598) and sovereign ruler (1598–1621) together with his wife Isabella of the Spanish Netherlands 163, 169, 171–3, 176, 179, 181, 184, 203, 212
ALBERTINA AGNES (1634–1696), daughter of Frederik Hendrik, wife (1652) of Willem Frederik 446 n.68
ALDRINGA, G., deputy of Groningen to the States-General 445
ALDRINGA, Wigbold van (1604–1644), deputy of Groningen to the States-General 262
ALTING, Lucas, deputy of Groningen to the States-General 359
AMALIA (1602–1675) countess of Solms-Braunfels, wife (1625) of Frederik Hendrik 283 n.189
AMAMA, Joachim van, Dutch captain 342
AMSTERDAM, burgomasters and city council of 42, 76, 198, 205, 213, 223, 226–7, 235, 237, 239, 241–2, 244, 251, 270, 273, 281–2, 303–4, 332, 336, 357, 359–60, 371, 408, 437, 441, 443, 447, 449, 458, 484, 488, 496–7, 509, 517
ANHALT, Christian von (1568–1630), commander of the troops paid by Brandenburg and Palatine-Neuburg in 1610 202–3
ANNE of Austria (1601–1666), queen of France (1615–1643), queen-dowager (1643–1651), sister of Philip IV of Spain 268
AQUILIUS, Tieleman, agent of the States-General with the French army 147
ARCHDUKES see Albert and Isabella
ARSKIN, Archibald, Dutch rittmaster 59
AYLVA, Hobbe, baron of (1696–1772), Dutch general officer 384
AYTONA, Francisco de Moncada (1586–1635), count of Osona and marquis of Aytona, Spanish general officer 236, 238–9

BAEL, Dieudonné de, weapons manufacturer based in Liège 401
BAERDT, Egbert van, deputy of Friesland to the States-General 313 n.37
BALFOUR, James, Dutch lieutenant in the Kirkpatrik regiment of foot 311
BAMPFIELD, Joseph, Dutch colonel and military adviser to Johan de Witt 316, 457
BAS, Dirk Jacobsz (1569–1637), burgomaster of Amsterdam 226
BAS, F. de, compiler of *Het Staatsche leger* 2
BAXTER, S.B., historian 306, 347
BEAUMONT, Simon van (1574–1654), deputy of Zeeland to the States-General 226
BEAUMONT, Simon van (1641–1726), clerk of the States of Holland from 1673 479
BELLEFONDS, Bernardin Gigault (1630–1694), marquis de, French *maréchal* 466
BENTINCK, Hans Willem (1649–1709), confidant of William III 505
BERGH, count Frederik van den (1559–1618), Spanish stadholder of Friesland, Groningen, Overijssel and Lingen from 1595 158
BERGH, count Hendrik van den (1573–1638), Spanish stadholder of Upper Gelderland (Opper-Gelre), commander of the army of Flanders from 1629 to 1632, entered Dutch service in 1632 212, 214–16, 219–22, 230, 232
BÉTHUNE, Leonidas de (†1603), colonel of a French regiment of foot in Dutch service 35
BEUNINGEN, Coenraad van (1622–1693), regent of Holland and diplomat 447, 503, 513
BEVEREN, Willem van (1556–1631), member of the town council of Dordrecht, field deputy 190, 226
BEVERNINGK, Hieronymus van (1614–1690), treasurer-general of the Union (1657–1666), deputy of Holland to the States-General 312, 437, 439–41, 452
BICKER, Andries (1586–1652), Amsterdam regent 223, 281, 303

INDEX OF PERSONAL NAMES AND INSTITUTIONS

BICKER, Cornelis (1592–1654), Amsterdam regent, brother of the above 281, 303
BINGHAM, John, English captain in Dutch service and translator of *The tacticks of Aelian* (1616) and *The art of embattailing an army, or The second part of Aelian's tacticks* (1629) 289–90
BIRKENFELD, Johann Karl (1638–1704), Prince-Count Palatine of, Dutch colonel 337, 339, 345
BLACK, Jeremy, historian 13
BOREEL, Jacob (1630–1697), Amsterdam regent, diplomat 509–10
BOSVELT, Adriaan van, field deputy of the States of Holland 333, 348, 462
BOTHWEL, Dutch captain 26
BOURGOGNE, Jacob, a Dutch *rouleur* or 'bounty-jumper' sentenced to run the gauntlet 337
BOURNONVILLE, Alexandre Hippolyte Balthasar de Hennin (1620–1690) prince de, Imperial field-marshal-general 472, 474–6, 483
BOVI, Jan, Dutch master pyrotechnician 143
BOXEL, Johan, Dutch captain-lieutenant and author of *Vertoogh van de krijghsoeffeninge* (1670) 15, 92
BREDEMUS, Salomon, Dutch lieutenant-colonel 348
BREDERODE, Johan Wolfert van (1599–1655), Dutch field-marshal 269–70, 275, 308–9, 407, 412, 431, 517
BRÉZÉ, Urbain de Maillé (1597–1650), marquis de, French *maréchal* 243–4, 248
BRODDEN, Melchior van, Dutch colonel 345
BROUCHOVEN, Jacob van (1577–1642), field deputy of the States of Holland 214
BROUCKE, Van de, clerk of Holland's treasury 80
BRUIJN, Jaap R., historian 71, 262 n.80, 307–8
BRUNSWICK-CELLE, Georg Wilhelm (1624–1705), duke of Hanover (1648–1665) and from 1665 duke of 417, 419–20, 430–1, 500, 502
BRUNSWICK-HANOVER, Johann Friedrich (1625–1679), duke of (1665–1679) 419
BRUNSWICK-OSNABRÜCK, Ernst August (1629–1698), Evangelical bishop of Osnabrück (1661–1698) 417, 419–20, 430–1, 499–500, 502
BRUNSWICK-OSNABRÜCK, Friedrich August (1661–1691), prince of, Dutch colonel 340

BRUNSWICK-WOLFENBÜTTEL, Christian (1599–1626), duke of, military enterpriser 41, 43, 208
BRUYNSTEIN, Johan, personal physician of William III 349
BUCQUOY, Charles Bonaventure de Longueval (1571–1621), count of, Spanish general officer 194–5
BURGERSDIJCK, Pieter (c. 1623–1691), field deputy of the States of Holland 333
BURMANIA, Poppo van (1603–1676), Dutch colonel 386
BURMANIA, Taco van, Dutch captain 342
BUZANVAL, Paul Choart (†1607), *seigneur* de, French ambassador at The Hague (1592–1607) 159
BYE, Joris de (†1628), treasurer-general of the Union (1588–1628) 117

CAESAR, Julius (100–44 BC), Roman general and statesman 140, 316
CALVO, Jean-Sauveur De (1625–1690), French commander of Maastricht (1676) 495
CAMER, Johan van der (†1669), deputy of Holland to the States-General 269
CAPELLEN, Alexander van der (1592–1656), regent of Gelderland, deputy to the States-General 120, 132, 208, 229, 244, 253, 259, 273 n.134, 276, 279, 285–6, 302–3, 318
CAPELLEN, Gerlach van der (1627–1685), son of the above 303
CAPELLEN, Henrik van der (†1659), brother of Alexander van der Capellen 285
CAPELLEN, Steffen Henrich van der, Dutch captain, a nephew of Alexander van der Capellen 318
CARDINAL-INFANTE see Ferdinand of Austria
CARLIER, Etienne, French intendant 423
CASTEL RODRIGO, Manuel de Moura y Cortereal, (†1661), marquis of, governor-general of the Spanish Netherlands (1644–1647) 276, 282
CATS, Jacob (1577–1660), Pensionary of Dordrecht (1623–1636), Grand Pensionary of Holland (1636–1651) 255
CATZ, Johan, ensign of Count Floris II of Culemborg's infantry company 53–4
CHAMILLY, Noël de Bouton (1636–1715), marquis de, French governor of Grave (1674) 386–7, 482–3
CHAMLAY, Jules-Louis Bolé 1650–1719), marquis de, French quartermaster-general and military advisor to Louis XIV 491

INDEX OF PERSONAL NAMES AND INSTITUTIONS

CHARLES I (1600–1649), king of England, Scotland and Ireland (1625–1649) 302, 405
CHARLES II (1630–1685), king of England, Scotland and Ireland (1660–1685) 302, 304, 405–6, 410, 415–16, 422, 425, 432–3, 467, 503, 505, 508–9
CHARLES II (1661–1700), 'Don Carlos', king of Spain (1665–1700) 411, 429, 461, 471, 476, 488, 499, 506–7, 509
CHARLES V (1500–1558), Holy Roman Emperor (1519–1556) 429
CHARLES X GUSTAV (1622–1660), king of Sweden (1654–1660) 407, 409–410
CHARLES XI (1655–1697), king of Sweden (1660–1697) 482, 507–8, 511
CHARNACÉ, Hercule, baron de (1588–1637), French envoy to The Hague (1635–1637) 235, 251
CHÂTILLON, Gaspar III de Coligny (1584–1646), duc de, French maréchal 243–4, 248, 263
CHAVIGNY, Léon le Bouthillier (1608–1652), count of, French secretary of state for foreign affairs 267
CHRISTIAN IV (1577–1648), king of Denmark (1588–1648) 212, 217, 270, 274
CLANT van Stedum, Edzard Jacob (1584–1648), deputy of Groningen to the States-General and a member of the Council of State 44, 145, 236
CLAUSEWITZ, Karl von (1780–1831), Prussian general officer and author of *Vom Kriege* 199, 444
CLEMENS VIII (1536–1605), pope (1592–1605) 184
COCQUIEL, Antoine de (c. 1545–1614), Spanish lieutenant-colonel, governor of Steenwijk (1592) 157
COEHOORN, Menno van (1641–1704), Dutch general officer, siege expert, artillerist and director-general of the fortifications (1695–1704) 354 n.189, 393–5
COLOGNE, Maximilian Heinrich of Bavaria (1621–1688), prince-bishop of Liège and elector of (1650–1688) 324, 331, 340, 407–8, 433, 436–7, 439, 441, 445–6, 448, 465–8, 470, 472, 499
CONDÉ, Louis II de Bourbon (1621–1686), duc d'Enghien, prince de, French maréchal 268, 434, 446, 471–7, 479, 481, 485–7, 489, 512
COPES, Willem, Dutch lieutenant-colonel, acting commander of Wesel 417 n.45, 422
CÓRDOBA, Fernández de (1585–1635), Spanish general officer 208
CORVISIER, A., historian 444
COUENDAEL, Agidius van, minister to William III's regiment of Dutch Guards 479 n.23
COUNCIL OF STATE of the Republic xiii, 24, 26–8, 30–3, 38, 44–50, 60, 64–6, 69–73, 79–82, 86, 93–4, 96, 119, 123, 137, 139, 148, 154–5, 157, 162, 186, 195, 213, 221 n.91, 232, 292, 301–3, 305–6, 309, 316–19, 321–3, 329–30, 335, 358, 368, 370, 375–6, 378, 380, 382, 401 n.128, 409, 412, 422, 426, 434, 436, 438, 501, 518, 523
CRÉQUI, François, marquis de (1624–1687), French maréchal 487
CROMWELL, Oliver (1599–1658), Lord Protector of the Commonwealth of England, Scotland and Ireland (1653–1658) 405
CULEMBORG, Floris II van Pallandt (1577–1639), count of, regent of Gelderland, deputy to the States-General, captain of a company of foot and rittmaster of a company of cuirassiers 23, 43, 52–3, 55, 61, 66–7, 76, 212, 225, 227, 240, 244, 256, 329

DANBY, Thomas Osborne (1631–1712), earl of, Lord Treasurer 505
DEGENFELT, Hannibal van, Dutch colonel 345
DEURSEN, A.Th. van, historian 161 n.46, 167 n.68, 181 n.110, 199
DON CARLOS *see* Charles II of Spain
DON JUAN of Austria (1629–1679), bastard son of Philip IV 429, 499
DORMANS, Eduard H.M., historian 2
DORP, *jonkheer* Frederik van (c. 1547–1612), governor of Ostend (March 1602–May 1603) 180
DORTH, *jonkheer* Diederik van, Dutch colonel 195
DRENTHE, Sheriff and regents of 25, 209, 230, 264, 309, 341
DURAS, Jacques Henri de Durfort (1626–1704), duc de, French general officer 454
DUSSEN, van der, Dutch captain 337
DUYCK, Anthonis (c. 1560–1629), advocate-fiscal of the Council of State (1589–1602), Grand Pensionary of Holland (1621–1629) 35, 37 n.63, 45–6, 49, 62, 87 n.4, 108 n.54, 125, 143, 156–7, 165, 178, 182, 206

EAST FRIESLAND, Georg Christian (1634–1665) of Cirksena, prince of (1660–1665) 411

ELIZABETH I (1533–1603), queen of England (1558–1603)   69, 152, 163, 166, 174, 186

ENGHIEN *see* Condé

ERENTREITER, Gerard, Dutch colonel   31 n.33, 226 n.111, 284

ERNST CASIMIR (1573–1632) count of Nassau-Dietz, Dutch field-marshal from 1607, stadholder and captain-general of Friesland (1620–1632), Groningen and Drenthe (1625–1632)   24, 35, 43, 50, 55, 61, 118, 145–6, 182, 190–1, 209–10, 212–16, 219–22, 224, 230

ESTRADES, Louis Godefroy, comte d' (1607–1686), French envoy at The Hague (1639–1640)   262–3, 274–7, 281

EUSKERCKEN, Johan (†1642), secretary to the Republic's ambassador in Paris (1634–1637)   147

EYBERGEN, Frederik (†1676), Dutch lieutenant-colonel (1672), colonel (1673)   341, 459

EYCK, Tobias van, adviser to Floris II Count of Culemborg   76

EYSINGA, Julius van (†1649), deputy of Friesland to the States-General   226

FAGEL, Gaspar (1634–1688), pensionary of Haarlem (1663–1670), *griffier* or clerk of the States-General (1670–1672), Grand Pensionary of Holland (1672–1688)   325, 327, 329, 331–3, 344–6, 349, 356, 360, 364, 370–1, 381, 386 n.83, 437–8, 440, 445, 447, 455, 457–8, 462, 469, 481, 484, 491, 494, 501, 518–19

FAGEL, Hendrik (1617–1690), *griffier* of the States-General (1672–1690)   359, 506

FARIAUX, Jacques de (1627–1695), general officer in Dutch service, commander of Maastricht (1673)   460

FARNESE *see* Parma

FERDINAND II (1578–1637), Holy Roman Emperor (1619–1637)   36, 207, 212, 218–19, 229, 247

FERDINAND III (1608–1657), Holy Roman Emperor (1637–1657)   278, 286

FERDINAND (1609–1641) of Austria, cardinal-infante of Spain, governor-general of the Spanish Netherlands (1632–1641)   64, 245–8, 252–5, 259–63, 265–6

FIJT, Pieter, *geappoincteerde* or invalid of Willem Lodewijk's Frisian regiment   61

FRANCKENBERG, Johan van Bawijr, lord of, Dutch rittmaster   65

FREDERICK V (1596–1632), elector palatine from 1610, king of Bohemia (1619–1620), the 'Winter King'   41, 44, 207

FREDERIK HENDRIK (1584–1647), count of Nassau and from 1625 prince of Orange, stadholder of Holland, Gelderland, Zeeland, Utrecht and Overijssel (1625–1647), general of the cavalry from 1603, and captain- and admiral-general of the Union from 1625   15–16, 24–5, 27–9, 34, 51, 55, 59, 64, 68, 76–7, 79–81, 83, 96, 100–1, 115, 118–23, 130–1, 138, 140, 142, 144–5, 190–1, 195, 206, 209–57, 259–88, 290, 295–7, 301–2, 308, 311, 316, 329, 339, 342, 361–2, 376, 380–1, 407, 450, 484, 516–17, 520–1

FRIEDRICH WILHELM (1620–1688), elector of Brandenburg (1640–1688), the 'Great Elector'   424–5, 445, 482, 484, 487–8, 494, 499, 507–8, 510–11

FRIESLAND, States of   25, 38, 69–70, 72, 81, 162, 193, 205, 219, 223, 264, 266, 268, 271, 279, 304, 309, 322, 330, 338, 340–2, 358 n.212, 406, 411, 415, 417, 443, 518

GALEN, Christoph Bernhard, *Freiherr von* (1606–1678), prince-bishop of Münster (1650–1678)   301, 306, 315, 329, 364, 407–8, 410–11, 414, 416, 419–20, 422, 424–7, 432–3, 436, 439, 445, 468, 500, 502, 516, 518

GASSION, Jean de (1609–1648), French *maréchal*   272, 275–7

GAYA, Louis de, French captain and author of the *Traité des armes* (1678)   400 n.123

FIELD DEPUTIES   31 n.33, 46, 48 n.118, 50, 118–19, 126–7, 130–1, 139, 141, 148 n.128, 187–8, 190–1, 196, 208, 214–16, 218, 220, 221 n.91, 226, 228, 230–3, 236–7 245–6, 248, 251, 254, 256, 260–1, 264, 269, 271–2, 275, 277, 284–5, 295, 323, 329, 333, 348, 351, 364, 388–9, 391, 420, 422–4, 427, 437, 440–1, 446 n.68, 462, 477, 486, 496, 501

GEELVINCK, Cornelis (1621–1689), field deputy of the States of Holland   333

GEER, Louis de (1587–1652), arms dealer   42

GELDERLAND, States of   70, 156, 159, 165, 193, 205–6, 208–9, 223, 226, 235, 303–4, 322, 329–30, 340–1, 358 n.212, 369, 417, 517–19

GENDT, Walraven, baron of (c. 1580–1644), Dutch colonel   31, 226 n.111

GENDT, Otto van (c. 1580–1640), lord of Dieden, Dutch colonel   221–2

GESAN, De (killed in action, 1593), Spanish commander of Geertruidenberg (1593)   161

GEYL, Pieter, historian   411

GHEYN, Jacob (II) de (1565–1629), engraver and artist   103

INDEX OF PERSONAL NAMES AND INSTITUTIONS

GHISTELLES, Pieter van (killed in action on 21 March 1604), Dutch governor of Ostend (20 December 1603–21 March 1604) 186 n.131

GLINSTRA, Epeus van (1605–1677), deputy of Friesland to the States-General 411, 415

GOCKINGA, Hendrik van (1624–1674), deputy of Groningen to the States-General 329

GOLTSTEIN, Reinier van, Dutch captain 222

GORGAS, Johann Georg, major-general in the army of the bishop of Münster 420–1

GRAMMONT, Antoine III (1604–1678) duc de, French *maréchal* 283, 285 n.205

GRISPERRE, Louis François de (executed 1673), Dutch colonel 345

GROBBENDONK, Anthonie Schetz, baron of, Spanish governor of 's-Hertogenbosch (1629) 218

GROENEWALDT, Georg, Dutch collector of the contributions 427

GRONINGEN, States of the City and Ommelands (rural environs) of 70, 145, 149, 161–2, 205, 209, 219, 223, 226, 230, 262, 264, 322, 330, 338, 340–2, 358 n.212, 359, 411, 415, 417, 443, 445, 518

GROOT, Cornelis de, *landdrost* or country sheriff of the Meijerij of 's-Hertogenbosch 313

GROOT, Hugo de (1583–1645), jurist 37, 313

GROOT, Pieter de (1615–1678), Dutch diplomat 443–4

GROOTHUYSEN, Johan Adolfsen, Dutch trooper in the company of Johan Maurits of Nassau-Siegen 312

GUSTAVUS II ADOLPHUS (1594–1632), king of Sweden (1611–1632) 7, 37, 113, 229, 234, 316, 397

HAERSOLTE, Arent Jurrien van (†1672), Dutch colonel 417, 419.

HAHLWEG, Werner, historian 3, 7–10, 87, 100 n.37

HALL, Bert S., historian 11

HAMEL BRUYNINCX, Gerard (1616–1691), Dutch envoy in Vienna (1670–1690) 481

HANNIBAL (247–183 BC), Carthaginian general 316

HARO y Sotomayor Guzman y Acevedo, Don Luis Mendez de (1598–1661), first minister of Philip IV of Spain 282

HARQUOS, Martin de Los, Spanish governor of Tienen (1635) 246

HART, Marjolein C. 't, historian 2

HASSELAER, Pieter Pietersz. (1583–1651), bailiff of Amsterdam 281

HAUBOIS, Cornelis (†1670), deputy of Friesland to the States-General 406

HAY, Alexander, Dutch lieutenant in the Kirkpatrik regiment of foot 311–12

HAY, ?, Dutch rittmaster 312

HEECKEREN, Jan de Roode van, Dutch captain, commander of the post near the Woerdens Verlaat (1672) 331

HEEMSKERCK, Coenraad van (1646–1702), Amsterdam regent, envoy extraordinary of the Republic to Brussels (1675) and to Madrid (1676) 373, 379, 484, 486–8

HEGAM, Jan Dircx van, *geappoincteerde* or invalid of Willem Lodewijk's regiment 61

HENDRIK CASIMIR I (1612–1640), stadholder and captain-general of Friesland, Groningen and Drenthe (1632–1640) 118, 230, 262–3

HENDRIK CASIMIR II (1657–1697), stadholder and captain-general of Friesland, Groningen and Drenthe (1664–1697) 325, 341–2, 354 n.189

HENRI DE BOURBON see Henry IV, king of France

HENRY III (1551–1589), king of France (1574–1589) 152, 154

HENRY IV (1553–1610), king of France (1589–1610), king of Navarre (1572–1610) 154, 159, 162, 165–7, 183, 197, 202

HERBERT, François (†1661), deputy of Holland to the States-General 269

HERTAING, Daniël de (†1625), *seigneur* de Marquette, last Dutch governor of Ostend (24 June 1604–22 September 1604) 189

HETTES, Haye, *geappoincteerde* or invalid of Willem Lodewijk's Frisian regiment 61

HEXHAM, Henry (c. 1585-c. 1650), English captain in Dutch service, author of *The Principles of the Art Militarie* (1637) and its translation into Dutch, *Principii ofte de eerste gronden van de oorloghskonste* (1642) 22–3, 113

HEYN, Piet (1577–1629), Dutch admiral 217

HINYOSSA, Alexander d' (beheaded 1672), Dutch captain 343

HOEUFFT, Diederik (1648–1719), Dutch rittmaster, liaison officer at the Spanish headquarters (1676) 351

HOEUFFT, Jean (†1651), Dutch envoy in Paris, 243, 253

HOLLAND, Delegated Councillors (*Gecommitteerde Raden*) of 48, 70, 75, 77–8, 305, 311–12, 333–4, 338, 345, 357, 360, 371, 401, 458, 477

HOLLAND, States of 3, 15, 23–4, 29, 40, 42, 68–9, 74–6, 78–80, 83, 96, 119, 152, 156, 205–6, 208, 213, 219, 223, 227, 251, 264, 267, 270, 279–81, 283–5, 287, 293, 297, 301–7, 309, 311–13, 318–19, 323–4, 330–4, 337–8, 340–1, 355–60, 369–71, 392, 401, 405–6, 410, 412, 415, 417, 427, 431, 437–8, 442–3, 445, 447, 449, 457–9, 479, 488, 502, 508, 517–20, 523

HON, Christoffel le, Dutch engineer and compiler of *Ordres van batailjen* (1672) 15, 516–17

HON, Johan le (killed in action 1632), Dutch engineer and father of the above 15 n.44

HONDIUS, Henricus (1573–1650), engraver and publisher 126 n.32

HORENKEN, Egbert, deputy of Groningen to the States-General 445

HORNES, Willem Adriaan van (†1694), Dutch general of the artillery 450–1

HOVE, Hendrik ten, commander of Fort Schenkenschans (1672) 440

HOXTER, Dirck Bogerts van, *geappoincteerde* or invalid of Willem Lodewijk's Frisian regiment 61

HUMIÈRES, Louis de Crevant (1628–1694), duc d', French *maréchal* 491, 495–6, 501, 505, 507

HUNDEBECK, Gaspar Richard, Dutch colonel 483

HUYGEN, Rutger, member of the Council of State 44

HUYGENS, Constantijn (1596–1687), secretary to Frederik Hendrik 101 n.38

HUYGENS, L., captain of the Frisian regiment of Willem Lodewijk 107

HYDE, Anna (†1671), first wife of James, duke of York 467

ISABELLA (1566–1633), daughter of Philip II of Spain, sovereign ruler of the Spanish Netherlands (1598–1621), governess-general (1621–1633) 171–2, 203, 212, 218, 224, 234

ISRAEL, Jonathan, historian 9 n. 21, 153 n.13, 243 n.4

ITTERSUM van de Oosterhof, Ernst van (†1681), Dutch colonel 414

JAMES I (1566–1625), king of Scotland (1567–1625) and of England (1603–1625) 36, 43, 187, 197

JAMES, duke of York (1633–1701), brother of Charles II of England 467, 505

JONG, Michiel A.G. de, historian 94 n.21

JOHANN VI (1535–1606), 'the Elder', count of Nassau 24, 187

JOHANN VII (1561–1623), 'the Middle', count of Nassau-Siegen 21, 24–5, 100, 102–4, 113, 143, 157–9, 521

JOHAN MAURITS (1604–1679), count of Nassau-Siegen and son of the above, Dutch officer, field-marshal (1668) and Brandenburgian stadholder of the duchy of Cleves from 1648 25, 309, 312, 322–6, 343–4, 366, 408, 417–24, 427, 431–3, 437, 442, 446, 448–9, 453–4, 456–8, 469, 518–20

JOHANN SIGISMUND (1572–1619), elector of Brandenburg (1608–1619) 201, 203

JORMAN, Jan Albert, Dutch colonel 345

JÜLICH, Johann Wilhelm (1562–1609), duke of 111, 201

KEMP, Jacob (killed during the siege of Groenlo, 1595), Dutch engineer 138–9

KIEN, Nicasius, commissioner of the victualling 127–8

KIEN, Nicolaas, commissioner of the victualling 247

KIEN, Thomas, commissioner of the victualling 414

KIRKPATRIK, Everwyne (killed in action 1677), Dutch major 439.

KIRKPATRIK, John (†1681), Dutch general officer, father of the above 311, 439

KNOOP, Mathijs Egberts, Dutch captain 32

KNOOP, W.J. (1811–1894), Dutch general officer and military-historical author 297

KNUYT, Johan de (1587–1654), deputy of Zeeland to the States-General 236, 239

KÖNIGSMARCK, Konrad Christoph, count of (1634–1673), Dutch general officer 331, 344, 458–9

KRIEX, Daniel, Dutch captain 344

KROENER, Bernhard, historian 12

LA CHASTRE, Claude baron de (1526–1614), French *maréchal* 203

LE BLOND, Guillaume (1704–1781), French mathematician and author of several military manuals 397, 444, 483

LE TELLIER, Michel (1603–1685), French secretary of state for war (1643–1677), chancellor of France (1677–1685) 314, 363, 433, 518

LEICESTER, Robert Dudley (1531–1588), earl of, governor- and captain-general of the Dutch provinces in revolt (1586–1587) 24, 69, 117, 152–3, 209

LEONIDAS, king of Sparta (488–480 BC) 451

LEOPOLD I (1640–1705), Holy Roman Emperor (1658–1705) 358–9, 379, 383, 411,

429, 431, 444–5, 448, 455, 461–2, 471–2, 474–5, 481–9, 507, 512
LEOPOLD (1586–1632), archduke, bishop of Strasbourg and Passau 202
LIÈGE, prince-bishop of, see Cologne
LIER, Willem van (1588–1649), lord of Oisterwijk, Dutch ambassador in Paris (1637–1648) 267, 280–1
LIEVENS, Kerst, burgomaster of Grave (1604) 41
LIMBURG STIRUM, Herman Otto, count of (c. 1592–1644), Dutch general officer 219
LIMBURG STIRUM, Joost, count of, Dutch colonel 30
LIMBURG STIRUM, Otto, count of (†1679), lord of Borculo, Dutch colonel 316, 407, 421
LIPSIUS, Justus (1547–1606), classical philologist and military theorist 3, 6–7
LORRAINE, Charles IV (1604–1675), duke of (1624–1633 and 1661–1670), Imperial army commander 235, 434, 461
LORRAINE, Charles V (1643–1690), duke of (1675–1690), Imperial army commander 487, 502, 511
LOUIS XIII (1601–1643), king of France (1610–1643) 12, 202, 224, 238, 240, 243–4, 251–3, 255, 260, 266–8, 288
LOUIS XIV (1638–1715), king of France from 1643, personal reign (1661–1715) xiv, 1, 7, 12, 18, 279, 297, 314–15, 361–2, 366–7, 383–4, 392, 395–6, 410–11, 425, 427, 429–37, 443–4, 446, 453, 455, 460–1, 465, 467–9, 470–4, 482, 485–7, 489–91, 493, 497–8, 500, 502–3, 505, 507–12, 515–16, 518, 522
LOUVOIS, François Michel Le Tellier (1639–1691), marquis de, French secretary of state for war (1662–1691) 314–15, 363, 375, 377, 395, 433, 444, 465, 489–91, 493, 498, 512, 518
LUXEMBOURG, François Henri de Montmorency-Bouteville (1628–1695), duke of, French general officer 446, 449–52, 454, 457–9, 462, 465–7, 482, 487, 498, 501, 503–4, 509–10
LYCKLAMA, Elias, Dutch captain 342

MACHADO, Moses alias Antonio Alvares (†1706), provediteur-generaal van den Staat (1672–1706) 366–73, 456
MAES, Cathelyna, sollicitrice-militair or financial agent for Count Floris II of Culemborg's infantry company 66
MANSFELD, Ernst (1580–1626) count of, military enterpriser 41–4, 208

MANSFELD, Peter Ernst, count of (1517–1604), interim governor-general of the Spanish Netherlands (1592–1594) 160–1
MARGARETHA THERESIA (1651–1673), sister of Charles II of Spain, wife (1666) of Emperor Leopold I 429, 431
MARIA d'Este, princess of Modena, second wife (1673) of James, duke of York 467, 505
MARIA de Medici (1573–1642), wife (1600) of Henry IV of France, regent for Louis XIII (1610–1617) 202
MARIA ANNA (1635–1696) of Austria, second wife of Philip IV of Spain and sister of Emperor Leopold I, queen dowager of Spain (1665–1677) 429, 499
MARIA THERESIA (1638–1683), eldest daughter of Philip IV of Spain, wife (1660) of Louis XIV of France 279–80, 297, 410–11, 430
MARIENBURGH, Willem, deputy of Overijssel to the States-General 239
MARTINET, Jean (killed in action 1672), inspector-general of the French infantry (from 1667) 315
MARY STUART (1631–1661), daughter of Charles I of England, wife (1641) of Stadholder Willem II 302
MARY STUART (1662–1694), daughter of James, duke of York, wife (1677) of Stadholder William III 505
MATHENESSE, Johan van (1596–1653), deputy of Holland to the States-General 269
MAURITS (1567–1625), count of Nassau, prince of Orange from 1618, stadholder of Holland and Zeeland (1585–1625), Overijssel and Utrecht (1590–1625), Gelderland (1591–1625), Groningen (1620–1625) and Drenthe (1620–1625), captain-general of Holland and Zeeland from 1587 and commander-in-chief of the Dutch army from 1590 3–4, 9, 15–16, 24–9, 32, 34–42, 46, 48 n.118, 50–1, 59–60, 63, 85–7, 91, 94, 96–7, 99–103, 105–6, 108, 111–13, 115, 117–18, 120–3, 125–6, 128–30, 137–41, 143–4, 146, 148–9, 151–3, 155–67, 169–71, 174–84, 186–200, 202–9, 215, 226, 240, 277 n.155, 289, 291, 295, 297, 302, 308, 311, 316–17, 339, 342, 361, 376, 379, 381, 399, 511, 516–17, 520–1
MAXIMILIAN I (1459–1519), Holy Roman Emperor (1493–1519) 21
MAXIMILIAN (1573–1651), duke of Bavaria (from 1597) and elector of Bavaria (from 1623) 203

MAZARIN, cardinal Jules (1602–1661), chief minister of France (1643–1661)   268, 279–81
MEER, *jonkheer* Jacob van der (†1604), Dutch governor of Ostend (April–June 1604)   185, 187
MEILLERAYE, Charles de la Porte (1602–1664), duke of, French *maréchal*   260, 263, 265.
MELO, Francisco de (1597–1651), count of Assumar, marquis of Tor de Laguna, viceroy of Sicily (1639–1641), governor-general of the Spanish Netherlands and commander-in-chief of the army of Flanders (1641–1644)   265–6, 268–72, 276
MENDOZA, Francisco de (1545–1623), admiral of Aragon, second-in-command of the army of Flanders   39, 62–3, 166–7, 169–70, 182
MONTALTO, French governor of Charleroi (1672)   456
MONTBAS, Jean Barton de Bret (1613–1696), vicomte de, Dutch colonel   313
MONTECUCCOLI, Ernesto, count of (c. 1580–1633), Imperial general   219, 221–2
MONTECUCCOLI, Raimondo (1609–1680), Imperial general   219, 448, 454–5, 465–7, 484, 487
MONTERREY and Fuentes, Juan Domingo de Zuñiga y Fonseca (1649–1716), count of, governor-general of the Spanish Netherlands (1670-January 1675)   368, 372, 436, 443, 453, 460, 465, 467, 471–7, 479, 485, 512
MOY, De, officer in the army of the bishop of Münster, commander of Coevorden (1672)   459
MUELEN, Elias van der (1720–1784), Dutch lieutenant   520
MUELEN, J. van der, Dutch ensign, 426
MULERT, Hendrik, Dutch captain   436
MUNDER, Borchard van, *geappoincteerde* or invalid of the Frisian regiment of Willem Lodewijk   61
MÜNSTER, prince-bishop of, *see* Galen
MUSCH, Cornelis (1593–1650), *griffier* or clerk of the States-General (1628–1650)   256

NAERSSEN, Revixit van, member of Holland's Delegated Councillors   359–60
NASSAU, Justinus (1559–1631) count of, Dutch officer and governor of Breda (1601–1625)   26, 209–10

NASSAU-LA LECK, Lodewijk (1604–1665) count of, lord of Beverweert, Dutch general officer   277
NASSAU-OUWERKERK, Hendrik van (1640–1708), rittmaster-commander of William III's Life Guards   349
NASSAU-SIEGEN, Johan Maurits, count of, *see* Johan Maurits
NASSAU-SIEGEN, Willem (1592–1642) count of, Dutch field-marshal   238–9, 247, 256–7, 259
NASSAU-SIEGEN, Willem Maurits (1649–1691), count of, Dutch colonel   345
NASSAU-ZUYLENSTEYN, Frederik van (1624–1672), Dutch general officer, killed in action near Woerden (1672)   450–2
NEVERS, Charles, duke of (1580–1637), claimant to the duchy of Mantua   217
NIEUWENAAR AND MEURS, Adolf, count of (c. 1545–1589), stadholder of Gelderland and Overijssel (1584–1589) and of Utrecht (1585–1589)   152
NOORDINGHEN, Dirck van, *solliciteur-militair* or financial agent for Count Floris II of Culemborg's company of cuirassiers   66–8
NOOT, Charles van der, Dutch governor of Ostend (March-early July 1601 and June–December 1603)   173–4
NYENBORCH van Naeltwijk, A., field deputy for Holland's Delegated Councillors   352, 477

OESTHEIM, Hans van, captain of Willem Lodewijk's Frisian regiment   107
OESTREICH, Gerhard, historian   3, 7
OLDENBARNEVELT, Johan van (1547–1619), Advocate of Holland (1586–1618)   23, 27, 69, 117–18, 128, 130, 148, 152, 156, 159, 162, 166–7, 169, 171, 181–2, 186–8, 197–9, 202, 205–6, 223, 239–40, 302
OLIVAREZ, Gaspar de Guzmán (1587–1645), first minister to Philip IV of Spain   212, 225
ONGER, Court, *geappoincteerde* or invalid of the Frisian regiment of Willem Lodewijk   61
ORLÉANS, Philippe (1640–1701), duc d', brother of Louis XIV of France, named *Monsieur*   490–1, 500–1
OSSORY, Daniël d' (beheaded 1672), Dutch governor of Rheinberg (1672)   343, 440
OVERIJSSEL, States of   3, 70, 159, 205–6, 209, 223, 229, 235, 304, 306, 322, 329–30, 336, 340–1, 358 n.212, 369, 417, 517–18

INDEX OF PERSONAL NAMES AND INSTITUTIONS

PADBORCH, Adolph van, captain-lieutenant of Count Floris II of Culemborg's infantry company 52, 55
PADBURCH, Willem, Dutch captain 344
PAEN, Louis, Dutch captain and author of the drill manual *Den korten weg tot de Nederlandsche militaire exercitie* (1679) 104
PAFFENRODE, Jacob van, Dutch lieutenant-colonel 332
PAIN ET VIN, Moise (c. 1620–1673), Dutch quartermaster-general, beheaded on William III's insistence 343, 459
PALM, François (†1674), Dutch lieutenant-colonel of a regiment of marines 346, 450–2, 463
PALATINE-NEUBURG, Philipp Wilhelm (1615–1690), duke of 494, 499
PALATINE-NEUBURG, Wolfgang Wilhelm (1581–1653), count of 201–3
PANIN, Dutch captain 337
PAPELAY, Alexander, Dutch captain 342
PAPPENHEIM, Gottfried Heinrich, count of (1594–1632), Imperial general 220 n.86, 231–4
PARFOUREUX, Dutch captain 29
PARKER, Geoffrey, historian 9–11, 13, 106 n.50, 112
PARMA, Alexander Farnese (1545–1592), duke of, governor-general of the Spanish Netherlands (1579–1592) 8, 151, 153–4, 156, 160, 207
PARROTT, David, historian 9, 12, 243 n.3, 294 n.14, 297
PAS, Philippe de Pracé du, French governor of Naarden (1673) 462
PAUW, Adriaen (1585–1653), Pensionary of Amsterdam (1611–1627), Grand Pensionary of Holland (1631–1636 and 1651–1653) 239–40, 406
PAUW, Reynier (1564–1636), burgomaster of Amsterdam 239
PEENE, Pieter van, official of the Council of State appointed in 1658 'for the dispatch of the patents' 306
PEREIRA, Jacob (†1707), *provediteur-generaal*, business associate of Machado 366, 368–73
PERJÉS, G., historian 383
PESTERS, Johan (1620–1703), Utrecht regent, pensionary of Maastricht, field deputy 329, 335, 359, 381, 383, 391–2, 454–5, 494, 497, 502–3, 506, 510
PHILIP II (1527–1598), king of Spain (1556–1598) xiii, 8, 151–4, 171–2
PHILIP III (1578–1621), king of Spain (1598–1621) 172, 185, 197–8, 207, 212

PHILIP IV (1605–1665), king of Spain (1621–1665) 212, 218, 240, 244–5, 262, 268, 279, 282, 285, 297, 411, 429
PICCARDT, Henric (1636–1712), syndic of the province of Groningen's Ommelands (rural environs) 341
PICCOLOMINI, Ottavio, prince of (1599–1656), Imperial general 247–8, 251, 259–60
PITHAN, Frederik van, Dutch major, governor of Jülich (1610–1622) 203, 207
POELHEKKE, J.J., historian 246
PRADEL, François de Vilanders et, commander of the French auxiliary corps (1665) 423
PUCHLER, Eustachius, Dutch colonel 101 n.38
PURCEL, Dutch captain 331
PUYSÉGUR, Jacques François de Chastenet (1655–1743), comte de, French quartermaster-general and author of *Art de la guerre, par principes et par règles* (1748; reprinted 1749) 249, 290, 363, 400, 403, 516

RAA, F.J.G. ten, compiler of *Het Staatsche leger* 2, 167 n.68, 253 n.48, 262 n.80, 398
RABENHAUPT, baron von Sucha, Karl (1602–1675), Dutch general officer 386, 389, 445, 481–2
RAMPERS, Arnold Jordan, *solliciteur-militair* or financial agent for Count Floris II of Culemborg's company of cuirassiers 67
RANDWIJCK, Arnold, baron of (1574–1641), deputy of Gelderland to the States-General 226
RANTZAU, Josias count of (1609–1650), French *maréchal* 275–7
READ, Dutch captain 68
REEDE-AMERONGEN, Godard van (1593–1641), deputy of Utrecht to the States-General 256.
REEDE-AMERONGEN, Godard Adriaan van (1621–1691), Utrecht regent, Dutch envoy in Berlin 335, 338, 347, 356, 374, 376, 391, 437–8, 441, 447, 452, 454–5, 458, 462, 479, 496, 503
REEDE-GINKEL, Godard van (1644–1703), Dutch general officer, son of the above 324–5, 331, 338, 347, 374, 376, 437–8, 441, 455, 462–3, 465–6, 477, 479–80, 503–4
REEDE-RENSWOUDE, Johan van (1593–1682), regent of Utrecht 450
RENNENBERG, Georges van Lalaing (c. 1550–1581), count of, stadholder of

INDEX OF PERSONAL NAMES AND INSTITUTIONS

Friesland (1577–1580), Groningen, Drenthe and Overijssel (1577–1581) 151

RHINEGRAVE, Frederik Magnus von Salm-Neufville (1607–1673), Waldgrave and, Dutch general officer and governor of Maastricht 309–10, 318, 320–1, 422, 437, 449, 460

RICHELIEU, Armand Jean Duplessis (1585–1642), duc de, chief minister of Louis XIII of France (1624–1642) 224–5, 235, 243, 251, 253, 260, 263, 265, 267–8, 288

ROBERT, Louis, French intendant during the Dutch War 509

ROBERTS, Michael, historian 3, 7, 9–10, 13, 112

ROCHEPÈRE, ? de, French commander of Oudenaarde (1674) 481

ROOCLAES, Willem, *solliciteur-militair* or financial agent for the company of Captain Read 68

ROORDA, Karel van (1609–1670), deputy of Friesland to the States-General 277

ROWEN, H.H., historian 306

RUDOLF II (1552–1612), Holy Roman Emperor (1576–1612) 36, 201

RUYSCH, Dutch commissary for the exchange of prisoners of war after the engagement at Kallo (1638) 64

RUYTER, Michiel Adriaansz. de (1607–1676), Dutch lieutenant-admiral-general 425, 443, 453, 461–2

SALM, Karel Florentijn von (†1676), Wald- and Rhinegrave von, Dutch colonel, son of the below 449

SALM-NEUFVILLE, Frederik Magnus von *see* Rhinegrave

SANTA CRUZ, Alvarez de Bazán, marquis of, Spanish general officer 227, 231

SANTEN, Johan van, Dutch governor of Wesel (1672) 440

SASBURCH, Thomas van (1611/12–1687), Dutch resident in Brussels (1656–1687) 359, 375, 489

SAVORNIN, Daniël de (1669–1739), Dutch general officer 521

SAVOY, François Thomas, prince of (1596–1656), Spanish general officer 244

SAXE, Maurice de (1696–1750), French *maréchal général des camps et armées* 458 n.126

SAXE-WEIMAR, Bernhard, duke of (1604–1639), military enterpriser in French pay 266–7

SCHADÉ, Gaspar (1623–1692), deputy of Utrecht to the States-General 440–1

SCHAEP, Gerard Simonsz (1598–1666), burgomaster of Amsterdam, 281

SCHAFFER, Goosen (1601–1637), deputy of Groningen to the States-General 226

SCHOMBERG, Friedrich Hermann, count of (1615–1690), French *maréchal* 491, 495–6

SCHULTEN, C.M., historian 2

SCHULTEN, J.W.M, historian 2

SCHWARTZENBERG and Hohenlansberg, Georg Wolfgang (1638–1674), baron of, Dutch colonel 414

SEDLNITZKY, *jonkheer* Pieter (†1610), lord of Soltenitz, Dutch general officer, sent on a mission to Ostend in 1601 177–8

SLANGENBURG, Frederik Johan van Baer (1646–1713), lord of, Dutch colonel 381

SLINGELANDT, Simon van (1664–1736), secretary of the Council of State (1690–1725), treasurer-general of the Union (1725–1727), Grand Pensionary of Holland (1727–1736), author of political works 305

SLOET, Bernard, deputy of Overijssel to the States-General 229

SMOUT or SMOUTSIUS, Adriaan Jorissen (c. 1580–1646), Counter-Remonstrant preacher in Amsterdam 223, 227, 241

SNAERTS, Dutch captain 344

SOLMS, Ernst, count of, Dutch colonel 51, 86–87

SOLMS, Georg Eberhard, count of (1568–1602), Dutch colonel 35, 163

SOLMS-BRAUNFELS, Heinrich Trajectinus, count of (1637–1693), Dutch colonel 329, 331, 450–1

SONNINO, P., historian 460

SOUCHES, Louis Raduit, comte de (1608–1683), Imperial field-marshal 472, 474–7, 479, 481, 483–4, 511–12

SPINOLA, Ambrogio (1569–1630), commander-in-chief of the army of Flanders (1604–1628) 121, 146, 149, 175, 184–5, 188–97, 199–200, 203–5, 207–10, 212, 240, 254

STANLEY, Sir William (1548–1630), English governor of Deventer (1587) 152

STATES-GENERAL of the Dutch Republic 15–17, 24, 27, 29–34, 36–44, 47, 49–52, 60, 63, 65, 68–73, 77, 83–6, 95, 117–19, 121, 123, 128–9, 137, 139, 141–2, 145–8, 153–5, 157, 159–65, 167, 169, 171, 173, 175–7, 179–80, 182, 184, 186–7, 190–3, 197–9, 202, 204, 208–9, 214–15, 217, 219, 221, 224, 226, 228–30, 232, 234–9, 242, 246, 255–7, 261–2, 267, 272–5, 277, 279–80, 283, 287, 292, 302–5, 307, 309, 316–17, 319, 321, 323–5, 329, 342, 346, 348–9, 351–2, 359,

361, 367, 370, 373–4, 379, 389, 391, 394–5, 405–6, 409–12, 415–17, 419–20, 422–4, 426–7, 431, 434–6, 438, 440–1, 445, 447, 450, 457, 460–2, 467–8, 471, 481, 484, 486, 499, 503–4, 506–9, 517
STATES-GENERAL of the Spanish Netherlands 234
STECKE, Diderik (†1689), Dutch colonel 325, 342–3
STEVIN, Simon (1548–1620), mathematician, engineer and quartermaster-general of the Dutch army 58, 97, 99, 100 n.37, 108, 112, 124–6, 139
STOCKHEIM, Johan van (†1674), Dutch colonel, commander of Weesp (1672) 332
SWARTZSTEIN, Godefroy Mom de, Dutch captain 338
SWOL, Jan, Dutch deserter 337

TARENTE et Talmont, Henri Charles de la Tremouille (†1672), prince de, Dutch general officer 414
TARGONE, Pompeo (1575-c. 1630), Italian engineer 184
TEMPEL, Olivier van den (1540–1603), head of military justice in the Dutch field army (1597) 62
TERESTEIN, Cornelis van (1579–1643), deputy of Holland to the States-General 119, 236
THONISZ., Pieter, gunsmith based in Dordrecht 96 n.29
TILLY, Jean t'Serclaes (1559–1632), count of, commander of the German Catholic League's army 217, 229, 294
TROMP, Maerten Harpertsz. (1598–1653), Dutch lieutenant-admiral 262
TURENNE, Henri de La Tour d'Auvergne (1611–1675), vicomte de, French *maréchal* 434–5, 446, 448, 465–6, 472–5, 483, 486–7, 489, 512
TURNOR, Margaretha (1613–1700), wife of Godard Adriaan van Reede-Amerongen 324 n.84, 438, 452

UTENHOVE, Gerrit van, Dutch colonel 337
UTRECHT, States of 3, 55 n.147, 60, 69–70, 205–6, 209, 223, 256, 286, 304, 322, 324 n.84, 330, 340–1, 358 n.212, 369, 417, 517–18

VALCKENIER, Gilles (1624–1680), burgomaster of Amsterdam 437–438, 447
VALKENIER, Petrus (1638–1712), author of *'t Verwerd Europa (Europe in Confusion)*, published in 1675 305, 468 n.169, 516

VASSY, Johan de, Dutch major, commander of Philippine 342
VAUBAN, Sébastien le Prestre (1633–1707), *seigneur* de, French fortifications engineer, siege expert and military adviser to Louis XIV 17, 361–2, 385, 391–2, 395–6, 461, 481, 491
VAUDEMONT, Charles Henri of Lorraine (1649–1723), prince de, Spanish general officer 477
VEGETIUS, Publius Flavius Vegetius Renatus, author of *De Re Militari* (late 4th century AD) 511
VEGHES, Claes, *geappoincteerde* or invalid of Willem Lodewijk's Frisian regiment 61
VELTDRIEL, Johan van (†1646), deputy of Friesland to the States-General 84, 273
VERDUGO, Francisco de (1536–1597), Spanish stadholder of Groningen, Drenthe and Overijssel (from 1581) 151, 154–61, 165
VERE, Sir Francis (1560–1609), English general in Dutch service, commander-in-chief of Ostend (July 1601–February 1602) 35, 106 n.50, 130, 139, 173–4, 176, 178–80, 182
VERVOU, Fredrich van (1550–1621), steward to Willem Lodewijk (1595–1605) and author of *Enige gedenckweerdige geschiedenissen* 125
VILLA HERMOSA, Carlos de Gurrea, Aragón y Borja (†1692), duke of, Spanish general and governor-general of the Spanish Netherlands (January 1675–1680) 351, 372–4, 379, 481, 485–9, 491, 493–6, 499–500, 502–9
VILLEROY, Nicolas de Neufville (1542–1617), marquis de, French minister of foreign affairs 202–3
VILLERS, Joost de Zoete (†1589), lord of, Dutch field-marshal 86
VRIES, Jacques de, captain of the Frisian regiment of Willem Lodewijk 107
VRIJBERGEN, Cornelis van, Dutch extraordinary envoy in Brussels 447

WAGEMAN, Jan Claesz., gunsmith in Dordrecht 96 n.29
WAGEVELT, Thonys Ruyter van, *geappoincteerde* or invalid of the Frisian regiment of Willem Lodewijk 61
WALDECK and Culemborg, Georg Friedrich, count of (1620–1692), Dutch field-marshal 325, 328–9, 345–6, 348–9, 363, 372–3, 376, 379, 381, 391, 399, 405, 419, 424, 445, 447–8, 450–6, 465–7, 469, 472–6, 483–4, 491, 493–500, 505–6, 519–20

WALLENSTEIN, Albrecht Wenzel Eusebius (1583–1634) baron von, Imperial army commander and military enterpriser 44, 217
WALTHA, Pieter van, deputy of Friesland to the States-General 236
WASSENAAR-OBDAM, Jacob van (1610–1665), Dutch lieutenant-admiral 416
WEEDE-DIJKVELD, Everard van (1626–1702), regent of Utrecht, field deputy and diplomat 351, 372, 374, 377, 388–9, 391, 496, 500–1, 506, 508–10
WEEDE-WALENBURG, George Johan van (1627–1696), Dutch colonel, brother of the above 348
WELDEREN, Johan van, captain-lieutenant of Count Floris II of Culemborg's company of cuirassiers 67
WIJN, J.W., historian 2–3, 96, 254
WIJNBERGEN, Ditmaer van (†1696), Dutch lieutenant-colonel, commander of Rees (1672) 343
WIJNBERGEN, Johan van, Dutch colonel 95 n.24, 221 n. 91, 284
WILLEM II (1626–1650), stadholder of Holland, Gelderland, Zeeland, Utrecht, Overijssel and Groningen (1647–1650), captain- and admiral-general of the Union 285–6, 302–5, 308, 316, 406, 517
WILLEM FREDERIK (1613–1664), count of Nassau-Dietz, stadholder and captain-general of Friesland (1640–1664) and of Groningen and Drenthe (1650–1664) 84, 118, 120, 137, 263–4, 266, 268–9, 271, 273 n.134, 275, 278, 280–1, 283, 303, 309, 321, 346, 412–15, 417, 426, 446 n.68, 518
WILLEM LODEWIJK (1560–1620), count of Nassau, stadholder and captain-general of Friesland and Groningen's Ommelands (1584–1620), of Drenthe (1593–1620) and of the city of Groningen and its Ommelands (1595–1620) 3, 5, 9, 15–16, 21, 24–5, 27–8, 32, 34–5, 38, 43, 48 n.118, 51, 59–60, 85–7, 91, 94, 100–3, 105–8, 111–13, 117–18, 120–3, 125–6, 130–1, 138, 140, 143, 146, 149, 152, 155–63, 165, 167, 169, 171, 175–6, 178–82, 187–8, 191, 193–7, 198–200, 203–4, 209, 240, 289, 291, 295, 297, 302, 317, 326, 361, 380, 397, 399, 511, 516–17, 520–1
WILLEM, ? de, receiver at the Amsterdam tax office 360
WILLIAM I, 'the Silent', prince of Orange (1533–1584), leader of the Revolt 3, 24, 151, 307, 438, 517

WILLIAM III (1650–1702), stadholder of Holland and Zeeland (1672–1702), Utrecht (1674–1702) and Gelderland and Overijssel (1675–1702), captain- and admiral-general of the Union (1672–1702) 120, 304, 306–7, 325–7, 329, 334, 336, 338, 340–9, 352–3, 356, 359, 361, 366–8, 371–3, 375, 379–81, 386–7, 389, 391–2, 394–5, 399, 401, 405–6, 410, 427, 438, 440–3, 445–58, 460–2, 465–7, 469, 471–7, 479, 481, 483–8, 491–505, 507–10, 512–13, 517–23
WIMMENUM, Amelis van den Bouchorst (†1669), lord of, member of Holland's Knighthood, deputy to the States-General 280
WIMMENUM, Nicolaes van den Bouchorst (†1641), lord of Noordwijk and, deputy of Holland to the States-General 226
WINGFIELD, John, English governor of Geertruidenberg (1589) 153
WIRTZ, Paulus (1612–1676), baron of Orneholm, field-marshal in the Dutch army 431, 456–7
WITH, Witte de (1599–1658), Dutch vice-admiral 274
WITSEN, Nicolaas (1641–1717), regent of Holland, field deputy 351, 371, 501
WITT, Cornelis de (1623–1672), regent of Holland and deputy of Holland to the States-General 323, 356, 425, 447
WITT, Johan de (1625–1672), Grand Pensionary of Holland (1653–1672) 306, 308–9, 312, 316, 323, 356, 406–8, 410–11, 416–17, 419, 423–7, 430–2, 439, 443, 447, 516–17
WORCKUM, Syrck Gerbrants, *geappoincteerde* or invalid of the Frisian regiment of Willem Lodewijk 61

YORK, Rowland, English commander of the redoubt before Zutphen (1587) 152
YVENS, Jan, Dutch officer, captain of the Frisian regiment of Willem Lodewijk 107
YVOY, Maximiliaan van Hangest Genlis (1621–1686), called d', Dutch quartermaster-general and engineer 387, 391

ZEELAND, States of 3, 69–70, 72, 149, 152, 156, 205, 209, 223–4, 226, 279, 282–3, 286, 301, 304, 309, 322, 330, 338, 340, 356, 358 n.212, 417, 443, 517–18

Index of Alliances, Peace Treaties, Land and Sea Battles, Rivers and Canals, Forts, Towns and Villages

Alliances and treaties
ACT OF HARMONY (1670)   438
ACT OF NAVIGATION (1651)   405, 410
ACT OF SECLUSION (1654)   405–6, 437
ALLIANCE OF THE HAGUE (1673), the Dutch Republic, the Holy Roman Emperor and Spain   462
ANGLO-DUTCH ALLIANCE (1678)   509
ANGLO-MÜNSTER ALLIANCE (1665)   416
'CLOSER ALLIANCE' (1634), France and the Dutch Republic   77, 83, 238–9, 252
DUTCH-BRANDENBURG ALLIANCE (1666)   424–5
DUTCH-BRANDENBURG ALLIANCE (1672)   445
DUTCH-BRUNSWICK ALLIANCE (1665)   420
DUTCH-IMPERIAL ALLIANCE (1672)   445
DUTCH-SPANISH ALLIANCE (1671)   436
FRANCO-DUTCH ALLIANCE (1635)   77, 80, 240, 242, 244, 251–2, 255, 261, 267, 270, 277, 282, 285, 287–8, 296
FRANCO-DUTCH ALLIANCE (1662)   410–11, 432
FRANCO-DUTCH DEFENSIVE TREATY (1608)   198
FRANCO-DUTCH SUBSIDY TREATIES (1630–1646)   225, 252, 255, 265, 268, 279, 281
FRANCO-SWEDISH ALLIANCE (1672)   482
PERPETUAL EDICT (1667)   438
'QUADRUPLE ALLIANCE' (1673), the Holy Roman Emperor, the Dutch Republic, Spain and the duke of Lorraine   461
SECRET TREATY OF DOVER (1670), France and Charles II of England   433
TREATY OF DORTMUND (1609), Brandenburg and Palatine-Neuburg   201
TREATY OF GREENWICH (1596), France, England and the Dutch Republic   164
TREATY OF NONESUCH (1585), England and the Dutch Republic   152
TREATY OF XANTEN (1614), Brandenburg, Palatine-Neuburg, Spain and the Dutch Republic   204
TRIPLE ALLIANCE (1668), England, the Dutch Republic and Sweden   315, 431–2
UNION OF UTRECHT (1579), rebellious Netherlandish provinces   16, 151, 166, 199, 278
VENETIAN-DUTCH DEFENSIVE TREATY (1619)   42

Peace treaties
AIX-LA-CHAPELLE (1668), Spain and France   315, 323, 355, 395, 432, 453, 491
BREDA (1667), the Dutch Republic and England   425
BRÖMSEBRO (1645), Denmark and Sweden   274
CHERASCO (1631), France and Spain   227, 229
CLEVES (1666), the Dutch Republic and Münster   315, 425, 427, 445
LONDON (1604), Spain and England   189, 197
LÜBECK (1629), Denmark and the Holy Roman Emperor   218–219
MÜNSTER (1648), European peace settlement   278–82, 285–6, 301, 313, 317, 329, 352, 396, 397, 405, 407, 412, 445, 516
NIJMEGEN (1678/79), France, the Dutch Republic, Spain and the Holy Roman Emperor   17, 301, 352, 360, 375, 395–6, 401, 403, 497, 507–11, 515, 521, 523
PYRENEES (1659), France and Spain   286, 314, 363, 410, 431, 462
RIJSWIJK (1697), France, the Dutch Republic, England and Spain   393–394
TWELVE YEARS' TRUCE (1621), Spain and the Dutch Republic   16, 36, 50, 60,

73, 96, 111, 120, 142, 198, 201–2, 205, 218, 240
VERVINS (1598), France and Spain   166–7, 197, 199
VOSSEM (1673), France and Brandenburg   460
WESTMINSTER (1654), England and the Dutch Republic   405, 407, 410
WESTMINSTER (1674), England and the Dutch Republic   467
WESTPHALIA see MÜNSTER

Land battles and engagements
BREITENFELD (1631), Swedes and the German Protestant princes defeat the German Catholic princes   229, 290, 294 n.14
CONSARBRUCK (1675), Lorraine-Brunswick army defeats the French   487
DESSAU BRIDGE (1626), Imperialists defeat Ernst von Mansfeld   44
FEHRBELLIN (1675), Brandenburgers defeat the Swedes   487
FLEURUS (1622), Ernst von Mansfeld and Duke Christian of Brunswick-Wolffenbüttel defeat the Spaniards   41, 208
FLEURUS (1690), French defeat the Dutch and English   401 n.127
HONNECOURT (1642), Spaniards defeat the French   266
HUY (1635), French defeat the Spaniards   244–5
KALLO (1638), engagement at, Spaniards defeat the Dutch   63–4, 256–7, 259, 272
LÜTZEN (1632), Swedish pyrrhic victory over the Imperialists   37, 234, 290
MONT-CASSEL (1677), French defeat the Dutch and Spaniards   334–5, 348–9, 359, 380–1, 383, 501, 503, 506, 512, 534
NIEUWPOORT (1600), Dutch defeat the Spaniards   63, 111, 120, 122, 128, 168–71, 176, 199, 335, 380, 525
NÖRDLINGEN (1634), Imperialists defeat the Swedes   266, 290
ROCROI (1643), French defeat the Spaniards   268, 290, 434
SAINT-DENIS (1678), Dutch defeat the French   349, 380, 509–10, 512, 534
ST GOTTHARD ABBEY (1664), Imperialists defeat the Ottomans   329, 448
SENEFFE (1674), undecided battle between the French and Dutch-Spanish-Imperial armies   327, 349, 351, 380, 477–9, 511–12, 534
SINZHEIM (1674), French defeat the Imperialists   475
THERMOPYLAE (480 BC), Persians defeat the Greeks   451
THIONVILLE (1639), Imperialists defeat the French   260
TURNHOUT (1597), Dutch annihilate the Spaniards   113, 164
WHITE MOUNTAIN (1620), Imperialists decisively defeat the Protestants in Bohemia   207
WOERDEN (1672), engagement at, the Dutch gain a moral victory over the French   331, 346, 449–53, 469

Sea battles
DOWNS (1639), Dutch defeat the Spaniards   262
FOUR DAYS' BATTLE (1666), Dutch defeat the English   425
LOWESTOFT (1665), English defeat the Dutch   416
MEDWAY (1667), Raid in the, Dutch destroy English fleet   425
SCHONEVELD (1673), Dutch tactical victory over the English and French   461
SLAAK (1631), Dutch destroy Spanish fleet   229
SOLE BAY (1672), Dutch tactical victory over the English and French   443
SOUND (1658), Dutch defeat the Swedes   409
TEXEL (1673), Dutch defeat the English and French   461–2
TWO DAYS' BATTLE (1666), or the St James's Day Battle, English defeat the Dutch   425

Rivers and canals
BRUSSELS CANAL   247
DEMER   122, 225, 247, 250, 296, 377
DENDER   493
DIEZE   217
DIJLE   122, 225, 246–8, 296.
EEMS see EMS
EMS   410–12, 414, 416, 424
ESCAUT see SCHELDT
GEET, GROTE and KLEINE   246
GHENT-BRUGES CANAL   147, 277, 286
GHENT CANAL   228, 265, 269, 271
IJSSEL   153, 155, 163, 167, 191, 194–7, 205, 207, 216, 218–22, 247, 325, 352, 365, 419, 421–2, 424, 432, 435, 437–41, 449, 466
LEIE   122, 147, 225, 265, 296
LEK   457
LYS see LEIE
MAAS see MEUSE

INDEX OF ALLIANCES, PEACE TREATIES ETC. 573

MEUSE 9, 130, 142, 154, 182, 190, 225, 227, 230–2, 247–8, 254, 261, 269, 271, 284, 318, 396, 407, 432, 436, 439, 442–3, 460, 462, 465–6, 472–6, 486, 491, 494–6, 498, 529
RHINE 40, 43–4, 122, 154, 156, 158, 161, 165, 167, 189–90, 192–4, 196, 201–2, 214, 226, 232, 234, 236–7, 247, 261, 267, 407, 432, 435–7, 439–40, 446–8, 454–5, 462, 465–6, 472, 474–5, 483–4, 486–7, 497–8, 529
RIJN see RHINE
RUHR 128
SAMBRE 504
SCHELDE see SCHELDT
SCHELDT 122, 129, 147, 176, 189–90, 198, 225, 246, 256, 259–60, 272, 275–6, 282, 286–7, 296, 461, 481
VISTULA 407
WAAL 154, 156, 167, 190, 194, 196–7, 207, 216, 219, 247, 443, 466
WEICHSEL see VISTULA

Forts, towns and villages (with year of siege)
AACHEN see AIX-LA-CHAPELLE
AALST (1667) 362, 431, 493
AARSCHOT 130, 248
AIRE (1641 and 1676) 265, 276, 387, 396, 495, 498, 507, 510
AIX-LA-CHAPELLE 204, 245
ALESIA (52 BC) 140
ALKMAAR 406
ALMELO 421
ALPHEN AAN DE RIJN 333, 345, 458
AMEIDE 457
AMERSFOORT 221–2, 448, 454, 465
AMIENS 165–6
AMSTERDAM 42, 44, 70, 73–6, 80, 82, 91, 237, 262, 281–2, 303, 332, 336, 351, 357, 360, 365–9, 398, 408, 441–2, 446, 449, 452, 458, 517
ANTWERP (1585) 64, 122, 129, 151, 187, 189, 198, 208, 225, 230, 236, 238, 240, 252, 255–6, 258–60, 264, 269–79, 281–4, 286–8, 291, 296–7, 366, 376, 500, 508
ARGENTEAU (1674), castle 473, 485
ARMENTIÈRES (1667) 431
ARNHEM 127, 156, 162, 219, 221–2, 365, 421, 440–1, 466, 468
ARRAS (1640) 263–4, 288, 375
ASSENEDE 263, 269
ATH (1667) 362, 375, 395–6, 431–2, 474, 476, 481, 485–6, 491, 503–5, 507, 510

BAPAUME 265
BEERTA 364
BERGEN IN HENEGOUWEN (Hainaut) see MONS
BERGEN OP ZOOM (1588 and 1622) 26, 41–2, 59, 136, 146, 149, 153–4, 189, 207–9, 212, 230, 260–1, 264–5, 269, 272, 275, 284, 296, 323, 361, 394–5, 431, 436, 444, 454–5
BERGUES (1646 and 1667) 283, 288, 362, 431
BERLIN 484
BESANÇON (1674) 473
BÉTHUNE (1645) 276, 288
BINCHE (1667) 362, 510
BLOKZIJL 344
BOCHOLT 220, 222, 424
BODEGRAVEN 331, 442, 458–9, 470
BOIS LE DUC see 'S-HERTOGENBOSCH
BOMMEL see ZALTBOMMEL
BONN (1673) 347–8, 367, 465–7, 470, 473
BORCULO 193, 407, 420–1, 425, 468
BORKEN 374
BOUCHAIN (1676) 375, 396, 491, 493, 507, 510, 522
BOURTANGE 193, 197
BOXTEL 218
BREDA (1624–1625, 1637) 26, 39, 41, 55, 130–1, 140, 144, 146, 154, 189, 208–10, 212, 216, 223, 229, 236, 238–40, 253–5, 264, 288, 291, 353, 362, 392, 395, 444, 461, 528–9
BREDEVOORT (1597) 62, 144, 166, 189, 192–3, 528
BREISACH (1638) 262
BREMEN 34, 44
BRILL see DEN BRIEL
BRUGES 147, 198, 225–6, 228, 238, 240, 253 n. 48, 259–60, 263, 265, 269, 271, 273, 275–8, 280, 282–4, 286–8, 296, 500, 508
BRUGGE see BRUGES
BRUMMEN 219
BRUSSELS 39–40, 64, 77, 147, 163, 171, 182–3, 189, 197–8, 202–3, 208, 218, 223–5, 227–9, 231, 234–5, 237, 240, 244–5, 247, 250, 259, 268–9, 286, 351, 372, 460, 472, 476, 486, 489, 493, 496, 500, 504–6, 508–10
BÜDERICH (1672) 407, 437, 439

CADIZ 163
CALAIS (1596) 163, 262
CALENBERG 417
CAMBRAI (1667 and 1677) 163, 362, 376, 396, 491, 498, 500–2, 507, 510
CASSEL 510
CHARLEMONT 498
CHARLEROI (1667, 1672 and 1677) 362, 379, 395–6, 431, 434, 453–6, 459, 465, 467, 473–7, 485, 491, 496, 499, 502–7, 510, 512
CHARLEVILLE-MÉZIÈRES 475
CHEB see EGER
CLEVES 31, 327, 408, 424
COESFELD 416, 421

COEVORDEN (1592 and 1672)   128, 151, 155, 158–9, 161, 191–3, 197, 395, 445, 459, 528
COLOGNE   165, 218, 267
CONDÉ (1676)   375, 396, 491, 505, 507, 510, 522
COPENHAGEN (1658)   409
COURTRAI (1646 and 1667)   147, 282, 288, 362, 394–6, 431–2, 460, 485, 491, 505, 507, 510
CREVECOEUR, fort   443

DAMME   190, 275, 284
DANZIG (1656)   407–9
DEINZE   495
DELFT   73, 80, 82, 96
DELFZIJL   151, 156, 422, 528
DEN BOSCH see 'S-HERTOGENBOSCH
DEN BRIEL, cautionary town   73, 80, 82, 152, 187, 443, 468
DENDERMONDE   275, 372, 486, 493, 503
DEN HAAG see THE HAGUE
DEVENTER   127, 152–3, 155, 180, 191–2, 194, 219–20, 224, 343, 412, 414–15, 420, 441, 528
DIEPENHEIM   421
DIEREN   219, 421
DIEST (1635)   197, 247–8, 250, 376–7
DIJLERSCHANS (1663 and 1664), fort   411–12, 414–15, 417, 426
DIKSMUIDE   496, 498
DINANT (1675)   475–6, 486, 489
DOESBURG   127, 162, 189, 191, 195–6, 219–20, 421–2, 441
DOETINCHEM (1598, 1599, 1665)   166–7, 189, 421
DOMMELEN   236
DOORNIK see TOURNAI
DORDRECHT   73, 80, 82, 94, 96 n.29, 156, 190, 205, 223, 226, 235, 251, 255, 275, 278
DORSTEN   436
DOUAI (1667)   265, 362, 395, 431, 476
DUFFEL   284
DUINKERKEN see DUNKIRK
DUNKIRK (1646)   72, 128, 167, 169, 181, 199, 213, 225–8, 238, 241, 243, 245, 251–5, 260, 262, 267–8, 271, 275–6, 281, 283–4, 288, 296
DÜLMEN   416
DÜSSELDORF   203, 436

EDAM   205, 406
EGER   461–2
EINDHOVEN   236
ELBURG   465
ELTEN   182
EMDEN   34, 162, 191, 220, 352, 407, 411
EMMERICH (1672)   54, 60 n.164, 204, 207, 222, 228, 407–8, 439
EMMERIK see EMMERICH

ENKHUIZEN   70, 73, 153, 205, 227, 406
ENSCHEDE   120, 166

FLUSHING see VLISSINGEN
FRANKFURT AM MAIN   448
FURNES see VEURNE

GDANSK see DANZIG
GEERTRUIDENBERG (1593)   138–9, 153–5, 160–1, 180, 189, 208, 239, 528
GELDER (1638)   40, 220, 240, 248, 257, 259, 264
GENNEP (1641)   257, 265, 267, 288, 529
GENT see GHENT
GERAARDSBERGEN   493
GHENT (1678)   198, 228, 240, 259–60, 265, 269, 271–3, 275–7, 282–4, 286–8, 296, 351, 359, 372, 474, 481, 486, 489, 493, 496, 507–8, 510
GOEJANVERWELLESLUIS   442
GORINCHEM   29, 73, 80, 82, 229, 442
GOUDA   73, 80, 82, 227, 458–9
GRAVE (1602, 1672 and 1674)   40–1, 137, 155, 176, 182, 218, 254, 367, 386–7, 389, 392–3, 395, 443, 462, 466, 468, 470, 481–3, 485, 528
GRAVELINES (1644)   270–1, 288
GREETSIEL   417
GROENLO (1597 and 1627)   127, 139–40, 159, 162–3, 165–6, 189, 192–3, 195–7, 199, 214–16, 241, 306, 309, 316, 409, 421, 426, 528–9
GRONINGEN (1594 and 1672)   49, 143, 151, 155–7, 159, 161, 191, 386, 395, 445–6, 528
GROVENBRUGGE   451
GULIK see JÜLICH

HAARLEM   8 n.20, 73, 80, 82, 223, 325, 344, 406
HALLE   486–7, 505–6
HAMONT   39
HARDERWIJK   441, 448–9, 465
HASSELT   194, 421
HEES   222
HERENTALS   130, 164, 221, 454, 467
'S-HERTOGENBOSCH (1601 and 1629)   11, 37, 65, 127, 131, 140–2, 144, 155, 176–8, 180, 184, 208, 217–18, 221–3, 234, 239, 241, 248, 253, 267, 282, 362, 365, 392, 395, 401 n.128, 444, 461–2, 529
HESDIN (1639)   260
HEUSDEN   127, 223
HILDESHEIM   448
HINDERDAM   332
HOEI see HUY
HOOGSTRATEN, castle   39–40, 130
HOORN   70, 153, 338

INDEX OF ALLIANCES, PEACE TREATIES ETC.

HULST (1596 and 1645)   155, 157, 163–4, 176, 214, 225, 238, 240, 252, 255, 260–1, 263–5, 268–9, 271, 273, 275, 277–8, 288, 291, 528–9
HUY (1675)   486, 489

IEPER see YPRES
IJZENDIJKE   137, 189–91, 228–9, 276
ISSELBURG   213

JÜLICH (1610 and 1621–1622)   126–7, 201–4, 207

KAISERSWERTH   436
KALKAR   214
KAMPEN   454, 465
KEPPEL   421
KERPEN (1673)   467
KIELDRECHT   214
KLEEF see CLEVES
KNODSENBURG, fort   156
KOBLENZ   448
KORTRIJK see COURTRAI
KREFELD   266

LA BASSÉE (1641 and 1642)   265–6
LAFELT   236
LANAKEN   231–2, 454, 496
LANDEN   474
LANDRECRIES (1637)   253, 288
LA ROCHELLE (1627–1628)   37, 472
LEERORT   407, 411
LEIDEN   3, 73, 80, 82, 139, 153, 223, 406, 458
LENS (1641 and 1642)   265–6
LE QUESNOY   474, 476
LEUVEN see LOUVAIN
LICHTENVOORDE   421
LIEFKENSHOEK, fort   64, 246, 256
LIÈGE (1675)   131, 230–2, 237, 391, 401, 473, 486, 489, 497
LIER   280, 284
LILLE (1667)   147, 265, 282, 295, 362, 395, 431
LILLERS (1645)   276, 288
LIMBACH   203
LIMBOURG (1632 and 1675)   119, 234, 486, 489, 510
LINGEN (1597 and 1605)   149, 162, 166, 191, 193–4, 196–7, 199, 214, 224, 414, 468, 528
LINNICH (1673)   467
LOCHEM (1665)   193, 195–6, 421, 424
LOEVESTEIN, castle   303, 443
LOKEREN   283
LONDON   152, 505
LOOSDRECHT   367
LOUVAIN (1635)   130, 246–8, 250–1, 287, 296, 351, 372, 376, 486
LOPIK   347, 397
LUIK see LIÈGE

MAASEIK   130, 231, 503
MAASSLUIS   227
MAASTRICHT (1632, 1673 and 1676)   15 n.44, 33 n.40, 122, 131, 137, 141, 148 n.129, 186, 204, 230–4, 236, 238–9, 241, 244–5, 247–8, 250, 254, 266, 284, 286, 296, 312, 318, 324 n.82, 329, 349, 361–2, 365, 367, 372, 379, 384–9, 391–3, 395, 407, 422, 435–7, 439, 446, 449, 453–5, 460–1, 465–6, 468, 470, 473, 482, 486, 494–7, 499, 503, 505, 507, 510, 512, 529
MADE   209
MAGDEBURG (1631)   145, 229
MALINES see MECHELEN
MARDYCK (1645 and 1646), fort   271, 275, 278, 283, 288
MARIAKERKE   277
MAUBEUGE   510
MECHELEN   132, 240, 284, 351, 376–7, 436, 473, 486, 505
MEERSSEN   232
MENEN   147, 395 n.104, 510
MENIN see MENEN
MEPPEL   158
MEPPEN   415
MEURS (1597)   165, 407
MIDDELBURG   178
MISERIA (1645), fort   275
MONS (1678)   252, 255, 351, 359, 380, 473–4, 476, 479, 486, 491, 493, 505–6, 508–10
MUIDEN   442, 446, 449
MÜNSTER (1657)   306, 408–10, 416

NAARDEN (1672 and 1673)   8 n.20, 325, 347, 352, 367, 392, 394, 399, 441, 448–9, 453–4, 462–5, 470
NAMEN see NAMUR
NAMUR (1692 and 1695)   208, 240, 252, 255, 266, 394, 395 n.104, 456, 473–6, 486–7, 489
NANCY   235
NAVAGNE (1674), castle   473, 485
NEUENHAUS   414
NEUSS   218, 266, 436, 467
NIEUW-AMSTERDAM (NEW YORK) (1664)   415
NIEUWERBRUG, sconce   343, 459
NIEUWPOORT   169, 394–5, 496, 508
NIJMEGEN   151, 155–7, 194, 230–2, 234–5, 248, 365, 443, 466, 468, 528
NINOVE   493

OLDENBURG   34
OLDENZAAL (1597, 1605, 1626 and 1665)   120, 145, 149, 151, 159, 166, 191, 193–4, 197, 199, 213–14, 241, 421, 528
OOSTENDE see OSTEND

OOSTERHOUT 160
OOTMARSUM (1597 and 1665) 120, 166, 421, 528
ORSOY (1632 and 1672) 234, 407, 436, 439
OSTEND (1601–1604) 32, 49, 54, 61, 63, 72, 128, 132, 135, 143–4, 151, 155, 167, 169–71, 173–89, 195, 197, 199, 253 n.48, 282, 394–5, 508, 528
OUDENAARDE (1667 and 1674) 362, 375, 395–6, 431–2, 460, 481, 484–5, 491, 505, 507, 510
OUDEWATER 8 n.20
OVERIJSE 247

PARIS 147, 154, 162, 243, 267, 268, 280, 434
PEER 454
PERNAMBUCO (Recife) 224, 235
PERWEZ 476
PHILIPPINE, fort 260, 263, 265, 269, 270, 342
PHILIPPSBURG (1676) 472, 475, 493, 497, 511
PURMEREND 205

RAMMEKENS, fort, cautionary town 132 n.66, 152, 253
REES (1672) 204, 207, 222, 343, 407, 439
RHEINBACH (1673) 347–8, 466, 470
RHEINBERG (1597, 1598, 1601, 1606 and 1672) 40, 141, 144, 165–6, 174–6, 190–7, 199, 202, 218, 229, 234–5, 261, 264, 266–7, 343, 407–8, 439–40, 468, 528–9
RIJNBERK see RHEINBERG
ROCROI 475
ROERMOND (1632 and 1637) 40–1, 220, 230–1, 239, 248, 254–5, 257, 261, 269, 271, 286, 486–7
ROOSENDAAL 223–5, 454, 473, 500
ROTTERDAM 70, 73, 80, 82, 223, 235, 251, 313, 454, 496
ROUVEEN 421
RUPELMONDE 275

SAINT-GERMAIN-EN-LAYE 434
SAINT-GHISLAIN (1677) 376, 498, 505–6, 510
SAINT-OMER (1638 and 1677) 255–6, 260, 265, 276, 381, 396, 498, 500–2, 507, 510
SAINT-QUENTIN 476
SAINT-TROND see SINT-TRUIDEN
SAINT-VENANT (1645) 276, 288
SASBACH 487
SAS VAN GENT (1644) 190, 269, 271–2, 275, 281, 283, 288, 342, 392, 529
SCHENKENSCHANS, fort (1635–1636 and 1672) 182, 248–9, 291, 440, 443
SCHIEDAM 73

SCHOONHOVEN 73, 442, 457
SEDAN 434
SINT-ANDRIES (1645), fort 145, 443
SINT-JORIS 277
SINT-TRUIDEN 129–30, 182
SINT-WINOKSBERGEN see BERGUES
SLUIS (1604) 32, 50, 144, 151, 153, 176, 187–8, 199, 271, 443, 468, 528
SOEST (County of Mark) 205
STEENBERGEN 230, 395
STEENWIJK (1592) 101, 141, 143, 151, 155–9, 528
STOCKEM 231
STRALEN 220, 230–1

TELGTE 416
TERHEIDEN 131
THE HAGUE 54, 66, 73–4, 87 n.4, 230, 235, 304, 344, 356, 458
THIONVILLE (1643) 240, 252, 255, 260, 268–9, 288, 502
TIENEN 130, 245–6, 248, 250, 287, 294, 474
TIRLEMONT see TIENEN
TOLEDO 499
TONGEREN 129–30
TOURNAI (1667) 362, 375, 395, 431, 481, 505
TRIER (1673 and 1675) 465, 487

UERDINGEN 266, 436
ULFT 421
UTRECHT 53–4, 206, 219, 221, 327, 344, 365, 367, 397, 441, 449–51, 454–5, 465–6, 482

VALENCIENNES (1667 and 1677) 362, 375–6, 396, 491, 493, 498, 500, 507, 510
VEGHEL 218
VENLO (1632, 1637 and 1646) 40, 141, 220, 229–31, 248, 254–5, 257, 261, 269, 271, 284, 286, 486
VEURNE (1646 and 1667) 283, 288, 362, 395 n.104, 431, 485
VIANEN 457
VILVOORDE 247, 474
VISÉ 231, 439
VLISSINGEN, cautionary town 132 n.66, 152, 253, 443, 468
VOORNE or Schans Ter Voorn, fort on the River Waal near Heerewaarden 443
VOSKAPEL 247, 250

WACHTENDONK (1605) 40, 192
WAREMME 496
WARENDORF 416
WARNETON 395 n.104, 510

INDEX OF ALLIANCES, PEACE TREATIES ETC.   577

WATERVLIET   190, 228
WEERT (1595)   139
WEESP   332
WESEL (1629 and 1672)   65, 196, 204–5, 208, 218–22, 237, 291, 343, 407–8, 417 n.45, 422, 439–40, 448
WESTERVOORT   219
WIJK BIJ DUURSTEDE   53–4
WILLEMSTAD   229
WOERDEN   449–51, 454, 459, 465
WOERDENS VERLAAT   331
WOUDRICHEM   29, 229
WOUW   454

XANTEN   202, 204

YPRES (1678)   359–60, 372, 375, 395 n.104, 396, 496, 498, 501, 503, 507–8, 510

ZALTBOMMEL (1599)   167, 443
ZEIST   443
ZEVENAAR   159
ZONS   266
ZUTPHEN   8 n.20, 49, 151–3, 155, 180, 192, 195, 219–21, 303, 316, 365, 395, 421–3, 432, 441, 466, 468, 528
ZWAMMERDAM   458–9, 470
ZWARTSLUIS   421, 454
ZWOLLE   158, 192, 194, 306, 365, 395, 420, 441

Warfare in History

The Battle of Hastings: Sources and Interpretations, *edited and introduced by Stephen Morillo*

Infantry Warfare in the Early Fourteenth Century: Discipline, Tactics, and Technology, *Kelly DeVries*

The Art of Warfare in Western Europe during the Middle Ages, from the Eighth Century to 1340 (second edition), *J.F. Verbruggen*

Knights and Peasants: The Hundred Years War in the French Countryside, *Nicholas Wright*

Society at War: The Experience of England and France during the Hundred Years War, *edited by Christopher Allmand*

The Circle of War in the Middle Ages: Essays on Medieval Military and Naval History, *edited by Donald J. Kagay and L.J. Andrew Villalon*

The Anglo-Scots Wars, 1513–1550: A Military History, *Gervase Phillips*

The Norwegian Invasion of England in 1066, *Kelly DeVries*

The Wars of Edward III: Sources and Interpretations, *edited by Clifford J. Rogers*

The Battle of Agincourt: Sources and Interpretations, *Anne Curry*

War Cruel and Sharp: English Strategy under Edward III, 1327–1360, *Clifford J. Rogers*

The Normans and their Adversaries at War: Essays in Memory of C. Warren Hollister, *edited by Richard P. Abels and Bernard S. Bachrach*

The Battle of the Golden Spurs (Courtrai, 11 July 1302): A Contribution to the History of Flanders' War of Liberation, 1297–1305, *J.F. Verbruggen*

War at Sea in the Middle Ages and the Renaissance, *edited by John B. Hattendorf and Richard W. Unger*

Swein Forkbeard's Invasions and the Danish Conquest of England, 991–1017, *Ian Howard*

Religion and the conduct of war, c.300–1215, *David S. Bachrach*

Warfare in Medieval Brabant, 1356–1406, *Sergio Boffa*

Renaissance Military Memoirs: War, History and Identity, 1450–1600, *Yuval Harari*

The Place of War in English History, 1066–1214, *J.O. Prestwich, edited by Michael Prestwich*

War and the Soldier in the Fourteenth Century, *Adrian R. Bell*

German War Planning, 1891–1914: Sources and Interpretations, *Terence Zuber*

The Battle of Crécy, 1346, *Andrew Ayton and Sir Philip Preston*

The Battle of Yorktown, 1781: A Reassessment, *John D. Grainger*

Special Operations in the Age of Chivalry, 1100–1550, *Yuval Noah Harari*

Women, Crusading and the Holy Land in Historical Narrative, *Natasha R. Hodgson*

The English Aristocracy at War: From the Welsh Wars of Edward I to the Battle of Bannockburn, *David Simpkin*

The Calais Garrison: War and Military Service in England, 1436–1558, *David Grummitt*

Renaissance France at War: Armies, Culture and Society, c. 1480–1560, *David Potter*